☞ W9-BGN-619

Clark Gable

Biography,
Filmography,
Bibliography

CHRYSTOPHER J. SPICER

McFarland & Company, Inc., Publishers
Jefferson, North Carolina, and London

Frontispiece: Clark Gable in 1955, while filming *The Tall Men.*

Library of Congress Cataloguing-in-Publication Data

Spicer, Chrystopher J.
    Clark Gable : biography, filmography, bibliography / Chrystopher J.
Spicer.
        p.   cm.
    Includes bibliographical references and index.
    ISBN 0-7864-1124-4 (softcover : 50# alkaline paper) ∞
    1. Gable, Clark, 1901–1960.   2. Motion picture actors and actresses —
United States — Biography.   3. Gable, Clark, 1901–1960 — Bio-
bibliography.   I. Title.
PN2287.G3 S75   2002
791.43'028'092 — dc21
    [B]   2001051198

British Library cataloguing data are available

Cover: Clark Gable at about the time he was filming *Betrayed* in 1954 *(Author collection)*

Manufactured in the United States of America

McFarland & Company, Inc., Publishers
  Box 611, Jefferson, North Carolina 28640
    www.mcfarlandpub.com

This book, which brought us
together, could be dedicated to
none other than my wife, Marcy.
It would never have been
completed without her inspiration,
her faith, and her help.

ACKNOWLEDGMENTS

Clark Gable was a man of international status. In researching his life I have been fortunate indeed to be assisted by people and organizations from many places around the world, and I would like to take this opportunity to thank them.

In the United States, I would like to thank Barbara Hall for her guidance through the vast collection at the Margaret Herrick Library of the Academy of Motion Pictures, Arts and Sciences; Ned Comstock of the Doheney Library at the University of Southern California for his help with access to the Constance McCormick Collection and other interview transcripts and articles ; Laura Kath of Mariah Marketing, and Vintage Hotels for their assistance with information about the Weasku Inn; Patrick and Annabel Curtis; Christi Welter (née Galvin), and to Sandy of the *Tribute to Clark Gable* web site who has uncomplainingly provided valuable assistance from her own extensive resources. I would also like to thank the Auburn-Cord-Duesenberg Museum in Indiana for their help with information about Clark's vehicles; Dr. Maurice Crane of the G. Robert Vincent Voice Library at Michigan State University for allowing me access to interviews with people who had known Clark; and Herb Bridges and the *Gone with the Wind* Answer Lady, Kathleen Mar-caccio, for their assistance and encouragement.

I will always be deeply grateful to the Microforms Department of the Boise State University Albertsons Library not only for their valuable assistance with periodical and newspaper research, but for introducing me to their assistant supervisor and then allowing me to remove her to the other side of the world. To her belongs the credit for much of this book's photographic and newspaper research. Really, she had no idea what she was getting into.

Clark Gable's home state was Ohio and many people there kindly donated their time to help. In Akron: the library staff of the *Beacon-Journal*; Robert Ethington, Fine Arts Division Manager at the Akron-Summit County Public Library; and John V. Miller, Director of Archival Services for the University of Akron. In the Ravenna area: Eleanor O'Connell, Loris Troyer, and the Ravenna *Record-Courier*; Don Evans and the Southeast Local School District; Virginia Jones of Diamond; Mary Ocheltree of Newton Falls; Wallace and Mary-Anne Wagner; Paul Shively; Denise French and Dorothy Knapp; David Hartley; Madeline Matjunas; and Pat J. Spano.

In Cadiz, Ohio, Clark's hometown, I cannot thank enough Michael Cope of the Clark Gable Foundation for his interest in and encouragement of this project from the beginning. I would also like to thank Nan Matten and all the ladies at the Clark Gable Birthplace Museum for making my time there so enjoyable. Special thanks also goes to Mr. Charles B. Wallace of the Harrison County, Ohio, Historical Society for his interest and information and for the Society's kind permission to use photographs from their collection.

In Oregon, I would like to thank the Portland Historical Society; Spring Quick, the Adult Services Librarian for the Silver Falls Library District in Silverton; and Mr. and Mrs. Abel Olsen in Astoria for their assistance with information about Clark's early theatrical career in Oregon.

I would also like to thank Tammy Wood-Behnke and Ed Shoemaker in Oklahoma for their research on the town of Bigheart; Jean Shanley of the Meadville, Pennsylvania, *Tribune* for information about Clark's family history there; and the Federal Bureau of Investigation archives in Washington, D.C.

In England, I would like to thank Ken Harbor, historian for the 351st Heavy Bomber Group Association; and Michael Downes of Oundle. I would also like to thank the 303rd Heavy Bomber Group Association for their assistance.

In Australia, I am grateful to the staff of the State Library of Victoria, the Victoria University Library, and of the Albert Park Library in Melbourne for their patient handling of requests for hard-to-find material.

When navigating a lengthy project like this, one goes through pools of calm when research can be found and words come readily, but for all of those times an author must also find his way through trackless deserts when there is a drought of knowledge and the rain of words ceases. In those times I have been grateful for support and encouragement from: the other three important women in my life — Miranda, Madeline and Alexa; the Sunday Morning Breakfast Club — Nick and Zara and Andrew and Francesca, and George and Julie of the Dundas Place Cafe who supplied us all; Eric Brand of the Windsor Hotel, Sue Chisam, Trisha Copeland, Captain Peter Janson of Rutherglen House, Lawrence Money, and all my friends with whom I work at Victoria University in Melbourne, who know all too well what it is like to work the hours we do and to try to have a life as well.

And often, in the early hours of the morning, I'm sure I felt Clark standing behind my chair reading over my shoulder and chuckling to himself.

CONTENTS

You see, the film studio ... is really the palace of the sixteenth century. There one sees what Shakespeare saw: the absolute power of the tyrant, the courtiers, the flatterers, the jesters, the cunningly ambitious intriguers. There are fantastically beautiful women, there are incompetent favourites. There are great men who are suddenly disgraced. There is the most insane extravagance, and unexpected parsimony over a few pence. There is enormous splendour which is a sham; and also horrible squalor hidden behind the scenery. There are vast schemes, abandoned because of some caprice. There are secrets which everybody knows and no one speaks of.

— Christopher Isherwood

PREFACE

In May of 1993, I sat one afternoon in a hotel room with Donald Spoto looking out over the city of Melbourne, Australia. We were talking about his recent biography of Marilyn Monroe and he happened to comment that, when he was researching her work with Clark Gable on *The Misfits,* information on Gable had been difficult to find. He had found, and I was surprised to learn, that at this time no biographies about the film star were in print, there were no collections of his documents in a library somewhere as source material, and there was only one book currently available that analyzed his contribution to over seventy films. We both agreed that someone should tackle the job of writing a new work about this man, who had played a vital part in the history of motion pictures for some thirty years. It was then that Donald uttered a challenge that consisted of only four words but which would change the course of my life: "You should do it."

However, doing anything about Clark's life had to wait for a while until there was space in my own. Three years later, while moving into another home, I came across the article I had written about my meeting with Donald, and I started to think again about Clark Gable. Phil Pianta, then the editor of *The Melburnian* magazine, provided valuable encouragement and unwavering faith that I could succeed, so I set out on my journey of discovery into the life of a legend.

There have been eight biographies published about Clark Gable, including one written by his last wife, Kathleen Gable, two books published about him and Carole Lombard, and two commentaries published about Gable's films. While some of these contain bibliographies, none contain notes as to the exact sources of information about Gable, so I have attempted here to trace as much of the story of his life as I could back to those original sources. This has not been an easy quest. Clark was the source of much legend even while he was still alive and, to be honest, he did his own fair share of promoting it. He would often rewrite his own autobiographical script, not necessarily for reasons of secrecy but more for the sake of providing an entertaining story. So, he would rarely recall events in his life the same way twice.

Possibly because so few Gable documents survived, the rumor began that Clark said very little about himself during his life and so, given he's no longer alive and that he left no diaries behind to examine, not much could be known about what went through his mind. However, although he was never interviewed at length on radio or television, Clark was interviewed by print media quite extensively during the thirties and fifties. He also spoke occasionally to his friends and fellow actors, few of whom, sadly, are still alive but many of whom, happily, left behind their memories in the form of interviews and published biographies. All these have left us, in fact, quite a legacy of Clark's thoughts and opinions.

I have set out here, then, to provide as much information as possible about the man Clark Gable, through his own voice and through the voices of those who knew him. I have sought to allow those voices to speak of him from their own point of view, and so not cast the shadow of an author's point of view too heavily.

While Clark was a man of his time, as most of us are, it would probably be more correct to say he was a man of his times. His acting career spanned over thirty years of motion picture history, including the introduction of sound, of color, and of wide-screen viewing, the development of censorship, the shift from shooting predominantly on an enclosed backlot or sound-stage to location shooting, and the rise and beginning of the fall of the big stu-

dios. So I have also placed Clark within the context of some of these developments, while trying not to lose focus on the man and his career.

I do not think that the definitive biography can ever be written of a life. Whether we are alive or not, we reveal ourselves over time to those who would discover us. There is always something else hidden in an attic, at the bottom of a drawer, in the corner of a basement, or on a dusty shelf at the back of a library archive that will allow the searcher to see more clearly through the dark glass. I would like to think that the information and references provided here will not be thought of as the last words on Clark Gable that can be written but that they may be a valuable signpost for future researchers. Reward us then, future writer, by using this material wisely to discover yet more about a man who became that rare combination of a king and a legend in his own time.

Chrystopher J. Spicer
Australia
August 2001

CHAPTER 1

BILLY THE KID

Frank Taylor, the producer of Clark Gable's last film *The Misfits*, once observed that "Clark Gable is a man de-classed. You can't guess in any way where he came from or what he was."[1] Certainly in 1960 most people didn't have to guess what Clark Gable was. To his peers and to his fans he was "the King" long before that title was applied to some slick-haired, swivel-hipped singer from Memphis. In theater since he was a teenager, and an Oscar winner at thirty-four, Clark wore his profession like one of his impeccably tailored suits. He had about him an air of success, of having reached the top of the heap and remained there, and of knowing that everyone was aware that was exactly where he belonged.

Women especially were aware. Clark was now married for the fifth time. His romances, whether fact or fiction, were already the stuff of legend. The story of Clark looking at a group photograph of MGM female stars one day and observing that he'd been to bed with them all was already in circulation. Now, as a fifty-nine-year-old married family man, women still found him magnetically attractive. On his way to *The Misfits'* Nevada film site, for example, he passed through Palm Springs and a waitress who served him there remarked later: "He looked so gorgeous, so

clean. He looked like chocolate melting in your mouth."[2]

Clark Gable didn't only look clean, he *was* clean. He showered several times a day, never using a tub because he couldn't bear to sit in dirty water. He shaved his chest and under his arms, and his bed linen was changed every day. He was invariably impeccably dressed in public. His suits and jackets were handmade for him at Dick Caroll's in Beverly Hills and at Brooks Brothers in New York, from where he would order them ten at a time. They were all arranged in his wardrobes by color and size and tagged with the purchase date.

For much of his career, he was one of the highest paid actors in the world. For the last part of his career he was *the* highest paid actor in the world. A cautiously wealthy man, he had most of his money sitting in bank savings accounts and tied up in percentage deals relating to his last few years of independent movie appearances, rather than investments in shares or property. Indeed, it was more than likely that anyone looking at this successful, confident and handsome man in 1960 would not have been able to guess from where he had come. That had been a very different place.

Clark Gable was born in Cadiz (pronounced KAA-dis locally), Ohio, a small town

Clark's reconstructed birthplace in Cadiz, Ohio. He was born on the upper floor of the original house that stood on this site. (Spicer Collection.)

of about three thousand. It hovers on the edge of the industrial belt of the Ohio Valley rather than on the plains of the Midwest, among oil wells, coal mines, and steel mills rather than corn fields and feed bins. Clark's family roots were not in this ground but, until he was twenty-one, Clark's life would be closely associated with something that was — oil.

His great-grandfather and great-grandmother, John Gable and Sarah Frankfield, had come west to Crawford County, Pennsylvania, from LeHigh County over near the Hudson River around 1825. Their forebears had probably migrated from Germany to America earlier in the eighteenth century. The Gables settled in Meadville, where John became a teamster hauling goods between Erie and Pittsburgh, and they eventually had seven children. The fourth of these was Charles Gable, who became a budding hotelier. He took over the Crawford House in Meadville in

1852 and then in March 1864, he purchased the Sherwood House, renovated it and renamed it the Gable House. Meanwhile, in 1857, he'd married Nancy Stainbrook. By 1863 Charles and Nancy had four children and were expecting a fifth, and they were in serious need of some extra room. So, they bought Charles' brother John's 170 acre farm just outside of town at the top of what is now known as Gable Hill, where they eventually rounded off the children at ten. William Henry Gable, Clark Gable's father, was the eighth child, born in 1870.[3]

Clark's mother was Addie Hershelman, a striking, dark-eyed brunette from whom Clark inherited his dark, wavy hair, his expressive eyes, and his determined jawline.[4] Her parents were farmer John Hershelman and Rosetta Clark. Like the Gables, Addie's Catholic descendants had also migrated to the area from Germany in the early nineteenth

century. Her grandparents, Jacob and Elizabeth Hershelman, had migrated to the United
States from their native Bavaria and then, in
1847, they and their four children had moved
from New York State to Vernon, Pennsylvania.[5]

The Hershelman family lost their
mother when Addie was seventeen, and as she
was the eldest daughter Addie took on the responsibility of caring for the children.[6] She
was still living at home in her early twenties
fulfilling her duty as the family's mother, well
on the way to being a spinster in those days,
when her life was changed by meeting Will
Gable. No one remembers how they met, but
it may have been through Addie's two
younger sisters Josephine and Mary who were
working around 1897 in the Kepler House in
Meadville.[7] Will regularly came back to town
to visit his family, and the sisters would probably have known or heard of this eligible
bachelor who was about the same age as
Addie. Perhaps they did a bit of matchmak-
ing.

Her father most likely had misgivings
about Addie's romance. Will had forsaken the
respectability of his family's hotel business
nearly ten years before for the adventure of
life as an oil-driller and wildcatter, probably
around the Titusville, Pennsylvania, area
where oil had been discovered. In this quiet
and conservative farming community, falling
for a wildcatter was the equivalent of eloping
with a riverboat gambler. Not only that, Will
was a Methodist and families around there
generally didn't mix religions. However, the
older Hershelman brothers had married
Protestant sisters, so at least Addie could make
some claim to precedent.

Addie had been plagued by a mysterious
illness lately, too, and it would have been only
natural for her family and friends to have
justifiable concerns about whether she could
cope with the physical strain of partnering a
man like Will and sharing his sort of life. Like
most of her family, but unlike Will, Addie was
interested in the arts and had shown early

*Clark's mother, Addie Hershelman Gable (1869–
1901), to whom he bore a close resemblance.*
(Harrison County Historical Society.)

promise of developing into an artist of some
potential. One story is that her parents sent
her off to Paris to study painting and hopefully
get Will Gable out of her system, only to have
her return after a year saying that her modest
talent did not justify spending more of her
family's money.[8] Against such odds Addie and
Will were married, probably early in 1900 because the census taken in June of that year
gives her years of marriage as zero.[9]

It was right about this time that oil was
discovered in eastern Ohio, and the richest
fields were found about twenty miles west of
the Ohio River in Harrison County, particularly on the John Bricker farm near Cadiz.
The nearest pool of experienced oil workers
was in northwestern Pennsylvania, and when
the news reached there with the speed of a
brushfire, across the state line they came in a

rush. By the second week of January 1900, there were five producing wells on the Bricker field with six more in the drilling.[10] Will Gable couldn't hold out any longer and joined the rush to Cadiz, a small county seat town on top of a hill where much the same number of people have always lived, where everybody knows everybody else, where it can be humid and hot in summer and below freezing in winter. To an older person it's the sort of town where you might want to settle down and stay; a younger person would more than likely want to get right on out of there to somewhere else.

Addie eventually joined Will later that year when he had found them both a place to live in a little house on Charleston Street, which led to the Bricker field. By now she was pregnant. Addie was very much in love with Will, but married life was not easy for her. Will was often away for days at a time with his oil-drilling equipment that he hired out. When he was home he tended to be uncommunicative and to drink quite a bit. The Gables got to know Tom and Jennie Reese, who lived in the lower-floor apartment of a two-story house across the street. Tom was a tool dresser and was soon often working with Will dressing bits for his drilling rig. With both their men away from home for extended periods, the two women quickly became good friends and Jennie looked after Addie as her pregnancy progressed.

Addie needed more care as her health declined, and she became a friend of the local doctor, John S. Campbell, a University of Michigan graduate and a skilled diagnostician with whom she could talk about painting and books. Concerned by her worsening condition, Campbell felt he had no choice but to advise her that she would be risking her life by having this child. She was thirty-one by now, and in those days that was mid-life and a dangerous age for a woman to venture into childbirth, especially for the first time. As a devout Catholic, Addie wanted to carry on, though. Perhaps she sensed that this child might be the only kind of future she would have.

Carole Lombard, Clark's third wife, would tell the story that once Addie had decided to go ahead she wrote and asked her sister Josie to come visit. When Josie arrived, Addie told her the happy news and of Dr. Campbell's fears for her survival if she was to have her baby. She then handed Josie a numbered series of eighteen letters that she had written to her unborn child, telling her that when the baby was old enough she was to read one letter to the child every six months. When the child was able to read, Josie was to give him one letter every six months. Addie was said to have made Josie swear to do this so that her baby would grow up knowing who his mother had been and of her hopes and desires for him.[11]

Demonstrating a feel for sensitive timing, the Gables' landlord chose this time to re-plaster the house. Fortunately the apartment above the Reeses was empty, and so the Gables gathered their few belongings and moved across the street into the top floor of the white timber house. Their new home consisted of three main rooms: a living room and bedroom at the front, each about twelve feet square, and a smaller kitchen area at the back with still smaller nursery and pantry rooms leading off it.[12] The only access to both front and rear doors, though, was by external staircases and as winter wore on and Addie grew heavier with her child, those steep stairs must have become more difficult to climb. With Will often out of town, Addie must have been largely confined to that apartment and to thoughts of her baby and its likely impact on her life.

Apparently she became so closely attuned to her unborn child that Addie felt when her baby was about to arrive. On the last day of January 1901, she told the iceman to leave extra ice in the box the next day because her baby would be born by then.[13] Sure enough, that night she went into labor. Fortunately, Will happened to be home and was able to hurry the short distance through a raging snowstorm to Dr. Campbell's house to fetch him for the delivery. It was a long and exhausting labor, and the hefty ten-and-a-half-pound boy finally arrived at 5:30 in the morning of February 1. Will would say later that "The kid, I always call him that, was a real he-man from the start. He was a regular blacksmith from the time he was born."[14] Already Will was thinking of his son's future, but it would be one over which he and his little blacksmith would sharply disagree.

Addie and Will settled on the name Clark, Addie's mother's family name, for their son. No middle name was recorded. Briefly, later in his life, he would turn Clark into his middle name by adding William in front of it. William Clark Gable did flow off the tongue a little more lyrically and perhaps it sounded more like a stage actor's name to him, grander maybe, more adult. Perhaps, too, combining names reminiscent of both his father and mother helped him feel connected to his origins at a time when he needed that foundation under his feet.

For some unknown reason, given that the Harrison County public offices were only a few blocks away, Clark's birth wasn't recorded until June 10 when the tax assessor made his annual call. Will might have had to leave town immediately after the birth to return to work, and Addie would have been too ill to venture down that flight of stairs in the middle of winter. When entering the baby's name in the register, the county records clerk first wrote both M and F in the gender columns, and then later crossed them out and re-entered M. Clark's entry is not the only one where this ambivalence occurs, and apparently the reason was that Dr. Campbell, who was delivering most babies in town at the time, had typically illegible doctor's handwriting. The clerk was unable to determine some babies' gender from the doctor's notes, and wrote in both to be on the safe side until it could be checked with Dr. Campbell personally.

As a baby, Clark already had his char-

Clark Gable's birth record in 1901. Both "M" and "F" were crossed out and replaced with "M."

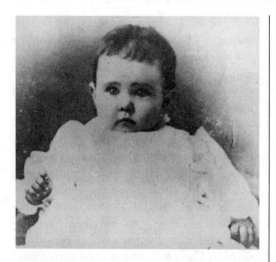

Clark Gable's earliest known photograph at eight to twelve months of age. (Harrison County Historical Society.)

acteristic broad hands and strong squared face with his mother's dark eyebrows and direct, penetrating gaze from large, sensitive eyes. He was able to sit up and do things for himself very early, and he was without doubt his father's pride and joy and the light of his mother's short life. Sadly, as her son grew bigger day by day, Addie's health rapidly worsened. Dr. Campbell visited her seven times during February. "She never did pick up after Clark was born," he recalled later. "She kept losing steadily." She was becoming weaker, was having convulsions and her personality began to change. Campbell eventually concluded she was suffering from a brain tumor, and in those days there was nothing anyone could do to prevent it killing her.[15]

In the spring the Reeses and the Gables moved into a duplex on Lincoln Avenue close to the train depot. The Bricker oil field was about finished and Tom and Will had to travel farther out by train now to find work. It was impossible for Will to care for his wife and their new baby full-time, and so Jennie Reese and a neighbor, Mrs. Hines, helped out.

Despite all Dr. Campbell could do,

Addie continued to deteriorate until her behavior became at times psychotic. While she was still lucid, Addie felt she had to do one last thing for her boy. Because there was no Catholic priest in Cadiz, a predominantly Protestant community, she had not been able to have her baby baptized. She pleaded with Will to have it done but the nearest parish was in Dennison, twenty-five miles away, and Will couldn't take the time off work needed to travel. A neighbor, John Conway, volunteered to take the baby over there instead, so Clark was baptized at the Immaculate Conception Church in Dennison on July 31 by Fr. Patrick M. Heery.[16]

As if she had been holding on until this task could be accomplished, Addie's mind now let go. Alarmed, Will brought his frail and confused wife back to her family in Meadville where she could receive the round-the-clock care she now needed, but it was to no avail. Although she rallied slightly for a while, the tumor kept growing and her convulsions and violent episodes increased in frequency. Finally she slipped away from them on November 14. Her grieving family laid Addie to rest by her mother in the little Chestnut Corners cemetery by the family church of St. Peters, in which she had sat on Sundays for much of her life. She was only thirty-one.

Once again, there was a delay in the recording procedure and her death was not officially noted until January 10, 1902, at which time her family also recorded Clark's birth in Meadville, apparently unaware it had already been recorded in Cadiz.

Clark, being the reticent person he was, tended to dismiss his childhood in a few words when interviewed later in his life. The few occasions when he did mention his mother seem to indicate a hardening of attitude about her as he grew older. In 1932 he said that whenever he thought of her, he had "a vague, sick feeling. She must have been fine. All her people were. My father told me she was beautiful and that she always talked of doing great things — some day. I wish I could have known her. I've always felt a great love for her, a sort of confused, helpless love for someone I owe everything to but have never seen."[17] Twenty-eight years later he was more dismissive, saying that he "never knew her. She was sick almost from the day I was born and she went back to her parents' home outside Meadville, Pennsylvania."[18]

The only person he might have talked to at any length about his mother was Carole Lombard, but unfortunately she died long before she might have told anyone what he'd said. Nevertheless, it would be a traumatic experience for any ten-month-old child to lose his mother under such circumstances. At that age Clark would have recognized Addie as his mother, yet not be old enough to comprehend why she would suddenly disappear. How does one explain the concept of death to a ten-month-old boy? It can't be done, of course, and has to wait until the child is older. In the meantime, what does a boy do with a vast sense of loss that he can't express because he doesn't have the vocabulary at that age?

Clark's answer may have been to internalize it all. That may go a long way in explaining

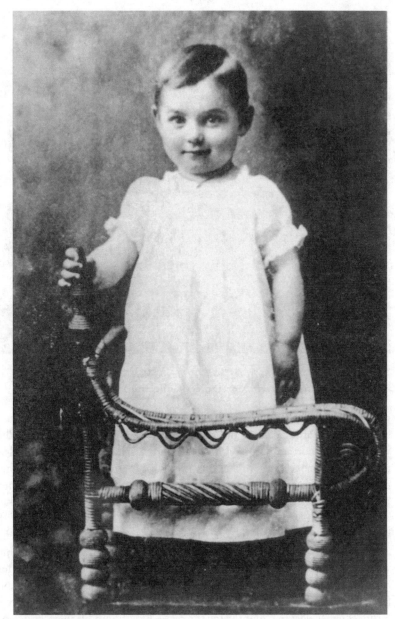

Eighteen-month-old Clark poses for a photograph with a dimpled smile that would later be famous. (Harrison County Historical Society.)

why he always seemed to be looking for a woman to take care of him. Indeed, he seemed to be unable to live without one. It might explain, too, why he referred to at least two of his wives as "Ma" or "Mother" as an affectionate name. The sudden loss of his mother and the sudden change in family circumstances that

The Gable family home built by Will Gable on Mill Street, Hopedale, Ohio, still looks much the same as it did when Clark lived there. (**Spicer Collection**).

resulted might also have caused him to lose his belief in the world as a safe and secure place, which is an important part of childhood innocence. He probably came to feel that the only constant thing in his world in which he could believe and trust was himself.

Will Gable was now faced with a problem. As much as he loved his son, his work as a drilling contractor was out in the field, which was no place for a baby. His own aspirations had taken him along the slow, grueling path from laborer to contractor, but he'd let his business go the last few months for the sake of his sick wife. Money must have been running low, and with no place of his own he had to make the difficult decision to leave his son behind while he got himself back on his financial feet again. So after the funeral was over he turned "the Kid," as he liked to call baby Clark, over to the care of Addie's family and left Meadville for Ohio to earn his living the only way he knew how.

Clark stayed briefly with Addie's sister Josie. Then, he was taken in by his uncle and aunt, Tom and Elizabeth Hershelman, who had no children. Will sent them about a hundred dollars a year to help out. By all accounts, they loved Clark as their own and he spent an idyllic few years on their farm.[19]

Ever looking for that oil well that would one day make him rich, Will washed up some time around late summer of the following year in Hopedale, only a few miles east of Cadiz, where he found lodging with the Dunlap family. Hopedale was experiencing its own oil boom by then, and new wells on nearby farms had drawn oil-men like Will to the town. Henry and Mariah Dunlap had five children — three boys and two girls — and Will developed a friendship with one of their two daughters, Jennie, who was about thirty-two and ran a successful business in the town as a milliner and dressmaker. Jennie was a tall, slender, gentle but strong-minded and independent woman who was always immaculately dressed. Indeed, one might say she was a walking advertisement for her talents and for her business. She could reproduce and be seen wearing the latest fashions first among the ladies of Hopedale.

Will was so impressed by Jennie Dunlap that he soon proposed, and they were married on April 16, 1903, in Hopedale.[20] Will wanted his family to be complete again and so, as soon as he could, he returned to Meadville to retrieve Clark. The Hershelmans, however, were reluctant to relinquish the boy to a father he hardly knew. Many tears were shed before father and son left to start their new life together.

Clark would come back often, though, to spend his summer holidays with his surviving grandmother Gable and grandfather Hershelman. Many years later he would still sense "a strange feeling of homesickness, a sort of unreasonable depression, whenever I have smelled the spicy odor of cooking tomatoes. It always calls to mind the picture of my kindly grandmother stirring a kettle of old-fashioned tomato ketchup over a coal-burning stove. I used to stand on a wooden stool and watch her.[21]

The Pennsylvania Dutch farmers took their lives, their work and their religion seriously, but where there might not have been a lot of laughter there was a lot of love for the young boy Clark. His grandparents rocked him to sleep, he would reminisce as an adult, "spanked me when necessary, did everything in their power to bring me up in the right way. I followed my grandfather wherever he went, lay under the maple trees, chased squirrels through the woods behind the house, learned to swim in the lake and slid down the warm hay in the big barn.[22]

Yet as the years went by these memories faded. Eventually, Clark would dismiss his childhood as having hardly been there at all.

CHAPTER 2

GROWING UP

If Cadiz was small, Hopedale was even smaller. Only about five hundred people lived there at the time. Even today it is still a one-store town you can drive around in about ten minutes. The new twentieth century before World War One, though, was a period of hope that matched the town's name, when it seemed possible that any small town might grow and prosper if only the right combination of events would happen. For a short time, with the discovery of oil on nearby farms, it seemed as though that right combination had happened. Will's drilling contracts took him near and far, from the wells on the nearby Spellacy, Irwin, and Stringer farms over to the Knoxville fields in adjacent Jefferson County and out as far as West Virginia. Hopedale had an efficient rail service that would take him away for the week and then bring him home on weekends. Once again, Clark embarked on family life largely without father.

Clark always referred to his stepmother as "Jennie Dunlap" rather than "Mother." On those later occasions when he did speak of his childhood to interviewers, which was rare, he remembered Jennie fondly as a wonderful woman whom he had liked immediately. "She was young and sweet," he said in 1932, "and she knew just the right way to treat a home-sick youngster. No real mother could have

been kinder or more affectionate than she was to me. She proved all through her life that I meant as much to her as though I had been her own. I think of her mighty often. You can't forget her type of woman. She was all goodness."[1]

Thirty-three years after those comments he still thought of her as a "wonderful woman who was very kind to me, a cultured and well-educated person. I was crazy about her."[2] He mused that "she must have loved me very much, because I was not a very nice little boy."[3] Clark was by all accounts quite a spoiled little boy; he was, after all, the only child in town with his own pool table. References to Jennie, though, were about the only mention he ever made later in his life of his extended family. As an adult, Clark spoke little of his childhood except to say how quickly he left it behind, never letting journalists forget that he'd left home at sixteen and, as far as he was concerned, had lifted himself after that by his own bootstraps. Few people would ever have known that Clark became part of a large family on his stepmother's side that took the young boy and his new mother into their home until Will could find a place for them. Jennie tried to make Clark's childhood as happy for him as she could, as if trying to make up for the sadness of his first year.

While working in West Virginia in August 1903, Will suddenly fell ill and returned home where he remained recuperating for a month. Perhaps that long period of rest gave Will time to do some thinking about providing for his family, because as soon as winter was over he purchased some land to build a home for them.

Clark continued to grow up as the center of attention in a house of doting adults. As such, he became more accustomed to receiving than to giving. At a time and place where few other children would have had such luxuries, Clark was dressed beautifully and was immaculately groomed. He had all the toys he wished, and at Christmas his stepmother would decorate a big tree for him and stack it with gifts. The Dunlaps were so proud of him they photographed him whenever they could. A photograph of him at age three in the Harrison County Historical Society shows a smartly dressed smiling boy in knickerbockers and stockings, wide collar over his cuffed shirt, peaked cap in one hand, and the reins of a wooden hobbyhorse purchased by Jennie's sister Mary Ella and her husband John held firmly in the other. Clark used to leave that hobbyhorse tied up to the bedpost at night. He was afraid of the dark, and the horse and a lantern comforted him.

That adored and cosseted childhood began its inevitable change in 1907 when Clark was enrolled for classes in the big, frame Hopedale schoolhouse right across Church Street from the Dunlap home. His primary teacher was Frances Thompson, popularly known as Aunt Fannie. She evidently saw a lot of potential in her new student, and she instilled in him an early appreciation of music and performance. He gave the recitation during the closing exercises of the 1907-1908 schoolyear, and he sang a solo and was in a duet for the exercises of 1909-1910. She recalled him as "one of the kindest and fairest youngsters I knew ... a very fine boy."[4]

Earning good money at steady work now, Will was once again prompted to do something about a home. In September, he finalized the purchase for $650 of a large, gently sloping allotment fronting Mill Street on the western side of Hopedale. Using the few days that he could spare when he wasn't working, Will was soon hard at work building the family home. Two years later they moved into their new, spacious, two-story, L-shaped timber house with three bedrooms upstairs, a gable roof, a wide front porch, and big bay window. It must have been a wonderful house for a little boy to be raised in, with lots of room to run around and full of smells from Jennie's cooking that would have drawn him into the kitchen to sit at the table, watch her, and talk.[5]

Will would typically arrive home from work on a Saturday afternoon, and then start to get reacquainted with his wife and son. Whenever Will picked up some extra money from a job, he would buy some special treat for Clark such as his bicycle, then a pool table. He would have to work at scrubbing all that oil and grease off his skin so he could look the part of Sunday School superintendent at the Hopedale Methodist Church. It didn't give him a lot of time to establish paternal authority around the house, but he soon found out that the quickest way to make Clark behave was to call him a sissy. In return, Clark figured that the best way to be when his father was around was invisible. Poor Jennie probably spent a lot of the weekend trying to help the two find enough common ground to get along with each other.

In 1910 Clark progressed to grades four, five, and six of the Intermediate Department under Miss Emma McMillen. She was a teacher who insisted on nothing but the best from her students, and Clark's response was to give the best performance he ever gave in school, although he was never wildly enthusiastic about the experience at any time. Even so, he finished sixth grade first in his class and was named a Scholarship Honor Pupil.[6]

Jennie always tried to help Clark learn at home, too. She read to him, taught him to sing, and tried to teach him to play the piano.

***Clark, champion hitter and second baseman, in the 1908 Hopedale Elementary School class photo-
graph. He would have been in the second grade.*** (Harrison County Historical Society.)

Jennie wanted to be sure that Clark would have the tools at hand by which he could discover the joys of learning for himself. She persuaded Will to invest in seventy-two volumes of the *Library of the World's Best Literature*, the complete works of Shakespeare in thirteen volumes, and then the *History of the Bible* in sixteen volumes! Clark evidently never read any of them in front of his father; years later Will told a reporter, "They were all in a bookcase right in front of him, but I never saw him open a single volume."[7] Then again, Will wasn't home all that much. Clark certainly did develop a love of literature as the years went by, eventually acquiring quite a sizable library in his house at Encino. Myrna Loy noted that by way of celebrating at the end of movies they had been working in, she and Clark would share a bottle of champagne and he would read poetry to her, "usually the sonnets of Shakespeare. He loved poetry and fine literature, and read beautifully, with great sensitivity, but he wouldn't dare let anybody else know it."[8]

This dichotomy was typical during Clark's childhood. Will taught him to swim in the local swimming hole, to fish, and to hunt and shoot expertly. He was proud of Clark's self-reliance. In his own way, Will loved his son very much. When Clark was ill, it was Will who went out and bought him the bananas he asked for. When a dog followed him home one day, he allowed Clark to keep it as a pet. Jennie, on the other hand, sent her stepson to music lessons when he was twelve where he learned to play the mellophone, or sliphorn, a type of French horn used in marching bands. Soon he could play that horn with such skill and sureness that he was invited to join the town brass band the following year. Clark recalled later how he swelled with pride when the audience applauded after his first performance and the band-leader, John Kyle, signalled they could take their bow. Clark thought, though, that "the audience should have taken the bow. They'd been through more than we had."[9] By now, people

Clark and his stepmother, Jennie Dunlap Gable, c. 1909. (Harrison County Historical Society.)

Clark standing proudly behind the drum of the Hopedale Brass Band, c. 1912. (Harrison County Historical Society.)

tended to forget Clark's age, because at nearly six feet tall and 150 pounds he was about the same size as everyone else in a parade.

Clark began to find his feet. He took part in athletics, played on the baseball team, and took part in the occasional school concert. He showed no signs of being shy about stepping forward in public unless his father was in the audience, and he had good reason. Will showed up at one performance in which Clark sang in a duet of "Silver Threads Amongst the Gold," and all he had to do to embarrass the boy after that was to hum the tune or incorporate the words of the title into whatever he was saying.

Clark never saw himself as popular. As a young boy, he probably felt about as awkward as he often looked. His first attempt to tell young Marjorie Miller that he liked her ground to a halt in a bout of nervous laughter and hair-pulling. "As a social light," he later admitted, "I didn't shine very brightly. I was an awkward, overgrown boy who never was quite sure what to do with his hands or feet. I liked girls, but I was afraid of them. I used to envy the boys who could walk up to

them and laugh and talk without blushing or stammering."[10]

Still, he was popular. Marjorie Miller, remembering that he would dare the girls to walk the railroad trestle with him, said: "Did I take that dare? Every time. I wouldn't miss it. And I remember one night we all decided to go buggy riding. There was a big snowstorm going on... . We came down a steep hill, the front wheel came off the buggy, the horse reared, and we all fell out in a snowdrift. Anyway, I sat on Clark's lap during that ride."[11] Clark's best friend was Andy Means, who was four years older and the son of the owner of the local Means Hotel. As youngsters in a small American town early in the twentieth century, Clark and Andy and their friends Lucille Kyle, Thelma Lewis and her brother Tom, Marjorie Miller and her brother Francis, Bill Henry, Mable Bell, and Daphne Reed probably rode bikes together, went fishing, had sodas at Jolley's Drug Store, and met up at church socials and parties.

Clark completed grades seven and eight of his schooling at the Hopedale Grammar School, an imposing two-story building with

A confident, relaxed Clark in his first year at Hopedale High, ninth grade, 1915-1916. (Second from right, second row from front. Thelma Lewis is second from the right in the row behind him. Tommy Lewis is next to Clark on the left. George Dunlap, superintendent, is first on the left in the back row.) (Harrison County Historical Society.)

a belltower, on the hill behind their house. The eighth grade was as much education as most Hopedale children got, but Jennie and Will had bigger plans for Clark and in September 1915, he enrolled as a freshman at Hopedale High School.

That year, Hopedale High had twenty-eight students, eight of whom had enrolled in Clark's year. There were three teachers, one of whom doubled as the principal and another as the superintendent.[12] It was a small group where everyone knew each other, helped out, and worked together. Pretty, redheaded Thelma Lewis often found herself helping Clark. In 1961 she recalled that "Clark was my first date. He was not particularly good-looking. His ears were too large. He was very lazy about school work. He would never do his homework, and I practically put him through his freshman year in high school by letting

him copy my Latin and algebra assignments."[13] Like most of us, Clark did well when he felt like it and badly when he didn't. As probably will happen to many of us, too, his school records survived him and show that he tended to swing from average scores to high scores from month to month. Among his subjects were math, English, Latin, and history, but his highest grades were in spelling.[14]

Thelma and Clark appeared together at the old Patton Opera House in Hopedale in at least one of their fellow classmates' dramatic productions, *The Arrival of Kitty*. Thelma played Kitty; Clark, in his first acting role, was a roustabout. She remembered him having a very good voice.[15]

Clark felt comfortable with the sound of words, so much so that despite his father's efforts to convince him that the quickest way to win an argument was to hit someone, he

Clark, in sunglasses, hanging out with friends at the Hopedale Depot. Marjorie Miller sits between him and Tommy Lewis. Thelma Lewis is on the left. (Harrison County Historical Society.)

preferred to talk his way out of trouble rather than fight, according to Andy Means, who later recalled that Clark also had the loudest voice of anyone in their neighborhood.[16] Despite his size, Clark was never a violent man. He preferred attempting to reason with someone, even if sometimes his reasoning could be a little short, sharp and one-sided, but being so big so early he rarely had to fight to get his opinion across. He was never afraid of other men. By his thirties, Clark had developed an air of assurance along with his size that seemed to imply a "rightness" about him and what he did. He would remain a man respected by a public in whose eyes he could do no wrong, nor would anything he wanted seem deniable.

Not that Clark ever expected people to give him anything. His father impressed a work ethic on his son very early that would stay with him. Clark always believed in earning his way in life. His first job was at age twelve earning fifty cents a week as a delivery boy at the local flour mill and, even as a wealthy man, he was still working a few days before he died.

In 1916, Will contracted to drill a well just outside of Hopedale. It meant he was at home during the week for the first time since he and Jennie were married. He'd been mostly traveling by train, but now he was working so close to home he bought himself a car. Just like any teenager would, Clark begged his father to teach him how to drive. His father recalled, "we went out where the road was wide and there wasn't much traffic and I put him behind the wheel. I put my arm around him to help drive but there was no need for that. He drove right off and that was the only driving lesson he ever had."[17]

For a while, with both parents home, Clark was happy. Then later that year, with little warning the safe ground of Clark's world shifted beneath his feet again. First, his close friend Andy Means announced that he and

The Gable farm at 3150 Alliance Road in the late 1960s. The house still looks much the same as it did when Clark lived there. (Courtesy of Wallace and Mary Ann Wagner.)

three other boys would be leaving in August to find work in the rubber factories of Akron. Life around town was never the same after they had gone, and as he drifted through the latter part of his tenth grade Clark's absences from school became more frequent. Rumors began to circulate that he was involved in an affair with a much older woman.[18] Jennie would naturally have been worried about her son and about the effect such a scandal would have on the family's reputation if these tales proved true.

The family was having enough problems as it was. Perhaps becoming a bit over-confident with the success he'd had so far, Will had made the mistake of going into a business deal over his head. He'd gone into partnership with two other oilmen as Hugas, Sutton, and Company to drill a well near town. Unfortunately it turned out to be a dry hole and Will lost everything — money, credit and equip-

ment. Nor was there much chance of him finding work on another rig anywhere near Hopedale now, either; the oil boom had passed by and been replaced by coal mining. Will and Jennie could see their family being attacked and, as families often do in such circumstances, they drew their wagons into a circle and considered their options. Will had no drilling equipment now, but even if he did the journey to find work would take him further away from his family than he probably wished to travel. Perhaps he thought that farming ran deeply enough in the ancestral veins for him to give it a go. Reluctantly he and Jennie realized they would have to sell their beloved home in order to raise sufficient money to invest in a farm somewhere up in northern Ohio, closer to the countryside with which Will was familiar. Perhaps out of loyalty to his family, Clark never mentioned these problems in later life. He always claimed doctors

Clark dressed in his Sunday best, at about seventeen, sitting on the front porch of the Alliance Road farmhouse. (Harrison County Historical Society.)

had advised his mother to move for her health.[19]

The Gables sold their Hopedale property in August of 1917 for $2900[20] and a few weeks later purchased the seventy-four acre Ensinger farm some seventy miles north near Ravenna, Ohio, just outside of Akron.[21] Clark and his mother were moved in by September 17 when he started attending grade eleven classes at Edinburg Centralized High School, only about three miles away. Serving the local township area, Edinburg High was a small school enrolling, with Clark, a total of 24 students that fall in grades nine, ten, and eleven. There were fourteen boys and ten girls aged between thirteen and seventeen. Clark was listed as being seventeen years old, but that was because they mistakenly wrote in his birthdate as 1900.[22]

Clark's life changed abruptly. There would be no more parties, church socials, or hanging out at the soda fountain with his friends. Mr. and Mrs. Ensinger continued to live in the farmhouse with Clark and Jennie, introducing them to how the farm worked and helping with the cooking and chores until Will could wind up his affairs in Hopedale and join them. They remembered Clark many years later as a big, quiet boy who loved caring for the horses on the farm, riding one the few miles to school at Edinburg.[23] Jennie joined the local church where she loved to sing in the choir, sometimes walking down the aisle and encouraging the congregation to sing with her, and she occasionally managed to persuade Clark to come with her and attend Sunday school. Clark commented in 1932 that he had loved being on the farm during those days with his stepmother because it had reminded him of his grandfather's farm back in Pennsylvania.[24]

Once his father arrived and the Ensingers moved out, however, Clark had to help around the farm when he got home from school and on the weekends, and he found coping with this new life in a new place increasingly difficult. Neighbors noticed that he always carried a lantern whenever he went anywhere at night, as if afraid of his own shadow. He would have been accustomed to a fairly comfortable middle-class life in a small town where he had lived most of his life, and it would have been very hard for him as a teenager to suddenly be uprooted and transplanted into a close-knit rural community. Self-consciously bigger and taller than his classmates, who would have had their own established cliques, the new boy in town had understandable problems with feeling accepted at Edinburg High. His absences increased from a couple of days in October to five during November, although he maintained a grade average of 81. At the end of November his name was stricken from the school roll.

For the next few weeks he worked with his father around the farm, leaving Clark with vivid if slightly exaggerated memories of "getting up at four in the morning every day of the year, spring, summer, fall, winter, and the winters were sure cold. I fed the hogs and the rest of the stock, plowed in the spring till every muscle ached, forked hay in the hot sun until I was sweating an impressive mop of calluses. I did what I was expected to do on the farm, but it takes a certain knack for farming in the old-fashioned way. I just didn't have what it takes."[25]

It wasn't that Clark didn't like hard work; he was to take on manual labor of one sort or another for a number of years yet. Even in later life it would have been difficult to find an actor with a more rigidly defined work ethic. Clark was all too aware, though, that life on a farm had its limitations. "I don't know where I'll end up," he declared to his friends Ralph and Carl Byers, "but it won't be here in Yale!"[26]

That Christmas, Clark returned to Hopedale to stay with the Dunlaps. He decided to remain there for a while, and took a job at the nearby Harmon Creek Coal Company hauling water for five dollars a day. It gave him time to do some thinking about his future. By the time he returned home in April of 1918, Clark had decided to join Andy Means in Akron in the fall.

Rubber has been the life-blood of Akron since Benjamin Goodrich set up his factory there in 1871 to take advantage of railway and canal junctions. With the rapid development of automobile production and the sharp escalation in the need for rubber goods during World War I providing an unprecedented industrial boom, Akron became known as the rubber capital of the world. Between 1910 and 1920 the city's population soared from 69,000 to 208,000, the greatest population growth during that period of any American city of over one hundred thousand people. During that same decade, rubber company employment jumped from twenty-two thousand to seventy thousand. Tire plants such as Miller, Firestone, and Goodyear lit up the sky twenty-four hours a day in a beacon that drew country boys into town from as far away as the southern states like moths. So many men came from below the Ohio River that the city became known as "Akron, the capital of West Virginia." The factories ate up labor as fast as it could be found; Goodyear alone was employing some thirty thousand people in 1920, and an experienced hand could make a fortune. By 1916 the rubber plants were paying thirty cents an hour to raw beginners and five to seven dollars an eight-hour shift to men who had been there a month. Factories worked three shifts, and some men would finish work in one plant and rush over to another plant in time to work the next shift.[27] Andy and then Clark figured it was high time to go to Akron before opportunity passed them by.

Although Jennie saw Clark's point of view, Will would have none of it. He thought that Clark would be more secure working on the land. The two men argued heatedly for weeks without budging an inch, each man's stubbornness only increasing that of the other. Jennie stayed on Clark's side though, and she eventually persuaded Will to let him go.

So Clark set off for Akron, probably like many other young men before and since, with nothing but a suitcase and the clothes he wore. Although he would visit a few times, he never went back home to live. He rarely returned to the town where he was raised, nor would he maintain ties with any of his family, with the exception of his father. His Aunt Ella would comment sadly many years later that "when John got so sick, I tried to get word to him but nothing happened, so the church and the neighbors had to tend to John's burying, and then take care of me. I've been sick just about ever since John went. Clark should have answered, with his own folks that brought him up needing him so much.[28]

But Clark had set out on his journey, and he never looked back. As a young boy, he had never given away many clues as to his choice of future career. Townsfolk were later mystified when he became a movie star. They remembered a quiet, unassuming, only child whose doting stepmother called "Clarkie."

Chapter 3

The Player

For many years, so the story goes, Clark held onto the boyhood dream of becoming a doctor when he grew up. This idea was supposedly planted when, at age eight, he had a run-in with a farm wagon. He had to have the gash in his head stitched, and to take Clark's mind off what was going on, the doctor showed him what he was carrying around in his black bag.[1] If he did have such a dream harbored within him, then it's more than likely that Clark would have seen going to Akron as the chance to do something about it at last. He'd have a better chance of finding a good job at which he could earn enough money to support himself while he studied part-time. Perhaps these were the dreams that went through his mind as his train pulled out of Ravenna on the first part of his journey toward a new life.

When Clark's train arrived at Union Station in Akron, Andy was late to meet him. So, there in the hub of the biggest city he'd ever been in, Clark sat and waited. "I had been warned of confidence men and city women," he recalled later, "so I put my suitcase between my feet and waited with wary vigilance. That hour in that strange station was the longest in my life. After all I was only sixteen, and it was my first trip away from home alone."[2]

Accustomed to the fresh air of the country, he would have been assailed by Akron's distinctive odor. "Boy, that smell of Akron!" Vicki Baum would write of her arrival at the same place. "It was the first thing that hit me square in the face when I came out of Union Station that morning; it's a funny smell, warm and sweetish and burned, and sticks to you like green rubber.... Seems they hadn't even had time to put in a decent sewer system, and you could smell that too ... the whole town was a jumble with too many folks crowded in, sweating, swearing and pushing each other out of the way."[3]

Andy soon arrived, though, and it must have been quite a reunion. It had been a while since the boyhood friends had seen each other and there must have been lots of news to discuss. Andy had located somewhere for Clark to room, too, and that would have been no easy matter. Due to the stampede of newcomers into Akron, predominantly young, single males, there was a profound shortage of living space. When you found one, a rented room could cost you between eight and fifteen dollars a week, some 40 percent above the going rate in other larger industrial cities. Many rooming houses operated on the same three-shift basis as the factories—when one worker rolled out of bed another rolled in. The situation was no better for families. Houses could not be built quick enough and basements, attics, garages and chicken coops were being hurriedly fixed up and rented for up to eighty dollars a month.[4]

Andy had found Clark a room at 1163 Getz Street with a family from Hopedale, the Williamsons. Clark was quickly accepted for a clerical position that paid ninety-five dollars a month in the time-keeping office at the Firestone rim plant. When the Williamsons eventually needed more space, he moved around the corner into the home of Lewis and Emily Grether, at 24 Steiner Avenue. Clark and Lewis, a pharmacist for the Haun Drug Company, eventually became quite friendly and would go fishing together. Clark would often hang out at the Haun drugstore on the corner of Main and Miller and help out behind the soda fountain counter.[5]

Clark may have been so busy keeping the wolf from the door that he never did enroll in studies as he had intended. One persistent story about Clark's early days was that he attended pre-med classes at night at the University of Akron.[6] For many years, his entry in *Who's Who in America* claimed that he had been educated at the University of Akron, and his father once stated that "he took a business course at night school at the University of Ohio (Akron)."[7] However, no evidence has been found that Clark was ever there.

Rather than women or education, Clark unexpectedly heard the call of another voice altogether — the theater. According to the writer Jim Tulley, there was a young actor named Eddie Grisdale working in the factory who struck up an aquaintance with Clark. Finally finding work in a play production at the Akron Music Hall, Grisdale handed in his notice.[8] Thinking there was a mistake in the hours for which he was collecting pay, Grisdale asked Clark if he could check the timesheets. Clark duly located the error and a grateful Grisdale promptly offered him a free ticket to the play and a backstage tour. So, that Saturday night Clark took his friend up on his generous offer and found himself seated in the Akron Music Hall watching the Ed

Clark Lilley–Pauline McLean Players performing *The Bird of Paradise*, Richard Walton Tully's romance about an American who falls in love with a native princess on an Hawaiian island. He eventually abandons her there and she commits suicide by leaping into a volcano. Needless to say, melodrama like that left hardly a dry eye in the house. The show with its tropical atmosphere, beautiful music, and seductive dances, had been popular wherever it played for some years.

Clark was entranced. He'd never seen anything so wonderful. It was as if lightning struck him right there on the spot. Perhaps he heard echoes of his brief childhood appearances on the school stage, or perhaps he saw a future that offered him an escape from the limitations of life in Ohio. Whatever went through his mind that night, Clark emerged from the darkness of that theater walking down an entirely different path than the one on which he'd walked in.

No matter which path he was on, though, he still had to eat. By the following year, Clark hadn't been able to persuade Firestone to raise his pay and so he left them to work in the time-keeping office of the Miller Tire and Rubber Company. Whenever he wasn't working, he haunted the stage door of the Music Hall. He even took to eating in the same diner in which the actors ate, and eventually he got to meet some of them. They introduced him to Pauline MacLean and her husband, leading man and troupe manager Ed Clark Lilley. From then on, they couldn't get rid of Clark who just kept hanging around backstage, willing to run errands and help with odd jobs. He always claimed later that he became the company's unpaid callboy. However, when Lilley was interviewed many years later he could recall that only once, maybe as a favor, they let Clark walk on to the stage carrying a spear.[9] In any case, that was all Clark needed to hear his calling. "I thought I'd die as I waited to go on," he remembered later. "When I didn't fall on my face, I thought I was an actor. It was all over then."[10] At all of eighteen, Clark had discovered what

Clark (far left), aged about 18, with fellow workers in the powerhouse at Miller Tire and Rubber, Akron, Ohio. (Photograph courtesy Lokken family.)

he wanted to be and nothing, not even chronic shyness and the self-doubt that he fought for most of his career, would ever change his mind.

Then, in November of 1919, Clark received the traumatic news that his stepmother's health had taken a turn for the worse. He left for home immediately. When he arrived, Clark and Will took her to the hospital but there was little the doctors could do. Her illness was diagnosed as incurable. Clark had to go back to Akron, but he returned frequently to visit until Jennie died on January 11, 1920. "Clark would come up every week to see her," his father said later. "Nobody can say that he wasn't good to his mother."[11] One of her last wishes was that the minister from Hopedale conduct her service, so Clark made the lonely journey to get him before Jennie was finally laid to rest in the Palmyra Cemetery. After it was all over, Will tried to persuade Clark to stay on, but he had no interest in farming now. He headed back to those precious footlights in Akron as soon as he could. Distance also probably helped him deal with his grief and great sense of loss. He would tell

writer and friend Adela Rogers St. Johns in 1932 that he thought Jennie was "the finest woman who ever lived ... with a great understanding of humanity. The gayety and beauty and joy of life came into our home with my stepmother. No matter how hard she worked, she always had time to laugh and sing and play. I didn't have any brothers or sisters, but she was like all three combined. Mother, brother, sister, and friend. I loved her."[12] As Will was to say many years later, "He filled her life and she filled his."[13]

By the beginning of 1920, the rubber industry boom was fading fast. Hundreds of workers were being laid off as production demand fell, and Clark and Andy were among them. Andy went home, but Clark stayed on and found work selling shirts and ties at Gates and Kittle's haberdashery and clothing store across the street from Haun's. Then he was laid off from there too, and times really got hard. He lived from day to day, picking up whatever work he could find, still hanging around the theater.

Will couldn't run the farm by himself

Jennie Dunlap Gable's grave in Palmyra cemetery. Will was eventually buried in California. (**Spicer Collection.**)

working in the theater, and it was mostly unpaid work at that. Will basically maintained that attitude for most of his life, even when Clark was earning big money. Will never really accepted Clark's career choice. "To the day he died," Clark once said, "my father could never get it through his head that acting was honorable work for a man. Even when I was making seventy-five hundred dollars a week, he stubbornly kept saying, 'What kind of a job is that for a fellow six feet tall, weighs 195 pounds?'"[14] For many years, Clark would continue to try and prove himself to his father. When asked how he felt after the successful 1932 premier of *Strange Interlude*, for example, Clark said that he was "wondering what my old man thinks of me."[15] Clark kept wondering and kept looking for that approval, but Will Gable would refuse to be impressed even when his son was the idol of millions and a wealthy man.

While Will stayed in Akron with his son for a few days, they had a photograph taken that survives today in the Harrison County, Ohio, Historical Society. There they are, standing shoulder to shoulder, dressed in their best suits. Clark is already noticeably taller than his father, with his mother's sleepy dark eyes, slicked-back hair that only accentuated those big ears that would cause so much later comment, and just a trace of a smile in the set of his mouth. His father's face with its penetrating gaze is set closer, sterner. Perhaps Will already knew he would have to admit defeat and catch the train for Tulsa alone. From there, he eventually ended

and regretfully had to put it on the market, but it didn't sell until spring. It must have been a long and lonely winter for him there with nothing but shadows and memories for company. Then in April it was sold. He was free to do what he knew best, and in 1920 the place where oil was bubbling out of the ground was Oklahoma.

Before he went south, Will stopped in Akron to try to persuade Clark to come with him. Clark had other plans, though, and attempted to explain to his father how his new-found career wouldn't possibly allow him to join Will on this new venture. Will could hardly believe that his big, handsome son who was going to be his future partner in his search for "black gold" was throwing his life away

Father and son, William and Clark Gable, photographed in Akron in 1920. (Harrison County Historical Society.)

up in a little Oklahoma town called Big-heart.[16]

That summer the Roaring Twenties were only whispering in Akron. There were so many people out of work the city was one long breadline, and Clark struggled to survive. For a while he ran errands and did odd jobs for the stock company, but even they were starting to feel the pinch and in mid-summer they moved on a few miles south to Canton. Clark wasn't invited to join them. With no prospect of steady work as summer began to cool, Clark must have felt his back up against the wall.

At this point, Clark may have decided to sink all the money he had left into one last try at theater work. There was certainly nothing happening in Akron, and so Clark may have decided to try for the place where things might still happen for him: New York and Broadway. Clark would later tell the story of how he got there to find he could only get odd-job work until he was hired as a callboy for a production of *The Jest* at the New Plymouth Theater, which opened September 19, 1919. Produced by Arthur Hopkins and starring John and Lionel Barrymore, the play ran for 179 performances. Clark used to say that it was through knocking on their doors with five-minute calls that he got to know the Barrymores, an aquaintance that would figure in his life a few years later. But after the run was all over, Clark would have been out on a very slender limb with no visible means of support.[17]

Neither Will nor Clark were men who ever readily admitted they had changed their minds about something. Both had reputations for being stubborn as mules. A friend of Clark's once said, "Clark inherited from his parents all the basic characteristics of the Germans. He was stubborn, methodical, immaculate, a perfectionist about his work. His father was the same way."[18] Typically then, when asked later in their lives about how Clark ended up working in an oil-drilling outfit with his father after being so adamant he wouldn't, both men claimed it was the other who instigated the move. Will's story was that Clark wrote him saying that he was on his way and that one day he just showed up and asked if his father could get find him work as a tool dresser, a driller's helper. Times were slow then, Will said, and that work wasn't to be had, but he found him work doing odd jobs around the drilling outfit.[19] Clark told

Joe Hyams in 1956, however, that Will wrote *him* saying that if Clark wanted to be an actor, Will would find him work, and that when Clark arrived his father had found him a job as a student tool dresser.[20]

In any case, Clark found himself at the end of 1919 in Bigheart, Oklahoma, doing just what he had always sworn he would never do, but discovering in a very hands-on way just how his father had supported his family all these years. Work around an oil-drilling rig was ugly, dirty, and physically brutalizing as the well pumps clanked and sucked around the clock. Crooked gamblers, con men, thieves, and whores were attracted into town by the smell of oil and money. Bars erupted into fights fueled by bootlegged booze that left men dead on the floor. The only good thing about it all was that if one became proficient at the tool-dressing trade, wages were a dollar an hour. It must have seemed like a nightmare to Clark, who could remember that time as clear as yesterday forty years later:

> It was a rough business. There were no geologists then. A contractor, like my father, would find a likely place, get someone to finance him and begin drilling a hole. We worked twelve hours on and twelve hours off. There was a sleeping tent and a cook tent and we had two men on each twelve-hour shift. The beds in the sleeping tent never got cold. I'd get up at midnight, and in the freezing cold I'd have to climb a rickety eighty-five-foot wooden tower in the driving wind, to oil the bearings on the rig. There was no light and it was pitch black, and even in World War II I was never so scared.
>
> In addition, I had to chop wood to keep up the steam in the boilers which were some distance away because if we hit gas or oil the fire would ignite it and we'd all be blown to bits. From time to time I had to "dress" the seven hundred pound bit which was drilling the hole. My job was to get the fire going and then, after the driller heated the bit to a white heat with a bellows, he'd tell me he was ready — a dresser wasn't supposed to know anything — and I'd have to swing at it with a sixteen-pound sledge-hammer to sharpen the cutting edges. I worked like this seven days a week, eight or nine weeks at a time.... I kept saying to myself, "There must be a better way

of making a living," but I didn't know how to go about it at the time.[21]

Clark started work weighing 165 pounds, but he soon muscled up to around 200 pounds. It was a hard-drinking, violent life amid mud and oil, which must have felt as if they were ingrained into one's very soul after a few weeks. It would have all been a shock for Clark, who hadn't had any on-site exposure to his father's work before, and he came to hate the dirt, the cold and the hostility of the local townsfolk towards the oilmen. "They paid me $12 a day," he said later, " but I would have been glad to trade it for my nothing-a-day job as callboy and general utility actor with the stock company. I hated the work, the place, and the people. I longed to get out of the Oklahoma desert country. But I stuck it out for a whole year."[22] There was that stubborn Gable pride again.

A completely unexpected windfall undoubtedly helped Clark stick it out. On January 30, 1921, his beloved grandfather John Hershelman died and, in time, the news reached Clark that John had left him three hundred dollars in his will.[23] That was a substantial sum in those times, even for someone with a steady job. It must have seemed like the windows of heaven had suddenly opened. The bad news was that Clark couldn't have the money until he turned twenty-one, according to the conditions of the will. Until then, a long year away, the money had to be held in trust with Will as executor. Having access to that much money at one time would finally give the young Clark the chance to break away from the oil-soaked life in which he was becoming mired.

Work wasn't always waiting for an oil-drilling contractor and his team, though, and Clark had to find other employment to supplement his income. He worked as a garage mechanic at fifty dollars a week, then as a sales assistant and book-keeper for a clothing store in Tulsa until he was laid off after five weeks. Then his father, who seemed to think that having Clark working in hell would make a man of him, found him work in an oil refinery cleaning stills. Once again, it was the sort of work which would have made an indelible impression on anyone's memory, as it did on Clark's:

> There is a certain amount of deposit, like asphalt, that settles in the bottom of those stills. You have to go in there and take that out. They let the boilers cool for twelve hours. You can stay in there for about two minutes. In two minutes, if you don't come out, they go in and drag you out. In a gang of eight men you start work every sixteen minutes. We cleaned out storage tanks too. You go in with a pick and shovel and they tie a rope around you. One man would go in at a time. I don't know how they work it now but then we'd work until we felt faint; it wasn't very long before you'd go hysterical....[24]

Will thought their companionship was the best thing ever and was really proud of his son. Clark's pride was all that kept him there. As 1921 drew to a close, his light at the end of this dark tunnel became his grandfather's legacy that would be waiting for him to collect back in Meadville on his twenty-first birthday. First, though, he would have to tell Will that all those dreams of working with his son were in vain because Clark intended to go back to acting.

The violent argument that ensued between the two equally stubborn men was ugly. Will could not understand why Clark didn't want to be in the same line of work; after all, in a job where strength and physique mattered, Clark had both to such a degree that he'd earned the respect of his father and workmates. Not only that, but in a period where jobs were hard to find, there was always work of some kind to be found in the oil industry. All Will could see was his crazy son giving everything away that his father had tried to set up for him. Clark, on the other hand, had briefly caught a glimpse of another life that beckoned him on, and nothing was going to stop him from reaching for it now. Will even offered to set Clark up in a clothing business that would be sure to profit in a busy oil town, but nothing would deter Clark from his course. In his typically understated way, all he would say about the confrontation in later years was that "we parted, not too friendly."[25]

So unfriendly was the parting that the two men would neither speak to, nor meet, each other again for many years. Seven years later Will was in San Angelo, Texas, about one hundred miles from Houston, where Clark was playing stock that summer. When one of his friends asked him why he hadn't gone over there to meet his son, Will replied that a hundred miles was a long way to travel just to see a show.[26] In 1932, ten years after that, Will would tell a reporter that the reason they still had not seen each other was that "We are both independent and it has just happened that our paths have gone in different directions. He has never asked nor expected anything from me and I never ask or expect anything from him. But we think a lot of each other."[27]

On February 1, 1922, Clark duly showed up at the courthouse in Meadville to collect his twenty-first birthday present of three hundred dollars. The man who left town soon after that now preferred to be called Billy Gable. He'd experimented with using different versions of his name before, signing himself W. Clarke Gable back when he was twelve, and appearing on the Edinburg high school roll as Clarke Gable a few years later. Perhaps this time he really wanted to emphasize his break with a part of his life; in any case, suffering a name like Clark among an oil-rig crew had probably given him a lot of incentive to change it.

The young Billy Gable seemed to inherit some of his father's restlessness and yearning for something better in life. However, where Will Gable saw his future in a Quixotic search for that one well at the end of an oily gusher, Billy Gable had seen just enough of the wider world through Jennie Dunlap's eyes and some schooling to search for more to satisfy needs of which his father would never be aware. In

the short time he'd hung around the Music Hall in Akron, Billy Gable had been given a brief glimpse into another world, a fairy-tale Arabian Nights just out of reach where he could be clean, where people would notice and respect him, where he'd have a regular job and salary, and where a small-town boy could become big-town rich. To a guy with nothing, that was something worth climbing a mountain for, and Billy Gable was a very determined climber. For many years, nothing and no one would be allowed to get in his way.

Having heard that traveling tent shows were hiring in Kansas City, which was the jumping-off point then for shows heading through the Midwest, Billy caught a train there and was hired by a show to work as stagehand, stablehand and roustabout for ten dollars a week. He also played cornet on street corners in a band with the other troupers to help drum up the townsfolk's interest in *Uncle Tom's Cabin, Camille, Hamlet*, or whatever they thought would pull a crowd in that night. "That was the most God-awful thing," Clark later recalled. "We used to climb into old clown suits and stand on the corner playing *Marching Through Georgia* to get them in."[28]

By late March the show was trapped by heavy snow in Butte, Montana, until the spring. As the snow melted away so did the troupe, who after a few weeks in such close quarters together probably had cabin fever and were only too ready to part company. Billy had become friendly with Phil, the pianist, who it turned out had an uncle in Bend, Oregon, so they rode boxcars for over three hundred miles only to find that the uncle had left town.

Once again Billy was cold, broke, and jobless in a strange place. Eventually he found work in a lumber mill, another hard, tough, physically brutal job he would never forget:

> I got a job piling green logs. Probably the toughest work I ever did. The logs were rough and heavy and I should have worn special gloves with leather palms, but I couldn't afford them. I'd tie into that lumber, and it was like

grabbing hold of sandpaper. I developed cuts in my hands and they'd get all stiff and they'd crack open. I'd almost go crazy from the pain. But I'd read somewhere that Jack Dempsey toughened up his hands by soaking them in salt water and vinegar and alum, too. That worked — until I got my first pay check and was able to afford a pair of gloves."[29]

He stuck it out until he had enough money to take him to Portland, where he found a much quieter job demonstrating rubber-lined neckties in the window of Meir and Frank's department store. He'd roll them up into a ball in his hands and then show passersby that the ties hadn't wrinkled.

Billy soon discovered he had lots in common with a young, handsome salesman there named Earle Larimore, who came from a long line of theater people. One of his aunts was Laura Hope Crews, a famous Broadway character actress whom Billy would meet many years later playing the part of Aunt Pittypat in a film called *Gone with the Wind*. Not suprisingly then, when he wasn't working behind a counter, Earle was directing and performing with a local theater group known as the Red Lantern Players. They were working on a production of *Nothing but the Truth*, and once again Clark attached himself to a theater troupe like glue and soaked up experience.

When Earle was offered a lead character role with what would become the Astoria Players Stock Company, Billy tagged along to the auditions. It was there that he met the very attractive Frances Doerfler, or Franz Dorfler as she preferred to be known. During that summer of 1922, Franz would come to symbolize a number of loves for Billy — love for love itself, love of the theater, love for the future. Unfortunately, all that love would still eventually leave Franz wondering if Billy had ever really loved *her*.

CHAPTER 4

FRANZ DORFLER

When Charles Samuels, author of *The King*, met Franz Dorfler in 1961, she was a sixty-two-year-old woman living alone in a house by the sea. She had probably not seen Clark for perhaps twenty years, and Clark had walked out on their romance nearly twenty years before that. Yet, Samuels says, "Miss Dorfler glows whenever she thinks about it. Her untroubled hazel eyes and her whole face light up with the enchanted smile one usually finds only on young faces."[1]

Franz never married after Clark left, and she wasn't the only one upon whom Clark had a similar effect. Josephine Dillon, his first wife, never married again, and neither did his second wife, Ria. All the women in Clark's life remained incredibly loyal after he had loved and left. Not one of them ever said a vindictive thing to the media about him or acted revengefully, yet Clark was never shy of informing a woman when he'd seen enough of her. On the whole though, Clark was gallantly polite and treated women with a lot of respect. In the early stages of his career, he was very willing to learn from the women he met.

In the summer of 1922 Franz Dorfler was, at twenty-two, slightly older than Billy. She countered her five feet, two inches with an elfin beauty, big bright eyes and a smile, and she wore her curly dark hair in a stylish bob.

Raised in a large and prosperous farming family in Silverton, Oregon, Franz had been convent educated and grew up a happy, loving girl, full of fun, who revealed an early liking for dressing up and play-acting. It was little surprise to her family when she rejected their suggestions to become a high-school teacher to pursue a career in the theater. For a while she had worked with small theater groups in Salem and other cities in western Oregon, and she had come to Portland to work as a chorus girl in the Lyric Theater. Then she had seen the advertisement for the stock company auditions.[2]

North of Portland, at the mouth of the Columbia River, is the port town of Astoria. A Scotsman there named Kirk McKean owned the Astoria Theater. He thought it was high time that Astoria had exposure to some culture. When he read of the Red Lantern Players' success with their latest production, he traveled to Portland to talk with Earle Larimore about being the leading man in a stock company McKean wanted to form. He'd already selected a director-manager named Rex Jewell, but he offered Larimore some chance of directing as well.[3] Larimore jumped at the chance, and tryouts were quickly scheduled to select the rest of the group that would eventually be known as the Astoria Players Stock

Company. Franz auditioned and was invited to join them, as was Larimore's sweetheart, Peggy Martin, as female lead, Dorita Cordero Jewell, Lucille Schumann, Perry Silvey, and Charles C. Chinn.[4] Poor Billy, on the other hand, couldn't read lines to save himself. Rex Jewell later recalled that "I had not the slightest desire to add him to the company. He seemed to me to lack the slightest gift for the stage with nothing, absolutely nothing, to offer either then or in the future. If anyone had suggested that Gable would one day be a great film star, I would have regarded them as either joking or mentally unbalanced."[5]

Apparently very taken by Franz from the moment he saw her, Billy had offered her a drink while she was waiting to go on. When she refused, he offered to walk her home. She again refused, but he waited for her anyway. "I didn't like him at first," she later wrote, "I thought him aggressive. But I had been raised in a convent, and although I loved it, I learned nothing about the world. I had never had a beau that I cared about before, so I resented him a little initially. But he was always as nice as he could be. A little forward, but charming."[6] They soon hit it off, though, and became close friends. Franz had never had so intense an admirer. Unlike his later, more confident, "I can have any woman anytime" approach, the young Billy was less sure of himself and so was more possessive and jealous. Within days he was professing to Franz that he loved her like no one else, and that he would leave town forever or even commit suicide in despair if Franz refused him.

Quiet and shy Franz had never had so much single-minded attention focused on her by a suitor, and she was quite swept off her feet. She couldn't help but love this young ardent dreamer too, and she surrendered to all the emotions that his words and attention aroused in her. So there was something akin to panic in the air as the time approached for the group to leave, and Rex Jewell still showed absolutely no inclination to take Billy along.

Finally, in desperation, Franz enlisted the help of their mutual friend Earle, and they both knocked on Jewell's door and pleaded Billy's case. Jewell, seeing that Franz and Billy were hopelessly in love, eventually relented under the combined onslaught and agreed that Billy could join them. So the small company of actors set sail for Astoria down the winding Columbia River aboard the old stern-wheeler *Bailey Gatzert*. Billy brought with him his only Brooks Brothers suit and a spare white shirt with French cuffs in a Gladstone bag. According to Franz, "He always wore French cuffs, even when he was penniless. For having so little, he always managed to look immaculate. I could never understand how he did it."[7] As the paddlesteamer plowed steadily downriver, the excited young actors looked out on riverbank scenery that had changed little from pioneer days. There were still towns for which the steamboat was the only access, stopping to pick up passengers and mail and dropping off stores and food, and there were still acres of virgin forest stretching along the mist-shrouded riverbanks. In such a romantic setting it seemed only fitting that love would be in the air. Earle was with his leading lady, Peggy Martin, and Billy and Franz were growing closer every day. The lovestruck foursome probably wouldn't have minded if the steamer had just kept sailing clear out to sea, but eventually it pulled into Astoria.

Old Cinderville, as Astoria was sometimes called by the locals, was first settled as Fort Astoria on the south bank of the Columbia River by a party of John Jacob Astor's fur trappers in 1811. Two years later, the British occupied the town. It was handed back to America in 1818, only to be burned to the ground three years later and largely abandoned, except for a few hermit trappers. In 1836 the writer Washington Irving immortalized the place in one of his books and it never looked back, becoming a deep-water port center. Astoria had reached its peak by 1922 with a population of fifteen thousand, predominantly of Finnish descent, mainly occupied with fishing or lumbering. Because immigration officers had been unable to spell the Finnish names, one of the local quirks was that about five thousand of the men in the town were called John Johnson. Another of the local quirks, that Finns are notoriously thrifty and hate to part with money, was one to which the Astoria Players management really should have paid attention.

Evidently in an attempt to make the troupe look more impressive than it really was, McKean and his partner Joseph Kelley gave a story to the local paper that there were more actors on their way from Los Angeles, but that they had been involved in a car accident and were delayed.[8] So, on the night of Saturday, July 15, 1922, the curtain went up before three hundred and fifty people on the Astoria Players' opening-night performance of the three-act comedy-drama *It Can't Be Done,* directed by Kelley. The night was going fine until partway through the second act when all the lights went out. The audience began to get restless and some booing and hissing started, so the quick-thinking McKean went onstage with a candle and kept everyone amused by singing Scottish songs. Silvey and Chinn followed him with some vaudeville until the desperate backstage crew got the lights working again, and the show went on. Despite all that, the following day *The Morning Astorian* showered their performances with compliments.

During the next two days, though, McKean began to hear rumors that the blackout might have been a hint from Astoria Light and Power concerning a certain outstanding bill that Kelley should have paid. When pressed on the subject, Kelley was far too quiet; the next morning he'd left town with all the takings. McKean called the actors together and suggested that the best way to work this out would be for them to all be paid on the basis of an equal division of whatever they would take in ticket sales.

George Lanigan didn't like the sound of the risk involved in that idea, and he left for Portland while he still had ticket money, leaving them one man short. There had been one extra man all along though, and an overstressed Rex Jewell had little option but to throw Billy Gable in at the deep end and give him what may well have been his first speaking roles on a stage since childhood.

On the following Wednesday night, the Astoria Players started a run of a piece Jewell called *Bits of Life.* It was made up of three one-act plays: a farce called *Are You a Mason?* a drama entitled *Dregs,* and a send-up of the old melodrama *The Villain Still Pursued Her.* In the first play Billy just had a walk-on, but in the second he was a detective, and in the last he was Billy Dressuitcase — a baby! As the biggest baby that audience had ever seen, he brought the house down.[9] The next Sunday and Monday, Jewell directed them in *When Women Rule,* starring Peggy Martin as the first woman mayor of Astoria. Billy played the part of Eliza Goober, the Negro cook. Once again the company received a favorable review.[10]

Meanwhile, Billy and Franz had been growing closer as they enjoyed each other's company. "He began to depend on me," Franz wrote later. "He seemed insecure because of past hardships, financial troubles, and had to be reassured that he was liked. Once he confided to me that his mother had died of epilepsy, and he was afraid of having inherited the disease."[11] Jewell would regularly threaten to fire Billy when he'd trip over a loose floorboard — or just his own feet — and stumble onstage or forget a line and fumble. Billy would get depressed for a bit, but then he'd put himself back together and keep working, usually with Franz's help. She thought it was so wonderful to have met such a kindred actor spirit, and felt that she was falling more in love with Clark daily. They couldn't bear to be apart from each other for a minute.

On Thursday they began a run of the well-known play, *Corinne of the Circus,*[12] in which Billy was the village doctor. The players' work was, said the local reviewer, "one of the finest bits of work that organization has presented since arriving in this city."[13] That night the actors actually found themselves taking curtain calls. They must have finally felt they were hitting their stride at last as an ensemble company.

For a while, it probably seemed a bit romantic to be starving artists, as the actors tried to carry on with only a trickle of money coming in. By this time they were rationing food and even going without meals. The ones they had were mainly of salmon given to them by kind-hearted fishermen and cooked by Mrs. Jewell. Occasionally, one of the prop boys would steal a few cans from the local market to try to keep them going, but it couldn't last.

On Sunday they started a run of *Blundering Billy*, in which Billy Gable, now billed as William Gable, had a part as an old sea captain. Ominously, few people came. On Wednesday, August 2, they had the opening night of their next play, *Mr. Bob*. William Gable took the role of an uncle from Japan. When they counted out the takings that night after the show, there was only enough for each player to receive $1.30.[14] It was the end. Sadly, Jewell had to tell the group that they couldn't go on any longer. Even worse though, the acting troupe was so broke that they were now stranded without even boat fare back to Portland.

The ever-resourceful Rex Jewell came up with a plan B. If they could give him a week, he proposed, he would organize venues in some towns so that they would be able to pay their way back upriver by touring another play. The actors agreed, and so they decided to re-group in Seaside, about twenty miles away on the coast, where they would be able to stay with Lucille Schumann's mother. When they arrived, however, they couldn't all fit in the house, and so they had to take turns sleeping indoors while the others wrapped themselves in blankets and slept around a campfire on the beach.

Franz recalled that one day, while she, Billy, Earle and Peggy were idling around the waterfront, a fortune-teller told her that her boyfriend would go much farther than Earle.

"He has something wonderful inside of him," she predicted, "something that others cannot see."[15] When she rejoined the others and told them what the woman had said, they all laughed. After all, at the time Earle was the one showing all the promise. The only reputation Billy had gained so far on the stage was for tripping over either his own feet or his own tongue.

Jewell did finally pull some rabbits out of a hat and succeeded in organizing their tour back up the Columbia River to Portland, playing *Corinne of the Circus* again in many of those little towns that they had passed so full of dreams and promise only a short time before. To minimize costs they would travel on the milk boats, the cheapest form of transportation there was. These were little more than barges that made shuttle runs up and down the river, picking up the milk cans that the farmers left out on the piers. The actors would have to sleep out on deck because there were no cabins. Even in these desperate times though, love flourished. Before they left Astoria, Billy and Franz announced their engagement. She wrote home that she was going to marry "Mr William C. Gable, an actor."[16]

However, much to everyone's dismay, Dorita Jewell decided to return to Portland ahead of them. Then Earle Larimore received an invitation from his aunt, Laura Hope Crews, to join the Jesse Bonstelle Stock Company in New York. It was regarded as one of the best companies in the country for young actors to train with and was a chance not to be missed.[17] Peggy Martin was heartbroken but not too heartbroken. Billy was sad but not that sad. As the only male actor without an allocated role, he would be a shoe-in for Earle's role of Joseph Amrocia Jones.

So the hardy little group of surviving actors set off back up the river, determined to bring *Corinne of the Circus* to whoever would sit still long enough to hear it and, of course, pay them some money for the privilege. They began their journey by crossing the Columbia at Astoria to the Washington side where they played in Ilwaco. Then they travelled upriver to Cathlamet, where Billy became the subject of much audience mirth when he stopped in the middle of his big love scene with the dying Corinne to allow some noisy lumberjacks, who had come in late, to find their seats. A couple of days later, the actors boarded another boat and steamed upriver again to perform in the Oregon town of Clatskanie. It was early fall, and nights on the river that far north quickly got cold. Franz and Billy took turns sleeping on one of the benches by the ship's rail so they could share Billy's coat. Franz grew worried about his health, which was deteriorating after months of hand-to-mouth living. "There was so little money in those days that we often had to choose between pie and soup for our meals when we could afford it," she later recalled.[18]

Love prevailed though, as it always will. Billy forgave her for burning his one spare shirt with the iron and showed her how to bleach out the burn with peroxide, explaining that it was an old trick a hobo had taught him. Despite enduring what must have been a very hard time, Franz remembered only that they were so happy, "We were almost oblivious to much of the bitterness. We were always together. And in recollection, it seems that Billy behaved much as a schoolboy in love for the first time. I found it hard to take a walk by myself without having to explain to him where I'd been. It felt strangely wonderful to be loved so passionately."[19]

Mr. Jewell was a never-say-die showman who tried everything he could to draw crowds. Ilwaco was nearly one hundred percent Finnish, so he bought Finnish hats and costumes in which the cast dressed for their performance. In other places, he prompted the audience to come up onto the stage and dance after the show. He'd usually manage to persuade the local ladies to put on refreshments for that evening's audience. On those nights the cast didn't mind at all if the numbers were down; that meant there would be all the more to eat for them.

Despite all they could do though, business stayed poor. The final blow came at Kelso, Washington, where Jewell had staked everything on a two-night run. What he did not know was that Kelso was in the middle of a war with the neighboring town of Longview. There had been murders, burnings and libel suits and, the night before they had arrived, a mob had broken into the Kelso church and locked out the pastor. With such melodrama freely available right out in the main street for all to see, very few people showed the slightest interest in seeing it being acted on a stage.[20] So, tired and hungry, the little group of actors finally straggled back into Portland, bankrupt in body, soul and pocket.

Even so, Clark retained fond memories of that period and of Earle Larimore. In a 1934 interview with *The Oregonian*'s Hollywood correspondent, Marie Canel, he said,

> I'm always trying to recapture some of the fun and the thrills I knew in those days. It was a carefree existence ... with a great deal of freedom and not too much thinking about tomorrow. If I had beans and doughnuts one day that was swell; whether I'd have them the next day didn't seem to matter....
>
> Believe me, Earle and I knew what the word "struggle" meant.... When I dunked doughnuts in the picture *It Happened One Night*, no director had to teach me how to do it. I knew blamed well, maybe too blamed well — I was an expert.... Earle and I often talked about successful actors, but it didn't dawn on either one of us that we'd ever amount to anything.[21]

On December 8, 1922, Old Cinderville lived up to its name when another fire wiped out a large section of the Astoria business district, including the Astoria Theater. It was about the only thing that hadn't happened to the actors while they were there and seemed a fitting symbol for the demise of the Astoria Players.

By the time they arrived back in Portland, Franz was still worried about Billy's health. He had lost a lot of weight skimping on meals, and his skin had taken on a decidedly unhealthy yellow color. Franz may well

Clark outside the music studio he and Franz rented in Portland in 1923.

have thought this would make an ideal excuse to bring him home to meet her family. They had never really approved of her choice of career, but they hadn't been able to talk the independent young woman out of it either. She was just chasing rainbows, they thought, and would soon come to her senses. So, having another actor in the family was not something to which they were really looking forward, and they awaited Billy's arrival with some misgivings. Billy's charm and high spirits won them over, though, despite them being a little startled by his uninhibited kissing of Franz in public.

To Billy, it must have felt as if he was back on the Hershelman's farm in Pennsylvania where he had spent so much time as a small boy. The Doerfler farm covered hundreds of rolling acres, with the big farmhouse the center of the family's life. Billy soon got his

healthy color back wandering through the fields and woods with Franz. They'd climb trees, leap into the haystacks, and wade in the streams. For a while, they were able to forget the dark side of the world that they had so recently endured and be carefree teenagers.

Feeling secure in this familiar environment, Billy begged Franz to marry him as soon as possible, but his level-headed fiancée was all too aware of the problems that they faced. For one thing, while her parents' attitude toward Billy had certainly improved, they still did not like the idea of their rainbow-chasing daughter marrying some penniless actor they hardly knew. For another thing, Franz couldn't see any immediate advantage in being married. She'd just had an all-too-recent taste of what it would be like for a couple of poor actors to eke out a living, and it was still a little bitter in her mouth. She wanted to be better established in

her own career before plunging into a partnership. Some ten years later she was to reflect in
some very modern words that "I just couldn't
make up my mind to marry him. When a girl
has a career in the back of her mind, she thinks
of marriage as something to be indulged in if
the career fails."[22]

Three weeks had drifted by in a haze of
dreams and dandelions when Franz decided it
was time they earned some money. So she
found Billy, her Aunt Pauline, her sister Bertha
and herself, work hop-picking a few miles
away near Independence, and she made sure
they took books so Billy could resume studying. Soon after they got back, Billy and Franz's
younger brother Fritz left for the coast to help
build a logging railroad along Haloff Creek,
near Brighton. They worked at clearing trails
and carrying the chain for a surveying team
from one of the eastern universities for a few
weeks, until they were forced into town by the
on-coming winter.

Billy's plans of Franz waiting around
while he made enough money to get married
took a beating that November, when she announced she was moving to Portland. She had
decided to move in with an older married
brother while she took singing lessons there.
Besides, as she no doubt pointed out, it wasn't
any farther for Billy to travel there to see her
than it had been for him to go to the farm.

With the money from his job with the
surveying team in his pocket, Billy could
afford to check into Room No. 5 at Mrs.
Charity Scott's Cottage Hotel on Silverton's
Main Street shortly after Thanksgiving 1922,
while he looked for more work. Relying on
his past experience, Billy did the rounds of the
timber companies. On December 5, he started
as Worker 243 with the Silver Falls Timber
Company loading rough lumber for shipping.
It paid three dollars and twenty cents an eight-
hour day and that month he earned sixty-five
dollars for his twenty days work.

The only work clothes Billy had were the
jodhpurs and riding boots he'd worn in
Corinne of the Circus. Needless to say, this un-

usual outfit drew some comment from the
tough Swedes who crewed the mill. Instead of
trying to hide or taking offence, Billy defused
the situation by making them laugh with
clowning around and imitations of them complete with exaggerated Swedish accents. That
he could get away with it says something
about his infectious, good-humored personality; these were big, dignified men who usually
took themselves and their work very seriously.
They promptly christened him "Billy the ham
actor."[23]

For a short time, Franz would come back
to Silverton on the weekends, and Billy would
walk the eight miles out to the farm to see her.
However, within a few weeks, Rex Jewell
offered Franz a job with a new musical company he had put together that was about to
leave to tour the Northwest for the next few
months. Billy was upset; it would mean they'd
be separated for Christmas. Franz was elated;
it was the break she'd been waiting for. They
promised to write every day.

They did, too. Sometimes Franz would
find two or three letters waiting for her that
had been posted on the same day. He would
write how lonely he was without her, and she
would write back how lonely she was without
him. Billy wasn't beyond occasionally consol-
ing himself with some female company at the
town dances though, and he soon gained a bit
of a reputation for his dancing and the attention he would shower on even the plainest girl
there.

Billy spent Christmas with the Doerfler
family on their farm. Between Christmas and
the new year, bad storms halted the mail trains
and he and Franz were out of touch for over
a week. His letters, when they finally caught
up with her, were full of hurt and certainty
that she had forgotten him. Franz quickly reassured him that he was never far from her
thoughts.[24]

Billy quit his work at the mill late in January of 1923 and moved to Portland, where he
found a job for eight weeks selling advertising space over the counter of the classifieds

department of *The Oregonian*. He later said that his main reason for taking the twelve dollars-a-week job was that he would be first to read the employment vacancies as they came in.[25] His plan paid off when a job came up as timekeeper for the local telephone company, Pacific Telephone and Telegraph. Billy was able to be the first one on their doorstep to get the job which kept food on his table for most of the remainder of his time in Portland.

Franz figured it was time she got Billy's mind back onto the stage, and so she convinced him to study voice by way of singing lessons with Lawrence Woodfrin. By June, Woodfrin considered Billy had progressed enough to give a Sunday concert at the Portland Hotel. As her sister Bertha was getting married that same week, Franz made the trip from Seattle, where she was currently playing, to hear Billy. He sang traditional songs like "Mother Macree" and "Mighty Like a Rose." His audience of mostly elderly ladies, who seldom missed these free concerts, were thoroughly charmed by his warm, rich baritone and applauded enthusiastically. Eleven years later, Clark commented that it was an experience he didn't think he would ever forget.[26] Franz wouldn't forget it either. "I thought I would burst with pride," she recalled. "This time when he asked me when we were going to be married, I answered 'at the end of the year.' We spent every moment together before I had to return to Seattle."[27]

Dazed with joy, Franz then unknowingly steered their little boat towards a waterfall. A few months later, a friend mentioned to Franz that a well-known Broadway actress and drama coach, Josephine Dillon, was going to start a theater group in Portland. Franz dashed off a letter to Billy right away, urging him to get in touch with Dillon as soon as possible about joining this group.[28]

Billy was as enthusiastic as Franz about the whole idea, especially when Dillon agreed to interview him. She listened to his audition, and then she told him the blunt truth. If Billy wanted to work with her, he would have to

start all over again. His acting until now had been with all the highly exaggerated movements and facial gestures used for stage melodrama that, incidentally, were also adopted from there for silent movies. To become a serious actor, Billy would have to do more than just learn lines and emote. He would have to learn control. He was, she told him, starting late in life to learn acting. If she was to accept him as a student, he would have to be totally committed to his study. She left him with no illusions about the big gamble they would both be taking and that she could by no means guarantee that they would win.

Billy took her at her word and plunged headlong into the theater life for which he had wished so long. At last, he wrote to Franz, people were taking him seriously as a student actor, and he poured out his hopes and dreams to her. This was the turning point in his young life, and Franz was really happy for him. It was the last time she would experience such happiness with Billy Gable, for she had introduced the man she loved to her nemesis.

Dillon knew that acting was about being physically fit as well as mentally alert. Billy still looked thin and sallow from his rough time on the boards with the Astoria Players, and so she put him on a special diet and sent him to a ranch on a vacation to restore his health. He probably did some pretty deep thinking while he was out there, and he may well have realised that it would be a long time before he could hope to provide for Franz after they were married. He would have to be totally focused on his acting study, and being married would only distract him from that single-minded devotion to his career that he was rapidly developing. For an instant, he and Franz had been at the same place in their lives at the same time, but just as quickly they had passed each other and their positions were becoming reversed.

Billy's letters to Franz now came farther apart, and she began to worry; it wasn't like him. She wrote him that she was coming home for Christmas and that they could be married

Franz Dorfler in the early 1940s.

starting a new life with Franz, Billy had decided to devote the next few years to studying acting with Josephine Dillon. He felt that without Josephine's help he would never get anywhere. Franz was in shock. "That shattered me," she later recalled. "I felt great physical pain. Unable to answer him, I quickly turned and ran away. The next four days, I could neither eat nor sleep. I would burst into tears each time my brother or sister-in-law tried to talk to me. Wanting to only die, I withdrew to the security of my parent's farm."[29]

Amazingly, Billy called the tortured woman on New Year's Eve to apologize and say that he wanted to marry her after all. They met again, but Franz could tell this was all about his sense of obligation, not about his feelings for her. Billy was just going through the motions to appease his conscience. She informed him that under the circumstances she thought it would be better if they officially broke off the engagement. Billy seemed relieved; after all, now he could feel that it was her doing, not his. He trotted out some lame story that a doctor had told him he couldn't get married. Franz said that she didn't think she would ever get married either. She never did.

then just as she had promised, but her assurances were already too late. She arrived in Portland on Christmas Eve and hurried to meet Billy at her brother's house, where there was a party. To her dismay, the reunion that she had been anticipating for so long was decidedly cool. She started to tell Billy about all her wedding plans, but he stopped her to say that even though he never would have believed this could happen, he really didn't feel the same way about her any longer. Rather than

CHAPTER 5

THE APPRENTICE

Born in Denver in 1884, and thus seventeen years older than Clark, Josephine Dillon was a slight, gentle, determined, and industrious woman from a family of six children.[1] She was educated in Californian public schools, then in Europe, finally graduating from Stanford University in 1908 at a time when few women had done so. Her father, Judge Henry Clay Dillon, became a district attorney credited with helping to shape state legislation protecting women's property rights. Her mother, Florence Hood Dillon, was prominent in local Southern Californian cultural life and presided over an eighteen-room homestead on the forty-acre Dillon ranch.[2]

After graduating, Josephine studied stage acting in Italy for a year. She eventually became quite a well-known actress in New York, and for a year was the leading lady of British actor Edward Everett Horton's stock company on Broadway.[3] Perhaps she then began to feel the strain of stage work, or maybe she felt she had gone as far as her talent could take her. In any case, Josephine apparently decided she would follow in the footsteps of her sister and take up coaching. It was while she was working at that in New York that a fellow teacher who had a studio in Portland persuaded Josephine she would do well there. So, Josephine packed her bags and traveled right across the country to Portland, where she rented a large old house and industriously converted the lower floor into a theater-studio and the upper floor into her apartment. She placed advertisements for her "school of the theater" in the local paper. Soon, the Little Theater, as it became known, was popular and fashionable with wealthy, cultured patrons.[4]

It was there in her Little Theater that Josephine Dillon met and began to work with the man who would change her life so drastically. In 1940, long after Clark had slipped out of her life, she wrote a book called *Modern Acting* in which she described the man who had walked into her studio nearly twenty years before as having "the furrowed forehead of a man who is overworked and undernourished. He had the straight-lipped, set mouth of the do-it-or-die character. He had the narrow, slit-eyed expression of the man who has had to fight things through alone, and who tells nothing."[5] They seem to have had little in common except driving ambition; he to learn everything he could necessary to become a successful actor and she to make a name for herself by turning him into one. She may not have counted on falling in love with him in the process, but she did, and by all accounts she remained in love with him for the rest of her life.

Though Clark might have been the man

41

who told nothing, Dillon did tell something in her own quiet way some sixty years later, four years after the love of her life had died. In 1964, Dillon's cousin Belva Hall became concerned about the elderly lady's health and persuaded Josephine to move in with her. She recalled later how proud Josephine still was of Gable when she would see him in a movie, and that she would talk about how hard she had worked to make that "big lug" picture material for the world to enjoy. "Josephine really loved Clark Gable," Hall said. "She carried a torch up to her dying day for him. That was her one and only real love. She always kept the very young picture of Clark in front of her, and she loved that until she passed away."[6]

Clark, on the other hand, seems to have been very ambivalent about his life with her, to say the least. When he talked in interviews about his early days, Clark was open about the struggles he had gone through, but he would never mention Josephine nor the help she had given him to survive those times.

Belva Hall noticed that Josephine always carried around a manuscript she was working on that she never let out of her sight, even sleeping with it under her pillow. When she left Hall's house for the hospital, Josephine knew she would never be back, and she gave the manuscript to Belva for safekeeping. This manuscript, which was eventually shown to writer Lyn Tornabene, recounted the story of a relationship between a young drama teacher named Julia Hood and a young actor named Mark Craven. Bearing in mind that Hood was Josephine's mother's maiden name, there appear to be remarkable parallels between Josephine's fictional characters and events and what evidently happened between her and Clark. As Clark never talked about this period at all, Josephine's voice speaking through that of her manuscript character Julia may be the only inside view that we have, however filtered, of the working relationship that became the first Gable marriage.

On the other hand, this also means that it is virtually impossible, given the lapse and the toll of time since these events, to distinguish between fact and fiction in much of this manuscript. So, while certainly interesting, the story that Josephine tells through Julia should be taken at its face value and not necessarily confused with fact. After all, by the time she wrote these words, Josephine would have had every right to be a very bitter woman as a result of Clark's apparent lack of love and appreciation for her. Perhaps she was letting her own opinion of Gable's actions at last be heard by naming her character Craven — a coward.

Josephine uses the device of having a reporter interview Julia Hood while seeking information about Mark Craven's background, which provides context and enables her story to be told in the first person. Julia tells of how a physically awkward but confident mannered Mark Craven joined her theatrical study group in Portland. This first night Julia's group is going to read *The Contrast* by Royall Tyler. As she talks to them about the early days of American drama when this play was written and performed, she notices that Mark Craven is entirely absorbed in what she has to say. Leaning forward intently, he seizes on every word as a chance to satisfy his hunger for the theater. "I looked at him then," she remembers, "really looked at him for the first time and I thought, "I will help him. I will give him my booklearning, and acting knowledge, and speech and a voice. This is the one!"[7] And so Julia, drawn like a moth to a flame, makes the decision that will change the course of her life. When Craven stays back after everyone leaves and asks if he can come over tomorrow to talk about acting, she agrees.

The next evening, the door bursts open and in he strides, hands in pockets, coattails flying, snap-brim hat pushed back on his head. He proceeds to pace up and down Julia's floor talking about his dreams of becoming a succesful actor. As she answers his questions, Julia is impressed by the force of his desires, his courage, and the strength of his will. She also feels a warmth around her heart.

Inexorably, Julia is drawn into a relation-

ship with Craven that grows more intense as he becomes absorbed in acting
and she becomes absorbed in him. He
quickly demonstrates his new skills at
the Womens' Club by giving a recitation of a long dramatic poem about a
starving poet who has lost his love and
welcomes death. The ladies adore both
the poem and the presenter. Billed as
William Gable, Clark did actually give
such a recital of Henry Murger's "Bal-
lad of Despair" with musical accompa-
niment for Portland's MacDowell Club
one Tuesday afternoon late in 1923.

As her coaching progresses, Julia
continues to be pleasantly surprised by
Craven's thirst for knowledge and
quick grasp of the principles she
teaches him. So quickly does he absorb
everything, in fact, that she soon tells
him she is sure that the time has come
for him to journey to the heart of his
dream, to Hollywood. Julia makes the
decision to close her studio and go on
ahead to Los Angeles to arrange everything.
Before she leaves, she arranges for Mark to
work with a stock company in Portland until
he can follow her out to the West Coast.

Josephine Dillon did arrange for Clark
to work with the Forest Taylor Stock Company in Portland before she left in the summer of 1924. Given her shrewd knowledge of
the arts scene in what was then a small city, it's
quite likely that Josephine was aware that it
was the same company with which Franz
Dorfler had been working for some months.
She may also have been aware that Clark had
remained in touch with Franz, much to
Franz's astonishment, at the same time as he
was keeping company with Josephine. Every
time he visited her, he would renew Franz's
hope for the two of them and expressed jealousy if he saw her with another man. Franz,
truly a remarkable woman, later recalled of
the woman who took the love of her life away,
"I could tell she was in love with him. But I
didn't hate her."[8]

Josephine Dillon, Clark's first wife and his mentor.

To her sorrow, Franz found Clark a
changed man once they were working in the
same company. More often than not, he
avoided her. Understandably sceptical of him
by now, Franz refused to let him get to her this
time. On the rare occasion when they accidentally bumped into each other offstage, she
escaped to her dressing room rather than confront him. She wasn't left on the rack very
long; Clark played only a couple of minor
roles, and Franz was almost glad when he left
after only a couple of weeks.[9]

From Clark's point of view though, he
was probably just going through the motions,
sleepwalking with his body on remote control
while his mind was already out on the coast.
All this time he had been dreaming of being
able to break away from small towns into big-
city life, to swap poverty for wealth, to be able
to wash away those memories of the filth, and
the grime, and the smell of oil. Now his
chance had come.

CHAPTER 6

BECOMING CLARK GABLE

Hollywood in 1924 was a town where thousands of people wanted to make it into the big time just as badly as William C. Gable did. The population had tripled in only a few years and hundreds of people turned out just to vie for extras' parts. One hundred thousand people had registered with Screen Service, the industry's largest employment agency, over the last six years. Of these, five had become stars. For those who could appreciate it, Hollywood was still a pretty place. There was no smog yet to screen the sun, and in the clear evenings the smell of citrus still drifted on the air from the orchards on the outskirts of town. Many weren't in a position to appreciate it though; the 1923 report of the Travelers Aid Society revealed that 20,000 people had requested assistance and most of them had come to town looking for work in the film industry, just like Mr. Gable.[1]

Once again, because there is no one who can shed any other light on the situation, Josephine Dillon's manuscript about the relationship between Julia Hood and Mark Craven is the only insight available into how she may have trained Clark and why they may have married.

Julia finds a small cottage on the same street where Tom Mix lives, and renovates and decorates it while she lives in a hotel. When she is done, she sends Mark fifty dollars for the fare. Before long, he is rushing across the hotel lobby to meet her. The next day, he goes out looking for work and gets a job in a garage. That night he knocks on her hotel door, flings himself into a chair and suggests that they get married. Julia agrees, but explains carefully to Mark that this partnership will be for the sake of their mutual interest in his career, not because they are under any illusions about love being involved. It will, in short, be very much a working relationship. Mark protests that he will love her for as long as she lives. Stunned, she offers to show him something and takes him out to see the cottage. Mark is touched by her gesture, and they decide to get married immediately.

In the real world, five months elapsed before Clark Gable and Josephine Dillon were married, during which time he lived in a hotel and she paid the bills. They were married by the Reverend H.W. Meadows in a quiet ceremony in his church office on December 18, 1924. Clark claimed he was a year older at twenty-four; Josephine claimed she was younger and thirty-four, but she was really forty.

Josephine always maintained that she and Gable were married "in name only." That might have been true, but it's a little difficult to imagine Clark staying away from any woman with whom he was living. It's more likely that admitting they shared some intimate moments may not have suited Josephine's later adopted role of martyr to the Gable Cause. So just like Julia and Mark's relationship, the first Mrs. Gable always portrayed her relationship as primarily a practical partnership to give Clark all the help possible to find a job and a career.

Times were tough in the Hollywood of the early 1920s; an ordinary extra's job paid only three dollars a day plus a box lunch. The pay for working in a costume supplied by the studio was seven dollars and fifty cents, but it rose to the giddy heights of ten dollars if you were a "dress extra" who owned their own evening clothes. Yet, you could get trampled in the rush whenever work was advertised. In July, 1924, *The Literary Digest* published a photo showing a crowd of 3,500 people clamouring for attention outside a casting office that had advertised for thirty-five![2] What price potential stardom?

For months Clark wore out shoe leather trying to get those sort of jobs, the only sort open to a complete unknown without an agent. As well as Central Casting, the studios had jobs available for whatever pictures in production needed extras that day, but getting that information required being in the crowd outside the gates when the calls for labor were announced. This was the origin of the term "cattle call." There were, however, many miles between Culver City, where Metro-Goldwyn-Mayer had just been created by a major merger, out to the San Fernando Valley and Universal, not to mention the other studios in between. It was necessary to be there first thing in the morning to be at the front of the line, and casting officers rarely knew until late what the needs would be for people the next day. Needless to say, Clark landed very few of those jobs. With virtually no money in his pocket, he had to cover most of the distance to find work on foot.

Because of the passing of time and the anonymity of the work, it is difficult to determine exactly which film is the first in which Clark appears as a lowly extra. It is often said to have been Ernst Lubitsch's *Forbidden Paradise*, made at Paramount and released on November 30, 1924,[3] or it could have been Universal's *The Great Diamond Robbery* starring Shirley Mason and directed by Denison Clift.[4] However, it is most likely an earlier 1924 P. B. Schulberg silent film titled *White Man*, directed by Louis J. Gasnier and starring Kenneth Harlan as the White Man and Alice Joyce as Lady Andrea Pellor. Clark appears as Lady Andrea's brother.

Advertisements for extras and bit players weren't known as cattle calls for nothing; that was pretty much how you were treated. Clark once recalled being initially selected as a day extra for *Forbidden Paradise* because of his height. He was ordered into a line-up, a process he disliked because it made him feel like a showhorse. As grenadier guards in tall hats and gold braid, they had to stand motionless at the back of the set during three long days of the shoot for seven dollars and fifty cents a day.

Even after he had become a star, Clark never forgot what it was like to be on the bottom rung of the ladder as an extra. "For years I couldn't get myself arrested in Hollywood," he would say, and he always made sure that extras were being treated right in his movies. He would sometimes go out of his way to be courteous to them and he couldn't bear to see them being pushed around.

At some point early in his search, William C. Gable made the decision to revert to the original form of his name, Clark Gable. One version of how this came about is that after they had purchased a shirt at Clark's Dollar Shirt Shop on Hollywood Boulevard, Josephine noticed the sign outside the store and remarked that it was a coincidence his name was Clark. She then suggested that it would be lucky to change his working name back to Clark.[5] He did. Perhaps he felt now that he had come full circle through the changes in his life, signified by the addition of an "e" here and a "William" there, and that he was ready to be Clark again. This time it must have felt right, for he never altered his name again.

Meanwhile, Josephine was training him to be the star she knew in her heart he would be one day, and that involved a lot of hard work by both parties. Josephine considered Clark's voice much too nervous and hard and, consequently, rather high-pitched. In her book *Modern Acting,* she writes of how Clark had to sit for hours at the piano, day after day, working his voice down a halfstep at a time until Josephine was satisfied that he had the right amount of depth and resonance in his voice for a big man. She would not be the only person to comment on this tendency during his career. As late as 1952, director Delmer Daves had to try and get Clark to lower his pitch while starring in *Never Let Me Go.* He recalls that Clark's reaction was, "Hell, this is my style." Daves exclaimed in frustration, "Oh forget style, Clark! I can talk like a tenor, or a second tenor, or I can talk like a baritone, and you have to do exactly the same thing. By God, if I want to I can talk a bass, but each one is honest. Clark, don't think you're being dishonest if you lower your voice range. You're a gutsy guy doing a gutsy part and you have to talk with a gutsy voice."[6] Clark duly found his gutsy voice for the part.

Josephine also helped Clark to even out his accent, which was a mixture of East and West, of farm and city, of Pennsylvania Dutch and Oregon logging camp, and she worked him through breathing exercises. She sent him on forced marches around the streets and up and down the cottage stairs to keep him fit. As he worked, she noticed that his face began to relax. As it did so, his soon-to-be famous smile became more apparent, and the physical awkwardness that had marred Billy Gable's early stage appearances became Clark Gable's muscular grace.

Clark had an inferiority complex a mile wide about his lack of education, so Josephine took it upon herself to broaden his outlook.

She took him as often as she could to the cinema so he could study the work of other actors. Then they would sit late into the night around the kitchen table analyzing what he had seen. She took him to concerts, so he could study the breathing and annunciation of great singers, and to art galleries so that he could appreciate artistic interpretation. She encouraged him to read the works of modern playwrights and the classics. Clark grew to love Shakespeare, and later in his life he still liked to recite long passages from *Hamlet* and *Romeo and Juliet.*

Josephine also introduced Clark to the social niceties, encouraging him to play golf on the local course and to be her escort at Hollywood parties and dinners where he could observe and make mental notes about the correct way to hand a lady a cocktail, to shake hands, to sit down, to stand up, and to engage in elegant small talk. When they returned home, she would get him to imitate what he'd seen. Josephine taught Clark how to manage his body language with dignity and how to act as though he were already a star, as though success was a foregone conclusion. Indeed, in the following year it all started to come together for him.

By the spring of 1925, Clark had not been able to find enough work in films to keep him in steady employment, nor a significant role that might convince him that his career should be the silver screen. Besides, all his voice training was going to waste in silent movies. So he returned to his first love, the stage, to supplement his income. Los Angeles was quite a center of live performance around this time, and there was no shortage of road companies in town auditioning for parts. Clark started to do the rounds.

It was about this time that he finally found himself a car. Clark, being the old mechanic that he was, had his eye on an old, broken-down, open-topped Roamer that had been sitting in an alley near where he lived for some time. The design of the Roamer was modeled after the Rolls-Royce, which might have had something to do with why it appealed to Clark, but there was little of the aristocratic left about this jalopy. The seats were torn, the tires had collapsed, and the owner had given up on trying to get it started. Clark offered the owner thirty-six dollars to be paid at three dollars a month, found a set of secondhand tires for twelve dollars while Josephine patched the upholstery, and he was on the road![7]

Clark heard that the husband-and-wife team of Louis O. MacLoon and Lillian Albertson's West Coast Road Company was holding auditions for *Romeo and Juliet*. Lillian Albertson had been renowned on Broadway for her success in a show called *Paid in Full* before moving into directing, with MacLoon as producer. Considering that Clark spent a good part of the next six years under Lillian's able, biting, yet affectionate direction, her influence on the development of his acting technique should not be ignored. While Josephine taught Clark a lot of theory, it was Lillian who directed Clark in putting that theory into practice on the unforgiving stage in play after play through a variety of roles.

This version of *Romeo and Juliet* would feature the strikingly beautiful Jane Cowl, who at forty-one would be playing the teenage Juliet. Given his love and study of Shakespeare, *Romeo and Juliet* was something Clark and Josephine figured he was ready for. What they hadn't figured on was that Jane Cowl was ready for Clark. At the height of her fame and power, Cowl usually got what or who she wanted. Boston-born, she had studied law at Columbia University until deciding in 1903 that she preferred the theater of the stage to that of the courtroom. In 1923, by then known as the most beautiful woman on the American stage, she had established a world record of 856 consecutive performances of *Romeo and Juliet*. Her Juliet had been called "the greatest in living memory," and she was now triumphantly touring the country.[8]

Lillian would recall that it all began because they needed some tall actors as soldiers.

"A big, awkward boy came walking down the aisle of the half-lit theatre toward the stage where we were rehearsing. Jane and I were talking over some stage details at the time. Both of us were struck simultaneously by his height.... Jane said, 'Look at that boy. He'll do. What's his name? He looks like he has something.'"[9] So Clark was hired on the spot as one of ten tall, broad-shouldered, walk-on soldiers. Lillian thought he was a bit thin and ungainly, but she was struck by the rugged quality of his physique and personality. Jane Cowl was also struck by Clark's rugged good looks. While he might have had only a minor role onstage, Clark was soon playing a major role offstage in her dressing room.

A week later the actor playing the role of Mercutio left the company, and Clark was asked to replace him because he knew the play so well. Lillian Albertson worked with him night after night trying to refine his movement and coordination on the stage. He was full of enormous energy and willingness to work, but he was very raw. His closest friend in the troupe, Eddie Woods, commented later that "Persons who knew Clark Gable only after he made his sensational success in Hollywood cannot imagine how clumsy and callow he was in those days. There were times when Lillian Albertson despaired of ever teaching him to walk properly across the stage. I remember sitting with her one day in the window of her office. She looked out and saw Gable crossing Hollywood Boulevard. "Look at that big, awkward galoot," she said. "Did you ever see any actor who walked more like a truck driver?"[10]

Although she remained to be impressed by his acting abilities, when casting for their next production, *What Price Glory?* Lillian decided to give Clark a chance in his first real character part with the company. She cast him in the role of Kiper, one of three roughnecks who knows he is somebody and doesn't mind telling the world about it.[11] Clark was still having trouble with the pitch of his voice, though, and he and Lillian put in some serious time working on lowering it to fit this tough-guy role. Josephine objected to the method by which Lillian was attempting to help him do this, though, and she became increasingly critical of Lillian's direction of Clark. Eventually, they became tired of Josephine's continual interference, and within a short time she was barred by the MacLoons from rehearsals.

Clark's Kiper was such a success after the play opened in Los Angeles in May that when one of the lead parts became vacant, that of Sergeant Quirt, Clark was invited to take over that role. He played it for fifteen weeks, and he was so successful that he went on to reprise the role in two other productions of the play within a year.

At the end of June the troupe headed for San Francisco. Having been up all night in a poker game, Woods and Gable took turns driving while the other slept. As they approached Santa Barbara, Clark noticed increasingly larger cracks in the road pavement, and he woke Eddie up to point them out and comment that the California road maintenance crews were falling down on the job. Eddie realized before too long, however, that they must have arrived at the tail of an earth tremor. He recalled later that Clark was absolutely fascinated by this close encounter with his first earthquake. "He might have been an archaeologist discovering a long-lost city," he said. "No detail was too small to be overlooked. We were there for hours." Eddie kept reminding Clark that they'd be late for the rehearsal and he was worried by the presence of militiamen on the lookout for looters, but "Clark just smiled his way past them everywhere."[12]

It had been a closer call for the two actors than they realized. The Santa Barbara earthquake, measuring 6.3 on the Richter scale, had arrived at 6:44 that morning of June 29, 1925, wreaking havoc on buildings and humanity alike as the earth shook for eighteen seconds. Twelve people died. The ocean receded. Tram lines twisted like Chinese noodles. The Old Mission's towers tumbled and

the ninety-room Arlington Hotel, a luxurious city show-piece, was completely destroyed. The Californian Hotel, which had only been open four days, lost its entire four floors of south wall leaving guests exposed in their beds. Only buildings such as the smaller Upham Hotel on De La Vina Street, built of more flexible redwood timbers, managed to survive with only the loss of a chimney or two.[13] It was later estimated the earthquake caused some $20 million worth of property damage.

After that dramatic start, the troupe went on to San Francisco and then north to Portland. Clark commented to Eddie that it felt strange to be back with a job and money in his pocket after spending so long in and around Portland broke and struggling to survive. After playing in Seattle and Vancouver, they returned to Los Angeles. In quick succession, Clark appeared in six plays for the MacLoons over the next two years: *Lullaby, The Copperhead, Lady Frederick, Madame X, Lucky Sam McCarver,* and *Chicago.*

In Edward Knoblock's *Lullaby,* Clark played a drunken sailor. Touring with this role eventually took him back to San Francisco's Curran Theater, where he had appeared in *What Price Glory?* One night, one of the troupe was drinking in a small nightclub they all went to after the show, when who should he see but an old friend. It was none other than Franz Dorfler. It turned out she was teaching dancing at the Bell Studios right across the street from the theater. Knowing of her friendship with Clark, he mentioned it to him the next day and Clark called her, saying that he would leave a ticket for her at the box office and asking her to meet him after the show. She agreed.

At no time during this meeting, or subsequent ones in the following years, did Clark ever seem to think it necessary to mention to Franz, for whom "he remained the love of my life," that he and Josephine were married. The first she knew anything about it was when he casually mentioned while visiting her in

Hollywood, where Franz eventually moved, that he was getting divorced. In one of the great understatements in the history of memoirs, she wrote of her reaction to what must have seemed like a bolt of lightning from a clear blue sky: "It surprised me, to say the least."[14] Although it would seem to be unusual behavior, such an omission is consistent with Clark's history of rewriting this part of his life when telling it to interviewers. It indicates how little he assimilated his relationship with Josephine into the context of his life and suggests that, perhaps already aware that he might have to leave his marriage behind one day, Clark had already mentally distanced himself from it.

Meanwhile, while Franz was dreaming of Clark, he was a busy man in someone else's dreams. After *Lullaby*, Clark went on to appear in 1926 as a prosecuting attorney in the last act of the play *Madame X*, starring Pauline Frederick. The same age as Jane Cowl, Fredrick was also renowned for her sensual beauty and for her topaz-colored eyes. In 1915, at 32, she had been one of the first Broadway stars to quit the stage for Hollywood, and being able to fluently move between mediums seemed to have only increased her popularity. On the opening night of *Madame X* in San Francisco, one of Pauline's most renowned roles, she received thirty-one curtain calls by the last of which both she and the audience were in tears.

The warmth of her personality and the sweetness of her nature belied a single-minded steeliness when Pauline wanted a particular man. It was generally conceded that once that man wandered within range, he had about as much chance of escaping as a deer caught in the headlights of an oncoming truck. Pauline had a reputation for playing women who find themselves in trouble despite their good intentions, and sometimes because of them, and to a large extent her life imitated her art. By the time she met Clark, her father had disowned her, and a young actor had hanged himself when told she did not love him. She had weathered three rough marriages, had managed to drive a New York newspaper publisher into bankruptcy, and she had been accused of breaking up so many happy homes that people had lost count.

Needless to say, Pauline was a woman driven by passion, and she apparently demonstrated no lack of it in young Clark's case. He would complain to Eddie about having to buy oysterettes, an aphrodisiac then sold in drugstores, groaning, "They talk about Al Jolson singing every song as though it would be the last of his life. This woman acts every night as though she never expected to see another man!"[15] He began to take Eddie with him when invited to her Sunset Boulevard mansion, pleading not to be left alone with her. However, there were side benefits. It was most probably Pauline who paid to have Clark's upper gold front teeth replaced with others more natural in appearance. Pauline and Clark continued to work together in *Lady Frederick* and then *Lucky Sam McCarver*, in which Clark plays the manager of the nightclub in which Pauline is a dancer. When the play closed, Pauline departed for London and further fame. Clark was left with an inscribed gold cigarette case that he treasured for many years.[16]

By this time, Clark had quietly separated from Josephine and had moved out of the house. Neither of them commented about it publicly at the time, nor did the public seem to notice. Josephine, on the other hand, would say quite a lot when she grew older. She would always maintain that Clark was never really interested in women, and they usually pursued him.[17] If that were the case, as Eddie Woods would recall, it was no wonder that "Despite his clumsiness, his unworldliness, and his lack of good looks, women even then were crazy about him. 'Lack of good looks' is putting it mildly. Gable was scrawny and looked half-starved. One could only say that women must have loved his lean and hungry look, but there was something else. We know what happened when he lost that lean and hungry look. Women loved him even more.... You couldn't help liking him. Just being with him made you feel good."[18] A few years later, writer and friend Adela Rogers St. Johns would discern that same appeal from a woman's point of view: "Women have been good luck to Clark Gable. To meet Clark is to meet the same man you see on the screen. That is true of few stars. He has the same smile. The same animal magnetism. The same charm which no psychologist has ever explained, but which probably got Eve in the Garden of Eden when she first saw Adam."[19]

Clark was thrilled that in his next play, *The Copperhead*, he got to appear with Lionel Barrymore. The story goes that the part came Clark's way mainly because Barrymore remembered him from his days as a callboy for *The Jest* in New York. The old actor did get irritated though, by Clark's tendency to still trip over his own feet and be just a tad absentminded on the stage. On one renowned occasion, Clark dropped his hat down what was supposed to be a forty-foot well, then reached in, picked it up, and put it back on his head. The audience fell over laughing, but *The Copperhead* wasn't supposed to be a comedy! Nevertheless, Barrymore was evidently impressed by the potential he saw in the young actor and would later play a major role in bringing Clark to the attention of movie studios. He advised Clark that no matter how straight the role he was playing, "never to play it straight, but always with a dash of character in it."[20] This would help Clark avoid playing a character as if to a rubber-stamp formula.

During 1925 and early 1926, Clark had continued to supplement his stage actor's income with work as a film extra. He got work in First National's *Declassee*, also released as *The Social Exile*, and then in F.B.O's *The Pacemakers* in August 1925, directed by Wesley Ruggles, but disappeared into the background of MGM's *The Merry Widow* the following month as an uncredited soldier. It must have been an entertaining experience working on the *Merry Widow* set, because from the very start director Eric von Stroheim and his female lead Mae Murray hated each other and frequently fought loudly and openly. Murray would make temperamental demands; von Stroheim would turn his back and stage whisper insults. Finally, reaching the end of her particular rope, Murray called the director a "dirty Hun." Von Stroheim promptly stormed off the set and wouldn't return. Louis B. Mayer replaced him with another director, whereupon the stagehands as one refused to work unless von Stroheim was reinstated. Eddie Mannix, a former bouncer who had just arrived to be Mayer's aide, unwisely clipped one of the gathered strikers on the jaw in an altercation, which didn't exactly smooth the path of negotiation. Eventually, Murray was persuaded to apologize and the film was completed.

During October, Clark worked in *The Plastic Age*, directed by Wesley Ruggles for B. P. Schulberg's Preferred Pictures.[21] Based on the 1922 novel by Dartmouth professor Percy Marks, *The Plastic Age* tells the story of a student who is at first lured into the hard-drinking, fast-living side of college life along with a female classmate, played by rising star Clara Bow, but who then reforms. Clark and the other male extras playing the college students would greet the sexy-looking "It" girl's appearance on the set each morning with wolf whistles. Although he would not have been aware of it at the time, history was being made as Clark looked on. *The Plastic Age* would prove to be the greatest success yet for Clara Bow, and it would make her famous. One of her costars in his first major film role was Luis Antonio Damaso de Alonso, whom Schulberg renamed Gilbert Roland for this film.[22] In February of the following year, Clark appeared in a small part as Archie West in one more silent film, *North Star*. The only whistling he did around a star on this set was for his costar, a dog called Strongheart![23]

By May of 1927, Clark was concentrating on acting on the stage and was appearing at

Clark as an extra in The Pacemakers *(1925), with hair plastered down and parted in the middle, standing behind Alberta Vaughn.* (Spicer Collection.)

the Music Box Theater in Los Angeles in *Chicago*, a humorous satire written by newspaperwoman Maureen Watkins. Once again, Louis MacLoon was the producer and Lillian Albertson was the stage director. Heeding Barrymore's advice, Clark turned the minor role of the reporter Jake into one that gained him a lot of attention by giving the role some individual character touches. Clark's costar was Nancy Carroll who later recalled that, though her role of Roxie Hart was the lead, "Gable really did think *Chicago* was *his* play. Clark was the first hat-on-the-back-of-his-head reporter in stage history unless I'm mistaken.... When people later spoke of Clark's stiff-legged stride as something new I was really surprised. Gable had it then."[24]

By the time the popular *Chicago* closed, movie scouts were waiting at the stage door. Nancy Carroll accepted a contract at Para-

mount.[25] However, when MGM scouts asked Clark whether he would be interested in coming back into the movies, he told them he was too disillusioned by his early experiences. The stage was where he wanted to be now. "With luck," he declared, "I can make it good on Broadway one day. Why waste my time and your money? I've tried movie work often enough to become convinced I have nothing Hollywood wants."[26]

So, it was on the stage he remained. Clark had two options open to him when the *Chicago* run was over. He could join the Houston stock company of Gene Lewis, which he wasn't very interested in doing, or he could do a season of personal appearances with actress Jean Davenport, which he was very interested in doing. Josephine, attempting to guide Clark's life as usual, gave fate a helping hand when she lied to Davenport over

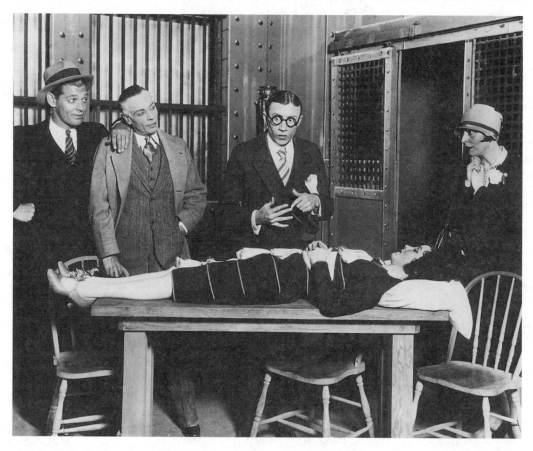

A scene from the 1925 Los Angeles stage production of Chicago. *Left to right: Gable, Barry Townly, Paul Fix, Nancy Carroll, Kay Campbell.* (Spicer Collection.)

the phone and said that Clark had already signed with someone else. "I don't think that Clark ever forgave me for that," she later wrote.[27]

In Houston, Lewis' stock company, with Clark as second lead for seventy-five dollars a week, did a different play every week in the Palace Theater. Working in a stock company was, in fact, just the sort of practice that Clark needed. Playing different parts so frequently across the whole spectrum, from comedy to tragedy, helped him extend the range of his talent. Stock audiences tended to be kinder and more tolerant too, and regulars would feel they got to know the actors, who in turn felt they could relax a bit and learn from their own mistakes and those of others. They felt more able to experiment with inflections and ges-

tures, trying them on for size as if buying new clothes.

Three months into the company's season the leading man quit. For the next twenty-five weeks, the world of Houston was at Clark's feet as he became the star of the show. His pay rose to two hundred dollars a week. People couldn't get enough of him. He was recognized in the street and asked for autographs, local ladies waited for him in his dressing room, and his fan mail started to pile up. Most of the city's female population became severely Gable-struck.

One of the many adoring young women who went to see Clark and sigh was a redheaded fourteen-year-old girl named George Anna Lucas, who preferred to be called Jana. She and her best friend had a terrible crush on

A scene from the stage production What Price Glory? *Clark is seated in the middle.*

him, but Jana didn't want her mother, Ria Franklin Prentiss Lucas Langham, to know about it. So she never said anything, even though she and her mother were very close. They were so close, in fact, that she was later very sure that Ria never met Clark personally in Houston even though Josephine, who infuriated Clark by following him there, would insinuate they had. In a 1936 letter, Josephine wrote that "In Houston he had met people who are now in his life. I was asked to step out, and I went to New York to fulfil my promise, saying that I would give him his divorce when he had accomplished what we set out to do — make a good actor of him."[28]

True to her word, Josephine eventually made contact in New York with producer Arthur Hopkins, who wanted to open *Machinal* in the Fall. Hopkins was a plump, kindly,

middle-aged mystic with a reputation among Broadway producers for his talent and his versatility. His productions of *Hamlet* and *Richard III* had proved that John Barrymore was one of the great actors of his time, but he also had to his credit melodramas such as *What Price Glory?* and farces such as *Annabelle*. As the female lead in *Machinal* he had already signed Hungarian-born Zita Johann, who held him in such esteem that she had opted for this part rather than sign a five-year contract with Universal. Worried because it was such a heavy part, Zita thought that she would need a well-known actor to support her in the role. Instead, Arthur found for her an unknown "Woolworth Romeo," none other than Clark Gable.

In the summer of 1928, Broadway was the place to be. All the important producers seemed to have stacks of green paper that they were willing to invest and spread around to keep those chorus lines kicking. Florenz Ziegfield alone was staging three musicals at the same time. Eugene O'Neill's *Strange Interlude* was breaking records for the Theatre Guild with Clark's old Astoria Players friend Earle Larimore in a lead role. The place was crowded with beautiful girls, hard drinkers, sports champions, pool halls, and dance halls. Not only that but one could now buy good booze, even if it was still bootlegged, that wouldn't send people blind.

Joy was definitely in the air, and Clark was no exception to the general feeling. As he strolled down the street, he was confident and just plain happy to have the chance to be in New York at all. Not only that, but he had money in his pocket, recommendations from the MacLoons, enthusiastic reviews from the Houston critics, and a job waiting for him! It felt to him as if he had been waiting to be here all his life

Within two weeks of his arrival Clark signed with major agency Chamberlain Brown, which at that time cast most of the Broadway shows, and then with Arthur Hopkins. Having settled in, he called Josephine and broke the news to her that they were through. He was tired of her interference and wanted her out of his life. Josephine, who had expected little else but who could at least say she had fulfilled her promise, retorted that he had better become a good actor because he was never going to be a man. Then she left for California.

Clark plunged into four weeks of rehearsal for *Machinal*. A dramatization by Sophie Treadwell of the recent Snyder-Gray murder case that had shocked the country, the script simply called Clark's character "a Man," but a man more devoid of moral scruples it would have been hard to devise. Clark played an adventurer who has an affair with a married mother and then leaves her to go to Mexico when he becomes bored. She murders her husband so she can join him there, but his response is to betray her by signing the statement that will send her to the electric chair.

Zita Johann was pleased with Clark's progress, particularly as he wasn't moody like other male leads with whom she'd worked, and he knew his lines thoroughly and didn't make mistakes. She and Clark got along well, too; he would even gallantly walk her home at night but they struck no sparks with each other. "He was genial, affable, lovable," she later remembered. "Nice. Bemused is the word for him. Bemused."[29]

Machinal opened at the Plymouth Theater on September 7, 1928. Received well by the critics, the play ran its full three-month season. Although Zita got all the rave reviews, critics had some good words to say for Clark too. *The New York Times* noted that he played his role as the "casual, good-humored lover without a hackneyed gesture." *The Morning Telegraph* enthused that he was "young, vigorous and brutally masculine."[30]

Clark's stepdaughter Jana believed it was during these three months that Clark met her mother, Ria, for the first time. Jana was on a visit to New York, visiting her mother, and they decided to go and see Clark in *Machinal* after noticing an advertisement in the newspaper. Ria's half-brother, Booth Franklin, was an actor, and he took them backstage and introduced them to Clark. About a month later, Jana recalls, she returned to New York and was amazed and delighted when her mother told her that she and Clark had been seeing a lot of each other. "I was extremely impressed and thought it was great," she recalls, "and I could tell that Mother was happy too."[31]

CHAPTER 7

CLARK AND RIA

Ria Franklin Prentiss Lucas Langham was a petite, strong-minded woman with exquisite taste and a fine sense of the proprieties. She had style, and she taught Clark as much about it as she could. Maria Franklin had been born in Kentucky in 1884 and raised in Macomb, Illinios, where she married William Prentiss at the tender age of 17. They had one son, but within four years their marriage fell apart.

By that time, her mother Anna had died and her father George was living on a ranch in Texas with his new wife, who hoped the dry air would help his tuberculosis. Ria took her son and moved there for a while, and then she went to live in Houston with an aunt and uncle. She worked in a jewelry store by day and studied bookkeeping at night. She eventually married Alfred Thomas Lucas, a wealthy contractor who was twenty-two years older. Three years later she gave birth to a daughter, George (Jana) Anna, and six years later had another son, Alfred Jr. In 1922 Lucas died, leaving Ria a rich woman.

She married Denzil Langham three years later, but this lasted only two years. In 1928 Ria's eldest boy, who was going to school in Hartford, Connecticut, fell very ill. It so happened that Jana also graduated from school that year, so Ria packed up and moved with the two children to a glamorous apartment on Eighty-first Street and Park Avenue in Manhattan.[1]

Machinal never bloomed into a hit play and closed in its twelfth week. After that, Clark couldn't find a job, and it was Ria who was there to provide his much-needed support as he sank into despair. Up until now, Clark's energies had been focused on making the right stage moves; Ria set out to teach him the right moves in the society to which she was accustomed, such as how to order in a good restaurant, how to develop a taste for elegant clothes which stayed with him all his life, and how to choose just the right drink for the right occasion. They made a very gracious pair, but the fancy exterior glossed over Clark's self-doubt and insecurity as 1928 drew to a close with no sign of work.

As if that weren't enough, Josephine wouldn't grant him a divorce because she didn't believe in it and, in any case, it wasn't she who wanted one. So grumbling all the way, Clark found a lawyer who could get him a Mexican divorce for $100, and then he boarded the next train west. Arriving in Los Angeles, Clark tried to persuade Josephine to sign the papers. "I knew he meant it," she recalled in 1932, "and I knew it was folly for me to try to dodge fate any longer. When he had mentioned divorce before, I had told him he didn't mean it.

I was trying to tell myself he didn't mean it. I had told him that if he ever came to me and made me actually believe he wanted to leave me, I would divorce him. Well, he had come."[2]

Determined and independent to the end, she still did it her way and filed for a separation on the grounds of desertion on March 28, 1929. The final divorce decree was granted a year later on April 1.[3] Clark rarely spoke about her again, commenting only in 1932, for example, that "She was a sweet woman. She was good to me. But we weren't suited — for marriage. I hope she's happy and I hope she thinks well of me."[4] So completely did he erase her name from accounts of his life, over the following years, that many people were surprised to discover she existed when the media rediscovered her as an elderly woman many years later.

Meanwhile, Clark returned to New York and Ria. He kept haunting the offices of his agents, Chamberlain and Lyman Brown, waiting for something to develop. Lyman Brown later recalled that, despite work being so hard to find, Clark was always so affable that "Chamberlain and I almost regretted it each time we found him a job. I can almost see him now, standing in a corner, watching the others with those friendly smiling eyes of his, taking everything in as though amused by it all…. In those days he wore a derby and carried a gold-headed cane. Always well-dressed of course and neat, fantastically neat and dapper." The Browns had a lot of faith in the attractiveness of the combination of roguishness and innocence that they saw revealed in Clark's personality. They also felt that another of his great attractions to an audience "was the mystery of what he was thinking and would be doing next. As an actor, it captured and held one's interest, even on the screen, even though you knew that the picture was completed and whatever he was going to say or do next had already been said or done. He aroused your emotions because you were not quite sure. It added greatly to the suspense of watching him."[5]

As Lyman Brown had noticed, Clark was an astute observer of people, studying them whenever he had the chance and storing what he saw for later use in his craft. He hated being idle. Even when he wasn't working, he rarely wasted his time. So with time on his hands at the moment, he took to visiting night court each evening where he observed that endless collection of criminals, strange and horrifying, petty and large, who had been arrested in the early hours of the morning after the police courts had closed. Each night Clark went to his own form of life class, where he studied to perfect his art.

In fact, he did this whenever he could. While making the trip to Los Angeles to see Josephine in early 1929 aboard the Twentieth Century Limited, Clark happened to bump into his old stage costar Nancy Carroll, now a movie star. As it happened, they arrived in Chicago on February 15, the day after the St. Valentine's Day Massacre. Facing a six-hour layover before their train left for the West Coast, Clark and Nancy both took advantage of the break to talk themselves into the police station so they could watch suspects being brought in for questioning about the shooting. While there, Gable was moved by the interrogation of some young African American boys who had been brought in about another murder. "In my whole life," Carroll remembered later, "I have never looked at a man so bursting with compassion."[6]

Late in the spring, after Clark had returned to New York, he was offered through the Browns the lead role in a George M. Cohan play called *Gambling*. He took the part but, after the play opened in Philadelphia and then moved to Atlantic City a few weeks later, Cohan became increasingly unhappy with both the script and Clark's performance. In the end, Cohan fired Clark, rewrote the play, and then he took over Clark's role when *Gambling* opened in New York. The Browns immediately found Clark another role in *Hawk Island*. In this Howard Irving Young play, Clark played the role of Gregory Sloane, host to a house party on a remote island. Bored and looking for excitement, he and a mystery writer concoct a fake murder that backfires when the writer is actually murdered and the police think Sloane did it. Critics thought Gable did a good job but the play, which opened September 16, 1929, folded after twenty-four performances. Clark went on to David Belasco's *Blind Windows,* but this little stinker closed quickly without getting out of Philadelphia. "I couldn't get a job," Clark recalled, "but at least I could see other actors at work and study their techniques.... All that winter I was on the outside looking in."[7]

Still, Clark and the Browns kept trying, and they found him a role in *Love, Honor and Betray* during March and April of 1930 at the Eltinge Theater in New York.[8] Alice Brady played a femme fatale who visits a cemetery, where she reunites with three men in her life: the youth she jilted, the millionaire she married, and her lover, who was played by Clark. By the end, Alice has her eye on her daughter's lover, the handsome chauffeur. This play didn't do much better than the others, closing after four weeks; critics commented that the set designer gave the best performance.[9] Clark said in 1932 that he and two other actors, George Brent and Robert Williams, used to sit around back-stage discussing their futures and swearing they would never go into the movies. Ironically, all three eventually did. "I think those months in New York were the happiest days of my life," he said. "I was doing exactly what I wanted to do. I was having a moderate degree of success in the theater. I worked hard and I played hard."[10] The problem was that Clark played harder than he worked. In the cold light of day, his degree of success was only moderate. Of the eighteen months he was in New York, he only found work for a total of about six. However, his luck was about to change.

Just before the end of his run with *Love, Honor and Betray,* Clark heard from his old theater producer friends, Lillian Albertson and Louis MacLoon. Lillian had developed a strong faith in Clark's potential, and now she thought he would be just right for the lead role in a play called *The Last Mile,* which Lillian and Louis wanted to bring out to the West Coast. As usual, Lillian would be directing and her husband Louis would be the producer.

The Last Mile, referring to the last walk of a condemned prisoner, was a disturbing play about a group of death-row inmates who attempt a last-minute breakout after one of them is executed, figuring they have nothing to lose. Failing to escape, they hole up in the prison with hostages they eventually kill while the police lay siege, exchange gunfire, and attempt to blast their way in with dynamite. The play, with Spencer Tracy in the lead role, was currently being performed to great acclaim on Broadway, where it had opened in January 1930. Lillian and Louis wanted Clark for the Tracy role of John "Killer" Mears, the leader of the prisoners' revolt. The controversial play was regarded at the time as a powerful indictment against capital punishment, and it had been attracting packed houses.[11]

Clark and Ria went to see the play. Tracy was so impressive that Clark came away saying the part was beyond him and that he wouldn't be able to do it justice.[12] It was an attitude that Clark demonstrated at regular intervals during his career, and typically the role in question would turn out to be not only a success but a major turning point for him. Despite giving the impression of being an adventurer, Clark actually preferred to play sure bets and liked his security. He may well have been influenced to keep both his feet so firmly on the ground by watching his father continually and unsuccessfully search for an ever-richer oil well always just over the horizon. Clark tended to be reluctant to venture into the unknown, and it was usually only after a lot of persuasion from an agent, wife or friend, or when forced against his will, that Clark would attempt something different by way of a role.

So, it was only after a lot of confidence-

Clark looking every inch the vicious "Killer" Mears in the 1930 Los Angeles stage production of The Last Mile. *(Spicer Collection.)*

boosting from Ria that Clark could finally be persuaded to sign with the MacLoons to play the role of Killer Mears. By now, he and Ria were married, having been very quietly united in New York only a couple of days after Clark's divorce had come through. Ria couldn't go to Los Angeles with him because the children were still in school. So with only four weeks to rehearse the role, Clark flew out to the West Coast alone. Probably as a means of increas-

ing public anticipation, rehearsals took place at the Majestic Theater behind locked doors and strict security. Clark discovered that two old buddies of his would be appearing with him: Paul Fix from *Chicago*, and Edward Woods from *What Price Glory?* and *Madame X.*

The Last Mile opened at the Majestic Theater in Los Angeles on Monday night, June 2, 1930, and took the town by storm. It rapidly became the fashionable play of the time that one just had see. Clark was acclaimed in a role in which he became part-man, part-animal caged in his cell, pacing it, gripping the bars in his huge hands as if he would pry them apart and leap into the audience. The harsh top-lighting cast deep shadows on his face as his voice snarled in hatred at his fate. The critics loved it. Harold Waight wrote in the *Hollywood Filmograph*, "Stark, terrific and stunning are adjectives beloved by critics, but none have been used with more right than in the description of that strange and bitter outpouring of human emotions known as *The Last Mile*…. As Killer Mears, the role that Spencer Tracy is now essaying in the New York production, [Clark Gable] portrays the leading character in the last two acts with verve and force."[13]

The Los Angeles Times drama critic Edwin Schallert wrote the next day that "*The Last Mile* is hot. It is vigorous stuff…. It dashes along with interest literally on fire…. It is clever, consistent and real…. The cast offers some distinctly notable performances. Those of Clark Gable and Edward Woods are decidedly the most impressive, and Gable's necessarily the most intense."[14] Schallert later commented that he saw all of Clark's Los Angeles stage performances and that none of them made any impression until he saw Clark play Killer Mears and "knock everyone in the audience between the eyes with the fierce, bloodthirsty, vindictive and blasphemous way he tore the part open."[15]

As a result of his instantly acknowledged success in the play, *The Los Angeles Times* published in its Sunday edition what is quite probably the first person-to-person interview with Clark Gable. Alma Whitaker's article remains interesting for its first insights into a prevailing trait of Clark's for many years. Evidently uncertain as to how people would relate to his newly developing image if they knew of his working class background, Clark would attempt to romanticize it, to gloss and to smooth out its roughness, to rewrite it in var-

ious ways as he would have liked it to be. Eventually, the stories would become so familiar in the telling that they became his life. Here, talking to Whitaker, Clark gives himself the education he never had by claiming to have graduated from a business course at Akron University, which in other interviews became a pre-med course. He tells Alma that he "ran off" with a traveling show playing northwest towns because he was "unhappy and unsatisfactory in business," which, he implies, was not selling ties but being employed by a father with status — "an Oklahoma oil man." And in the end, it's not Josephine who directs him to Los Angeles but the driving ambition of "getting into the movies."[16] Poor Josephine. Barely a year in the past and without whose help and encouragement Clark might never have left Portland, she was already relegated to the dustbin of Gable history.

Apart from the critics, one member of the audience who was also apparently impressed was Lionel Barrymore, who no doubt would have been marveling at how far Clark had come from the bumbling actor with whom he'd worked in *The Copperhead*. According to Barrymore, in his dual capacity of actor-director at MGM he was scheduled to direct a film by the name of *Never the Twain Shall Meet*. Impressed by Clark's lean and hungry resemblance to boxer Jack Dempsey, he called Clark and invited him to screen test for a part. Clark was hesitant, having made a number of earlier unsuccessful attempts to work in the movies. However, Barrymore was persuasive and Clark agreed to the test. "I had him wear nothing but some orchids and a lei or something, and a blossom behind his ear," Barrymore told Cameron Shipp in 1950. "I made three or four scenes and had Gable stick out his chest in all of them." Thoroughly impressed with Clark's performance, he had Irving Thalberg view the test, but Thalberg just viewed it and, "nodding his head in an indefinite negative," walked out. Barrymore felt ashamed to call Clark and then never went ahead with the film anyway. Some time later, arriving on the set of *A Free Soul*, he was surprised to see none other than Clark Gable giving a woman who turns out to be Norma Shearer, Mrs. Irving Thalberg no less, "one of the longest kisses on screen record." Clark then made the highly unlikely claim that the day after he'd seen the test Thalberg had put him under contract.[17]

Like many Gable tales, this one evolved over time. Clark's first version of this story went on record in 1936. When he reported to the studio, he says, it was only to discover that Barrymore was away on location. As they were already set up to shoot *Bird of Paradise*, however, the studio decided to go ahead with the test and had Clark made up as a native Hawaiian. "They seemed to know what they were doing," he says, "and I stood like Old Dobbin being harnessed to the shay as they covered my body with a dark make-up, dressed me in a few square inches of cloth, put a wig on me, a knife in one hand, and a gardenia behind one ear. Then they stood me in front of a camera and told me to do something. The only thing I could think of was to run and hide. The next day Lionel called up: 'The executives looked at your test and the blankety-blankety-blank-blank fools don't think you're any good. But I do.'" Then, according to this version, Clark made another test of a scene from *The Last Mile* for Mervyn Le Roy, but he was again turned down. Clark claimed he borrowed the film of that test, showed it to a third group of executives and was again refused, but that agent Ruth Collier was in the audience and offered to represent him.[18]

Here we have the pro-active Clark, seeking to take charge of his own destiny. Perhaps its no coincidence that Clark claims his test was for *Bird of Paradise*. This was the pivotal theater production he had seen back in Akron as a frustrated small-town teenager that had so changed his outlook on life, and it was apparently quite similar in its romantic Polynesian setting to *Never the Twain Shall Meet*.

Over the following twenty years, the story continued to evolve. Talking to writer Pete Martin, a less self-conscious Clark had Barrymore as an active participant, but still had him directing the wrong movie:

> I went out to MGM and Lionel said, "Go over to make-up." I went over and they curled my hair…. Then I went over to wardrobe, where they stripped me and gave me a G-string. The sound stage where they were making the test was a long way off. I am no exhibitionist and I was embarrassed making that trek….
> When I showed up on that MGM soundstage, I asked Lionel, "What is this? Why am I curly-haired and half-naked?"
> "I'm directing *The Bird of Paradise*," he told me, "and I want you to play the native boy in it." A prop man stuck a hibiscus behind one of my ears, shoved a knife in my G-string, and there I was, creeping through the bushes, looking for a girl. Lionel had made a big thing out of "these actors out here can't talk," but he'd given me nothing to say throughout the test. Then my test was sent in for Irving Thalberg to look at. He called Lionel in and said, "You can't put that man in a picture. Look at him!"
> Lionel said loyally, "He's a good stage actor. He's young, but he'll be alright." Irving said, "Not for my money he won't. Look at his big bat-like ears."
> Fortunately a woman agent had seen me and believed in me enough to sell me to Pathe for awhile.[19]

According to legend then, because it is not until many years later that Clark's ears come into this story (they weren't even mentioned in Barrymore's own version of it), Thalberg was at the head of a long line of people who were to comment about the Gable ears. Paul Fix, who appeared with Clark in some of those early plays, observed that his ears "stuck out like barn doors," and claimed that Clark had them surgically altered.[20] Clark always denied this, saying that they had looked more prominent when he was young because he was so much thinner.[21] Mervyn LeRoy would claim that he wanted Clark for the lead in Warner Brothers' version of *Little Caesar* but that Jack Warner knocked the suggestion back because he thought Clark's ears were too big. Myron Selznick, who was Vivien Leigh's agent for *Gone with the Wind,* was said to have commented to a friend that Clark had ears like two spoons. Ben Piazza, who was MGM's casting director during the 1930s, supposedly pointed out that Clark's ears made him look like a giant sugar bowl. On the other hand, Milton Berle joked at an Academy Awards dinner that Clark should get an award for the "Best Ears of Our Lives."[22]

Ruth Collier assigned her assistant Minna Wallis, producer-director Hall Wallis' sister, to look after Clark as a client. Minna promptly found him a part in a Pathé western that would pay $750 a week. Despite all his intentions to stay on the stage, Clark never went back to Broadway.

Clark was tested and accepted for the part of a young, tough cowboy in *The Painted Desert*, provided he could ride. Clark declared he'd been born on a horse and signed on the dotted line with an option for a long-term contract. He was stretching the truth just a little. While he might have ridden a farm horse a few times to school back in Ohio, Clark had never actually been in a western-style saddle on a genuine galloper. He would need to learn to be a proficient cowboy rider in the two weeks before shooting started.

Minna drove him out to the Griffith Park Riding Academy, where Clark was handed over to Art Wilson, a former cowboy from Montana. In 1932 Art recounted his experience with Clark to Adela Rogers St. Johns, journalist, screenwriter, and eventually one of Clark's close friends.

> First day he come out here, I took a look at him, and I says to myself, "Art, he's a big devil and he ought to make a rider, but, hell — he's an actor. Chances are he'll be thinking about his face."... I says, "How much time can you give me every day?" He grins and says, "Art, I ain't got a thing in the world to do. Write your own ticket."
>
> Well, right then I'm beginning to weaken, what with him admittin' to plowin' and that grin ... but I says to myself, "Art, don't get excited. Lots of folks are OK when they got both feet on the ground, but they turn yellow when they see how far down it is from the back of a horse."

> Well, anyhow, I took a good safe cow pony I had, that I knowed had more sense than most men. Gable gets on top of him. An' I took 'em up on top of a hill in Griffith Park. I knowed that hill and I knowed that pony. But Gable didn't. So I says, "Now come on down after me." I wanted to find out, right off, if he had guts. I started down lickety-cut and I yells at Gable, "Come on down, brother!" And he come! Right down that hill just as fast as that pony could carry him.... Say, when he got to the bottom he was laughing like a kid. "I'm still on top," he says.
>
> Le' me tell you something. I know, and a horse knows, when a man's afraid.... That Gable don't no more know the meaning of fear than a mountain lion. I give him the works too. At the end of two weeks he could pick up a handkerchief going full tilt. He could get on and off a big horse running. There's western stars around can't do that yet. He's got a body that's just about perfect — balance, strength, everything.... He's got the guts of an army mule, and he's in there in the pinches.

A few days after he started work on location in Arizona, Clark sent Art a telegram which read: "The first thing I had to do was ride down a hill fast. Got away with it OK. Thanks, Kid."[23]

Clark was on the payroll for seventeen weeks for *The Painted Desert*, and riding down a hill fast wasn't all that he got away with. He was in a cowboy posse that rode headlong into a stunt explosion when the side of a mountain was blown up, rather ironically by Clark's character Brett, and debris flew the wrong way because of a fault in the rock strata. "The mountain, instead of collapsing, leapt out at us," Clark recalled five years later. "Stones as large as grand pianos were blown a mile. One man was killed and twenty-eight were injured. I was knocked down by a tornado of loose dirt, but no rock touched me."[24] Clark claimed that his horse had a premonition something was wrong and shied away before the mountain-side came down on their heads. It was just as well he was a novice rider, Clark commented. "If I'd had more brains than that horse I might have forced him to run ahead with the others and we'd both have been blown to hell."[25]

The Painted Desert *(1931). J. Ferrell MacDonald, Clark Gable, Helen Twelvetrees.* (Spicer Collection.)

Directed by Howard Higgin and starring William Boyd (only five years away from starting his career as Hopalong Cassidy) and Helen Twelvetrees, *The Painted Desert* was a B-grade western in which Clark plays the part of a leering heavy. Without the mustache to give it a hard edge, his smile has a Cheshire cat quality about it that adds an air of feline menace to his bad guy role. He spits the very ordinary lines out of the corner of his mouth; a villain who seems to hiss at himself. Despite Clark's hard work though, *The Painted Desert* was just another production-line matinee Western after all. Much to his chagrin, the critics ignored his presence in it in favor of the scenery.

His mood was lightened, though, by Ria's decision to move west to be with him. She and the two youngest children, seventeen-year-old Jana and eleven-year-old Al, settled into the Ravenswood Apartments in Hollywood. Jana was old enough to lead her own busy life, attending UCLA and visiting friends back in Houston. She didn't refer to Clark as her father or stepfather, just "Clark" while he called her "Sister." They had liked each other from the moment they had met, though, and they had fun getting to know each other on those occasions when they were both home. "Clark could charm everyone," she later recalled, "regardless of age or station in life. And for a person who had not had any more education than he had, he was very smart. He could listen to your conversation and the next day repeat back exactly what you had said."[26] To Al, on the other hand, Clark was his father. They shared ballgames and days out with each other. Clark was his friend and mentor.

Clark moved on to First National for his second film, *Night Nurse*, directed by William "Wild Bill" Wellman, in which Clark plays a villainous black-uniformed chauffeur.[27] Along

Clark and Ria Gable. (Spicer Collection.)

with the other house staff, the chauffeur plots to starve to death two angelic little rich girls whose trust fund will then go to their mother, whom he plans to marry. However, the evil plan is foiled by the girl's nurse, Lora Hart, played by a young Barbara Stanwyck.[28] Her reward is to be punched unconscious by the chauffeur and threatened with death, so giving Stanwyck the dubious honor of being one of the trio of women, along with Norma Shearer and Vivien Leigh, with whom Clark was famously violent during his film career.

Bill Wellman was a strong-minded, versatile director with sharp blue eyes. A quick thinker with an even quicker fist, he had been a pilot in World War I and still had a plate in his head from a dogfight injury that some people thought made him just a little crazy. He and Clark got along well on this shoot, although they would have a notorious run-in while working on *Call of the Wild* together. Stanwyck always said that she thought Wellman was "a wonderful man," not vain like many directors, and she worked successfully with him on a number of films.[29]

By the time *The Painted Desert* was released in January of 1931, delayed by Pathé's financial problems, Clark had moved on. His agent, Minna Wallis, had finally persuaded Irving Thalberg at Metro-Goldwyn-Mayer to sit still long enough to view another screen test of Clark which this time had been personally supervised by, and rehearsed with, Lionel Barrymore. Thalberg was a hard man to impress, but he knew that Minna had begun negotiations with RKO over Clark. That and Minna's excellent hustling finally convinced Thalberg to take Clark on board and on December 4, 1930, Clark signed a one-year contract with MGM for $650 a week.[30] For the studio, it was a win-win situation. Even if Clark did not turn out to be a major star and the studio did not renew his contract at the end of the year, the chances were that they would recoup their $33,800 investment on the basis that at least a couple of the films released would pay off. If he did turn out to be a hit, they would have an option on him already. For Gable, $33,800 was more money than he could then imagine.

So Clark Gable became a part of the studio system, a system that basically controlled an actor's life no matter which of the Big Five studios one worked for, and which was still in place into the 1950s. To a studio, a star was not so much an employee as a combination of child and investment real estate, and the studio took upon itself the dual roles of parent and property owner. The more they invested in the star, the more they regarded the star as quite literally and personally belonging to them.

It should be said, however, that in many cases this was no shotgun marriage. Both bride and groom, more often than not, went quite willingly to the altar to be wedded for life, albeit there were some divorces later. For many film stars, the rise up the ladder of fame happened at a speed that left them helplessly off-balance in a world that was quite foreign, even to those who had some theatrical background. As is still the case, though, many film actors of the thirties had no theatrical training at all and were often, quite literally, plucked off the street. Many, like Clark, came from small Midwest towns with not even much experience of life in a big city, let alone potentially becoming an idol of millions of people. Compared to some, Clark handled it all with remarkable calmness. With no idea of how to cope with the madness into which they were flung headlong, most actors of the period were only too glad to have the studio's parental and protective control of their lives. Give or take a few trade-offs to other studios, and a brief period of independence towards the end of his career, even an unhappy and occasionally rebellious Clark Gable was to remain within the security of MGM for most of his working life.

Although the MGM studio, with its instantly recognizable symbol of a roaring lion, was so large and famous that it could easily be assumed to be an independent West Coast company, it was actually a subsidiary of the larger New York organization Loew's Inc. Loew's was such a successful corporation that, unlike other major studios, it did not lose money and so never had to be re-organized during the Great Depression era or during the 1940s. In 1904, Marcus Loew had formed the People's Vaudeville Company to tender what was known as nickel vaudeville shows, a combination of filmed and live entertainment. His business grew rapidly, mainly due to his willingness to diversify into concessions at amusement parks and his shrewd insight that one could be sure of a theater putting on your shows if you owned the theater.

In February 1910, Loew's Consolidated Enterprises went public with a $200,000 stock issue. Loew assumed the presidency of the new organization, and Nicholas Schenck became secretary-treasurer. Loew's continued a slow but sure expansion, but it was still an organization primarily involved with vaudeville. That changed, however, after World War I. Unlike competitors such as Famous Players–Lasky and First National, who had their own production companies, Loew's was being forced to pay increasingly higher rates to rent the movies they showed. They couldn't help but notice that these movies were rapidly becoming more popular with audiences than the vaudeville acts teamed with them. So, in 1919, they began talks with a film distribution company known as Metro Pictures.

Metro had been formed in 1915 to distribute the films of five small studios. The rapid rise to fame of a small group of actors from these studios, Francis X. Bushman, Mary Miles Minter, and Ethel and Lionel Barrymore, had enabled Metro to finance all their activities from profits alone for the company's first two years. After that, Metro was able to incorporate with a two-and-a-half million dollar capital base and take over the five studios. Unfortunately, that was the best that Metro could do, and from that peak they slid downhill into deeper debt. In 1920, Loew's agreed to take over Metro and finance their debt.

Loew's Inc., as they now were, expanded rapidly across the full spectrum of film production, distribution, and exhibition. By mid-decade, they owned more than one hundred theaters, including their flagship 3500-seat Loew's State theater in Times Square, that opened in 1921, and the 5000-seat Capital Theater, near Times Square, which was at that time the largest theater in the United States. The Capital had come to them courtesy of their takeover in 1924 of another ailing company, Goldwyn Pictures, based in Culver City, California. Loew's hired former Metro executive Louis B. Mayer to manage this expanded production facility, which was named Metro-Goldwyn-Mayer that same year. Within three years MGM became one of Hollywood's major studios, but Loew's continued to resist the use of sound which had been introduced by Warner Brothers in 1926. All too soon, though, it became obvious Loew's would not remain in the race without it. In 1928 they, United Artists, and Paramount signed a rights-and-equipment deal with Western Electric. Within twelve months, MGM was making talkies to be shown in Loew's newly wired theaters.

They never looked back. In 1930, Loew's profit of fourteen-and-a-half million dollars set a corporate record that lasted for sixteen years as they continued to make money while others lost it during the Depression. As they became an international motion-picture corporation, with over 120 subsidiaries and 150 theaters, Loew's succeeded in dominating the industry.

One of those subsidiaries was the rapidly expanding Metro-Goldwyn-Mayer Film Corporation. By 1932, the studio covered over fifty-three acres of Culver City, housed in eighteen permanent buildings and using twenty-two standing sets. Before the decade was out, it would expand to sixty-six acres and add five more soundstages, as well as processing laboratories and offices. MGM's production staff exceeded six thousand and their average film budget was $500,000. By 1949, the MGM lot covered 168 acres with twenty-seven soundstages. Their film-processing labs could process 150,000 feet in twenty-four hours, and their property rooms contained more than fifteen thousand pieces. Their dubbing studios in Barcelona, Paris, and Rome enabled them to have international distribution in a number of languages.

Loew's was managed by a seven-member executive team headed by Nicholas Schenck that was remarkable for its continuity; with the exception of David Bernstein, all stayed on until well into the television era. This was probably in no small part due to their salary packages which were also remarkable, including not only a handsome salary figure but also a fixed percentage of the corporation's profits. In 1941, for example, overseas manager Arthur Loew received $3,000 a week plus five percent of the overseas profits. Schenck, known in the industry as "The General," who stayed in the chair until he was seventy-five, received $2,500 a week plus two-and-a-half percent of the net corporate profit, which meant that in the long run he received more. J. Robert Rubin was Schenck's liaison with MGM, smoothing the often rough road of relations with bosses Mayer (1924–1948) and Dore Schary (1948–1954), and bidding for screen rights for books, plays and musicals.[31]

For most of Clark Gable's career, MGM was continuously presided over by one man, Louis B. Mayer, the highest-paid American executive of the 1930s. Like Loew's, MGM was managed by a team of highly paid specialists who remained with the company over long periods of time. Directly below Mayer on the company ladder were four key decision makers. General manager Edgar (Eddie) Mannix joined Mayer in 1925 and stayed for some thirty years. Labor-relations specialist Benjamin Thau, with MGM from 1929 to 1956, handled labor and union problems and negotiated contracts. Production specialist Sam Katz and distribution expert Al Lichtman had joined from Paramount and United Artists respectively in the mid–1930s, and they were directly responsible to Schenck. In fact, despite Mayer's apparent tight control of the studio, neither he nor the other executives made many major decisions without running them by Schenck.

Below these four executives in the corporate structure were the five producers in charge of specific types of film. They also participated in the profit-sharing, a system that had been set up by Mayer in 1933. These were Harry Rapf (1924–1948), who specialized in

sentimental films such as *Lassie*; Hunt Stromberg (1924–1942), who specialized in dramas and musicals; Bernard Hyman (1924–1942), who supervised jungle films such as *Tarzan* and then moved to more literary material such as *The Good Earth*; Lawrence Weingarten (1927–1968), who began with comedies and then moved to the Tracy-Hepburn movies, and Mervyn LeRoy (1938–1956), who was a producer-director of prestige films such as *Waterloo Bridge* and who frequently credited himself with "discovering" Clark Gable.

Two other important additions, of course, were David O. Selznick and Irving Thalberg. Selznick first worked there from 1926 to 1927, and then he returned in 1933 as Mayer's son-in-law to stand in for an ailing Thalberg. When Thalberg recovered, Selznick moved on to his own company. Prior to the institution of the unit-producer system, Thalberg and Mayer approved everything between them. After 1933, Thalberg became the special projects producer, involved in such films as *The Barretts of Wimpole Street* and *Mutiny on the Bounty*, until his untimely death in 1936.

Schenck was a conservative man, and MGM's output reflected that. Until after the Great Depression they were the least diversified of the Big Five studios. After that, they made up for lost time and diversified quite widely, but Loew's relatively small theater chain meant they had to produce feature films that would primarily be attractive to other distributors. There were not enough Loew's theaters to ensure a profit for a film playing in them alone. With this necessity driving them on, MGM eventually collected the biggest stable of stars and produced a larger percentage of top-grossing films than any other studio, always with an eye on public recognition and resulting popularity and profits. MGM, in fact, became highly dependant on the very star system they went to great lengths to create.

During the early 1930s, MGM's stars were predominantly women such as Norma Shearer, Joan Crawford, Greta Garbo, and perhaps most interesting of all, Marie Dressler, who became the studio's top star at the age of sixty-one and won an Academy Award. The late 1930s and early 1940s, however, saw a change in public preference with the rise in popularity of MGM's male stars. The top three of these were Mickey Rooney, Clark Gable, and Spencer Tracy. Rooney's popularity was unbeatable; he ranked number one at the box office for three successive years, which neither Gable nor Tracy could achieve. Clark lasted longer in the top ten, though, from 1932 until 1942, and then returning after he came out of the army. People could not seem to accept Rooney as an adult after World War II, and his contract was terminated in 1948, when Clark was still number seven.

By January of 1932, having weathered the advent of sound and the stock-market crash, Metro-Goldwyn-Mayer would be worth over twenty-five million dollars and would continue to expand and prosper. Its colonnaded main gate led into fifty-three acres of magic kingdom, long before one was ever dreamed of in Annaheim, dominated by twenty-two sound stages built back-to-back. One of them had what was reputed to be the largest proscenium stage west of Broadway for filming musicals and theatrical spectacles. Another, one hundred feet wide and two hundred and fifty long, was for exterior scenes. To the left of the main gate loomed the three floors of the executive building and the wardrobe building, which housed tailors' workshops, designers'

studios and storage for over ten thousand costumes. Nearby were the publicity building and casting office, and across the street was the commissary — dining rooms, lunch counters and soda fountains which served an average of a thousand meals a day, seven thousand during heavy production.

Directors Row rose two stories beside the commissary, and around the corner in the fan-mail department seven clerks sorted some thirty-eight thousand letters a month. Dressing Room Row was where the lesser actors prepared themselves for work, whereas the major stars had their own Spanish-style bungalows. The MGM lot also contained the studio's own schoolhouse for the child stars, dance and music rehearsal studios, recording stages and studios, and a projection room where the "rushes" were previewed.

The property department and carpentry shops that used more than three million feet of lumber a year lined MGM's own railroad spur. Beyond them was the vast back-lot, cities within a city — jungle villages, Western main streets, Parisian departments, and medieval castles. Even the studio power plant was of municipal proportions. Able to supply 2.5 million kilowatts of electricity a year, its connected load of thirty-five thousand horsepower could have lit up a town the size of Reno, Nevada.

The end result that really mattered ? Fifty million feet of exposed film a year.

CHAPTER 8

NEW MAN, NEW WORLD

By the end of 1931 Clark Gable was a star. He'd earned every bit of the accolade, having worked in ten movies that year, nine for MGM. It's unlikely that Clark ever made another annual contribution to film history equal to this body of work. In one year he laid the foundation for the next thirty years of his career. After this, he would never be out of the public eye. Writer Ben Hecht, attempting to analyze Clark's enduring popularity, wrote that people liked Clark because he stayed as remote as a king should be, yet they could also see that he was the same man he was on the screen. In Hecht's opinion, Clark was venerated because "he didn't louse up the mental picture the movie-goers had of him, as did Erroll Flynn and many of the others by getting drunk and wallowing in the gutter, by getting in barroom brawls and scandalous love affairs…. Clark Gable was all America at its best…. He was America's dream of itself, a symbol of courage, indomitable against the greatest of odds. But he was also a human being, kind, likeable, a guy right out of the life all around the fans who worshipped him."[1]

Clark's first movie in 1931 was *The Easiest Way*, directed by Jack Conway with whom Clark would make six films, and starring Constance Bennett, a willowy blonde who had begun in silent movies.[2] Bennett's character,

Laura, chooses the easiest way of rising from the slums by becoming the mistress of an advertising-agency owner. Her family shares the money, but criticizes the means by which she earns it. Her older sister Peg wants to take her into her home, but her laundryman husband, played by Clark, refuses. Eventually Laura is abandoned by everyone and takes to prostitution to survive. It was not a big part for Clark but, on the whole, critics thought Clark shone in it. Temporarily rescued here from a series of gangster and bad-guy roles, Clark looks young, dimpled and charming, an ordinary working-class hero with a lot of sex appeal. Audiences loved him, and the fan mail started to pile up.

Clark was having a lot of trouble believing that his career was going anywhere, though. Used to ensemble acting in small theater troupes, Clark felt like a small fish in a very big pond among the hundreds of people working at MGM. He petulantly complained to his old friend Franz Dorfler that neither Constance Bennett nor the director knew he was alive and that everyone at the studio hated him. Franz was, he declared, his only friend in town. Franz, tired of San Francisco's fog, had moved south to sunnier Los Angeles late in 1930. Clark had found out she was in town and regularly came over for dinner and a chat. In all that time he had not bothered to mention the small detail that he was married to Josephine Dillon, until one night he surprised Franz by saying he was getting a divorce, justifying it by saying he was tired of Josephine playing Mrs. God. Nor did he apparently think it important to tell Franz that he was intending to marry again as soon as the divorce came through. Poor Franz, who had gone though hell and back when they split up, but who had never really gotten over the man, still found that she was in love with him. Although she had other offers, Franz felt she couldn't marry someone else while she still loved Clark. She was enchanted with him, she would recall, "and sometimes when he would talk of the progress he was making, I just sat there looking and listening with mouth open, thinking, 'Oh, you wonderful thing,' which I suppose is what he wanted."[3]

However, as the year got under way and Clark rushed from film to film, becoming more involved in his new role as a wealthy married man, he forgot Franz all over again and no longer came by to see her. They were not to meet again until 1937 under very different circumstances.

Meanwhile, Clark had been forming another relationship that was to become both professionally and personally important to him for the duration of his career with MGM. In November 1930, Minna Wallis invited Clark to a party at her apartment. There she introduced him to Howard Strickling, a tall man with a stutter who was soon to become director of the MGM publicity department. Strickling had been a publicist since 1919, working with Valentino, Barrymore, and Garbo, so by now there was not much he didn't know about actors' foibles. Strickling could vividly remember the meeting with Clark years later:

He was the biggest man I ever saw. His hands were tremendous. His feet were tremendous. He had a tremendous big head. His ears were tremendous. He was the biggest guy I ever knew and I would say one of the most pow-

erful. One of his great fears, I learned as I got to know him, was that he would hurt somebody. Physically. He never did. He always knew he had this tremendous strength, but he never used it.

I thought, "Gee whiz, what a tremendous guy. What a hell of a man." There was nothing effeminate about him. Nothing actorish. He came in, you know, sat down in a chair, and right away you could see he knew how to handle people. When Gable gave an interview, he would know more about you than you would know about him. If you walked in and started talking to him, before you knew it you were talking about yourself and liking it. From the very first time he talked to me, he was interested in me.[4]

Both men quickly developed a mutual interest in each other, in fact, and remained friends for the rest of Clark's life. Professionally, they were beneficial to each other. Strickling smoothed the way for Clark as a buffer between him and the equally bluntly spoken and opinionated Mayer. In turn, his facility in handling Clark, and Clark's dependence on him to handle studio, press and fan problems, made Strickling pretty much indispensable to MGM. Strickling had the rare ability to be loyal simultaneously to his bosses and to their employees whose interests he served. He was both a company man and Clark's trusted and admired friend.

A studio publicity man in those days was also a security guard, a nursemaid, a go-between, a counselor, and a cover-up expert for the stars in his care. Mayer once said that his stars were like precious stones that he invested in, cleaned, and polished, and put in a safe. However, in reality, Mayer's assets didn't stay locked up; they walked out of the gate every night. Someone had to make sure they were back in the safe the next morning, and that's where Strickling and his department came in. Stars were unique assets. If a star wasn't quite working out in a picture, they couldn't just be fired and replaced. Where could another Barrymore be found, after all, or Garbo, or Shearer? So it was part of Strickling's job to pour oil on such troubled waters and see that everyone stayed happy, or at least working undisturbed on their respective films.

Another part of Strickling and his publicity department's job was the packaging of a star. The studio would make a decision as to what sort of image its star should have, and that would be who the star became. Clark came to MGM with all the qualifications there were to be the man's man; after all, as well as being a trained actor, Clark had been at various times an oil driller, a lumberjack, a hobo, and a mechanic. He was literate, polite, elegant, and a gentleman. He had the build and face to be any or all of these. He could be dressed down or up equally as well. Better still, Clark had no clear-cut image of himself to conflict with all this. With everything to gain and nothing to lose, he was along for the ride and loving it.

Eventually, Clark's image became so close to the real man that after a while he disappeared into it, much like the later John Wayne. As his life went on, there became less and less difference between the Clark on the screen and the Clark off the screen. He became the person people expected him to be. Someone who works at the same job for a prolonged period of time often becomes identifiable with that job outside the workplace. Their personal characteristics might reveal something of their work, or they may have chosen an occupation which suits those characteristics. In much the same way, Clark eventually became so closely identifiable with his screen persona, especially after *Gone with the Wind*, that in the end one could perceive only minor differences. Often, the mingling of real man and screen character was quite deliberate. Many of Clark's roles were written specifically for him, tailored like his handmade suits to fit so closely to his personality as to seem part of it. He might be wearing a different costume, be called another name, be kissing a blond, or a brunette, or a redhead on a ship, or in a mansion, or on a ranch, but Clark Gable remained essentially and recognizably Clark Gable. In a sense, he became his own myth.

"He liked the image and fit into it," Strickling would say later. "He was willing to be molded. He wanted to be a star. He wanted to be a success."[5]

Clark put a lot of work into that success. After the places he'd been and the jobs he'd had, Clark was no stranger to the film actor's discipline of fourteen-hour days, of rising before dawn, of exercise, or of schedules. He could get along with a crew as easily as he could a director, if not better. Only the risk of losing all his money and becoming poor again would ever worry Clark, and that got to be less of a worry the longer he stayed in the business and the more assets he accrued. If worst came to worst, he would say, he could always go back to being a mechanic, and he threatened to do so more than once. The likelihood of that happening, though, became less as he grew older, wealthier, and more accustomed to living a life comfortably cushioned against most of fate's whims.

All this was still ahead of him, however, as Clark joined Joan Crawford to work in Harry Beaumont's *Dance, Fools, Dance*.[6] At this point, MGM was still seeing Clark as a villain and a heavy, and they proceeded to cast him in six consecutive "black-hat" roles. In *Dance, Fools, Dance*, Clark plays a bootlegger whose gang is infiltrated by journalist Crawford, who is trying to find out who murdered a fellow reporter. She discovers that her brother, who is one of the gang, did the deed. All hell breaks loose.

Clark and Crawford had not met before and were wary of each other. Clark complained to Strickling that as Crawford was a major star, he would look like "a jerk" alongside her and that she would probably just laugh at him. Crawford, on the other hand, thought that she might be left looking silly because Clark's stage training would give him an edge with acting technique. As it happened, something entirely different occurred that neither of them could have predicted.

For the rest of her life, Crawford was

never backwards in coming forward about the sexual magnetism that she and Clark felt the first time they held each other on-set. As she said later in her autobiography, "He played Jack Luva, the gangster heavy, and in one scene where Clark grabbed me and threatened the life of my brother, his nearness had such impact my knees buckled. If he hadn't held me by both shoulders, I'd have dropped."[7] It was the start of an off-and-on relationship that would endure many years, two marriages, and a death. She adored him and, she said, the feeling was mutual. "We were attracted to each other instantly. I had what he wanted and he had what I wanted. Call it chemistry, call it love at first sight, or physical attraction. What's the difference? The electricity between us sparked on the screen. It wasn't just acting; we meant every damn kiss and embrace. God, we both had balls in those days!"[8]

They were, though, both married at the time, and Clark never had a history of playing around with seriously married women. He had too much respect for home happiness, having had such a brief taste of it, to be a home wrecker. Apart from that, Crawford was connected to serious Hollywood royalty, and involvement with her was not to be taken lightly. Born Lucille Fay LeSueur in 1905 in San Antonio, Texas, she had learned to dance in the local opera house, which her stepfather owned. She was sent to boarding school which she left at sixteen to eventually become a chorine in New York. An MGM talent scout spotted here there, and she was tested and sent to Hollywood. In 1928, after a series of minor roles and a name change, Crawford persuaded producer Hunt Stromberg to give her the lead in *Our Dancing Daughters*. The role made her a star. When she was twenty-one, Crawford met the charming and wealthy Douglas Fairbanks, Jr., whose father was married to Mary Pickford, and they eloped to New York to marry in 1929. Back in Hollywood, he socialized around the pool while she continued to work despite his protests. In 1931, Crawford earned some $145,000 to his $72,000. By the

time she met Clark, she was feeling both bored and ignored.

For now, though, their passion was largely confined to the set. *Dance, Fools, Dance* was reviewed as a good film but not a great one. When it was all over, Clark and Crawford went their separate ways. Clark was briefly loaned out to First National to continue his series of gangster roles in a minor film called *The Finger Points,* in which he's a gangster boss who has been manipulating the press. He has a journalist executed for publishing a story about him. *Variety*'s comment that the gangster role was "portrayed characteristically" by Clark seems to indicate that people were already becoming used to seeing him in this kind of role.[9]

Then it was back to MGM for *The Secret Six*, in which he plays for the first time on film another role for which he would become well-known, that of the newspaper reporter. *The Secret Six*, and many another gangster and jailhouse film, was spawned in the wake of the success of MGM's *The Big House* (1930), for which writer Frances Marion had won an Academy Award.[10] Hoping she would be inspired to repeat that success, Thalberg had sent Marion to Chicago to research story ideas. She found one within the pages of *The Saturday Evening Post* where she read that, in a city where people distrusted the allegiance of the police, a small group of leading citizens met in secret to arrange their own justice for criminals.

Marion had married the director of *The Big House*, George Hill, while production was in progress, only to discover that he was a secret and compulsive alcoholic prone to violence. They had consequently separated in January 1931, but had continued their working partnership on this new project. Thalberg was pleased with the leading roles Marion had written for Wallace Beery and Lewis Stone, but he asked if she could also fill out the minor leads for two of his new contract actors, Clark Gable and Jean Harlow. This was the first, but by no means the last, film in which Gable and

Harlow were to be partnered in her tragically short career. Born Harlean Carpenter in 1911, Jean Harlow had borrowed her mother's maiden name and begun her film career as an extra in Hal Roach comedies in 1928. Two years later, she gained a combination of fame and notoriety with her appearance in a film produced by Howard Hughes for United Artists called *Hell's Angels*, in which she uttered a line that would long outlive her: "Pardon me while I slip into something more comfortable." Perhaps Clark saw in this young woman, who never wore underwear and who spoke her mind, something of his own devil-may-care forthrightness. He and Harlow soon became close friends.

Impressed by Clark's potential, ever since she had seen him on the Broadway stage in *Machinal* two years before, Frances Marion enlarged his role of investigative reporter Carl with each rewrite of *The Secret Six*, building the love interest around him instead of actor John Mack Brown. When Thalberg showed signs of resistance to her changes, Marion quietly fell back on her favorite method of writing into a "heavy" role some traits that would appeal to the female audience. As women watched Clark's reporter save the life of a young woman while investigating gangland murders, Marion wanted them to think that here was a man who could still be saved by the influence of a good woman.[11]

It worked. Critics praised *The Secret Six* for its action and slick direction, and once again they wrote that Clark did good work in it. However, the film was accused of being overly violent and of glamorizing the underworld, and parts of it were censored. Marion had to completely rewrite the ending when the Hays Office objected that the death of Scorpio (Beery) under the hooves of stampeding stockyard cattle was too arbitrary. Instead formal justice had to be seen being served, and so a reluctant Marion substituted a quick anti-climactic arrest scene. Even so, *The Secret Six* was still eventually banned in New Jersey, where it was held responsible for the shooting death of a child while playing "Secret Six" with friends and loaded guns.[12] Clark's reputation gained a shading of notoriety as a result.

Acting with Gable, in the role of baby-faced killer Johny Franks, was another young actor just off the New York train named Ralph Bellamy. Both of them were having trouble comprehending their good luck at the time, and one night over dinner Clark confided his doubts: "This can't last. I've got a room at the Castle Argyll (an inexpensive hotel at the top of Vine) and a second-hand Ford. I'm socking away everything I can and I'm not buying anything I can't put on 'The Chief.' This just can't last."[13] Clark was never under any illusions as to the short shelflife that one could have in his profession. His own nickname for himself was "Joe Lucky," and he would often comment that he was just a man who happened to be in the right place at the right time.[14] Larry Barbier, the head of MGM's still department and a friend of Clark's, once commented, "He was afraid that his luck would end and he would be poor again.... Every once in a while he'd say to me, 'Larry, I'm a lucky sonuvabitch.' That's the way he approached it. To him it was all luck. And he figured it could suddenly change."[15]

Indeed, Clark was frequently reminded of the fickleness of that luck in the fates of his fellow actors. His next film role came about, in fact, as a direct result of fate taking a hand in the career of actor John Mack Brown, with whom he'd worked in *The Secret Six*. Brown and his costar Joan Crawford had finished most of their work on a film called *Complete Surrender*, the story of a Salvation Army worker who gives up religion for the love of a fallen woman. Mayer took one look at Brown's acting, compared notes with the Crawford-Gable performance in *Dance, Fools, Dance*, and promptly ordered Brown's part cut and the film reshot with Clark in his place.

The new version was called *Laughing Sinners*. Once again, Clark and Crawford were directed by Harry Beaumont. By the time this film shoot was finished, though, it could have been said by the more moralistic that the "laughing sinners" were Clark and Crawford, who were discovering that their developing relationship was becoming difficult to restrain. "I was falling into a trap," she recalled later, "that I warned young girls about — not to fall in love with their leading man. Boy, I had to eat those words, but they tasted very sweet." They both felt, too, that there was a lot in common with elements of their pasts. They had both started from the bottom of the acting ladder, "nobodies transformed into somebodies by Hollywood, and married to people who had tried to change us. We asked for it, bought it, had to live with it, but we were scared shitless. He was relieved to know I felt the same, even though I was a star and he wasn't. God, how we talked and sometimes cried.... Clark was the first one I could talk to candidly in Hollywood."[16]

Unfortunately the critics did not cry over this soapie. The *New York Times* summed it all up by finding Clark's performance "rather unconvincing."[17] Clark still didn't register with audiences as a romantic lead; most people seemed to think that the combination of his bulk and that smooth, feline smile gave his character a certain air of menace rather than suavity.

It was Clarence Brown, who would direct eight Gable films, who finally realized that the key to Clark's popularity might lie in combining those elements of menace and suavity in Clark's onscreen personality in such a way that they would be attractive.[18] Previously, there had been a sharp distinction between romantic leads who were invariably smooth, mannered, morally acceptable gentlemen, and the unethical villains who were cruel, physically powerful, violent thugs. Creating a physically violent and unethical lead character who was also good-looking and attractive to women would give Clark's character a certain raw edge. It would give to his romance a quality of "tough love" that would be different and distinctive.

Norma Shearer, actress wife of Irving Thalberg, had read Adela Rogers St. Johns' novel *A Free Soul*. She was fascinated by the story and especially by the role of the free-spirited daughter, who meets a ruthless but charming gangster with whom she falls in love. Shearer enthusiastically pushed for Thalberg to have it made as her next film, claiming that the story was so strong it would top anything she'd done so far.[19] However, because of its racy plot Thalberg could foresee possible problems with censorship, and he wasn't as enthusiastic about the idea. So, Shearer enlisted the help of *The Secret Six* screenwriter Frances Marion and of St. Johns herself to pressure Thalberg to do it. Thirty years later, St. Johns recollected that she "had written that novel from my heart, and I wanted it on the screen."[20]

Given that St. Johns' father, Earl Rogers, had been a hard-drinking, colorful criminal lawyer who tended to win his cases with the help of theatrical trials and who encouraged his daughter to be independent with a mind of her own, there is more than a little autobiographical flavor to the story.[21] It's a moralistic tale about a wealthy lawyer, Steven, who won't stop drinking long enough to be a father to his independent and high-spirited daughter Jan. She leaves her fiancé and runs off with a ruthless gambler, Ace, whose virility excites her. Her father refuses to let her marry him. At first bedazzled by Ace, Jan begins to see him for the thug he is as he becomes increasingly violent with her. Eventually her former fiancé intervenes, but in the ensuing row he kills Ace. Jan pleads with her father to defend him, and so at the trial Steven confesses that that he did the crime. One of Ace's mob duly seeks revenge by gunning him down. Steven dies in Jan's arms knowing she has forgiven him.

According to St. Johns, the original casting choice for Ace was John Gilbert, the great silent-movie hero, but his career and his health had declined rapidly after the introduction of sound and by this time he was a sick man.[22]

St. Johns recalls that director Clarence Brown called her one morning to let her know that Thalberg thought Clark Gable would be an ideal replacement for Gilbert. It may well have been Frances Marion, who had been very enthusiastic about Clark's talents since his work in *The Secret Six,* who influenced Thalberg. In any case, as neither Brown nor St. Johns had actually met Clark, Brown suggested that St. Johns invite Clark to her house by the beach at Malibu, talk to him, and see what she thought of him. St. Johns could then let Brown know whether she considered Clark an appropriate choice for the Ace role.

Clark came to Malibu as soon as he could. "Young Gable sat down on the edge of his chair and studied me gravely," St. Johns wrote a few months later. "He didn't look very happy. He looked bored and rather sulky. I could see thoughts unwinding in the back of his head. What was expected of him? Women!" Suddenly St. Johns realized why he'd be thinking this. It was evening, and she had a fire lit and candles burning. To make matters worse she was dressed in French silk lounging pajamas, which were all the rage then in Malibu, and she was stretched out on the couch in what must have seemed an inviting fashion because she had been sitting at the typewriter most of the day. Fortunately, right about then her husband came downstairs and kissed her before he noticed Clark was in the room. "The look of joy and relief that spread over Clark's face was unconscious and simply swell," St. Johns recalled. "He took a deep breath, removed his coat and vest, remarked that he preferred his gin straight instead of gummed up with pineapple juice and cherries, and the evening began to look like a success." When St. Johns revealed that she just happened to have some bootleg gin in her basement, Clark laughed and a life-time friendship began.

St. Johns sat back that night and listened to Clark talk enthusiastically to her husband on what would become quite a theme of his during the 1930s. "If I had a hundred dollars

a week, sure, for the rest of my life, I wouldn't stay here another minute," Clark claimed. "I'd go places. I'd start around the world. I'd go where I pleased and stay as long as I pleased." As St. Johns listened, she decided she liked Clark's yearning and love of beauty. She found herself wondering if success would coarsen him and if in "a few years from now, he'd still care about trees and horses and high snow." She wondered whether Clark could handle the Siren call of wealth and fame that gets into the blood, and the appeal of flattery for which the need, like a drug, can grow out of control. Clark reassured her that he was not a child: "I've been in the theater for twelve years. I've been hungry. I'm cautious about money because in poverty I've learned how valuable it is. I know you can be a hero today and a bum tomorrow. I give myself five years — no more. I'm grateful as hell for that.... It's swell to be alive. There's a kick in things when you're down, fighting to get up. There's a kick when you're on top. And there's the whole damn world still to see."[23]

Buckling under all the pressure, Thalberg bought the rights for *A Free Soul.* John Meehan was instructed to stick as closely to the original when writing the screenplay and to retain as much of the sexual intrigue as could get by the Hays Office. Clark got the part of Ace, and Lionel Barrymore played Steven, for which he won the 1931 Academy Award for Best Actor.[24]

A Free Soul was supposed to improve Norma Shearer's career, but Clark's portrayal of tough love in response to Shearer's character's lust started to run away with the picture. In response to this, Thalberg may have influenced Brown to deliberately emphasize Ace's harshness by having him physically push Jan around. Thalberg would have hoped that audience revulsion at such harsh treatment would prevent Clark stealing the film from Shearer. However, if that was the case, the move didn't work and the plan backfired. American women went wild for lines such as, "You're an idiot — a spoiled silly brat that needs a hairbrush now and then." They laid the old-fashioned tender and romantic hero to rest with hardly a tear in their eye as they clamored for this new tough man who would call the shots and put a dame in her place when she got out of line. Trying to figure it all out, Jimmy Quirk theorized in a November 1931 *Photoplay* article, "Why Women Go Crazy About Clark Gable," that it was "that uncertainty about him, that self-assuredness, that indifference that interests women. He is like a magnet that both attracts and repels. That complex mystery, woman, is baffled by a greater mystery than her own — a man she cannot understand."

By no means was Shearer left in anyone's shadow, though. No one who could wear sheer silk gowns without a bra like Norma could possibly be ignored. Clark certainly couldn't do it. "Damn, the dame doesn't wear any underwear in her scenes," he exclaimed to Eddie Mannix at one point. "Is she doing it in the interests of realism or what?"[25] Commentators certainly couldn't do it, either. While considering she was excellent in the role, *Photoplay* declared in July 1931, "Norma's clothes are breathtaking in their daring, but you couldn't get away with them in your drawing room." Shearer, sexually frustrated in her marriage to Thalberg, burns up the screen with a glowing fire of uninhibited sensuality as she turns come-hither eyes on Clark and purrs, "C'mon, put 'em around me." And he does, sweeping her up in his arms, light as a feather, foreshadowing a later scene in another story involving Scarlett O'Hara and a long flight of red-carpeted stairs.

Of course, the inevitable rumors started about Clark and Shearer, but despite her marriage difficulties she always stayed loyal to Thalberg. Still, according to Frances Marion, kissing Clark would make any woman's hormones dance, and Shearer's were no exception: "After some extra-heavy kissing scenes, she wandered off toward her dressing room looking flushed and faint," she recalled. "Gable had that effect on all of them."[26]

Clark did indeed have that effect. Although Barrymore caught the attention of reviewers, Clark caught the attention of the viewers, and the fan mail stacked up at MGM. People waited outside the gates in hope that they could get an autograph or just a glimpse of him. Word went around the studio that he had Thalberg's attention. As if to verify that, Clark was offered a new contract although he still had five months to go on the old one. He was offered $1,150 a week, with $500 a week to be placed in trust.[27] Clark's value was at last being recognized, even if only in monetary terms.

Although Clark's name appeared at the top of the bill for the first time in his next movie, *Sporting Blood*, this piece of "horses and nonsense," as *Time* called it, did absolutely nothing to further his career. Released at the same time as the earlier *Night Nurse* in August, they were both mercifully buried by the popularity of *A Free Soul*, which the respective studios were trying to cash in on.[28] Barbara Stanwyck gave a graphic example of how the shift in Clark's popularity became apparent: "Our dandy little opus hit Broadway the first day billed as Ben Lyon and Barbara Stanwyck in *Night Nurse*. The second day it was Ben Lyon, Barbara Stanwyck and Clark Gable in *Night Nurse*. And the fourth day all you could see were black letters three feet high which simply said 'Clark Gable' and left poor Ben and me out completely."[29]

It was at some time between the shooting of *A Free Soul* and *Sporting Blood* when someone waved the red flag that Clark and Ria's New York marriage wasn't legal in California. There were hints that they may have married in New York before the Californian divorce decree came into effect, perhaps due to different periods of time being required in the two states. Clark promptly applied for a license on June 13 in Santa Ana under the name of William Clark Gable. If he was trying to keep the situation under wraps, it seems odd that the levelheaded Clark would choose this town. Santa Ana was the customary Hollywood marriage altar, and the press had it covered. They were onto this juicy morsel like hungry sharks circling a raft of sleeping shipwreck survivors. Ria and Clark, who had as yet no real idea of the asking price of fame, were not yet awake to notice them. Howard Strickling was a worried man with, as it turned out, due cause.

Clark and Ria were married at the Santa Ana courthouse at 9:30 on the morning of June 19. By the time they emerged ten minutes later, the press had the place surrounded. Clark stayed cool under the barrage, but Ria went to pieces, tearfully pleading with the reporters not to print the story. Of course, they went right ahead and wrote it up anyway. When she collected herself, Ria was so mortified that she never again gave an interview. She appeared with Clark at functions and premieres, but she let him do the talking. For a while there, though, he wouldn't talk either. The ever-hungry press, who wanted to see him as a great lover rather than a great husband, eventually got tired and went looking for someone who would talk. They found Josephine Dillon.

By this time, the former Mrs. Gable was living on very little money in Hollywood, still doing voice training. Once the press pack sniffed her out, they began circling her as well, scenting the possibility of inflicting a few wounds on Clark and drawing some blood. They were not able to inflict any serious damage, though, because Josephine would never say anything directly against Clark. So, they made a nuisance of themselves by pressuring her and by drawing comparisons between Clark's current status and high pay and Josephine's poverty.

Eventually, the besieged woman sought a way out and wrote to Louis B. Mayer in August 1931 that, due to circumstances, she had been persuaded to accept one of the many offers she had received for her story. She had agreed, she wrote, because there had been no attempt by Clark "to repay me in any way for the hours and years of careful instruction and coaching that he received from me and the money he cost me, nor has he shown the slightest concern for the heartaches and humiliations he has brought into my life." Having justified herself, Josephine then gently slid her knife between Mayer's ribs. Although she insisted that she bore MGM no ill will, such publication, she pointed out, will "probably damage one of your properties. If you would rather buy this story from me than have me sell it for publication, I am willing to agree not to give out any information about Gable while he is in your employ other than through your office." She wanted both MGM and Clark to acknowledge the help and coaching she gave Clark.[30]

Always a man who wanted to be in control of his public relations, Mayer evidently arranged with Clark to pay Josephine two hundred dollars a month to stay quiet. Whether Josephine eventually couldn't hold out any longer at the enticements being waved under her nose or whether Clark just got tired of paying her might never be known for sure, but in July of the following year Clark instructed that her checks be stopped because of interviews that she had allegedly given to the press without permission. Josephine denied everything, but when it became clear that no more money would be forthcoming she proceeded, rather like the Ancient Mariner, to stop everyone who ventured near to recount her tragic tale.

Strickling and the publicity department reluctantly concluded that, given this situation, perhaps it might be worthwhile giving Clark the chance to reply in his own words. The problem was that when asked a straight question, Clark was likely to give an honest answer. This gave the purveyors of fantasy more than a few nightmares. Rather than spin a fairytale of lights and glamour when asked how he got to be a star, Clark would grin wryly and comment, "I just got lucky, I guess." Clark was under no illusions and considered that he was where he was because he happened to be in the right place at the right time. He understood clearly that at any moment it could be the wrong time, and he would be back there on the street, doing the rounds looking for work in crowd scenes again.

But reality was not what studio public relations was about. Rather than talk, Clark was encouraged by the publicity department to pick up a fishing rod or a gun. Clark, who preferred to be out of the publicity limelight anyway, didn't need a lot of encouraging. His interest in guns and hunting had already been prompted by two of his friends: Buster Keaton and Mary Astor's second husband, Dr. Franklyn Thorpe.[31] When Gable complained to Keaton that he "liked women all right, but not all the time" and asked for suggestions as to what else to do, Keaton supposedly said, "Go shoot deer, or fish for marlin."[32] Invited to the Astor's home for dinner one night with Ria, Clark admired Dr. Thorpe's impressive gun collection, and the upshot of that was a hunting trip to the Sierras. They slept on the ground in sleeping bags, and when they came back Clark promptly bought some of the best camping equipment money could find. After that, Clark and his companions hunted in style all over the West, but Clark was usually more interested in the outdoor living than killing anything. In particular, he hated to shoot deer. Dr. Thorpe recalled that Clark was not a precision shot, "but a fast shooter. He would never shoot an animal while it was standing, only while it was running. Once Clark drew a bead on a buck then put his gun down, saying: 'I would have got him if the son-of-a-gun hadn't looked at me.' Gable also insisted always on doing his share of the work. He would help ... unharness the horses, put up the tents and skin the animals."[33]

Hunting and fishing soon became Clark's preferred way of relaxing between movies, and before long the Great Outdoors was part of his image. Clark's favorite fishing was along the Rogue River in Oregon where he'd stay, sometimes alone, sometimes with Ria, at the Weasku Inn owned by renowned fly-fisherman William E. "Rainbow" Gibson and his wife Peggie. Over the years he grew close to the Gibsons and their three daughters, Sybil, Carol and Vee Alice. The log lodge and cabins that formed the Weasku Inn had been built between 1923 and 1924 for Albert and Sarah Smith on the banks of the Rogue River, downstream from the Savage Rapids Dam. The Gibsons, frequent guests who had fallen in love with the Inn, had bought it in 1927 when the Smiths retired, and the Inn rapidly become popular with Hollywood personalities, writers, and politicians for its salmon and trout fishing and potential for quiet relaxation.

In spring and fall, for much of his life, Clark could be found at the Inn challenging salmon and steelhead on the Rogue. He had such a high opinion of cook Alice Everand's food that Clark could typically be heard at badly catered Hollywood parties commenting that he'd rather be eating flapjacks at the Weasku Inn.

Such became his passion for the outdoors that Clark came to define people he knew by whether they shared that love. His best friends were men who could hunt and shoot with him. Unfortunately, although Ria went with him on many trips, bunked down in sleeping bags, and cooking over an open fire, she could never quite reach the point of picking up a gun or a rod and reel. She never did become the sporting buddy with whom Clark could have shared his adventures. "Ria was typically society," Sybil Gibson would recall. "She didn't fish, just sat around and waited for Clark."[34]

Clark needed to relax. He worked hard, leaving home around five in the morning and returning after seven at night six days a week. Some weeks he would work Sundays as well. He lost weight. His stepdaughter Jana recalled later that she could remember so well "sitting at the table and Clark not wanting to visit or talk. The rest of us would just carry on with sort of light conversation which he would never enter into. Mother would say, 'He's so tired.' And he would shove his chair back before we were through and excuse himself. He was moody. Maybe for several days at a

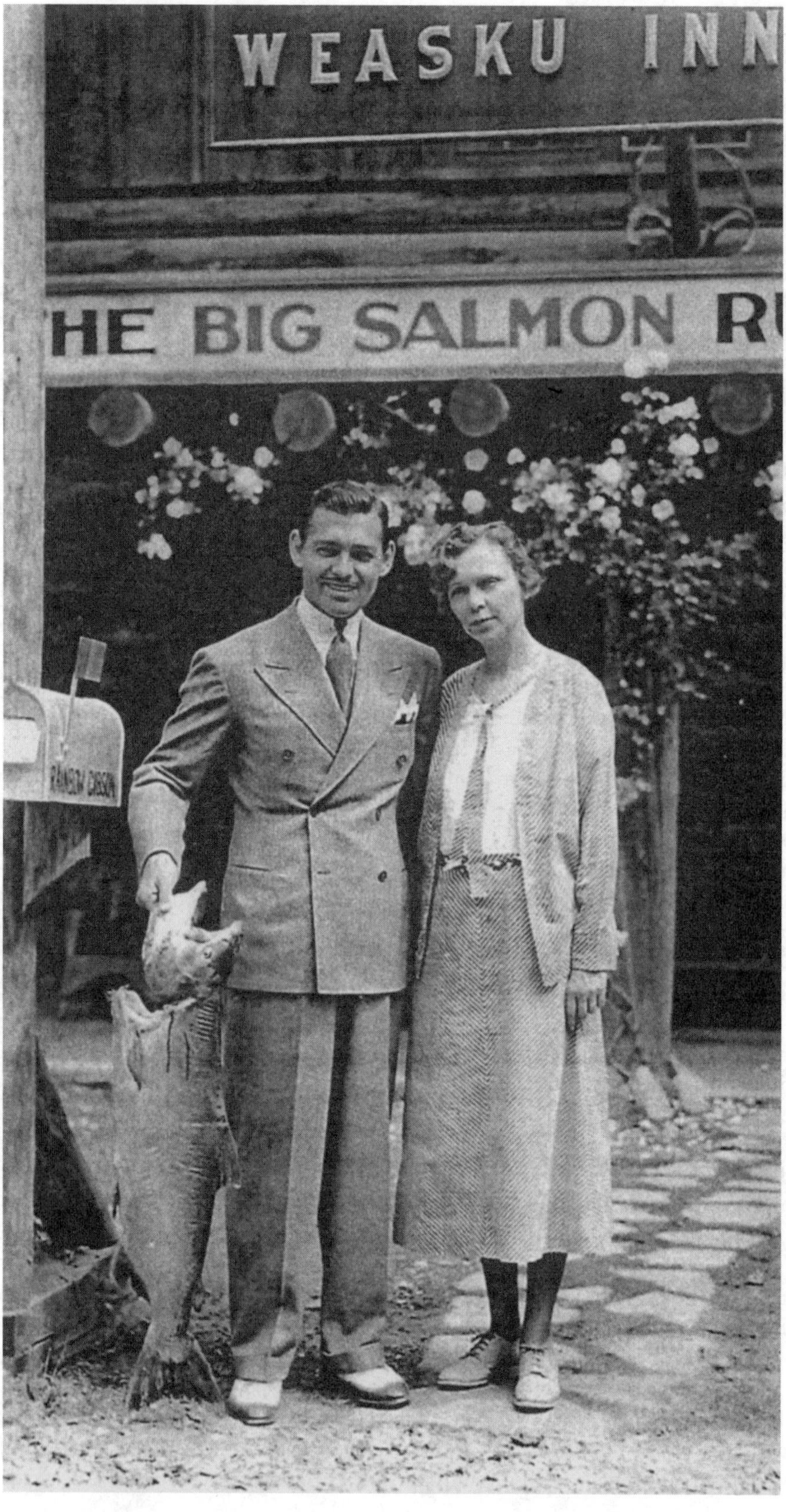
WEASKU INN
HE BIG SALMON RU

Above: The Weasku Inn at Grants Pass, Oregon, on the Rogue River was Clark's favorite recreation spot. Opposite page: Clark proudly holding one of his catches while he stands with Mrs. Gibson outside the Weasku Inn. (**Photographs courtesy Laura Kath and Vintage Hotels.**)

time."[35] Clark took to wearing clothes only a few times and then throwing them away. He bought a sports car, and then sold it not long after. He took up polo only to be told by the studio not to play because it was too dangerous. He took up photography instead. With the prize within his reach, Clark could not appreciate how close he was. With every reason to be a happy man, he was not and was open to suggestions. Very soon, some came by.

CHAPTER 9

POSSESSED

It was while Clark was enjoying his new-found sport of hunting in the summer of 1931 that he read he was going to appear with Greta Garbo in her new movie *Susan Lennox: Her Rise and Fall*, which would be directed by Robert Z. Leonard.[1] The news ruined his trip, and he was not a happy man on his return to Hollywood, as much because he hadn't been consulted as because he had difficulty imagining he'd be able to strike any sparks that would melt the famous Ice Princess. He was also no doubt just a tad intimidated by acting alongside the great Garbo, whose technique and focus were legend.[2]

What Clark thought in this case, however, made absolutely no difference. This was a command performance. Rumor had it that Garbo had pressured Irving Thalberg, whose first choice had been John Gilbert, to cast Clark as her costar and no one, least of all him, was about to say no. However, her request had more to do with his looks and status than his acting ability. Garbo's image was romantic, but it was an untouchable romanticism. There'd be no heat of desire here, and no attention-drawing embraces that would steal any scenes away from the star. However, the concept of a passionless Clark Gable was just a little bit hard to swallow by all concerned. The screenplay chewed up over twenty writers, shooting ran two weeks over schedule, and Garbo walked out six times.

Indeed, it is difficult to imagine a couple less likely to pair in real life than Garbo and Gable, and that's pretty much how it came across by the second half of the film. Garbo simply fails to be credible as Helga, a "fallen woman" escaping an abusive fiancé, who as Susie Lennox joins a circus by bedding the owner, becomes the mistress of a politician who abandons her, and finally hits rock-bottom in a Panamanian brothel. Clark plays engineer Rodney Spencer, who at first gives Susie shelter and tries to help her but in the end refuses to accept her sleeping around and humiliation of him. "Every time a man would come along, I'd wonder," he pouts. Quite understandably, both Rodney and Clark seem to become increasingly awkward and frustrated by Susie's rejections of him and Garbo's upstaging antics as the movie unspools. As Rene Jordan so astutely comments,

> After Garbo sneakily dampens the effect of his drinking-bout tirade with a marvelously dolorous gesture of covering his glass with a trembling hand, Gable goes into a tantrum that now seems not entirely the character's. He stomps out, grabs a persistent prostitute who has been propositioning him, and flings her down a flight of stairs into the bar. It is very possible he had Garbo-Lennox in mind."[3]

Even the dialogue is enough to drive people to drink. Only Garbo could have pronounced lines like, "This hurt we have inflicted on one another has become a bond neither of us can break," with anything like conviction and a straight face. Apparently she might have been laughing on the inside, though. The film curator at the New York Museum of Modern Art, Richard Griffith, recalled that while he and Garbo were watching her films he noticed it was *Susan Lennox* that most amused her. She would get a laugh out of satirizing herself, emoting lines such as, "R-r-odney, when will this painful love of ours ever die."[4] Maybe some witty Hollywood screenwriter seized their chance to pen in a last word for Clark, and perhaps themselves, in the final scenes. When the legendarily bisexual Garbo declares that "We are two cripples clinging together for salvation," Clark looks her right in the eye and sneers, "You have a very queer view of things."

The Garbo-Gable partnership was so strange it nearly worked. Critics gave it fairly favorable reviews, although giving most of their attention to Garbo as she would have intended. *Susan Lennox* made a tidy profit, enough for MGM to consider pairing Garbo with Clark again in the forthcoming *Red Dust*, although that plan never eventuated.[5] In the end it was, after all, an indication of Clark's steady rise in studio status that a star of Garbo's magnitude had requested his presence and, always the observer, Clark learned a lot by just watching how Garbo dealt with her time and with the studio. He was impressed that she only worked an eight-hour day and had a clause in her contract allowing her to go home at 5:00 P.M. He stored that away in his memory as a goal, and many years later he demonstrated his star power by having the same clause written into his own contract.

During the summer, Clark and Ria moved into a rented house on San Ysidro in Beverley Hills. Their neighbors were Frederic March and his wife; Douglas Fairbanks and his wife, Mary Pickford, lived not far away at Pickfair. Ria could at last entertain the way she'd always wanted, but Clark often complained about having to dress for dinner after a long day's filming. He also complained about the cost of their newer, richer lifestyle. The man who was now paying eight thousand dollars a year in income tax could recall only too vividly when he would have been doing very well indeed if that were his entire earnings for a year. He once said to his friend Dr. Thorpe of Ria's dinner parties, "I never sit down to eat in my home without hearing at least nine sets of jawbones crunching food."[6]

Ria, though, was merely living the life to which she was accustomed. She was not the sort of woman to play second fiddle to her famous husband, and entertaining well was really her way of seeking recognition in her own right. Adela Rogers St. Johns eventually met Ria at a bridge party at the Barrymores and, after noting that she gave no interviews, received few callers, and never discussed Clark, wrote that this "regal and aristocratic beauty," with eyes that were "dark and sad and a little wistful," suggested Park Avenue and the "well-groomed woman of the world. She suggests the woman who has always had money, who has always worn smart clothes.... But the world of pictures is new to her. When she married Clark Gable ... she stepped into a land and a people as strange to her as China. Somehow it gives you a feeling of her loneliness to see her. Her job is a tough one. But she has a determination, a will, which should see her through."[7]

As much as Ria loved Clark, she would often overplay her hand in front of his friends. Nothing would irritate Clark more. Dr. Thorpe recalled that he was drinking with Clark in a hotel bar one evening when, to his surprise, Ria sailed in and began to issue Clark instructions about her dinner party the next night. She informed Clark that he should at least try and greet the guests as if he was pleased to see them. Clark replied wearily, "Ria, you should know these people care nothing for me. They do not come to see me.

They come to see Clark Gable, a label, a name in lights on theater marquees. Up to a year ago I couldn't buy myself a job in this town or even get myself arrested. The day I lose my popularity you won't be able to get them to the house without a police warrant." Thorpe thought that while Ria listened to Clark's words, though, it was if she was listening to a child.[8]

Clark was absolutely the wrong person to treat this way. Stubborn as a Pennsylvania Dutch mule, he could be just as ornery and did not like being told what to do. Whereas Ria was a very methodical, orderly, and fastidious person, Clark did most things on the spur of the moment. This exasperated her. While Clark would ask his friends for their advice and help, he did not like being told how to live his life. That leaves only a very fine line for a friend to tread. Of his five wives, only Carole and Kay managed to walk it successfully.

As much as he might have had problems with Ria, Clark doted on his stepchildren, Jana and Al. When Jana was old enough, he gave her an allowance of $100 a month and bought her a two-door Ford. Then he made her his secretary and paid her another $100 a month for that. He consciously tried to be a father to her, but he sometimes came off as being just a tad overprotective. When she was seventeen, her parents arranged to have her portrait painted, but Clark accompanied her to every sitting because he didn't think the artist was someone who could be trusted alone with her. He didn't approve of her first serious boyfriend either, and he ended the relationship by seizing a poker and chasing the young man out of the house.[9]

On the whole, Clark and Ria shared very little and had few interests in common. Ria was always busy. She moved in a constant social circle, shopping, lunching and playing bridge with friends, and frequently going to horse races. She also arranged screen tests for young actors, promoted designers she admired, and cultivated people she thought

would help Clark's career. He, on the other hand, would suffer it all, but preferred the outdoor life with a couple of hunting buddies as soon as he could get out the studio gate. "I believe," Ria once said, "that Clark liked me, but he never loved me. I knew when I met Clark that the difference in our ages would count against me, but I wanted him, even if just for a short while."[10] It was going to be shorter than she thought.

Clark's next movie was *Possessed* with Joan Crawford again. By all accounts, including Joan's, they certainly were possessed with each other during this shoot. By now, Joan's marriage was on the rocks, and Clark was not happy with his. This time, the barriers came down that had previously held them back. Many years later Crawford wrote that she was lonely and dejected over the failure of her marriage. She and Clark took to arriving on the set earlier than the others every morning, "just to have a little more time with each other. In the picture, we were madly in love. When the scenes ended, the emotion didn't — we were each playing characters very close to our own.... Occasionally we'd break away early, go for a quiet ride along the sea. And all day we'd seek each other's eyes. It was glorious and hopeless. There seemed nothing we could do about it. There was no chance for us."

There certainly wasn't. Crawford wept every night all the way home, and she lost interest in parties and socializing. She would go out on long drives late at night, and she and Clark would meet on some deserted beach and talk for hours. Crawford would claim later that she and Clark went as far as discussing marriage and that he wanted to start divorce proceedings as soon as possible. However, she said, "I dared not ruin the dreams. I'd rather live with them unfulfilled than have them broken."

Although they tried to keep their feelings for each other out of the public eye, Hollywood was the same small town then that it can be now. Rumors were soon flying, and cryptic lines appeared in the gossip columns. To make matters worse, Crawford was in the uncomfortable position of knowing Ria Gable socially, meeting her at parties and occasionally lunching with her. Crawford "felt like a heel cherishing this emotion for her husband. I wouldn't have hurt her for the world…. It was like living over a lighted powder keg, but it was worth it."[11]

Ria happened to think Clark was worth it too, however, and quiet as she was by nature she proved a very determined woman who refused to lay down and throw this fight. She also had MGM's active support, even if it was more a matter of public relations as usual. After all, they had just gone to some trouble to ensure that Clark and Ria were legally married, and they didn't have to crunch many numbers to know that Clark and the studio would be faced with a major public-relations disaster if Clark left Ria so soon. He was a father to her children as well as a husband. Inevitably, some of the mud that would fly as a result of a divorce would stick to Clark, and he'd emerge with it all over his face.

So the MGM public-relations team organized a coast-to-coast publicity tour for Ria and the children as the Gable family. While they were away, Mayer called Clark into his office and informed him that the relationship with Crawford was to end forthwith or Mayer would see to it personally that he did no more acting in Hollywood. Mayer doing his interpretation of God handing down the Ten Commandments was a force to be reckoned with, and Clark had to tell Crawford they better let things cool down for a while. *Possessed* was finished in a record twenty-seven shooting days. Clark welcomed his family back. Then it was Crawford's turn to sit in front of that big desk on its platform, looking up at Mayer while he handed down the Word: the Word was no more Gable! Crawford wept for weeks. She asked for Clark to costar with her in her next film, *Letty Lynton*, but Mayer refused. She had to make do with Robert Montgomery instead. She was then thrown a lead

in *Grand Hotel* by way of compensation. She and Clark would work together again, though, and they would see each other again. Their friendship would remain close and a source of speculation for many years, well after Carole Lombard's death.

Although there is no record that Clark was ever very concerned with such issues, *Possessed* was the first of his movies to find itself embroiled in the rapidly heating water of movie censorship, and it would not be his only one. The debate over how much films influence behavior has been waged ever since moving images first flickered across hung bedsheets. It is still a subject for heated discussion, although it frequently now involves the medium of computer video games. By 1907 there were three thousand nickelodeons luring two million customers daily in the United States; by 1910, there were ten thousand nickelodeons.[12] While the modern perception might be that most silent movies were of the Charlie Chaplin or Keystone Cops comedy genre, these were really only part of the output. Movies were born during the height of the Progressive reform movement in America. In the light of that philosophy, many of them indulged in social commentary and criticized Victorian values and work practices. However, there was a conservative side to this movement. While the Progressives freed workers with an eight-hour day, for example, they expected that increased leisure time would be used to restore American ideals in their purer form, and they were against anything that might corrupt this enlightening process. Churches, too, became concerned about the corrupting influence of the movies. Canon William Shaefe Chase, rector of Christ Church in Brooklyn, campaigned against the movies for three decades, claiming they were the "greatest enemy of civilization."[13]

Agitation for legislation to control this new "vice" grew. In 1907, Chicago enacted America's first movie-censorship ordnance, requiring all exhibitors to obtain a permit from the superintendent of police for public exhibition of a film. Two years later, the movie industry retaliated with their first legal challenge in *Block v. Chicago* concerning the historically accurate *Night Riders* and *The James Boys*. However, the court swept their case aside with a judgment that the state had a constitutional right to protect citizens because these movies depicted obscene and immoral events that would corrupt the public, especially children. It was a spark that would ignite a brushfire. By 1909, the National Board of Review had been formed. However, many states claimed it was too liberal and continued to enact their own legislation, culminating in the industry's Supreme Court challenge to restrictive Ohio legislation in 1915. Once again, the legislature sided with moral guardians, recognizing the movies' potential to be a force for evil, and reinforcing the need for regulative legislation. The movie industry quickly saw that the only way they could avoid massive restriction was to censor their own product.

By the 1920s it was Hollywood's fortune, or misfortune, to be the major interpreter of the postwar liberated lifestyle, the Jazz Age. Women had voting rights and birth control. They were moving out of the home in large numbers into the workforce. More liberal attitudes toward sex, marriage, and divorce were being depicted by such stars as Clara Bow, Greta Garbo, Norma Shearer, and Gloria Swanson. Men became subjects of sexual passion for women who felt free to express their desires in a manner unacceptable in prewar society. Conservatives felt that movies were responsible for advocating this shift in American values, and they criticized the Board of Review for not being restrictive enough. Then came a number of Hollywood scandals, including the Fatty Arbuckle rape and murder trial and the murder of director William Desmond Taylor, which only reinforced the public's views.

Alarmed, and with strict censorship bills already being enacted in New York, the movie industry made a step toward self-regulation with the formation of the Motion Pictures and Producers Association of America in January 1922. The head of this organization was a Midwestern Presbyterian elder and Mason, William Harrison Hays, chairman of the Republican National Committee and former postmaster general. His office in New York became known simply as the Hays Office. Although he became the byword for censorship, Hays was always just a paid employee of the movie industry involved in regulating the product of his own employers to avoid antagonizing the strong antimovie lobby as much as possible.

Until 1929 this lobby was led largely by Protestants, but with the introduction of "talkies" the Catholic church quickly became concerned with the increased capacity of the movies for moral corruption. Martin Quigley, Catholic publisher of the industry trade journal *Exhibitors World-Herald*, began to agitate for movies to be regulated during production via a code. Thus, if moral issues had already been dealt with by the time a movie was released, there would be no need for government panels to judge whether they could be exhibited. The church, with its twenty million members concentrated in urban areas and with its own press readership of six million, was in a unique position to influence the public. Cardinal George Mundelein of Chicago advocated that Father Daniel Lord SJ, professor of dramatics at St. Louis University, work with Quigley to draft the code. They were joined by Joseph I. Breen, a radically conservative and anti–Semitic Catholic writer and public-relations expert.

By November 1929 they had drafted a Catholic morality code for movies that would govern what the American public saw on the screen for the next three decades. They wanted to emphasize that the family, the government, and the church were the cornerstones of an ordered American society and that the movies should reflect the success and happiness that would be the result of respecting this structure. They wanted the code to reflect the moral responsibility they felt moviemakers had to educate a universal audience, the majority of whom they believed could not tell fantasy from reality. To ensure that the power of the movies was used for the common good, then, it had to be controlled and regulated. The basic premise of the code was that no picture should lower the moral standards of the viewer. No film should be in sympathy with a criminal or an adulterer, nor should it confuse the issue of right or wrong. The sanctity of marriage and family should be upheld. Law and government should not be ridiculed or shown to be less than fair and protective, whether it concern politics, the courts, or the police. Basically, the code forbade the movies from questioning the veracity of modern social values and standards. While some nineteenth-century thinkers would have applauded the document, it was hopelessly out of touch with the twentieth-century creative mind. It resulted in films that denied reality, presenting a utopian view of life that certainly lacked box-office appeal.

When the draft was shown to Hays, he said, "My eyes nearly popped out when I read it. This was the very thing I had been looking for."[14] On February 10, 1930, Lord, Quigley, Hays and his West Coast representative Jason Joys, met with Irving Thalberg, Jack Warner, Jesse Lasky, and Bud Schulberg from Paramount, and Sol Wertzel from Fox and convinced them that it was what they were looking for too. The movie men probably saw some very good reasons why they should accept a code that turned them into defenders of the status quo. First, regulation would rest firmly with the Hays Office and not with the government, nor with some Protestant-Catholic religious coalition lobby. Second, movie production rests on fragile financial foundations, and the possibility for Catholic pressure to be placed on bankers back in New York could not be ignored. Third, they had all been living with some sort of restriction for a long time, and if they disagreed with the Hays Office about a cut, then a board of producers could review it. For the next four years Hays and the movie industry argued about whether the code was just a set of guidelines (producers' view) or a literal prescription (Hays' view). The battle was engaged over whether Hollywood should challenge traditional moral and social values or educate the audience about them — and to what extent and by what methods and genres it would challenge or educate.

Certainly for the first three years of the 1930s, Hollywood seems to have decided to challenge. It produced thousands of feet of film concerned with divorce, adultery, prostitution, and promiscuous behavior. When films such as *Madame Satan, Blonde Venus, Call Her Savage, Faithless, Private Lives*, and *Safe in Hell* were released, the Hays Office found most of its recommendations ignored. It's not surprising that Thalberg and Joy clashed heatedly over MGM's production of *Possessed*, which was based on the stage version of Edgar Selwyn's *Mirage* and was after all another "kept woman" story. Joy thought that it showed adultery in much too positive a light and wanted Thalberg to drop the entire project. Thalberg refused, stating that he did not see the subject of adultery as violating the code. There would be no nudity, he reassured Joy, and the whole relationship would be shown in good taste, to the extent of some dialogue lines in which Crawford would emphasize how important marriage was to her. Getting nowhere, Joy appealed to Hays in New York, who discussed the matter with MGM senior executive Nicholas Schenck. For once, Schenck refused to get involved, and the film was eventually produced the way Thalberg wanted.[15] *Possessed* played throughout the country without significant protest.

However, it was quickly becoming all too evident to Hays, Lord, and many other self-imposed guardians of morality throughout the country, that any realistic discussion of changing moral values had absolutely no place in mass entertainment. It would not be long before another of Clark's films became the subject of heated debate.

MGM threw Clark straight into his next movie, *Hell Divers*, with hardly time to get his breath back. Costarring Wallace Beery and directed by George Hill, both of whom had worked with Clark in *The Secret Six*, it's an action story about two rival military pilots. It was the last Gable release for 1931 and not a very successful one, following on the heels of a number of other naval and pilot movies. There was too much of an age and character difference between Beery and Clark to make for a successful duo, and any romantic interests were sacrificed too early to maintain the public's interest.

Overall, though, 1931 had been a very successful year for Clark's career, and he had every reason to be in a confident mood. Although received in mixed fashion, none of Clark's movies for MGM had lost money. He'd been in steady demand with rapidly rising popularity, and he was probably beginning to think that the studio might start treating him with some recognition of his status. Clark was understandably a very tired man under a lot of pressure. Then he found out that MGM was about to trade him off again to play yet another unsuitable role at the request of another actress with powerful connections.

This time it was Marion Davies, mistress of William Randolph Hearst. She was later unfortunately and satirically immortalized by Orson Welles as the jigsaw-puzzling Susan Alexander, mistress of Citizen Kane. However, whereas that lady couldn't sing, Davies certainly could act. A witty and talented comedienne and a brilliant mimic, Davies had been in movies since 1917. She would have quite probably been a star in her own right without Hearst's heavy-handed help.[16] Her early films, such as *When Knighthood Was in Flower* were released through Paramount. However, in 1923 Hearst moved his Cosmopolitan production company, created especially for Davies, to MGM where she had a two-story, fourteen-room bungalow as her dressing-room. She had gone on to make three

films, all directed by King Vidor: *The Patsy*, *Show People*, and *Not So Dumb*. These had made her very popular, even though the advent of sound caused her to worry about her stammer. Thalberg had wanted to team Clark and Davies in her 1931 movie *Five and Ten*, but she had insisted on Leslie Howard instead. Without realizing that Clark was sitting behind her, she told Thalberg after they had screened the test that he looked too much like boxer Jack Dempsey to carry the role of a society man. Thalberg said she'd regret the decision, as Clark was going to be "the biggest sensation in the world." Clark had wanted the part and, needless to say, was not impressed. A few days later he met Davies on the lot. "I'm the pug," he said. "Remember me? I'm Jack Dempsey."[17]

Despite Davies' excellent reputation and connections, Clark was not happy at being requisitioned for *Polly of the Circus* like one of the costumes by someone who thought he looked like a heavyweight boxer, nor was he happy being stuck in the role of a priest in a remake of a stage chestnut he could recall from his Astoria Players days. His agent, Minna Wallis, recollected that Clark called her in a really bad mood after hearing the news and said, "I don't want to do this bloody thing." They went into a meeting with Mayer and Hearst that went on until 2:00 A.M. without success. Clark was adamant that he wouldn't do it. In desperation, Hearst even offered to buy him a new $10,000 car, but Clark still refused to have anything to do with the picture until it was rewritten. Finally, Mayer and Hearst surrendered and agreed to a rewrite in which Clark's role would be changed to that of a Protestant clergyman.[18]

It didn't matter. The picture still stank. Clark walked off after the first day, and he and Minna went into hiding in Palm Springs, attempting to hold out for a raise of $2,000 a week. It was, and has been many times since, a typical star actor's ploy. Once a picture or play is in production the management is over a barrel, provided one is big enough that the audience is paying primarily to see them in the role. It wasn't only this film that Clark was griping about, though. He felt, with some justification, that MGM had worked him very hard for a large profit in which he'd had no share so far. However, MGM had fallen short of its projected production figure for 1931, and its profits were down by $1 million as a result. Mayer refused to play Clark's chess game. He informed them that if Clark didn't return immediately, he'd be suspended for so long people would forget his name. Clark refused to budge and a stalemate ensued.

Then Marion Davies waded in; she wanted her movie back and got Hearst to persuade Mayer to draw up a new contract for Clark. From January 22, 1932, he would be on $2,000 a week for two years. Aware that he'd not only triumphed in a time of adversity but that his star value had been acknowledged, albeit grudgingly, Clark went back to work a happy and richer man. It was just as well; the money would take the sting out of the flop *Polly* turned out to be. Accustomed to seeing Clark in roles of dubious reputation and virtue, critics found this sudden switch to him being a man of the cloth hard to take seriously in a film where he nurses a literally fallen circus trapeze star back to health and wins her heart with no violence or sex involved.

Despite this fracas, Davies and Clark remained good friends. She tended to stay at her Santa Monica beach house, while the thirty-four-years-older Hearst preferred his castle at San Simeon. So Davies had a lot of her life to herself. She and Hearst sincerely loved each other for three decades, but she also liked the company of young men closer to her own age. She and Clark would drink together, stroll along Ocean Front Walk, and ride the roller coaster at Venice Amusement Park. She would invite Clark to her dinner parties, at one of which in 1933 she introduced him to George Bernard Shaw.

Meanwhile, the studio had been having problems with someone else's contract, namely John Gilbert. Once again, Clark would see an example of how fleeting fame could be. Gilbert, at $520,000 a year, was still the highest-paid actor in the movies. Yet the shortcomings of his voice, revealed when the famous silent-movie romantic lead uttered his first words on the screen in 1929, had begun a downhill career slide that was only accelerating with the passing of time and his drinking.

A play by Wilson Collison, titled *Red Dust,* had been sitting on the MGM shelves since 1930 as a fifteen page treatment of a "very purple melodrama about a poor little slaving whore," gathering quite a bit of dust of its own. At various times, Joan Crawford and Norma Shearer had been considered for the lead until John Lee Mahin and Paul Bern settled on turning it into a comedy starring Jean Harlow and John Gilbert. They announced on July 14, 1932, that Hunt Stromberg would supervise production, John Lee Mahin would be the screenwriter, and Jacques Feyder would direct. Mayer had recently purchased Harlow from Howard Hughes' Caddo Company for $30,000 and had her on contract at $1,250 a week, which would increase to $4,000 a week over the next six years. Consequently, he was keen to put her in something that would make her worth his while very quickly. Her starring role in *Red-Headed Woman* earlier that year had proved to be just controversial enough to ensure its firm success, and so the studio's theory for *Red Dust* was that costarring Harlow with Gilbert would help his ailing image. Gilbert was not a well man and had lost a lot of his confidence. MGM was growing more hesitant by the month about putting him into a major film.[19]

Costume and makeup tests began in late July, while Mahin continued working on the script. Mahin was to claim later that it was he who saw Clark in a new film and who went to Stromberg about how much better Clark would be with Harlow than Gilbert. "There's this guy, my God, he's got the eyes of a woman and the build of a bull," he raved. "He and Harlow will be a natural."[20] Stromberg agreed, but they would need a stronger, more macho director. So the older Feyder was replaced with the younger Victor Fleming. Then, the script had to be further rewritten to suit Clark. Production did not resume until August 19.

Red Dust was the first major film to make use of Clark's wry, self-deprecating way of undercutting his own romantic seriousness. He refused to take himself completely seriously, making himself more human and less of a superman in the process. While Gilbert had fallen from grace because audiences couldn't believe that their perfectly romantic god turned out to have a very mortally flawed voice, Clark played right from the start on his own human foibles. His scripts allowed women to be frustrated by him, annoyed at him, and even to make jokes at his expense. In *Red Dust*, Mary Astor's character becomes so frustrated by him that she actually shoots him. Clark might succeed in wooing a woman by the end of a movie, but it was often only after a battle of words, wits, and wills. Clark excelled on film when he met his match in a woman, as he did in real life. With a couple of notable exceptions, women would tend to appear constantly before Clark during his life like ripe fruit on the vine. He had only to reach out and pick them, and for a man of his independence that was hardly challenging. The best of Clark was brought out by someone who would refuse to be awed by him, who would treat him the same as anyone else, and who would give him back as good as they got. To their credit, and to their advantage, both Carole Lombard and Kay Spreckels did just that. In many ways, Clark was like a little boy who enjoys testing people to discover where the boundaries lie. The people who had his respect established boundaries.

While Clark and Jean Harlow hadn't struck any sparks in their earlier film, *The Secret Six*, they burned up celluloid in *Red Dust*. Like Norma Shearer, Harlow preferred the no-bra look under her sheer gowns, but she went one step farther by rubbing ice over her nipples before going before the cameras.[21] There

is no record that Clark voiced the objections this time that he had done with Shearer. The heat got so intense onscreen that the usual rumors did the rounds, and have continued to do so, that there was something going on between them offscreen. Mary Astor recalled that their behavior together was very physical, that they "seemed to be wrestling all the time. He was holding on to her or Jean was hanging on to Clark, pulling, tugging or romping ... always touching each other."[22] However, Clarence Sinclair Bull, the renowned production still photographer, observed that "They'd kid around and wrestle until I'd say 'lets heat up the negative.' And they burned it clear through. I've never seen two actors make love so convincingly without being in love."[23]

The relationship between Clark and Harlow was never other than platonic. To each of them, both the only children in their Midwest families, the other was the sibling they never had. Both had been trade-marked as sex objects and, though to a certain extent accepting of that, both were largely embarrassed by it too. With neither of them very confident of their acting ability at this stage of their lives, they found that kidding around and playing pranks with the other could help them forget their stress and boost their confidence in much the same way that Clark found he could behave later with Carole Lombard. Although Harlow came on as being a woman of blazing sexuality she, like Clark, had tired very quickly of being treated as a sexual object. She once said in an interview: "Believe me, the real Jean Harlow has nothing in common with the shadow one. Sex is something that is all very well on the screen, but more than a mild nuisance off it."[24] MGM executive Paul Bern, whom she had just married in July, courted her, looked after her, read to her and sent her flowers; in short, he treated her like a normal woman instead of the source of sex-on-demand that most men seemed to see her. Clark, who also treated her like a human being, remained lifelong friends with Jean and his attitude towards "Baby," as everyone used to call her, was always protective.

In *Red Dust,* Clark has the role of Dennis Carson, the manager of an Indo-Chinese rubber plantation who finds himself giving shelter to Vantine (Harlow), a prostitute on the run from police. He is just beginning to be attracted by her sensitivity and kindness when the boat arrives bearing a sick engineer, Willis (Gene Raymond), and his wife Barbara (Mary Astor). Carson finds himself falling for the more sophisticated and genteel Barbara. When Willis is well, he sends him up the river to work on a bridge so he can have her to himself. Willis returns feeling better than ever and full of praise for Carson, who promptly feels like a heel for romancing his wife. He takes up with Vantine again to turn Barbara against him and succeeds only too well — Barbara shoots him. When Willis rushes in, Vantine says that Barbara shot in self-defense to protect herself against Carson's advances. As Vantine digs the bullet out of Carson, he realizes that he really loves her. They remain behind together as Willis and Barbara leave.

The entire plantation, eight separate rooms built around a central compound complete with working river, was constructed on a huge MGM soundstage with overhead plumbing installed to provide monsoon rain. All that water created an incredible, muddy mess. Once the lights were turned on, the hot and steamy conditions were quite real. Live moths were released before each take to ensure authenticity, despite an alarming death toll as they constantly flew into the lights. Victor Fleming, a tall, tough, no-nonsense director, kept things moving and on schedule. In general, he was respected for that. One knew exactly where one stood with him, and everyone got along very well on the set. Gene Raymond and Clark actually belonged to the same duck club in Bakersfield, and they would go off shooting and playing cards together.

On September 4, toward the end of the shoot, Clark was away hunting and fishing with Marino Bello, Harlow's shady stepfather. Jean was staying with her mother, which she did regularly. The next morning, Paul Bern was found by his servants dead in his home of a severe gunshot wound to the head, pistol by his side, setting off one of the biggest scandals in MGM's history. Thalberg had the unwanted task of telling the new bride she was now a widow. In true big studio style, MGM did a masterly job of managing damage control and burying the facts. Consequently, decades of rumor and innuendo ensued. It is now evident that Bern was probably either murdered by, or committed suicide because of his mentally unstable first wife, Dorothy Millette, who herself committed suicide barely twenty-four hours later.

A brave Harlow summoned up tremendous reserves of courage and strength and sent herself back to work on September 12, the day after her husband's ashes were interred.[25] She did this out of consideration for Clark and her fellow workers, for her own peace of mind, and because she had heard the rumors already circulating that Mayer had made overtures to Joan Crawford and Tallulah Bankhead about picking up her role in case she couldn't return. Her first scene was where Clark finds her bathing naked in the rain barrel. When he asks her what she thinks she's doing, she was to reply: "Don't you know? I'm La Flamme and I drive men mad." John Lee Mahin recalled that when she came to that line, "she looked over to me and said, 'I don't have to say that, do I?' and I said, 'I'm sure you don't.' The line was cut."[26] For the next three days, she splashed around seminude in that rain barrel while Clark teased and dunked her. Little usable film was shot, but the ice was broken and serious shooting soon resumed.

Red Dust was finished quickly by the beginning of October and released on October 22, probably to cash in on the scandal and at the same time to help take the public's mind off it. It was an unqualified success. Along with

Tugboat Annie and *Grand Hotel,* it made up the trio of MGM's biggest profitmakers for the year. *Red Dust* basically created what would be an oft-repeated Gable character: the guy who might be briefly impressed by a lady, but who is enduringly amused, attracted, and frequently loved by the tart with the heart of gold. *Red Dust* also created for Clark the ideal woman onscreen, the pal with whom he could also enjoy great sex as an added bonus, for whom he started to search off it. The power of Clark and Harlow's onscreen attraction has endowed *Red Dust* with a long-standing steamy reputation, so it is worthwhile to quickly take a look at how the film's eroticism works.

Even though the film was made before enforcement of the Hays Production Code came into effect in 1934, this was still an era where the sexual act was suggested rather than seen on film. It could be said that movies were all the more imaginative and witty for that. When Carson pulls Vantine to him after she has broken down his reserve, the camera pans to a squawking parrot rather than to entwined bodies. As Barbara prepares to take a bath and Carson is revealed to be spying on her, a tiger prowls in the nearby jungle, and the breaking monsoon echoes the inner tempest of her passionate desire as Carson literally sweeps her off her feet. The later *Casablanca* would cut to an airport control tower at a similar moment, and we have the even-later *From Here to Eternity* to thank for eternalizing crashing waves as a motif. Finally, the only place left to go with this increasingly outdated tradition of sexual symbols would be the satire of Steve Martin's treatment of it in his *Dead Men Don't Wear Plaid.*

Interestingly, in *Red Dust* it is not Vantine's sometimes near-naked beauty or eroticism that sways Carson, as much as the similarity of their characters and her willingness to put up with him, look after him, and share life with him. They are more like an innocent pair of children playing together. At the end of the film, she is actually seen reading a children's bedtime story about a rabbit to him. Carson is more sexually attracted by the aloof Barbara, an intolerable, snobbish bitch who has never been seduced before by a real man and whose aloofness is a mask for smoldering sexual desire. It was a typical Astor role that she played a number of times, most famously in *The Maltese Falcon.*[27] While Vantine is seen more than once in soft-focus with her platinum hair framing her head like a halo, the camera luxuriously wanders over Barbara's body and dwells on her perfection, sensuality, and desirability. Carson's passion for her is animalistic, symbolized by the tiger. When he is faced with the choice of telling her husband or shooting the tiger, Carson kills the beast and — by extension — his desire for Barbara. He chooses Vantine, the "good mate," and the playfulness of pure sexuality over the tainted lust of his desire for Barbara. It's an interesting slant on a moral fable, as many of Clark's films are.[28]

The quality of Harlow's comic style in particular seemed to take critics by surprise. *Time* put it down as "effortless vulgarity, humor, and slovenliness." It was kind of a backhanded compliment. Richard Watts, Jr., wrote in *The New York Herald Tribune* that "In the new film she is called upon to go in for the playing of amiably sardonic comedy and, by managing it with a shrewd and engagingly humorous skill, she proves herself a really deft comedienne."[29] Harlow, with whom Clark had initially been reluctant to star because of her onscreen reputation and who lost her husband right in the middle of the shoot, had bravely seized her part and streetwalked it right up to him.

The critics might have been analyzing Harlow, but they and the audience were looking at Clark. *Red Dust* did a great deal for Clark's macho image. For most of the film he is damp and unshaven, with his collar undone and his sleeves rolled up, and occasionally has no shirt at all. *Film Daily* stated the obvious in commenting that he came across "tough, ruthless, hard-boiled yet retaining a sense of decency."[30] Tough was the right word. In the climactic scene, where Carson confronts Barbara, Clark rages: "I'm not a one-woman man. I never have been, and I never will be. If you want to take your turn..." Barbara accepts the offer and shoots him. He clutches his side and snarls back, "All right. If it makes you feel any better." They don't make them like that anymore.

CHAPTER 10

QUIET INTERLUDE

In 1928, Irving Thalberg and Norma Shearer had gone to see Eugene O'Neill's play *Strange Interlude* in New York. Ever since then, Thalberg had been thinking about how to turn it into a film. It was a daunting prospect. The play ran five hours, so long that a dinner break was inserted into the performance. O'Neill had used stream-of-consciousness techniques where characters masked their true feelings and thoughts while speaking to each other but revealed them in asides spoken to the audience. It would also be the first main-stream Hollywood attempt to deal with Freudian sexual themes, although it is debatable how aware Thalberg was of this.

The play centers on the life of neurotic Nina Leeds, who cannot forgive her father — whom she loved perhaps a little too closely as a young girl — for preventing her marriage to her beau, who was then killed in war. It is only after she marries impotent Sam Evans, to spite her father, that her new mother-in-law reveals insanity runs in the family, sensational stuff in those days when it was still believed insanity could be genetically inherited. In an attempt to introduce new genes into the old pool, she has a fruitful affair with the local doctor, Ned Darrell. She allows her husband to believe the ensuing child, Gordon, is his. As Gordon grows up, Nina loves him in turn too closely

and possessively, so much so that she is furious when she discovers he cares for someone else, when he announces his engagement. Sam has a stroke, and Nina and Ned realize they will have to continue to put aside their feelings for each other to care for this man who has trusted them both.

To make a marketable movie out of this Wagnerian soap opera that covered about forty years in the lives of its characters, the plot of *Strange Interlude* had to be distilled to a comprehensible 110 minutes. O'Neill refused to have anything to do with such a project and thought they were all in way over their heads. "God help *them*—and God help *me*," he reportedly told his wife.[1] Even L. B. Mayer predicted it would be a fiasco. Seven writers came and went on the project before Bess Meredyth and C. Gardner Sullivan took it on and refused to throw in the towel. They should have. Although Sullivan was a veteran screenwriter from silent-movie days who had worked on *Hell's Hinges,* and Meredyth had written the screenplay for *Laughing Sinners,* neither of them was of the caliber to improve upon O'Neill. To make matters worse, Thalberg uncharacteristically miscued with his choice of director. Afraid the film would come off as being too literary and over the audience's heads, he hired the commercially successful but far from creative Robert Z. Leonard. "Bob is competent and reliable," he told Norma, "and we can control him — which is the important thing."[2] Lee Garmes was called in for the photography and was told by Thalberg to make Norma and "the whole shebang look good — if we fail on the other counts, we'll have some glamour to fall back on — hopefully."[3]

Clark was brought aboard for *Strange Interlude* purely with the box office in mind. Nobody, including Leonard, seriously thought he could handle the complexities of the Ned Darrell character. Even Clark nursed doubts. "All I do is get mad and look worried all through it," he complained to Leonard at one point. "Can't I smile and be affable and romantic once in a while?"[4] The plot did not give him much room and neither did Shearer, who did her best to exercise control over as much of the production as she could. In the scene where she descends the stairs to the hallway to greet her lover and her husband, for example, Leonard was satisfied with the second take. Norma demanded twenty more, until she had wrung every nuance from it. Her queenly rule extended even beyond the camera. Maureen O'Sullivan, who played the daughter-in-law role, recalled that "Norma spoke very little to me, but Clark was kind and attentive. I didn't even notice she noticed this — but she did and didn't like it. She sent a message asking him to spend less time with me on the set."[5]

Once Mayer found out that as part of the plot Shearer would have an illegitimate child by Clark, though, he positively brightened. "Hell," he exclaimed to Clark when he knocked on Mayer's door looking for a sympathetic ear for his troubles, "you're knocking *up* Norma in this one — you only knocked her in a *chair* the last time out. The fans will eat it up!"[6]

The fans did eat it up, briefly, until word got around that this Gable-Shearer pairing packed none of the wallop of the previous one. Then the boxoffice died. *Strange Interlude* lost $90,000. One of the main reasons for the film's failure is that Leonard failed to cope with the "aside" problem effectively. For most of its time, the film is leaden, self-conscious, and wordy. Even critics didn't seem to know quite what to make of the film, aware of its significance as an O'Neill vehicle on the one hand, yet not happy with the performances on the other. John Gammie in the *London Film Weekly* said that "Clark Gable's personality shines steadfastly through the misty atmosphere of mixed psychology."[7] On the other hand, Alexander Bashky writing in *The Nation* summed up the case for the prosecution, charging that the film was "hardly a feather in the producer's cap. It conforms faithfully to its Hollywood type of an un-inspired cross-breed of the stage and screen, and it is badly mis-cast in its two principal parts. Neither the beautiful but cold Norma Shearer, nor the uncouth Clark Gable are the actors for the parts of Nina and Darrell."[8]

Strange Interlude had a gala premiere at Graumann's Chinese Theatre in the fall of 1932, followed by an all-star party at the Coconut Grove with the Thalbergs and the Gables at the table of honor. By now, Clark and Ria were living in the fishbowl that a movie star calls home. They had to move from their San Ysidro home to a two-story colonial in Brentwood because of the number of women that gathered outside the gates. It didn't stop there, though; women fought to be near him wherever he went and would for many more years to come. Stars such as Clark, ordinary people suddenly plunged into the chaos of fame, needed people like Howard Strickling for some very good reasons. As Strickling put it, "There were twenty Hollywood columnists, there were fifteen fan magazines, there were all kinds of photographers. There was such a great demand for the stars. Someone had to channel all that, you know? Otherwise they'd get themselves in jams or things. Everything they did was news. There were so many demands on their time. So many requests for them to go to parties. Clark would talk to me and say: 'What will I do? So and so wants me to go to so and so.' I'd help them duck things."⁹

As added insurance just in case the stars did slip through the net and get themselves into "jams or things," MGM had its own police force of eighty-seven uniformed patrolmen and two plainclothes detectives, supervised by four captains, an inspector, and chief Whitey Hendry. It was, in fact, a larger force than the local Culver City one. If any of the stars got themselves involved in a crime, in a loud brawl with some wronged woman, or just collapsed from too much drink or drugs, it was Hendry's job to get to the scene and clean up the mess before the local cops got there. It was Strickling's or Ralph Wheelright's job to deal with the press. Consequently, they had contacts everywhere who would make sure they heard the bad news first. The Gable house staff, like the staff of other stars, had orders that if there were any trouble, they were to dial Hendry and Strickling first.

It was toward the end of 1932 that Clark first met someone who would later change his life, although there were no clues as to such far-reaching consequences at the time. William Hearst and Marion Davies' film company was still attached to MGM, and Davies wanted to make a film with Bing Crosby, who was currently under contract to Paramount. Hearst persuaded Mayer to offer Clark in trade for Crosby. So Clark duly arrived at Paramount to work in the film *No Man of Her Own* with a vivacious blonde named Carole Lombard.

Jane Alice Peters had been born into a wealthy Fort Wayne, Indiana, family on October 6, 1908, but her safe, secure world vanished like waking from a dream when her parents divorced when she was seven. Her mother took Jane and her two older brothers to live in Los Angeles. They grew up close, with Jane developing a tough, competitive edge as she fought to stay on an equal footing with her brothers. She played the same sports as they did, baseball, football, and swimming, eventually winning medals in track and field. She

developed a keen sense of fair play and equality. She was thrown into her first movie at twelve when director Allan Dwan visited their neighbors and noticed Jane typically boxing with her brothers in their yard. He was so taken with the feisty blonde that he obtained her mother's permission to cast her as Monte Blue's sister in *A Perfect Crime*. The three days' of work only paid $50, but it set up her goal.

Three years later when she graduated from junior high, her mother enrolled her in drama school. When she turned sixteen, she was screentested by Fox and promptly hired to play the thirty-three-year-old Edmund Lowe's wife in *Marriage in Transit*. Fox thought her name too ordinary, so she took Lombard from her neighbors, and her mother consulted a numerologist to settle on the name Carol. The final "e" was added accidentally by Fox in 1930 in advertising for *Safety in Numbers*. Carole left it that way, saying it was lucky.

It was while costarring with cowboy star Charles (Buck) Jones and his crew that Carole developed her reputation for both her riding and her profanity skills. Carole's extensive and devastatingly appropriate vocabulary was her favorite way of shocking people, but profanity was also her self-protection, her method of keeping the wolfpack at bay and of letting them know she was one blonde who could look after herself. However, to Fox she was just another starlet, and for a while her career stalled.

Then in 1926 she was thrown through the windshield of her boyfriend's Bugatti in an accident. Her face was cut down her left cheek to the corner of her mouth. The surgeon warned against using an anesthetic because it would relax her facial muscles and she could be disfigured when the wound healed. So, she had the fourteen stitches done without it. Her eyelids were then taped, and she was not allowed to move a muscle in her face for ten days. Despite all that, when the bandages were removed, she was scarred. Carole retreated from public view and refused to see anyone for months. Gradually, the scar faded, and with careful photography, good lighting, and makeup (and later some plastic surgery), it became hardly noticeable.

Her mother found Carole work with the Mack Sennett studio, where she appeared in thirteen of their slapstick comedies, effectively providing her with some excellent training for the success she would later achieve in later, more major films for bigger studios. It was at Sennett that she met Madalynne Fields, or "Fieldsie" as she became known, who would eventually become her best friend, secretary, and personal assistant. When the Sennett studio closed, Carole moved to Pathé. Unlike many other actors, she made an easy transition to sound. In June 1930, Fieldsie helped her negotiate a five-year contract with Paramount.

Now Carole had the backing of a big studio to help her career. Paramount looked after their contract players and enrolled her in drama, voice, and dance classes to make up for her lack of stage experience. Her fourth film was *Man of the World*, in which she played a wealthy debutante alongside William Powell. As they worked, she fell in love with this experienced, sophisticated, witty actor. Sixteen years older than Carole, he was everything she aspired to be. Paramount approved of the match, and promptly starred them together again in *Ladies' Man*. After living together for eight months because Carole wasn't sure their age difference would work out, they married June 26, 1931, at her home.

The union boosted her social and their financial positions; their combined income was about $6,000 a week in the middle of the Great Depression. Carole was still young and a party girl, however, and didn't take to being the mistress of a household with a lot of responsibility. Powell, on the other hand, worked hard at cultivating his cultured and suave onscreen image in real life. She once complained that "the son of a bitch is acting even when he takes his pajamas off."[10] He didn't approve of her extensive cursing vocabulary, which Carole would revert to deliberately just to annoy him.

So when Carole met Clark Gable on the set of *No Man of Her Own*, she was too involved with personal problems to take much more than a professional interest in him. It was a pity, in a way, because this was the first and last time they appeared in a film together. Carole was extremely popular with her fellow workers; Adolph Zukor, the head of Paramount, once said that if anyone should be titled "queen of the lot" it should be Carole Lombard.[11] On the one hand, she was ambitious and driven with a keen eye for good public relations; once a size sixteen, she had worked herself down to a very slim size twelve with the help of a masseuse, a rubber diet girdle, and lots of exercise. On the other hand, Carole was a completely natural, independent young woman, devoid of pretense and bitchiness, who was interested in everybody and who never left one in any doubt as to exactly what was on her mind. At the wrap party, Carole gave Clark a big ham with his picture on it. Not to be outdone, he presented her with a pair of oversize, fluffy ballet slippers into which, he thought, she might grow.

No Man of Her Own, directed by Wesley Ruggles, featured Clark as a smooth, big-city conman, Babe Stewart, who fleeces wealthy businessmen in rigged card games.[12] Finding himself under close observation from a persistent detective, Stewart leaves the city for a small town until the heat dies down. There he becomes infatuated with the local librarian (Lombard) who is desperate to get out of her stifling environment. He pretends to be a wealthy businessman to impress her, and he does such a good job of it that they get married. When they return to the city, Stewart avoids telling his wife about his real occupation. More clever than he gives her credit for, she eventually connects the dots, figures it out, and alters the card stack in one of his games, causing him to lose. Arrested for running a crooked card game, Stewart realizes that he is tired of this life, and he decides to take his ninety days in jail. However, he tells his wife that he's going to South America. One of his ex-girlfriends tells her the truth, though, and when he gets out, she's waiting for him, realizing he's reformed.

Despite the regeneration theme of a bad man changed by the love of a good woman, that censorship firebrand Father Lord could not see past all those ill-treated women of Babe's, the seduction of innocence, the glorification of a rogue, and, oh yes, the naked shower scenes. He must have been thinking of that seductive shot, from the shoulders up, of Lombard showering alone behind a glass screen in a shower cap and being shocked by Clark opening the door. He then half-closes it and talks from behind it. Nevertheless, Lord burned up his typewriter telling Hays that the movie was "filthy" and "violated every possible article" of the code, that it featured seduction and bedroom scenes "with every possible detail," requiring the women in the film to undress and shower "evidently for the men in the audience." He was beginning to believe, he said, that movie producers must own stock in lingerie companies. In his view, the entire picture "was a sin." Perhaps Lord was upset that virtuous small-town life is shown to be so stultifying that Lombard's character can't wait to get away. It probably didn't help that he evidently saw the picture on a Sunday afternoon, and the audience members were enjoying themselves.[13]

Not surprisingly, Lord's attack shocked Hays and Joy. They, with just about everyone else, could clearly see that it was a picture in which love and goodness won. Consequently, the film did well in Midwest centers such as Lincoln, Nebraska, and St. Louis where it was reported, "Gable's getting them as usual." It brought in $38,000 in one week in Chicago, where the cost of seats ranged from thirty-five to seventy-five cents.[14] No reviewers mentioned showers, seductions, or silk underwear.

Toward the end of 1932 two events coincided that would affect Clark's career profoundly. David O. Selznick, L.B. Mayer's son-in-law who had been vice-president of production at the small RKO studio, decided not to renew his contract with them, which had expired at the end of October. Then in December, MGM's executive producer, Irving Thalberg, had a heart attack and left to recuperate in Germany. Thalberg had been upset and unsettled by the death of Paul Bern in September, and he had a number of battles with Schenk over his salary in an effort to protect his wife and daughter if anything should happen to him. In the end, he was allowed to invest in Loew's stock. Selznick immediately entered into negotiations with MGM to take over from Thalberg. He was offered $4,000 a week for two years to make between six and ten films a year. They would be credited as "Produced by David O. Selznick," and if Thalberg came back before the contract expired, he could not interfere. Selznick agreed and began work at MGM on February 14, 1933.

It was not a happy move. Thalberg had been popular with cast and crew alike, and a legend quickly developed that turned his illness into martyrdom for the cause of quality moviemaking in the face of Mayer's commercialism. Selznick was seen as the hitman, the son-in-law who also rises, and not to be trusted. As this hostility bit deeper, Selznick slipped into deep depression and began gambling heavily; in March alone he lost nearly $3,000.[15]

Possibly because he had bigger things on his mind, then, Selznick paid little attention to finding appropriate films for Clark. In his first one for 1933, *White Sister*, Clark looks more like he's trying to avoid accidentally crushing Helen Hayes than being passionate with her. The implausibility of the whole story doesn't help, either, despite being screenwritten by Donald Ogden Stewart and directed by Victor Fleming. During the war an Italian princess (Hayes) is told that her lover (Gable) was killed on active duty as a pilot. In despair she enters a convent. However, he was only taken prisoner, and two years later he escapes and searches for her. By the time he finds her, though, she has taken her final vows, and it's all too late. Despite the best heat that the Gable blowtorch could produce, it fails to thaw the ice out of the White Sister, and that was unbelievable enough in itself to any woman in the audience. As he leaves the convent without her, he is struck down by an exploding bomb and dies in her arms, repenting of having tried to seduce her away from her vocation. Needless to say, Clark had problems getting into the part, and the audience had problems suspending their disbelief. The whole exercise was not a success.

His next film, *Hold Your Man*, teamed him again with his friend Jean Harlow and looked more promising, if only because he was escaping Selznick for Sam Wood.[16] However, in its final version the film suffers from a deliberately moralistic ending that gives it a curiously schizophrenic feel. The first two-thirds simply do not sit well with the rest. It is as if this pair, who steamed up the jungle in *Red Dust*, are sat down in front of stern parents and told to behave themselves. They start out well enough as a pair of partners in crime. On the run from the police, Eddie (Clark) hides in Ruby's (Harlow) apartment. She leads the cops off the scent by claiming Eddie is her husband. She takes to frequenting his nightclub, and they soon become lovers. In an effort to hold him, Ruby involves him in what was known as the "badger game." She brings home a man, Eddie arrives claiming to be her brother, and they then blackmail him. But Eddie gets carried away and hits one of Ruby's marks a bit too hard, accidentally killing him. Eddie runs off, and Ruby is run into reform school.

Now that's probably about where it all should have ended, and it probably would have if *Hold Your Man* had been made three years earlier. By now, however, MGM was all too aware of Hays and Lord looking over its shoulder, sensitive to moral sensibilities that decreed that this pair be reformed before the end credits. So when Ruby discovers she's pregnant and gets the news to Eddie, he races

back one step ahead of the law and pleads for the jail chaplain to marry them before the cops arrive to drag the couple apart. Due to a clever lawyer and a pledge to go straight, Eddie serves only a short sentence. Wife and baby are waiting for him when he gets out, and they set out together to start a new life. It all comes across as a bit forced, and the critics were not fooled. Harlow and Clark were giving the audience the characters expected of them by now though, and a happy ending was all part of the fairy tale.

Clark and Jean Harlow had a happy time working on the film. Anita Loos, who co-wrote the script along with Howard Emmett Rogers, recalled that when Clark and Jean were together they turned work into play. Jean would bring out her Victrola, as she usually did on a set, and played dance tunes. She and Clark set up a giant jigsaw puzzle in a corner and worked on it between takes, much to the enjoyment of the crew who kept stealing pieces. Jean called Clark "you big Ohio hillbilly," and he called her "the chromium blonde." They played pranks on each other and on whoever would happen to be passing by, and they even staged a mock feud for a hapless reporter, yelling insults at each other while Jean threw shoes at Clark. Loos was not fooled. "Underneath the jibes," she observed about the pair, "lies deep friendship and respect."[17]

Sadly, Clark's career had one step farther to slide back before he could move forward. In an effort to repeat the success of the all-star *Grand Hotel*, Mayer pushed ahead with making *Night Flight*, based on the novel by Antoine de St. Exupéry and directed by Clarence Brown. As well as Clark, the film featured an excellent cast, including both Barrymore brothers, Helen Hayes, Robert Montgomery, and Myrna Loy. It wasted the lot.

Clark plays an Air Express pilot who is forced by an iron-willed boss to continue flying routes at night even though the company board has disagreed with the practice. The pilot never returns, and the manager has to be the one to bring the news to the pilot's wife. For practically the entire film, Clark does nothing but sit in a plane cockpit with little to say. Even he said later that it was only a minor part. The best that could be said about *Night Flight* was that the flying sequences were novel and technically interesting for the time. The only role of any real weight is that of John Barrymore's Riviere, the man who has to make the tough decisions.[18] The film's main problem is that there are too many people in too many small roles. Unlike *Grand Hotel*, there is very little in the way of human relationships connecting those roles for the audience to care about the characters' motivations and fate and, thus, to hold their interest for the film's eighty-four minutes. Indeed, many of the cast never met. Although this was Myrna Loy's first film with Clark, she never came face-to-face with him, or virtually anyone else for that matter, on the set. "We did that picture in bits and pieces," she remembered, "episodes with different characters who never met. I didn't see Jack or Helen or anyone except Bill Gargan.... We had a very nice scene as he goes off on a fatal flight, which everyone seems to do in that picture."[19] Just like Clark's plane, *Night Flight* runs out of fuel and crashes.

Myrna Loy was actually introduced to Clark off the set by Minna Wallis, who was Myrna's agent at the time. Minna was taking Clark and Ria to the annual Mayfair Ball at the Ambassador and asked Myrna if she would like to go along and finally meet Clark. Myrna agreed. "By that time he was hot, the big rage," she recalled, "all the women in Hollywood ... were talking about him. I'd heard he was always on the make at the studio, after everyone, snapping garters left and right."[20] However, he was the perfect gentleman that night until they reached her front door after the dance. As she unlocked the door, Clark kissed her so hard on the neck that he left a mark. Myrna, alarmed because Ria was still in the car and she didn't feel Clark had done the right thing, promptly pushed him off the porch into a hedge. Clark just stumbled off laughing, leaving Myrna to storm into the house. Some time would pass before they spoke to each other again.

By the time he finished work on *Night Flight*, Clark had starred in three movies within six months and was exhausted. He told the studio he needed a break, and it agreed to give him four weeks to do what he loved best: hunting and fishing. At first he thought of going to Europe, but he realized he would get little time to relax in the light of public attention. So Clark, who jumped at any chance to take a fast car out on the open road, decided instead that he and Ria would team up with studio public-relations man Joe Sherman and his wife to drive north into the Canadian Rockies to Banff and Lake Louise. They set off toward the end of June, stopping first at Grants Pass, just over the California border in Oregon, to stay with the Gibsons and successfully fish for Chinook salmon on the Rogue River. On June 23 they arrived in Portland and moved into the Multnomah Hotel, at the foot of the picturesque Multnomah Falls a few miles out of town along the Columbia Highway. From there they drove to Seattle, Vancouver, and then Banff. A couple of weeks later they returned to Seattle, loaded the cars on a ship for San Francisco, and drove back to Hollywood.

They returned just in time for Clark to go into the hospital on July 20 to have his tonsils removed. Never one to lie around, Clark was quickly out of bed and heading into the wilderness toward Jackson's Hole, Wyoming, with his friend Dr. Thorpe. Earlier in the year they had been out this way when Clark was attacked by such severe abdominal pain that Thorpe stopped and treated him with ice packs until they could return home. By then, Clark felt better and waved off Thorpe's recommendations to get it checked out. This time around they no sooner reached Jackson's Hole than Clark was felled with pain again. Thorpe knew he had a red-hot appendix on his hands. Clark objected to returning, though, until Thorpe reminded him that if Clark died out there Thorpe would probably have to leave town.

Reluctantly, Clark agreed to turn around. It took them two days to drive back, and he was in pain all the way. Thorpe drove straight to Cedars of Lebanon Hospital and operated the next day, August 1, none too soon. "When it came out, his appendix looked like a dirty piece of pork," he remembered. Clark's one stipulation about his hospital stay was that they find him a pretty nurse. Dr. Thorpe would never accept payment from Clark for saving his life. So Clark presented him with a Mathe-Tissot watch inscribed, "To my pal, Dr. Thorpe." The doctor wore it until it fell apart.[21]

It was the end of August before Clark resumed work. It's quite possible that he may have had another medical problem attended to during his stay in the hospital: his teeth. Like most people, once Clark found a good dentist he went back to the same man for most of his life. His dentist was George Hollenbach, Jr. Many years later his widow claimed that her husband had to remove most of Clark's teeth in one sitting in the early 1930s because his teeth had rotted and his gums became diseased. It would have been very convenient to have such a drastic procedure done while Clark was already in the hospital, and that way it could be concealed from the press as well. It took a month, Mrs. Hollenbach said, for the gums to heal so that partial dentures could be fitted and attached to his back teeth. This was about the only interval during this period when Clark is out of sight for that length of time.[22]

All in all, 1933 was just not going to be Clark's year. As if he didn't have enough on his plate already, before the year was out both his father and his ex-wife showed up, the former in person and the latter in print. Will Gable and his son had not spoken to each other since Clark had stormed out of Bigheart, Oklahoma, eleven years ago. Will hadn't been lost, though; various enterprising journalists had

managed to track him down for interviews over the last few years. It was just that they weren't speaking to each other, being the two stubborn Pennsylvania Dutchmen that they were. Clark's stepdaughter Jana claimed that Ria heard that Will was in California and was instrumental in bringing father and son together: "Mother was a great family person and she believed in family ties. She thought that Clark's father should be welcomed and have a place in our home."[23] Will was not well and didn't have any money, so they let him have Jana's younger brother's room and put in another bathroom. He stayed with them for about a year. Clark put up with the situation, but the two men didn't exactly grow to appreciate each other. Will remained contemptuous of his son's career and having him around with that attitude tended to make Clark doubt himself more than he usually did.

Then half-way through the year, when he wasn't in great physical shape, his ex-wife Josephine showed up as the author of two "Open Letters to Clark Gable from His Former Wife" in *Motion Picture*. Just when Clark was feeling most unsure of his career after a couple of bad films — and it never did take much to shake his confidence — Josephine waded in with a few critiques. She commented that his voice had "less variety of tone quality in your later pictures ... and you are using a hard brittle quality." She advised him against becoming lazy and letting the microphone do all the work. "Make that man you are playing talk the way that man would in real life," she instructed, always the teacher.

Having worked over his voice, Josephine then started in on his acting style in her second letter. No wonder Clark went straight into the hospital! To be just admired on the screen was not enough, she admonished, wagging a figurative finger. She reminded him that "to act is to arouse in your audience the same emotions you are supposed to be feeling in the part you are playing. If people in the audience are not included in the varying emotions of the story, they don't get their money's worth, and they soon cool off." She reminded him that in *White Sister*, probably the last film about which he wanted to be reminded, "you are still doing those funny things with your mouth to make your dimples show" and that such mannerisms merely distracted the audience's attention from the story to him. However, she did compliment him on his entrances and the way he moved, commenting that all those exercises she had put him through had obviously paid off. She concluded that he should return to the simple, straightforward acting of his earlier movies and focus more on presenting the character rather than Clark Gable.[24]

At the end of August, Clark started work on *Dancing Lady* with Joan Crawford. Produced by Selznick and directed by Robert Z. Leonard, it featured costumes by Adrian, music of Richard Rodgers and Lorenz Hart, and the film debuts of Fred Astaire and Nelson Eddy. With his body bruised by the doctors and his ego still bruised by Josephine, especially after having nothing to do for a few weeks except lie in bed and think about what she said, Clark would not have been feeling very happy or secure at the time.

After a number of unsuccessful attempts to revive their marriage, Joan Crawford and Douglas Fairbanks, Jr., were divorced on May 13 that year. Although Crawford and Clark had had their passionate moments, had unsuccessfully battled with Mayer to stay together, and had once sworn they would marry as soon as they were able, now that the track was clear Clark hesitated at the final hurdle of divorcing Ria. After all, she would want a considerable settlement, and Clark always went into a panic at the thought of parting with money. There would also be family involved — the only time this would be the case with Clark — and probably a lot of detrimental publicity as a result. He shied away from the final jump.

While Clark was hesitating, Crawford met Franchot Tone, an educated and experienced stage actor from a wealthy family.[25] They had starred together as brother and sister in his second film for MGM, *Today We Live*, earlier that year. Tone later claimed that when he saw Crawford, it was love at first sight.[26] They were certainly immediately drawn to each other. Of course, it would not have been beyond Mayer, who had a vested interest in keeping Crawford and Clark apart, to make sure she and Franchot were cast together in *Dancing Lady*. Clark would have heard the studio gossip and, probably peeved at sensing she was not warming to his embraces the way she had in the past, was soon complaining that he was tired of these "gigolo" roles, tired of playing up to (and being billed beneath, of course) studio queens. He felt that he was being typecast as just another good-looking leading man, like Franchot Tone for example, and wasn't being given the chance to develop characters that stood out on their own as individuals rather than as just escorts. Perhaps Josephine's comments about thinking deeply over his future roles and giving really fine work were haunting him a bit. In any case, Clark griped, until everyone got sick of hearing about his hard luck.

He needn't have worried. Critics and audiences alike loved *Dancing Lady* and, especially, the chance to see Clark dance for the first time. He played a Broadway musical director who takes Crawford's dancer character under his wing. Together they fight attempts to close the show, and they make it a success. So was the film. "Perhaps it should have been called "Dancing Man" to introduce the new Clark Gable," enthused *Time*.[27]

Nevertheless, Mayer thought it was high time Clark was brought down a peg or two and reminded of just who was the boss on the lot. Typically, he had in mind just the way to go about that.

CHAPTER 11

IT HAPPENED ONE YEAR

The year Clark reached out his big hands and took hold of his Holy Grail was 1934, but he hadn't started down the path toward it willingly. He had been given a swift kick onto it by L. B. Mayer, who had decided Clark needed bringing into line. Typically with what would become his greatest successes, Clark stomped off down the path grumbling all the way.

As director Frank Capra would say many years later in his memoirs, what was amazing about *It Happened One Night* was not that it achieved the status of a classic film but that it ever got made at all. That it did, he said, only went to prove that "the only rule in filmmaking is that there *are* no rules, and the only prediction is that *all* predictions are by guess and by God until the film plays in theaters."[1] The sixth of seven children in a working-class family, Frank Capra put himself through college and graduated from Cal Tech with a degree in chemical engineering just as World War I erupted. He taught engineering for the army but was left with only itinerant work after the war, until he picked up an odd job making movie shorts in 1921 and began his apprenticeship in moviemaking. He worked his way up through editing and comedy writing until, by 1926, he was directing for the Sennett studios. From there he went to Hearst in 1927.

The following year Capra started directing at Columbia, where he had remained successfully developing the romantic-comedy genre, starting in 1930 with Barbara Stanwyck's first major film, *Ladies of Leisure.*

During 1933 two short stories by the pulp-fiction writer Samuel Hopkins Adams were published about young single women traveling on buses. Capra claims he read the second story, "Night Bus," in the August edition of *Cosmopolitan* while waiting in a Palm Springs barbershop one day. Sensing a possible movie script in the story about a runaway heiress and an inventor meeting on a bus, Capra prompted Columbia studios to buy it for $5,000. After that, he claims he forgot all about it.[2] He certainly forgot about Adams, who received hardly any recognition for his contribution to Capra's career and to film history. MGM forgot all about the story too, which would come back to haunt them. By reason of their relationship with Hearst and his Cosmopolitan Pictures, MGM had first option on all stories that appeared in *Cosmopolitan* magazine. The studio story department had recommended "Night Bus," but L.B. Mayer turned it down because he didn't like the way the millionaire father was portrayed.

On October 18 of the previous year,

Thalberg had done a deal with Harry Cohn over at Columbia to borrow Capra to direct *Soviet*, a pet project of Thalberg. In return, MGM would pay Cohn $50,000 and loan him a male star. Thalberg had been interested in the socialist movement as a boy and had wanted to make a movie about the people of the Soviet Union for some time. Pre–World War II America didn't know much about the post-revolutionary Soviet Union and so Thalberg and Capra, rather idealistically side-stepping political issues, wanted to show them the human side of world events. Budgeted at $750,000, *Soviet* would be a film about the common Russian man, a story of the survival of the fittest, a "tremendous melodrama" for which Capra was given "the dream cast of all time," he told Richard Glatzer in 1973.[3] Wallace Beery would play the role of a commissar saddled with the job of building a great dam. Marie Dressler would be his patient, loving wife, and Joan Crawford would play a politically-minded assistant commissar. Clark Gable would take the role of an American engineer sent over to manage the project. There would be a battle of wills between the commissar's methods and those of the American engineer, and a battle of ideology as a romance developed between Gable and Crawford, all played out against the drama of the dam's construction.

Then on Christmas Day, with preproduction well advanced, Thalberg had his heart attack and went off to recuperate for several months. The deeply conservative L. B. Mayer had come to believe that a film that could potentially be accused of disseminating Communist propaganda was political dynamite waiting to go off. He brought in Selznick to replace Thalberg, and he took the opportunity to cancel Thalberg's projects. MGM made the announcement that they were postponing work on *Soviet* indefinitely in the last week of February. A disgruntled Clark, who had started to work his way into his part, was left at a loss. A deeply hurt Capra, having just seen four months' work go down the drain, re-

turned bitterly to Columbia and to Harry Cohn, who still figured that MGM owed him a major name actor as his end of the deal.

Nevertheless, Capra's next project for Columbia was the hugely successful *Lady for a Day*, a critical and commercial hit. When the dust had settled, Capra started looking around for another potential success. Roosevelt's fireside chats and his social safety net for those hit hard in the Depression was lifting the public mood, and so had Mae West's redoubtable, suggestive, strong female screen image. Maybe, Capra thought, the time was right for the type of devil-may-care movie heroine that he thought could be made out of the heiress in "Night Bus."

So in the fall of 1933, Capra, his pregnant wife Lu, their six-month-old son Frank Jr., and writing partner Robert Riskin moved into the Desert Inn at Palm Springs to work on the "Night Bus" script. Riskin and Capra had begun working together after Capra had based his movie *Miracle Woman* on a Riskin play in 1931. Despite some intense work on the "Night Bus" script, and retitling it as *It Happened One Night* because Cohn didn't like the word "bus," their efforts drew a storm of criticism from studio executives when Capra and Riskin brought it back to Columbia. Weren't Capra and Riskin aware, they complained, that MGM had only recently released a Robert Montgomery "bus picture," *Fugitive Lovers*, that had bombed badly? It was not the time, the bean-counters admonished, for a picture with such a similar theme. However, Capra eventually persuaded Cohn that it would work.

Then they discovered that the rumor mill had been grinding out stories foretelling doom for the project which were scaring away potential stars. Myrna Loy, Miriam Hopkins, Margaret Sullivan, and Constance Bennett all turned the script down. Myrna Loy admitted later that she took flak for years for refusing to do that picture. "But," she claims in self-defense, "they sent me the worst script ever, completely different from the one they shot....

That girl was unplayable as originally written."[4] Bette Davis and Carole Lombard couldn't be involved because of schedule conflicts.

In the face of so many rejections Capra started to lose confidence, thinking that maybe there were inherent problems with the script. Story-editor friend Myles Connolly suggested some character changes that would render the leads as more sympathetic people with whom the audience could identify. Rather than having the female lead be a brat because she was an heiress, he suggested she be rewritten to be a brat because she was *bored* with being an heiress. The male lead role had evolved from being an infrequently employed college-educated chemist to a vagabond painter, but Connolly suggested the part should be rewritten as a crusading reporter at odds with his stubborn editor, but eager to win back his job. It would, in other words, be a "taming of the shrew" story with a shrew worth taming and a tamer to whom the audience could relate as just an ordinary Joe like them. Here was a workingclass hero, one of nature's gentleman, who could still attain to winning a spoiled heiress and turning her into a loveable woman. That the audience could also relate the story to the scandalous current events of Woolworth heiress Barbara Hutton's marriage to the shady Prince Mdivani against her father's will would probably not have escaped Capra or Riskin, either.

This time Capra and Riskin thought they had it in the bag. Even Cohn was impressed when he reread the new script, and he promptly reminded MGM they owed him on that *Soviet* loan-out deal. MGM refused to loan Cohn's first choice, Robert Montgomery, but Mayer said he had a star that he wanted to punish because he had asked for more money; Cohn could have Clark Gable. Cohn jumped at the chance but Capra, who had only heard of Clark in the context of his early "heavy" roles, was not happy about the choice. He remained to be convinced that Clark would be appropriate for a light comedy role.

According to Capra, nothing about his first meeting with Clark changed that opinion. He claims that Clark arrived to pick up his script very drunk and very angry about being exiled to "Siberia," as he called Columbia, and that he left Capra's office in much the same condition.[5] It could be that Capra is making an allusion to this first meeting when he has Clark drunk in his first scene in the film. Clark himself said in 1936 that he hadn't wanted the assignment, "for the whole thing looked sour…. After I read Robert Riskin's script, and before production began, I had a change of heart. One thing I liked about it was that at no time was I called upon to beat up Miss Colbert."[6] Twenty years later he elaborated on his "change of heart" to writer Pete Martin. Capra didn't know, Clark said, "that I felt I'd just been swept out of MGM's executive offices with the morning's trash. I took home the script of *It Happened One Night* and I read it. I had a couple of drinks and I thought, 'It can't be that good. I'd better look at it later.' I had dinner and read it again. It was still good. The next morning I called Frank and said, 'Look, I want to apologize for my behavior yesterday. I was rude and I had no reason to be. You've got a fine script. Why you've chosen me to be in it I don't know. You've never seen me play comedy on the screen."[7]

Once Clark was confirmed as the male lead, Cohn and Capra felt a lot more positive about being able to secure a female co-star. Cohn suggested Claudette Colbert at Paramount. Colbert, who had been born Lily Emilie Chauchoin in Paris in 1903, had come to Paramount's Hollywood studios from New York in 1930 after a successful New York stage and film career cut short by the Great Depression.[8] She had languished around the lot for a while before Cecil B. DeMille rejuvenated her career and her notoriety by casting her as Emperor Nero's lascivious wife Poppaea in his *Sign of the Cross* (1933). Her famous scene where she bathed naked in a tub filled with ass's milk had attracted legions of new admirers for her, and she never looked back. Even so, her principal renown was as a light comic actress with a witty, sophisticated polish. It was for this reason that she had sprung to Cohn's mind. He had heard, he told Capra, that Colbert liked money and that Paramount currently owed her a four-week break, which she was preparing to take. Cohn suggested to Capra that he could propose to Colbert the possibility of earning some extra money by working for Columbia during this period.

On November 21 Capra and Riskin knocked on Claudette Colbert's door, behind which they found her industriously packing for her vacation at Sun Valley with L. B. Mayer's daughter Edie Goetz. As far as Colbert was concerned, she had earned this break, and nothing was going to interest her less than the suggestion of more work. It didn't help that she had never forgiven Capra over his direction of her disastrous first film, *For the Love of Mike*, which had so appalled her that she had thought seriously about never making another. It was no wonder that Capra was, as Colbert's friend Leonard Gershe once put it, "the one director she really hated."[9] However, it is always surprising how much success can modify the memory; later in her life, after *It Happened One Night* had become so famous, Colbert would say that she had considered it a pleasure to work in the film because she had admired Capra so much.[10]

To get rid of Capra and Riskin, Colbert demanded double her current salary of $25,000 a picture and a completion date of December 23. Capra phoned Cohn then and there and, to Colbert's shock, they agreed with her conditions on the spot and signed her.[11] It was an accurate call by Capra who was well aware of where Colbert's allegiances lay; she was, he once commented perceptively, "lovely and feminine as they come, with a mind as bright as a dollar and a French appreciation of its luster."[12] Shrewd and self-promoting, Colbert undoubtedly saw the advantage in appearing in a film with a name costar in a role that would put her ahead of her female con-

temporaries, who had refused to take advantage of such an opportunity.

Capra began shooting the next week on a $325,000 budget, hampered by his tight schedule and winter exteriors. He shot very fast, trying for single takes as much as possible. Joe Walker later recalled that "The image of Clark, the strength in his face that we came to know later, had not yet come through on camera. He was still very young-looking, and we had to light him carefully."[13] The hours were long and hard, and there were occasions that they worked all night. "The bus scenes were very difficult," remembered Walker, "because we didn't have 'breakaways' in those days. We had to shoot in the cramped quarters inside an actual bus."[14] According to Colbert, one of the few scenes that Capra did reshoot was her entry into the motor-camp cabin that Peter rents for both of them. She played the scene, she said, "with bravado as if she [Ellie] knew what time it was." Capra wanted her to appear more scared and dismayed, forced to spend the night in a cabin with a strange man.[15]

Despite the stress of the schedule and working conditions, the cast got along well. There was a lot of clowning around and ad-libbing. "Clark broke up — take after take — in some of the scenes," Colbert recalled.[16] While shooting the "Walls of Jericho" scene, where Clark and she are separated by a blanket thrown over a clothesline hung through the middle of the cabin, she became conscious of a delay. Waiting on her side of the blanket wall, she asked what was wrong. "Well," said Capra, coming around from the other side, "there seems to be slight problem and Clark wants to know what can be done about it." When Colbert put her head around the blanket, it was to see Clark on his back under his covers, smirking, with a large bulge rising from between his legs. He had taken a potato masher and propped it up there. Colbert laughed hard.[17] Capra always believed that *It Happened One Night* was the only picture in which Clark was ever allowed to play himself, "the fun-loving, boyish, attractive he-man rogue that was the *real* Gable."[18]

Yet initially, Clark was not sure that he could handle a light comedy role, and he told two slightly but revealingly different versions over the years of a conversation with Capra about his fears. In 1936 he claimed that, upon saying to Capra that he wasn't sure he was suitable for the role, Capra told him that he'd call the picture off after four days if Clark still didn't think it was working. In 1957, a more self-assured Clark remembered that conversation as *he* saying to Capra that if after "three or four days" Capra didn't like Clark's work, then Clark would harbor no ill feeling if Capra called the whole thing off. There is an intriguing shift of power between the two versions. Earlier in his career, with post–Oscar hindsight and ego, Clark evidently felt it necessary to suggest that he had the power to cause directors to halt work on a film just because he had doubts about his role. In the latter years of his life, comfortable with his senior status, Clark felt able to admit that as a male lead being punished by exile to a minor studio in the early thirties, it was more likely that the director would have stopped work on the picture and sacked *him* if he hadn't been suitable.

The "Daring Young Man on the Flying Trapeze" song in which everyone joins on the bus was just a duet written in to relieve the monotony of the bus journey through the rain. But Capra noticed that as the two hillbillies sang, the bus cast would spontaneously sing along. It gave him an idea. Ordering more cameras to cover close, medium, and long shots simultaneously, he shot the entire scene in one take with no rehearsal, telling them all to just join in and sing any way they felt like it. As the cameras rolled, he sat back and laughed as, "One by one the actors shed their inhibitions and became nutty show-offs. They sang, danced, made up their own verses. But all joined as one in the chorus, holding on to the 'Oh!' until their faces were blue. Gable lost his truculence—he joined the singing.

The 'brat' lost her 'brattiness'—she joined in the fun.... They were children again—rollicking and romping like lambs in springtime. And Gable and Colbert rollicked with them."[19]

That may not have been the only occasion Colbert and Clark rollicked together. Leonard Gershe once asked her if she had liked Gable. "Darling," Colbert replied, "I did go all the way with him. Does that answer your question?"[20] On another occasion she was heard to pass favorable judgment on the size of Clark's male anatomy. So the "Walls of Jericho" may have fallen between the pair well before they did in the film, and the result perhaps added some ingredients to the successful chemistry between them.

Still, Colbert didn't let anyone forget that they were being driven by her schedule and that, personally, she couldn't wait to get out of there. She worried, she pouted, and she harassed Capra about her part. For what became one of the film's most famous scenes, for example, Colbert refused to pull up her dress and show off her leg as a hitchhiking lure until Capra brought in a double. Colbert took one look at the substitute and exclaimed, "Get her out of here. I'll do it. That's not *my* leg!"[21] In that later "Walls of Jericho" scene, Colbert flatly refused to even partially undress in front of the camera. So Capra devised what was in the end a more subtle and tantalizing scene, during which Clark sees only underwear being draped over the top of the concealing blanket. "She was a tartar," Capra admitted, "but a cute one."[22]

In step with the gender confusion of the times, when men had lost their jobs while women were entering the workforce, Capra has Clark and Colbert go through some interesting role reversals in this film. Colbert moves from powerful heiress to homeless waif; Clark moves from reporter to higher-status protector. Playing Clark against his established "heavy" MGM image, Capra has him buying groceries, setting the breakfast table, and cooking the eggs. Colbert, on the other hand, demonstrates a better hitchhiking technique by showing some leg, tossing off a Mae West line from *I'm No Angel*, "I've got a system all my own," when Clark's manly techniques have failed. Here was what audiences had been waiting for. Here is a hero suitable for the Depression. As Elizabeth Kendall points out, Clark's Peter Warne, "unlike outdated stereotypes, has no pretences to social power. He's broke; he's out of a job; he can't even run fast enough to catch the guy who stole Ellie's suitcase. He's a surprisingly frank embodiment of the ineffectuality of the American male in the face of the Depression."[23]

In the end, Capra got his picture finished on time, and Colbert got her skiing holiday in Sun Valley.[24] Capra had *It Happened One Night* edited at two hours for the previews, then found he was so tired of the negative comments that still dogged him about the film that he left it that length just to have it finished and out of the way. A few days later there was such a fiasco at the Academy Awards ceremony over his earlier picture, *Lady for a Day,* that he dismissed any thoughts about the "bus picture" for quite a while.[25]

Meanwhile, when Clark walked back through the MGM gates after his short exile, he found his status the same as ever — just another leading man. To remind him of that, the studio ordered him to shave his moustache and put him to work as a dedicated, unsmiling intern alongside Myrna Loy amid the medical melodrama of *Men in White*. Myrna was a little apprehensive about working with Clark after their incident on her front porch some time back, and her intuition proved justified because Clark refused to speak with her off-camera. Eventually, though, they reconciled and became good friends during the seven films in which they worked together. "It seems incredible that we were never lovers," she later reminisced. "We never were; just friends. Clark was very gentle with me. I was like a little sister. He could also get very annoyed with me. I was very unrealistic, he

thought — always falling in love. I guess he wasn't my type."[26]

Instead, it seems that he thought his type was more Elizabeth Allan, a beautiful young English actress in the role of a student nurse who finds herself pregnant after a brief affair with Clark's Dr. Ferguson. Desperately ill after a botched abortion, she is rushed to the hospital, where Ferguson vainly attempts to save her. She dies after telling Ferguson's superficial and rich fiancée (Loy) that she shouldn't blame him for what he did. Myrna later claimed that Allan and Clark had quite a serious thing going during the film shoot. Clark would take coffee and doughnuts to her every morning, walking right by Myrna without saying anything. "We managed to be convincing lovers on-camera," she recalled, "which wasn't easy while he virtually ignored me."[27]

While the critics liked the new, serious Clark when *Men in White* opened in March, 1934, audiences stayed away. They wanted to see a different Clark. *It Happened One Night* had set a house record for an opening day at Radio City Music Hall in New York on February 23. In its first week, the film had grossed $90,000. However, by the end of the second week the gross had slipped to $75,000, and so the film had gone to local theaters. Somewhere out there in the suburbs and the small towns, something quite unanticipated occurred. Neighbor spoke to neighbor; work-mate laughed with work-mate by the water cooler about what a great movie this was. Through word-of-mouth, *It Happened One Night* became a must-see film. Before they knew it, Columbia had a hit on their hands.

At the time *Men in White* opened, MGM seems not to have realized that a public punched to the canvas by the Great Depression needed some laughs to forget its troubles and climb back on its feet. "Depression? Who knew there was a Depression?" commented Anita Loos, the novelist and scriptwriter who had come out to Hollywood in 1931 from New York. "We didn't know anything that was going on, we were working too hard.... [E]verybody was so busy you didn't have time to do anything except work and worry about work."[28] Well, as far as audiences were concerned, watching *It Happened One Night* helped them get up off that canvas to their feet. One could stay warm in a theater when there was no fuel to heat the house, and laughter could help a father or mother forget how to feed a hungry family for just a little while. After watching *It Happened One Night*, people came out of theaters feeling better about life. They would share with their friends just how much fun the film was, and the next thing they were all standing in line to see it again and again. They kept on standing in line so much that *It Happened One Night* made 1934 the most profitable year for Columbia since 1929. At a time when one third of the nation's theaters were dark, and other studios struggled to make ends meet, Columbia reported net earnings of $1,008,870 for their fiscal year ending June 30, a gain of well over a quarter of a million dollars on the previous year. The film brought in a million dollars in film rental for its initial lease alone.[29] According to the terms of his contract negotiated before making *Lady for a Day*, Capra duly received 10 percent of *It Happened One Night*'s net profit. Clark just got salary.

To sell *Men in White* in the face of such competition, MGM sent Clark on his first nationwide tour, ironically to publicize one movie in which he was starring to try and draw audiences away from another movie in which he was starring. For Clark, who up until now had led a fairly sheltered life in Hollywood under the watchful eye of studio public relations and security personnel, it was a terrifying experience. Thanks to *It Happened One Night*, Clark's popularity had rapidly escalated. Insulated within the walled city of MGM, he had little idea of how much in demand he really was, especially with female fans, and of what that meant in terms of how physically close hundreds of them at a time really wanted to be to him. In Kansas City,

twenty-five hundred screaming women stampeded toward him at the railway station. They climbed onto the tracks and over coal cars to try to get to him. In Baltimore, one love-struck fan ambushed him in the elevator, kissing him and nibbling his ears. In one hotel, he woke up to find the chambermaid leaning over him stroking his cheek. Another girl begged him to autograph her bra, which she then obligingly took off and held out to him.

Needless to say, all this female adoration did not impress Ria one little bit, especially when she found herself repeatedly having to defend their marriage against rumors it was in trouble. Suddenly their roles were reversed, and she might as well not have been there. Clark didn't need her to choose clothes for him any more; store managers fell over themselves to show him their best. He didn't need her advice in restaurants where he was feted and where women hovered at the table just to be in his presence. When they went out to the theater, it was Clark who was the focus of the society pages, who stood between acts so audiences could applaud him. No longer could they walk down the street and just be together. Whenever and wherever Clark appeared, crowds would gather, reaching for him, pulling off his buttons and his cufflinks, stealing his handkerchiefs, grabbing for locks of his hair, screaming and calling for his autograph.

Finally, just to round off the whole affair of the rival movies, Clark arrived in New York in late February 1934, for appearances at the Capitol Theater only to find himself supporting *It Happened One Night* as it opened at Radio City Music Hall. *Men in White* had been held back from New York movie theaters because the stage version was still playing on Broadway. Emerging from the Capitol, having seen Gable in person, women wept in the street. Norbert Lusk, writing for the *Los Angeles Times*, put Clark's popularity down to his

making friends instead of repelling them. He has exerted himself to respond to interest in him wherever he has found it. Consequently, audiences have the enthusiastic vibrations of personal friends, whispering, buzzing, giggling, leaning forward in their seats, and even gaining the stage at the conclusion of his act. All this may not be the tribute of great art, but it is undeniable approval of the democratic majority.[30]

Be that as it may, so much friendliness to so many would be a strain on anyone after a while. Clark was no doubt thankful to shake the dust of New York off his feet on March 7, when he began the journey back to Hollywood and the shelter of the studio. There he found them, as usual, out of touch with what the public really wanted to see of him. MGM had taken a step back into his past to cast Clark as a gangster again, albeit a good one, in *Manhattan Melodrama*.

In this film the bad guy becomes a good guy by nobly going to the electric chair, knowing that his death will save the marriage and career of his former love, played once again by Myrna Loy, and his childhood friend (William Powell) who has become the district attorney.[31] The basic plot of friends growing up in a poor neighborhood who find different ways out was well-known then and has remained so since. One takes the high road, the other (in this case, Clark) the low, and a third one covers all the bases by becoming a priest. Columnist Mollie Merrick complained in *The San Francisco Chronicle* about how cliched and frustrating it all was. "The eyes of Hollywood are on Clark Gable," she wrote. "Here is one of the most promising players in the motion picture profession — the man chosen by the public, not by the producer." Yet when his own studio previewed its latest effort on Clark's behalf, she continued, all they could present was:

> First — a trashy old story which incorporated all the banal and outmoded angles of gang, political and "Sidewalks of New York" stories.
> Second — The dullest dialogue to ever hamper an already painfully familiar theme.
> Third — Clark Gable surrounded with a group of good actors, all of whom tried in their embarrassed way to make something out of nothing, to read sorry old cliches with a

new fresh intonation and to infuse some spirit of freshness into a stale situation.
> This isn't the way to make a star.... It isn't even fair to the public who pay their money to see a good picture.... It's unfair to a lot of competent people to miscast them in a maudlin mix-up of all the stories you've ever seen since "Little Caesar" and "Public Enemy."[32]

However, other critics liked the film and the way Clark came across in it. "Gable manages his exacting role with power and appeal," said *Film Daily*, and *The Hollywood Reporter* commented that Clark was "back to the type of role that he does best: a do-gooder gangster. And he comes off great."[33] Even gangsters, surely the most demanding critics, enjoyed watching Clark be a gangster; *Manhattan Melodrama* gained a certain notoriety as the film John Dillinger broke cover to see in Chicago the night of July 22, when he was shot down by the FBI as he left the Biograph Theater. Perhaps the *Chronicle's* Mollie Merrick appreciated the irony when, a few months later, *Manhattan Melodrama* walked away with the 1934 Academy Award for Best Story.

Four years in the future, in a film called *Broadway Melody of 1938*, a young Judy Garland sang "You Made Me Love You" to a photograph of Clark. In breathless words that tumbled out between the choruses she would say, "And then in that picture with Joan Crawford I cried and cried because you loved her so much and you couldn't have her — not until the end of the picture, anyway." That pretty well summed up the typical Crawford-Gable movie relationship — Clark would ever-resourcefully pursue Joan Crawford, who faded into the distance the harder he ran toward her.

In *Chained*, when Mike (Gable) meets Dianne (Crawford) aboard a cruise ship, he can't have her because she is already the mistress of a wealthy businessman, Field (Otto Kruger). They are waiting for Field's wife to agree to a divorce. She falls in love with Mike, but gives him up to marry Field out of the loyalty she feels for him. Later, Mike meets Dianne by chance. She confesses she loves him, but she will remain loyal to her husband. Mike follows her home and tells Field the truth. Field graciously sets Dianne free to be with Mike. The film was directed by Clarence Brown and written by John Lee Mahin, two men who knew Gable and Crawford well. It was the perfect vehicle for them both. Audiences and critics alike approved. It was the first film in which Crawford worked with cameraman George Folsey, who designed lighting specifically for her using a key light and diffused filter. As a result, her best features are accentuated so well that Crawford's loveliness in some scenes is nothing short of breathtaking, leaving no mystery as to why Clark pursues her.

Studio executives were so enthusiastic about the success of *Chained* that they teamed Clark, Crawford, and Folsey together again in *Forsaking All Others* as soon as possible. This was one of the first MGM scripts written by Joe Mankiewicz, who had joined the production team of Bernard Hyman the year before. Originally a film journalist in Berlin, Mankiewicz had come to Hollywood in 1929, where he wrote titles for Paramount silents before graduating to dialogue when sound arrived. Working from someone else's story or play, screenwriters would usually fashion a script with specific actors in mind. *Forsaking All Others* was originally written for Loretta Young and George Brent, but then Hyman was so impressed by Crawford and Clark's popularity that he changed his mind. To his terror, Mankiewicz was told that he would have to take the first script he had written for major stars and go read it to Crawford, who would never consider a role until it had been read aloud to her first. Fortunately for his future career, Crawford laughed, especially at the witty Robert Montgomery line: "I could build a fire by rubbing two boy scouts together."[34]

Once again, in *Forsaking All Others*, Clark can't have Crawford until the end of the movie. Here she's a childhood playmate about to marry someone else, only to be jilted at the altar. She is consoled by Jeff (Clark), until a year later, when she is thrown together with her old boyfriend by chance, and they pledge to marry again. Understandably, Jeff leaves town to board a ship, the bride-to-be realizes her mistake at the last minute, and this time it is she who jilts the fiancé to join Jeff on the ship. Fortunately, most of the critics took Crawford's cue and laughed too, but the film wasn't quite the success of *Chained*. It had a strong cast that carried it well, but many people thought Clark went too far over the light comic line here and was a little too jokey for their taste.

As usual, the studio didn't take the hint. At the beginning of 1935 they paired him in *After Office Hours* with Constance Bennett, with whom he had last appeared at the beginning of his career in *The Easiest Way*. Here, Clark has the role of a newspaper editor who persuades Bennett's character to act as an undercover lure to trick her boyfriend into confessing to murder. Audiences liked it, but it was just another piece of light entertainment. Critics such as John Gammie in the *London Film Weekly* started to mutter that it was about time Clark was given a straight role into which he could sink his talented teeth. Because the audience laughed at Clark Gable in *It Happened One Night* and *Forsaking All Others,* he wrote:

> the idea now seems to be that he should clown as much as he possibly can. Which is really a pity. This would have been a better picture if Gable had been allowed to do some straight acting. As it is, he is compelled almost to burlesque his part of a tough, New York newspaper editor.[35]

They were about to have their wishes granted in an unexpected way. *Forsaking All Others* was released Christmas week, and its success quickly became part of the excitement generated by the runaway-train popularity of *It Happened One Night,* culminating in Clark's nomination for a Best Actor Academy Award on February 23. That his bared-chest scene in the film pulled the rug out from under the American undershirt industry is now legend.

Clark with his Best Actor Oscar for his role in It Happened One Night, presented at the Academy Awards in February 1935.

Clark always claimed ignorance: "I didn't know what I was doing to the undershirt people," he said in 1957. "That was just the way I lived. I hadn't worn an undershirt since I'd started school. They made me feel hemmed in and smothered."[36] Men had begun to wear Gable mustaches and trenchcoats. Buslines reported a passenger boom (especially among female passengers) equivalent to the current boom in cruise-ship traveling brought about by the popularity of *Titanic*. Clark, as usual, went around saying it was all just a streak of luck that had happened by chance and that it could all be over for him tomorrow. It hadn't even begun.

At 8:00 P.M. on February 27, 1935, more than one thousand people were seated in the Biltmore Hotel's dining room, the Biltmore Bowl, for the Academy Award presentations. Another six thousand stood in the lobby and foyer. Thousands more stood in the street. The polls had closed at 5:00 P.M., and frantic

counting of the votes had been going on since then. Clark hadn't wanted to go, but he bowed to pressure from Ria and Jana and squeezed himself into an uncomfortable, stiff collar and dinner jacket. Claudette Colbert was so sure Bette Davis would win the Best Actress award for *Of Human Bondage* that she hadn't bothered to turn up at all, and she was boarding a train for New York.[37] Irvin S. Cobb was the master of Ceremonies for the occasion, opening for the first time what has become the now-traditional sealed envelopes with contents guaranteed secret by Price Waterhouse.

It Happened One Night was nominated in five categories: Best Actor, Best Actress, Best Director, Best Screenplay Adaptation, and Best Picture. There had been only three nominees for Best Actor, all from MGM: Clark, William Powell for his role as Witty detective Nick Charles in *The Thin Man*,[38] and Frank Morgan for his sixteenth-century Duke of Florence, Alessandro, in Gregory La Cava's *Affairs of Cellini*.[39] Clark wasn't even considered as a sentimental favorite; after all, none of the previous seven Oscar winners had been from a comedy. Claudette Colbert had been nominated for Best Actress, along with Norma Shearer for her performance as the invalid Elizabeth Browning in *The Barretts of Wimpole Street* and Metropolitan Opera soprano Grace Moore as American opera singer Mary Barrett in *One Night of Love*. *It Happened One Night* was considered an underdog among the twelve films being considered for Best Picture in what had been a banner year.[40] Frank Capra was nominated for Best Director, as had Victor Schertzinger for *One Night of Love* and W. S. Van Dyke for *The Thin Man*.

Almost before the audience realized, *It Happened One Night* began to sweep the awards. Robert Riskin picked up Best Screenplay Adaption. Then Frank Capra was finally able to collect that elusive award for Best Director and for Columbia's first Best Picture. Soon, Cobb was shouting into the microphone, "You guessed it! It's something that …" and the audience jubilantly shouted back, "happened one night!"[41] By now, Columbia was searching desperately for its female star. Three studio men sped to the railway station, hustled Colbert off her train (which then waited thirty minutes for her), and raced with her back to the Biltmore in time for her to appear onstage — still dressed in her brown wool traveling suit and hat — to tearfully collect her Best Actress Award from seven-year-old Shirley Temple. "I could say a lot more," she said, "but a cab is waiting, so I'll just say thank you." A stunned Clark could only get out, "Thank you!" as he collected his Best Actor statuette. Vance King, one of the publicity men, commented later that as he led Clark off the stage he could hear him muttering under his breath, "I'm still going to wear the same size hat. I'm still going to wear the same size hat."[42]

This was the first Oscar sweep of all five top award categories: Picture, Actor, Actress, Director, and Adaptation. It was also the first time in Academy history that male and female leads from the same film won their respective top awards. It would be 1975 before another film, *One Flew over the Cuckoo's Nest*, would gain all five top awards, followed by only one other film: *The Silence of the Lambs* in 1991.[43] Clark would be nominated twice again, for *Mutiny on the Bounty* and *Gone with the Wind*, but he would not win another award.

Ten years later a six-year-old boy named Richard Lang, the son of Carole Lombard's close friend Fieldsie Lang, was playing with his toy car in Clark's study in the house at Encino. Finding an old statue on Clark's desk, he spent the afternoon using it as a target for his car. When it came time to leave, he picked it up, took it to Clark, and asked if he wanted it. Clark smiled and said no, Richard was welcome to it. Recognizing what the statue was, his mother was horrified and told Richard to put it back at once. Clark just patted him on the head and told him to keep it. Looking up, he said to Mrs. Lang, "Having it doesn't mean anything; earning it does."[44]

CHAPTER 12

CALL OF THE WILD

Some six weeks before Clark walked onto that stage at the Biltmore, he'd set out on another journey that would eventually have a profound impact on people's lives, some of whom were not even born yet. On January 15, 1935, after being held up for twenty-four hours to finish some last-minute work on *After Office Hours*,[1] Clark boarded a Southern Pacific train in Los Angeles bound for Portland, Seattle, and farther north to Mount Baker in northern Washington. He was on his way to meet with director "Wild Bill" Wellman and a large contingent of cast and crew at the Mt. Baker Lodge in Heather Meadows to do location shooting for the movie of Jack London's *Call of the Wild*. When the train pulled into Portland at 8:00 A.M. the next day, some reporters roused the unshaven Clark out of bed for an interview. "You would think a great movie star, awakened out of a sound sleep by a trio of drab, colorless reporters would be a crab," commented *The Oregonian* journalist. Instead, the star surprised them by inviting them in and sitting down for a chat as though they were all old friends. Clark was excited about being back in Portland after so many years, and he reminisced about his time there in the logging camp at Silverton and working in the classified-advertising department of *The Oregonian*. He was also excited

about going to Tahiti next to work in *Mutiny on the Bounty*. "That's a great story," he enthused, "and think of the jump! From the snowcapped peak of Mount Baker to the lovely dreamland of Tahiti. Oh boy, that's something." Put on the spot about who might be his favorite actress, Clark rather unsurprisingly nominated Joan Crawford. Finally they got around to asking him what he thought about starring in *Call of the Wild*. "I'm not the star in this play," he cheerfully complained. "A dog is the star in it."[2]

As it turned out, both Clark and the dog were completely upstaged by the weather. Blizzard after blizzard repeatedly snowed them in, cutting them off for days at a time until plows could clear the road. It was so cold that the oil in the cameras froze. Food and tempers ran short. Clark became uncharacteristically careless about his punctuality on the set and about his lines. Before long, with conditions being as stressful as they were, Wellman's temper ran out. He told Peter Lawford in 1975 that he did something he should never have done:

I got mad and lost my temper in front of the whole crew, and I told him what I thought about him. I said, "You're coming in here at eleven o'clock when the call is at nine. The property men and all of the grips are freezing their so-and-so's off, and me too. Now you're a big guy, and I only weigh 150 pounds, but you make your living with your face, and I don't. I just stand here behind the camera and no one gives a damn what I look like. My 150 pounds has been well-educated in the French Foreign Legion, and it's a dirty 150 pounds. I can assure you that I might go to the hospital, but you'll be a different-looking guy!"

I wasn't afraid, but I was wondering.... [H]e was a big man, after all ... but nothing happened. He sorta turned and walked away, and we went on. But it was Mr. Gable and Mr. Wellman from then on.[3]

It was soon obvious to just about everyone on the shoot that the reason why Clark couldn't keep his mind on the job was because his mind was somewhere else, or to be more specific, on someone else. That someone was his twenty-three year-old costar, Loretta Young.

Loretta, whose name was originally Gretchen, was born January 6, 1913. Her mother, Gladys Royal, had married the handsome and dashing John Earle Young in 1907 in Denver, when they were both nineteen. By 1910 there were two daughters, Polly Ann and Elizabeth Jane, and the now Roman Catholic family moved to Salt Lake City, where Gretchen was born. The last child, John Royal Young, came along a year later. By then, the Young marriage was not doing well due to Mr. Young's roving eye for the ladies. Eventually, Gladys took the children and moved to her sister's house in Los Angeles. Her brother-in-law, Ernest Traxler, was a production manager and assistant director for the Famous Players–Lasky Studio, soon to be Paramount. Before long, all four children were being employed as extras in silent movies. For a while, their father lived with them again until Gladys found him with the maid and ordered him out of the house. He left, and they never saw him alive again. In 1990, Loretta explained that her own marriages failed because she thought her husbands "would take care of me the way my father should have and didn't."[4]

Without a father, the family fell on hard times. Gladys opened a boarding house to make ends meet. It helped, but they remained poor. Loretta grew up with a desire to rise above her circumstances. Many years later she would remember that "I was six when I knew I was going to be a movie star. Not an actress, a star."[5] In 1923, Gladys married George Belzer, a bank examiner. Two years later, Georgiana was born. The girls were all educated in Catholic convent schools and then went into the movies. Elizabeth became known as Sally Blane. Gretchen's first role was at fourteen in a film starring Colleen Moore, who became her friend and role model.[6] It was Colleen who suggested the name Loretta, after her doll, Laurita. Loretta never looked back; in 1928 alone she appeared in six movies and was earning $250 a week. By the early 1930s she was earning $1,000 a week and, along with the family, was living in a large colonial mansion in Bel Air that her mother had designed.

In 1930, she was seventeen and starring in *The Second Floor Mystery*. Loretta eloped with her twenty-five year-old costar Grant Withers. The marriage lasted nine months. During that time she consulted with a Jesuit priest, and he said some words to her that obviously stayed in her mind to influence her later actions. He told her that given the occupation she was in, it could be difficult to distinguish real life from the acted life and that she could just be playing at being married. He reminded her that she lived a very public life, and her actions were being watched and emulated by other young people. From then on, Loretta carefully controlled her public life.

Her private life, however, was a very different matter. In 1933 she and her costar Spencer Tracy fell in love while making *Man's Castle*. At the time she was a divorced woman of twenty living at home, and he was a separated father of two. They were both Catholics, however, and the church refused to recognize divorce. The relationship was doomed. In 1934 Tracy reconciled with his wife.

By 1935, when Loretta Young and Clark Gable met on the slopes of Mt. Baker, they were both acclaimed film stars, although her Academy Award was yet to come.[7] Although twelve years younger than Clark, who celebrated his thirty-fourth birthday up there in the snow, Loretta had been acting for some eighteen years and was just emerging from a failed marriage and a broken romance.[8] Clark's second marriage was already heading for the rocks. They were a pair of emotionally vulnerable people cut off from the outside world, acting out being in love on camera with no escape from each other when the cameras stopped rolling. What happened was fairly inevitable.

Loretta took her own camera with her on the shoot, and the film has survived to show their developing tenderness for each other. With camera in hand she sneaks up behind Clark and catches him when he turns, sticking his tongue out at her; the camera zooms in and captures his face in close-up. In another scene he blows kisses at her. In another, they are caught sitting with their legs entwined in each other's, bundled in furs, looking into each other's eyes and so deep in conversation that they don't even notice the camera.[9]

By the time they came down the mountain barely a week before the Academy Awards, an avalanche of rumor about how close their relationship may have become had snowballed into town ahead of them. Ria Gable, for one, was not a happy woman about it. However, the occasion of the Academy Awards gave her a chance to be seen in public with Clark and make some attempt to lay rumor to rest. Then, Loretta Young discovered she was pregnant. "She said the tryst happened on the train coming home," Young's biographer Joan Wester Anderson commented. "She fully expected to date him when they got home, but she told him that sex would not be a part of it. He said that was all right."[10]

The Hollywood of 1934 was not the Hollywood it had been five years earlier. The Production Code Administration, a branch of the Hays Office, had been set up to oversee the reform of movie and actor morality in Hollywood. Contracts now contained a "morality clause" that gave a studio the power to void an actor's contract in the event of sexual scandal.

The devoutly Catholic Loretta, divorced and pregnant to a married man, found herself in a whole world of trouble that conflicted with her ethics and had the potential to destroy her career.

Loretta was already late to begin work in *The Crusades* at Paramount, and Clark was due to leave any day for Catalina Island to begin exterior shooting for *Mutiny on the Bounty*. She and Clark were still seeing each other, but the first person she turned to was her mother, Gladys, and there she found not recrimination but a staunch ally. In early March 1935 the two women met with Clark at the Young house. According to Loretta, on hearing the news he would be a father he turned to Gladys and said, "I thought she knew how to take care of herself. After all, she had been a married woman."[11] They all agreed that total secrecy was an absolute necessity. Two star careers and reputations were at risk. At this point, they both loved each other in their own way, and neither had any wish to inflict on the other the appalling damage that public exposure would bring.

Once over his shock, Clark was deeply concerned about Loretta's welfare and predicament. He offered to do whatever he could to help. Gladys and Loretta agreed to keep him informed. A blanket of silence then descended over the whole situation and remained there, smothering it completely, until the baby grew up to be a mother herself. Only then was she finally told the whole story by her mother about who she was.

Within a few days, Clark and Ria separated and he moved into the Beverly Wiltshire Hotel. If Clark ever told Ria about this whole affair, or if she ever later divined the nature of the final catalyst in the break-up of their marriage, then no one ever revealed the secret. Ria was typically too well-mannered to ever say anything about it. There is little doubt, though, that Clark and Ria's marriage had been gradually eroded little by little over the years. This could have been the last big wave under which it finally crumbled.

Adela Rogers St. Johns always claimed that she knew "positively" that Ria had left Clark, and summed the situation up in the words of the poet Edna Millay: "'Tis not love's going that dims my days, but that it died in little ways." Ria had said to her, she claimed: "Sometimes I think that Clark ought to be free.... Clark is definitely a man's man; he's not domestic. He doesn't like conforming to social obligations and things like that. He works very hard and no matter how hard I try, I cannot give him complete freedom. It can't be done in marriage. Sometimes I think he would be happier on his own." In retrospect, Ria may have finally realized the mistake of attempting to give a man caviar when all he wants is corned beef and cabbage. She was a rich, cultured and highly educated woman who had tried to provide an environment of elegance and taste for the matinee idol of the day. She had surrounded him with the best of everything and with the best of everyone. Despite gossip, innuendo, Joan Crawford, and screaming female fans who tore at Clark's clothing, the graceful Ria remained a lady who neither saw, heard nor spoke evil. Even Clark himself had said that as far as he was concerned she was close to being the perfect wife.[12]

She wasn't close enough though, and in the end Ria's kind of life was not what Clark really wanted. Although Clark was always a gentleman, there was still a lot of the independent traveling workman about him. He didn't care if dinner was not on time, and when he did eat he didn't want to be sitting around a silver service table with a bunch of socialites, nor did he appreciate having to go out to some party when he had just arrived home, tired from work. He wouldn't have minded if Ria had broken a vase over his head one night because she caught him out kissing some starlet who had been chasing him. In fact, he would probably have got quite a kick out of the fracas. Clark's marriage had finally become an old suit that just didn't fit him comfortably any more. Then came that fateful message to meet Loretta and Gladys.

Loretta started work on *The Crusades*. She and Clark stayed in telephone contact, using a code in case anyone overheard them. Ironically, now that they were free to see each other, Loretta became too frightened and now refused to meet Clark in public. "He kept calling and calling, wanting to see me," she recalled, "and I kept telling him to go away, go away. I was so terrified someone would see us together. All I could think of was keeping him away."[13] In desperation, Clark visited the set of *The Crusades* one day just so he could be near her.

By June, Loretta's pregnancy was difficult to conceal any longer. She and Gladys told the studio they were going to take a European holiday. When they returned, Loretta retired to a small house in Venice, California, where she could stay secluded and under the care of the family doctor, who notified 20th Century-Fox that Loretta was too ill to return to work. Clark began formal separation proceedings from Ria, who began calling Loretta to beg her to quell rumors about being pregnant. That, of course, is just what Loretta could not do. Neither would she see Clark, telling him instead that he should leave town so that the gossip could settle down. He left for South America, but the gossip didn't settle; it got worse.

Finally, on November 6, 1935, a blonde, blue-eyed daughter that Loretta named Judith was born. Clark received an anonymous telegram notifying him what had happened. He read it, tore it into pieces, and flushed them down the toilet. When he arrived back in Los Angeles on November 18, telling reporters he was now formally separated from Ria, he called Loretta and asked to see Judith. She lied to him and said she had sent the baby away. On December 27, Loretta had Judith baptized as Mary Judith Clark at St. Paul the Apostle Roman Catholic Church in Westwood. The baptismal certificate lists the father as William Clark. For many years to come, all that would be missing would be the last name: Gable.

In January, Loretta went back to work,

leaving Judy in the care of a nanny. Clark would visit to see his daughter whenever he could. However, the risk of discovery was always present, so in July, Loretta decided on a desperate step. She placed Judy in St. Elizabeth's Infant Hospital, an orphanage and home for unwed mothers run by the Sisters of Charity of St. Vincent de Paul in San Francisco.

By November, two of Loretta's sisters had had children. Evidently, Loretta thought this would be a good time to rewrite a daughter of her own back into the script of her life. For the next few months she dropped hints to the press about how much she would love a daughter. Then, in June 1937 she gave Louella Parsons the story that she had adopted two daughters. A month later she leaked the news that one girl had been taken back by her family. Very conveniently, Judy could now live with her birth mother as an adopted child, and the public was left totally confused. Quite a few people in Hollywood, though, weren't confused at all about the girl with the dimpled grin and the big ears that stood out from her head. When Judy was seven, she underwent surgery to have those telltale ears altered.

Judy grew up not knowing Loretta was her birth mother or that Clark Gable was her father. Fifteen years went by before Judy met Clark, in person, and then there he was standing in her hallway one summer day. He was starring in *Key to the City* with Loretta, who invited him to stay and talk with Judy. Without knowing her true relationship with him, Judy sat with her father on a couch in the large living room and talked about her school, her ballet lessons, her boyfriend, and her life: "It seemed strange for him to be interested in me at all, but I knew that he was, and I trusted what I felt from him.... He was warm, and considerate and caring.... I liked his interest in me; I didn't understand it, but I genuinely

enjoyed it. I answered his questions freely because something told me he needed to know everything I could tell him about myself. This wasn't just polite conversation on his part. He was there with me because it was something he wanted to do, and I responded as genuinely and honestly as I could. It never occurred to me to ask him any questions or even to ask how he knew who I was. But as I sat there it did occur to me that he had actually been waiting for me to walk in the front door and that he had known when I was due home."[14]

Judy only saw Clark once again, briefly, as he stood in the open door of a soundstage watching her. He said, "Hi, Slim," to her mother and left. Later, Judy would wonder how many times he had watched her without her seeing him. It wasn't until just before her marriage to Joe Tinney in 1958, when Joe told her he knew who her father was, that she realized she knew it too, deep down, and that one day the issue would have to be resolved. But Clark died before she could talk to him about it.

In 1966, after much angst and illness, Young finally admitted to her daughter that Clark was her father. Judy asked her if she had any regrets. "I think the biggest regret I have in my life," Young replied, "is that I didn't get your father to marry me."[15] However, Young flatly refused to ever publicly acknowledge that Clark was Judy's father, and she and Judy were estranged for a number of years during and after the writing and publication of Judy's book, *Uncommon Knowledge*. They were finally reconciled in 1997.

It would not be until after her death from cancer, on August 12, 2000, that Young made public her life-long secret. Through her biographer, Joan Wester Anderson, Young finally confirmed that she and Clark Gable were the birth-parents of Judy Lewis.[16]

CHAPTER 13

UNCHARTED SEAS

To the Clark Gable of early April 1935, however, leaning back in his dressing-room chair being made up as Captain Gaskell of the grungy tramp steamer, *Kin Lung*, the life of Judy Lewis was part of an unimaginable future. He had enough problems to keep him preoccupied. As usual, one of those worries was money.

Clark's father had begun courting his brother's widow, Edna. Typically, Will had no money. Clark had been supporting him and helping him by letting him live with them, but this could hardly continue once Will was married. So, Clark made arrangements to buy a house for him and to give Will a living allowance of $500 a month. Clark also paid for a new marker to be erected over his mother Addie's grave in Pennsylvania.[1]

Clark wasn't exactly hard up at this point. Not long after he'd finished work on *It Happened One Night*, Clark had changed agents from Minna Wallis to Phil Berg of Berg/Allenberg. Phil Berg always maintained he bought the contract from Minna for $25,000. Minna always denied he did, claiming that Clark had been unhappy, that they had talked it over, and though she was hurt after having been his agent from the beginning of his career, they had agreed Clark should go. Minna and Clark stayed close friends, in any case,

much as they had always been. As usual, there was talk as to exactly how friendly they became. Adela Rogers St. Johns said that Minna was a "slim, gypsy-like young girl" who saw Clark "with the eyes of a woman."[2] Barbara Sinatra once commented a little more tartly that when Minna was casting director at Warner Brothers, "she had all the stars go through her casting couch."[3] Maybe Minna was different as an agent. Maybe Barbara was just having a bad day. In the mid-1970s Minna put it rather more delicately, if not ambiguously: "It was a relationship that is difficult to explain. I adored him, just adored him. He was sweet and wonderful to me always.... He came to my house a lot because we were very dear and very close."[4]

Phil Berg negotiated a new contract. Clark's salary went to $3,000 a week, and he was recognized as one of MGM's sixteen stars with his own dressing room, handpicked crew, and a seat at what was known as the Directors' Table in the commissary. Designed by studio set designer Cedric Gibbons, the green-and-chrome MGM commissary served lunch to twelve hundred people a day on average. There were so many people needing to eat that the various film companies broke for meals on a rostered schedule. People tended to gather at various tables according to their occupation, so that there was a writer's table, a make-up table, and a publicity table, for example, or an entire film company might sit together if they got along particularly well. A certain amount of social status was attached to the various tables, and one was expected to be aware of the ranking. There were some rebels, though; Ava Gardner, for example, would flout tradition by typically sitting with the drivers and grips. The Directors' Table was the peak of the social pyramid, a large table on a screened porch attached to the main dining area. Some thirty men might gather around it to eat, including directors, department heads, and Spencer Tracy, Robert Taylor, and Clark Gable. No woman ever sat there. At the end of every meal a cage containing three dice was passed around, and the man who rolled the low number paid. Being the center of attention wore thin on Clark, though, and he would often dine in his dressing room or drive off to a restaurant somewhere. He would sometimes sink into one of his "black moods" and when he wasn't talking or hadn't shaved, people knew to keep away from him.

During Easter of 1935, Clark fulfilled a promise he had made to his stepdaughter, Jana, to be at her wedding in Houston, Texas, to give her away to Dr. Thomas Burke. Jana had accordingly planned the event to fit into a gap between Clark's work commitments. For a while during that trip, Clark may have wished he hadn't made that promise. On the way to Houston, Clark's plane made a stopover at Fort Worth's Meacham Field, where he took the opportunity to have breakfast at the airport café with his buddy, Fort Worth press columnist Jack Gordon. By the time he was due to leave, word had spread that he was there, and he was met at the door by a pack of more than 500 adoring women fans.

He bravely started to push through the throng, maintaining his smile, while one woman snatched the feather from his Tyrolean-style hat, another whipped the handkerchief from his jacket pocket, and someone pulled on his necktie until he nearly choked.

He lost his practiced composure though, when one brave enterprising young thing attempted to remove the belt from his pants. "Oh, no!" he howled, "Not that!" and covered the remaining few yards to the plane's door in a last great burst of strength. A stewardess slammed the door behind him and the plane flew on to Dallas' Love Field. There, no doubt to his relief, only a couple of young girls awaited him. After a short time Clark's plane took off again, and they flew on to Houston.

Jana was Episcopalian, but she couldn't be married in church during Lent and so the wedding was held in the home of a friend. "Everyone was agog because Clark Gable was coming to give the bride away," Jana recalled. "Frankly, when my engagement was announced some of my friends didn't even know that Clark was my stepfather.... I laughingly said that I'd have to put a red sash around the white dress so that they could see the bride."[5] Clark paid for Jana's trousseau, and he presented her with a diamond bracelet that Ria had designed.

Unfortunately, the *Dallas Morning News* had let it slip that Clark would be returning to Dallas' Love Field on March 17, aboard the 6.45 P.M. Bowen Airlines flight, where he would have to wait for several hours before transferring to an American Airlines plane. To pass the time while waiting, he'd planned to go with Jack Gordon to the Southwestern Exposition to see the horse show and then have supper at the Melrose Hotel. It wasn't to be. The newspaper had given Clark's adoring female fans time to make other plans for him. Only quick action by the pilot avoided casualties when eight *thousand* women, teenagers and dowagers together, rushed the runway as soon as the plane's wheels touched the tarmac. The Melrose Hotel manager, Mr. W. H. Oglesbee, tried to get through the mob in his car to rescue Clark, only to have the doors forced open by women who crowded in with him. Temple Bowen, the airline president who was aboard Clark's plane with his wife, stepped out to remonstrate only to be picked up and crowd-surfed over the women's heads to be landed on the other side of the pack. Women climbed onto the wings and pounded on the windows; they sat on the wheels and clung to the propellers. In the end, a force of some forty-five National Guardsmen had, with great difficulty, to forcibly remove them and clear a path so the plane could take off again. Mr. Bowen never made it back on board. He had to watch forlornly from a safe place as his wife and Clark Gable lifted into the air towards Fort Worth without him.

The frustrated women milled about like longhorns waiting for an excuse to stampede. A rumor had the Gable plane circling, waiting for an all clear to land again. Suddenly, a similar plane was seen to be touching down on the other side of the airport and the mob rushed it, only to find it was an American Airlines flight carrying an astounded Gertrude Stein from Chicago. Like Gable, she opted for discretion and stayed on board. Unfortunately, the taxi driver dispatched to pick her up bore a faint resemblance to the departed Mr. Gable. Mr. Owens, the driver, was promptly ambushed and stripped naked by the crowd, who even pulled out tufts of his hair. Finally accepting that Clark had gone, many women dashed back into the terminal to buy tickets for the next flight to Fort Worth, while others ran outside and crowded into anything that would get them there on wheels. Several hundred boarded the next train out. Clark must have retained mixed feelings about Texas for years.[6]

Jana would see him again only once, in 1938 when she was visiting her mother in Beverly Hills. Clark called and said he would like to see her and her son Tom, who was two at the time. So he sent a car to bring them to the studio. She remembered that during their visit Clark asked her if her husband had wanted Tom to be a boy. "I said, 'Yes,' and he said, 'I've never understood why men want sons. If I ever had a child then maybe I could be convinced.' I thought that was so strange for him to say, I really did. He picked Tom up, and

just seemed to be pleased with the whole visit. And that's the last time I saw him."[7]

With Tay Garnett directing, filming for *China Seas* began in late April 1935. Clark was once more teamed with his friend Jean Harlow.[8] MGM had bought the rights for Crosbie Garstin's 1930 rousing adventure novel some years before, then promptly filed it in the "too hard" basket until Irving Thalberg seized upon it as his chance to escape from making highbrow films into escapist thrillers. The script went through the typewriters of a number of hacks before landing with a dull thud on the desk of those two veteran scriptwriters, John Lee Mahin and James Kevin McGuinness. They were horrified to find that not only had the whole story been changed almost beyond recognition, but that whole chunks of the script had been lifted entirely from Somerset Maugham and Mark Twain.

From this mess, they crafted a better story about a ship's captain, two women who are vying for his attention, and a pirate. Clark was cast as Captain Gaskell, Rosalind Russell[9] and Harlow as the women, and Wallace Beery as the disreputable James McArdle. It was the first time Clark and Jean had teamed with Beery since *The Secret Six* in 1931, and the press made much of it.[10] But Beery's abrasive personality, not improved by his drinking habits, had alienated too many people for too long, and the cast didn't have much to do with him. Harlow and Clark were leaders in a prank that saw him presented with a wooden cake for his birthday, then a cotton-wool cake by way of apology. Beery was not amused.[11]

China Seas still holds up well today. It has something of a James Bond feel about its handsome male lead and its action, sex appeal, Asian villains, and beautiful women. Harlow once again found herself playing a lady of dubious reputation, Dolly Portland (known as China Doll, "the gal that drives men mad"), who is in love with Captain Gaskell (Gable). He is not happy to find her aboard his ship heading across the China Sea with a cargo of gold and troublesome passengers, including Gaskell's fiancée, Sybil (Rosalind Russell). Dolly drowns her sorrows in a drinking contest with the villainous McArdle (Beery) and cleans him out when she wins. The ship is caught in a typhoon. By the time it's over, Dolly has figured out that McArdle is there to steal the gold, and she attempts to warn Gaskell. He doesn't believe her. In revenge, she steals the ship's armory key for McArdle. He brings in a group of Malay pirates, and a battle takes place that Gaskell loses. He is captured and tortured. However, the battle turns when the third officer blows up the pirate junk, the pirates are defeated, and Gaskell is rescued. Realizing his mistake with Dolly, he agrees to testify on her behalf at her trial. Dolly will get her man when she gets out.

Shooting started in late April and went on for about two months. A lot of money was poured into the project, and Thalberg made a total nuisance of himself, hanging around, getting in everyone's way, making sure the i's were dotted and the t's crossed. Clark was tense because of his separation and Loretta's pregnancy, and Beery was being protective about his four-year-old daughter, Carol Anne, who was making her acting debut in the film. It was enough to give the cast and crew a bad case of the jitters, and there were a few close calls on the set. During one of the typhoon sequences, the special-effects crew mistimed the release of one of the fifty-ton waves of water, and it swept Clark and Jean's stunt doubles, Chick Collins and Loretta Rush, right off their feet. They narrowly missed getting swept into live electrical cables.

However, everyone managed to survive more or less intact, and the film was an outstanding success. "If any one member of the cast were to be singled out as outstanding, it would be Clark Gable," glowed *The New York Times*. "It is one of his most convincing portrayals."[12] Jean Harlow's popularity soared along with that of the film, and as a measure of this she was featured on the August 19 cover of *Time* magazine. Up until then, during its

twelve years, *Time* had accorded that honor to only six female actors, all stage stars. To his credit, the unknown author of the accompanying article not only describes her as the "U.S. embodiment of sex appeal" but also as intelligent and serious about her career. They attribute a quote to her that could sum up the situation of any woman actor who finds her physical attributes making it difficult for men to look her in the eye: "My God, must I always wear a low-cut dress to be important?"[13]

On July 29, Clark signed a new seven-year contract with MGM retroactive to December 13 the previous year. That must have given him quite a tidy sum in back pay. By the end of 1935, Clark was running second only to Shirley Temple in movie exhibitor's polls, which ranked in terms of audience pulling power. His new contract, then, reflected the recognition of his status by MGM and their recognition of the worth of their investment in him as a commodity and asset.[14]

Some of the contract terms are interesting today for their insight into the conditions under which Clark and other stars typically worked, bearing in mind that Clark was one of MGM's major stars. In a forecast of the value of other media, Clark would be expected to not only "render his services" as an actor in films but also on radio and on television. This was not a bad prediction by the studio lawyers in 1935. The studio had sole and complete rights to Clark's work and to the use of his name, his image, his voice, and to information about him. They also retained the right to use a double to stand in for him or for his voice at any time. They could loan him out to whomever they liked and insure him as their property. Not only would he not get any benefit from the studio policy if he were injured, if he were badly injured or facially disfigured, they had the right to suspend him indefinitely without compensation. He could not expect any assistance if the studio burned down or was hit by an earthquake, or if strike action closed it or the majority of Loew's theaters. In any of those events, the contract would be suspended for six weeks; after that, MGM could tear it up and sack him. Of course, Clark had no right of refusal; he had to appear in any movie in which he was ordered to appear, otherwise the studio could suspend him without pay until he changed his mind, during which time he couldn't work for anyone else. If he returned to work, they could then extend the period of his contract for that same length of time with no extra pay. A prolonged refusal would result in them suing him for the amount of their estimated loss.

In return for MGM basically owning him body and soul, Clark was to be billed as either the star or costar of any film in which he appeared. On marquees, billboards, and advertising, his name would appear in type larger than that of everyone else. In financial terms, Clark's brand of stardom translated to $4,000 a week for three years, $4,500 a week for two years, and $5,000 a week for the final two years. For those staggering sums of money, considering the United States was only just beginning to emerge from the Great Depression, Clark would be available to work forty weeks of the year, during which time he would make at least three films. If he made more than three, he would be paid $25,000 a picture.[15]

Unlike modern contract provisions, there is no mention of Clark getting a percentage of film profits. Phil Berg was known to prefer cash to percentages in his deals. In any case, MGM and 20th Century–Fox had a joint agreement not to give any stars percentages and to blackball anyone who even asked.[16] What Clark received was seven years of security with a guaranteed rest period every year. To Clark, his relaxation time was just as, if not slightly more important than his work time. He would have a structured and tiered income in much the same sense as someone signing on as a corporate executive, and in a way, that is how Clark saw himself. The final touch would be the nine-to-five workday agreement that was still in his future. Clark appreciated what he did, but it was as work well done, not as art for art's sake. He always

had a very acute perception that he had fallen on his feet, that he was just a lucky man. To him, a contract was a way of locking all that luck away into a very safe vault where it couldn't be taken away from him. It would be a much older and wiser man who, many years later, would realize that security can be a gilded cage.

When asked, Clark would usually nominate two films as his favorites: *It Happened One Night* and *Mutiny on the Bounty*. Typically, he had to be dragged by the neck into both of them, as was the case with a number of his movies. Irving Thalberg wanted him for the role of Fletcher Christian in *Mutiny*, but these two equally stubborn men "bumped heads," as Clark would so eloquently put it twenty years later, over this casting. What primarily upset Clark was that he would have to wear knee britches ("more than I could stomach"), shave off his mustache, have his hair drawn back into a short tail, and be an American voice adrift in a sea of British accents.[17] Clark was quite reasonably worried that audiences would not accept him in a role so radically different from how they were accustomed to seeing him. He felt strongly that neither his looks nor his voice would be appropriate, and he told Thalberg so in no uncertain terms: "'You have guided me right many times, Irving,' I said, 'But not this time. I can't do this. The public will never believe me as a first mate in the British navy. I'd be more believable as a first mate of a Puget Sound scow.'"[18] On the other hand, what Clark would not have told anyone was if the knee britches and ponytail costuming brought to mind all those cracks he had been hearing from his father for years about how unmanly acting was as a profession. He might also have been concerned about the standard of both his acting and his voice against that of Charles Laughton, whose reputation preceded him and who would be playing Captain Bligh in what became one of the defining roles of his career.[19]

With all those concerns on his mind, it

is hardly surprising that Clark initially said no. For a while, a deadlock ensued over the matter that was eventually broken by, of all people, not a senior studio executive but the head of MGM's story department, Kate Corbaley. This kindly, white-haired woman came up to Clark one day and told him that he was making a mistake, that she had read the script, and that Clark was perfect for the part. The role called for maleness and independence, she said, and those elements would be far more important to the role than whether Clark was seen in britches or a three-cornered hat. She told him that, in her opinion, it had all the signs of being a big picture in which Clark would be the hero, not the heavy. Clark didn't agree with her entirely, but he agreed enough to finally tell a relieved Thalberg he would take the role.[20]

The rights to *Mutiny* had originally been purchased from the novel's authors, Charles Nordhoff and James Norman Hall, by actor, writer, and director Frank Lloyd, who had intended taking the Bligh part himself.[21] Irving Thalberg, with the help of a substantial fee, persuaded Lloyd to direct instead and gained the rights for MGM. One of Lloyd's stage trademarks was his bushy eyebrows, so it's probably no accident that Laughton, who had a wickedly satiric sense of humor, adopted them as part of his Bligh characterization.[22]

It was a long and arduous shoot over some eighty-eight days, mostly around Catalina Island aboard a replica *Bounty*, although much of Bligh's small-boat scenes were done later in a studio tank. Laughton and Thalberg both feuded with Lloyd over his roughshod handling of the cast. Nevertheless, Clark always reveled in the outdoors and had a lot of fun working in the film. He would say a year later that it had been "like a voyage of companionable men on a private yacht. We were at sea all day and between scenes swam, fished, shot sharks, and learned to scramble up the lines to the flag, 180 feet above the waterline."[23]

After the sun went down, though, there wasn't much to do to stay amused. The principal actors all retired to their separate residences and didn't associate with each other much. During the week Clark would be reading for the next day's shooting, but by the weekend he was tired of that. He typically preferred to socialize with the crew anyway. So on Saturday nights they would all board a water taxi and head to Avalon to sit in the tavern, drink, swap yarns, and play poker. Returning in the early hours of one Sunday morning, the drunk ferry captain ran the boat into a rock, and it started to sink. The first priority the group had was to get a life belt on Clark, but by then Mont Westmore, the makeup man, had made a raft of them all and was preparing to float away, complaining that he couldn't swim and Clark could. As they all wrestled him for lifebelts, another boat showed up to the rescue. When they landed, Mont said, "I'm sorry Clark. I wasn't trying to drown you. I was only thinking of my kids, see. I didn't want them to grow up fatherless." "You're a noble man, Westmore," hissed the dripping Clark through false teeth clenched together because the salt water had dissolved the adhesive.[24]

While waiting to leave harbor one day aboard the *Bounty*, Clark and the rest of the company were surprised by the sudden appearance of the local hand-drawn fire wagon being pushed by four men down the hill as fast as they could go, siren screaming. Standing on top and urging them on was Laughton in full Bligh regalia. When they skidded to a stop, Laughton stepped down and marched across the gangplank with a very dignified, "Right on time, I trust." His car had broken down, and having called the fire truck by mistake, he had managed to persuade them to take him to the ship.[25]

Laughton, with his ambiguous sexuality, seemed unsettled by Clark's all-too-evident masculinity. He unsettled Clark in turn by reinventing a Laughton characteristic as a Bligh trait — that of not looking Fletcher Christian in the eye when he spoke to him. It threw Clark completely off his stride, and he would be driven to storming off the set in frustration, complaining that Laughton was cutting him out of the scene.[26] With a female costar, Clark tended to rely on his charm, if not his reputation, to establish rapport. With a male costar, Clark would typically attempt to establish a friendship off screen on which to base his onscreen working relationship. He preferred friendships with "real men," and a "real man" to Clark was one who hunted, shot, and fished like he did and who would look one right in the eye as a sign of directness and honesty. That way, Clark could know the person with whom he was working and, feeling safer with the devil he knew, could react to that person on the set much as he would if they met on the street in real life. Clark was a man of method, of order, of structure, and in that lay his security.

Laughton, on the other hand, acted self-contained and self-centered. As Bligh, the talented but strict sea captain to whom rules have become the entire universe with no room for humanity, he refuses to participate in Christian's universe by speaking not *to* him, but rather off to one side, into the sea. Bligh's soul is trapped by itself; he punishes himself as much as others, prepared to journey into hell for the sake of his code. "When I have a part like Bligh," he once told a journalist, "I hate the man's guts so much that I always have to stop myself overacting and be real. Parts like that make me physically sick."[27] His problem was to strike balance, and so effectively did Laughton strike it here that the watcher wants not only to condemn Bligh but to help him.

By the time they finished shooting the small-boat scenes, though, it wasn't just Bligh that needed help. For ten days they floated around the studio tank, tossed about by wires that rocked the boat. They were toasted by big arc lights that imitated the tropical sun until their makeup ran. Then Lloyd discovered that Eddie Quillan was acting the part of a crewman who had stayed on the *Bounty*, so they had to start all over without him. "We

have conquered the sea," cries Bligh at the end of the voyage, and cast and crew were said to have wept. It is not hard to imagine why.

All this theory was beyond the essentially practical Clark, however, and when he would stomp off the set complaining, Laughton would retire, hurt, to his bungalow. Shooting would grind to a halt. Thalberg would fly in by seaplane and yell at Lloyd, who would yell back. As it happened, all this conflict and tension rather ironically worked with the atmosphere of the film. After all, Bligh and Christian weren't supposed to be getting along nicely; they were two men from opposite ends of the rank and class scale of their time, in violent opposition over the treatment of their fellow man. As a result, their relationship in the film contains all the tense, underlying complexity of the actors' off screen relationship. It would be, in the end, perhaps Clark's most successful in-depth treatment of a character until much later in his career. "Fletcher Christian is a brilliant characterization," wrote John Gammie in the *London Film Weekly*. "It is a fine natural performance, full of those small touches that make a character live."[28] Clark was nominated for the 1935 Best Actor Academy Award for his performance. Although he didn't win an individual award, he did win in a way; *Mutiny on the Bounty* was awarded Best Picture.

When he emerged from work on *Mutiny*, it was to find that Loretta Young still did not want to see him, even so close to their baby's birth, and he was feeling more distant from Ria than ever. Neither did he feel *Mutiny* had gone well for him. "I told everybody who'd listen," he said, " 'I stink in it!'"[29] Probably in an effort to get as far away from his troubles as he could, Clark agreed to a South American promotional tour. Perhaps he just thought it would be a quiet break in a part of the world where he wouldn't be so famous. How wrong he was! On October 2 he arrived in Managua, Nicaragua, on his way to Rio de Janeiro. He was given a personal audience by Maria Sacasa, the president's daughter, and was mobbed by wildly cheering crowds. In Santiago, Chile, and then in Rio, crowds invaded airfields and mobbed him in the streets, where they would tear off his coat, his tie, his cuff links, even his handkerchiefs out of his pockets. Special police details guarded his hotel door to prevent fans from stealing personal effects from his room or climbing into his bed. In the meantime, Thalberg had reviewed *Mutiny on the Bounty* and sent Clark a telegram that read, "The movie is wonderful. We're proud of it. You'll like yourself in it."[30] If there was one person Clark trusted, it was Thalberg. Finally he could believe he'd done good work.

So closely was attention focused on Clark that even happily married women were forced to deny interest. When he left Buenos Aires for New York on a Pan American Airways flight on October 20, some journalist desperate for a story noticed that actress Lupe Valez was due to board the same plane later in Rio. Married to actor Johnny Weismuller at the time, Lupe had to produce her husband's telegrams saying how much he missed her as proof that she wasn't about to have some airborne secret assignation with Clark. "I am interested only in my husband," she protested vigorously.[31] Neither Clark nor Lupe arrived on that plane, however, but they steamed into New York harbor on a liner called the *Pan America* on November 8, two weeks later. The lonesome Weismuller couldn't wait for the ship to dock; he hired a boat and raced out to meet his wife the minute the liner came over the horizon. No one was there to greet Clark, except the usual shark pool of hungry journalists wanting to know if the rumors of his impending divorce were true. Ria had retreated to Texas while he'd been gone. Clark evasively stated that any decision would be hers.

News about that decision wasn't far off. On the night of November 14, Ria officially confirmed an MGM announcement made earlier that day. She and Clark had indeed separated, she stated, and she planned to seek a divorce soon. The reason she diplomatically gave was that Clark's heavy work schedule had placed too much of a strain on their marriage. "Difficulties in our domestic life arose because Mr. Gable has to work so long, hard, and tensely in his movie roles," she said.[32]

It was work that Clark continued to do. Having made a movie essentially for his male audience, Clark was handed back to the ladies for the light soap opera of *Wife vs. Secretary.* Directed again by Clarence Brown and based on the Faith Baldwin novel *Office Wife* (a much better title), this film is about a jealous wife who presumes her husband is having an affair with his beautiful personal assistant. He isn't, but her suspicions nearly destroy their marriage until the personal assistant confronts the wife personally and points out how close she is to losing everything.

Together again with both Jean Harlow and Myrna Loy, Clark was in the unique position of working with two women who were good friends but with whom he had no romantic ties, and he looks the happier for it. In fact, they all do. Loy and Harlow were quite close friends, despite having met only a short time before when Harlow had accompanied Powell while he and Loy appeared on Louella Parsons' radio show. Both Midwesterners, the two women found they had much in common, including their sense of humor. Harlow was thrilled to find they would be working together at last, and what would otherwise be a lightweight romance carries more weight because of their excellent work together. Myrna Loy would later insist that the character of personal assistant Helen Wilson, capable and intelligent with an amused air of indulgence, was very close to the real Jean Harlow. In something of a role reversal for both women, Helen Wilson remains a very proper character while Clarence Brown brings out the wife's sexuality with subtle use of double entendres and ambiguity. Loy always said that her role was the sexiest wife she had ever played.[33]

This is, incidentally, the first role that Harlow played in her natural hair color, in contrast to the brassy platinum blonde for which she had been famous. Jean's happiness at finally being allowed to act herself was apparent to everyone during the shoot and in the quality of her performance. Many still think that this is Harlow's best dramatic role. "I felt more real than I had ever felt," she commented to a reporter afterwards. "If I *feel* more real, then I am likely to *act* more real."[34]

A young Jimmy Stewart took three days off from playing his first lead role in *Next Time We Love* to appear briefly in *Wife vs. Secretary* as the secretary's boyfriend, an amiable young man who is mystified by Whitey's all-consuming passion for her job.[35] Stewart remained impressed ever after by Harlow's memory skills; he noticed that she could quickly scan a page of dialogue and then act her way through it. He was also impressed by her kissing skills. When they first rehearsed the scene where she finds Stewart waiting up for her, asleep in his car, he recalled that Harlow took charge of the kissing: "It was then I knew that I'd never really been kissed before. There were six rehearsals, and the kissing gained each time in interest and enthusiasm. By the time we shot the scene, my psychology was all wrinkled. She was a stunning girl with a dress so low cut you had to bend down to pick it up, and I was just a guy from Pennsylvania. I'll always remember Jean as being warm, lively, and wonderfully constructed.... Her dresses were tight and she wore nothing under them."[36]

Neither Clark nor Loy nor Stewart could have guessed that such a lively spirit had less than two years to live.

CHAPTER 14

LIFT UP YOUR GOLDEN GATE

As 1936 began, the world was at Clark's feet. His status was assured, his popularity was unbounded, and he had no romantic ties. It was his time to party, and he did it as much, as hard, and with as many women as he could. He knew right where he was when it came to charming women: at the top of the ladder. After all, by now he'd had a great deal of practice in a lot of movies. Joan Crawford once observed that Clark "knew what he would get back from a woman when he gave her the right look; he'd seen that reaction too often on the screen not to know. And he loved it if there was a new woman around and he could walk into a room and hear her sigh."[1] Clark was now that most desired of men, a man who was safe to be with because he was married but with whom it was safe to play because he was at the same time single. Clark accepted all women quite unblushingly as his due reward for living a public life. If one was going to have to live in a fishbowl, he seems to have reasoned, then one might as well give the onlookers something to talk about and have as much fun doing it as was possible. Clark's favorite fun at this time of his life was women. "He adored women," Joan Blondell recalled, "not in a lechy way; he loved beauty.... His eyes would sparkle when he saw a beautiful woman, and if he liked you he let you know

it.... He affected all females, unless they were dead."[2]

Howard Strickling, having been with Clark to many a party in his capacity as MGM publicist and watchdog, once described Clark's approach to a woman: "The first thing he always did, you know, he'd look her over. She'd know damn well that he was sizing her up head to foot. And he was looking at her eyes and he was looking at her lips ... and she'd wonder what this guy was thinking about. He'd ask her a lot of questions about herself, or something about her dress. Or why do you wear your hair like that? And he'd have a few laughs with her. If he sensed she didn't respond the way he expected, he might clam up a bit. But mostly, they responded."[3] Clark dated whom he chose when he chose. He was seen with young socialites such as Mary Taylor in New York, and he even pursued a very reluctant Mary Pickford for a while, who would say years later that she regretted turning him down. He was seen a lot with British actress Elizabeth Allan. On the other hand, he was also seen with a filly of a different kind: a racehorse he owned called Beverly Hills.

It was also a time, however, when Hollywood was being examined more and more closely under the microscope of morality. Clark would be blindsided by this changing

126

attitude from an unexpected direction. In 1933 the Catholic Church had launched the Legion of Decency for which millions of members signed pledges, or were obliged to take an oral pledge in church, that they would boycott movies the church declared immoral on their own rating scale. Some dioceses went so far as to inform parishioners it would be a mortal sin for them to attend a movie on the banned list.

On top of that, during the year nine volumes known collectively as the Payne Studies were published by the Motion Picture Research Council after four years of research. The studies attempted to prove that movies did affect children, but no more than did other cultural influences. However, the one-volume summary, published as *Our Movie-Made Children*, claimed that movies adversely affected children and had helped shape a race of criminals. It became a sensational best-seller, sweeping common sense aside. By the following year, the Legion of Decency had spread like a forest-fire across the country, and by midyear some seven million Catholics in America had sworn to uphold the Legion of Decency pledge.[4] It was a formidable weight of organized public opinion. In response, Hays installed Joseph Breen, a pugnacious Irish-Catholic former journalist and rabid anti–Semite who knew nothing about movie production, as head of the Production Code Administration and, thus, the chief censor for the Hays Office in Hollywood.

Breen would write and rewrite the Code over the next few years until it went much further than Lord's original to demand that movies contain sufficient good to compensate for any depiction of evil. There must be characters that spoke for moral behavior to compensate for, and counteract those, who spoke or acted with evil intent. Characters' actions must be clearly seen and signaled for the audience as either right or wrong. Ambiguity or moral confusion would cease to exist as far as Breen was concerned; the movies were no place for moral or ethical debate. Movies

should result in clear moral lessons involving punishment and, if possible, regeneration. From now on, movies would have to carry the Production Code Administration seal to indicate they had been approved for the tender eyes and innocent consciences of Americans.

Clark may have been criticized in terms of acting performance, but rarely had he ever been, or would he be, attacked personally. However, in March 1935, Clark had come under criticism from what must have been a totally unexpected direction for him: his boyhood home of Hopedale. There, at a meeting of the local Parent-Teacher Association, the new twenty-five-year-old pastor of the Hopedale Methodist Church where Clark had gone to Sunday school had risen to his feet and said some harsh words about the town hero. Children who went to see Clark Gable on the screen, said the Reverend Samuel J. Williams, were "mingling in the society of Hollywood stars who glorify perverted love. How many of you parents would like for your children to duplicate Gable's love scenes? Clark Gable has brought no real credit to Hopedale." The citizens promptly got stirred up in that otherwise quiet backwater and vigorously defended their local boy. The Presbyterian minister said people had a right to earn an honest living. Mr. Bell, the mayor, hastily protested that Hopedale looked up to Clark "as its first citizen."[5]

A short time later, the Reverend Williams actually came to Hollywood with the same message and attempted to meet the actor, but Clark wouldn't be drawn. Then in August, who should get into the act but none other than Josephine Dillon who on visiting Cadiz told people that if only Reverend Williams had asked her, she would gladly have given him all the help she could. She agreed, she said, that "Clark would be a mighty influence on young people, just as Douglas Fairbanks was with the Boy Scouts. But in Hollywood all the devious safeguards they put about their stars gave him about as much chance as a man in a whirlpool. Clark at heart is religious, but he can't be himself. Rev. Williams calls it 'movie madness,' but I call it Hollywood hypnosis."[6] Clark must have breathed a sigh of relief when the whole issue seemed to die a natural death after that.

Believe it or not, there were some women, albeit very few, whom Clark simply could not stand. He could never abide columnists Sheila Graham and Dorothy Manners, nor did he ever seem to warm to Greer Garson or to actor and singer Jeanette MacDonald. Unfortunately, Jeanette MacDonald was planning to be his next costar. A woman of very independent spirit, MacDonald had grown tired of MGM's attempts to dictate the boundaries of her career. She wanted to expand into formats other than operetta, knowing that she was quite capable of carrying a film without a male singing partner. When Clark heard that she wanted him to appear with her in *San Francisco*, he swore that he would never do it. He refused to read even an outline. He hated to be sung at, he declared; after all, he couldn't sing back and defend himself. "Hell," he reportedly exclaimed to Eddie Mannix, "when she [MacDonald] starts to sing nobody gets a chance. I'm not going to be a stooge for her while she sings in a big beautiful close-up and the camera shoots the back of my neck!"[7] MacDonald's manner could also come across as being quite superior, and Clark disliked anyone, especially women, who had their nose in the air.

Nothing daunted, MacDonald set out to prove her commitment to Clark and to the project by doing the almost unthinkable in Hollywood. She took unpaid leave from MGM, which promptly put on hold its current project being developed for her and Nelson Eddy, *Maytime*. More importantly for MacDonald though, her action opened up her schedule so that any time at which Clark became available would be the right time for her. Clark was impressed. He respected anyone who could be that dedicated where money was concerned. Besides, once he got around to reading a treatment, the character of Blackie Norton was so close to Clark's personality it

might have been written for him. In fact, in a way it had been, although Anita Loos was originally inspired by someone else entirely.

Loos, who had come from a theatrical family, sold her first film script when she was twenty-three. A very experienced writer, who sold thirty-eight film scripts in 1913 alone for from $15 to $50 each, Loos started work with D. W. Griffith at Fine Arts–Triangle in 1915. The following year she teamed up with writer and director John Emerson there to write nine scripts for Douglas Fairbanks. When Fairbanks went to Famous Players–Lasky in 1917, he took Loos and Emerson with him. After Fairbanks moved on to other things, Loos and Emerson transferred to Famous Players' New York studios, where they worked with Marion Davies and Norma Talmadge, the actress wife of Joe Schenck. The Schenck brothers, Joe and Nicholas, were the partners of Marcus Loew; Nicholas eventually rose to head MGM, while Joe became the New York corporate connection between MGM and its parent company, Loew's. In 1920, Loos and Emerson were married at Schenck's estate on Long Island. In 1923 they began writing for Broadway, and two years later Loos published the unbelievably successful *Gentlemen Prefer Blondes*. By 1929, it had been reprinted nineteen times and had earned her over one million dollars. It was adapted for the stage, and the first film version was in 1928 with Ruth Taylor as Lorelei Lee.

In 1931, Loos accepted an offer of $1,000 a week from Irving Thalberg to work at MGM, where she found herself working alongside F. Scott Fitzgerald and her friend, writer and "ideas man" Wilson Mizner, whom she had first met in Palm Beach in 1927. Her first assignment was the Jean Harlow movie *Redheaded Woman*, and in 1932 she worked on the Harlow and Gable film *Hold Your Man*. Later that year Emerson joined her after receiving a producing offer from Thalberg. The following year Mizner, with whom Loos had become close friends, died from alcohol and heart problems.

Loos teamed up with writer and concept

An original sheet-music cover of the song "Would You," sung by Jeanette MacDonald from the movie San Francisco. *It was orginally purchased from Gable's Song Shoppe in the Gable's Department Store (unknown location).* (Spicer Collection.)

developer Robert "Hoppy" Hopkins in 1935. Like Mizner and Loos, Hopkins had lived in San Francisco and in his case, the Barbary Coast area in particular. Screenwriters Hopkins, Loos, Johnny Mahin, and Howard Emmett Rogers often met at a small cafe just outside the studio walls to eat and talk freely, rather than in the commissary. Whenever possible, they were joined by Spencer Tracy and Clark, whom Loos had got to know well while working on *Hold Your Man*. So, it is really no surprise that she would have Clark in mind when she and Hoppy hatched their screenplay idea. Besides, Loos always had a fond spot for Clark ever since she had encountered him at an MGM drinking fountain washing his dentures, whereupon he had looked up with a grin and lisped through his caved-in lips, "Look, America's thweetheart."[8]

Hopkins and Loos made a rather unique team because only Loos used to actually put pen to paper. Hoppy, who apparently bore a remarkable resemblance to conductor Leopold Stokowski, was employed as a dialogue extemporizer and creative thinker; whenever directors found themselves stuck for lines of dialogue in the middle of a scene, they would call for Hoppy, who would come up with them on the spot. He would sometimes come up with plot ideas too, but his language was so staccato and violently colorful that he usually needed a translator, which is where Loos would step in. The two friends would often reminisce about their time in San Francisco and people they had known, such as Mizner. One day, while walking around the studio lot, they came up with the idea of writing a screenplay that would celebrate their departed friend and the city for which they pined. According to Loos, Hoppy's succinct summary of their new screen-play's plot was, "Okay, there's this canary who thinks her cunt's just for piss and this cocksucker of a priest and this brass-balled gambler who get thrown together during the earthquake."[9] Blackie eventually realizes all he needs is a woman like Mary, but will she be found amongst the survivors? After

Loos understandably cleaned Hoppy's version up somewhat, they pitched it to Thalberg, who agreed it sounded like a viable project for Clark.

Although based on Loos' memories of Mizner, she wrote the character of Blackie Norton for Clark. In what Loos described as an "unadulterated soap opera," Norton is the "brass-balled gambler" who runs a casino in the Barbary Coast area (as Mizner used to do).[10] He rather bemusedly hires Mary Black (MacDonald), a singer down on her luck, and is intrigued to discover that she really is the good, honest girl she claims to be. Mary is also taken under the wing of the local priest, Father Tim Mullin (Tracy), who gives her a chance to use her voice in the church choir on Sundays. Blackie is running for city supervisor and attempting to get a fire ordinance passed that would condemn many Barbary Coast buildings, but would save lives. He is opposed by crooked landlord Burley (Jack Holt), who lures Mary away from Blackie with the offer of singing in the local opera house. Despite a marriage offer from Blackie, who has fallen in love with her, Mary becomes engaged to Burley. Then the 1906 earthquake strikes, just in time to prevent Mary marrying the wrong man. Blackie spends two days searching the ruins before he finds her singing (no surprises there) a hymn to survivors. Blackie sees the light, although it has taken one of the worst natural cataclysms of all time to do it, and he rather unconvincingly becomes converted, seeming to lose those round brass things in the process. Even director Van Dyke seems to have considered that as Blackie sinks to his knees and thanks God, he needed a close-up in which he says, "I really mean it."

As Loos continued to hand in drafts at regular intervals for Thalberg to read, he became convinced that Spencer Tracy would be the most suitable person for the role of the priest. However, studio politics decreed who was going to play the role of Mary Black. Although Loos had written the part with Grace Moore in mind, Moore was not under contract to MGM, whereas lyric soprano Jeanette Mac-Donald was. Besides, Louis B. Mayer had been thoroughly infatuated with MacDonald for some time.

Mayer had personally signed the talented Philadelphia-born singer and dancer two years ago, probably to prevent her contracting with Thalberg, whom she knew. Having been on stage since childhood, MacDonald had become a Broadway star in the late twenties.[11] In 1929, Ernst Lubitsch saw a Paramount screen test she had done and starred her in his film *Love Parade*. During the next three years she appeared in a series of musicals and light comedies, but MacDonald grew dissatisfied with her career progress and went to Europe, where she met Thalberg and his wife Norma Shearer.

When the Rogers and Hart film *I Married an Angel* was put on hold by the Hays Office because it had an angel losing her virtue to a mortal man, MGM had to find another starring vehicle for MacDonald. The studio chose *The Cat and the Fiddle*, followed closely by *The Merry Widow* in 1934.[12] The following year she was teamed for the first time with Nelson Eddy in *Naughty Marietta*, after which her popularity was assured. MacDonald had a voice that ranged nearly three octaves, and she had a mind of her own. She refused to wear false eyelashes or heavy makeup, and she opted for wigs rather than have the hair that she loved tampered with by studio hairdressers. Mayer could be mesmerized by ladies of wide-eyed innocence who had style and presence, and MacDonald was no exception. She was fully aware, however, that the power of beauty had its limitations.

By March 1935, MGM had taken no action about *San Francisco*. Still convinced about the worth of the project, MacDonald went over Mayer's head with a letter to Felix Feist, MGM's general manager of sales and distribution based at Loew's New York head office. She wanted to broaden the range of her appeal, she wrote, and was convinced that the film roles fitted her and Clark "like a pair of gloves," yet the studio kept refusing to change Clark's schedule so that he would be available to appear with her. Feist responded that he would look for an opening to talk the project up.

It took the combined weight of Feist, Mayer, MacDonald, Hopkins, and Loos to finally persuade the stubborn Clark to take the part of Blackie Norton. An unsympathetic Mayer, in his typically blunt fashion, had to remind Clark of just who was paying him an obscene amount of money every week and of what life could be like without that. Clark duly, if grumpily, showed up for work. He retained a kind of smirky disdain for MacDonald that in the end worked in with his character's attitude, although his indifference to her upset MacDonald to the point of tears on occasion.

No sooner were the actors in place, however, when Thalberg reluctantly decided that his declining health, combined with his increasing commitment to making *The Good Earth*, would not allow him to supervise the production of *San Francisco* personally. He suggested that Loos' husband, Emerson, co-produce with Thalberg's right-hand man, Bernard Hyman. Emerson agreed for a two-year contract and $1,250 a week. *San Francisco* went into production on St. Valentine's Day, 1936.

Clark really has two costars in this film, for *San Francisco* is the first of the Gable-Tracy partnerships. Tracy and Clark were friendly, but it was an uneasy relationship at best, somewhere between being, as Renee Jordan puts it, "competitive companions and friendly enemies."[13] They had started out competing with each other on stage. Clark became a success on the West Coast with the role of Killer Mears in the play *The Last Mile* that Spencer had been successful with on the East Coast, and they had quietly been competing ever since. Clark, an extrovert who had to really work at emoting, was known to envy the introverted Tracy's ability to be able to let his emotions smolder onscreen beneath a deadpan expression. Tracy, on the other hand, may have coveted Clark's handsome sexual magnetism, but being the epitome of the very private person that he was, he rarely gave away what he thought. Twenty-four years later, while making *The Misfits*, Clark would comment to writer and Tracy biographer Bill Davidson that, in his opinion, Clark had got as close to Tracy as anybody could. They did a lot of drinking together, he said, "and when a guy boozes with a friend he usually lets his hair down and lets you know something about what's going on inside his noggin. But not Spence. It was like he had a curtain in there. He was a guy with a lot of things bothering him, but he never lifted that curtain to let me know what was buggin' him."[14]

According to Davidson, Tracy was working in *San Francisco* at the same time as he was working in Fritz Lang's *Fury,* and he rather enjoyed escaping to the much easier-going atmosphere of the former to escape Lang's Teutonic meticulousness and obsessiveness on the set of the latter. Like Clark, though, Tracy had had his own doubts about his role in the film. "I had a tough time deciding whether or not to get myself out of the part," he said later. "I thought of how my father had wanted me to be a priest, and wondered if it would be sacrilegious for me to *play* a priest. All of my Catholic training and background rolled around in my head, but then I figured Dad would have liked it, and I threw myself into the role."[15]

Relations between Clark and MacDonald, however, continued to deteriorate. Just to demonstrate how unhappy he was about being press-ganged into the film, Clark showed up for his first scenes with MacDonald reeking so heavily of garlic that she could barely stand to be near him. Things went downhill from there. After a week's work MacDonald wrote in a letter that Clark was a mess and that she had "never been more disappointed in anyone in my life! It seems (according to Mayer) that he is very jealous of me and acts very sulky if I get more attention on the set than he....

Gable acts as tho' he were really too bored to play the scenes with me. Typical *ham*."[16] For the next six weeks, Clark and Jeannette kept up a show of cordiality, but once offcamera they were two equally strong-minded people who just kept on bumping heads. The punctual Clark liked to start work at nine sharp, and it didn't help matters when Van Dyke granted MacDonald an extra hour to get ready. MacDonald actually respected Clark's acting a great deal, but she simply couldn't bring herself to tell him. She had wanted him in the film with her because she thought him just right for the part, more so than William Powell and Robert Young whom she had turned down. In what surely was the understatement of the shoot, MGM publicist Emily Torchia concluded: "They were not kindred spirits."[17]

Director W.S. Van Dyke had worked with MacDonald the year before in *Naughty Marietta* and earlier that year in *Rose Marie*. Known around the studio as "One Take Woody," he traditionally brought in pictures underschedule and, mainly for that reason, underbudget . Van Dyke proved no exception on this occasion. He moved a bit too quickly for Anita Loos' taste, however, for whom this movie was close to the heart. When she found her suggestions that some scenes be reshot were ignored by Van Dyke, Anita went to Hyman and complained that quality was being sacrificed in the name of economy. When Hyman's reply was that Van Dyke never did a second take, Loos promptly reminded him that Thalberg had earned a reputation for always being willing to do so however many takes it took until he achieved the best-quality product he possibly could. Hyman took her point and some reshooting took place.

That didn't, however, keep Loos any quieter. When she saw the first rushes of the earthquake scenes, Loos tore into Hyman again about how tame and faked they looked, suggesting that Emerson could replace Van Dyke and do a better job. Hyman rejected the substitution, but he agreed the earthquake did need some work for authenticity's sake. Before the cameras rolled for the reshoot, Van Dyke exhorted actors and extras to get into the spirit of the catastrophe, to run for their lives as walls fell around them and to help their friends do the same. It worked; in fact one of the extras became so carried away that he grabbed hold of Loos, flung her over his shoulder and carried her out of the disintegrating saloon. She later commented regretfully that as she hadn't been in costume, she had to be edited out, "which was unfortunate since nobody shrieked as realistically as I did!"[18]

There were quite a few shrieks among the audiences too, as walls crumbled, San Francisco fell into ruins, and good triumphed over evil. The effects were so realistic that at the San Francisco premiere some 1906 survivors became ill and had to leave the theater. People have always loved a disaster movie, though, and this one pushed out *The Great Ziegfeld* to make MGM's biggest profit for 1936. In fact, *San Francisco*, which cost only $1,300,000 to produce, became MGM's greatest money-maker worldwide prior to *Gone with the Wind* with gross receipts of $5,273,000.[19] It received *six* Oscar nominations including Best Picture, Best Director, and Best Original Screen Story (a category since eliminated). The latter was in Hopkins' name, though, not that of Loos because her credit was for the screenplay which ironically was not nominated. Spencer Tracy's efforts were rewarded with his, not Clark's, nomination for Best Actor, although he lost to Paul Muni for his work in *The Story of Louis Pasteur*. Tracy's consolation prize was that *San Francisco* turned him into a popular star.

It's a pity there wasn't an Academy Award category at the time for Best Song, because it would have been won by Jeanette Macdonald for the movie's rousing and hugely popular hit tune, oddly enough also called "San Francisco."[20] Written by Bronislaw Kaper and Walter Jurman, with lyrics by Gus Kahn, the song's popularity has held on into the present in its home city.[21] On May 15, 1984, it became, along with Tony Bennett's more sentimental "I Left My Heart in San Francisco," one of the two official city songs. Ten days after the earthquake of October 1989, World Series baseball fans stood in Candlestick Park for a minute of silence to commemorate those who had lost their lives. Then, as if to celebrate the renewed spirit of their city, they broke out into a spirited rendering of "San Francisco."

In September 1936 an earthquake of a different sort shook MGM. After attending an outdoor concert, Irving Thalberg caught a chill that developed into pneumonia. Within a week, he was dead. Things would never be the same at the studio again. By then, neither Clark's life nor that of Carole Lombard would be the same again either.

After working together in *No Man of Her Own* in 1932, Clark and Carole had gone their separate ways. Involved in their own lives and their own relationships, they had not had time to think of love. Four years later, they were in very different places. Clark was now separated from Ria; Carole's twenty-eight-month marriage to William Powell had ended in 1933, and her relationship with singer Russ Columbo had been brought to a tragic close the following year when he was killed in a shooting accident. Carole was now one of Paramount's leading comediennes after her success in *Twentieth Century* and *Hands Across the Table*, and she also had a reputation as a socialite who in real life was every bit as madcap as she was onscreen.

On Saturday night, January 26, 1936, the Mayfair Club of Hollywood hosted the White Mayfair Ball, so called because all the women were requested to wear white gowns and the men white tie and tails, at Victor Hugo's in Beverly Hills. Carole, who was better known for presiding over her own wacky parties where her house might be turned into a hospital ward or even stripped bare, had persuaded club president David Selznick to let her be the hostess for the ball to prove that she, too, could be elegant. She had arrived early at the ball, escorted by Cesar Romero because she had quarreled earlier that week with her usual date, screenwriter Robert Riskin. Her table was near the entrance so she could have a full view of the room, which was decorated all in white. The ball's 350 guests included just about every major star, director, and film executive in town.

Clark, escorting singer Edie Adams, who often dubbed for some of the stars whose voices weren't quite up to it, arrived with Marion Davies' group which included her lover, William Randolph Hearst, and columnist Louella Parsons. Davies was president of the Motion Picture Relief Fund, the beneficiaries of the ball. Lombard greeted the party warmly as they walked through the doors. Any chance of further conversation between she and Clark died almost as soon as it started, however, as Carole caught sight of Norma Shearer arriving behind them dressed entirely in red! Unable to eject Shearer because of her status as Thalberg's wife, Carole had to seek refuge in the ladies' room while she calmed down. She had only just sat down at her table again when Clark came over. Using the nickname he had given her while they were on the *No Man of Her Own* set, he grinned and said, "I go for you, Ma." She looked at him, caught a bit off-guard for a minute, and then quipped back, "I really go for you too, Pa." And away they went onto the dance floor. Marion Davies, watching Carole teaching Clark to dance the rumba a while later, for which she was famous, turned to columnist Louella Parsons and said: "Those two were made for each other. Wouldn't it be great if they fell in love?"[22]

It wouldn't happen this night. Clark offered to take Carole for a ride in his big Duesenberg during the night to get some fresh air but, angered after she refused his invitation to come up to his Beverly Wiltshire room for a drink, he quickly drove her back to the ball. They both arrived in a bad mood. Carole soon had to separate him from Lyle Talbot with whom Clark was about to fight, then Clark had to dissuade Carole from punching Norma Shearer, with whom she was still piqued over the red dress. They ended up dancing again in each other's arms by the end of the night, though, and when Carole invited Clark back to her house, he must have thought that at last his chance had come for them to be alone together. He was out of luck. Instead, Carole had a few friends around, and she wanted Clark to help entertain. That was not what was on his mind; he made an excuse and left in a huff. Carole probably watched him drive off laughing that knowing laugh of hers. She was far too intelligent and independent a woman to be just another one-night stand with Clark Gable.

The next morning Clark opened his eyes in amazement to see an open birdcage and a pair of white doves flying around his room. When he finally caught them, he found a note tied to one dove's leg: "How about it? Carole." She had bribed a hotel porter to quietly release the doves in Clark's room. He phoned Carole to thank her and to tell her he had nowhere to put the birds. She said she would keep them, and he could come out every Sunday to feed them. She sent her butler to pick them up.[23]

It was two weeks before they saw each other again, at a gag party organized by Clark for Donald Ogden Stuart's wife, who was recovering from a nervous breakdown. Everyone was to turn up in evening dress in the middle of the day. Clark was at the door welcoming guests when suddenly an ambulance tore up the drive with siren wailing. It screeched to a halt outside the door. To Clark's horror, the attendants opened the doors and wheeled out a stretcher with Carole stretched on it, apparently unconscious. Everyone gathered around it concerned when suddenly Carole sat up, laughing. Few people, including Clark, were amused. Carole, in her usual blunt manner, wanted to know what was the matter with everyone. Before long, she and Clark were shouting at each other. She walked off; he fumed. Eventually, he attempted to make up by suggesting that they play tennis in their evening clothes, and so that was how they spent the afternoon, running back and forth, tripping over each other, and laughing helplessly. When they tired out finally, she threw her arms around him and kissed him.

As Valentine's Day approached, Carole was in a quandary. She knew Clark liked big, fast cars, but what do you get a guy who is piqued because his Duesenberg might not be quite as long as Gary Cooper's? Then she came up with the answer. On Valentine's Day morning, Clark was at MGM rehearsing for *San Francisco* when he was called to the soundstage door. There sitting outside was a decrepit Model T Ford, springs poking through the seats, painted brilliant white with red hearts all over it. Tied to the steering wheel was a note that read, "You're driving me crazy." He had no trouble guessing who had written it. He called Carole to thank her and asked her to dinner at the Trocadero. She wore her best champagne-colored gown for their first official date. When she opened the door, there was Clark sitting outside in the Model T. She climbed graciously in, and they laughed all the way there.

Their romance developed slowly, both of them having been hurt before, both of them sensing that this relationship could be important and not wanting to rush it. Clark seemed to take pleasure in finding his match at last. Unlike his two previous partners who had been much older, Carole was only a few years younger. She had her own career, being pretty much his female equivalent at Paramount in terms of star value, and had her own income and property. She was independent by nature, too, and she could stand up for herself and give him back as good as he gave. Clark had never really known what it was like to have a lasting and meaningful relationship with a woman who was his peer. Carole would give him that chance.

On the other hand, there's little doubt that Carole saw a number of advantages in being Mrs. Clark Gable, as any red-blooded woman at the time would have. Seizing the opportunity with which fate presented her, Carole set out to be just the sort of woman whom Clark would want, even learning how to shoot so she could go along on hunting trips and be one of the boys. Having lost his mother while a baby, Clark seemed to be searching for a woman who could be the perfect balance of mother and companion to him and Carole seemed to sense that need, gradually making herself over into that image. She may also have perceptively observed that his last two wives had let Clark live independently of them and do pretty much what he liked, so she may well have figured on making herself so indispensable to him that he would be unable to feel complete without her.

They made a very stylish couple when dancing at the Trocadero or the Coconut Grove. Clark was always immaculately turned out in his tailored clothes, and Carole was probably the best-dressed woman in Hollywood, wearing clothes by Travis Banton, Paramount's head stylist. When they were working, which they were both doing pretty much flat out for most of that year, Saturday was the only night they could go out together. When they did, the flashbulbs would be blinding. So, Sundays they preferred to get away from everyone and would usually go horseriding, or to rodeos and horseshows. They usually went out by themselves because they had few friends in common for a long time, until people realized that this was going to be a serious relationship.

Carole was a curious mixture of a very beautiful, gracious woman who still felt she had to use language that would turn air blue, possibly as a defense mechanism or in an effort to reassure the predominantly male film crews of the time how much she could be one of the boys. Johnny Mahin claimed that her choice of words used to sometimes embarrass him so much he'd leave the room: "It was always fuck and shit, fuck and shit. Clark loved it. He'd laugh; never try to stop her. She'd never swear if there was someone visiting on the set; she was always very careful. It was only around who she felt was a pal, or the crew and the grips."[24] Carole was certainly never a woman of convention and Clark did indeed love her for it, never seeming to tire of recounting "Carole stories." Many years later, for example, he would tell A.E. Hotchner that, when Carole and he went duckhunting for the first time, it was too foggy that early in the morning to see either geese.or ducks. When Clark pointed out that you just had to wait until it cleared, Carole suggested she could think of something better to do. They made love twice in that duck blind, which Clark recalled was not an easy thing to do.[25]

Monday morning it would be back to work at their respective studios, though, working on different movies at different times. While Clark was involved with *San Francisco*, Carol started work on *My Man Godfrey*, thanks to the efforts of her former husband and costar William Powell, who had insisted no one else could do the lead comedienne role as well as Carole. Powell was currently in the middle of his relationship with Clark's close friend Jean Harlow. If that wasn't enough to demonstrate what a small town Hollywood could be, the role of Carole's mother was being played by Alice Brady, who had had an affair with Clark when they were on Broadway together. By the time Carole was done with that shoot, Clark had started work on *Cain and Mabel*.

Earlier in 1936, William Randolph Hearst had moved his Cosmopolitan production company from MGM to Warner Brothers studios, where he devised pictures that would enhance his actress lover Marion Davies' reputation as a singer and dancer. Louis B. Mayer still owed him a favor, so once again Clark was traded, thankfully for the last time, at Davies' request. In *Cain and Mabel*, directed by Lloyd Bacon who had made *42nd Street*, Clark is a down-and-out boxer and Davies a down-and-out singer and dancer.[26] They both have the same problem: no audience for their shows. They meet when Clark is kept awake by her tapdancing, and they proceed to hate each other on sight until they eventually fall for each other.

The overlavish (if not over-the-top) musical numbers were staged by Bobby Connolly, who had worked with Busby Berkeley. In the wedding scene, Davies wears a Venetian wedding dress consisting of 185 yards of satin and lace. She stands alongside Clark in front of a ninety-foot-high organ with 160 pipes, each adorned by a bridesmaid. As it plays, the organ spews forth dozens of tap-dancing maidens playing assorted musical instruments. Frank Westmore claims that it was the brainchild of his older brother, Perc, who was then creative-effects senior executive at Warner Brothers and Marion's personal make-up man. After Perc had gone through the whole concept in front of Jack Warner, Busby Berkeley, Davies, and Hearst, he gained their enthusiastic support. However, Berkeley complained that they had no soundstage big enough in which to set it all up. Right then and there, Hearst said he would put up the needed $100,000 to raise Sound Stage Seven's roof thirty feet, and it has been that way ever since.[27]

Cain and Mabel has the unique distinction of being the last film for which Clark shaved his mustache, apparently at the specific request of Davies, who claimed that she couldn't kiss him because it tickled too much. The film's distinction for Davies was the unbelievable heat she endured while dressed in heavy costumes. She recalled that "It was 148 degrees up in the flies, where the electricians were, and 122 on the stage. The girls would faint on the set, even though they had those big aeroplane propellers with ice in front of them. They would faint like dead flies. I had on a fur costume and had to do dances.... They had to put ice on my wrists and chain me to the rail.... Finally, it took ladders to get me down. The costume alone weighed about fifty-six pounds.... It was Purgatory."[28] Clark could always be relied upon to bring ice cream every day for everyone.

The bright spot in an otherwise mundane film is the wonderfully acerbic Laird Doyle di-

Clark and the baby cougar he captured and brought back from the Kaibab Forest in Arizona, as a present for Carole in 1937. He is wearing the long sideburns he grew for Parnell.

alogue with which Clark and Davies fling insults at each other. Clark on Davies' dance steps, for example: "If the galloping you do is dancing, I've seen better ballet in a horse show." Unfortunately, people figured there were better movies to see too, and *Cain and Mabel* bombed. The plot was trite, the musical numbers overdone, and Clark and Davies were miscast anyway. Discouraged, and tired of being continually criticized, Davies made only one more movie and then retired to be the companion of the man she cared about most.

Left to right: *Clark filming* Love on the Run, *Spencer Tracy, filming* Captains Courageous, *Robert Taylor, filming* Camille, *and William Powell, filming* After the Thin Man, *meet on the MGM lot in 1936.*

She would say in 1951 that she would have preferred to stay on the stage and not go into movies, and did not think she had any real talent. She claimed she had never seen *Citizen Kane* and was not angry with Orson Welles.[29]

When the shoot wrapped, Clark was ready to relax. He left to go hunting on the Kaibab Plateau, along the northern rim of the Grand Canyon. Carole loved animals and asked him to bring her back something cute and cuddly. He certainly did; he came back with a very cuddly seventy-five pound cougar cub that had wandered into the camp one night. It was a fine idea for a few days, until the cub started to dine on Carole's domestic menagerie, at which point it was off to the MGM Zoo for the cougar.

By this time the success of *My Man Godfrey* had made Carole famous, and some shrewd renegotiation of her contract with Paramount ensued. Earlier in the year, the studio had considered not renewing her contract because of her flagging popularity. Now she had them over a barrel. Her new fee of $150,000 a picture made her the highest-paid female star in Hollywood. She was given concessions that even Clark could only dream of at this point in his career. She was allowed to choose her director, her main crew, her hairdresser, and her makeup artist. She was allowed to make one independent picture a year. But probably most important to her current situation, she forced them to remove the "morals clause" from her contract which had given them the right to sack her on grounds of "moral turpitude," such as being involved in a relationship with a married man.[30]

Clark must have had to smile very tightly and say how pleased he was for her. As MGM's exclusive property, he could make no decisions as to what films he appeared in or who worked with him in them. As if to reinforce that, Clark was handed yet another movie destined for a dusty shelf, *Love on the Run*, a poor imitation of *It Happened One Night*. Even the plot was the same. Heiress runs away, teams up with a newspaper reporter, and they eventually fall in love. Just the locations were different: the Fontainebleau Palace instead of a motel, and an ox-cart instead of a bus. Despite the John Lee Mahin screenplay, the whole thing was far too derivative for its ancestry to go unnoticed. W.S. Van Dyke was no Capra, and Joan Crawford couldn't reach the standard of Colbert as a comedienne.

By the time it was all over, Thalberg had died, and an era at MGM was over. Clark had always been ambivalent about Thalberg, who was more involved in promoting the careers of the studio's female stars that that of Clark until he had tried to make amends with *Mutiny on the Bounty*. That had worked, but Clark always had the suspicion he'd been cheated out of earlier fame. Nevertheless, Clark accepted the offer to be an usher at his funeral. Thalberg's death left Mayer in absolute control of MGM. Earlier that year, Mayer's son-in-law, David Selznick, had purchased the rights to Margaret Mitchell's novel *Gone with the Wind*. With Thalberg gone, Mayer and Selznick were soon involved in what would be some two years of intrigue and maneuvering that would take place before the film could be made. And caught right in the middle would be Clark Gable.

CHAPTER 15

WHO DO YOU THINK YOU ARE, CLARK GABLE?

By 1937, Clark had reached a level of fame and popularity that in this day and age might more likely be attained by teenage music idols or sports stars. The public loved him unconditionally. That popular expression of the time about whether a person thought they were Clark Gable says a lot about the level of perfection people awarded him. The only rival in his importance to MGM was possibly Shirley Temple, and her appeal was to a different audience. In the words of photographer Clarence Bull, Clark was "the big rock in the studio foundation."[1]

Being such a big rock, though, also meant he was a big investment for MGM and, like any investment, Clark had to be protected. Fieldsie's son, Richard Lang, says, "The secret of Clark surviving his own fame was that he was protected by the people around him. If a building was falling, for whatever reason, they would throw themselves over him."[2] Clark thought he was free, when in fact he flew within a gilded cage.

It was a very brightly gilded cage, though. In a U.S. Treasury Report released to the press, his salary for the 1935 financial year was revealed to have been $211,533, compared to the highest corporate salary reported of $193,128 paid to G.W. Mason, president of the Kelvinator Refrigerator Company in Detroit.[3] On January 4, 1937, the film trade magazine *Boxoffice* announced that according to their national poll, Clark was the most popular film star across the country, followed by Shirley Temple. However, the results of the annual movie-exhibitors poll conducted by the *Motion Picture Herald*, for the period September 1, 1936, to August 31, 1937, placed Shirley Temple in the lead, followed by Clark.[4] Either way, Clark's star was certainly in the heavens even if his feet briefly rested in cement. One of the physical milestones of public esteem for Hollywood stars since 1927 has been to have their foot and or handprints pressed into the cement paving in the forecourt of Grauman's Chinese Theater on Hollywood Boulevard. On January 20, it was Clark's turn. The largest crowd that had ever assembled for one of these events turned out to watch him do it, a record that stood until Doris Day added her prints in 1961.

Perhaps having all these people acting as if Clark could do no wrong persuaded MGM that it was time Clark was given a project that would prove his worth as a serious actor. The problem was that at MGM it had been Thal-

A debonair Mr. Gable with the look that sent women swooning all over the world, c. 1937. (Spicer Collection.)

Sid Grauman and director W.S. Van Dyke look on as a theater artist helps Clark immortalize his hands in wet cement outside the Chinese Theater on Hollywood Boulevard, February 15, 1937.

berg who had embodied all the taste in the selection of such serious projects. Without him, they had no guide through the woods and, consequently, they became badly lost.

The studio decided that their serious project for Clark would be *Parnell*, a former Broadway hit play by Elsie T. Shauffler about the love of the Irish Nationalist leader for married woman Katie O'Shea. Clark even agreed to work with the academic director John Stahl.[5] This project had all the indications of being a prestige picture of monumental stuffiness, and Joan Crawford promptly pleaded out when offered the female lead. Clark, apparently blinded to the fact that a woman who regarded herself his friend was trying to drop him a hint, was so offended by Joan's decision that he refused to speak to her

until they worked in *Strange Cargo* together in 1940. Instead, Myrna Loy was given the role. She would later defy the doomsayers by commenting that, in her opinion, Clark was "wonderful" in the title role. "The best love scene he ever played is in that picture," she said. "It's the first meeting between Parnell and Katie, when he talks about having seen her in a white dress at the opera. It's a beautiful scene. You can feel the beginning of this love that would rock the British Empire."[6]

Clark initially liked the film too, but neither the critics nor the public did. In a rare circumstance for a Gable movie, MGM lost money at the boxoffice with *Parnell*. Clark was judged to be profoundly mis-cast in a role that didn't suit him, which Myrna Loy refutes. "Clark gave a subdued, sustained performance

Now for the feet! Clark balances on Sid Grauman's shoulder.

Clark's signature and imprints as they look today. Clark wrote "To Sid / A Great Guy." (Spicer Collection.)

as Parnell," she protests, "which apparently was the problem. He had been so typed as those red-blooded Blackie Nortons that the public didn't want to be reminded that he was an actor. They went after the macho stuff.... We were actors for God's sake. We couldn't be Blackie Norton or Nora Charles all the time!"[7] Myrna Loy also ran into her share of criticism over her role in the film. People were so used to seeing her as the bright and breezy, ultimate 1930s wife in *The Thin Man* series that they couldn't adjust to her as a nineteenth-century mistress. According to Loy, disgruntled fans wrote in to MGM "by the thousands."

Well before it was known by that name, Clark seems to be attempting some method acting in his efforts to *become* Parnell instead of doing what he usually did, molding the character to fit Clark Gable. He actually changes his accent, something that he could never be persuaded to do again even when it

became an issue for *Gone with the Wind*. It was Clark's one attempt to break the mold and be a serious actor who could be successful in a variety of roles, but he was so burned by the critics and dissuaded by public opinion after *Parnell* that he would never go back there again. At this point in his career, he gave every indication of being able to cope with that level of acting. That he evidently never felt he could cope with it in the future may have been one of motion picture history's great losses. Even Rhett Butler would be an extension of the kind of character everybody expected from him, and he would eventually believe that playing that expected distilled essence of maleness was all he could do. From here on he seemed to adopt that succinct philosophy of a later macho hero, Clint Eastwood: "A man's got to know his limitations."

A shocked Clark would remain positively paranoid about repeating the public errors of *Parnell* for the rest of his life. Carole didn't help,

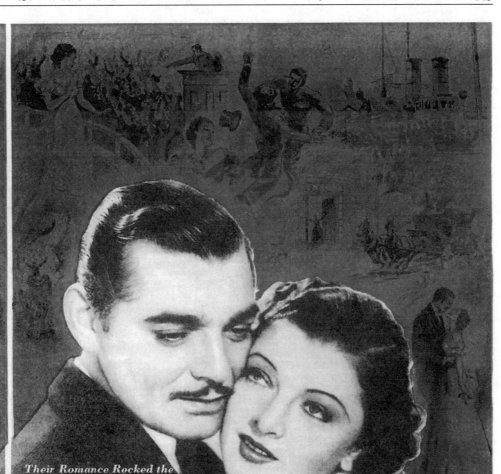

Their Romance Rocked the Foundations of an Empire!

THE MOST *Powerful* LOVE STORY EVER FILMED!
...Of a Patriot Who Lost a Country When He Found a Woman

You thought "San Francisco" was exciting — but wait! You'll be thrilled to your finger-tips when this mighty drama comes thundering from the screen. A fiery romance with your two favorite stars!...CLARK GABLE—courageous, masterful leader of a fighting nation . . .

MYRNA LOY—the bewitching beauty in whose arms he forgot the pain of leadership . . .

Answering the call of millions of picture-goers M-G-M has brought them together in the most dramatic heart-stabbing love story of our time!

CLARK GABLE · MYRNA LOY
IN
PARNELL

A Metro-Goldwyn-Mayer production based on the great stage play that thrilled Broadway for months, with EDNA MAY OLIVER, BILLIE BURKE, and a great M-G-M cast. Directed and produced by John Stahl.

An original advertisement for the release of "Parnell," June 1937. (Spicer Collection.)

Clark with his payroll sheet from The Merry Widow *showing his wage of $7.50 per day in 1925.*

either; whenever she figured Clark's head was starting to look like it might not fit through the door, she would whisper, "Remember *Parnell*." It was the hangover of embarrassment from this movie that kept Clark from wanting to have anything to do with *Gone with the Wind*, as it became clearer as the year went by that he would come under enormous pressure from the public to take the role of Rhett Butler. He refused to accept that the role was a good idea until well into the shoot, and he had to be threatened and cajoled into participating in the one movie most responsible for perpetuating his fame into the present day.

Trying to focus on the character of Parnell could not have been easy for Clark when everything was going well. Right in the middle of his work on the film, however, he was handed a problem-package that must have made concentrating on his role very difficult indeed. Unbeknown to everyone else it must have brought with it a lot of very private pain, because of the parallels with his life of which few people were aware.

Considering that during Clark's career as a screen idol he was involved with quite a number of women, very little mud was ever thrown at him. Other well-known actors who dated far fewer women, or for that matter actresses who dated far fewer men, were involved in far more scandal. Ingrid Bergman, for example, was publicly crucified over only one romantic episode. One reason for this could have been that Clark tended to be so patently, and occasionally embarrassingly, honest about himself that interviewers simply didn't have the heart to dig up dirt on him. Clark came across as just a decent, ordinary guy doing a job, just like them. Naturally curious, he was genuinely interested in people he met, and journalists would soon find themselves answering *his* questions. They came away with empty notebooks, realizing only later that they had been the ones who'd been interviewed. On the other hand, while Clark might have been open about himself, he was notoriously private about his domestic life. Clark never kissed and told, and women seemed to appreciate that to the extent of returning the favor.

Then there was also the matter of *whom* Clark chose to be with. It's quite possible, although it could never be accurately estimated, that Clark made love to hundreds of women during his lifetime. Most of them were not movie stars, but women from ordinary walks of life such as waitresses, secretaries, continuity girls, and more than a few hookers. Clark took his one-night stands where he found them, which in his case could mean hiding in his closet, climbing through his hotel window, or even waiting in his bed when he got back to his room. It was not as if he ever had to look very far, really, or send out a search party. Sex for Clark was like w a n d e r i n g through an orchard where fruit hung ripely from branches waiting to be picked, and he regarded the picking as his due reward for hard and honest work. He was never less than honest about what that sexual o c c a s i o n amounted to, and women seemed to appreciate that honesty. None said a derogatory word about him.

Even some men were remarkably understanding. When Douglas Fairbanks, Jr., finally discovered that his wife, Joan Crawford, and Clark were having an affair (even though Clark had

A 1937 ad for the new Dodge Convertible Coupe, featuring Clark. (Spicer Collection.)

been a friend and a guest in their house, and even though he and Joan had used the dressing room that was her wedding present from

Clark planning a hunting trip after finishing Parnell *in 1937.*

Douglas), Fairbanks still regarded Clark as, "such a nice guy that even in my private distress I couldn't blame him."[8] Other men were not so accomodating. When Anthony Quinn found out on his honeymoon night that his wife, Katherine de Mille, had previously lost her virginity to Clark, he beat her until she ran from the house. Quinn remained "insane with jealousy" for some time.[9] Still, no exposés recounting lurid details of Clark's sex life or lovers were published while he was alive, and that had as much to do with the respect people had for him as it had to do with the efficient MGM public-relations team. In an era when paternity cases were not unusual events for some Hollywood stars, only one case concerning Clark ever got into court.

A few years previously, an English mother named Violet Norton had gone to the movies in her local theater in Billercay, Essex. There on the screen she saw a man who apparently looked to her so like Frank Billings, her long-lost lover and the father of her daughter Gwendoline, that she came to believe the two men were one and the same. In 1922 she had been living with Frank Norton when Billings moved into the farm next door to raise chickens. Soon Violet and Billings became lovers, and the result was Gwendoline. By the time his daughter was born, however, Billings had disappeared to America, promising that he would send for her. He never did, and although it was Norton who signed Gwendoline's birth certificate and married Violet two years later, she had over the years built a fantasy around the man she called her "fairy prince," always believing she would find him again. Watching Clark in that theater, Violet Norton convinced herself that she had finally discovered what had become of Frank Billlings.

So in 1932, Violet wrote to Clark asking him to acknowledge his daughter and to contribute some assistance, but he thought the letter so "fantastic" that he threw it away. Undaunted, Violet seems to have then decided to wage a long-term campaign to obtain the recognition she considered Gwendoline should rightly be accorded. Her first step was to move them both to the Canadian city of Winnipeg, in late 1935. Violet then wrote to Clark again in March 1936, reminding him of their affair and that he was Gwendoline's father. "You are free and so am I," she wrote. "Nobody needs know. Let us go away together as I am a difference (sic) to when you knew me. I am fully of pep and romance."[10]

Receiving no answer, Violet then resorted to her backup plan and placed advertisements in American movie magazines, offering to make any actor who would support her Gwendoline's godfather. She also wrote to Mae West, apparently because she thought Gwendoline looked a bit like her, offering to make her the child's godmother if Mae would support their cause. With no results from those quarters, the resourceful mother then wrote to the Los Angeles District Attorney and the British Consul asking for their assistance. She offered her story to various newspaper columnists. Finally, she somehow persuaded seventy-five-year-old Frank Kienan (or Keenan), a Winnipeg boarding-house operator, to finance Violet and the thirteen-year-old Gwendoline to travel to Los Angeles in December 1936.

There, Violet hired Jack L. Smith, a private detective, to put pressure on Clark and MGM to admit Gwendoline was his daughter. Smith approached the secretary of the Motion Picture Producers Association and Ralph Wheelwright, a studio press agent, with the suggestion that a trust fund of $150,000 be quietly set up for Gwendoline to avoid unfavorable publicity. "A nasty mess has arisen concerning Clark Gable…. I want to protect the movie industry which would suffer if Gable's name were smeared all over the papers," Wheelwright would state Smith told him. Wheelwright said his reply was that the studio and Clark considered the "whole thing a preposterous frame-up," and that Smith agreed but had figured he would be able to get some of the trust-fund money.[11]

At this point, MGM evidently decided the whole matter had gone far enough. The studio notified the District Attorney's office which, it turned out, had been keeping its eye on Violet Norton anyway.

Violet Wells Norton, garrulous, buxom, gray-haired, and forty-seven, was duly arrested and charged, along with Smith and Kienan, by a grand jury on January 27 with conspiracy to extort money from Clark and with mail fraud. Despite hammering on the door of the grand jury room, Norton was denied leave to speak before them. Reporters were certainly willing to listen to her, though, and she informed them that along with recognition for her daughter she wanted recognition as a playwright. "The smallest 'e could do for me and little Gwen," she proclaimed, "would be to buy me plys. I've wrote (sic) four of 'em. …They was all about 'im an' me in Bellercay fourteen years ago." If only he would confront them, Violet suggested, he would "bryke (sic) down in a trice."[12] Clark declined the invitation, but he did appear before the grand jury and proved to their satisfaction that he was selling neckties in Portland, or trimming trees in a Silverton timber mill, at the time Violet was claiming he was fathering children in England. Norton, Smith, and Keenan were all duly indicted. Violet remained in jail, with bail set at $2,500, until the case came to trial before Judge George Cosgrove and an all-male jury on April 20.

Probably because of the stress of trying to cope with work and this case at the same time, Clark fell ill with influenza. He was due back on the *Parnell* set on his thirty-sixth birthday, February 1, and in an effort to cheer him up

MGM decided to throw him a surprise party. The studio asked Arthur Freed to produce some musical entertainment. He and arranger Roger Edens decided to turn the occasion to young Judy Garland's benefit and have her serenade Clark with a special birthday song. Born into a vaudeville family as Frances Gumm, and onstage with her sisters from the age of three, Judy Garland had been signed by MGM in 1935 at the age of thirteen. Since then, the studio had basically ignored her except for a brief Fox loan-out. L.B. Mayer would be present for this party, and Garland's friends figured this would be an ideal occasion to remind him of how talented she was. Judy argued with arranger Roger Edens about which song to perform. She wanted to do Ethel Merman's "Drums in My Heart," which would not have suited her age. The more girlish Judy could appear, her friends reasoned, the more favorably she would appear to Mayer, who saw himself as the eternal father-figure. He had adored Deanna Durbin's dreamily adolescent rendering of "Someone to Care Over Me" in *Three Smart Girls*, for example.

To resolve the issue, Eden adapted an arrangement based on the old Harold Arlen song "Let's Fall in Love" called "You Made Me Love You." Written for a Carmel Myers monologue that she had performed on the Rudy Vallee radio show, it was called, "Gee, Mr. Gable," and played out a chambermaid's dream of meeting Clark. Edens rewrote the monologue as, "Dear Mr. Gable," playing humorously on the in-joke of Violet Norton's letters to Clark. There was further irony in the similarity of Judy's and Gwendoline Norton's ages. Judy was not at all sure how Clark would take the joke, and she initially protested doing the song. Edens told her it would work as long as she maintained an entirely innocent attitude while singing it.

So on February 1, when Clark and Carole walked back onto the *Parnell* set after lunch, they found the entire cast and crew assembled with MGM executives. A piano

flourish drew attention to the corner of the stage, where Judy was sitting on top of the upright, by her own admission "trembling like a leaf … stage frightened for the first time. [But] I gave it all I had because I admire him so." She needn't have worried. By the last lines the crowd was cheering, and Gable had tears in his eyes as he made his way over to her. "He put his arms around me and said, 'You're the sweetest girl I ever saw in my life,'" Judy remembered. "Looking at him up close, my knees almost caved in. And then *I* cried, and it was simply heavenly." Clark would later say about the experience that "I was in a hell of a state in my life [at the time] and hated making *Parnell*. When little Judy was brought on the set to sing, I just about dropped. I was so surprised and really touched."[13]

Although it was Judy's first step toward legend, both she and Clark would be less touched by the song over the years as they both endured repeat performances. In February 1949, Judy would find herself sitting alongside Ava Gardner while they sat with other MGM stars for the studio's silver anniversary group photograph. Clark, who was sitting on the other side of Ava, took the opportunity of a break to lean across and whisper to Judy with a wry grin: "You goddamned brat. You've ruined every one of my birthdays. They bring you out of the wallpaper to sing that song, and it's a pain in the ass." Judy would say later that she only really began to like him from that day because he had finally "leveled" with her about it.[14]

By the time the trial got underway in April, witnesses had come to Clark's aid from every quarter. Late in February, an unsigned letter turned up purporting to be from Frank Billings, admitting that he was the father of Gwendoline and claiming that he looked like Clark Gable. From the northwest, *The Oregonian*'s payroll clerk Margaret Leisure, Meier & Frank stockman Chris Nielsen, surveyor Ernest Nelson, and Silver Falls Timber Company president M. C. Woodward made the long journey down the coast to testify. The star witness, however, would be no less than Clark's long-ago sweetheart Franz Dorfler.

Clark was first up to bat on the opening day of the trial, and hundreds of women besieged the federal building hoping to catch a glimpse of him, despite Clark and his father, Will, arriving an hour early. In answer to government prosecutor John Powell's questions, Clark calmly denied that he had ever been in England, nor had he seen Violet or Gwendoline before, nor was he Gwendoline's father. He had been working in Oregon during 1922 and 1923, he said. Morris Lavine, Violet's defense attorney, said in cross-examination that she had acted in good faith, truly believing that Clark was the father because of the close resemblance. She could thus be considered justified in her course of action, he stated. He then moved for an acquittal, but the judge allowed the trial to proceed.

On the following day Clark, who was still being forced to seek shelter behind locked doors from the crowds of female spectators, was only required to identify some old copies of his paychecks tendered by the manager of the Silver Falls Timber Company as evidence he'd been there at the time Violet claimed he was in England. As he had the day before, Clark refused to look at Violet, much less recognize her, although she would stare steadily at him for minutes at a time. Each of the Oregonians testified he'd been working for their respective companies over that period. Letters were submitted. Wheelwright talked about his conversation with Smith. Then Gwendoline, the girl caught in the middle of all this mess, took the stand to say that Kienan had put up the money to bring her and her mother to Los Angeles.

Up until now, despite the prosecution's persistent efforts, Clark had refused to allow Violet Norton anywhere near him. However, her lawyer finally won his point that only with close-range identification would she finally be able to decide whether Clark was Frank Billings or not. So late that day, the courtroom held its collective breath as Violet approached close enough to Clark to touch him.

She didn't, though, content to stare intently into his face and then down his body to his feet, which she had said she needed to see bare. Needless to say, Clark kept his shoes firmly on and calmly looked back at her without expression. Then she stepped back and nodded her head vigorously to confirm to everyone that she was sure this was Frank Billings before her. A low titter rippled across the crowded room. Her cause was lost.

After deliberating for an hour and fifty-five minutes the following afternoon, the jury announced that they had found Violet guilty on the charge of misuse of the U.S. mail but not guilty on the charge of conspiracy. Violet showed no emotion. Neither Clark nor Gwendoline were there. Judge Cosgrave set sentencing for early May.

That weekend, the irrepressible Violet still regaled reporters with her story. "I'm innocent of the charge," she declared. She went on to say that she still thought Clark was the father and that he should submit to blood tests to decide the paternity issue. Her counsel said that he had been given leave to apply for probation on the grounds Violet go back to Canada and drop the whole thing but he sighed that she was still eager to appeal and keep on fighting the courts. By this time Frank Billings' brother Harry, a London fireman, had told reporters in England that although there was some resemblance between the two men, they were definitely not the same person.

Violet Norton was sentenced on May 10 to serve one year in jail for mail fraud. Judge Cosgrave handed the matter over to federal immigration authorities with the expectation that she would be deported back to Canada after serving her time. She was never heard of again.

The trial did benefit two people, though, being the means by which they gained jobs at MGM. Franz Dorfler was identified early as a key witness in the trial because it had been her parents' farm on which Clark was working at the time Violet Norton was claiming he was making love to her on a farm in Essex. As Clark had lost touch with Franz by then, al-

Clark on a hunting trip in the Santa Barbara mountains just before starting Saratoga *in 1937.*

though he figured she was still somewhere in Los Angeles, his lawyers put in quite a bit of time and effort locating her. Finally they found her right under their noses. For a while she had been working in a dress shop in Hollywood, but then that had closed. Finding it hard to make ends meet, Franz found work as a domestic cook in the kitchen of none other than Bert Allenberg, the other partner in the agency handling Clark. The Allenbergs paid her well, but it made for long, hard days of work that had taken their toll on the still delicately beautiful Franz's health. Perhaps still feeling a pang of guilt, and no doubt grateful for her help, Clark decided to help her in return. Knowing she was not doing very well financially, Clark found her work at MGM in some small singing and dancing roles. Sadly, their friendship gradually drifted apart. When she was laid off from the studio during World War II, Franz was too proud to ask Clark for help. Once she left the studio, she wrote later, "I never saw Clark again. I never went to his pictures because I knew him. I knew all of his expressions, his gestures, the raising of one eyebrow, the crooked smile, the dimples, and his wink. He never really changed. A bit polished, but still the same." She then went on to offer some rather astute analysis of Clark and of how she felt about him. He got what he wanted, she said, "but he had to work hard for it. He married two women he didn't love to further his career, and that's something I couldn't have done. But then he did a number of things I didn't think were right. He had a lot of hard times, and he drank a lot, but he managed to win in the end. He never took advantage of me, and I've always respected him for that. I just wish that things had worked out better for us."[15]

The other person whose career was changed was journalist Otto Winkler who had been working for the *Los Angeles Examiner* covering the trial. Apparently Clark was so impressed with his work that he asked Howard Strickling to give him a job in the publicity department. Otto became Clark's personal publicity and public-relations man, and a close friendship grew up between them. Sadly, that friendship would one day be a factor in Otto's death.

Letters such as Violet Norton's were not the only ones that Clark received during his career blaming him for a marriage breakup, inviting him out, asking him for help with someone's career, or attempting to extort money from him by violent means. It was something that went on throughout Clark's career, and stars still have to deal with it today. Unfortunately, it is one of those debits balancing the credits of public fame. Clark's fan mail was opened at the studio, and any suspicious letters were as a rule handed over to the FBI for assessment and, if necessary, investigation. Only letters that threatened bodily harm, kidnapping, or actual extortion were usually regarded as arrestable offenses. In other cases the G-men would more than likely just give out some stern warnings.

In October 1937, for example, MGM handed over to the FBI a letter from a young lady who purported to be a "true, loving friend" of Clark's in Barberton, Ohio. She was so friendly that she threatened to have a young male associate, whom she said they had in common, tell a story about some dark aspect of Clark's past to the press if Clark did not arrange an introduction for her with a Hollywood director or producer. The young lady obligingly included her return address. She was traced to a hotel in East Liverpool, Ohio, where she was working as a prostitute. No doubt thoroughly frightened to have a pair of FBI agents at her door, she confessed to writing the letter out of desperation with little thought as to the consequences. The agents seemed satisfied that she had no actual information and intended no real harm, nor did she seem aware of the penalties that she could have incurred, so they were content with issuing a warning.

In February the following year, however, the studio forwarded a much more serious note to the FBI. Addressed from Fonda, Iowa, the few roughly printed lines ordered Clark to send the writer $1,000 if "you value your life" because the young woman writer needed the money for her family's farm. FBI inquiries revealed that a thirty-year-old eccentric farm laborer, Gaylord Forsyth, had written the letter using the name of a girl to whom he was attracted but who had rejected him. "I did it for spite," he confessed. "I fell in love with her but she wouldn't pay any attention to me." Forsyth was promptly arrested.

Sometimes the FBI could act on information received to head off an offensive item. Due to a voluntary confession from an Illinois insane asylum escapee, a forewarned FBI intercepted a postcard addressed to Clark demanding $5,000 in March 1939. The FBI made sure the writer was restored to their comfortably padded environment, from where any more letters would be closely observed before being mailed.

Then there were the downright mysterious letters. In August 1940, MGM forwarded a potentially ominous letter to the FBI in which a man who identified himself only as "an ex-convict now going straight" claimed he'd heard of an elaborate kidnap scheme. He wrote that he had recently met an old convict buddy from Folsom Prison who had invited him to be part of a kidnap plan. Fake police officers in a stolen patrol car would pull Clark and Carole over late one night, as they returned home from a party, and seize them. They would be taken to a house where Carole would be secured to a bed, underneath which would be a time bomb. The following morning Clark would be shown the bomb, which would be set for twelve noon. He would have until then to raise $15,000 or the bomb would detonate. After that, the kidnappers intended to move on to Barbara Stanwyck and Robert Taylor. By the time FBI agents called at the address mentioned in the letter, though, its writer had vanished. Quiet and well-behaved, the six-foot tall, gray-eyed man had arrived in June, the proprietor of the rooming house said, and had been working as a mechanic somewhere until she discovered his room empty on September 4. Despite a comprehensive search of Los Angeles records, no trace of him was ever found, nor did any kidnap attempt take place. At least, none that anyone ever spoke about.[16]

As a motion picture star, Clark was also in demand for radio theater shows which banked on the recognizability of his voice and his name. A modern equivalent might be a guest appearance in an episode of a popular television series. It kept the star's name familiar to the audience, and it often linked a sponsor and the star's use of their product. Clark's

contract allowed him to appear in four or five radio plays a year. One benefit for him personally was that these plays gave him an opportunity to go back to his stage roots, to exercise some theatrical muscles that had not been used for a while, and work in the kind of serious drama that MGM and his adoring movie audiences never seemed willing to let him attempt.

Clark's first appearance in a full-length radio play was in *His Misleading Lady* on the night of November 11, 1935. It was part of the Lux Radio Theatre series, sponsored by Lever Brothers and their Lux Soap product, which had begun in 1934 on the NBC Blue Network broadcast out of New York City. After running out of Broadway play scripts to use, the program moved to Los Angeles the following year. On Monday night, June 1, 1936, Clark could be heard co-starring with Marlene Dietrich in *The Legionnaire and the Lady* in the first Lux Radio Theatre show to be broadcast from their theater on Hollywood Boulevard. Produced by Cecil B. DeMille, the show took place before a live audience, which on this night included such celebrities as Joan Blondell, Gary Cooper, Al Jolson, Franchot Tone, and Frederic March. Eventually, the series became so popular that at some time or another virtually every major Hollywood star of the thirties made an appearance on it. In 1936 alone the audience for the show was estimated at 40 million, and some film stars confessed they were frightened to be heard before an audience of that magnitude. Over its twenty-one-year history it put to air versions of every major play and film of the time and probably quite a few minor ones, going through approximately 52,000 pages of scripts.

Clark proved as much a star on radio as he was on screen and was asked to launch Columbia's Camel Caravan radio show for $6,500 and all the Camel cigarettes he could smoke. He duly appeared in *Men in White* with Madeleine Carroll. The August 1936 edition of *Time* commented on how easy-going and informal Clark sounded on the air, and it credited him with breaking a Hollywood taboo by having a real audience in the studio to create truly live theater. On October 20, he was heard in the Caravan series as George Washington in Maxwell Anderson's play *Valley Forge*. Then, early the next year on April 5, Clark appeared in another Lux Radio Theatre production, *A Farewell to Arms*, with Josephine Hutchinson and Adolphe Menjou.

Clark's radio bookings were handled by Corney Jackson, from Phil Berg's agency, who once recalled an example of Clark's natural kindness. On this particular night they had an hour to spare before they were due at the radio studio, and they stopped at a roadside stand to get a hamburger and a milk shake. When the girl brought Clark's order around to his side of the car, she was so flustered at seeing who was there that she dropped the entire tray right down the front of Clark's light gray suit into his lap. She burst into tears but Clark just laughed and told her not to worry about it.[17]

Lux had a cap of $5,000 for any star appearing in their shows, but Clark had told Corney that his fee would be $7500. Lux wouldn't relent, and so on at least one occasion Corney had to make up the $2500 out of his own pocket. That afternoon when they went to the tennis club, Clark put his arm around Corney's shoulders and gave him the check back. "I was just letting you sweat it for awhile," he said with a laugh.[18] Unlike some of the other stars, Clark never argued about where his name came in the billing. He was quite happy to have it announced last — which, incidentally, is usually the name people remember.

Clark did three further appearances for Lux Theatre. On September 27, he was heard in their production of *Cimarron* with Virginia Bruce. Then, on November 14, 1938, he played Jean Laffite in *The Buccaneer*. His final radio appearance for Lux was *It Happened One Night*, for which he and Claudette Colbert were reunited to reprise their award-winning

roles one last time on March 20, 1939. A genuine cross-country bus driver, Harold Bernam, played himself in the show.

In October, Clark changed radio networks to Columbia (CBS) and their Screen Guild Theater, which was initially sponsored by Gulf. Over the next ten years he was heard in a series of productions that included *Red Dust* with Ann Sothern (October 6, 1940), *China Seas* with Lucille Ball (December 4, 1944), and *Homecoming* with Lana Turner (October 6, 1949).

Clark had been scheduled to begin wardrobe and costume testing for *Saratoga* in March 1937. For the sixth time he would be costarring with his good friend Jean Harlow. The lineup for this horse-racing drama was nothing short of impressive. The experienced and capable Jack Conway would be directing, and the script was written by Anita Loos and Robert Hopkins. Cast members included Lionel Barrymore, Cliff Edwards (later known as the voice of Jimmy Cricket), Margaret Hamilton (later the *Wizard of Oz*'s Wicked Witch of the West), Hattie McDaniel (future Oscar winner as Mammy in *Gone with the Wind*), Frank Morgan (later the Wizard in the *Wizard of Oz*), and Walter Pidgeon (later to be in *Command Decision*).

Work on the film had to wait, however, when Jean was ordered back into the hospital at the end of March because she had developed blood poisoning after all four of her wisdom teeth were extracted. There was no such thing as antibiotics in those days; they handed out painkillers and waited to see what would happen. Myrna Loy, for one, had noticed Jean hadn't been looking well for some time. In the fall of 1936, Loy and Powell had taken Jean with them to San Francisco while they were filming *After the Thin Man* there. They had stayed at the St. Francis Hotel, Myrna and Jean in one room and Powell downstairs in another. The two women got to know each other well, and Myrna noticed that "Jean tired easily and in the mornings her usually snow-white skin sometimes seemed slate-gray. I sensed that she was a sick girl." Concerned, she had a doctor friend of hers confirm her observation with a preliminary diagnosis of a blood disorder, but Jean never took advantage of the appointments Loy made for her to get help.[19]

The tooth infection eventually seemed to clear up, and Jean was ready to begin work in April. By then Clark was tangled up with the Violet Norton case, but the studio was chomping at the bit and could wait no longer. Shooting began on April 22. That was the day that Clark was in court testifying as to his whereabouts fifteen years ago, so Clark quite understandably appears tired and thinner in this film. Jean was also feeling tense, being in that position film stars sometimes find themselves in of appearing in a horse saga when you're not too keen on horses. She wrote to a New York fan she knew well, "I am jittery because I have horses on all sides of me and surrounding me all day long, and I am scared to death of them. But I hope to survive."[20] The film is essentially a complicated love triangle. Jean plays Carol Clayton, a horse-breeding heiress, and Clark is Duke Bradley, a bookie. Carol is flat broke and trying to save her farm, and Duke wants to scam her rich fiancé out of his money. However, Carol refuses to be indebted and tries to honestly come by the cash, falling for Duke as she does so. As every honest woman should, Carol wins both the horse race and the race for her man.

As shooting wore on into mid–May, people started to notice Jean was tiring visibly and couldn't seem to keep warm. She began sleeping in her dressing room rather than face the drive home at night. On May 20 she was shooting a scene with Walter Pidgeon when she doubled up, complaining of acute abdominal pain. She stayed home the next day while she was checked out by a doctor. His diagnosis was that she had a cold and perhaps a slight gall bladder infection. It was nothing to worry about, he said. Everyone tried to cheer her up when she returned to the set. To the huge appreciation of the crew, Clark sprang an anniversary gag to celebrate six years of their working together, sweeping Jean into a prolonged passionate embrace instead of the peck on the cheek called for in the script.

On Saturday, May 29, Jean and Clark were shooting the scene in the train compartment where she confesses she loves Duke. Kneeling right next to her head, Clark noticed she looked seriously ill. Trying to stand up, she sagged against him, and he could feel she had broken into a cold sweat. Tenderly he lowered his friend onto a sofa. William Powell was called from the nearby set of *Double Wedding* and rushed over, ordering her taken home. Her mother hurried back from Catalina, where she'd been on holiday, and the doctor was called again. Once more he could only give the same diagnosis.

What none of them realized was that Jean's kidneys had been slowly failing for nine months and had finally stopped functioning under attack from infection. In an era long before anyone would have dreamed of dialysis or transplants, there was simply nothing anyone could do for her. On the night of June 6, Jean slipped into a coma and was admitted to Good Samaritan Hospital, where she died the next morning without regaining consciousness. Word of her death reached the *Saratoga* set just after noon, when Jack Conway came back from a phone call to tell Clark, Anita Loos, and Walter Pidgeon, "Oh, my God, Baby's gone." Clark, overcome with grief, went home. Writer Harry Ruskin said years later, "The day Baby died there wasn't a sound in the commissary for three hours. Not one goddam sound."[21]

Jean was laid out in a silver and bronze coffin dressed in her pink mousseline-de-soie negligee she wears in *Saratoga*. Fifteen thousand dollars worth of flowers filled the Wee Kirk O' the Heather church at Glendale for her service on June 9; it could only hold two hundred and fifty mourners including Carole and Clark, who was one of the pallbearers. Horrified by the crowds of people crushing against the gates, Carole made Clark promise he'd never let her funeral deteriorate into such a circus if anything were to happen to her. That Saturday, Jean was interred in a room of multicolored marble purchased for her by William Powell in the Great Mausoleum at Forest Lawn.[22]

While stars had certainly died previously, no major MGM female star had ever done so in the middle of making a picture, and the studio was caught on the wrong foot without a contingency plan.[23] Eventually the studio concluded that they would have to re-shoot the whole film substituting blond, sixteen-years-old Virginia Grey, whom they had under contract for $75 a week, for Jean. However, there was an outcry over this decision by Jean's fans and the press, who rightly pointed out that Jean had completed about two-thirds of the necessary footage. MGM compromised by reallocating dialogue or shooting around all but five crucial scenes. Geraldine Dvorak, whose face slightly resembled Jean, was used in these scenes for close-ups where her face was partially hidden or where she could be shot from behind. Dancer Mary Dees, dressed in Jean's gowns, was used for long shots. Paula Winslowe rather indifferently dubbed some sixteen lines of dialogue.

"I was terribly nervous when they called me about the test," Virginia Grey recalled later. "I'd been told Clark was a real lady-killer, and I was on my guard. He's not going to get anywhere with me, I said to myself. To my astonishment he was very businesslike and such a gentleman. He was so kind and helped me so much that I felt I had a real friend."[24] Grey did have a real friend. She made such an impression on Clark that he found her a part in his next film, *Test Pilot*, and never forgot her. They stayed in touch, and after Carole's death they grew quite close. Ironically, another actor's future career would also be given a push by *Saratoga*. Jean was to have been traded to Fox to play the female lead in the period piece *In Old Chicago*, and in return MGM was to be loaned Shirley Temple for *The Wizard of Oz*. Instead, MGM used its own starlet, Judy Garland.

The remainder of filming and postproduction was rushed as MGM hurried to capitalize on the public's response to Jean's death. *Saratoga* was finally released July 23. It has its eerie moments. Wearing the negligee in which she was buried, Jean is examined by a doctor in one scene and complains that there is really nothing wrong with her. In another, her maid warns that her health will suffer if she keeps working so hard. In the railway carriage, only a few minutes before she collapsed, Clark bends over her and says, "Hey, you've got a fever. You all right? You had me scared there for a minute."

THE KING

It was actually another studio that, somewhat indirectly, was responsible for giving Clark a title that stayed with him for the rest of his life. In the end he seemed to give up trying to get away from it, and he just accepted the senior rank with a wry grin as his due reward.

It was Harry Brand, the publicity director at 20th Century–Fox, who in the fall of 1937 suggested to Ed Sullivan, who was covering Hollywood for the *Chicago Tribune–New York Daily News* syndicate, that Ed run a contest in the syndicate papers for king and queen of the movies.

Each of the fifty-five key city papers in the syndicate handled the balloting. Twenty million votes were cast. For a week the papers tried to create as much suspense as possible about what the outcome of the voting would be, but they were essentially discussing the vote for the queen. No one was in any real doubt about who would be elected king.

Clark was indeed chosen by the people, a long way in front of Robert Taylor. Myrna Loy was elected queen, mainly on the basis of her popularity as Nora Charles in the *Thin Man* series of movies. William Powell, who came in fourth in the King votes, sent Loy a long florist's box filled with sour grapes and a note that read, "With love from William IV."

Loretta Young came in second for queen; maybe she should have been given a runner-up title such as princess. Carole was nowhere in sight on the list.

For the king and queen, a formal graduation ceremony was held at MGM with Ed Sullivan as master of ceremonies. Each tin-and-purple velvet crown was decorated with the mastheads of the respective newspapers.

After that, Clark called Myrna Loy "Queenie," which she thought made her sound like she worked in a Western saloon. "We never took that stuff seriously," she said, "any more than we did the box-office polls that kept placing us in the top ten during those years. Funny, but those measures and titles didn't mean as much to us as you might imagine.... We were serious about our work, studying and observing, learning our craft, but we were having a ball. As Clark said later, 'We never expected to be legends.'"[1]

But a legend Clark became. After this a subtle shift seemed to take place in the public mind and in that of his fellow actors and crew. They had always thought Clark was the best in his profession and now this title seemed to confirm that for them. However fake the title might have been, however much of a publicity stunt the whole exercise was, there was nothing fake about the vote of

Clark and John Barrymore skeet shooting in 1937.

Appearing tired and much thinner after a tough 1937, an unsmiling Clark attempts to look friendly with his boss, L.B. Mayer, at Clark's birthday party in 1938.

Three Clark Gable pins sold at various stages of his career to eager fans. (Spicer Collection.)

twenty million people indicating who they thought was at the top of the ladder.

So for the rest of his life, and even after his death, Clark would be referred to as "the King." As he grew older, especially in the last decade of his life, he seemed to grow into the role of an elder statesman of the acting pro-fession, of being a wise old king who could impart wisdom from his experience. It would be experience tinged heavily with tragedy, however, a tragedy that would mark and divide his life much as being elected king marked and divided his acting career.

CHAPTER 17

FRANKLY MY DEAR...

Clark did not want to be in *Gone with the Wind*, but the king was checked by public opinion. There was no one in the American public mind but Clark Gable who could be Rhett Butler. It was discussed and decided on the street corners, over the radio, and in the newspaper columns. After all, Rhett was described as tall, broad-shouldered, powerful, and graceful, with dark hair, a mustache, and a way of looking at women as if they were naked. According to the terms of her contract with Selznick, author Margaret Mitchell did not have any input into who was to play Rhett, nor did she ever express a desire to influence the decision. Although she never stated them publicly, apparently her personal choices were either Charles Boyer or the Western star Jack Holt. When she heard it was to be Clark, though, she happily commented, "He ought to be a landslide."[1]

Understandably wary of appearing in any more costume dramas after the failure of *Parnell*, Clark did not feel at all comfortable with having such a popular role forced on him under these circumstances. As he said in a later interview, he was only too aware that people did not just read the best-selling novel *Gone with the Wind*, "they lived it. They visualized its characters, and they formed passionate convictions about them…. I thought, 'All of them

have already played Rhett in their minds; suppose I don't come up with what they already have me doing.' … It was a challenge. I enjoyed it from that point of view. But my chin was out to there. I knew what people expected of me and suppose I didn't produce?"[2] Movies about the Civil War hadn't been producing, either. The last major effort, *So Red the Rose* (1935), starring Margaret Sullivan, had been a box-office failure. Legend has it that when the *Wind* story was pitched to L.B. Mayer and he called in Thalberg for an opinion, Thalberg commented, "Forget it, Louis. No Civil War picture ever made a nickel."[3]

While Mayer may have hesitated about involving his studio in *Gone with the Wind*, he had no problem with involving Clark. He could hardly believe his luck. In the studio system of the 1930s, an actor was a studio's property. The movie-going public had decided that they would not be satisfied with anyone else but Clark in the role of Rhett Butler and, even if Mayer's son-in-law David O. Selznick was family, Mayer was going to take bids at the great Gable auction. However, he was unable to have an auction without a property for sale. So, aware of Clark's reluctance to be Rhett, Mayer dangled a financial carrot in front of his stubborn star. He offered to sweeten the deal by providing Clark with enough money to open property-settlement negotiations with Ria. "I will give Ria $500,000 if she will give Gable his divorce," he proposed to David, "on the condition that he make this film and that you give MGM half of it."[4]

The mere thought of MGM wanting nothing less than half of the financial interest in his precious film was a body blow that Selznick attempted to avoid. During 1937 and 1938 he had a series of discussions with United Artists and Warner Brothers, as well as MGM, concerning financing Selznick International Pictures' production of *Gone with the Wind*. Despite being under pressure to contract Clark to play the male lead, Selznick also considered some of the options that he had with that decision. As early as May 1936 he had discussions with Ronald Coleman about playing Rhett, and amongst other possibilities as time went on was Gary Cooper. In frustration, Selznick's thoughts even turned to the dead. "We have buried the man who should have been Rhett Butler," he once groused to John Gilbert's widow.[5]

His last serious alternative was Errol Flynn. Warner Brothers and Flynn were the main competitors to MGM and Gable right down to the line, losing out only because Selznick thought Loew's Inc. would market the film more widely and effectively, nor was he entirely convinced Flynn had quite the same box-office pull as Clark.

Eventually, faced with almost $400,000 already invested in the project, a falling bank balance, and a public who had cast their vote for Clark Gable, Selznick accepted MGM's final terms. MGM's parent company, Loew's Inc., would be the distributors, and profits on distribution would be split fifty-fifty after Loew's had deducted their fee of 20 percent. In return, MGM would loan Clark to Selznick International and infuse *Gone with the Wind*'s budget with $1,250,000, estimated then to be half the production cost. However, if the budget went over $2.5 million, Selznick International would be responsible for all of it. After

seven years, seventy-five percent of the film would belong to Selznick International and twenty-five percent to MGM.[6] On top of that, Selznick would also be paying Clark's salary of $4,500 a week, probably the highest salary being paid to an American film actor at that time. MGM and Selznick International signed a deal memorandum on August 5, then David Selznick signed the contract on August 25, 1938, with Al Lichtman, Loew's Inc. vice-president. Clark and L.B. Mayer looked on, and then posed for the publicity photograph admiring the document.

Shooting would have to begin no later than January 1939, to fit in with Clark's availability. However, it was going to be a while before any cameras started rolling. While in agreement about who should play Rhett, the voice of the people was not so forthcoming when it came to Scarlett O'Hara. That selection would turn out to be a long, dusty road. It was also going to take a while to marshal the forces necessary to produce such a cinematic epic. In any case, Selznick could not release *Gone with the Wind* for distribution with Loew's until his distribution contract with United Artists ended in about a year.

So in the meantime, Gable was given the lead in *Test Pilot* with Myrna Loy, Spencer Tracy and Lionel Barrymore, directed by Victor Fleming. Clark played Jim Lane, a test pilot for the Drake Aeroplane Company who loves living life on the edge with the dutiful support of his mechanic, Gunner (Tracy). While testing the new Drake Bullet, he crashes on a farm, falls for the farmer's daughter Ann (Loy), marries her, and takes her back East with him. While testing a new bomber with Gunner, loaded with sandbags to simulate a bomb load, they crash. Gunner saves Jim's life, pushing him out before the plane hits the ground at the expense of his own life.

Test Pilot, with its actual footage of aerial races and use of well-known pilots of the day, provides quite an archival record of aerial history. Standing in for the Drake Bullet is

Clark in Test Pilot *from a British cigarette card titled "My Favourite Part." No. 24 in a series of 48 issued by Gallaher Ltd., London and Belfast.* (Spicer Collection.)

a Marcoux-Bromberg, also known as the Silver Bullet or R-3, flown in all but the close-ups by its race pilot, Earl Ortman. Clark's character of Jim Lane was probably modeled in part on Ortman, who was a well-known test pilot for civilian and military aircraft from the mid–1930s to the late 1940s and was a record-holding race pilot. He once did diving tests from ten thousand feet to a thousand feet for the military in an HM-1 experimental plane at increasing speeds until the wings literally ripped off, then he bailed out and survived. Not surprisingly, like Clark's Jim Lane, he was said to be a heavy drinker and smoker and inclined to be a bit edgy.

Development of the low-wing, single-engine racing plane that came to be known as the Marcoux-Bromberg began in 1933 for the MacRobertson Race from England to Australia. After a fatal crash and a lot of experimentation with the design, the Marcoux-Bromberg, now sporting a powerful Pratt and Whitney Twin Wasp Jr. engine, was flown by Ortman in the 1935 and 1936 National Air Races in Los Angeles and Cleveland. In 1937, Ortman flew second in the Thompson Trophy race, and it was the ensuing public attention that brought plane and pilot to the attention of MGM. The race scenes were shot over the actual course at Cleveland Airport, with planes flown by a number of famous Thompson Trophy pilots such as Paul Mantz, who was also one of the unit directors, and Frank Tomick. The Marcoux-Bromberg was fitted with a smoke generator under the fuselage to imitate engine trouble for the crash scene. The military plane scenes were shot at Langley and March Fields using the new Boeing YB-17.[7]

Clark thoroughly enjoyed himself making the testosterone-driven *Test Pilot.* He was surrounded by high-powered engines and the men who played with them, such as Al Menasco, an engineer and former World War I test pilot who helped to put the collection of planes together for the film and who became one of Clark's lifelong friends. The on-set jokes pretty much reflected the atmosphere. One day, two of the guys introduced Clark to a pretty young woman who was actually a call girl, but whom they claimed was an ardent fan. They talked Clark into inviting the girl to his dressing room for lunch. As soon as the door shut behind them, she fell to her knees and, unbuttoning his pants, exposed him. Then, laughing, she ran out. Clark was so surprised he was still sitting there unbuttoned when his friends burst in to tell him he'd been had. Even Carole sent Clark a box on the first day labeled, "Too hot to handle," containing some pornographic pictures and a pair of asbestos gloves.[8]

By now costar Myrna Loy and Clark were like brother and sister. They developed a unique relationship that helped them work closely together. She recalled that "He had a moment when he talked about the girl in the blue dress — the sky. The scene terrified him, scared him to death. He got so upset when we shot it that I had to keep reassuring him, comforting him…. He was afraid it would make him appear too soft. He had this macho thing strapped on him and he couldn't get out of it."[9]

They all had nicknames for each other. Clark was "King," Myrna Loy was "Queenie," Tracy was the "Iron Duke," and Victor Fleming was "the Monk." Spencer Tracy and Clark got along fairly well, Clark commented admiringly that "the guy is good and there's no one in the business who can touch him, so you're a fool to try."[10] The quality of Tracy's work set a standard to which Clark felt he had to measure up, especially in the film's more tender and lyrical moments with which Clark had difficulty feeling entirely comfortable. With Clark in envy of Tracy's acting reputation and Tracy coveting Clark's standing with the studio and the public, their offhand comments to each other sometimes had bite. Tracy would refer to Clark as "Your Majesty," or Clark would call Tracy a "Wisconsin ham." Tracy might counter that with a "What about *Parnell?*" Tracy was never entirely happy with his role. "I was getting tired of being the good-guy schnook while Gable had all the scenes with the girl," he once said. He compensated by upstaging Clark wherever he could, and he took flagrant advantage of his *Test Pilot* death scene. A frustrated Clark complained loudly to Fleming that "the son-of-a-bitch is a slower dier than Cagney. At the rate he's going, it's going to take him four reels to kick off."[11]

MGM took some flagrant advantage themselves. Capitalizing on the success of *Test Pilot*, they immediately teamed Clark and Myrna Loy in another aerial picture, *Too Hot to Handle*. This time Myrna Loy takes the pilot's role, striking a blow for women's equality. Myrna actually knew quite a bit about flying, although she had never piloted a plane by herself. She'd played another aviatrix in *Wings in the Dark* in the early 1930s, for which

she'd been personally coached in the air by Amelia Earhart and test pilot and stunt flier Paul Mantz. Clark plays another of his reporter roles, that of ace newsreel cameraman Chris Hunter, who is not above a bit of creative camerawork when the real story doesn't present itself in time for his deadline. In the process of creating one story, he causes Alma Harding (Loy) to crash her plane. Thinking he arrived to save her from her burning plane, Alma starts to fall for her hero until she finds out he was faking it all and loses faith in him. To make it up to her, he and a rival cameraman (Walter Pidgeon) help Harding search for her long-lost brother in South America. Eventually, after some hair-raising escapades, Hunter rescues the brother from the voodoo-inspired natives, managing to scoop his rival with his film of their adventures.

At least one hair-raising, or rather hair-burning, adventure occurred during the plane wreck scene, when Chris Hunter drags Alma Harding out of the burning wreck. The story was released to the press that the fire got out of control and that Clark dragged Myrna Loy out of real danger. She claimed in her memoirs that it all happened too fast for her to be able to say for sure whether the fire was real or the whole thing a publicity stunt.[12] Either way, Clark got a lot of good press over the incident.

It could have been a ploy to keep Clark in the public eye while its attention was otherwise being seized by the search for the woman who would play Scarlett O'Hara in *Gone with the Wind*. Most actresses under forty at the time were on a list of prospects that included such favorites as Tallulah Bankhead, Bette Davis, Katharine Hepburn, and Norma Shearer. Selznick, though, wanted to prevent *Gone with the Wind* from becoming a star vehicle, just another Hepburn or Davis picture. He wanted to cast a relatively unknown face as Scarlett, but he still wanted that face to be of an actress who would have enough skill and experience to easily carry the considerable demands of the role. So, with the help of over a hundred talent scouts spread across the country and any number of radio announcers and newspaper reporters, not to mention the opinionated general public, the search for Scarlett that had begun in 1936 continued into December 1938. By then some fourteen hundred prospects had been interviewed, involving ninety screen tests and thirty-five actresses, 142,000 feet of black-and-white film, 13,000 feet of Technicolor film, and $92,000.[13]

Meanwhile, a young English actress by the name of Vivien Leigh had become fascinated by *Gone with the Wind* when the book was published there in time for Christmas of 1936. Having broken her ankle on the Kitzbuhel ski slopes while on holiday, Leigh had read the book while recuperating. Convinced she could play Scarlett O'Hara, Leigh promptly lobbied her agent John Glidding to bring her to the attention of David Selznick via her role in *Fire Over England*. Although shot in August 1936, it was about to be released in England on February 25, and it would open in New York on March 4. Whether Glidding acted rapidly, or perhaps he had heard from his brother Myron, Selznick seems to have given the name Leigh momentary consideration. On February 3, 1937, he cabled to his New York office manager Kate Brown that "I have no enthusiasm for Vivien Leigh. Maybe I will have, but as yet have never even seen photograph of her. Will be seeing *Fire Over England* shortly, at which time will of course see Leigh."[14] Myron Selznick, David's brother and the man who legend has it invented the traditional 10 percent agent's cut, was by now the American agent of Laurence Olivier, with whom Leigh was having a passionate affair. He had been in England while *Fire Over England* was being made, and he may have been instrumental in seeing that a print of the film was rushed to Culver City by air a few days prior to its release.

Such discouraging words only seemed to make Vivien more determined though, in true Scarlett manner. Caroline Lejeune, the *Ob-*

server's film critic, later recalled a conversation about the casting of *Gone with the Wind* during the London shoot of *Twenty-One Days* in mid–1937. Somebody suggested Olivier play Rhett Butler, but he laughed it off. The discussion then went on "until the new girl, Vivien Leigh, brought it to a sudden stop. She drew herself up on the rainswept deck, all five feet nothing of her, pulled a coat snug around her shoulders and stunned us with the sibylline utterance, "Larry won't play Rhett Butler, but *I* shall play Scarlett O'Hara. Wait and see."[15] In the autumn of 1937, Vivien was loaned to MGM for their first film made in England, *A Yank at Oxford*, starring Robert Taylor. Her friend, Eve Phillips, believed that Vivien in effect did a screen test for *Gone with the Wind*, playing the role of Elsa Craddock "as saucy and sexual, like an imperious modern-day Cleopatra ... an English version of Scarlett O'Hara."[16]

Clark would have time to work on one more picture before he would disappear into *Gone with the Wind*. For over two years, he had wanted to play the lead in the film version of Robert Sherwood's play *Idiot's Delight*, which would be directed by Clarence Brown and would costar Norma Shearer, with whom Clark had previously worked in *Free Soul* in 1931. In late 1935, Clark and Clarence Brown flew out to New York for a break. With time on their hands one night, they decided to go see Lynn Fontanne and Alfred Lunt star in a new play, *Idiot's Delight*. Brown made it on time, but Clark was held up by fans who stormed his taxi, and he missed the first act. So when the show was over, the entire cast re-performed that first act of the play just for Clark and Brown. Clark was struck by Lunt's role. He thought it would not only suit him in a movie version of the play, but it would also open up his acting range and demonstrate a broader capability to the audience. However, in trying to put the movie together MGM ran headlong into a political minefield. *Idiot's Delight* became a case study in how Hays' and Breen's Production Code Administration could use their code to squelch political ideas that differed from their concept of mainstream thinking.

Robert Sherwood was a journalist and writer who opposed war and violence, having been gassed and wounded during World War I. In 1935, he had captured national attention with his play *The Petrified Forest*, and then in 1936 he won the first of four Pulitzer Prizes for his antifascist, antiwar drama *Idiot's Delight*. Set in a small hotel near the Swiss border, the play deals with how the onset of World War I affects various people in the hotel who are trying to cross the border into Switzerland. One of them, an American arms merchant who has conspired to start the war to make a profit, makes sure his "Russian" mistress Irene is refused a visa because she knows too much about his activities. Another American, Harry Van, who is traveling with a troupe of entertainers called Les Girls, discovers Irene is a woman with whom he had a passionate but brief affair many years ago in America. They rediscover their love and remain in the hotel after the others have fled, only to be killed when a stray bomb hits the building.

The play's controversial message that war is an "idiot's delight," and its inferences to the involvement of munitions corporations promoting the business of war, did not sit well on the eve of yet another war. Neither did the play's strident antifascist sentiments mix well with United States and Italian diplomacy. As a result, the conservative Breen was prompted to discourage one studio after another from making a film version, until only MGM persisted in their desire to go ahead. At that point, Breen switched tactics to forcing political correctness on the studio. The Italian government was very unhappy about the possible ramifications of a film version of the play. The Italian ambassador duly notified Hays that the film would be banned in Italy and, consequently, in other European countries with diplomatic ties, if it were released. Hunt Stromberg, the film's producer who had paid $125,000 for the rights, finally agreed in des-

peration to give the It[...] Neither he nor Hays c[...] they were getting them[...]

MGM figured on [...] help them out of this j[...] play's author, Robert S[...] dust settled, a very alter[...] version of the play had emerged as a film script from his pen, no doubt aided and abetted by the additional $135,000 that MGM paid him to lighten the blackness of his ink and the bleakness of his vision.[17] The antifascist sentiment and much of the antiwar sentiment had been airbrushed out. What had been a profound political statement was now essentially a love story. The film's lovers would meet in an anonymous country whose troops wore generic uniforms and where characters spoke Esperanto to avoid any hint of nationality.[18] The focus was no longer on the folly of war, but on the intrigue of whom the mysterious Countess Irene would turn out to be and whether the lovers would survive. Of course, in the film version they do. In order to move the film along and make it less wordy, events would now take place using 167 scenes on 42 sets instead of the former play's three acts that were all set within an Alpine hotel lobby. Photographer Bill Daniels would estimate later that his camera traveled twenty-six miles around just one of the sets.[19]

In June 1938, Breen personally took the script to Italy to show it to Ambassador Caracciolo, from where it was eventually approved by Il Duce himself. From when Stromberg first contacted Breen, it had taken twenty-six months for the Hays Office to ensure that an important social commentary against war was neutered into a song-and-dance love story. In 1935, Breen had reported to Hays that 23.5 percent of total Hollywood production for that year fell into the social commentary category. By 1941, Hays could proudly inform a Senate committee that they had reduced that figure to 5 percent.[20]

By the time he rewrote the script, Sherwood knew that Clark would be playing the lead. Consequently, he fitted the script for him

neatly as if it had been one of Clark's tailored suits, letting Clark's comic talent shine
through in his portrayal of the lovable phony,
Harry the hoofer. However, what Clark didn't
know until he was handed the script on October 15 was that more dance sequences had
been written in. "When I read the script,"
Clark said, "I let out a squawk that must have
been heard from one end of the San Fernando
Valley to the other.... They not only had me
doing a song-and-dance act with six chorus
girls that runs for sixteen pages of script, but
added a couple of jokers. One was a vaudeville
routine … the other was a chorus boy number in tails and top hat."[21] A little waltzing
was about all the dancing Clark's size 11-C feet
and 190-pound body had ever done, but he set
out to improve that with his characteristic
stubborn determination.

Carole, frequently breaking up with
laughter, helped dance director George King
train Clark for the next six weeks for the sequences that included his three minutes and
fifty seconds of "Puttin' on the Ritz" tap routine. Clark could usually laugh at himself too,
though, and was rarely short of a wisecrack
on or off camera. When Clarence Brown directed him to hold onto a trapeze with his
teeth, Clark shot back, "Sure, but what do I
hold onto my teeth with?" Still, Clark was so
self-conscious of what the media could make
of his efforts that the studio stationed security
guards at the sound-stage doors while he
worked night and day and on weekends.

Clark needed all his humor on this shoot
to cope with Carole's jealousy. Despite wanting to be with Clark, Carole didn't cope well
with having too much time on her hands, and
so she agreed to costar in Selznick's *Made for
Each Other*, in which a young Jimmy Stewart
has a small part. It proved to be a good vehicle for her talents and career, and she and
Clark always seemed to get along better when
they were both working. However, it also
meant she could only be on-set to keep an eye
on her Clark when she was done with work for
the day. She was all too aware that the attrac-

tive and available Norma Shearer, now known
around Hollywood as the "Merry Widow,"
and whom Carole had never quite forgiven for
wearing that red dress to the White Mayfair
Ball, was with Clark for more of the day than
she was. That didn't sit well with her at all,
and she took to lashing out at whoever came
within range. On one occasion she targeted a
dancer in the Les Girls chorus line, loudly
telling Clarence Brown in her typically tact-
ful fashion to "Get that whore out of here!"
claiming she had seen the chorine make a pass
at Clark at a party. Evidently and probably
quite fortunately, given her mood, Carole
didn't notice Virginia Grey's presence in the
same chorus line.[22]

As part of her campaign to make sure
everyone knew Clark was hers, Carole sent
him more of her gag gifts to celebrate his success in his dancing scenes, including a span-
gled tutu with Clark's initials on the front, a
pair of size 11-C ballet shoes, and even a bunch
of pansies. It was her way of acknowledging,
as many people have done since, that in the
end Clark had pulled off no mean feat for any
entertainer. Not only does he tap, but he sings
and twirls his hat and cane — somewhat equivalent to learning how to pat yourself on the
head while rubbing your stomach as you dance
in time! As George King commented, "Bur-
lesquing a dance number is not as simple as it
looks. To start with, Clark learned the dance
straight until he could do it in his sleep. Then
we added the jitterbug touches. Next he had
to sing "Puttin' on the Ritz" while dancing. Finally he coordinated his singing and dancing,
working with a straw hat and a cane. If you
think that's simple, try it sometime!"[23] There
were compensations, though. The first scene
shot was of Harry kissing four girls. After four
takes and sixteen kisses Clarence Brown
cracked: "That's the way all of Clark's pictures
ought to start. Print it!" Then he added: "All
right. Lets have one more take." When a surprised Clark asked why, Brown chuckled with
an innocent look on his face, "Oh, this one's
for the girls."[24]

Carole often sent roses to Clark when he was working. She delivered these personally to the Idiot's Delight *set.*

The Encino ranch house.

When it came time to shoot the sequences, word had got around and the sound stage was packed. All twenty-one cast members showed up, along with every member of the crew, and there in the front row sat Carole. After the first take, two bellboys appeared bearing huge bouquets from her and Norma Shearer. Carole turned to King and congratulated him, saying she would never have believed it possible. "You're a miracle man," she marveled. It would take another two days' work to complete shooting the entire sequence, after which Clark swore he would do no more dancing in front of the cameras. Maybe it was just as well that he didn't know about a certain Southern ball yet.

Unlike Carole, Clark gave gifts so rarely that each one was a memorable event to those concerned. Not long after Carole had given him the famous Valentine car, for example, Clark had spent over $1,000 having it painted black and the engine tweaked. The result was a fast car that could handle one hundred miles-an-hour speeds with ease. Like all his cars, he eventually tired of it, but when Larry Barbier, who was in charge of MGM's still department, asked if he could buy it for his teenage son, Clark initially said no. He didn't

want Barbier's son to kill himself in it, he said. Some time later Barbier helped Clark to find a station wagon to use for his hunting trips. Clark drove them both in it to the Department of Motor Vehicles, and when they got there he asked Barbier for a dollar, commenting that he was going to sign his old black car over to him but he'd be darned if he would pay the transfer fee as well! [25]

As soon as she finished work on *Made for Each Other*, Carole started looking for a house for the two of them. Clark thought her place in Bel-Air was too small, and he had always dreamed of having a farm or a ranch where he could indulge in his love of the outdoors. Carole wasn't as taken with the idea, but she was willing to go along for Clark's sake. She had looked at a lot of places when she heard that a friend of theirs, director Raoul Walsh, wanted to sell his twenty-acre ranch in Encino in the San Fernando Valley. Clark and Carole had previously visited the beautiful property, set among rolling hills, several times and had fond memories of it. The main house was two stories, with tall clinker-brick chimneys. Styled after a Connecticut farmhouse, it looked older than its thirteen years. There was a stable, a barn, a workshop, garage, and lots of trees that included a citrus orchard. When they looked over the property, Carole surprised Clark by giving the house a detailed and workmanlike inspection, measuring the kitchen, testing the water pressure and the toilets, and examining the wall beams for termites. As she dashed about the house making plans, her enthusiasm was so infectious that Clark caught her up in his arms and declared, "I've always wanted a place like this. It will be the first home I've had since I was a boy that I can truly call my own. Ma, I think we're going to be very happy here."[26] Lombard agreed and handed over the $50,000 Walsh was asking. They couldn't move in just yet, though. For one thing there was work to be done on the house; for another, they weren't married.

Attitudes about unmarried couples, or couples married to someone else, living together were much more conservative in 1938 than in present society. This couldn't have been more glaringly spotlighted than when the January 1939 issue of *Photoplay* published an article titled "Hollywood's Unmarried Husbands and Wives," which discussed what had been the previously private lives of Robert Taylor and Barbara Stanwyck, Charles Chaplin and Paulette Goddard, Constance Bennett and Gilbert Roland, George Raft and Virginia Pine, and none other than Clark Gable and Carole Lombard. When it went on sale in late December 1938, the issue sold out in hours. It was the most outspoken article published on the stars of the time, and newspapers mined quotes from it for days, blowing the topic up into a national scandal. "Unwed couples they might be termed," announced the article, "but they go everywhere together, do everything in pairs.... They build houses near each other ... father and mother each other's children.... Yet to the world, their official status is 'just friends'. No more."

Noting that Carole had largely given up her busy social life for riding and shooting or just staying home with Clark in the house they had bought, the article's author (widely rumored to be Sheila Graham) commented that they just struck up "a Hollywood twosome. Nobody said: 'I do!' ... Yes, Carole Lombard is a changed woman since she tied up with Clark Gable. But her name is still Carole Lombard.... Clark is still officially a married man. Every now and then negotiations for a divorce are started, but, until something happens in court, Ria Gable is still the only wife the law of the land allows Clark Gable."[27]

Robert Taylor and Clark both worked for MGM. As his eyes frantically scanned the article's lines, Louis B. Mayer could already see the wood being stacked for some burnings at the stake of public morality, and he was not in the business of providing that sort of amusement. As the breast-beating memos started to arrive from the Hays Office during the following days, Mayer abandoned his support of Ria Gable in favor of encouraging Clark to marry Carole as quickly as possible. It wasn't that Mayer had doubts he could handle the situation; after all, he'd buried any number of star scandals over the years. Rather, Mayer was more concerned over the potential impact of scandal on Clark's forthcoming role in *Gone with the Wind*, and thus on how such scandal might affect Mayer's substantial investment in the film. Clark's main excuse so far for not filing for divorce from Ria was that he wouldn't be able to cope financially with what his wife would demand for a settlement without MGM's help. Mayer had cleverly been using the possibility of such help as a carrot held in front of Clark to steer him, but he realized that now would be the time to reward Clark in this small way so that they could reach for the big prize. So Mayer duly offered to pay Clark an advance against his future contract renewal, still two years away, giving Clark some extra money but at the same time putting Clark in his debt and guaranteeing that Clark would have to sign up again for more years of service with MGM.

Shooting of *Gone with the Wind* began on December 10, 1938, when old sets on the RKO "forty acres" back lot were torched to simulate the burning of the Atlanta rail yards and, at the same time, to make way for new set construction for the picture. It was during this event that the legendary meeting between Vivien Leigh and David Selznick occurred. With her sights still set on the role of Scarlett O'Hara, Vivien had followed Laurence Olivier to the U.S. at the end of November, where he was to play Heathcliffe in William Wyler's film of *Wuthering Heights*. As actor Stewart Granger recalled, "She had two passions, her love for Larry and her determination to play Scarlett O'Hara.... We all thought she was nuts to think she had a ghost of a chance."[28] That summer Vivien had starred in four favorably reviewed films that had played in New York, but Selznick had continued to resist testing her because he assumed that the South would never accept an English woman as Scarlett.

On the other hand, Vivien, Myron Selznick, and Olivier were equally convinced that she was just the person for the part. All of them may have played their part in having Vivien's and David's paths cross at just the right moment. Myron's office always kept precise track of Vivien's location. Maxine Graybill, Myron's secretary, recalled that Larry and Vivien turned up at the office just before six p.m. At a suggestion from Larry that they go visit David, Myron got on the phone and said, "David, I'm looking at Scarlett. We're coming right out."[29] So, using the dramatic setting of burning buildings against a night sky to best advantage, Myron introduced her to David as her face was lit by the glow of the dying flames. Smitten on the spot, David had director George Cukor test Vivien a few days later. On Christmas Day, at a brunch at Cukor's house, Leigh was told she had the part and on January 16 she was signed for $1,250 a week for a guaranteed sixteen weeks on a seven-year contract. She started work at nine the next morning. With overages, Vivien would finally collect a very ordinary $25,000 for 125 days work, much the same as she would have earned working in England.

Clark, on the other hand, would be paid $121,454 for just 71 days.[30] Selznick need not have worried over Leigh's nationality. The Daughters of the Confederacy summed up the South's feelings when they heard the news about Scarlett: "Better an English girl than a Yankee."[31]

Of course, Clark had not so much been selected to be in *Gone with the Wind* as drafted for it. He might have been the king, but he was also a slave to the system that created him. He initially felt so insecure with the role that he nearly wrote Margaret Mitchell letting her know that he considered himself the worst possible choice for Rhett. His own personal recommendation was Ronald Coleman.[32] He drew back into himself by way of protection against these feelings during preproduction, and that caused him to come across as quite aloof. While he endured solo screen tests dressed in his leather jacket, he didn't bother to show for costume fittings or to meet with any of the other actors and test with them. Clark had no ear for accent, either, and found adopting the Southern inflection as readily as Leigh very difficult. Susan Myrick, Margaret Mitchell's friend and fellow writer hired as a Southern technical advisor, kept trying to work with Clark on his accent even while shooting was in progress. She found it almost impossible to get rid of his heavy Midwestern "r." It was yet another worry for Clark, that he might sound foolish as well as look it. Then, he discovered a way out. "The thing that worried me most about my role," he would say later, "was saying my lines like I had been reared at some mammy's knee. About the second day on the picture, I met a girl on the set who was from Charleston, South Carolina. You know, the place Rhett hailed from. You would have sworn she was Scotch. That was how she talked. I asked, 'Does everyone in Charleston talk the way you do?' She said, 'Everybody.' From that day on, I relaxed. I had the perfect alibi, in case anybody didn't think my Southern accent wasn't thick enough. I was from Charleston, suh.'"[33]

Clark officially went on the *Gone with the Wind* payroll on January 23, 1939. Two days before, Ria had finally announced from Las Vegas that she would file suit early in March for divorce on grounds of mental cruelty after she established the required six weeks residence in Nevada.[34] When Clark had announced on December 13 that he was ready to seek a divorce, having reached an amicable property settlement with Ria of $286,000, it was the last straw for the woman who had waited for two years hoping he'd come back one day. Considering that Clark had done her wrong, Ria had refused to seek a divorce, expecting to collect her due reward when Clark would ask her for one. The settlement had to be approved by a California court before any divorce proceedings could start. Now that approval had been granted, Ria wasted no time.

Neither had Carole's agent Myron Selznick, who had been busy negotiating a two-year, four-movie deal with RKO that made Carole one of the first Hollywood stars to be paid a percentage of the profits on top of her $150,000 salary. It would be many years before Clark was offered such an incentive, and he would remain disillusioned with MGM that he was never offered a similar percentage deal for *Gone with the Wind*. Carole's first picture under her new contract was *In Name Only* with Cary Grant, coincidentally the story of a woman in love with an unhappily married man whose mercenary wife refuses to grant him a divorce. A frustrated Carole put Clark on notice that if his divorce mess wasn't straightened out by the time she started the film, she was going to offer Ria the role of the mercenary wife. Nevertheless, when Clark opened the door to his large, mobile dressing room with its knotted pine walls and red leather sofa and armchair on the morning of that first day on the set, it was to see that Carole had draped the mirror with a string of stuffed doves to symbolize her wish for peace for her man. On the dresser was a beautifully wrapped little package that contained a knitted "cock-warmer" and a note: "Don't let it get cold. Bring it home hot for me."[35] Selznick, with good reason but under-estimating Clark's professionalism, would become really worried that Clark would leave the set unannounced to marry Carole.

As if all this wasn't enough, by the time Clark stepped into the Bazaar scene on the sixth day of shooting, his first day, his aloofness during preproduction had allowed director George Cukor and Vivien Leigh to build exactly the sort of personal working relationship that reinforced Clark's insecurities. George Cukor was a fine, experienced, gay director. Because of the rewarding working relationships that he developed with his female leads, he had a reputation as a "woman's director." Writer Ben Hecht commented that, in his opinion, "Cukor was an exceptional man. He didn't know anything except one thing. He didn't know anything about stories; he didn't know anything about directing, sets, and technique. He had a flair for women acting. He knew how a woman should sit down, dress, smile. He was able to make women seem a little brighter, more sophisticated than they were, and that was about the only talent he had."[36]

However, this is being a little harsh on Cukor who, after all, successfully directed major male stars such as Lionel Barrymore, Robert Taylor, and Cary Grant. More to the point was that, while Selznick had originally seen *Gone with the Wind* as a romantic drama dominated by a strong woman's role, hence the need for Cukor, now his vision was that of a vast action epic that needed to move forward rapidly on a broad scale, and Cukor was not an action-picture director. He liked to take his time, building mood and layers of character detail, but with this picture Selznick simply didn't have that time. Although there have been claims that Clark felt so uncomfortable working with Cukor that he failed to turn up for work on some days,[37] no evidence of absences appears in production records.[38] Both Selznick and Cukor always denied that Gable ever mentioned a change of director to them personally, Selznick stating that "This

Clark, Vivien Leigh, and Victor Fleming chat while Vivien takes a break during filming of Gone with
the Wind.

was reported to me as his [Clark's] feeling, but he never mentioned it to me nor criticized Cukor. He worked with each of the directors just as personally."[39] Cukor's opinion about Clark was that "As stars went he was powerful, but that was little better than impotence in those days," implying that he was doubtful Clark even had the power to cause such a significant personnel change to be made.[40] Rumors that Clark had Cukor removed because Cukor knew something unsavory about his past have never proved to be anything other than idle gossip, and were certainly never based on anything Cukor, Clark, Selznick, or anyone else associated with *Gone with the Wind* ever said.[41]

There were, in fact, quite a few reasons why Clark was not a happy man on the set, other than whatever he felt about George Cukor. For one thing, Clark always liked to be

impeccably outfitted on or off the set, and he quickly discovered that his *Gone with the Wind* costumes were badly fitted, tending to wrinkle or bag if he didn't stand absolutely erect. The picture's costume designer was Walter Plunkett, who had been RKO's top designer and was one of Hollywood's most experienced people in the business. He had a reputation for creativity, research, and authenticity when it came to period costume. Clark was, however, physically the biggest star of his time, and he had further complicated the costumer's task by consistently refusing to turn up for his fittings. As late as April 17, noticing that Clark's costume problems had not been corrected, Selznick fired off a furious memo to wardrobe master Edward Lambert that blazed, "A more ill-fitting and unbecoming group of suits I've never seen on a laboring man, much less than a star!"[42] Consequently,

Clark was allowed to bring in his own personal tailor, Eddie Schmidt, to make a new Rhett Butler wardrobe.[43]

Then, Clark had to dance with Leigh in some of his first scenes. Clark was certainly a practiced dancer by now, thanks to his work for *Idiot's Delight*, but to enable the camera to circle the couple smoothly while they were waltzing through the crowd, a circular platform and cage on wheels had been constructed to which the camera was attached. It was pulled along and rotated at the same time, creating the illusion of Clark and Leigh spinning smoothly around in a waltz. Clark didn't feel comfortable with this moving platform, thinking that it made him look as though he was a bit of a klutz when in fact he wasn't one.

Clark was discovering, too, that the role of Rhett was harder to play than he had anticipated. While there was a buildup to Scarlett, Rhett's scenes were all climaxes in which he represented drama and action every time he appeared. He didn't figure in any of the battle scenes, being a guy who hated war, and he wasn't in the toughest of the siege of Atlanta shots. "What I was fighting for," he would comment later,

> was to hold my own in the first half of the picture — which is all Vivian's — because I felt that after the scene with the baby, Bonnie, Rhett could control the end of the film. That scene where Bonnie dies, and the scene where I strike Scarlett and she accidentally tumbles down stairs, thus losing her unborn child, were the two that worried me most.
>
> The problem of Rhett, to me, was that although he reads like a tough guy and by his actions is frequently not admirable, actually he is a man who is practically broken by love. His scenes away from Scarlett make him a heavy and his scenes with her make him almost a weakling. My problem was to make him, despite that, a man people would respect.[44]

Although Clark and Leigh treated each other with a cool friendliness off-camera, Clark was a little disconcerted by Leigh's blue streak in her language while still maintaining the tones of a lady of the manor. On the first day of production, for example, when a lighting hitch held up shooting, Leigh had delicately inquired, "What the hell are they fucking around for?"[45] She also had a tendency to arrive late on occasion; something that rubbed Clark, a stickler for punctuality, completely the wrong way.

Leigh could learn lines quicker than he could, too, and they were attempting to cope with a script that was a living thing, changing and growing every day as Selznick supervised rewrites overnight. Director, crew, and actors would frequently be faced with a script in the morning that was different than the day before. Ultimately, it was this situation more than any other with which Cukor felt he couldn't work any longer. He'd looked at rushes for days and felt he was failing. He knew he was a good director and the actors were good actors, and so he became more convinced as time went by that the constantly and continuously rewritten script was the problem. In the end, he announced to Selznick that he could work no longer if the script wasn't better, and that he wanted the original Sidney Howard script reinstated. Selznick replied that as director Cukor was no author and that it was as producer that Selznick was the judge of a good script. Cukor shot back that he was too good a director to have his name go out on a lousy picture and that if they didn't go back to the Howard script he'd quit.[46] Selznick accepted his offer, and Cukor was formally dismissed on Monday morning, February 13, nineteen days into production.[47] What only Selznick probably knew, though, was that the option for renewal of Cukor's contract had expired on February 11.[48] Despite all the innuendo, Clark really had very little if anything to do with Cukor leaving.

Victor Fleming, who had replaced Richard Thorpe as director two weeks into MGM's *The Wizard of Oz* shoot, was reassigned to *Gone with the Wind* by Mayer, who insisted that because of MGM's stake in the picture, Selznick use one of Mayer's directors this time.[49] Mayer also knew that Fleming was friends with Clark, having directed him in *Red Dust* and *Test Pilot*. In fact, there was a story that Strickling had based the studio's public image of Clark on Fleming's character. He too was tough, handsome, and forthright, and his forte was action films in which old-fashioned male virtues were vigorously projected. He took one look at what he had to work with for *Gone with the Wind* and promptly informed Selznick that "you haven't got a fucking script."[50] As writer Ben Hecht recalled in 1959: "David had done a hundred brilliant things for this movie…. The only thing he'd overlooked, in his great perfection mania, was a script. It's hard to remember that a script is also necessary when you have all those other producer jobs to do."[51] The shoot was shut down for two weeks while Selznick and Fleming consulted with Hecht in an effort to put something on paper that Fleming could use. They went at it eighteen hours a day for a week, at which point Hecht couldn't take it anymore and fled.

Finally, after two panic-stricken weeks, Selznick and his new director were as ready as they were ever going to be. When shooting resumed on March 2, Fleming came onto the set "like Cagney sneering at rookie cops."[52] Being friends with Clark, he tended to favor him a bit while bearing down harder on Leigh, which tended to bring out her sharper and bitchier side in her performance. Fleming nicknamed her "Fiddle-de-dee" and demanded she show more cleavage, which didn't help.[53] On the other hand, Fleming was attempting the frustrating exercise of shooting a script that was still being almost continuously rewritten by Selznick overnight and sometimes actually on-set. Working days started to stretch out over ten hours, six days a week. Pressure built.

Two days later, Ria filed her divorce petition in Las Vegas. Clark had deserted her in October 1935, she said, and had never re-turned. The divorce was granted in a five-minute hearing before District Judge William Orr. Clark was not present. When contacted for comment, Carole had no hesitation in happily informing everybody that she and Clark could soon be sneaking away to get quietly married as soon as Clark could get some days off.[54] Ria spent the day in bed crying inconsolably. MGM, in their usual sympathetic manner, sent a publicist over to watch her in case she said anything uncomplimentary to the press that would damage public relations for *Gone with the Wind*.

Carole and Clark had, meanwhile, been receiving advertising material and letters from just about every hotel, airline, and major restaurant suggesting when and where would be ideal for their wedding. Carole was telling everyone she knew her fears about the wedding degenerating into a "fucking circus." It had quickly become apparent to the pair that the only way they would have any privacy for their occasion was in a remote and secret place.

Then, at about three in the afternoon of Tuesday, March 28, Clark had finished his scenes and was taking off his make-up when the assistant director came over and told him he wouldn't be needed the next day. Clark immediately called Carole and discovered she wasn't scheduled to begin work until the following week. Hardly able to believe their luck, and knowing that a premiere of *The Story of Alexander Graham Bell* would attract the Hollywood press corps away to San Francisco for twenty-four hours, Clark and Carole figured this was a chance not to be missed. Clark immediately called Otto Winkler and Howard Strickling to the house and told them the marriage was on. It so happened that Winkler, who had been scouting locations for Clark just in case, had married his wife Jill the week before in the very quiet town of Kingman, Arizona, and he suggested that town would be the ideal spot.[55] It would be out of the way, but not too far. They would be able to drive the eight hundred-mile round-trip in Otto's car, which had new license plates and so wouldn't be spotted, and be back in time to hold a press conference on Thursday. It would be a tight squeeze with no time for a wedding night.

Very early the next morning, the coconspirators met at the Winklers' house. With a change of clothes in their bags, Clark and Carole crowded into the single seat of Otto Winkler's small blue De Soto coupe dressed in their shabbiest to avoid being recognized, and they left town. However, Clark had unwittingly given them away already. Having lost his way trying to get to the Winklers' house, he had asked a milkman for directions, who had recognized him immediately. He lost no time tipping the press off. Finding the birds already flown by the time they got there, the journalists laid siege to the house and awaited their return.

Meanwhile, Clark and Winkler spelled each other with the driving on the long trip. Clark kept muttering that he couldn't believe the day had finally come, and every few minutes he'd check his pocket to make sure he still had the twelve-dollar platinum wedding band he'd had waiting for some four months. Carole just clung to his arm quietly happy. Whenever they pulled in to a station for gas, Winkler would get out and distract the attendant with conversation, insisting that they didn't need their dusty windshield cleaned. Just before they crossed into Arizona, Carole decided there had to be flowers for the wedding. Winkler stopped and bought a corsage of pink roses and lily-of-the-valley for her and carnation boutonnieres for Clark and himself.

They arrived at Kingman Town Hall at 4 p.m. The clerk, Viola Olsen, didn't look up as she slid the forms across the counter, but when it came time for her to countersign the documents, and she finally saw who had signed them, she was so startled that she blotted her own signature. She escorted them to the local First Methodist-Episcopal Church, but the minister, Reverend Kenneth Engel, wasn't home. A frantic search ensued through the town's streets until they found him and got him back to the parsonage. When his wife came in with her arms full of groceries, she was so surprised to be introduced to Carole and Clark that she dropped everything on the floor. Eventually, Clark was able to change into his blue serge suit, white shirt, and printed tie. Carole dressed in a light gray suit with padded shoulders and delicately tapered waist, designed by Irene, with a gray-and-white polka-dot vest.

When they were ready, the small party of bride and groom, minister, Winkler the best man, and witness Howard Cate who was principal of Kingman High, walked sedately to the church where they entered to the sound of the minister's wife playing the Wedding March on the organ. The ceremony was an emotional one. Carole cried, and even Clark got so flustered that he gave the minister the band before he was asked for it.[56] Afterward they just had time for Carole to call her mother and for Clark to wire his father, neither of whom had known their plans, before they were back in the car headed for Los Angeles. On the way they stopped so Winkler could wire details of the wedding to the MGM publicity department and Carole could wire Louella Parsons the words, "Married this afternoon. Carole and Clark."[57] They had their "wedding breakfast" at the Harvey House in Needles late that night, where they startled customers by setting up at one end of the counter and ordering the biggest steaks in the house.

When they arrived back in Bel-Air at 4 a.m., Carole's family and Fieldsie were there to greet them. Carole laughed when she found her brothers had hung a shotgun over the bed. After only a few hours' rest, they nervously made their grand entrance down the staircase into the melee of their first press conference as a married couple. Clark told reporters they would be too busy with their various movie commitments to take a honeymoon, but they intended to take a break in New York to see the World's Fair. Carole confessed that she

Clark and Carole on the patio steps of the Encino house the morning after their wedding.

could cook "damn well," but even after three years she didn't know what Clark's favorite dishes were. They remained silent on questions about children and family, but later Carole commented over the phone to Louella Parsons that "I'll work for a few more years and then I want a family. I'll let Pa be the star and I'll stay home and darn the socks and look after the kids."[58]

Under the circumstances, Selznick waxed generous and gave Clark an extra day off. So, at ten in the morning of the 31st, Clark reported back on the set for what he thought would be the prison sequence. Instead, Fleming started singing, "Happy Bridegroom to You," and a thousand extras joined in. No work was accomplished that day. Instead everyone sat around, talked, relaxed and played card games or backgammon. "Nice festive honeymoon atmosphere," said Clark with a broad grin.[59]

By April the budget for *Gone with the Wind* had blown out to $3,300,000 from the earlier projection of $2,400,000 due in large part to new scenes being written that required extra sets. This new figure still did not allow for some of the movie's final scenes.[60] The pressure onset grew. On eight days between April 19 and May 24, shooting schedules went over twelve hours. Actors suffered from heat exhaustion in their Victorian costumes on the brilliantly lit sound stages as the weather began to warm up. Called in again for some more rewriting, Sidney Howard, the original scriptwriter, wrote to his wife that Fleming was taking "four shots of something a day to keep him going and another shot or so to fix him so he can sleep after the day's stimulation. Selznick is bent double with permanent, and I should think chronic, indigestion. Half the staff look, talk and behave as though they were on the verge of breakdowns.... It is impossible to get a decision on anything.... I say "What do you want, David?" and David has not the faintest idea."[61]

At one point there was panic when Leigh declared herself pregnant. It turned out to be a false alarm, but Selznick banned Olivier from the set to avoid any possibility of repetition. Leigh, a woman with quite a driving sexual need, became just a tad frustrated as the days dragged on. "It is really very miserable and going very slowly," she wrote, "I was a *fool* to have done it."[62] In her few relaxed moments, she took to playing a game with houseguests called "Killing Babies," in which the winner was the person who could successfully mime the most creative or bizarre method of murdering an infant.[63] When she managed to escape to meet up with Olivier in a Kansas City hotel on one occasion, as she so delicately put it, "we went upstairs and we fucked and we fucked and we fucked the whole weekend."[64] Leigh came to passionately hate Fleming as much as he hated her. Clark came to hate Selznick, who would not let well enough alone and was always interfering in everything. He came, however, to view Leigh with the amused wariness of a Rhett around Scarlett. He grew to admire her self-assurance, she to admire his professionalism. He taught her how to play Backgammon; she taught him how to play Battleship and they could often be seen in a corner between setups involved in one or the other. At the end of the day, in her hurry to be reunited with Olivier, it would usually be Leigh who could persuade cast and crew to do just one more take.

Clark's most difficult scene, personally, was when Scarlett suffers a miscarriage after falling down the stairs. Clark feared that being seen in tears over the tragedy would damage the credibility of his masculine tough-guy image and that the audience would just laugh. Fleming tried to persuade him that crying would only increase the audience's sympathy for his character, but Clark wasn't easily convinced. The night before the scene was to be shot, he was so nervous he couldn't sleep because of stomach cramps, and Carole had to sit up with him. That morning, Clark stomped around his dressing room threatening to quit and become a farmer, and he tried to persuade Fleming to cut the scene or at least have it rewritten. Eventually, they compromised by shooting the scene twice. First they did it with Clark's back to the camera. Then they did it showing his face full of remorse and eyes wet with tears. Later, when Clark saw the rushes, he burst out: "I don't believe it! What the hell happened?" Carole's opinion would always be that it was his best acting.[65]

Suddenly the explosion everyone had been dreading went off. Relations between Fleming and Leigh had been deteriorating noticeably. Fleming had been growing depressed about the film, confiding at one time to Clark that he had considered driving over a cliff on the way to work. In rehearsal on April 29 he was trying to encourage Leigh to put more bitchiness into her lines. Leigh kept protesting that she couldn't be a bitch. Finally, in utter frustration, Fleming shouted: "Miss Leigh, you can stick this script up your royal British ass!" and he stormed off the set.[66]

Fleming remained away for sixteen days, claiming illness. Sam Wood was hired to replace him. In the meantime, Selznick's money ran out. MGM refused to come to the rescue, family affiliations notwithstanding, so Selznick's friend and partner in Selznick International Pictures, Jock Whitney, bailed him out by securing a $1,000,000 loan for the picture. Fleming eventually returned, perhaps because Wood was doing such a good job, and cast and crew rallied.

Understandably, with so many people together for so long in arduous circumstances, quite a bit of gag-pulling and wisecracking went on, although not too much while the cameras were rolling as Technicolor film was far too expensive to waste on gag shots. In any case, there was the ever-present eagle eye of David Selznick, who doesn't seem to have been a man for onset joking around. Still, humor is a great reliever of stress, and there was certainly more than enough of that spread around, so some gags here and there were pretty much inevitable. Olivia de Havilland and Clark had been rehearsing the scene where Rhett picks up Melanie Hamilton Wilkes and carries her downstairs to a waiting buggy to escape from Atlanta. The strapping Clark was hardly noticing the 105-pound de Havilland in his arms, vowing it was a pleasant task, so she decided to test him out. Just before the final rehearsal, she had some stagehands conceal a large thirty-pound weight used for anchoring scenery within the folds of the quilt wrapped around her. Needless to say, a red-faced Clark couldn't budge her when the time came. When she finally stood up and let the weight fall out, Clark laughed as hard as everyone else.[67] Victor Fleming also couldn't resist a joke on Clark's strength. He had Clark do retake after retake carrying Vivien Leigh up that long flight of stairs. Leigh was in on the gag, and she made it look as though she ruined each take. Clark became exhausted and frustrated, but he kept going. Finally Fleming broke down and confessed, "The first take was fine, Clark; the others were just for laughs."

Clark of course wasn't above a gag or two of his own. In the scene where he and Mammy are making up past differences after the birth of Bonnie over a bottle of bourbon, Clark waited until a lighting break was called and then quietly replaced the tea in the bottle with real Scotch. When shooting resumed, Mammy took a big swig and whooped and coughed all over the place while cast and crew fell about laughing for ten minutes.[68]

Filming was now split between five units and it rushed on until finally, like all things, it came to an end. The wrap party was held on June 27 on Stage 5. A huge buffet supper was laid out along with drinks, and dancing went on until late hours. Carole, wearing her silver fox coat, came with Clark. By then, all units had exposed some eighty-one hours of Technicolor film and the cost stood at $3,576,000. David O. Selznick had about $20,000 left in the bank. By the time the last bills were in, the cost would be closer to $4,250,000. The film in its edited form would stand at 220 minutes long.[69]

It seems fitting that one of the last battles fought in *Gone with the Wind* would be over its most remembered line, Rhett's "Frankly, my dear, I don't give a damn." Sydney Howard had added "Frankly" to Margaret Mitchell's original words, but the real battle was over the "damn." Joseph Breen was not going to allow this word under Section Five of the Code, which stated that, "Pointed profanity (this includes the words, God, Lord, Jesus, Christ — unless used reverently — Hell, S.O.B., *damn*, Gawd) or every other profane or vulgar expression, however used, is expressly forbidden."[70] Selznick was concerned that removing the word would diminish both the picture's fidelity to the book and the impact of his carefully orchestrated conclusion. So, in mid–October he went over Breen's head and wrote to Hays protesting that "this line is remembered, loved and looked forward to by millions.... A great deal of the force and drama is dependant on that word.... This word as used in the picture is not an oath or a curse, but a vulgarism, and it is so described in the Oxford English Dictionary."[71] He pointed out that a number of popular women's magazines freely used the word as such, and that preview audiences had already expressed disappointment at the word's omission. Hays was also made aware that if he refused to overrule Breen, then a meeting would take place of the New York major studio heads to consider the matter. That turned out to be unnecessary; Hays agreed with Selznick's letter and permitted the word with the proviso of a face-saving $5,000 fine for technically breaching the Code.

The world premiere of *Gone with the Wind* took place December 15 at Loew's Grand Theatre in Atlanta. Planning rapidly took on the epic scale of the movie. As Kay Brown so aptly put it, "Sherman's march through Georgia will be nothing compared with Selznick's."[72] Mayer took one look at the reputations at stake and imposed his own publicity team on the production in the form of Howard Dietz and Howard Strickling, who in turn had the willing help of Atlanta's mayor, William B. Hartsfield, and Georgia's governor, E.D. Rivers. They planned to turn Atlanta into one giant advertisement for the movie. Rivers declared December 15 a state-wide holiday to mark the premiere, and Hartsfield organized three days of Atlanta festivities.

The prospect of all those crowds horrified the private and reticent Clark, who knew what it was like to be physically attacked by a horde of screaming fans. Then when he learned that his friend Victor Fleming had boycotted the premiere because of increasing animosity between he and Selznick, Clark declared that he would boycott the whole affair as well. MGM did not persuade Clark to change his mind until the last minute. Even Selznick was cool on the parade idea, though. Writing to Kay Brown, he protested, "After all, we have only made a motion picture and we are only motion picture people, and the concept of a town receiving us as though we had just licked the Germans is something that I for one will not go through with. You wouldn't get me into one of those cars for a million bucks and my guess is you won't get Gable into any of them either. It is our suggestion that Gable's plane arrive secretly."[73]

There was no chance of that happening. When Clark and Carole's American Airlines DC-3, with "GONE WITH THE WIND" painted on the side, touched down in Tucson, Arizona, after the first leg of the journey, a huge crowd was waiting. While Carole stayed on the plane Clark, who had a hangover after drinking with Fleming the previous night, good-naturedly asked the crowd to let him through so he could get some breakfast for them both at the cafe.

The rest of the film company, with the exceptions of Leslie Howard, who had also boycotted, and Hattie McDaniel who was denied a place in the proceedings by segregation-minded civic authorities who would not allow Selznick to even have her picture in the premiere's program, was aboard another plane which touched down on the Wednesday ahead of the Gables at the Atlanta airfield. They were met by some 300,000 people and entered Atlanta in a triumphal motorcade.

So when Clark and Carole landed at 3:30 p.m. on Thursday, December 14, their arrival was anything but secret. They were met by another huge crowd. In their own motorcade, they drove the seven miles from the airfield down a flag-decked Peachtree Street, where the cheering crowds were six deep, on into the heart of Atlanta. Even Clark was astonished at their reception, his face reflecting incredulity and amazement as he took off his hat and waved, laughing, to the crowd. The parade ended at the Georgian Terrace Hotel, where they were met by the governors of five southern states. Of course, there had to be speeches. Clark's was last, but it was greeted with thunderous applause and rebel yells. That night they were guests of honor at the Junior League Ball, where Clark danced with Mayor Hartsfield's daughter. At least one debutante fainted when introduced to him.

The next day, Mayor Hartsfield sneaked Clark and Carole out the hotel's back door for a private visit to the gigantic and lifelike Battle of Atlanta Cyclorama at Grant Park, where they were photographed walking along railway tracks while a silent war raged behind them. Luncheons and receptions followed. Clark and Selznick were made honorary colonels in the Georgia National Guard. At the Atlanta Women's Press Club reception at the Piedmont Driving Club, Margaret Mitchell finally met Clark for the first time. As a lot of people were when they first met the author, Clark was struck by her diminutive size. His first impulse was to sit down with her so she wouldn't have to strain to look up at him. Then the crowd started to press in as flashbulbs popped. Catching her eye, Clark grinned, jumped up, and spirited Mitchell into the nearby ladies' room, firmly shutting the door behind them. There, they finally got to talk for a short time. Afterward Clark was smitten, commenting more than once that she was "the most interesting woman I've ever met." That evening, he told the thousands gathered in the street outside the klieg-lit Loew's Grand Theatre for the premiere that,

"This is Margaret Mitchell's night and Atlanta's night. I want to see the picture just as you see it. Please, Atlanta, allow me to see *Gone with the Wind* tonight just as a spectator."[74]

As the curtain rose and Scarlett O'Hara became immersed in her fight to keep her home, so too did the 2,031-strong audience become immersed in the story of their South. They cheered and cried, hissed and stomped, and let out rebel yells as they took the movie to heart. When it was over, Mitchell was called to the stage, where she thanked Selznick, "on behalf of me and my poor Scarlett," for bringing her book to life. All told, this production had cost Mayer and Selznick about $100,000, but no one regretted a cent.

Clark, Carole, and the others packed and left the next day. However, they would all meet again twice more — in New York, where Leigh announced her engagement to Olivier, and at Fox's Carthay Circle Theatre in Los Angeles on December 28. Carole wore a princess-like gold lame evening gown and cape designed by Irene. Will Gable, who flatly refused to wear a tuxedo, and Edna accepted Clark's invitation to be there, the only time Will ever attended one of Clark's first nights. By this time, Clark and Carole must have been a little bored, having seen this movie one or two times before. Along with Marion Davies and director Raoul Walsh, they retired to the lobby part-way through the picture. They found some seats away from everyone in which to relax in the theater office. The staff was watching the movie, and no one was answering the phones, so at Clark's instigation the team of Gable, Lombard, Davies, and Walsh mischievously took over the job. As people called asking for reservations, one or another of the quartet informed them that performances were full for the next six months and no seats could be had. "We had a good time," Davies recalled later.[75] That pretty much summed up the general reaction from public and critics.

It did not, however, sum up the feelings

of a number of people associated with making the picture. Clark would remain unhappy for the rest of his life that he was never offered a percentage of *Gone with the Wind* profits nor, like just about everyone else involved, did he win an Oscar for his role. It would be many years before he spoke to Selznick again. Vivien Leigh, who did win an Oscar, never thought much of it or her role, which she would parody during her World War II troop performances. She used her Oscar as a doorstop.

Clark and Carole came to the twelfth annual Academy Awards in February 1940, anyway. Of a record-breaking eight Oscars, ten counting William Cameron Menzies' special award for his use of color and Selznick's Thalberg Award,[76] by far the loudest ovation was for Hattie McDaniel's award for Best Supporting Actress. It was the first ever for an African American performer, and it was to be the last for twenty-four years.

As Irene Selznick recalled in 1983: "Hollywood seemed to rejoice with us. It was their movie, too, and they were the better for it."[77]

CHAPTER 18

THE HOUSE OF
THE TWO GABLES

While all the *Gone with the Wind* fuss was going on, Clark and Carole had been concentrating on setting their new home in order. They had moved into their white, gable-roofed house in July 1939, and it didn't take long for Hollywood wits to christen it "the House of the Two Gables." It was an unpretentious house for two such major stars, with none of the flamboyant touches other star's homes had that shouted their occupant's importance. Carole had seen it as a family home from the start, and Clark always proudly gave her full credit for her work on it.

The house was entered through a small wood-paneled lobby. On the left was a stairway, and on the right was the living room, which was painted white and entirely carpeted in sunny yellow. The pair of skirted Lawson sofas was also yellow, along with a pair of club chairs in green and a pair of wing chairs in red linen. It was a bright room filled with sunlight through four large multipaned windows draped in white, green, and red flowered linen. On the other side of the room was an antique cabinet holding a collection of pitchers. The room had a large, open fireplace and was always filled with fresh flowers in large vases, but was otherwise uncluttered; Clark

hated things like newspapers and magazines to accumulate, and neither he nor Carole were great collectors of bric-a-brac or mementoes.

Behind the living room was Clark's gun room. One entire thirty-foot wall was taken up by a large glass case containing the one thing he did collect: guns. At the time they moved in there were over fifty, including many antique pistols and rifles, and these were constantly being added to by gifts from his friends. Comfy couches and lounge chairs were grouped together, making it the perfect men's cigar and brandy room.

The gun collection was the subject of drama for Clark and Carole later that summer of 1939, when Clark surprised a teenager in the process of stealing one of them. Clark had been working outside, but he went back upstairs to remove a ring that was bothering him. Looking in a mirror, he saw a door open behind him and a man walk through it without seeing him. Clark promptly hit him. Then, after wrestling one of his own guns from the thief, Clark dragged him downstairs by the collar. He was only a kid, and the sympathetic Clark might have settled for him apologizing, but the thief refused to and made another break for the door. Clark floored him again

Clark's study in the Encino house. The deer head was one of his prized trophies.

and called the police. It turned out the kid had slept in Clark's car inside the garage the previous night with the boxer watchdog, which ever after Clark called "Old Dependable." Clark didn't seem too bothered by it all but, as he admitted, "he might have given me a bad time if he had seen me in my dressing room before I saw him."[1] It gave Carole a bad scare, though, reminding her of Russ Colombo's accidental shooting.

The dining room, entered through sliding doors from the living room, had a very different feel. Cool and dark rather than bright and sunny, the vast room felt more like a tavern, with a large open bar along one wall and a whitewashed brick fireplace on the other. The walls were of natural pine, the floors were polished oak, and all the chairs were plain wooden captain's chairs. The only splash of bright color in the room was from Carole's collection of rare pink Staffordshire in wooden hutches. It was the only pink in the house, being a color that Clark didn't like at all. Over the long dining table, which could seat ten, was a chandelier made of old oil lamps. For formal occasions Carole would set the table with their Spode china and Waterford crystal, but otherwise they preferred to entertain friends on their large screened patio. The dining table had belonged to Clark, but it wasn't weathered enough for Carole's taste, so she sent it to a refinisher who left it outside. Every so often, Clark and Carole would go over to see how the table was doing and would proceed to help it along by pouring water over it, stubbing cigarettes on it, and beating it with chains. When it was eventually repolished, it was a thing of beauty.

There was an immense kitchen with a room-sized walk-in refrigerator and all the

Clark and Carole relaxing after lunch on the patio with their two Siamese cats.

latest appliances. That's not to say Carole actually cooked, of course. There was a house staff of three: Jessie the cook and Juanita the maid, who both left for a while only to be so unsuccessfully replaced that they gladly re-turned, and Rufus Martin the butler-valet who remained with Clark for the rest of his life. Then there was Fred, the ranch caretaker, who lived with his wife in their own cottage on the property. On Jessie's Sundays off or for

A September 1941 Good Housekeeping *ad for Lux soap, featuring Carole.*

Clark and Carole at a premiere.

big parties, Carole would order from the Brown Derby. Jessie was a large woman whose Southern cooking was known all over the valley. Clark loved good solid down-home cooking: steak, roast beef, stewed chicken and dumplings, spare ribs and baked beans, devil's food cake, and homemade ice cream. Dinner was never served before nine because, once home from the studio, Clark liked to take care of all his affairs, maybe go through some scripts and unwind with a few drinks before he sat down.

Their joint personal assistant was Jean Garceau, who had become Carole's personal assistant in October 1938, but took over that job for them both after they were married. After Carole's death, she stayed on to work for Clark for many years. Jean handled their income, investments, bills, and accounts. She prepared their tax statements, hired house staff, looked after travel arrangements, sorted and answered their mail, and did anything else left over that would probably fall into the category of general troubleshooting. She had come to Carole from the Myron Selznick agency, where she had been Carole's contact person. Madalynne Fields, or "Fieldsie" as Carole always called her, had been Carole's previous assistant, manager, friend, alter ego and roommate, but she left to marry Walter Lang. Jean had hesitated, knowing it would be a tall order to fill, but she accepted the offer and moved into an office in Carole's Tudor-style house on St. Cloud Road. When they moved into the Encino house, Jean once again had her own office, decorated in yellow and blue, and it became the nerve center of their personal, business, studio, and ranch affairs when the Gables were home. Clark and Carole called her "Jeanie" and treated her as one of the family, but to her Clark was always "Mr. G."

Upstairs, two adjoining bedroom suites occupied the whole floor; there was no guest room. Clark's was brown and beige; Carole's was white and blue, and both were carpeted in off-white wool. Clark had a double bed with tufted leather headboard; Carole's was a fully flounced mahogany four-poster with matching bedside tables. Bookcases and a small bar were built-in behind Clark's bed, and he also had an old pine desk from the set of *Gone with the Wind* that Selznick had given to him as a gift to mark the end of the film shoot. Carole's room contained a full-sized concert harp. Clark's beige marble bathroom had no tub, only a shower, and glass shelves holding antique bottles. Carole's white marble bathroom with its adjoining dressing room was given the full Hollywood treatment of white fur on the floor, crystal chandeliers, and fixtures of white marble and silver. Carole liked to call it "the most elegant shit-house in the San Fernando Valley."[2]

She was equally as blunt about Clark as a lover in real life, compared to how he seemed to be on the big screen, commenting to a friend, "My God, you know how I love Pa, but I can't say he's a helluva good lay."[3] She laid the blame, as it were, on his previous encounters with women, who were just glad to be in bed with Clark Gable; it had all been too easy, and he'd never had to be too concerned before with developing a loving relationship where both people were equally concerned and interested with the other's sexuality. Clark was very tender and giving with Carole, though, and she with him. Their relationship developed, but sex was evidently not a predominant element.

Carole had a longstanding reputation for her blunt language and blue streak in her vocabulary, but Clark could be as disapproving of it as he had been with Vivien Leigh, especially when she aimed her words at someone in particular. The day they were moving in, the plumber told Carole and Clark that they might not be finished working for a few days. When Carole expressed her opinions in a few choice phrases, Clark pulled her to one side and said to her, "Listen, baby, if there's any cussing to be done, I'm man enough to do it myself." Carole threw her arms around him, burst into tears, and cried, "I've waited a long time for someone to do that. Oh Pa, I'm glad I love you. I'm so glad I married you."[4]

That first summer they rode horses in the late afternoon, Clark's a sorrel named Sonny and Carole's a bay named Melody. They would sit and watch the sun set from their patio, Clark sipping Scotch and Carole with a Coca-Cola. There could be no doubt for anyone who knew the couple, though, who was the real star. "Clark comes first," Carole said to Jean Garceau, "I want to be ready to go anywhere, do anything Clark wants to do."[5] Carole made it clear to the house staff that they were to cater to whatever made Clark happy. One of the things that kept him happy was that the house could pass a white-glove inspection any time of the day. It kept her happy, too; Carole had a long-standing reputation for liking everything in its place. When she traveled, her clothing was packed systematically so that she could lay hands on anything she might want day or night, including the first-aid kit. If passengers became sick on the plane in which she was traveling, she could be at their side quicker than the flight attendants. Playing tennis, she would always be dressed in the fashionable outfit of the moment, right down to the correct coat to throw over her shoulders after the game, and she'd be carrying a spare pair of shoes.

With a big garage to work in, Clark could once again indulge in his hobby of tinkering with cars, usually large, fast ones, and the occasional motorcycle. Always one to comment that if his career ever went bad he could go back to making a living as a mechanic, Clark enjoyed being both in and under the many cars he owned at various times, usually another one every year. He had a Jaguar SS Tourer in the early 1930s, and then in 1949 he took proud delivery of the new Jaguar XK 120. It was the fastest production car in the world at the time, and Clark personally proved it could do its advertised 125 mph. He also owned at least two Packards: a 1932 standard-eight convertible and a 1938 straight-eight Roadster with a body custom

finished by Hibbard and Darrin, which was said to have been a birthday present from Carole.[6] Then there were various Fords, Chryslers, and Lincolns, often "loaned" by a car company so they could brag that Clark was driving one of their cars.

However, Clark's most distinctive vehicles were his Duesenbergs, regarded as the most luxurious and expensive cars of their time.[7] In the mid–1930s Clark had the unique distinction of having two "Duesies" in his garage. His JN Convertible Coupe had a custom body built for him by coachbuilders Bohman and Schwartz in Pasadena, and its total cost would probably have been between $15,000 and $18,000, a staggering price for a car in a period still feeling the effects of the Depression. A new Auburn family sedan, for example, could have been purchased then for around $1,000, while a snappy new Cord convertible would have cost just over $2,000.[8] The JN was powered by a Lycoming straight-eight and could achieve speeds over 115 mph. Clark's other Duesenberg was a red and silver supercharged SJ Roadster on publicity loan from the Duesenberg company. Only two of these were ever built. The other SJ, owned by Gary Cooper, had an engine that developed over 400 horsepower and was said to be the largest and fastest ever installed in any Model J intended for domestic use.[9]

Clark apparently developed a liking for Mercedes automobiles later in his life. He owned a 1955 300SL Gullwing, ordered new and probably the first to be owned in Hollywood at the time, and a 1956 300SC Cabriolet. Manufactured between 1955 and 1958, the Cabriolet was regarded as one of the most luxurious vehicles on the market, at a cost of around $16,000. It had a fuel-injected Einspritz engine, and its chrome parts were handcrafted and individually numbered to match each car. It even came with matching luggage and a personally engraved St. Christopher statue on the dashboard.[10]

For their first Christmas in the house, Carole bought the biggest tree she could find,

Clark posing happily with his 1932 Packard convertible.

had it sprayed white, and decorated it herself with lights and silver ornaments. Clark's gift to her was a ruby heart on a gold chain that she wore ever afterward. She gave him a set of monogrammed pajamas and a matching robe, made to her own design, of heavy, off-white silk from a roll of the last silk to come out of China before the Japanese invasion.

Andy Devine, one of their friends, once said of Carole and Clark that to spend time with them at their home was like "a day in the sun." They didn't feel the need to have a show-piece house as a symbol of their status. Number 4525 Petit Avenue, Encino, was a home in which they could be their own low-key selves and into which their friends were welcome. Carole and Clark weren't part of the Hollywood party circle with a large group of hangers-on always around. They were just Ma and Pa Gable with a small circle of close devoted friends. "He was a pretty private guy," added Devine, "and when he came home there was a certain group of people he liked to be with, people with whom he liked to say he could take his shoes off."[11]

Some of these friends were Carole's and some were Clark's, and they included Fieldsie and Walter Lang; Al Menasco, Clark's friend from *Test Pilot*, and his wife; Harry Fleisch-mann of the Bakersfield Duck Club and his wife Nan; Buster Collier who knew Carole from her days as a Sennett girl and his wife Stevie; Tuffy Goff and his wife Liz, and the Devines. The latter two couples were ranch people like the Gables. Howard and Gail Strickling lived nearby, too, on their ranch where they raised chickens.

Carole didn't let settling down get in the

Clark's 1935 Duesenberg SJ Roadster, one of only two ever built. Auburn Cord Duesenberg Museum.

way of her antics. Andy Devine recalls them all setting out for a picnic at the Pomona County Fair, not knowing that Carole had secretly sent her butler on ahead with the station wagon. When they arrived it was to find the picnic all set out on red tablecloths waiting for them. A guest at one of Fred MacMurray's parties recalls that he had a large fishpond around which, on this occasion, about thirty guests were sitting. It was very hot and Carole, who was wearing a long white gown, suddenly jumped into the pond to cool off. Clark laughed and laughed, saying: "Isn't she wonderful? Isn't she darling? Isn't she marvelous?" Carole eventually climbed out and went inside, only to return dressed in Fred's pajamas.[12]

The one thing with which Carole and Clark were not happy, however, was the lack of children. Carole's failure to conceive worried her a lot, and her New Year's resolution for 1940 was to become pregnant.[13] She had

always been plagued by menstrual problems, but her doctors told her that while conceiving would probably be difficult, it shouldn't be impossible. She became joyfully pregnant at least once, only to find at her next medical examination that she had miscarried, probably while horseback riding. Consequently, her doctor told her that if she really was serious about having a child, she would almost certainly have to give up much of her outdoor life and her acting career. Neither idea sat well; her outdoor life was something she shared with Clark and which she did not want to forego. She was still contractually tied to RKO for two more pictures, and so for the moment she kept working. She compromised, however, by eventually giving up riding.

Given *Gone with the Wind*'s overpowering presence for a large part of 1939, that year came to a close while Clark was working on a more spiritual and mystical film titled *Strange Cargo*, in which Clark was reunited with Joan

Clark with his 1935 Duesenberg J Bohman and Schwartz convertible coupe. Auburn Cord Duesen-berg Museum.

Crawford. Produced by Joseph L. Mankiewicz and directed by Frank Borzage,[14] with a script by Anita Loos and Lawrence Hazard based on Richard Sale's book *Not Too Narrow, Not Too Deep*, it is the story of a group of convicts who escape through the jungle from a New Guinea penal colony. After they are joined by another fugitive, Verne (Gable), and his prostitute girl-friend Julie (Crawford), Verne takes over as leader. However, the group falls under the influence of another member, the Christ-like Cambreau (Ian Hunter), who becomes each man's conscience in turn before they die a re-pentant death. In the end, as the Production Code decreed should be the case, the influence of good triumphs over that of evil, and so even Verne eventually succumbs to Cambreau's

influence. He agrees to abandon his escape and return to serve out the rest of his prison sentence, while Julie sacrifices herself for love to wait for him. Under the sensitive guidance of Borzage, Clark, Crawford and a supporting cast that included Albert Dekker, Peter Lorre,[15] and Paul Lukas turned in strong per-formances.

Clark and Crawford had not been on speaking terms since she turned down the lead in *Parnell*, saying that the script was "boring and pretentious."[16] However, he sent her red roses on the first day of the *Strange Cargo* shoot, as was his custom with his leading ladies, and all was forgiven and their friend-ship resumed. They spent a lot of time play-ing ball on the Pismo Beach location with the

Clark concentrating hard as he tinkers with an engine.

crew while they waited for fog to clear. Some days it refused to clear at all, so consequently much of the film was finally shot on a sound-stage. However, Clark had to do so much shouting while standing around in cold water and being hit with spray that he wound up in hospital briefly with laryngitis just before Christmas.

By now, both Clark and Carole were stars of sufficient stature to be able to select their own personal crew. Clark's would remain with him for the majority of his career. It included close friend Lew Smith, his stand-in, a big man who was about the same height and coloring as Clark, and Stan Campbell, his makeup man who had been with him since *San Francisco*. Stan often didn't have a great deal to do because Clark, unlike a lot of stars, preferred to wear as little makeup as possible. Crawford often tried to persuade him to wear more, but Clark would just laugh her makeup suggestions off. Carole's personal people were her hairdresser, Loretta Francel (nicknamed "Bucket" for some reason lost in time), her manicurist Peggy Mercer, her stand-in Betty, and her dress designer Irene, who made all Carole's clothes for on and off the set after she left Paramount. Carole also requested that Pat Drew, an electrician who had lost a leg in an aircraft accident, work on all her pictures.

So, as the new year began, the man who used to say he never got anything for which he hadn't worked was a fortunate man who had everything he could want, and he knew it. By now, Clark and Carole were very comfortable financially. On January 25, 1940, Clark signed a new seven-year contract with MGM that would bring him $5,000 a week to begin with, increasing to $7,500 a week. It was estimated that the money would add up to over $2,000,000 by the end of the contract.[17] To put that in another perspective, as *Saturday Evening Post* writer P. J. McEvoy pointed out, Clark earned as much for ten weeks of acting as President Roosevelt was paid to run the country for a year. That, he said, was quite unfair because F.D.R. was, after all, the better actor. Clark insisted, as usual, that he was just "Joe Lucky."[18]

According to the terms of this contract, though, he was more than just a lucky man; he was finally officially recognized by MGM as the star he was. His workday hours were now stipulated as between 9 a.m. and 6 p.m. for a minimum of forty weeks a year. He would now have a guaranteed eight-week break every year between September 1 and December 1. For the first three years of the contract he would be required to appear in no more than three films a year with a two-week break between them. For the next four years it would be no more than two films with a four-week break between them. Clark's name was to appear before any other costar in all film credits and advertising. No longer would

MGM be able to loan him out, nor could they force him to make personal appearances, and they would supply him with first-class accommodation and transportation while on location. However, the studio's catch was Clause Twenty-six, which stated that Clark would make himself available at all times in Los Angeles or any other place that the studio designated. This meant that Strickling or Mannix had to know where the studio's prime investment could be reached all day, every day, all year. As compensation, this would be the first of Clark's contracts with a self-destruct clause; he would have the option to terminate his own employment after five years if he so desired.

Clause Twenty-six caught up with Clark and Carole almost immediately, albeit quite accidentally. When Clark had finished work on *Strange Cargo* in late January, he and Carole decided to go on a belated honeymoon to one of their favorite hideaways, La Grulla Gun Club near Ensenada, about sixty-five miles south of the Mexican border. They drove down in Clark's new Dodge wagon, which he had fitted out especially for hunting trips, with their friends the Fleischmanns who had a duck club near Bakersfield where they spent a lot of time. Having no luck at La Grulla, they drove farther south to another club and then decided to return on February 1, Clark's birthday. Before long it started to pour with rain, and the wagon became stuck in mud on the narrow mountain road. They figured there was nothing to do but get into their sleeping bags and wait the night out, but not before eating a supper of lobster and birthday cake. Meanwhile, back at La Grulla, panic set in when the famous couple did not return. Word reached Hollywood, newspapers printed large headlines, and a frantic Strickling ordered Otto Winkler to fly south immediately. The next morning the Gable party was pulled out by a passing truck and reached La Grulla just as Winkler was about to start out with a search party.

Carole's annual salary at this time averaged around $150,000, on top of which she was receiving a percentage of picture profits, quite a drop from her publicized $465,000 in 1937. Both she and Clark also made several radio appearances a year at $5,000 a time. Writer Henry Pringle did some figuring that year for the *Ladies' Home Journal* about the financial standing of the Gable household, estimating Clark and Carole's combined gross annual incomes to conservatively be around $550,000, without factoring in any investment returns. Based on that figure, Pringle estimated they had a combined income of probably only $125,000 a year after tax.

A common assumption is that the large figures stars of this period commanded automatically meant that they were extremely wealthy, but this was not necessarily so. Income tax commonly consumed up to 70 to 80 percent of their money, which was why it was also common for many of them to be in trouble for trying to avoid paying those taxes. Unlike people with inherited wealth, movie stars could not escape payment through tax-exempt securities. Not only that, but those high figures were usually only paid for a short period when the star was at their peak. Clark was paid a consistently large amount of money during a remarkably long career, and for that he was indeed, as he frequently said, very lucky. So the Gables did not entertain in a big way, unlike many other star households. In Hollywood terms they lived quite conservatively, probably spending an estimated $16,000 a year on living expenses, including $3,600 on servant's wages and only $2,400 on food because of the farm, $1,200 a year on property taxes, $7,200 a year on utilities and maintenance, and around $1,500 on car repair and maintenance for the year.[19]

By way of comparison, the following year *Look* magazine did an analysis of just where an average actor's money could go. The article made the interesting observations that Nicholas Schenck stated in 1937 on oath that he had to borrow money to pay taxes when his salary went over $400,000, and that it was on record that Louis B. Mayer had paid

$1,108,352 in taxes in one year alone. Using the example of an anonymous female actor who earned $3,000 a week, or $220,000 a year, the article estimated $75,100 of that disappeared in state and federal taxes. Another $58,600 went in payments to her agent, business manager, private secretary, public relations person and private maid. Another $23,000 went into house payments, $18,300 to household expenses including staff, $6,300 on clothes, $4,300 on the car, $5,400 on personal expenses such as doctor, dentist, and lunches, and $1,200 went to charity. That left the grand total of $27,800 for life insurance, savings and investments.[20] A big salary, then, usually meant a lifestyle account to match. Still, a single person able to clear nearly $28,000 as disposable income in those days had quite a respectable amount of money indeed.

Clark's first movie for 1940 was *Boomtown* with Spencer Tracy, Claudette Colbert, and Hedy Lamarr. A big adventure story of oil-field wildcatters whose partnership and friendship eventually survives the tolls of too much black gold, bad business deals, and good women (each other's), it must have been a subject close to Clark's heart and a film that he evidently enjoyed. Carole, however, was more concerned with not letting Lamarr get close to Clark's heart. After all, Hedy already had quite a heady reputation after her notoriously naked appearance in the 1933 Czech film *Ecstasy*, and Carole was all too aware of Clarke's weakness for pretty women.[21] She could be tolerant about his minor dalliances, but she drew the line at anything involving a major leading lady. So on the day his love scene with Lamarr was being shot, Carole made a point of visiting the set dressed in an expensive suit, fur stole, and hat just to make the point that she could outclass any costar anytime.

Boomtown was Clark's third and last appearance with Tracy. They had both become stars who were now too important, not to mention too expensive, to put together in one movie. Besides, Tracy was getting tired of playing second fiddle to Clark. While rehearsing one of their fight scenes, Clark was practicing with Tracy's stand-in. Apparently unnerved by being asked to take a swing at the king, the stand-in mistimed his punch and actually landed it, knocking Clark down and breaking his top plate, sending false teeth everywhere and badly splitting his top lip. There was no way of shooting around Clark at this late stage, so everything had to be put on hold while his teeth were fixed and his lip healed, costing the film an extra $50,000. Carole reminded Clark that he was even more qualified now for the nickname with which Douglas Fairbanks Jr. had christened him some time ago: "the toothless wonder."[22]

By the time Clark finished with *Boomtown*, Carole had begun *They Knew What They Wanted*, directed by Garson Kanin, in which she played one of her best dramatic roles as the mail-order bride of Charles Laughton. Although Carole respected Laughton's abilities as an actor, she detested him as a person. She had it written into her contract that under no circumstances would she be required to kiss him. Laughton was still in tyrannical Captain Bligh mode, and Kanin, Carole, and he fought and argued for the duration of the movie. Some of the scenes were shot on location in the Napa Valley, and Carole brought Clark along for these, probably enjoying the opportunity for some moral support. They stayed in a private home, were able to find the time for some hunting and fishing together, and were even taught how to tread grapes by the locals.

Returning home they found that, unlike Carole, MGM had liked the Gable-Lamarr partnership and so teamed them again in *Comrade X*, directed by King Vidor,[23] a story about a cynical newspaper reporter (Gable) who has been smuggling embarrassing stories about the government out of Russia. His cover is blown by a hotel porter, who can only be silenced if Clark smuggles the porter's daughter out of the country. The only way she can get a passport is for them to be married. They're arrested before they can leave and are sentenced to death, but they escape and make it home to the joys of capitalism and the Dodgers.

Clark thought that Hedy Lamarr was absolutely beautiful, but he used to joke with her rather than make passes at her. She used to spend a lot of what he and Stan Campbell considered was wasted time making up her face and doing her hair. Both of them thought she was beautiful enough to not be concerned with artificial enhancement. "C'mon," Clark would say to her, "forget your face. Let's do some acting."[24] The critics agreed with MGM that Gable and Lamarr made a great pair, but Carole was no longer concerned. The doctors had once again told her that she wasn't pregnant. Depressed, Carole considered doing only one more picture and then perhaps retiring. Typically, she cheered herself up by plunging back into work.

She discovered that Alfred Hitchcock was hanging around RKO unemployed and charmed him into directing her in a comedy, *Mr. and Mrs. Smith*. She probably didn't have to work too hard to persuade him; he was always partial to an elegant, well-spoken blond, but it was certainly a departure of style for him even then. As usual, Carole couldn't resist a gag. Not long before, Hitchcock had provoked a few outraged reactions by commenting that actors were just cattle. When he came onto the set on his first morning, he found Carole had set up a cattle pen inside which were three calves labeled as the three leads, Carole, Robert Montgomery, and Gene Raymond. Hitchcock is, of course, renowned for his trademark of appearing somewhere in each of his films, and here he's mistaken for a beggar by Robert Montgomery and given a dime. Carole directed the brief scene where he appears. Then, getting some revenge on the perfectionist Hitchcock for his endless takes, she ordered a few herself so he could experience just a little of the receiving end.

Once it was all over, she settled down to being with Clark as much as possible. They went duck shooting down to Baja, California.

When that proved disappointing, they called Paul Mantz, Gable's flying buddy from *Test Pilot* to fly them up into the mountains around Laguna Hanson in his twin-engine amphibian plane. They had better luck there, but when it came time to leave they ran into trouble trying to fly off the tree-circled lake in the heavily loaded plane. They had to abort the first takeoff, leave a few things behind, and try again. As the treetops skimmed by just under the wings as they lifted off, a pale Carole turned to Clark and said intuitively, "Please, let's never travel in separate planes. Whenever I fly, I want you with me."[25] Only once again would she fly anywhere without Clark.

The day after Christmas, Clark and Carole left Hollywood by train for Johns Hopkins Medical Center in Baltimore. According to Jean Garceau, the visit was prompted by a recurrent shoulder injury of Clark's from when a wall of wooden bricks had fallen on him during *San Francisco* a few years before,[26] although newspapers put it down to a horse fall.

Arriving in Washington on December 29, they were invited by President Roosevelt to be present for one of his fireside chats to the nation that night. Sitting in the front row next to the Secretary of State and the President's mother, Clark and Carole were moved at the sight of the wheelchair bound leader. Roosevelt preferred not to be seen in public in his chair, and his disability was always played down by the media, so it was probably something of a shock for Carole and Clark to be confronted by it. It was to be one of Roo-

sevelt's greatest speeches, envisioning the United States as the "arsenal of democracy." Afterward, he chatted with the Gables for some thirty minutes, questioning Clark about the making of *Gone with the Wind* and thanking Carole for her public support of the income tax system. One wonders if they exchanged opinions on whether Roosevelt should ask for a raise. The President was interested in their views as to how the movie industry could help the war effort, if it came to that. Carole, expressing her hopes that war would not eventuate, suggested that they could perhaps be involved in voluntary efforts such as selling war bonds. It would be a fateful proposal.

The next day, the Gables drove to Baltimore, and Clark went into Johns Hopkins for treatment. However, friends of the Gables would later say that Carole also took advantage of this visit to consult gynecologists there about her conception difficulties.[27] To everyone's surprise, Clark's doctor, Louis Hamman, discovered that his shoulder problem was actually being aggravated by a severe tooth infection. So on January 2, Clark underwent dental surgery to remove the tooth and clean the infection. Carole's doctors, however, could find nothing seriously wrong with her. They suggested that, although they could carry out some minor surgery that could possibly improve matters, it might pay to wait until they were sure that all this wasn't a Clark difficulty rather than a Carole one.

CHAPTER 19

AS GOOD AS IT GETS

Carole and Clark had been together five years in March 1941, when they celebrated their second wedding anniversary. Clark was making *They Met in Bombay* at the time, and Carole organized a party for him on the set, catered by the Brown Derby. Everything served and given was in pairs or doubles. She had earlier thrown a fortieth birthday party for him at the ranch.

They Met in Bombay, directed by Clarence Brown, was adapted by Anita Loos, Edwin Justus Mayer and Leon Gordon from a Franz Kafka story originally titled "Unholy Partners." It was the last of the five Gable films that Loos either wrote or collaborated on in her years at MGM. There could have been a sixth, which would have been titled *The Great Canadian*, which Loos wrote in 1938 for Clark and Mae West, but she couldn't convince West that the role of a female manager of an ice-hockey team would be suitable for her. West suggested that Rosalind Russell would be better in the part, but MGM shelved the script.[1] They had, however, kept Russell in mind. They now teamed her and Clark, for the first time since *China Seas*, as two crooks chasing a lost diamond, pursued by the law. They fall in love eventually, of course, but there's a twist to the tale when, while disguised as an officer, Clark's character is sent on a mission and dec-

orated. By and large it was accepted by the public as just another lightweight farce. The *Hollywood Reporter* considered "preposterous ... hardly a strong enough word for the fictional conveniences of the plot," and that the "poetic verbiage ... meant to be romantic utterances missed the values a believable love theme might have added to surrounding absurdities."[2]

Russell enjoyed working with Clark and commented on how "there wasn't all this clinching and awkwardness. His rhythm and timing were much like a ballet dancer's." Actually, director Delmer Daves was said to have timed Clark's rhythm when he directed him in 1952 and found he maintained a one-two-three-kiss beat.[3] Russell had a maid who was very clever at hand-stitching leather gloves. No doubt having heard of Carole's legendary interest in Clark's leading ladies, she frequently sent home pairs with Clark for Carole, who evidently appreciated the conciliatory gesture.

The Gables now jointly suffered those hazards of fame that had been plaguing Clark for many years. Their ranch had quickly been drawn onto the maps of Hollywood stars' homes, and their privacy was being increasingly invaded. Tour buses would just motor right by the property so people could gawk at the house, and Clark had been approached by tour drivers about allowing them to come right up the driveway. They had found fans wandering the property and on occasions had called the MGM police to remove them. On one notable occasion Clark had run in from the fields where he'd been working, exclaiming that there was a woman after him. Jean and Martin rushed outside to find that a bleached blond in a riding outfit had made herself comfortable on one of the patio lounges and declared that she wasn't leaving until she was introduced to Mr. Gable. Jean called Whitey Hendry, who sent some of the MGM police. When they arrived, the woman played hide-and-seek with them through the trees until they tagged her and took her away.[4]

To no one's surprise, Jean kept a "mad woman" file to head any major trouble off at the pass. Although the studios dealt with mail addressed to either Clark or Carole there, piles of mail still arrived at the house for them, which Jean diligently sorted through to weed out the threatening or soliciting letters from the genuine fan mail which Clark always appreciated. People would send gifts such as pipes, bookends, handkerchiefs, and even clocks to Clark and Carole. These were usually all given to charity. Jean would then reply with a thank you note from Clark. By March 1940, Clark had been forced to erect an electric gate, and he soon added a chain-link fence with "No Trespassing" signs around the previously open front of the property to maintain their privacy. The gate bell would ring in Jean's office, and she would screen visitors, becoming proficient at telling lovelorn women that Mr. Gable was busy and couldn't spare the time to see them right now.

As time went on, Carole became increasingly concerned that no work was coming her way. Her contract with RKO was not renewed, and Gable's dislike of Selznick still hung like a cloud in the air, preventing her from seeking help from that quarter. She began to blame Myron Selznick for it all, and she sought release from her contract with him,

which wasn't due to expire until 1943. He refused, and the matter went to court for arbitration where it stayed for some time. Just as Myron had invented the commissioned agent, Carole was the first female actor, through her lawyer W. I. Gilbert, to pioneer legal redress against such an agent and to break an agency contract. During the proceedings, a small contractual quirk came to light. When they drew up the document Carole, as a gag, had inserted a clause awarding *her* 10 percent of *Myron's* earnings, and he'd signed it without noticing the change. Carole got her release, but had to pay costs and compensation of $26,500 to Myron against lost commission, and Myron would still collect a percentage on films he had negotiated for her in the past. She signed up with a new agent, Nat Wolff, and clinched a deal for two films that would start in the fall, *To Be or Not to Be*, and *They All Kissed the Bride*.

Anticipating the lackluster reviews for *Bombay* that it received, Clark plunged straight into playing Candy Johnson, a heartless, fast-talking, frontier gambler and conman in *Honky Tonk*, who finds the right woman for whom to have a heart, a beautiful but proper Boston belle, Lucy. Her father, unbeknown to Lucy, is also a conman, and he and Candy go into partnership to take over running a town. Lucy and Candy marry, but when her father is murdered, she loses her baby. Candy runs the bad guys out of town, but his operation is busted. He leaves town too, leaving Lucy to be taken care of by an anonymous fortune. Love reigns supreme, though, and she follows him. Directed by Jack Conway and costarring Lana Turner, in her first star billing role, with Frank Morgan and Albert Dekker again, *Honky Tonk* is, as *Variety* put it so well, "a lively, lusty Western that makes you wish you had been there."[5] Studio executives hadn't wanted Clark there originally, though, and he had to stick his neck out and fight for the role. Chill Wills played Clark's partner in card sharking and taught him a lot of the card tricks that they used in the film, with which Clark used to frequently entertain his friends.

Right from the start, rumors were rampant that the onscreen sparks between Clark and Turner were being struck off-screen as well. Carole, true to form, went off about the stories to Clark and anyone who would listen, threatening to come to the set and kick ass all over the place. After all, the blond and voluptuous Turner was only twenty-one at the time, eleven years younger than Carole and nineteen years younger than Clark, and Carole was well aware of her husband's weaknesses. Turner would say later, however, that she had "revered" Clark because of his status and that while their working relationship was pleasant, it never developed into a close friendship. She graciously gave Carole the benefit of the doubt in believing the "rampant press speculations about fireworks on the set between the two powerful sex symbols Gable and I were supposed to be." The day Carole first showed up on the set, she recalled, "my knees went watery and I became so flustered that I excused myself and fled to my dressing trailer" where she remained until she was called. By that time, Carole had gone. When Turner later apologized to Clark, "that famous smile lit up his face and he said simply, 'I understand.'"[6] After that, Carole made a habit of just happening to show up whenever Clark was filming a love scene with Turner, and she was once reported to have snapped at her, "Don't mind me, Lana. I know you must be having a tough time. Pappy's not very good in a clinch."[7] Understandably, both Clark and Turner developed the jitters, and eventually studio executives made it very plain to Carole that she was not welcome on the set.

Filming was finished unusually quickly, and to make it plain where matters stood after it was over, the Gables made the rare move of attending the premiere together and visibly held hands throughout. As far as the studio was concerned, though, even if nothing was going on in real life something hot was sure happening on the screen. Consequently, they made plans to pair Turner and Clark up again soon.

Feeling the need for a break, Clark and Carole left Los Angeles for their favorite spot on the Rogue River, the Weasku Inn, to spend time together hunting and fishing. However, they found the river heavily clouded with silt and mud. The fish had sensibly gone elsewhere. The locals had not, and Clark was kept busy signing autographs. Finally, they decided to leave on May 15. Hearing that the Gables were about to depart, three fur-clad Oregon Cavewomen, Marie Dean, Doris Colgan, and Frankie Rineharger, Caveman E. C. Westergren, and Chief Bighorn E. K. Miller rushed over to present the Gables with jawbone "passports" to the area. Clark accepted the gifts, although he refused to be photographed doing so, saying that his contract did not allow him to appear in gag pictures. While Clark was at the Rogue River, a man named Milton Dickinson was fined by the local Justice of the Peace for fishing with two poles, which was illegal in Oregon. His defense was that he was tending one of them for Clark, but he was more likely substituting for George "Gabby" Hayes, who was also there at the same time and who paid the fine.[8]

The Gables drove to Crescent City, California, from where they flew south to Lake Mead, near Las Vegas, Nevada. They hired a cabin cruiser there and, not needing to touch shore for a few days, they at last found the peace and quiet they needed. Those incidents, however, were harbingers of things to come.

In fall, when the duck season opened, the Gables and their friends the Fleischmans took a plane for Watertown, South Dakota. They didn't make it that far; bad weather grounded them in Albuquerque. The airline put them on a train to Kansas City, where they were put up at the Muehlbach Hotel. Clark, by now thoroughly disgruntled and unable to avoid being fussed over by hotel staff, got on the phone to the airline and chewed them out. The airline only had a large transcontinental plane available, but it put them on it and they eventually arrived in Watertown at two in the morning. Dedicated hunters that they were, they were out at the blinds at dawn ready to shoot. Everybody shot their limits for the day. By that night, however, word had leaked out as to their whereabouts in the town. They were besieged by fans, and the phone rang incessantly. The next day Clark bought a Ford, loaded them all in it, and drove straight home into a media storm over impending separation rumors.[9] As a result, they both swore that as soon as Carole finished her next picture they would sell the ranch and move somewhere where they could be alone together. They looked around for a while as far away as Arizona, but in the end they couldn't bring themselves to leave the place they loved.

Their ranch at Encino became Clark and Carole's retreat and their life. They seldom went out anywhere, totally happy in each other's company. "We die if we have to go out of an evening," Carole said.[10] They played poker or backgammon for penny stakes and read a lot. Clark liked mysteries, and Carole read extensively with an eye to books that might make good properties for scripts. They held occasional parties for their friends and played pranks on each other. Sometimes they combined the two. One night the guests arrived to find the patio set out for a twelve-piece orchestra with instruments and music stands, but no musicians. Instead, while Clark sat in on drums, Fred MacMurray played sax, Buster Collier sat in on piano, Spencer Tracy picked up the bass, and Dick Powell and Robert Taylor joined the brass section with Carole on trumpet.

One morning when Clark opened the barn door, an angry cow charged and butted him across the yard. At dinner that night Carole presented him with a red toreador's costume. Clark did some thinking. Carole had just had an expensive riding outfit made for her by her friend and designer Irene. A few nights later Clark announced at dinner that he had found her just the horse to go with it and that it would be delivered the next morn-

ing. When Carole ran out the door the next day, there standing in the yard was a decrepit, sway-backed, old nag that Clark had rented for the day![11] Late one evening they were sitting on the patio, as they usually did whenever they got the chance, watching the sun set. "Ma," Clark turned to her and said, "we're lucky people. We've got this ranch and while its not going to support us it feels like a ranch and it smells and looks like a ranch. It's not just animals and hay. We've got the house just fixed to suit us and we've both got good jobs, good friends, money in the bank and our health. God's been good to us. Can you think of anything you want that you haven't got?" Carole took a slow sip of her Coca-Cola and then replied, "Pa, to tell you the truth, I could do with a couple of loads of manure if we're going to do any good with those fruit trees."[12]

They both knew, though, what the one thing was that Carole really wanted and hadn't been able to have. As 1941 drew to a close Carole, with the support of her mother, turned to religion to alleviate her depression over not being able to have a child. Carole's mother was interested in the occult and Eastern religions and was a member of the Bah'ai faith. Not many people knew of Carole's search for some meaning, but one day she asked their friend, Adela Rogers St. Johns, whether she believed in God. Upon being assured that their visitor did believe, Carole commented that she had always thought of God as being "in the mountains and the desert. I don't think God is a softie either. In the end it's better if people are forced back into — well — being right before they're too far gone. I think your temple is your everyday living." Then, apparently without any sense of prediction, Carole said that she never saw herself as growing old, and that she had no mental images of how she would look in the future or of what she would do. While she saw herself with a small baby, she did not see them together when the baby had grown up. "I like it when the going gets tough," she commented, "if you wait for everything to be just right in your life you'll never get any happiness. You have to fight for it and get it anyway. The minute you start fighting for anything, you've won. The end doesn't matter.... There's got to be something after all this — after this life — where you can use all you've learned here, or nothing makes any sense."[13]

When the Japanese attacked Pearl Harbor on December 7, 1941, Carole wanted to fight for what she believed in. Remembering their recent conversation with President Roosevelt, she and Clark sent a letter the next day volunteering to do whatever they could to help their country. Carole's advance plan was for her to join the Red Cross or one of the women's armed services branches and for Clark to enlist. Clark wasn't quite so quick to jump at that idea; after all, at forty-one he was a tad older than the usual age for enlisting. Apart from that, he'd put in years of hard work to achieve his present comfortable life and top-of-the-heap $7,500 a week, and he wasn't about to risk it all.

Carole went back to work on the set of *To Be or Not to Be* with Jack Benny, but she wasn't her usual joking self. About a week later a reply came back from Roosevelt to their letter. To Carole's disappointment, he wrote that they would best serve their country by continuing to appear in films and so help public morale. Carole wouldn't take no for an answer, though, and kept badgering Clark. He had MGM's support, but they probably had more mercenary than patriotic reasons. While young Mickey Rooney had been classified 1-A for the draft, which they were appealing on grounds of essentiality, any involvement by Clark would be voluntary because of his age. The studio was not about to approve the loss of their major investment in such a risky venture as staying alive in a war zone.

To reinforce their point of view, MGM assigned Clark to a new picture beginning production in early 1942, *Somewhere I'll Find You*, and then blotted their copybook with Carole by co-starring Clark with Lana Turner again. Resignedly, Carole signed on for Co-

lumbia's *They All Kissed the Bride* during the same period rather than be home without the man she loved so much.

One thing that she could join Clark in, however, was the Hollywood Victory Committee, which was set up three days after the Pearl Harbor attack to enlist the movie industry's support for the war effort. Because of his eminent status, Clark was elected chairman of the Screen Actors Division, and the first meeting at the Beverly Wiltshire Hotel on December 22, 1941, had enough screen actors there to look like Academy Awards night. Clark spoke to the large crowd about the goals of the Committee and urged them to volunteer their services. A coordinating team of fifteen was chosen: Clark, Jack Benny, Charles Boyer, Claudette Colbert, Ronald Coleman, Gary Cooper, Bette Davis, Irene Dunne, John Garfield, Cary Grant, Bob Hope, Myrna Loy, Tyrone Power, Ginger Rogers, and Rosalind Russell.

Carole indulged in her usual gift giving at the on-set wrap party when shooting finished for *To Be or Not to Be* on Christmas Eve. Then she left with Clark for MGM where he was hosting entertainment for servicemen. The Gables' own celebrations were more conservative; instead of a gift, most friends received a card saying that a donation had been made in their name to the Red Cross. They saved their presents for each other and for Jean Garceau and her husband, to whom they gave an early-American bedroom set. Clark gave Carole a pair of ruby and diamond clips to match her ring and ruby heart; she gave him a slim gold cigarette case inscribed: "Pa — Dear — I love you — Ma."

New Year celebrations were very quiet. News from the war front wasn't good. Hong Kong had fallen to the Japanese; London was being bombed. Congress had passed new legislation that all men between eighteen and sixty-four should register for the draft, although only those between twenty and forty-four were immediately eligible. MGM now couldn't continue to actively discourage Clark from service, although they lobbied for him to take a commission and a quiet desk job. Carole fumed when she heard that and said he should enlist as a private instead on principle.

One of the first requests the Hollywood Victory Committee received when it reconvened that year was for a star to promote the sale of U.S. defense bonds in Indiana. Carole, a native Hoosier from Fort Wayne, was an obvious nomination. The request came to Clark as head of the committee, and he gave his ok. Frustrated at not being able to take up a rifle herself, Carole was only too glad to seize this chance to do something for her country in its time of need. Clark was unable to go along because of his commitment to making the Washington trip and to starting *Somewhere I'll Find You* on schedule. So Carole's mother, Mrs. Elizabeth Peters, said she'd go. At the last minute Cornwall Jackson, one of Clark's agents, couldn't go in his place, and so Clark asked their friend Otto Winkler from MGM to accompany Carol instead.

Carole ordered a new street coat, a dress, and a strapless black velvet evening gown with a silver fox cape from her designer friend Irene, and she bought a new outfit for her mother. On the way to Indianapolis she stopped off at Salt Lake City and Chicago to give speeches and press interviews in support of war bonds.

When the train pulled out from Los Angeles' Union Station on January 12, 1942, with Carole on board, Clark was not there to wave goodbye. Both Jean Garceau's and MGM's explanation for Clark's absence was that Clark had gone to Washington to discuss his military future with officials there, including U.S. Air Force General "Hap" Arnold, and that Carole unfortunately had to leave the day before Clark's return.[14] However, Carole had certainly not been happy about Clark working with Lana Turner again in his forthcoming film. She had also been hearing rumors for a while that Clark was being seen with another young MGM actress. They may have quarreled about this situation before Clark left,

and it's possible he had walked out.[15] In any case, he wasn't there, and Carole was clearly upset. As she left the house, she handed Garceau a series of notes that she'd written for Clark, one for each day she would be away. Hugging and kissing her, the usually undemonstrative Carole said: "Take care of my old man for me, will you, Jeanie? You know you'll be working with him more and more now."[16] Clark returned home the next day. Carole called him from Salt Lake City to tell him about the huge crowd that had gathered despite the freezing weather. Then she called again from Ogden and from Chicago.

They reached Indianapolis on January 15 and went immediately to the state capitol for a flag raising ceremony. It was the same flag that had flown over the White House the day the United States declared war on Japan. As it unfurled into the air, Carole raised her hand with her fingers in a victory salute and shouted: "Heads up, hands up, America! Lets give them a cheer that can be heard in Tokyo and Berlin!"

Three thousand people were lined up in the lobby to buy bonds. As she took their money, Carole gave each person a receipt on which was her autographed picture and the words, "Thank you for joining with me in this vital crusade to make America strong." That night Carole appeared on the stage of the Cadle Tabernacle, where three military bands and a color guard contributed to what must have been a moving and memorable experience for the ten thousand people there. An African American choir sang the Lord's Prayer. Carole stood in her strapless black gown and long black gloves, and as the audience joined her in *The Star-Spangled Banner*, accompanied by the bands and a pipe organ, she was so overcome that tears ran down her face. Will H. Hays, who had been so unimpressed by her appearance in that article about unmarried Hollywood couples, was so impressed by this appearance that he wired Clark, "Great day here. Carole was perfect. Really, she was magnificent. They sold in this one day

$2,017,534 worth of Defense Bonds and Stamps, with a quota of only $500,000. Everyone deeply grateful."[17]

Later that night, after all the spectacle was over, an exhausted Carole suggested that they fly home rather than return by train. She had been away from home too long and couldn't wait to see Clark again. She may have figured in advance that would be the case and that she would want to reach home quickly. Despite having a round-trip train ticket, she had only given Jean Garceau five notes instead of seven or eight that would have covered the longer train-trip period, and she had told a reporter in Salt Lake City that she planned to be back for the *To Be or Not to Be* premiere on January 18.[18] Arriving at the airfield at four a.m., they found that the first plane out would have no room to sleep. Winkler suggested that they would be able to sleep better on a train and arrive more rested. Carole's mother also suggested they not take the flight; a devout believer in astrology and numerology, she added the numbers concerning the name of the pilot, the number of the flight, and the registration of the plane and didn't like the results. Carole laughed and suggested they toss a coin for the decision, tails for the plane. Winkler produced a quarter; they tossed, and it came down tails. At the airport, she told *Life* photographer Myron Davis that, though strongly urged to go by rail, she had been "unable to face three days on the choo-choo train." The downside of flying would be that when she got home, she said, she would probably have to "flop into bed and sleep for twelve hours."[19] They flew out of Indianapolis on TWA Flight 3.

This flight had originated in New York and still had a few stops to make. At midmorning she wired Jean from Kansas City, saying she was dead-tired and eager to be home. Winkler wired Clark to meet them at Los Angeles Airport at eight that evening. Their last stop was Las Vegas. By the time the plane took off just after 7 p.m., fifteen of the seats were occupied by Ferry Command pilots and personnel. Only one other civilian, Mrs.

Lois Hamilton, was aboard with Carole, her mother, and Winkler, making a total of nineteen passengers. There were three crew members: Captain Wayne Williams with fourteen years of flying experience, copilot Morgan A. Gillette, and hostess Alice Getz.

As the plane's wheels were leaving the runway, Clark was at home making sure everything was just right for her return. He'd finished his first day of shooting on *Somewhere I'll Find You* that day and he and good friend Larry Barbier, one of the MGM publicity team, had driven out to the airport to check on Carole's arrival time. Barbier went in, only to find officials evasive about the plane's location. Sensing something might be wrong, he told Clark to go home and that he would call him there when he had news. Clark had invited Carole's brothers and Otto's wife back for dinner with he and Carole. True to form, he had a gag ready for Carole, too. When Clark had returned on January 13, he found a buxom blond mannequin that Carole had left tucked into their bed with a note pinned to it that read, "So you won't be lonely." It was kind of a hint not to get too friendly with Lana Turner, and perhaps any others, while Carole was away. In return, Clark, Robert Sterling (cast as his brother in the film), and Lew Smith made up a male dummy, complete with prominent erect penis, which Clark took home and tucked into Carole's bed. The table was set, fresh flowers were everywhere, and the house looked beautiful. Then the telephone rang. He picked it up. It was Barbier. Carole's plane had gone down at about 7:30 p.m.

Meanwhile, Barbier had called Eddie Mannix and Howard Strickling, who told him to charter a plane, and then Barbier called Clark. The first person Clark thought of turning to was Jean, who said she'd be right over, and then he called Fieldsie, who reminded him that a plane Carole had been flying in had at one time actually caught fire and she had survived that. When Clark told her that Strickling was on his way to the airport and

Ralph Wheelwright was driving to pick him and Jill Winkler up, though, she realized that the studio thought something serious had happened. She drove over to the Gables' place to wait for news.

As they rushed to the airport all they heard from the radio was ominous news. There was still no word about the plane and its passengers since workers at the Blue Diamond mine had seen a flash in the sky and then heard an explosion about thirty miles southwest of Las Vegas. "It was then," Ruth Waterbury wrote, "that Gable paid one of the prices of fame, the inability to get even the most horrible news quietly and privately."[20] Clark had to walk through a crowded airport that went silent the moment he came through the door, and endure all those eyes on his grief. Because of wartime regulations, officials made Mannix sign for the plane before it could take off, only to land again to pick up Strickling who had just rushed through the gate. It must have seemed like forever to Clark before the plane touched down in Las Vegas. Howard Strickling recalled, "Clark was the biggest man I ever knew, in every way.... In the plane that night I thought he was going to squash me. He was so tense, you know, because he had sensed what had happened. You knew you shouldn't talk to him. You knew not to say, 'It's going to be all right,' or, 'I'm sorry.'"[21]

Once they touched down in Las Vegas, they all went straight to the sheriff's office. There they found the mayor, Howell Garrison, and a group of deputies, local people, and military police from Nellis Air Force Base huddled over maps, plotting the best way up the rugged slopes towards the crash site. A Western Airlines pilot, Art Cheney, said that he had seen a fire burning on Table Rock Mountain, one of the high peaks of the 8,000 foot-high Charleston Range between Nevada and Death Valley, as he had flown over it. Ralph Wheelwright would recall that Clark's face went white, as if he knew then that there was little hope.[22]

Two ambulances went out from Las Vegas, followed by twenty-five cars and trucks of soldiers, police, cowboys, miners, Indian guides and anyone else who knew anything about that remote spot where there was no road, only snow-covered foot trails. They readied packhorses and stretchers, and then waited at the tiny hamlet of Goodsprings until daybreak. Predictions were that it could be twenty-four hours before they located the crash site and brought news back. Clark, feeling helpless, started out with a search party but the terrain grew too rough for the horses, and with no replacement mounts they had to turn back. Doing something was his way of handling the savage grief that kept welling up, threatening to overwhelm him, and that he kept pushing down, way down inside. One of the men who were there that night said later: "Imagine the biggest, strongest, most vicious animal hurt, cut to pieces — well, that's how he was that night."[23] They suggested that, instead, Clark should wait in case they brought Carole back and he wasn't there to meet her. So he waited at the El Rancho Vegas hotel with Jill Winkler, Stuart Peters, and Howard Strickling for hours, pacing back and forth, trembling like some big caged beast.

Eddie Mannix and Ralph Wheelwright joined the small second search party that set out at dawn on January 17. Shoes were shredded on the rugged terrain as they waded for miles through waist-high snow and struggled along inclines that were sometimes so steep the slope was only a foot from their faces. When their party located the crash site in a ravine six hundred feet below the summit at about 10 a.m., there was little of anything or anyone left. Off-course and 1,800 feet below the correct altitude, the plane had flown straight into the rock wall of the peak two hundred feet from the summit at 150 mph, exploding into tiny pieces that had slid down into the ravine, scattering so far that the surrounding woods had been set alight in one gigantic funeral pyre. Ira Galdner, an Associated Press photographer, said that it looked like "someone had taken a toy airplane and smashed it against a big rock."[24] Which of the bodies was actually Carole's was determined by a very educated guess by Mannix and Wheelwright. It would have to be confirmed later with the help of her dental records. Which of the bodies were even military, civilian, or crew could only be distinguished by buttons and scraps of cloth. The pilot's briefcase was found three hundred feet away.

On the way down, Mannix and Wheelwright found a lone telegraph station and sent a wire to Clark to let him know that there had been no survivors. Clark had impatiently driven up into the foothills early that morning, but hearing no news had returned to the hotel. When he was told what the wire said, he merely moaned tiredly, "Oh God!" When asked what he was going to do, Clark shook himself as if to shoulder away the shock and then said he would wait until they brought her down.[25] After that, he stayed quiet and calm, but he wouldn't eat or sleep.

Despite everything that could be done, there was some looting of the wreck. A gunnery-school recruit quietly approached Wheelwright later, offering a small piece of one of Carole's ruby and diamond clips, saying he should get something for it. Wheelwright suggested jail if he didn't hand it over.[26] Then, without saying how he came by it, he took the jewelry fragment and gave it to the big man who held it tight in his hands. With the help of Army officers, all the personal articles taken from the wreck were eventually recovered.

Clark's friend Al Menasco arrived, as did Spencer Tracy, to offer support. Clark asked if Al could drive him out to the foot of the mountain, from where they could see the spot the plane had gone down. When they got there, Al explained to Clark what he thought, in his pilot's experience, might have happened, and that seemed to help. Then Clark stepped out of the car, walked off a ways, and just stood there looking off into the distance at that snow-covered peak for a long time. He was probably saying goodbye; he could have been asking for answers, but in any case he never told anyone. He had no way of knowing that one day, nearly at the end of everything, he would come full circle and again find himself looking out into the distance toward Table Rock Mountain.

CHAPTER 20

AFTER THE DANCE

The man who came away from that mountain, said his friend Adela Rogers St. Johns, "was a blind giant, maimed, wounded almost to death, trying afterward to find his way in darkness."[1] For many years to come, Clark would be haunted by Carole's ghost and would go through the motions of living, until he again found happiness toward the end of his life.

It was two days after the crash before Carole's body and those of eight others could be brought down off that mountain and taken to Las Vegas. The bodies had to be wrapped in Army blankets and lifted by hand and ropes four hundred feet to the top of a cliff, then carried for miles down narrow trails on horseback to the tiny community of Goodsprings in the foothills, where they were transferred to vehicles. Carole's body was the first to be positively identified. A hastily convened coroner's inquiry officially confirmed her cause of death. Wheelwright thought that Clark shouldn't have to endure such a traumatic task, so he officially identified Carole. Only when that was done did Clark first venture from his hotel room, where he had been since Saturday, to choose Carole's casket and to make a drive out into the foothills to talk to the men who were waiting there for the rest of the bodies to arrive. Then he returned to base camp and

helped serve food to the exhausted men as they returned. The story is often repeated that on seeing one of the men gumming a steak he gave the sheriff a $100 bill to buy him some teeth.

By the night of January 20 all the bodies had been retrieved. Clark proceeded to make arrangements for the transport of Carole's, her mother's, and Otto Winkler's bodies back to Los Angeles.

Carole's death was mourned across the nation. President Roosevelt wired Clark the following words of consolation:

> Mrs. Roosevelt and I are deeply distressed. Carole was our friend, our guest in happier days. She brought great joy to all who knew her and to the millions who knew her only as a great artist. She gave unselfishly of her time and talent to serve her government in peace and in war. She loved her country. She is and always will be a star, one we shall never forget nor cease to be grateful to. Deepest sympathy.[2]

Later FDR awarded Carole a medal as the first woman to be killed in action in defense of her country. Secretary of the Treasury Morgenthau wired his sympathy, and *The New York Times* editorialized that "Like the Army pilots who fell from the burning plane with her, she too dies in the service of her country."[3]

In Los Angeles, stillness descended over the movie studios at noon on January 19 as "Taps" was sounded in her memory. The preview of her movie with Jack Benny, *To Be or Not to Be*, was canceled, but United Artists insisted they would release it in mid–February as scheduled after changing the advertising theme. Ernst Lubitsch decided to cut Carole's now sadly ironic line to Jack Benny: "What can happen to a woman in the air?"[4]

Many of her friends and colleagues expressed their shock and sorrow. Fieldsie was reported prostrate with grief. Robert Taylor said it was all "too terrible." Ginger Rogers said that the world had lost a star who "had brought joy to millions and her associates have lost a wonderful friend." Marlene Dietrich lamented, "We grieve, all of us, in Hollywood." Spencer Tracy seemed to sum up the feelings of everyone when he added, "So little can be put into words when a tragedy of this kind strikes."[5] In Washington, the Senate halted its schedule of business to hear Republican Senator Willis from Carole's home state of Indiana rise and speak in her honor. Not to be outdone, his Democrat counterpart, Louis Ludlow, read into the Congressional record Carole's final speech in Indianapolis, which asked the public to purchase defense bonds.

CBS radio commentator Elmer Davis became a voice in the wilderness, crying rather cynically that America still seemed to be a country where even in wartime the death of a movie star could be given greater attention than the deaths of the fifteen fliers in the plane with her at the time. After all, the group included two brothers and had been called "the honor roll of the command." It wasn't the right time to be cynical. Davis caught the edge of Walter Winchell's angry tongue for his pains and retired from the field.

There was some speculation, quickly refuted at the Civil Aeronautics Authority hearing into the accident, that because those personnel were aboard, the crash might have been the result of sabotage. In due course, the official investigation put the accident down to pilot error. All instruments and flight documentation had been destroyed in the explosion, and in those days there were no "black boxes" in cockpits to record what might have happened. With such a lack of evidence, it has remained uncertain as to exactly why the experienced pilot of the TWA plane was flying seven miles northwest from his correct course and below a safe altitude that night.

All of which would have been of little comfort to Clark, watching through unseeing eyes as the countryside unrolled like some vast, dark tapestry outside his train window. That long, lonely journey back to Los Angeles with the three wooden caskets in the baggage car must have seemed endless. To avoid the crowds waiting at the Los Angeles station, Clark was met at Colton by MGM people with an ambulance to take the caskets to Forest Lawn and a limousine to take him back to his friend Al Menasco's home in San Gabriel.

Carole had been horrified by the public spectacle surrounding her friend Jean Harlow's death and funeral. Consequently, the very first clause in her will requested that "no person other than my immediate family and the persons who shall prepare my remains for interment be permitted to view my remains after death has been pronounced. I further request a private funeral and that I be clothed in white and placed in a modestly priced crypt in Forest Lawn Memorial Park, Glendale, California."[6] Despite the army being in favor of a military funeral because of the nature of her mission, Clark obeyed Carole's wishes to the letter with the one exception that she could not have anticipated: that it would be a double funeral for her and her mother.

So on January 21, 1942, a service for both women was held in the Church of the Recessional at Forest Lawn Memorial Park. Only a small, select group of reporters was admitted for the simple ceremony. There were just forty-six mourners, including Mr. and Mrs. Jack Benny, William Randolph Hearst and Marion Davies, Mr. and Mrs. Ernst Lubitsch, William Powell, Spencer Tracy, Myrna Loy,

Will Gable, and Carole's three aunts. The identical, gray, closed coffins were covered in gardenias and orchids. Floral tributes by the truckload had been arriving for hours before the funeral. Following Carole's instructions, the Methodist minister Dr. Gordon C. Chapman read from John 14 and Psalm 23, then recited a short poem that was a favorite of the two women:

> The dark threads are as needful
> In the Weaver's skillful hand,
> As the threads of gold and silver
> In the pattern He has planned

and a quotation from the Persian philosopher Baha'u'llah: "I have made death even as glad tidings unto thee. Why dost thou mourn at its approach?"[7] Clark sat next to Carole's brothers, Frederick and Stuart Peters, solemn-faced and dry-eyed behind dark glasses. When the service was over, the coffins of the two women were carried down the slope to the Sanctuary of Trust in the Great Mausoleum, where they were laid to rest side by side. "Each was," Dr. Chapman said, "in fact what she seemed to be, devoted, generous, gifted, kind. Each shouldered life's responsibilities with resolution and rare goodwill. Each accepted life's genuine pleasures with glad and grateful hearts."[8]

It wasn't until Clark returned to the ranch after the funeral for the first time and Jean Garceau handed him Carole's last note that he finally allowed grief and tears to take him for a while. It was as well they did because the next day he had to sit through Otto Winkler's funeral as well. Clark blamed himself for Winkler's death, having asked him to accompany Carole as a personal favor. Consequently, he promised Winkler's widow that he would do all he could for her.

Then came the sad business of settling Carole's estate. Clark waived the right to sue the airline. Carole's will was opened on January 24. She had left everything, except for some insurance annuities, to Clark. Filed with the county clerk three days later, the will was admitted to probate on February 10. Contrary to reports that Clark became a wealthy man through inheriting over $500,000 from Carole's estate, the inheritance tax appraiser's report dated October 26, 1943, values her total estate at $296,417, including nearly $89,000 in bank accounts, close to $24,000 in stocks, real estate valued at $23,450 and an estimated $75,000 interest in five RKO pictures, courtesy of her contractual arrangements. However, not included in that valuation total until the taxation assessment was completed were figures relating to her four life insurance policies, which had a total face value of over $118,000, but which were only assessed in terms of taxable annuities at $82,389. This may be where some of the confusion has arisen over the estate's value.

In any case, there were three major factors that greatly reduced the estate's financial worth. First, there were taxes and expenses of well over $170,000. Second, only two of the insurance policies were payable to Clark. A $10,000 policy was payable to Carole's life-long friend Fieldsie, and a $25,000 policy was payable in equal amounts to Carole's two brothers. Last but not least, Myron Selznick made a successful $27,500 claim on the estate owed to him from the judgment of Carole's lawsuit. The final valuation of Carole's total estate, then, was put at $208,286, of which Clark's share was only $179,879. However, it would take another four years, no doubt complicated by Clark's overseas duty, before all the business of the estate administration was finally completed and Clark's petition for distribution of Carole's estate was finally allowed. This could explain reports that Clark made a shrine of Carole's room, leaving everything exactly as it was. Clark was not a morbid person given to enshrining anything; he was one for getting on with life. He simply would not have been able to legally do anything with Carole's personal effects until 1946.

However, there were some things he could do. Otto Winkler had always planned to build a house on land across from the Stricklings. Clark told his widow, Jill, to go ahead and that he would finance it. Carole had also owned a number of acres of land on which lived a retired couple from Indiana, who had been close to her. Clark continued to care for them, and when he eventually sold the land some years later he made sure another lot was purchased and a comparable home built there for them.

Production on the sadly ironically titled *Somewhere I'll Find You* was shut down for a month to give Clark some time to recover. Joan Crawford substituted, unsuccessfully, in what would have been Carole's next starring role in *They All Kissed the Bride*, costarring Melvyn Douglas, with the understanding that all of her $112,500 salary would go to charity.[9] However, some Hollywood cynics saw that as just an attempt by Crawford to reinstate her relationship with Clark now that Carole was gone.

Clark, meanwhile, was a lost man. For three weeks he retired to where he had always found peace, with his friends the Gibsons at the Weasku Inn on the Rogue River in Oregon, where he slept in his usual room at the top of the stairs and fished out in the river. Sadly, "Rainbow" Gibson had died in 1938, but Peggie and the three girls had carried on running the resort. Even here, though, he couldn't escape memories of good times he and Carole had shared together. At the time, Sybil Gibson was twenty-five. "Clark worshipped Carole and her death was very hard on him," she recalled later. "I liked Carole a lot; she was a good partner for him."[10]

Eventually he had to return home, where he would walk around the ranch, aimlessly looking at the garden, stop by the stables to console Carole's horse Melody in the stable, or just sit in the Dodge wagon in the garage that he and Carole had bought for their camping trips. He never drove it again. For a while Clark talked about selling the ranch and half-heartedly looked at some other houses, but in the end he didn't seem to seriously want to leave the place where he'd found so much happiness.

Always a man who believed in the ethic of work, Clark plunged back into acting again with a determination to take his mind off his loss. Before he returned to the MGM studios and the set of *Somewhere I'll Find You* on February 23, though, he expressed a wish that the title be changed because of its associations for him. The studio, however, were all too aware that the public would make their own associations with the title. While they made a show of using the name *Red Light* while the film was in production, they couldn't in the long term resist the lure of marketing appeal and reverted to the movie's original title for its release in August 1942. One of those unique films overtaken by events in which fact weighs heavily on the fiction, *Somewhere I'll Find You* bore more than its fair share of irony. Produced, like *Honky Tonk*, by Pandro S. Berman and directed by Wesley Ruggles, who had directed Clark and Carole in their only film together, this picture tells a love-triangle story of two brother journalists who compete for the love of another female correspondent during the Japanese invasion of the Far East and Bataan. The situation is tragically resolved when the younger brother is killed in action. Consequently, the script said a lot about death and heroism. When Clark on his return heard that it was being rewritten to save him from potential pain, he bravely insisted that it be left as it was.

Lana Turner, his costar, recalled that Louis B. Mayer called her into his office as they were about to resume shooting and told her that the situation could be very trying all round. He advised her to be very patient with Clark and that "if his mind should wander, don't be upset, you just be ready at all times. If he wants to come in earlier, you be there before him. If he wants to work through lunch, do it. A lot of the pressure of this picture will be riding on your shoulders. We're trying to arrange for people to go home with him for dinner. If he should ask you, go."[11] Clark did invite her for dinner one night, and she went. He was polite and cordial, and they avoided talking about Carole. After dinner, Clark showed Turner his gun collection and how he had been restoring and polishing some of the pieces. Then he had the studio limousine take her home. "After that evening my esteem for him grew even greater," she commented. "He was the consummate professional. No wonder they called him the King."[12]

He talked to others, though, in particular to his close friends Adela Rogers St. Johns and to Joan Crawford. St. Johns later wrote that Clark felt that most people were uncomfortable talking about someone who had died, but he felt that talking about Carole would in his own way keep her alive through memory. He didn't want to forget his great love.[13] Joan Crawford sent Clark a note that if he wanted to talk, she would be there for him as he had once been there for her. Talk he did one night while she listened, knitted, and kept the ice bucket filled. She advised him to stop feeling guilty because he hadn't gone on that trip with Carole. "The next day I received twelve dozen red roses with the longest stems I had ever seen," she recalled. "For the next four or five months Clark stopped by the house every single day. He wasn't the gay romantic Clark I had first known, he wasn't the easygoing Clark, he was a moody man who needed friendship."[14]

It certainly didn't help his frame of mind when *To Be or Not to Be* was released, and the media was full all over again with tributes to Carole lauding her performance and mourning her premature death with patriotic fervor. A navy air squadron being recruited in central Indiana was named "The Lombardiers," and they painted Carole's profile superimposed on a map of Indiana on their fuselages. Souvenir magazines were published, mythologizing the story of the Gables' life together. Clark took to drinking a little more heavily than usual while he sat up alone late into the night running Carole's movies. In June he made a rare public appearance to attend the funeral of John Barrymore, who had done so much to help Carole's career when they had appeared together in *Twentieth Century*. Inevitably, much about Clark changed. "He seemed to tap deep reservoirs of strength within himself which carried him through," recalled Jean Garceau. "There was a new maturity about him, often an almost spiritual quality in his face, and we all felt a stronger man was emerging from this tragic experience."[15]

From the day before Carole's funeral, Clark had made his future intentions clear. "There is nothing left for me in Hollywood now. I cannot stay there," he was quoted as telling friends, adding that he would apply to serve in the air corps as soon as possible.[16] For the moment, the studio bided their time and waited to see which way the wind would keep blowing. They offered to star him in a film about flying ace Eddie Rickenbacker, but Clark, remembering all those words he'd had with Carole, couldn't see himself now doing anything but the real thing for his country. He began to seriously investigate the military service options open to him. The air corps initially told him he was too old for active-service enlistment, but he kept insisting that was what he wanted to do. "I don't want to sell bonds, I don't want to make speeches and I don't want to entertain," he said. "I just want to be sent where the going is tough."[17] When he went there, he took Carole with him. The only part of her that came back from that mountain, the piece of her ruby and diamond clip, was in a small gold box that Clark wore on a chain around his neck.

CAPTAIN GABLE

It was a chance meeting with U. S. Army Air Force Captain Luke Smith in a restaurant in Phoenix, Arizona, that gave Clark Gable a clue as to which tough area to head toward. Smith commented that the AAF was finding it difficult to recruit gunners. Everyone wanted a piece of the glory that rubbed off onto pilots. If Clark could join the AAF as a gunner, he'd be doing a lot for the morale and recruitment among the ordinary guys of the bomber crews.

At first the thought of their major star actually going into real combat gave MGM heart failure. In fact, they had done their best to divert the AAF's attention away from him. On January 23, the Lieutenant General Chief of the AAF, Henry H. ("Hap") Arnold, had sent Clark a wire via MGM that he had a specific job in mind for Clark in the air force if he wanted to take them up on the offer.[1] MGM promptly buried the wire in a file, and Clark never saw it. Late in May, Clark's draft board sent Eddie Mannix a notice that Clark was being considered, and Eddie tried desperately to have the matter deferred. The studio legal department swung into action to prepare an affidavit pointing out how essential Clark was to the war effort right where he was, working for MGM.

However, Clark had plans and was making preparations of his own. He talked over with Jean how to keep the ranch running in his absence, and he made provision for the staff. Martin was found a job in a defense plant; Jessie went to another place as a cook. All but fifteen of the chickens were sold, and the cars were jacked up on blocks in the garage. Late in July, Clark personally offered his services to the AAF. He went through his physical exam in early August after a delay in order to have needed dental work done. On August 11 the War Department notified Eddie Mannix that Clark had been accepted. That same day, Lieutenant James M. Stewart became a bomber pilot at the Albuquerque air base.

The following day, Ralph Wheelwright drove Clark to the Los Angeles recruiting office to be sworn in. Half a floor of the Federal Building was roped off and guarded to keep the ceremony as quiet as possible. Clark, who had rejected offers to take a commission, was sworn in as Private Gable (SN 19125741) by Colonel Malcolm Andruss. When Clark raised his hand to swear that he would serve his country with honor, his emotion was such that it shook noticeably.

Taking the oath immediately after Clark was studio cameraman Andrew J. McIntyre. Changing tack swiftly, the MGM spin doctors

Clark being sworn in as a buck private by Colonel Malcolm Andruss, August 12, 1942, in the Los Angeles Federal Building. (Spicer collection.)

had realized what they could do with the story of a $357,000-a-year star making the ultimate sacrifice for his country for about $800 a year.[2] Of course, what they left out of the story was that Clark wasn't sacrificing quite that much. After all, a star still had a life style to which he had become accustomed to which he would expect to return. So MGM quietly arranged an annual "service salary" for him of $150,000, just to make sure he returned to them.[3] However, Clark was probably more concerned that the extra money would allow him to keep his ranch and have the staff look after it for him while he was away. After he had gone, Jean brought home Clark's personal effects from the studio dressing room. She didn't mention to him that she found another note to Clark from Carole. She put it away in his safe-deposit box to await his return.

Clark was sent to the Officer Candidate School in Miami, Florida. Word slipped out about his travel route, and he was mobbed by hordes of fans at every stop. At Houston, a huge crowd of screaming women delayed the departure of his train. When Clark and his fellow trainees arrived in New Orleans on August 15, they encountered the same reception. Hundreds of women had begun to gather at the station as word had spread of his approach. When he finally managed to break through the throng and find a taxi to take him to his Florida train, it was only to find it had left without him. Women continued to follow him around the city as he waited for the next train to leave that night. He reached camp at Miami Beach the next day to discover that the AAF public-relations machine had turned his first haircut into a media spectacle. He had to unhappily endure the removal of the nation's most famous mustache being recorded for posterity. Then a sergeant tossed him his uniform. Holding up the baggy pants, Clark looked at him quizzically and was gruffly told that both he and the pants would shrink a bit.

At forty-one, Clark was older than the average officer candidate. Although reasonably fit and a big man, he'd been doing a bit of drinking lately and had slipped out of condition. The king was about to be reminded of life back among the common folk.

Life in OCS was tough, not least because Clark had started ten days behind the rest of his class. Reveille was at 4:15 a.m. and there was a morning march before breakfast. There were drills and exercise routines and more marching. There were floors and latrines to scrub and insulting remarks from officers who regarded a star recruit as fair game. Even his fellow recruits were a little wary of him, until one morning in the washroom he took out his upper false-teeth plate and, waving it in the air in what would have been a familiar gesture to some of his friends, called out: "Look at the King of Hollywood! Sure looks like the Jack now, don't he?"[4] After that, they were on his side, coming to appreciate him as they got to know him better and realizing that he just wanted to be accepted. One of his fellow candidates said later that "Gable did not like people to paw him or yes him. But he would do anything for you. Once I was sick and he saw that I was fed.... We borrowed from each other and always paid each other back.[5]

What also made it more difficult for Clark were the ever-present female fans. They would line the fences to watch him train, and they would try to get into the hotel that was serving as a barracks. His roommate, Sergeant Hyman Grossman, wrote home in early September that Clark might be moved to another wing of the building because "there are too many entrances.... There are loads of women every morning watching us march — looking for Gable. Mr. Gable is not a young chicken and the heat here is really tough on him, and on top of that he's been taking those shots, which are plenty tough."[6]

One fellow recruit who remembered Clark vividly that summer was writer A. E. Hotchner, who was also undergoing, as he so eloquently put it, "thirteen weeks of the most grueling physical and mental hell imaginable.... We were kept in a constant state of nervous and physical exhaustion, the purpose being to crack us if they possibly could and wash us out as potential officers."[7] Every day at 4 p.m., when the temperature was well over the century mark, all candidates were paraded at attention in full equipment for extended periods. If somebody fainted once, it was a demerit; if he fainted twice, he was washed out. If anyone fainted during the parade march, the ranks were not to break stride even if it meant stepping on the fallen man. Ambulances, or "meat wagons" as they were known, circled the parade ground like vultures picking up the unconscious and battered bodies.

Hotchner had entered OCS a few weeks before Clark, and although he had seen him from a distance, he'd never met him. Walking down the street toward the Olympic Hotel one day, where they were quartered, he came upon a tired and sweaty Clark slumped on a bus-stop bench with one shoe off and a very badly blistered foot bared. Clark asked him if he had a needle with which he could lance them. Hotchner had, but taking one look at those blisters the size of quarters he recommended Clark seek proper medical attention. Clark replied that there'd be too much fuss if he did. "I understood," Hotchner later recalled. "If you're Clark Gable you're not allowed to get blisters. The heroic seaman of the *Mutiny on the Bounty* would not get blisters." They operated on the spot. Later, over a Coke at the canteen, Clark admitted that until he had arrived at OCS, "I thought I was in pretty good shape.... That hike today, my backpack felt like four hundred pounds. My legs were gone.... The heat's really getting to me and I've got twelve weeks to go. I really don't know if I'll make it.... Maybe they want to [flunk me] just to demonstrate that OCS is so tough and impartial they can even flunk Clark Gable."[8]

They survived, though. Hotchner met Clark once more a few weeks later when they were paired up for a midnight to 4 a.m. patrol along a beach. They were instructed to shoot anyone on the beach who didn't know the password "American eagle." No one crossed their path, however, and after a couple of hours of monotonous sand patrolling they took a break. Carefully cupping a hand around his glowing cigarette, Clark commented that while they'd been marching up and down he'd been thinking about Carole, and he started to talk about some of their time together. He told the story about them making love in the duck blind, and he talked about the time Carole had jumped into Fred MacMurray's fishpond in her evening gown. He remembered the gags they'd pulled on each other, the gifts they'd exchanged, the picnics they'd shared, and the Sundays they'd spent on the ranch just being themselves. "He made a funny little sound," recalled Hotchner, "I thought he was chortling over the incidents, but then in the moonlight I could see his tears.... What I did understand was the enormous love Gable had had for this woman."[9] As Clark wept, he told Hotchner that he knew exactly what little they had found of Carole on the mountain. Reaching inside his shirt, he showed Hotchner the piece of her earrings that had been found up there and which Clark always kept with him, along with her picture in a locket he had made by fitting a metal cover to his dog-tag. Then their break was over, and they had to resume patrolling. After that night, Hotchner never saw Clark again.

As examinations loomed, Clark, a high-school dropout from the tenth grade, became worried that he wouldn't be able to get through class-work in such areas as military law, transportation, and supply. It would mean embarrassment on a national scale if he ended up being transferred back to the infantry because he couldn't pass officers' exams. It was his actor's training that eventually helped him; he was so used to memorizing lines from a page of script that he could quickly memorize the mimeographed sheets they were given to study for tests. He would wait until lights out and then retire unseen to the bathrooms, where he would study in a cubicle for hours in his bathrobe.

His system worked; Clark graduated seven-hundredth in a class of 2,600 on October 28. He took the oath with his classmates of 42-E, accepting his commission as Second Lieutenant Gable, 0565390. By then, he was so well liked and admired by his class-mates that they had asked him to respond to Lieutenant General "Hap" Arnold's address, during which Clark said: "The important thing, the proud thing, I've learned about us is that we are men.... Soon we will wear the uniforms of officers. How we will look in them is not important. How we wear them is a lot more important."[10]

Clark then proceeded to Tyndall Field, near Panama City, the closest gunnery school in Florida to Miami, to study something he at last knew more than a little about: firing guns. He was still finding actual flying a bit hard to cope with, for obvious reasons. He grew his mustache back, had his uniforms tailored for him, and he looked every inch the well-groomed air force officer. On the occasions when he came into Panama City, one of Clark's favorite dining places was Mattie's Tavern in St. Andrews, famous for its hush puppies, fried chicken, steaks and seafood. However, word about his arrival had spread quickly through Panama City, despite efforts to keep it quiet, and Clark's fans followed him persistently, asking for autographs and even buying up his dinner checks. Eventually a frustrated Clark and the AAF issued a notice stating that "Lieutenant Gable will appreciate it if the public will not interfere with his training. He wishes to be treated like every other member of the service."[11] While on base, Clark practiced firing rifles, and .30 and .50 caliber machine guns. He and his classmates were repeatedly drilled on enemy aircraft identification. Models and silhouettes of planes were mounted in conspicuous places all over the base, hanging from the ceilings of squadron day rooms, the mess hall, and wash-rooms.

Clark couldn't wait to be back at the ranch for Christmas. On December 18 he called Jeanie and asked her to meet him at the airport the next morning at 11 a.m., as he didn't want to let the studio know in case they made a big publicity deal out of his leave. All Clark wanted after his crowded months of training was some rest and peace and quiet. Flying over Texas, his plane had engine trouble. For a few moments, he might have wondered if his life would end in the same way as Carole's. Jeanie was still there waiting for him when his plane finally got in at seven that night. He spent time around the ranch and saw only his father and a few close friends with whom, inevitably, his conversation would turn to Carole and his memories of her.

Jill Winkler invited Clark over for a dinner party one night, quietly making sure that Virginia Grey just happened to be there helping decorate the tree when Clark arrived. It had been years since Clark and Virginia had seen each other, and they spent the evening renewing a friendship that would endure for many more. When he was due to return to duty, prior to Christmas Day, Jean drove him back to the airfield. He was flying out in a B-17, and he gave her a guided tour. After walking her back to the car, he sat with her for a few minutes quietly. Then turning to her, he said, "Jeanie, you know I have everything in the world anyone could want but one thing. All I really need and want is Ma."[12]

Clark was awarded his silver wings by Colonel W. A. Maxwell when he graduated from gunnery school as a first lieutenant on January 6, 1943. "They have blood in their eyes," he said of his classmates. "They want to see some action, and of course I want to see some action too."[13] Before long, he would see quite enough. Four days later he arrived at his first posting, Fort George Wright in Spokane, Washington, where the Second Air Force trained and organized bomber crews for combat duty. On January 28, he was assigned to the 508th Squadron of Colonel William Hatcher's 351st Heavy Bombardment Group, of the Eighth Air Force's First Air Division, then based at Pueblo, Colorado.[14]

The following month, General "Hap" Arnold and General Luther S. Smith, AAF Director of Training, confirmed that Clark would be producing a training film on the daily activities of a typical heavy bombardment group, with special emphasis on gunners. There had been alarming casualties among aerial gunners, and the AAF hoped that a training film featuring such a famous personality would stimulate interest in recruitment. Clark informed Hatcher that he wanted Lee Mahin, who had been the scriptwriter for *Too Hot to Handle* and *Boom Town*, as writer for the film. Mahin, however, was serving happily in combat intelligence and had no desire to be anywhere else. Hatcher flew Clark to New Mexico to collect the unwilling Mahin, who commented later that Clark looked a little stunned by the whole thing, as though he wasn't yet sure he could pull this new role off. To Mahin, he was "an actor worrying about his role, really. He had a role to play, dammit. He was America's hero going out to help, to be with the kids, none of whom believed he would do anything at all."[15]

In fact, no one really believed Clark would be doing anything. None of the 351st, from Hatcher on down to the grease-monkeys, seriously thought Clark Gable was ever going to put himself in a position where he would actually get shot at when they got to Europe. As far as they were concerned, Clark was going to have to prove his capability in combat situations and, typically, he did just that.

Within days after the 351st's mid–April arrival at the Peterborough Air Base in Polebrook, about eighty miles north of London, Clark was right in the thick of the action where he wanted to be.[16] While they were waiting for the 351st to become fully operational, some of the senior officers along with Clark drove over to nearby Molesworth to fly

Clark Gable with the crew of the B-17F bomber 8 Ball MK2, *lead crew for Mission #33 to Antwerp by the 303rd Bomber Group, 4 May 1943. (L-r: Sgt. William Mulgrew, Sgt. Richard Fortunak, T/Sgt. Roman Zaorski, Sgt. Murel Murphy, Lt. Robert Yonkman, Lt. Col. William Hatcher (co-pilot), Capt. William Calhoun (pilot), Lt. Joseph Strickland, T/Sgt. Charles Terry, S/Sgt. Willard Stevens, and Capt. Clark Gable.* **(Photograph courtesy of the 303rd Bomber Group Association.)**

some missions with crews of the 303rd Heavy Bomber Group, the "Hell's Angels." The 303rd had arrived towards the end of the previous year and were already seasoned bombing veterans, with valuable experience they could share with the newcomers.[17] Clark was invited to fly on his first mission with Colonel Hatcher, who would be in the copilot's seat on board a 303rd B17, *8 Ball*, piloted by Captain William R. Calhoun Jr. on a bombing run to Antwerp.[18] By modern standards a B-17 was not a big airplane, only 74 feet long with a wingspan of 103 feet. Flying flat-out and empty, its maximum speed was 300 miles an hour. With a full bomb-load and crew of ten, four officers (pilot, copilot, bombardier, navigator) and six gunners including an engineer and radio operator (top turret, ball turret, waist and tail), speed was reduced to around 200 miles an hour at an altitude of 20,000–25,000 feet. The B-17 had been christened the "Flying Fortress" because of its heavy

armament of .30 and .50 caliber machine guns. Nevertheless, the B-17F was known by the German Luftwaffe to have a profound weakness when attacked head-on and a nasty habit of catching on fire when hit.[19] Clark was not flying "milk runs." Flying on bombing missions in a gunner's position, which had the worst casualty statistics of any crew position, he was in real danger every time he went up. During various missions, shells went right through the fuselage next to him. *Ain't It Gruesome*, for example, was hit over fifteen times while Clark was flying in it. When they saw that Clark was prepared to face their danger, his fellow-fliers accepted Clark as one of them.

His English fans accepted him just as whole-heartedly as their American counterparts. It did take the people of the nearby village of Oundle some time to become accustomed to seeing a famous Hollywood personality strolling down the High Street,

Capt. William R. Calhoun with Clark Gable, 4 May 1943, after Mission #33 to Antwerp by the 8 Ball Mark 2, 303rd Bomber Group. Calhoun had been pilot on the mission. (Photograph courtesy of the 303rd Bomber Group Association.)

Clark appeared in dress uniform in this popular and widely issued wartime public relations photograph, summer 1943.

but they found Clark affable and obliging. He could be seen touring around on his motorcycle, drinking in local pubs such as the King's Arms or the Rose & Crown, and he became a keen softball player. He would stop and chat, sign autographs for school boys, stop by the Market Place tailor to have a button sewn back on his jacket, and keep his shooting skills honed by targeting rooks on local farmland. Lorna Sloan still clearly remembers the day Clark dropped by with some of his friends for an afternoon tea that eventually became quite a party. "There was a shortage of booze in those days," she recalls, "and so we took Clark along to the George here on the corner. We had a great big enamel jug and went to fill it up — and poor old Mrs. Marriott who kept the pub opened the hatch and saw Clark Gable there and nearly passed out!" She remembered Clark as basically a "very quiet retiring sort of a chap, though, who didn't want to be recognized at all."[20]

Clark, dressed in the flying suit he wore as a gunner, admiring the Flying Fortress Delta Rebel.

Outside of the local area, it was a different story. His periods of leave were usually spent in London where he was in demand for dinners and functions with the press, military brass, English aristocracy, and other celebrities. During July he joined with Bob Hope, Frances Langford, and Tony Romano for a show at Polebrook's Red Cross Club. As usual, he was often mobbed by over-enthusiastic fans; Mahin recalled having to literally pull women off Clark's back when they went into Blackpool.[21] The enemy also recognized his popularity; according to General Ira Eaker, two captured German fliers informed him that Hermann Goering offered a promotion and a month's leave to any pilot who could bring Gable back alive to a German airbase.[22] Typically, Clark refused to listen to suggestions that he carry false identification papers, claiming that his face was too instantly recognizable. He declared that he would rather go down with his plane than be captured alive and exhibited in Germany.

In comparison with the average bomber crewman though, Clark's monthly missions did not amount to a heavy flying schedule. In the meantime, he and Mahin and the five-man film crew, Captain Andy McIntyre as first cameraman, Lt. Howard Voss as sound man, M/Sgt. Merlin Toti as film assistant, and M/Sgt. Robert Boles as operating cameraman, were busy touring airfields and interviewing and filming returned bomber crews and wounded personnel. Like all of his work, Clark treated this job professionally, rising at 7 a.m. to be off in his jeep to work by 8:30 a.m., seven days a week. On at least one occasion, he waxed a tad too enthusiastic about his gunnery for the sake of public relations. During his first press conference, some seven weeks after his arrival in England, he climbed into a B-17 waist gunner's position and fired off a few rounds into an embankment to demonstrate to the assembled press how easy it all was. A bullet glanced off a rock and embedded itself in the plane's wing. One of the journalists dryly noted that had it deflected in the other direction, few might have remained alive to tell the story.[23]

Clark did most of his aerial filming on board Lt. Theodore Argiropoulos' plane, *Argonaut 3* (29851 YB-J). He flew with them to Villacoublay on June 26, and on July 24 he flew in the same plane to Heroya, Norway, with Lt. Robert W. Burns. It would be this plane and crew that would feature in what would become *Combat America*, the end product of Clark's work and the only film that he would direct. As the name suggests, there were

three planes. The first *Argonaut* (29821 YB-F), was badly damaged on May 14. *Argonaut 2* (29817 YB-D), was shot down with Lt. King on June 28. *Argonaut 3* would eventually have to be abandoned over Norfolk by Lt. Argiropoulos and his crew, due to damage on October 10. Despite the loss of the three planes, the entire crew amazingly survived all their missions intact.

By the middle of August, Clark was back in the air again, flying on a raid into Germany on August 12. He flew in Captain John B. Carroway's bomber, *Ain't It Gruesome* (29863 RQ-Y), probably in the daylight attacks on the synthetic oil plants at Gelsenkirchen and Wesseling in which twenty-five bombers were lost.[24] The plane came back riddled with holes, having been attacked five times by fighters. On September 23 he flew in Major John R. Blaylock's B-17 *Duchess* (29925 TU-L) in a raid on Nantes, in France. During this mission, they came under such heavy attack that Clark once more left his camera to help man the guns. This fifth raid was his last, and he was awarded the Air Medal on October 4 for "exceptionally meritorious achievement" and his "courage, coolness and skill" while under fire.[25] McIntyre and Boles were also awarded medals for their work under combat conditions.

Clark had been flying in such hazardous situations that some people had begun to wonder if he didn't have something of a death wish. Frank Capra later claimed that he had a conversation one night with Clark's commanding officer, which would have been Colonel Hatcher, in London in the lobby of Grosvenor House. Noting that Clark looked as though air force life was agreeing with him, he asked how Clark was doing. The officer revealed that Clark was "scaring hell out of us, that's how he's doing. The damn fool insists on being a rear gunner on every bombing mission. Public relations, my eye! He's a hot potato! And I'm pulling every string to get him out of my command. Guy gives me the willies. Know what I think? Gable's *trying* to get himself killed. Yeah! So he can join up with his wife."[26]

It is little surprise then, that Clark Gable and the "Little Hollywood Group," as the film crew had come to call themselves, were put on notice to be sent Stateside after barely six months in England. They had shot fifty thousand feet of film. Clark denied he'd been any sort of a hero and was, he said, just happy to be going home, having earned the respect of his peers.

He returned home only to find that the AAF had forgotten why they had sent him off to England in the first place. Anyway, they no longer had a gunner problem. His adoring public hadn't forgotten him, though. When Clark visited the Pentagon on October 27 for what was supposed to be a routine press conference, the predominantly female staff all tried to fit into the corridors at the same time just to catch a glimpse of him. Clark was pretty much free to work where he chose, so he returned on November 2 to the place he knew best, MGM, where in December they negotiated a continuation of his pre-war contract until its expiry in three years. For $7,500 a week he would make two pictures a year. The contract would come into effect when he left the AAF.

In January 1944, Gable, Mahin, and editor Blanche Sewell set to work to make something out of their fifty thousand feet of unwanted combat footage. The result was four air force training films,[27] and one major promotional film, *Combat America*, that didn't see general release in theaters because the Office of War Information claimed it paralleled the film *Memphis Belle* too closely. The actual reason may well have been *Combat America*'s over-the-shoulder realism and grainy style. While it is quite similar to current "real-life TV" styling, it was very different to the patriotic glamorization of war that OWI preferred the general public to see. John Huston had exactly the same problem with his documentaries about shell-shocked and traumatized soldiers. *Combat America* was eventually

released in 16mm for use in training, and in clubs and wartime factories. While necessarily patriotic in tone, it gives the general public back home an insight into the training and day-to-day life of bomber crews. The film pulls no punches, with interviews of wounded airmen and live combat footage showing bombers under attack and being shot down while on missions. As it was meant to, the film focuses on gunners, in particular gunner T/Sgt. Kenneth Huls from Okalahoma and T/Sgt. Philip Hulse from Springfield, Missouri, the top turret gunner of the *Argonaut 3*. Huls confirmed that the film really came to grips with how the war had been from their perspective. While never a commercial film in the same league as *Memphis Belle*, *Combat America* survives as a fascinating historical insight into the personal side of World War II aerial combat.

However, Clark was now much too valuable a commodity to ever be allowed to see active service again, and he remained an unhappily grounded public relations tool for the rest of his service time. On January 8, 1944, he was badly shaken when rear-ended by another car on Hollywood Boulevard. He was by all accounts only faintly impressed when he was promoted to Major on June 1, given that the AAF then promptly confirmed reports he had been placed on the inactive list and that he would probably be returned to civilian status shortly. Eleven days later, on June 12, Clark's honorable discharge papers were signed by a certain Captain Ronald Reagan of the AAF Personnel Office in Culver City.

Ironically, not long after his period of service ended, Clark was reminded of how it had begun when he had the sad duty of speaking at the launching of the Liberty ship, *Carole Lombard,* at the Terminal Island Docks of the California Shipbuilding Corporation in Wilmington. On January 15, 1944, fifteen thousand workers and guests heard Clark speak of the importance of the Liberty ships in the war. After Irene Dunn, a close friend of Carole's, broke the traditional bottle of cham-

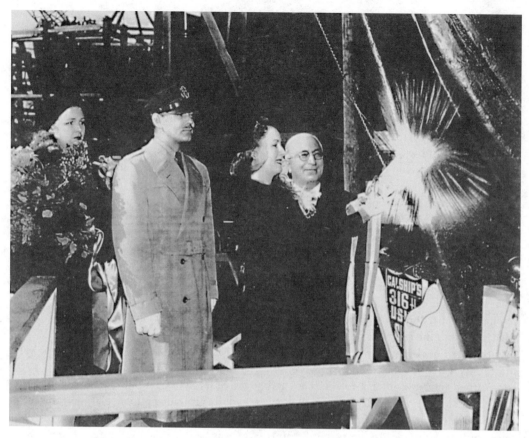

Irene Dunn breaks the bottle to launch the liberty ship Carole Lombard *on January 15, 1944. On either side are Mrs. Walter Lang, Clark, and L.B. Mayer.*

pagne over the ship's bow, Clark stood at attention saluting, watching with tears running down his face as the ship bearing the name of the woman he'd truly loved slipped away from him, just as Carole had slipped away.

CHAPTER 22

SOMEWHERE I'LL FIND YOU

In the strange new world of 1944, MGM didn't seem to know quite what to do with Clark Gable. The stars in the studio's heaven had moved, and worlds had turned if not collided. Everything was bigger now, but not necessarily better. MGM covered 120 acres with a wardrobe department that could handle more than 5,000 people a day. Even the studio police department now had over fifty men working in it. Clark must have felt like Rip Van Winkle returning home to find that an age had passed in what seemed like the blink of an eye, and now there were few familiar faces to be seen. Crawford, Garbo, Loy, MacDonald, and Shearer were gone; only Lana Turner had stayed. In their place were the likes of June Allyson, Judy Garland, Greer Garson, Katherine Hepburn, Margaret O'Brien, and Elizabeth Taylor, most of whom had been children in the 1930s.

There had been administrative changes at MGM, too. Mayer was now so involved in breeding racehorses that he rarely showed up at the office anymore, and the studio was essentially being managed by committee, or "bureaucratic dictatorship" as writer Frances Marion termed it.[1] Eddie Mannix and a couple of executives essentially managed the studio. Two key producers had gone: Hunt Stromberg because of illness and Bernie Hyman because of a fatal heart attack. They had been replaced by Pandro S. Berman, who had been with RKO, and Joe Pasternak from Universal. Whereas Thalberg had produced forty-five films a year with half-a-dozen supervisors, it now took forty producers to achieve the same output. Nor had their attitudes to women's roles improved with the times; of almost forty directors the studio had under contract, Dorothy Arzner was the only woman.

With Americans flocking in droves to see anything on the screen that would take their minds off the war and whether Johnny was going to come marching home some year, the studio was practically running itself. No one was feeling particularly creatively challenged. Musicals and lighthearted family fare were the typical order of the day.

The other problem was that by now people saw Clark as a combination of St. George and King Arthur. He was a legend who had slain dragons, but he was now a king tragically without his queen, who had returned from his crusade a hero only to find the kingmakers dubious about his future role. There seemed to be no script worthy of his attention; there seemed to be nothing for the once and future king to do. Clark's friend Adela Rogers St. Johns was hired as his story consultant, but even she had problems finding a suitable vehicle for him. Clark tried to describe for her what he saw as his place in the public eye. They saw him scared and in trouble, he said, "but coming out fighting…. They see life with a high price tag on it, but they get an idea that no price is too high if its life…. The things a man has to have are hope and confidence in himself against the odds, and sometimes he needs somebody, his pal, or his mother, or his wife, or God to give him that confidence. He's got to have some inner standards worth fighting for or there won't be any way to bring him into conflict. And he must be ready to choose death before dishonor without making too much song and dance about it."[2]

Nevertheless, MGM couldn't ignore Clark's value to them. Estimates were that so far his films for the studio had grossed $275 million. For twelve consecutive years prior to his entering the AAF, Clark had placed among the top ten box-office favorites; his nearest male rival had been Gary Cooper. Finally, in May 1945, a desperate studio threw Clark into a film called *Adventure*, which had originally been intended as former child star Freddie Bartholomew's comeback vehicle. Clark's old friend Victor Fleming would direct, and Greer Garson was costarring. "Gable's back and Garson's got him!" shouted the advertising slogan created by MGM publicist Emily Torchia. Garson might have had a grip on Clark, but Clark didn't have a grip on either her or the film, for a number of reasons. As he told Louella Parsons in 1947, "I blame myself as much as anyone that it wasn't as good as my earlier movies. I had war jitters. Like every other guy back from the service, I was nervous and restless. I was pressing too hard. We were all pressing too hard. Result — it was all very depressing. When it was over I realized that I would have to get away and fight this thing out for myself."[3]

Probably as part of trying to deal with his loneliness, Clark was drinking heavily. His other costar, Joan Blondell, later recalled that he perspired a lot and that his head would

tremble noticeably when Clark was under pressure.[4] David Niven blamed the shaking on the Dexadrine that Clark was using to fight the weight he was putting on from drinking. He observed that on his return Clark "seemed to have lost interest in making pictures." After all, after fighting in a war, "it seemed so childish for a fully-grown man to put on makeup and spend the day playing charades."[5] Jimmy Stewart, on his return from flying twenty missions, was likewise physically and emotionally devastated as a result of his experiences. There was gray in his hair, and he had aged noticeably. He couldn't sleep because of nightmares, suffered from digestive problems due to stress and anxiety, flatly refused for decades to discuss what he'd been through, and accepted only one post-war film role as an officer in uniform in a war zone. Clark, too, would never speak of what he'd experienced up there. Colonel Ramsay Potts, commander of the 453rd Bombardment Group, once summed it all up in these words: "I think that the experience was so profound and the danger so great that you would feel when talking to people who hadn't experienced it that maybe they'll think I'm exaggerating, maybe they'll think I'm bragging, maybe they'll think that I'm trying to make this out to be more than it really was. But the fact of the matter is that it was an extremely hazardous, dangerous task every damned day you went on one of these missions."[6]

Having been away from the film business for some three years, Clark had lost a lot of his working momentum and his skills were rusty. Prior to the war he had worked on movies practically one after the other; this was the longest break between pictures he'd ever had, and it was going to take him a while to get back up to speed again. Then, of course, unlike Niven and Stewart's return into the arms of family, Clark had only an empty house to come back to. For a long time while he was in the service, it must have been easy for Clark to say to himself that Carole hadn't really died, that she was still back there waiting for him

Ready to roll for Adventure *in 1945. L.B. Mayer, Greer Garson, Clark, and Victor Fleming.* (Spicer Collection.)

like everyone's wife and girlfriend. It would not have been until he arrived back to a house where many of her things were still set out in her bedroom and bathroom as though she would walk through the door any minute, but where she was never going to walk through any door again, that the emptiness of it all must have hit him very hard indeed.

For his own sake he had to find his way back into his life and his work without her, and it would take him a while to find the right path. However, he did. "Every picture I make," he would later comment, "every experience of my private life, every lesson I learn are the keys to my future. And I have faith in it."[7]

Clark would have needed a lot of faith to find the key to his future in *Adventure*. Adapted from a novel by Clyde Brion Davis called *The Anointed*, it was a project about which Clark had reservations from the beginning. He had asked Frances Marion her opin-

ion of the script when he had been handed it. She promptly told both he and Fleming that she thought Clark's role was a "mishmash" that offered him "no scenes of cumulative drama or comedy."[8] Clark plays a sailor, Harry, who wanders into the San Francisco Public Library one day with his good friend Mudgin (Tom Mitchell). They are searching for, of all things, Mudgin's soul which has wandered off because Mudgin promised God he'd reform when he was shipwrecked and, of course, once rescued he's done no such thing. Instead of Mudgin's soul they find icy, prim, librarian Emily (Garson). Harry melts her heart, though, and they eventually elope to Reno and marry, to the amazement of her party-girl flatmate (Blondell). The thirties Clark would have gone for blonde bombshell Blondell; the postwar older, wiser, and more moral Clark goes for ex-Mrs. Miniver Garson.[9] While Emily is serious, for Harry it's all a lark. He goes back to sea, leaving Emily who threatens to divorce him. Mudgin rebukes Harry and is then fatally injured in an accident. His dying words send Harry back to Emily just in time for his first-ever prayers to revive their stillborn baby.

Unfortunately, such turn-arounds in the behavior of Clark's characters never really ring true, and this one is less convincing than Blackie Norton's earthquake-prompted conversion at the end of *San Francisco.* They're all patterned on that well-used Mayer and Hays, Old Testament template of sin-retribution-redemption. Somehow it's that whole redemption thing that just doesn't jell with the Gable characters. They seem, after all, to be having so much good honest fun being such unrepentant sinners that the whole concept of them asking divine forgiveness for merely being their charmingly roguish selves always feels forced and implausible. The audience is being asked to suspend just a bit too much disbelief.

Adventure had other problems, too. Vic Fleming was a director of action films, not philosophical ones, and the picture suffers from his heavy hand. Sparks simply fail to strike between Clark and Greer Garson. Clark is at his best onscreen with warm, earthy girls like Jean Harlow, Ava Gardner, and Lana Turner. He had a lot of trouble relating to the more prim and refined type, such as Jeanette McDonald and, as it happened, Greer Garson. MGM publicist Emily Torchia recalled, "Gable and Garson never hit it off. He'd look at her as if she weren't there ... when I saw him put on that regal chill with other women, it was like fifty degrees below zero."[10] Clark was never happy with *Adventure,* and would later grouse that, "I didn't like it from the first. I suffered through five and a half months making it and the public suffered through two and a half hours seeing it."[11]

However, the public didn't seem to suffer enough to prevent the film doing moderately well at the box office to the tune of some $4,500,000, mainly because of its star appeal and some favorable critical comments. *Time,* for example, although noting that the film

"was clearly carpentered to the old Gable formula," considered that it generated "as bright a piece of cinema comedy as has shown up this season."[12] Maybe there hadn't been much bright comedy that season.

After it was over, Clark felt he needed some time out and left for some fishing at his favorite place, the Weasku Inn along the Rogue River, where he'd become quite interested in the second Gibson daughter, Carol, who was then in her early twenties. During their many fishing and rafting expeditions along the river, the two had become close friends, and Clark had come to call Carol his "girl on the Rogue." Her sister Vee recalled in 1998 that their relationship grew "pretty serious there for awhile. In fact, although nobody would believe it, Clark did ask Carol to marry him, and she refused. At the time he said that he didn't want to have any children, and he was quite a bit older than her, too." By now, Clark had come to like the area so much that he purchased some thirty-eight acres in 1945 that included his favorite fishing spot, the Pierce Riffle. He was such a fixture around the Inn, where the Gibsons treated him like one of the family, that many people actually thought he was a part owner. He'd call Vee "Junior," sit down with Peggie and the girls and their step-father, Ced Hefferan, around the kitchen table for a lunch of corned beef, red Bermuda onions and dill pickles, and then help out with the dishes.[13]

When he returned to Encino, Clark gradually started to become more social. It was if he'd gotten something out of his system up on the river and now he was ready to start being with people again. He had brought a love of motorcycles back with him from England, and soon became part of a bunch of middle-aged motorcycle riders that included friends such as Ward Bond, Andy Devine, Vic Fleming, Al Menasco, Bill Wellman, Keenan Wynn, and Howard Hawks. With them, Clark could feel one of the guys again. With little patience for out-of-date equipment, he owned a number of meticulously maintained bikes over the years, including a Square Four Arial, a 1941 Harley Davidson 61 cubic-inch Knucklehead Twin, and a Triumph Trophy.[14] The group would convene on Sundays in the driveway of Hawk's home in Morago Drive before heading out. Competition among them was not necessarily over who had the fastest, but who had the shiniest bike, so they called themselves the Morago Spit and Polish Club. Hawks even had sweatshirts printed up for them. Even so, the Club did like to let the bikes out on straight, empty roads where one of their favorite games was playing high-speed tag at ninety miles an hour.[15] Clark had a solid reputation for his excellent riding that was respected widely in Hollywood right down to the younger actors. James Dean once commented that he was "a real hot shoe," and went on to explain that, "When you ride you wear a steel sole that fits over the bottom of your boot. When you round a corner, you put that foot on the ground. If you can really ride, you're called a hot shoe. Gable rides like crazy."[16]

Clark's ride through his next few movies, though, was nowhere near that hot. His work was certainly professional enough but rarely inspired. Opinion was, and still is, divided as to the merit of many of his 1950s movies, but much of this difference of opinion is because critics are prone to forget that one is looking at a very different man than the prewar Clark Gable. For one thing, he had been matured by his war experiences and by Carole's death, both physically and mentally. For another, despite initially being sadder and lonelier in his private life, he was more confident and assured about his professional status. As far as his adoring public was concerned, that status was set in concrete.

However, long-term contractual ties to the studio, coupled with both their and the public's rather set opinions about what roles they preferred to see him in, meant much of that concrete was set around Clark's feet. For the next few years Clark would pay a price for such security. Having pushed him to the top, MGM then seemed to leave him up there without a lot of support in terms of the right movie vehicles with which to sustain the growth and development of his acting ability. Clark would continue to stroll easily and pleasantly onscreen, though at times unhappy and frustrated off-screen, and walk through the work that the studio gave him, always professional, occasionally a little out of his depth, but rarely tested. MGM was content to reap due rewards and maintain Clark's status quo as much as possible, without risking any box-office returns by being too creative. Clark would continue secure as the king at MGM with no serious contenders for his throne.

On the other hand, his security now gave a mature Clark assurance to speak his mind about how unhappy he was with the way MGM failed to nurture his career. In typical Clark fashion, he dealt with his frustration by holding MGM ransom over his contract. If he was going to be treated badly, at least he would extract as much money out of them and lighten his working day as much as he possibly could. In reality, though, Clark and MGM always had rather a Faustian deal going. Clark may have certainly sold his soul to the studio, and admittedly they worked him hard for a few years for long hours. On the other hand, he was always well paid for work that never seemed to unduly stress him in times when many people suffered severe hardship. He rapidly became a wealthy man who could afford to have a lifestyle that most of the people who watched his films could only dream of living. He was famous and loved by the public and by more women than he knew what to do with. He was married five times to women who all loved him and who, with the possible exception of Josephine Dillon, never said a bitter word about him even after he walked out on three of them because they either didn't live up to his expectations or his changing career image. In short, he may have traded his ordinary life to a devil of a studio for the price of some hard labor, but he was given a hell of a reward.

Still, Clark was so unhappy with the way *Adventure* had turned out that he evidently stood on his status and declared that the revised postwar Gable's career would not be treated in this way. For nearly a year, the studio kept paying Clark thousands of dollars while attempted to interest him in a suitable script. At one point they prematurely announced he would star in a film called *Lucky Baldwin*, but Clark refused to go ahead with that. Adding pressure to this stalemate, too, was the ticking clock of Clark's contract. His current seven-year deal was due to expire in 1947. He couldn't keep refusing to work indefinitely. Already rumors were circulating that he was about to retire. On the other hand, MGM was not in good financial condition and could not afford to let a major earner for them slip through their fingers. They needed him back. So, once again, Faust and the Devil sat down to fashion a deal.

For some time, the studio had been trying to persuade Clark to accept the lead role of Vic Norman in *The Hucksters*, based on Frederic Wakeman's runaway best-selling novel for which they had handed over a hefty $200,000 for the rights. It was a brave decision on their part for, in those pre-television times, *The Hucksters* was a scathing satire on the ethics and methods of the radio-advertising industry. The studio must have been aware that many of the book's characters were immediately recognizable to those working in advertising at the time the book was published. Like his antihero Vic Norman, Frederic Wakeman was a war veteran who had gone into the advertising industry only to leave disillusioned by its methods.[17] He had put all his disgust into his character of Evan L. Evans, the president of Beautee Soap, one of the most unlikable heads of business since Dickens created Scrooge. Rumored to be based on George Washington Hill, the Lucky Strike cigarette baron, Evans is portrayed in a wonderfully skin-crawling way by Sydney Greenstreet, who makes a memorable entrance when he hawks loudly and spits messily on

top of a boardroom table to begin a conference.

Clark, however, was not impressed at all by his first reading of *The Hucksters*. It "is filthy and it isn't entertainment," he declared.[18] He objected that the advertising agency boss, Mr. Kimberly, was always cheating on his wife. In particular, however, he was offended that his love interest, Mrs. Dorrence, would be an unfaithful wife cheating on her army-officer husband. He also did not like the way the character of the cynical, disillusioned Vic Norman had been written, feeling that he would come across as "a heel." So the script went back to producer Arthur Hornblow and screenwriters Edward Chodorov, George Welles and Luther Davis for further tweaking. It took some months and a few rewrites, but they eventually appeased Clark's war-veteran sensitivities by having the officer honorably killed in action so that Deborah Kerr would now be playing an honest widow whom Vic Norman rather dishonestly uses, initially, to endorse Beautee Soap and thus get his foot in Evans' door.

Vic is a cynical former advertising executive just out of the Army who returns to his interrupted career only to find himself working for Kimberly (who was rewritten to be merely an amiable if somewhat lecherous drunk played by Adolphe Menjou) on Evans' Beautee Soap advertising campaign. Evans is an abusive and manipulative client who cares only that people hear about his product, not about people themselves as either customers or staff. Despite setbacks, Vic does such a great job on the Beautee Soap radio advertising campaign that Evans offers him a job. Vic, however, finds at last that he has ethics and leaves the job and his career behind. Mrs. Dorrence's honesty and ethics have intrigued Vic. Instead of putting her aside as he has with other women, he ends up falling in love with her.

Finally, Clark was satisfied and agreed to do the film. Then he made a few other stipulations before signing away his life for another few years. After all, as he once said to Z. Wayne Griffin, "I don't like money — any more than the air I breathe."[19] On November 3, 1946, nearly a year after the release of *Adventure,* MGM announced that Clark had signed a new contract, but it kept a watertight lid on any leaks about the contract's advantageous terms for as long as it could, probably just in case any other stars got ideas. Just after he started work on *The Hucksters* in January, though, Clark revealed to *The New York Times* columnist Thomas Brady that his new contract was for nine years at $7,500 a week. The extended term of what would customarily be a seven-year contract was apparently so that Clark would be able to take advantage of the studio's pension plan to provide him with an income if he chose to retire at around fifty-five.[20] Dan Fowler, writing in *Look,* added that the new contract provided Clark with provisions for bonuses and, at long last, percentage cuts from film grosses, and that it also specified he be consulted about the producer, director, cast, and story. He was now expected to complete only one picture a year, although he would often do more, with at least a four-month break between pictures.[21] It seems highly likely that it was this contract that at last gave Clark that long-awaited personal recognition of his status by allowing him to finish work at 5 p.m.[22] It was what he had been waiting for all those years; at last he could look out at the world from the same peak as Garbo had climbed all those years before.

Heading off retirement rumors that had started because of his long period away from work, Clark finally began work on *The Hucksters.* His female costars were the twenty-four-year-old Ava Gardner and the one-year-older English actor Deborah Kerr in her first American role. Kerr had been brought out from England by Mayer ("Her name will rhyme with star and not with cur," he had said) to give him some leverage against the headstrong Greer Garson. He had placed Kerr on a seven-year contract starting at $3,000 a week and scaling up to $7,000 for the last two years.

Those were very close to Clark's 1940 contract terms, and it's possible that news filtering out about Kerr's terms, coinciding with Clark's own contract renewal, could have prolonged and complicated the negotiations. A few years later, Kerr would finally get her chance to play that original character of an army wife embroiled in an affair in the 1953 film *From Here to Eternity,* for which she earned an Oscar nomination and an eternal place in film love-scene history for her steamy embraces amid the surf with Burt Lancaster.

Clark had been impressed by the young Ava Gardner's earlier work in *Whistle Stop* and *The Killers.* He pushed for her to appear with him in *The Hucksters,* playing a sultry nightclub singer who was an old flame. Ava was in turn impressed that Clark actually sat down with her in her apartment before filming began to talk with her, "a little nobody," about the role. "But that was Clark," she said later, "down-to-earth, informal, liking people, helping them, and all done with style."[23] Clark liked Ava because of her forthright manner and language; like Carole, Ava could use "fuck" in a sentence with the same free-spirited variety of explicit emphasis. He prophesied to Louella Parsons that Ava would go far, "perhaps as far as Jean Harlow or Lana Turner. Ava just has what it takes. The first day we worked on *The Hucksters* I was worried about her. It was at my suggestion that she had accepted such a small role, and I wondered if I had done right in urging her…. Then I took a look at the rushes. 'Gable, my boy,' I said to myself, 'Every man for himself. That girl's good.'"[24]

So Clark took Ava under his wing, as it were, helping and encouraging her whenever he could. When it came time for Ava to do her nightclub performance scene, it was late and everyone had gone home. She would have to sing romantically to an empty nightclub set, a daunting prospect. Just as she was about to begin, who should step out of the shadows but Clark carrying a chair. Reversing it, he set it in front of her between the tables and sat down, leaning on his arms across the chair back, listening as she sang even though it wouldn't be her voice that eventually went on the soundtrack. Sometimes, Ava would realize just who she was kissing in a scene and all her coolness and collection would fly right off the set. Suddenly, the thought would hit her that, "*This is Clark Gable!* My mind would be completely blown. Every line, every direction, every little nuance suggested by director Jack Conway, it would go right out of my head. But in some magical Gable way, Clark would understand that, bless him. He'd lean in a bit, all those crow's feet at the corners of his eyes crinkling, his face beaming, and he'd whisper, "Hey, kid, where are we? You stuck? Let me give you a lead." He was always trying to calm me down, always telling me, "You don't see yourself as an actress, and I don't see myself as an actor. That makes us even."[25]

When *The Hucksters* was released on August 27, 1947, critics loved the movie and all three stars' performances in it. The *Hollywood Reporter* summed up the general feeling: "Clark Gable zooms back to the pre-eminent place he held in Hollywood with this smash performance."[26]

Opinion was divided again, however, for Clark's first 1948 film, *Homecoming*. Based on a Sydney Kingsley story titled "The Return of Ulysses," the plot concerns a self-centered society doctor, Ulysses (Gable), who learns the true meaning of humanity through his experiences as a medical officer during the war and through his love for his nurse assistant (Lana Turner), who is eventually killed helping others. He returns home to his wife, Penny (Anne Baxter), and community a changed man.

Despite the advertising that paired Gable and Turner as "the team that generates steam," they didn't generate a whole lot in this imitation epic. *Homecoming* was directed by Mervyn LeRoy, who had always wanted to work with Clark.[27] Many years later LeRoy laid claim in his memoirs to actually having been the one who discovered Clark in the 1930s, despite Clark always having given that

honor to Barrymore, if to anyone. Perhaps LeRoy wanted to lay a smoke screen to conceal the evidence that the first chance he got to direct Clark produced a fairly mediocre performance. Nevertheless, the movie went a long way toward reassuring all those wartime Penelopes that no matter what their husbands may have done while away, they would return home to their waiting families better men for the experience, and so it did fairly well at the box office. The New York critics who rated the film one of the ten worst for 1948 were obviously not as easily impressed.

Clark had returned from his own Trojan War to a Hollywood that was not the same place of austerity as the rest of the nation. It was a party town, and there were no shortage of spots at which to party. There were restaurants such as Chasens, Romanoffs, Ciros, and the Mocambo in which to have a good time, and stars such as Betty Grable, Veronica Lake, Carol Landis, Rita Hayworth, and Anne Sheridan with which to be seen having it. The prewar Clark had been a quiet, ambitious guy who was also married for most of his Hollywood time. The new postwar Clark found himself with time on his hands and in high social demand. He was now willing to take advantage of both to take his mind off his troubles. For the next few years he would keep Hollywood playing guessing games trying to figure out who he might marry next.

Apart from Virginia Grey, the three women who played a major role in Clark's life around this time were Kay Williams, Anita Colby, and Dolly O'Brien. Clark had met Dolly O'Brien at the Stork Club in New York in late 1944, and they had hit it off immediately. Known for her offbeat wit and elegance, she was six years older than Clark, blond, blue-eyed and very, very rich. Her ex-husband was yeast millionaire Julius Fleischmann, and the divorce settlement was rumored to be around $5 million. When she traveled by train, she took her own water, her silk sheets, and one of the great traveling wardrobes of all time. The two of them knew each other for a

An original ad for Homecoming, *released May 28, 1948.* (Spicer Collection.)

number of years, and Clark fell for her enough to ask her to marry him. However, she turned him down, and to his intense hurt and disappointment she went on to marry someone else.

Kay Williams was born Kathleen Gretchen in Erie, Pennsylvania, only about sixty miles from Clark's parents' hometown of Meadville, where in the late thirties she married Parker Capps. Arriving in Hollywood in 1942 after modeling in New York, she picked up a stock contract at MGM. "I acted in a few pictures, but very badly," she later admitted. "I remember getting screen credit in only one movie. But I never liked acting very much. I just wasn't interested in it."[28] Kathleen was a strikingly elegant and animated blond with dancing, light-blue eyes and exquisite taste in clothes, who already had a reputation for her intelligence, her tact and discretion, and her sound judgment. She could be brisk and breezy with throwaway lines, yet she could also be thoughtful and attentive.

One day she got a call from studio executive Benny Thau, who told her that they were giving a farewell party for Clark who was going into the Army. He asked her if she would be Clark's dinner partner. Kay, however, was in the middle of a messy divorce from her second husband, cattle millionaire Martin de Alzaga, and didn't feel like being anyone's partner right then. She turned the invitation down, then turned it down again when Eddie Mannix called a few minutes later, then turned it down again when Thau called a second time. "Apparently," she wrote later, "they just couldn't believe that a young unknown contract player ... would turn down a chance for a date with Clark Gable."[29]

Six months later, home on leave, Clark called her himself and invited her to his home for dinner. Having now been granted her divorce, Kay felt more settled and better able to accept this time. What was going to be an elegant occasion, though, was turned into comedy when Jessie, Clark's beloved cook, tripped over the rug on the way into the dining room carrying the roast and fell. The gravy landed in Kay's lap, and the roast landed between the jaws of Bobby, the retriever, who promptly made off with it. Helpless with laughter, they cleaned up and then shared Kay's bacon and eggs.

For the next twelve months Clark and Kay were good friends, playing tennis and golf, horse riding and fishing together. The pair had much in common, coming from similar rural backgrounds, despite their sophisticated veneers. "Its probably difficult to associate a model and someone who was practically a resident of El Morocco and several other New York clubs with a gal from the farm," she once said, "but that's what I am — a farm girl. I love the earth and I love a home…. I love this place where I live because of its garden as much as anything else. I love the smell of the morning dew on the grass. I love the wind that sweeps in from the sea in the late afternoon. I feel like racing to meet it when I come home from the studio. I'd rather watch a beautiful golden sunset than the best act in the best nightclub in the world."[30]

Is it any surprise that Clark was attracted? They were seen together at restaurants, clubs, and parties and the inevitable rumors circulated about a passionate affair, even that they would get married. John Lee Mahin recalled many years later that "they used to come to my house for dinner, dating like a couple of youngsters. But it was one of those things. After a couple goes together for a while they either get married or go their separate ways. Kay was very much in love with him, but Clark was afraid of marrying again."[31] According to Kay, though, she was a little cooler than that. She would write later that they were not deeply in love that year, using the word "simpatico" to describe their warm, friendly relationship. One night Clark called her to say that he was going to New York and then on location for a picture. "Just as we were winding up our pleasant conversation," Kay recalled, "Clark remarked lightly, 'Please, Kathleen, don't get married again.' We both laughed, then in the same casual tone I replied,

'May I say the same to you, my dear — and bon voyage.' So that was that. Clark didn't write me — not even a scribbled postcard — or telephone me for the next ten years. Nor did I make any attempt to contact him.... I believe we were both guided by fate — and fate decreed we needed a little more time."[32] Kay did get married again, though, becoming for some unexplained reason the fifth wife of sugar magnate Adolph Spreckels, whose four previous wives had all successfully accused him of serious physical abuse.[33] Kay would prove no exception.

Anita Colby, another friend of Clark's, was a rare Hollywood woman. Not only was she a renowned beauty and a famous ex-model (perhaps the first to be known as "The Face"), but by the time she was thirty, Anita had become a $100,000-a-year executive with Selznick Productions. She was still known to be nobody's woman. A friend of Kay Williams and Jennifer Jones, she invited herself to a party at David Selznick's house specifically to meet Clark. She persuaded Joseph Cotten to introduce her, danced with Clark most of the night, and from then on was seen on his arm often. Anita was excited about being seen with Clark, but he seemed to her "the loneliest, most insecure man in the world" who was so nervous at parties and functions that he would shake "so much I thought he was going to drop dead."[34] Anita always denied being in love or having an affair with Clark, and she was customarily one of a group with Clark when they went anywhere. However, they were close friends and she enjoyed being a trusted confidante with whom Clark could talk freely and openly. It was to her that he poured out how he felt about Dolly O'Brien.

Like Carole had been, Anita was quite a quirky gift giver. Clark decided to have a pool installed; typically he didn't want it for himself, but he thought it would provide entertainment for his friends and their children when they visited. Carole had known how Clark hated mess and dirt, and she had been careful to have any work done when he was away. Without her, he had to put up with it, and having to do that kept him in a permanent foul mood for three months. Finally, the pool was completed and filled, and Anita presented Clark with a dinghy in which to row around it which she had named "King III" so the salesclerk would think Clark had a pool big enough for a small flotilla.

Then, on holiday in New York after he'd finished work on *Homecoming*, Clark happened to meet Standard Oil heiress Mary Millicent Huddleston Rogers Salm Von Hoogstraeton Peralda-Ramos Balcom. The very independent Millicent Rogers, as she was called by her friends, was a dark-haired, pale-eyed jewelry creator and collector of designer fashion in her mid–forties who promptly fell madly in love with Clark and pursued him for a year. Unfortunately, she discussed her feelings once too often with a columnist and fell out of favor with Clark, who tolerated publicity about his working life, but who guarded and treasured his private life closely. With her romantic hopes dashed, Rogers stitched her broken heart to her sleeve in the following haunting letter that she forwarded to both Clark and columnist Hedda Hopper:

> My darling Clark,
>   I want to thank you, my dear, for taking care of me last year, for the happiness and pleasure of the days and hours spent with you; for the kind, sweet things you have said to me and done for me in so many ways, none of which I shall forget.
>   You are a perfectionist, as I am; therefore I hope you will not altogether forget me, that some part and moments of me will remain in you and come back to you now and then, bringing pleasure with them and a feeling of warmth. For myself, you will always be a measure by which I shall judge what a true man should be. As I never found such a one before you, so I believe I shall never find such a man again. Suffice that I have known him and that he lives.
>   You gave me happiness when I was with you, a happiness because of you that I only thought might exist, but which until then I never felt. Be certain that I shall remember it. The love I have for you is like a rock. It was great last year. Now it is a foundation upon which a life is being built.

I followed you last night as you took your young friend home. I am glad that you kissed and that I saw you do it, because now I know that you have someone close to you and that you will have enough warmth beside you. Above all things on this earth I want happiness for you.

I am sorry that I failed you. I hope that I have made you laugh a little now and then; that even my long skinniness has at times given you pleasure; that when you held me I gave you all that a man could want. That was my desire, that I should always be as you wished me to be. Love is like birth; an agony of bringing forth. Had you so wished it, my pleasure would have been to give you my life to shape and mould to yours, not as a common gift of words but as a choice to follow you. As I shall do now, alone.

You told me once that you would never hurt me. That has been true, even last night. I have failed because of my inadequacy of complete faith, engendered by my own desires, by my own selfishness, my own inability to be patient and wait like a lady. I have always found life so short, so terrifyingly uncertain.

God bless you, most darling Darling. Be gentle with yourself. Allow yourself happiness. There is no paying life in advance for what it will do to you. It asks of one's unarmored heart, and one must give in. There is no other way. When you find happiness, take it. Don't question too much.

Goodbye, my Clark. I love you as I always shall.[35]

Thanks to Hedda Hopper, who published this letter years later, the only known copy of a love letter to Clark was preserved. Perhaps that was exactly what the very astute Rogers anticipated and why she forwarded a copy to Hopper; maybe it was Rogers' way of having the last word after all. Her words make for an interesting study of how a woman who was otherwise renowned for having an independent, even somewhat notoriously willful, mind of her own was so willing to completely surrender that independence just to be with Clark. He tended to have that effect on women, despite advocating that he preferred women who were "special and distinctive." In much the same way as did both Carole and Kay, the two women with whom Clark had the most successful relationships, Rogers will-

ingly offered, with nuances of religious fervor, to give Clark "my life to shape and mould to yours ... as a choice to follow you." As she said she would, Rogers lived alone for the remaining few years of her life until her death in Taos, New Mexico, in 1952.

Although Dolly O'Brien had divorced her fourth husband and was back within Clark's social circle by now, they were never more than good friends. "We live in two different worlds," Dolly once explained. "You're a rich actor, I'm a rich woman. You like the outdoors, hunting and fishing, but I'm a luxury-loving baby. Your life, frankly, would bore me to death."[36] It was Anita Colby whom Clark stunned with a proposal a short time after his split with Millicent Rogers. She never saw it coming. They had been close friends for some time; he respected her, took her to parties, got a bit jealous about her, and had been concerned for her when she was sick. Anita was very fond of him and was concerned for him too, and they could share some laughs when he was depressed. However, Anita had no idea he felt that deeply about her. Tired of Hollywood life, she was about to go home to New York. Clark dropped by to say goodbye and, evidently unwilling to face the days ahead without his close friend, begged her to consider staying with him. He informed her that as he'd been baptized a Catholic, he could go to the church and have his other marriages annulled. They could have a wonderful life together. Anita, just wanting to go home and not considering herself ready for marriage, could only wonder, "How do you say no to Clark Gable? I also told him he drank too much — he drank Scotch in vases by that time — and he said, "That's because I'm lonely." Poor darling. He was so ready for marriage. I said to him, "Please don't get married right now; you're so anxious, you might make a mistake." He assured me he wouldn't and said he'd see me soon in New York. After I left he wrote me, "The sun has gone from California."[37]

CHAPTER 23

LADY SYLVIA

In late May 1946, Primula Niven (or Primmie as she was popularly known) was killed in a tragic accident during a Sunday night play party at Tyrone and Annabella Power's house. She was only twenty-five. During a game called "Sardines," for which the lights are turned out and then everyone finds a hiding place until there is none left for the last person, Primmie opened a door that she presumed in the darkness led into a closet. Instead, it opened onto the basement stairs and she plummeted to the floor below, receiving such severe head injuries that she died the following night. Clark and Primmie had been friends all her married life, and her death in this manner must have seemed to him as much a pointless whim of fate as that of his own wife.

David Niven and Clark had first met in 1934 when Niven was a poor, young actor earning some money as a deckhand on the *Konig*, a forty-five-foot spear fishing boat that Clark had chartered to take him fishing for marlin. Six months later, Niven landed a small contract with MGM. He was at the 1935 Academy Awards, sitting at a table across from Clark and Ria, when Clark spotted him and came over to wish him luck and advise him not to give up fishing. Niven's first speaking role was in *Barbary Coast*. Clark, who was

working at the studio finishing *Call of the Wild* and who was typically mindful of young actors, came over to the set on Niven's first morning on the job to wish him well. From then on they became close friends, often going fishing together on the Rogue River when the twenty-pound steelhead were running, and playing lots of golf. Needless to say, they talked a lot about acting. "I worked like a son of a bitch to learn a few tricks," Clark once told him, "and I fight like a steer to avoid getting stuck with parts I can't play."[1]

By 1943, Niven had enlisted, returned to England to join his regiment, married Primmie, and was a proud father. When Clark arrived to join his AAF bomber group, he discovered Niven was living only a short distance away, so their friendship resumed until Niven embarked for Normandy. Primmie was a great comfort to Clark as he tried to cope with Carole's loss. One evening she came into the garden to find Clark sitting there on an upturned wheelbarrow, weeping, and she just put her arms around him and held him.[2] He never forgot her kindness. Six weeks after the Nivens arrived back in Hollywood, Clark took them north to Pebble Beach, where he had rented bungalows at the Country Club for a weekend of relaxation. Primmie had written her father, saying it was the happiest she had been in her life. Two days after they returned, she was dead.

Now it was Clark's turn to comfort a shocked and grieving David Niven, who wrote later that "I don't know how people can get through periods of great tragedy without friends to cushion and comfort them.... During that long period of utter despair, Clark was endlessly thoughtful and helpful, and he checked up constantly to see I was all right. Without my realizing it, he was drawing on his own awful experience to steer me through mine."[3]

It is often said that tragedies come in threes. A short time later, Will Gable's wife, Edna, had a heart attack and was bedridden. Clark made a point of going over to see her as often as he could. Despite all doctors could do, though, her condition steadily deteriorated, and she died on June 19. Clark, Will, and Jean Garceau went to her small, quiet funeral at Hollywood Cemetery. Will became quite depressed after that, especially as Clark began planning a trip to Europe. It must have been reminiscent for him of those lonely years after Jennie had died and Clark had gone to Oregon.

A few days later, Clark left for New York, from where he sailed on July 12, 1948, aboard the *Queen Mary*. Anita Colby and Slim Hawkes came down to see him off. Slim was director Howard Hawks's ex-wife; soon to marry Leland Hayward, she was a vivacious and fascinating woman consistently on the ten best-dressed women list. She and Clark had been good friends since his Sundays with the Moraga motorcycle club after the war. As a mark of their fondness for each other, Clark was godfather to her three-year-old daughter, Kitty. Two lonely people at the time they met, Clark still missing Carole and Slim tired of Hawks' infidelities, they often talked over lunch and found they shared mutual interests in the outdoors and horseback riding. Despite Slim's efforts to get Clark and Leland Hayward to like each other, the two strongly competitive men mistrusted each other's motives

on sight. Clark called Leland "Rah-rah Boy" because of his college haircut, while Leland's favorite name for Clark was "Kewpie Doll."

Clark wanted Slim to go with him to Europe, but she had already decided she was deeply in love with Leland and was going to remain in New York. The only way she could break this news to Clark in private was to walk up the gangplank with him onto the *Queen Mary* and into his stateroom. "Clark didn't seem at all surprised," Slim recalled later. "He didn't carry on. All he said was, 'I'm against it. I just think it's all wrong for you.' It was a grown-up scene and not at all mushy." So deep in conversation were they, though, that the bell to go ashore had rung and they hadn't heard it. The ship waited while Slim was found and hurried ashore. Convinced Clark had been proposing marriage to Slim, the press contingent had been going crazy with anticipation. Slim found herself having to deny any proposal had happened. Some time later, Clark sent her a postcard from Europe that simply said: "You were wonderful."[4]

His friend Dolly O'Brien was there to meet him when the ship docked in France, as were the Stricklands. He stayed in the hotel at Deauville for a while, playing at the casino, and attended a dinner party with Dolly given by Elsa Maxwell at the home of the Fellowes-Jordans at Aaribeau, near Cannes. Guests included Tyrone Power, Jack Warner, Virginia and Darryl Zannuck, and the Duke and Duchess of Windsor. For a while, he and the Duke were golfing partners. Clark stayed in Paris, then hired a car and valet and drove to Switzerland. Three weeks after disembarking in France, as he pulled up at his Swiss hotel still feeling the wind on his face, Clark was greeted with a message from Howard Strickling notifying him of the third tragedy: his father had died of a heart attack on August 4, aged seventy-eight, less than two months after Edna had died.

The man whom no one had been able to persuade to board an aircraft since he had stepped out of his last bomber sailed on the next liner for New York and stayed mourning in his stateroom until the ship docked. Once again Clark, Howard Strickling, and Jean Garceau went to another small, quiet funeral, this time in Bakersfield.

Clark refused to hold onto the house he had had built for his father as an investment, preferring to sell it at a loss for cash in hand. Clark always wanted his money right where he could see it, holding it in a number of bank accounts rather than investing it in California's postwar land boom like many other Hollywood people were doing. "You can't get your money in a hurry if it's tied up in real estate," he would say.[5] He would customarily carry $1,000 in cash on him rather than a checkbook for similar reasons. Cautious and frugal, he also resisted advice to incorporate, as quite a few stars had lately. Jean finally persuaded him to invest $25,000 in stocks, but that was as far as he would go.

Clark had returned to MGM to find the situation there had deteriorated alarmingly, and he was concerned about his future. That year, MGM's profits came in at only a little over $4 million, the lowest since 1933. Even worse, once production costs were figured in, they found themselves $6.5 million in the red.[6] Things were so bad Mayer had to auction his racehorses and look around for another production head. He chose a forty-three-year-old Easterner, Dore Schary. Mayer should have stayed with picking horses.

Schary's and Clark's methods could not have been farther apart. Schary liked the concept of "message movies"; Clark liked a simple, solid, entertaining story. Clark was also a member of the Motion Picture Alliance for the Preservation of American Ideals (MPA), the body that was formed to ensure that communism did not gain a foothold in the motion picture industry. Never very interested in politics at any time, the conservative Clark was not an active anticommunist but had joined this widely disparate organization largely because it had been cofounded by his good friend John Lee Mahin and because a number

of his actor friends such as Ward Bond were involved. Clark was evidently not a union man, though; the Conference of Studio Unions blacklisted him and many other leading actors for crossing picket lines outside studios.[7] The CSU informed its members nationwide to boycott blacklisted artists' films, but there is no evidence that the ban had any serious impact on Clark's box-office figures. One of the MPA's other co-founders was MGM executive, writer, and producer James McGuinness, who considered Dore Schary a deep shade of pink. Consequently, McGuinness hampered Schary and created as much friction as he could before eventually leaving MGM with two other executives, but not before the studio was essentially split into pro-Schary and anti-Schary camps. Clark was left somewhere in the middle, not disliking Schary but not trusting him as much as he had Selznick.

Schary didn't help matters when his first suggestion for a Gable film was *Quo Vadis*. Clark promptly refused to appear in a film where he'd be wearing a skirt. Instead, toward the end of 1948, Clark started work on *Command Decision*, a unique movie for him in that it consisted of an all-male cast in the major roles. Based on a successful Broadway play by William Wister Haines set almost entirely on an air force base, there would be no customary Gable romantic interest here to appeal to a wide audience.

Directed by Sam Wood, the film of *Command Decision* stuck closely to the original play and did well, considering it is quite wordy in parts because of that stage heritage. General Dennis (Gable) finds himself in unpopular command of Operation Stitch, a series of daylight bombing raids over Germany during World War II to wipe out production of their new jet fighter. The loss of bombers carrying out these raids is prohibitive. Dennis' superior, General Kane (Walter Pidgeon), can see both his friend's career and the future of daylight bombing at risk. The situation reaches a crisis when mission leader Colonel Ted Martin

(John Hodiak) reveals that instead of bombing Schweinhafen, they bombed a similar town. They will have to go back. Fifty bombers are lost this time, including Martin, and a congressional committee forces Kane to replace Dennis. However, his successor Garnet goes ahead and orders the completion of the Operation, proving Dennis right in the end.

It is interesting that critics, including Adela Rogers St. John, tended to agree that Clark's best scene was one that was written into the film script and was not in the original play. It takes place outside of the otherwise completely interior setting. In it, Clark tries to talk down a damaged bomber being flown by the bombardier with the rest of the crew dead or wounded. It's a magnificent piece of tense drama, all the more so considering that it was presumably shot with Clark looking at nothing in particular; the aircraft scenes would have been cut in later. While Clark excelled in being this sort of officer, tough and strong while all hell was breaking loose, he wasn't quite as good at being the thinking general struggling with the metaphysics of guilt, having sent a few men to certain death to save the lives of the many. Nevertheless, Clark was able to bring to this role a great deal of personal experience indeed; it may have been the closest he got to successful "method" acting. It all must have felt very close to home.

As a favor in return for Dore Schary's promise of better scripts, the first film that Clark did for him was *Any Number Can Play*, a gambling soap opera directed by Mervyn LeRoy early in 1949. Clark plays a casino owner who manages to win back his wife and son's love and approval, prevent a suicide, foil the robbery of his business, and finally deliberately lose a game so that the casino can be owned by its employees. He and his family then live happily ever after. Does it sound a little tangled and contrived? The critics and the public thought so too, and they stayed away from it.

While he was working on this film, Clark struck up a friendship with that other matinee idol with a flashing smile and slim mustache, Errol Flynn, who was on loan to MGM at the time. They often ate lunch together at a nearby saloon that showed films of old prizefights. Clark later observed to Wayne Griffin that Flynn was killing himself by smoking so much "just the same as I'm killing myself." When Griffin's response was to agree that Clark wasn't getting any younger either and it might be worthwhile to cut down on his smoking and drinking, Clark merely replied, "You paddle your canoe, and I'll paddle mine."[8]

During Clark's four-month vacation, he and Z. Wayne Griffin tried to interest Schary in a script in which they both held an interest. When the project was presented to Schary as a package with Clark as star and Griffin as producer, Schary liked the concept and offered $137,000, providing Clark work for his contract salary. When Griffin went back to Clark, he suggested they go for $200,000. To Griffin's utter skepticism, Clark told him to ask for $500,000. This was not a game at which Clark had a good track record, and he should have quit while he was ahead. Predictably, Schary laughed them out of his office, and Griffin had to buy back Clark's interest.[9]

Meanwhile, there were still plenty of women in Clark's life. He was still friends with Joan Crawford and would drop by to see her. Two years earlier, they had attended the opening of the California Cabana Club together, fueling rumors of romance, but the timing never seemed to be right for them to be anything more than just good friends. For awhile, he was seen out with Joan Harrison, an attractive English woman who worked for Alfred Hitchcock. He found himself having to avoid Paulette Goddard, on the other hand, who developed a huge crush on him. David Niven introduced him to Ida Lupino, and Clark would often drop by to sit around and talk about his memories of Carole and his regret that they had not had any children. Gossip columnists such as Hedda Hopper were having the year of their lives suggesting who might be the next Mrs. Gable, while Clark denied everything and insisted he just sat home and watched television or played cards with a few of the boys. "He's got a sensitive quality you'd never suspect," said long-time friend Virginia Gray. "He asks where you'd like to go and what you'd like to do. He knows when you want to talk and when you don't. And when you don't, he doesn't prod you, and keep after you. He is understanding and has lots of feeling. He's lonesome. Everybody tries to tell him what to do, how to run his life, what pictures to make. His nature makes him listen to everybody and weigh things carefully. The result is he's been stung and stung badly a few times, so he tries to withdraw." [10]

During that year, he often withdrew very quietly to a suite at the Bel Air Hotel, apparently just to get some time to be with himself away from prying eyes. Clark had a new Jaguar XK-120, shipped out directly from the factory in England and the first to be seen in California, if not the entire United States. Sometimes he would take it way out into the desert at the high speeds of around 120 mph that it was designed to reach. Out there alone, he started to think again about what it would be like to retire.

Patrick Curtis tells a great story about Clark and that Jaguar. Curtis' father used to act in Westerns for Republic studios. On Saturdays, the cowboy heroes would work half a day, then join their fellow heroes from PRC, Lone Star, and Monogram to lay the dust in their throats at the Smokehouse Restaurant. Then, they would move on to the Curtis house for the weekly poker game. One hot Saturday in July, young Curtis opened the door to find Ward Bond and Victor Jory on the step. They were early, so Curtis went to get his bike so he could go fetch his dad and the rest of the cowboys. Then he heard the most incredible sound coming down the street, like nothing he had ever heard before, "sort of like a P-51 fighter plane. I ran to the curb as the most wonderful car I had ever seen came around the corner. Low, long and very loud, it was dark green with no top. The driver was smiling and waving as the car slid to the curb with a low rumble coming from its dual exhausts. Clark Gable, the King of Hollywood had arrived.... 'Hop in and I'll give you a ride,' said the King." Curtis did. It was three blocks down through the curves of Valley Spring Lane to the restaurant and Clark wanted to see what it would do. He let it out all the way. What it did do was scare Curtis so badly he peed his pants! When they pulled up to the restaurant portico, Clark threw Curtis his soft leather sports coat, telling him to put it on and mind the car while Clark went in. Within minutes the cowboys had surrounded the car and Curtis, whose potential humiliation was now averted due to a considerate king. [11]

Clark never did retire, mainly because he became bored very easily. Besides, he never felt he had enough money, so later that year he started work on his second film for Schary, *Key to the City*, directed by George Sidney. [12] It was produced by his friend Z. Wayne Griffin, who persuaded him to take the part of a mayor who meets another mayor (Loretta Young) at a convention in San Francisco. In a comedy of misperception, their innocent escapades together are perceived as being altogether more significant by others, and they spend much of the time nearly being thrown in jail. Much as in *It Happened One Night*, this is also something of a road movie, during which the pair gradually fall in love as they survive their experiences. They eventually get married, and in true 1940s spirit Young's character surrenders her political career in favor of his to become a homemaker. It was a film very similar in flavor to many of Clark's 1930s comedies in which he got a chance to get some laughs, to be tough and virile, and to sweep a woman off her feet with his charm.

In one scene, they were sitting on a park bench on the soundstage, supposedly in San Francisco, surrounded by swirling fog being

Clark in his light-grey 1949 XK 120 Jaguar.

pumped out by fog machines. During their conversation, Loretta edges toward Clark, who edges away. Not being able to see in the fog, Clark kept edging and suddenly disappeared out of sight off the end of the bench. For a minute there was silence. Then from out of the fog came Clark's ghostly baritone: "Guess we need a longer bench." Everyone fell over laughing. But Griffin didn't think it so funny when Clark's insistence on his five p.m. finishing time slowed shooting down a lot because they had to close the set. Having fought so hard and waited so long for this indicator of his status, though, Clark felt he had no choice but to stick by the clause in his contract.

When it was all over Young and her husband threw a "thank God it's over" wrap party. Right in the middle of it came the news that cast member Frank Morgan, whose association with Clark went all the way back to

Saratoga in 1937, had suddenly died. Clark left at once to see if he could be of any help to Frank's widow. At the funeral, he was a pall-bearer.

Perhaps the death of such a long-time associate emphasized to Clark how lonely he was. Virginia Gray had said very perceptively earlier that year, "I think he'll get married some day. Deep down in his heart that's what he wants to do. The right girl will come along."[13] One morning during the week before Christmas that year, Clark called Jean Garceau and, after asking her if she was sitting down, informed her that he was going to marry Syl. Her startled response, to be echoed down a long line of women correspondents, lovers, friends, and fans was: "Syl *who*?"

Syl "who" was Lady Sylvia Ashley Fairbanks Stanley of Alderley, recent widow of Douglas Fairbanks Sr. Sylvia's name might as

Ad for Key to the City, *released on Clark's birthday in 1950.* (Spicer Collection.)

well have been Cinderella. Born in England and the daughter of a footman, as a teenager she worked as a living mannequin in a dressmaker's shop. The tall, slim, elegant girl soon became known as "Silky" because long, slinky, silk negligees looked so good on her. Sylvia's heart was set on a stage career rather than modeling, however, and in 1926 she joined the London chorus line of *Midnight Follies*. Her beauty stood out in a crowd, and she was soon invited to all the right places and introduced to all the right people. Inevitably, one of them fell madly in love with her, but Lord Ashley's parents, the Earl and Countess of Shaftsbury, balked at their son's announcement that he actually intended to marry her. They refused to have anything to do with the idea. So the pair eloped and were married in February 1927. Just as inevitably, they separated less than two years later, although they weren't divorced until 1934.

Ashley upset a very large applecart indeed when he named Douglas Fairbanks Sr. as correspondent in the divorce proceedings, because Fairbanks was still married to Mary Pickford at the time. Sylvia and Fairbanks were married in Paris in 1936 and lived relatively happily until his sudden death of a heart attack in 1939. His will left Sylvia an estate reputedly worth around $2 million. In January 1944, Sylvia married British Navy Lieutenant Commander Edward John, the sixth Baron Stanley, in Boston. However, he went to sea and she went to London. Four years later, he sued for divorce on the grounds of desertion. Sylvia then came back to live in the house in Santa Monica that Fairbanks had left her.

Sylvia and Clark had first met when she was Mrs. Fairbanks. When they began to be seen in each other's company at parties in that fall of 1949, no one gave it much thought. They just seemed to be friends renewing an old acquaintance. Clark said later that in fact they'd "been going around together for two or three years."[14] Columnist Elsa Maxwell claimed in 1952 that she had been instrumental in getting them together three years

earlier, when she introduced them to each other as dancing partners at her New York ball.[15]

They were seen regularly at all the well-known restaurants such as Romanoff's, and it was evident that she was blithely letting Clark pursue her instead of what was more usually the other way around. Her technique seemed to work; perhaps Clark was attracted at the time by what he couldn't readily have. In any case, some deep water was apparently running rather quickly below a deceptively still surface. It was probably on Sunday, December 18, when Clark proposed to Sylvia while they were out driving. He said later that he'd been thinking about doing it for some time. Although he was "scared to death" she'd say no, Sylvia said yes, "as fast as I knew how. I wouldn't give him any time to change his mind."[16] Clark then called Howard Strickling and asked him to be the best man, and Sylvia called relatives to let them know the news.

On Monday night, Clark and Sylvia drove to the Alisal Ranch, a dude ranch near Solvang, some thirty miles north of Santa Barbara, that was popular with movie people and owned by friends of Clark, Lynn Gilham and his wife. They stayed in separate cottages overnight, and the next morning they drove a hundred miles north to San Luis Obispo to obtain the marriage license, Clark giving his age as forty-eight and Sylvia as thirty-nine. Up until then, they had managed to avoid attention, but the clerk at the marriage office gave them away to the press, who were waiting for them by the time they returned to the ranch. Clark and Sylvia were married by the Reverend Aage Moller, pastor of the local Danish Lutheran Church, in the ranch-house living room at 3:15 p.m. before twenty-five relatives and ranch guests dressed in their best boots, jeans, and ten-gallon hats. Clark slipped a simple platinum band on Sylvia's finger and then kissed her. The ranch hands were all invited in for champagne and cake, which Sylvia cut with a Japanese sword that one of the hands had as a souvenir. Then,

A wedding photo of Clark and Lady Sylvia Ashley in December 1949. (Spicer Collection.)

Clark and Sylvia cutting the cake after their surprise wedding at the Alisal Ranch near Solvang, California.

letting everyone think they were going north to San Francisco, they doubled back and spent their honeymoon night at Clark's Encino house.

The next day the happy newlyweds finally drove to San Francisco to board the Matson liner *Lurline* at Pier 32, bound for Hawaii with seven hundred passengers. By then the word was out in a big way, their departure having been advertised in the press. The pier, the ship's corridors, and even their C-deck suite 245 (two bedrooms, a sitting room and a private deck), were jammed with hundreds of people, mostly women of all ages. The ship was scheduled to leave at midnight. When Clark and Sylvia drove onto the pier a little after 11 p.m., they were escorted by police on motorcycles.

As they left the car, they were surrounded by ten police officers who formed a flying wedge to push people out of the way so the Gables could reach a small, roped-off area where they were officially welcomed by Matson Line officials. As they were being welcomed aboard, hundreds of screaming women suddenly materialized from out of the night and descended on the hapless pair like an incoming floodtide. What *The New York Times* called a "near-riot" then ensued. People were trampled or pinned against walls as the Gables were swept towards their suite in a stampede of nearly a thousand people that gave the shocked Sylvia a foretaste of what it was going to mean to be Mrs. Gable.[17] As Carolyn Anspacher of the *San Francisco Chronicle* wryly observed, the elegant blond promptly lost "her look of cool, calm happiness." Once the Gables were finally insinuated into their suite, the crowd tried to beat the door down. To pacify them, Clark and Sylvia held a brief press conference, for a few selected journalists in their cabin, timed to wind up just as the ship's warning whistle sounded. Their relief to get some peace and quiet must have been tangible. The last woman was ushered off the ship sobbing hysterically, "I could kiss that man's feet." That the ship was able to leave anywhere near its scheduled departure time of midnight, Anspacher observed, was "one of the minor miracles of this Christmas season."[18] As a media event, the Gable wedding had caused quite a ruckus, considering there had been competition from another wedding of a slightly different kind. That week Dick Tracy and Tess Trueheart finally tied the knot after an eighteen-year relationship before about 43 million readers of the comics section in the *San Francisco Chronicle* and some 350 other newspapers. Now *that* was a full church!

Clark and Sylvia might have been tempted to think that now they were going to get some peace. If so, it must have come as an unpleasant surprise to look out at the Hawaiian docks four days later and realize that there weren't one thousand people waiting for them here — there were *ten* thousand! It took most of the Honolulu police force to hold the crowd back and another motorcycle escort to enable the Gables to drive off the dock. Howard Strickling and his wife, Gail, had flown in ahead of Clark and Sylvia and had found them a romantic honeymoon house with a private beach. There at last they found time for themselves, sunning on the beach, going for rides in outrigger canoes, or in Clark's case playing a lot of golf. She took to calling him "Bird," and he would usually refer to her as "Syl." At the same time, they were never short of enough invitations to socialize with local people, so they could pick and choose. Three weeks later, looking tanned and relaxed, they returned on the same ship to a much chillier and quieter San Francisco and headed home in a Cadillac convertible to the ranch in Encino.

Sylvia soon had her own housemaid, Elizabeth, move in to take over the housekeeping from Jean Garceau, who was only too glad to relinquish that part of her work. Elizabeth brought along Sylvia's Manchester terrier, Minnie, to add to the ranch menagerie. Up until now, Jean had been working out of an office at Clark's house, but some changes would have to be made now that there were

Clark and Sylvia arriving in Hawaii on their whirlwind honeymoon.

two people living there. Sylvia really had no space of her own other than her bedroom, so she suggested that Jean's office become a sitting room and that they build Jean an office at her own home. Jean thought that was a great idea; the move would give her more time at home with her own family, and Clark and Sylvia would have more privacy. Sylvia also wanted to have extra space for guests, so a two-bedroom guest house was built on the property at the same time. After about a month had gone by, however, Clark figured

the work-from-home scheme wasn't working. He moved Jean back onto the ranch and into the guesthouse.

Perhaps as a way of respecting Clark's memories of Carole, Sylvia made few changes to the main house, apart from moving in some of her English antiques, which she had shipped over, and her priceless collection of rose quartz. However, she did redecorate her bedroom, which of course was Carole's, in pink and white, and pink was known not to be one of Clark's favorite colors. Sylvia took quite a delight in planning all the menus and introducing Clark to some continental flavors and tastes. She was also a true English garden-lover and soon had four large, landscaped rose gardens put in, with another one at Jean's house to provide flowers year-round.

Clark asked Jean if she could help Sylvia with her legal affairs, and Jean soon found she certainly needed it. Sylvia might have been a wealthy woman, but she could use very little of it in America. By and large her funds had all been frozen in England, and she was in constant communication with enough lawyers back there to keep a courthouse busy. Needless to say, having been the wife of a pair of aristocrats, Sylvia had developed fine tastes in clothes and jewelry. A large part of the latter had been stolen in Europe the year before, but she still had enough to stun Jean when it came time for her collection to be displayed for insurance appraisal.

Once settled, Clark and Sylvia began to entertain again and to socialize. Sylvia was friends with many of the English and European Hollywood families and stars, including the Nivens, the Colmans, Fred Astaire, Charles Boyer, Louis Jordan, and of course the Fairbanks. They would often go out to dinners and parties at the homes of Tyrone Power, Gary Cooper, and Ray Milland, or with Gloria Swanson, Clifton Webb, Cole Porter, Joan Fontaine, and Sonja Henie and her husband.

In the middle of May, Clark and Sylvia left for Indianapolis, where location shooting would take place for *To Please a Lady*, a race-car movie the plot of which would be echoed a few decades later in Tom Cruise's *Days of Thunder*. Clark's character Mike crashes and kills another driver in a midget car race. Barbara Stanwyck is a journalist, instead of Nicole Kidman's doctor, who gets Mike banned because of the circumstances. Rather than quit, Mike takes to sideshow stunt driving to raise enough money to buy a full-size car. Mike and Stanwyck's journalist meet again and eventually fall in love, only to be held apart both by her fear he will be involved in another accident and by his failure to understand her attitude. During the Memorial Day race at Indianapolis Speedway, Mike lets another car go by him and spins out into the rough rather than risk another accident, earning Stanwyck's approval and love.

This was director Clarence Brown's eighth film with Clark, their first having been *A Free Soul* back in 1931, and they would make only one more together. With only one other director, Jack Conway, did Clark preserve a similar lengthy working relationship, making six films between 1931's *The Easiest Way* and 1947's *The Hucksters*. Clark and Brown probably got along so well because Brown never placed strong demands on him as to how a scene should be played. He preferred to let the actors rehearse without him to develop their own feel for the scene, then he would make any suggestions very quietly on the set, never raising his voice. He was typically so quiet that actors would have to come over to his chair to hear what he had to say. Hal Rosson was responsible for photography on this movie, as he had been on fourteen of Clark's films beginning with *Sporting Blood* in 1931. Rosson shot footage during the rolling start and laps of the actual Memorial Day race. They had Clark drive one of the cars, a Curtis, during the rolling start with the pace car out in front, so they would have scenes of him as a driver. Then they continued to shoot much of the race to use as background. Barbara Stanwyck was chosen "Queen of the Race," which was in reality won by Johnny Parsons. Ted Scott, a midget car racing driver who had trained as a stuntman, was Clark's double in the actual car racing scenes.[19]

Given Clark's avid love of sports and high-speed cars, it was his ideal movie, and he had a ball. It was probably also the time when he and Sylvia were happiest. Clark's friend Al Menasco, a car fan as well, came along with his son to watch the race, as did Sylvia's nephew Timothy Bleck (to whom Rosson was godfather), and Sylvia set up a kitchen in their hotel suite and insisted on feeding them all.

The film was a great success. Many people saw this role as Clark's return at last to the character with whom they were familiar: the rough, tough, dirty-faced bad-guy-with-a-heart-of-gold who can slap a woman and still earn her love by the end of the movie through some heroic self-sacrifice. Barbara Stanwyck had received some hard words from Clark at the beginning of both their movie careers back in 1931's *Night Nurse*. This was Clark's third famous bit of forceful female byplay during his career, if you count all the physical tension between Rhett and Scarlett implied in that "I could crush your head like an egg" grip of his big hands around her head. In a way, the distortion of Leigh's face as Clark gradually increases the pressure is more frightening than the slap across Stanwyck's face.

After they were finished in Indianapolis, Clark returned home while Sylvia flew to Europe to get some of her tangled legal affairs straightened. By the time she got back three weeks later, Clark and Jean had begun making preparations for a six-week stay in Durango, Colorado, while shooting *Across the Wide Missouri*, so Clark and Sylvia could leave on July 28. As he preferred to do, Clark drove across the desert alone. Sylvia went by train with the luggage and her dog, Minnie.

The 325 cast and crew took over the El Rancho Encantado, occupying the cabins. Sylvia immediately set about making the two-room Gable log cabin into a home, hanging curtains and planting grass and trees outside, for which Clark came in for no end of jokes among the crew. She started cooking in the cabin, but Clark never liked being treated differently or separately than the rest of the crew, and they were soon eating with everyone else at the long tables in the huge mess tent, that could hold the entire company at one sitting. Clark couldn't resist the closeness of all those mountain streams full of fish just waiting to be hooked, and he would grab a rod as soon as there was a break. Sylvia gave it a shot, but thereafter preferred to sit alongside the stream and paint. Every evening they would

go riding together, Clark on his quarterhorse stallion, Steel, that he used in the movie.

Across the Wide Missouri, along with *Broken Arrow*, is one of the rare films of the period that treated Native Americans sympathetically. It would be a long wait from here until the 1970s and films such as *Soldier Blue*, *Little Big Man*, and *A Man Called Horse* attempted to appreciate the Native American culture and its head-on clash with, and betrayal by, the Western world. As a later film of Clark's, *Wide Missouri* is also replete with references to his earlier films. It was directed by William Wellman, who after his run-in with a very romantically distracted Clark on the *Call of the Wild* shoot was just a little worried, needlessly as it turned out, that Clark might refuse to work with him again. Clark's hard-drinking trapper friend is played by Adolphe Menjou, whose association with him also went all the way back to 1931 and *The Easiest Way*, although Menjou was already a star by then. The Native American chief is played just a little incongruously by Jack Holt, Blackie Norton's rival in *San Francisco*.

Unfortunately, although Clark probably thought a well-tried action director might be just the man to maintain the momentum of the film, *Across the Wide Missouri* comes across as a curiously slow and truncated film. If it were made now, one would suspect it was the pilot for a television series, because the film has the feeling of an episode badly needing a sequel that would tell how trapper Flint Mitchell's infant son grew up and came to be narrating this story of his and his parent's origins. Just when it has at last succeeded in drawing the audience in and involving them in these people's lives, the film suddenly ends. Beaver trapper Flint (Gable) marries a young Native American woman, hoping the union will prove convenient in giving him an edge with her militant tribe. She guides Flint's trappers over a longer but safe route into her country, they win the approval of her grandfather the chief, build a stockade for the winter, and they start trapping. Flint falls in love with his wife, and she bears him a son, which influences Flint to lead the trappers out and then return to live with his wife and her family. But a vengeful trapper kills the chief and starts a running war, during which Flint's wife is killed. When peace finally is made, Flint and his son return to live with the tribe.

However, how does the son come to receive such a good education, become part of Western civilization, and get to narrate a movie about his childhood? It's all a mystery, and while audiences and critics can appreciate a good mystery in a film, they usually don't appreciate the film being a mystery itself. People expect movies to tie up loose ends, and *Wide Missouri* left just a few too many dangling to entirely satisfy. When critics start saying nice things about Technicolor, impressive scenery, and interesting authenticity, it is what they are very politely not saying about the acting that is significant.

MGM was apparently horrified with the hundreds of feet of slow, lyrical, semidocumentary material with which Wellman returned from a very expensive location shoot, and it ordered the film pared down to seventy-eight minutes of action sequences and vignettes. From them emerges the first glimpse of the noble, wise Old Man of the Outdoors figure who is gradually being overtaken by modern times that would come to full fruition in *The Misfits* almost a decade later.

A LONE STAR

While Clark was working on *Across the Wide Missouri*, Wayne Griffin would drive with him to the location most days, and they would discuss the problems Clark was having with the studio finding him suitable scripts. Clark was already having doubts about whether he would sign another contract with MGM, and in the meantime he wanted to experiment with independent production. So in September they announced they would be setting up an independent production company, Sylvia Productions, to make three films. The first would be *Lone Star*, followed by *The Novel Husband* and *The Big Moose*, all of which would be released through MGM.[1] It was a great dream but, as so often happens, it would be overtaken by a harsh reality.

Al Menasco had bought a lovely ranch in the Napa Valley that year, and he and his wife asked Clark and Sylvia to spend Thanksgiving with them. Sylvia, who was making less of a pretence about liking the great outdoors since their return from the Missouri location, was reluctant to go, but she finally went at Clark's urging. Once there, she seemed to relax and be having a good time. Al told Clark the neighboring land was for sale, and Clark authorized Al to bid $75,000 for it on his behalf. Al asked him what Sylvia would think of that idea, and Clark replied shortly, "That won't make any difference." It was only a small thundercloud on the horizon, but Al could sense a bigger storm building behind it.[2]

In December, Clark and Sylvia left for Nassau in Bermuda to spend Christmas with friends. When they returned to the ranch in mid-January, Jean Garceau thought they no longer looked very happy. For his birthday the previous year, Sylvia had invited mostly their European friends for a formal dinner. This time around she wanted to do something special and more casual that Clark would be sure to like, so she consulted Jean on his favorite food, and Jean nominated stewed chicken and dumplings. Maybe it says something about how close they weren't that after a year of marriage, Sylvia was consulting Clark's secretary about what his food preferences were.

It was not going to be either Sylvia's or Clark's night. They had just hired a new cook and, despite Clark's hesitancy about inviting people for dinner until they discovered how the new cook would work out, Sylvia considered she could cope and went right ahead and invited the Menascos, the Stricklings, the Adrians, the Griffins, and Merle Oberon. The house looked beautiful with fires set and fresh flowers everywhere. Dinner was served, and so was trouble.

The new cook had prepared the chicken

the day before and had not refrigerated it at the right temperature. Overnight, it went bad. Rather than look for a quick alternative when she realized the entire dinner was in jeopardy, the frightened cook panicked and served the chicken. It was quite apparent what had happened once it was on the table by the smell. Some of the women sniffed their perfumed handkerchiefs while the men tucked in bravely, but Clark was so embarrassed that he left the table for his room, not to return until later in the evening. By then everyone had recovered and were sitting around telling jokes about their own dining fiascos and laughing hilariously.[3]

However, Clark remained an unhappy man and, perhaps thinking a few months ahead, decided not to go ahead with his production company. Instead, they sold the *Lone Star* rights they had purchased for $100,000 to MGM as a starring vehicle for Clark. Shooting was scheduled for May. Griffin would still produce, Vincent Sherman would direct, Ava Gardner would costar and, for the last time, Hal Rosson would be in charge of photography.[4] It would be another physically demanding outdoor shoot for Clark, so in early April he checked into Cedars of Lebanon Hospital for a complete physical. When he checked out a few days later, he left for Arizona. Sylvia had also gone into hospital for minor surgery. When she came home, she headed straight to Griffin's office and poured out a tale of woe about how Clark wanted a divorce and how she would do anything to keep him.

Rumors were already flying. According to Hedda Hopper, Clark had come right out and said to Sylvia while they were dressing for a party that he thought their marriage was a mistake, that he didn't care much for her British ways, and that he didn't like being married anymore and wanted a divorce as soon as possible. However, Hopper claimed, Sylvia told her she was "still stuck on the guy" and hoped for reconciliation.[5] By April 18 the studio was forced to issue a statement that there had been "a marital spat" but that separation

was not being considered.[6] A few days later Sylvia left for Nassau, telling reporters that she was going to look at some property she and Clark were considering purchasing, but it's quite probable that Clark had already been to see his lawyers.

She returned in May, but the situation had not improved in her absence. Clark locked her out of the Encino house and had the locks changed. Finally admitting defeat, Sylvia sued for divorce on May 31 in the Santa Monica courthouse on grounds of mental cruelty. She had only taken this step, said her well-known lawyer Jerry Geisler, "with deepest reluctance and under severe pressure and after all her attempts at reconciliation proved fruitless," and she was merely asking for an equitable property settlement.[7] The next day she sailed out into the Pacific aboard the schooner *Pioneer* with her friends the George Vanderbilts, accompanying them on a six-month scientific expedition. When they reached Honolulu twelve days later she wouldn't meet curious reporters, leaving Vanderbilt to inform them that "she is feeling terrible."[8]

Not many people were surprised at the split. David Niven, for example, had always thought Clark and Sylvia were a high risk combination because "Clark was a selfish man. Sylvia was a selfish woman ... so far — a standoff. Clark was a man's man, but Sylvia was a man's woman ... a red light. Clark lived for the open air, blood sports, the big country and large dogs. Sylvia was devoted to the great indoors, to her milky, white skin, her flawless complexion, loathed the thought of animals being slaughtered, was happiest among the chattering chic of cafe society ... Possible friction points could possibly have been welded into a great happiness by their mutual devotion to laughter had it not been for a further divergence. Clark was close with a buck while Sylvia adored spending money."[9] Hedda Hopper said that their patterns of life "had been set in a different mould." She recalled sitting behind the couple at Sam Goldwyn's house one night watching *All About Eve*. While

Hopper thought it was pretty exciting, she noticed that "it didn't excite Sylvia. If she opened her purse once, took out a comb, combed her golden hair, she did it a dozen times. When she wasn't combing her hair, she was applying lipstick and powder and checking her compact. She would whisper in Clark's ear like a schoolgirl."[10] You can almost hear Hopper sniffing her disapproval.

On June 5, Clark filed an answer to Sylvia's petition, denying mental cruelty and her claim to community property. She already had a fortune of more than $1 million, he replied, and so she needed no financial assistance from him. Clark pointed out that they owned no property jointly; all their earnings had gone to pay bills.

About this time, Clark joined the crew to begin shooting *Lone Star*. Broderick Crawford was playing the villain, and he, Clark, Wayne Griffin, and director Vincent Sherman all had a lot of fun in the process. One night after the four of them had gotten a little drunk while having dinner in a room at Chasen's restaurant, they figured the big fight scene in the film needed some rehearsal and just tore the place apart. The next day, sobered and a bit remorseful at what they had done to their friend's establishment, they offered to pay for all the damage. To remind them all of the occasion, Dave Chasen had little boxing-glove cufflinks made for each of the quartet. A few days later Clark and a few of the technicians wired Griffin's new Cadillac to blow a bit of smoke when he started it up, but they got a little enthusiastic, and the resulting explosion broke all the spark plugs and buckled the hood. When Griffin staggered out of the cab with his face blackened by oil and smoke, Clark laughed so hard he fell over. Nevertheless, he blamed himself for the damage and had the car totally repaired.

Vincent Sherman later claimed that Griffin cautioned him to be mindful of Clark's creeping Parkinson's disease that caused his head to shake if he became tired or tense, or if a pose had to be held too long. This is one of the very rare times anyone mentioned this disease in relation to Clark, so whether he did suffer from it is an interesting question to consider. It would certainly explain the trembling head and shaking hands that many people put down to Clark's drinking. On the other hand, even a few years later he was evidently not having trouble with remembering lines or with walking. It might be that Griffin, being the friend that he was, could have been running a smoke screen for the increasingly visible effects in an aging Clark of years of steady drinking. As Clark once said to Sherman, "I'm past fifty. They say life begins at forty, but they've got no fucking slogans for after fifty."[11]

Lone Star, in which Clark plays a Texas adventurer employed by Andrew Jackson to persuade Sam Houston to change his mind about signing a treaty with Mexico over Texas annexation, is a competent but mediocre film. As Bosley Crowther commented in *The New York Times* the following year, "It isn't art and it isn't history precisely, but the producers have Mr. Gable tussling with assorted villains, and the prettiest gal north of the Rio Grande, so it probably doesn't matter, after all."[12] Ava Gardner, who costarred immediately after finishing work on *Show Boat*, seems to have also agreed that the film didn't matter too. She idolized Clark, yet she did not consider *Lone Star* significant enough to rate a mention in her autobiography other than in the filmography. Clark was so unhappy over the result, and over what he saw as the declining standard of story being offered to him by his current agents, that after talking the matter over with Wayne Griffin he had discussions with Lew Wasserman and George Chasin of MCA. As a result, they became his representatives.

When Sylvia returned from Honolulu, she went to live at her beach house. Clark kept calling, suggesting she could come get her things if she wasn't going to live at the ranch, and Sylvia would agree but never do anything. Finally, Clark moved out himself to live at Glenbrook Lodge in Lake Tahoe, Nevada, to establish residency in that state. Wary, with due cause, of California community property laws, he had his driver's license and all his bank accounts transferred and started to investigate purchasing some land.

Having established residence in Nevada, Clark filed for divorce six weeks later, on October 4. Through his attorney, W. I. Gilbert, he in turn alleged "extreme mental cruelty." A Nevada divorce had to be filed, Clark said, because "no agreement could be reached on Mrs. Gable's unreasonable and exorbitant financial demands." No community property existed any longer, he claimed, because they had spent more than he had earned during their marriage. Sylvia's reaction the next day through her attorney was predictable. Clark's allegations and alimony offer were ridiculous, she fumed, stating that their property-settlement negotiations had broken down because Clark had refused to disclose his income tax returns to prove his allegations.[13] That would have been typical of Clark, who never wanted anyone to know exactly how much money he had. Hedda Hopper, claiming that Clark once told her no woman would ever get a penny out of him, told the story about a friend of Sylvia's who arrived at the Gable ranch only to find Sylvia seated at the table signing checks. On inquiring why she was doing it rather than Jean Garceau, Sylvia replied that these were for her share of the expenses. She complained that, apart from a diamond-studded collar that she and Clark bought for Sylvia's dog, Clark had never bought her any presents.[14] Her attorneys declared that Sylvia would seek her day in court to hear Clark's explanation of why a larger settlement figure was not being offered.

When Glenbrook closed for the season in late fall, Clark moved to the Flying M. E. Ranch in Carson City, which became his official Nevada address. He soon met a young attractive divorcee there, Natalie Thompson, and they kept close company into the New Year. Then Sylvia and her lawyers obtained an injunction against Clark's divorce action, and she left for Nassau again. As it was no longer

necessary for him to remain in Nevada, Clark returned to California. Natalie followed him a little later to "see her mother," and they were seen together quite a bit. Clark worked around the ranch and started some spring plowing while he waited to find out when the divorce would come to trial.

Having heard that Sylvia was returning from Nassau, Clark left for New York the day after his birthday, with the Griffins along for moral support, to reopen property negotiations with her. She had injured her ankle in a car accident on the island and had checked into Doctors Hospital, where Clark and Wayne found her in a wheelchair. To Wayne's surprise, the two were just like old friends who hadn't seen each other for a while. When they dropped by again the next day, Clark was so reluctant to leave, and he and Sylvia were getting along so well, that Wayne felt sure they would reconcile.

While they were in New York, Wayne had been asked to persuade Clark to appear at Madison Square Garden to speak at a rally in support of General Eisenhower running for president. Clark, who hated getting tangled up in politics, had been difficult to persuade, but Wayne had finally succeeded. That afternoon they went to see Sylvia again, and once again she and Clark chatted just like old friends. At Wayne's prompting, Sylvia finally said that she didn't want to cause any trouble or extended legal problems, and she just wanted to work out an arrangement that was fair all around.

Wayne finally got Clark to the rally. Clark sat on the stage in a ring of dignitaries and other film stars. The highlight was to be a broadcast conversation between Clark and Eisenhower, who was at the other end of a trans-Atlantic phone hookup. Clark had been given a long script, but after reading it he had tossed it aside and said he would have to talk in his own words. When the host announced that this was "being beamed to you, General, to let you know that the people want "Ike" for their leader," Clark said, "General, I'm sure that if you were here at this rally, there would be no doubt in your mind that your fellow Americans want you as their next president. If you decide to run, that's how it will be, for you will win."[15] For some time after, people would comment on how much Clark's voice and laugh sounded like Eisenhower's.

As friendly as they were, Clark and Sylvia did not get back together, and they reached an out-of-court settlement. Wayne accompanied her into the Santa Monica court on April 21, 1952, where she was granted an uncontested interlocutory divorce. As alimony, she would receive ten percent of Clark's income for the first year, then seven percent for the next four or until she remarried. The property settlement was $6,002.46. Hedda Hopper, in her usual inimitable style, attempted to analyze the situation. It wasn't that Clark couldn't hold his women, she wrote, it was that they couldn't hold him, and he "grew away" from them. According to her, Clark was simply not ready for this marriage and had gone into it for all the wrong reasons, including looking for another Carole. A week before Sylvia's filing for divorce, Hopper said, Clark had commented that, "after I lost Carole I became a lone wolf. I liked my life that way. I liked my own home. I don't like a family underfoot — not even my own. And while Sylvia's sister and her children didn't live much at the ranch, they were there a good deal of the time. A man's home is his castle, even though mine happens to be a rather simple ranch." Hopper figured that, though Sylvia had tried, she had too many airs and graces for Clark and had wanted to make too many changes by way of refining the rough, tough gent that he was, while he considered that he was too old and too set in his ways for that. While they had both come from the poor side of town, were both ambitious, and had three previous marriages each that had contributed to their social status, Clark and Sylvia had ended up very different people at heart.[16]

Clark didn't sit around the ranch moping for too long. He'd always wanted to com- plete the European trip that had been cut short by his father's death. When MCA negotiated a deal for him to appear in the film *Never Let Me Go,* which would be shot in England, he seized the chance to leave early. On May 6 he left for France on the *Liberte* , after a farewell party attended by French Line officials. On his arrival in Paris he moved into the Hotel Lancaster, from where he telephoned Jean to tell her how beautiful Paris was. He had read the script for a film to be called *Mogambo* on the way over and was very enthusiastic about it, especially since John Ford would be directing.

Ford, one of the most famous directors of his time but also with a reputation as "one of the crustiest sons-of-bitches ever to direct a film," had been approached in the summer of 1952 by producer Sam Zimbalist to direct a re- make of *Red Dust,* the 1936 classic that had starred Gable and Harlow. Zimbalist, a tough, no-nonsense movie man, had commissioned John Lee Mahin to rewrite his own 1936 script, which had in turn been based on a Wilson Collison play. In the process, the setting had been moved from the French Indo-Chi- nese jungle to the British East-African one, and the title had been changed to a Swahili word said to mean "to speak of love." Mahin had, of course, also rewritten the male lead role for Clark. This time, though, instead of being a rubber plantation manager, Clark's character would be an animal trapper named Vic Marswell, possibly as a homage to the late Vic Fleming, who had directed *Red Dust.* Otherwise, the basic plot line was much the same. Ava Gardner would take the old Jean Harlow role, although Ford would have pre- ferred Maureen O'Hara. Choosing a succes- sor to Mary Astor proved a little more prob- lematic. The studio preferred Deborah Kerr, but Ford disagreed; they then suggested Greer Garson, whom both Ford and Zimbalist ve- toed. Ford then surprised everyone by sug- gesting Grace Kelly, who at that time had ap- peared in only the minor *Fourteen Hours* and as Gary Cooper's drab Quaker wife in *High*

Noon. Ford was impressed by her quality and class, and he personally directed a color test of Kelly to prove to Dore Schary that she would be right for the part. He agreed. and she was promptly signed for her first studio contract.

Ford, who had never seen the original *Red Dust*, had only just emerged from a very troubled time with the Republic studio, and he had very commercial and pragmatic reasons for taking on this project. It gave him the chance to once again be working on a big-budget film for a major studio, in this case an MGM-British coproduction with a mostly English crew and a cast of very competent professionals. He liked the script, he liked the professional way the project was being put together, and he'd never been to that part of Africa — "so, I just did it."[17] Determined to make the film look as realistic as possible, Ford began preparations to take the entire film shoot to Africa.

Paris being the romantic city that it is, it wasn't long before Clark found some romance in the very lovely, slim, and well-educated form of Schiaparelli model Suzanne Dadolle d'Abadie, who was soon being seen constantly in his company. She was reported to be "taming" him, taking him to the opera, to museums and recitals, and boating with him on the Seine.

However, Clark had to eventually leave behind the romantic Paris spring, and a tearful Suzanne, and move to the more uncomfortable London of mid-June to begin work on *Never Let Me Go* at MGM's Boreham Wood Studios. Staying at the Dorchester Hotel, however, no doubt improved the comfort factor. Directed by Delmer Daves and based on the novel *Came the Dawn* by George Froescher, the story of *Never Let Me Go* concerns a Russian ballerina (Gene Tierney) who marries an American foreign correspondent (Gable) based in Moscow in 1945. He is suddenly deported and forced to leave his wife behind. He eventually resorts to impersonating a Russian officer to enable him to get back into the country to help his wife escape. Daves

used the interesting and then-novel technique of inserting actual newsreel footage for backgrounds and filler to give the film an authentic feel and context.

Clark enjoyed working with Gene Tierney, and she with him. After brief modeling and stage careers, the sleek, svelte, and breathtakingly beautiful Tierney had begun her career at barely 20 in the 1940 Fritz Lang film *The Return of Frank James*. She was rapidly escalated to stardom with her Oscar-nominated performance in *Leave Her to Heaven* (1944) and her role in *Laura* (1944). Her name was already associated romantically with Oleg Cassini, Howard Hughes, and Jack Kennedy. She was in England on loan to MGM from 20th Century–Fox to appear in *Plymouth Adventurer*, when director Clarence Brown had taken the opportunity to produce *Never Let Me Go* and asked her if she was interested in the role of the Russian ballerina. It was a physically demanding part, requiring Tierney at thirty-two to take two hours of ballet lessons every day for six weeks before and during the shoot. Her feet became badly swollen and blistered. Perhaps recalling only too well how that felt from his days of OTS training in Miami, Clark was not only kind and considerate but brought back a special salve ointment for her from one of his trips to Paris.

Tierney's mother, who was traveling with her at the time, was eager for her daughter and Clark to get together. However, although they went out for dinner together a few times, Tierney felt there was too much of an age difference, and she was too put off by her mother's eagerness. Not only that, she was starting to be conscious of the mental affects of the bouts of depression that were beginning to cloud her mind. Clark would spend most of their time together talking about Carole and "for all his he-man, no-undershirt screen image," she recalls, "I saw him as sweet and gentle, a hard crust with a soft center. I thought that quality was what came across on the screen and made him adored by so many."[18]

Having bought a new Jaguar in which to

drive out to the studio from the hotel, Clark grew to like it so much that he instructed Jean Garceau to sell the one at home because he intended bringing this one back with him. The weather turned bad, and *Never Let Me Go* began to run badly behind schedule. Much of the "rescue" scenes, being shot off the coast of Cornwall, were delayed due to rain. Clark began to find London too dull. He took to flying to Paris on the weekends to see Suzanne, and they celebrated Bastille Day together. On the whole, critics were kind to the movie when it was finally released in May the following year, although some felt it was a tad long on words and slow with action.

When shooting was over, Clark decided to waive his usual four-month rest period between films and to make the journey to Africa and *Mogambo* into a short vacation instead. While he was having some of his costumes made in London, he wired Jean to send him some more suits. Clark had a detailed memory for exactly where and when each of his many suits had been made, and he had them tagged and racked accordingly, as well as by color and material, in his huge closets. When asking Jean to locate one, he would just tell her for which color and date tag to search.[19]

Clark left London on September 20 for France. He had the Jaguar flown across the English Channel and proceeded to drive across country into Switzerland where he couldn't resist staying at Villa d'Este on Lake Como for three weeks playing golf. He arrived in Rome in mid-October, where he enjoyed just being an ordinary tourist and sightseeing the ruins and churches, but his fun was cut short by a wire from Sam Zimbalist, *Mogambo*'s producer, who recommended he leave Rome for East Africa by the end of the month at the latest. The Mau Mau situation was getting worse in Kenya and had everyone concerned. In August, Jim Havens, the excellent second-unit director with whom Ford had worked on *They Were Expendable*, had begun a six-week survey of East African locations. As a result,

Mogambo would be shot on the Serengeti Plain, in what was then Tanganyika, because of the huge herds of grazing animals, and at the Kagera River in Uganda because of its spectacular waterfalls and rapids. However, in the course of his extensive traveling, Havens had become aware of the potential hazards of the developing Mau Mau native rebellion to drive out the white farmers. People were getting murdered in their beds out there. The farmers were consequently armed to the teeth and protected by British troops often backed by tanks. So, Havens advised Ford that it might not be a good idea to tempt fate by remaining in the area any longer than absolutely necessary.

Clark put his beloved car in storage, and on October 31 boarded a British Airways Comet for Nairobi, Grace Kelly, Ava Gardner, John Ford, and a safari of hundreds.

Headquarters for the film company had been set up at the New Stanley Hotel in Nairobi and there, when he arrived on November 2, Clark met up with director John Ford. Although they had known each other socially for years, this would be the first time they had worked together. While waiting for the rest of the cast to arrive, Clark and Ford flew sixty miles upriver to Mount Kenya to visit Carr Hartley, who specialized in trapping animals for circuses and who would be catching the animals that would be seen in the film. For Clark, of course, as with many people, the words Africa and hunting were synonymous. He had ten of his guns and some hunting outfits flown in by MGM. Carr took him out shooting and Clark was in heaven, although he was to become somewhat disillusioned with it all by the end of his stay.

A week later Ava Gardner and Frank Sinatra, who had been married for a year, arrived followed by Grace Kelly. Ava was once again thrilled to have the chance to work with Clark, whom she could remember seeing in *Red Dust* when she was a young girl sneaking into the theater balcony in Smithfield, Virginia.[20]

Mogambo was the biggest African film venture to that time. Scheduled for a sixty-seven-day location shoot, its logistics were mind-boggling. MGM had put together what amounted to the largest safari East Africa had ever seen. Consequently, there wasn't a vehicle to be had anywhere in that part of the country. It took eight days to travel in more than fifty trucks the thousand miles to the Kagera River through country where daytime temperatures could reach 130 degrees. There the crew set up a camp of some three hundred tents, including accommodation and dining quarters, a wardrobe department where three copies of each costume were stored, a makeup tent, a recreation tent, a hospital tent complete with X-ray facilities, and a jail tent — just in case. MGM also built an eighteen-hundred-yard airstrip there in five days so that supplies and mail could be flown in and film stock flown out. The whole site was guarded by a thirty-man police force, which could call on the nearby Lancashire Fusiliers and the Queens African Rifles in case of serious trouble, and every cast member was issued a weapon. Just by way of thinking of everything, according to Ava, MGM had even set aside an expense item to pay local witchdoctors for casting favorable spells.[21]

The first setup was for the scene where a leopard walks into Ava's tent. Apparently nobody told the leopard about this line-up, and he just didn't feel like responding to his cues. It was a catchy attitude, and soon Ava and then Clark were fumbling their lines. Finally, Ford had a scene he could print, only to be told the key light had blown at the last minute. That meant the scene would have to be reshot. Ava got up off the bed and said, "Oh, that was a real fuck-up. We goofed everything." Ford took it personally and lost his temper, ranting at her that if she thought she could do it better, she could change places with him. It was all brought to an abrupt halt when Clark put his arm around her, gave her shoulders a squeeze, and then walked off the set without a word, shutting it down. An hour later, after everyone had cooled down, Ford reshot the scene in one take.[22] It was an omen of things to come.

Ford, almost sixty years old and feeling the strain of carrying this enormous and lengthy project on his shoulders, remained prickly and soon he and Clark were having their problems. As professionals, their styles were quite different; as kings, they were equal in their own domains. While Ford preferred to move quickly and to have the last word, Clark was a careful and methodical actor who liked to know exactly what he was saying and where he would be before he walked onto the set. He did not like spontaneous script changes and preferred to be able to study and learn the script before filming began. Ford's attitude to a script, on the other hand, was fluid. As he once groused to Grace Kelly when she took up a scripted position, "We're shooting a movie, not the script."[23] When interrupted in the middle of a scene, rather than pick up from his last words Clark considered it necessary for his continuity to go back to the beginning of the scene and start over, something Ford thought a criminal waste of time. More importantly, Clark expected to be granted the status to which he was accustomed, and if he didn't think a scene was his best he preferred to do it again. Ford considered none of his decisions were open for discussion.

Despite these theatrics of power, however, the eyes of cast, crew, and columnists alike were not on Clark and Ava-as-Jean this time around. They were speculatively following the nature of the relationship between Clark and the young Grace Kelly. Although she had appeared on Broadway and in television drama, *Mogambo* was Kelly's first work while under a long-term contract to MGM. Upon receiving the news she had got the part, Kelly's first call had been to her mother. "Guess what I'm going to do next?" she gushed. "I'm going to Africa ... *with Clark Gable*!" "Clark Gable?" was the response from a society-conscious mother to her twenty-three-year-old daughter in 1952. "All the way to Africa with him? How can I allow you to go over there by yourself? What will people say? Do you think its proper?"[24] Even Clark told Louella Parsons later that Kelly should never have been allowed over without a chaperone.

By all accounts they both had something to be concerned about. "Grace was mad for Clark," her sister Lizanne once commented. [25] Ava Gardner wrote that, "As far as romance was concerned, Clark's eyes were quite definitely on Gracie and her's, for that matter, were on him…. Gracie was a good Catholic girl, and she was having a hard time feeling the way she did about Clark. Not to mention that being in Africa, with exotic flora and fauna all over the place, and Clark, strong and smiling and completely at home, only made her love him more."[26] Gore Vidal, in his own inimitable fashion, was a little more blunt about the situation: "Grace almost always laid the leading man. She was famous for that in this town. One of the few she failed to was Clark Gable," he said, and went on to tell how Clark finally had to resort to getting her completely drunk one night over a moonlit dinner, to the point where she threw up, to try and dispel her romantic notions.[27]

Throughout the shoot, Grace was never far away from Clark's side, although usually with a good reason. When a puzzled Clark once questioned her as to why she would want to tag along on his early morning hunting expeditions, she said, "It's the strangeness and excitement of it all. I want to be able to tell my grandchildren about it some day."[28] Whatever Grace may have felt, Clark tended to treat her like a daughter whom he needed to watch over, care for, and advise. Grace took to calling him "Ba," the Swahili word for father, and that may well have reminded him of Carole calling him Pa.

Like Carole, Grace had a tough, earthy private side that evidently impressed both Clark and Ava. The two women became close friends after they celebrated each other's birthdays on location, Grace on November 12 and Ava on Christmas Eve, and remained so for many years afterwards. Grace seemed to delight in being shocked by Ava, who in turn seemed to take delight in shocking anyone she could. The British Governor of Uganda invited Gardner and Sinatra, Kelly, Donald Sinden, Ford, and Clark to spend a weekend at the Governor's house in Entebbe. When they arrived, Ford did the introductions. "Ava," he said, "Why don't you tell the Governor what you see in this one-hundred-and-ten-pound runt?" Ava looked at him steadily and replied, "Well, there's only ten pounds of Frank but there's a hundred-and-ten pounds of cock!"[29] Gore Vidal used to repeat another Ava story that Sam Zimbalist had told him: "The location was full of these tall Watusis, beautiful warriors that had been hired as extras, wearing their breechclouts. The girls were walking along and Ava said to Grace, 'I wonder if their cocks are as big as people say? Have you ever seen a black cock?' Grace turned purple, of course, and said, 'Stop that! Don't talk like that!' Ava said, 'That's funny — neither have I,' and with that she reached over and pulled up the breechclout of one of the Watusis, who gave a big grin as this huge cock flopped out. By then Grace had turned absolutely blue. Ava just let go of the breechclout, turned to Grace and commented, 'Frank's is bigger than that.'"[30]

After some coaching, and it took a lot, Grace could eventually drink around the campfire with everyone else. She would sometimes go wandering off though, especially if hurt about something, and Clark would look at Ava and say, "Sugar, where has she gone? This is Africa. You can't just go running off in Africa." He wouldn't take the bait, though, and he would send Ava out to look for Grace.[31] Once he came across Grace reading Hemingway's *The Snows of Kilimanjaro* and crying. When he asked her about her tears, she said it was so beautiful because she'd just been reading the lines about the leopard and had looked up to see a lion walking by. Clark came back shaking his head, impressed by a young woman who could sit there watching a lion stroll by her rather than run screaming back to camp.[32]

Everyone, not just Grace, had their chance for wild encounters, and there were injuries and personal problems aplenty. Ava became pregnant and had to be flown out at one point for hospitalization.[33] A bad-tempered rhino took exception to Grace, Clark, and Ava's Jeep on one occasion, punching holes in it and nearly overturning it. They escaped, but three crew members were later killed when their Jeep crashed on a jungle track. A close call took place during a love scene between Clark and Grace, at an idyllic spot that Ford had picked out on a cliff point overlooking the Rift Valley. After the first take, as Ford went to talk to the actors, Clark took a step back and slid twenty feet down a slope towards the edge. Ford calmly sat down while a sweating Clark was hauled back up on the end of a rope, and then chided him gently about not being immediately willing to do a second take.[34] The oppressive heat, the mosquitoes, or one of many and various nasty tropical illnesses eventually took their toll on everybody, including John Ford. As the shoot progressed, his eyesight deteriorated alarmingly and he suffered from amoebic dysentery.[35] His mood understandingly became blacker as he wore down, and eventually he began to look for ways to cut the African location time. He rewrote several dialogue scenes so they could be shot as interiors back in England. Some scenes that showed animals and people together were altered so that they could also be done back in England using rear-projected background footage, shot later by a second and third unit team under the direction of Yakima Canutt. In late January 1953 he brought the group back to Nairobi and from there to London.

Completion work on *Mogambo* went on there for most of February. It was not made any easier by clashes of will between Clark and Ford. They had been hardly speaking to each other by the time they left Africa as it was and

now, with nothing to distract either of these two equally strong-minded and stubborn individuals, hostility broke out into the open. After shooting one love scene between Clark and Ava, for example, Ford had begun to move onto the next setup when Clark told him he thought he could do the scene better and that they should do it again. "Ok, Clark, *you* do it again," Ford replied, and putting everyone back into position he sat down beside the camera and called, "Action." Clark started the scene but then realized he hadn't heard those other three crucial words, "roll 'em," and "speed." Looking over, he saw Ford had a sly grin on his face. "Well," Ford chuckled, "I said *you* could play it, I didn't say *I* was going to shoot it."[36] Clark stormed off the set and refused to speak to Ford again. Finally Sam Zimbalist took him aside and said, "Look, Clark, Ford's a tyrant. He's been used to John Wayne. When you get in there you just say 'Yes, Coach' and everything will be okay."[37] An uneasy truce was maintained. Clark ended up admiring Ford's work — but it was from a great distance.

Clark had moved into the Connaught Hotel and had his Jaguar shipped back to him. He found London dull and the weather terrible, but at least he was being kept busy at the studio with publicity interviews and discussions about future projects. George Chasin of MCA flew over to discuss an MGM film called *Holland Deep*, which the studio would want to shoot on location in Holland, and he wanted to sound out Clark's thoughts on extending his contract for two years. However, Clark was still mulling over forming an independent production company, and he didn't want to make any final decisions until he'd had a chance to have a well-earned break in Europe with Al and Julie Menasco.

Work on *Mogambo* was finally completed by mid-April. As a vehicle for two well-known stars and some picturesque wildlife, the film would eventually do what it was supposed to do and make a lot of money. Produced at a cost of $3.1 million, *Mogambo*'s worldwide gross would be $8.2 million.[38] It contains, though, only a faint shadow of Clark's previous performance in the more torrid and sexually charged atmosphere of *Red Dust*.

Clark saw Grace Kelly off to New York at the London airport on the nineteenth. She was spotted in tears by the media as she said goodbye to Clark. A long time later she would reveal, "I was very fond of Clark Gable.... Perhaps, if there hadn't been so much of an age discrepancy things might have been different."[39]

He left immediately with the Menascos for Paris. For the next month the three of them hit all the tourist high spots as they toured France, Switzerland, and Italy, occasionally joined by Suzane Dadolle and then Wayne and Elinor Griffin in Florence. "It was interesting to note Clark's pleasure and enthusiasm for the cultural side," Wayne later told Jean Garceau. "He seemed eager to broaden his knowledge of people, places, and things."[40] At the end of May, Clark's divorce decree came through. Nothing daunted, he continued on with his own travel after the Menascos sailed for home, this time stopping in small towns as he slowly made his way back to Paris. He would call Jean every now and then just to let her know where he was. "I might as well make the most of this trip, Jean," he said once. "I don't ever expect to see any of this again."[41]

By July, he had established himself at the Hotel Raphael in Paris and was studying the script of *Holland Deep*, which by now had been edited and tightened up. This would be another Sam Zimbalist production, directed by Gottfried Reinhardt and costarring Lana Turner and Victor Mature. It is the story of a Dutch intelligence officer, Deventer (Gable), who is captured by the Germans during World War II, only to be dramatically rescued by an underground resistance group led by a man called The Scarf (Mature). Against his better judgment, Deventer is ordered to train a female operative in England (Turner), with whom he falls in love and then has to send back into Holland. However, he becomes convinced she has betrayed them, and he sets off to hunt her down, only to discover that The Scarf is the real traitor.

With positive encouragement from George Chasin and Jean, and high hopes for Rienhardt's direction and seeing as how he was in Europe anyway, Clark finally decided to take on the film. However, he had become more and more unhappy with the management at MGM and was sure that this would be his last film for them. He shipped his beloved Jaguar back home and went to London for story conferences and wardrobe fittings.

Taking as much advantage of Clark's star presence as they could, the studio decided to stage a week-long goodwill tour of Holland. MGM assigned Paul Mills of the London office and Emily Torchia from Culver City to travel with Clark and handle the public relations. On September 23 they embarked on KLM for Amsterdam, where they were met by huge crowds and the inevitable press receptions. From there, accompanied by police escorts, they progressed to Delft and then to Rotterdam, where Clark was presented with two lion cubs named Mogambo and Gable. The procession then made its way to the town square of Maastricht, where Clark was met by eight thousand cheering people and a parade of tanks and guns to celebrate the arrival of Allied troops during the War. Champagne toasts were given and speeches made thanking the Americans for liberating the townsfolk from the Nazis. Clark then rose and expressed his gratitude for the welcome, claiming kinship with the Dutch through his mother, Addie Hershelman. It was a very worthy piece of public relations himself, considering her ancestry was more likely to have been German. The crowd loved it though and cheered madly, and a pretty girl was chosen to kiss Clark. They pushed on through Utrecht, The Hague, and other cities on their tour, which was an outstanding success as these enterprises go. Clark commanded respect wherever he went, even something akin to awe a lot of the time, and he wasn't jostled.

Clark at about the time he was filming Betrayed *in 1954.*

Eventually they arrived back in Amsterdam, where they met up with the rest of the cast and crew and settled down to work on *Betrayed*, as it was now called, in earnest. Lana Turner, who had just married ex-Tarzan Lex Barker on September 8, always held Clark in high esteem, and the two got along well. The company moved around various locations, attracting crowds wherever they went. When they were working near Arnhem, Clark and *Collier's* photographer Martin Harris decided to test just how recognizable the star was. Clark dressed up, or rather down, as a local barge hand and wandered around the streets of the town. He stopped by fruit stands, leaned on lampposts, mingled with crowds. Nothing happened. It was over an hour before a pair of young women on bicycles did an incredulous U-turn and pedaled back to get his autograph. "Fine walk," Clark grinned ruefully. "I feel like a has-been."[42]

As Clark's last work for MGM, *Betrayed* is good but not remarkable. Clark strides through the film with a grim look on his face most of the time and a "lets hurry along and get this over with" attitude. His underplayed style contrasts sharply with Mature's larger-than-life melodramatics and Turner's edgy emotions, and they don't sit easily with each other. Consequently, a lot of hard work goes into generating a few romantic sparks. However, *Betrayed* is interesting from a technical point of view for its extensive use of outdoor location shooting, which was still relatively uncommon in the early 1950s, and for the use of Eastman color stock, which produces more subdued and shaded tones rather than the bright primaries of Technicolor, giving much of the film the look of a Rembrandt painting.

When studio shooting in London finished, Clark flew home for Christmas. Jean had the house redecorated, converting Sylvia's sitting room back into a library for Clark and painting over "that damned pink," as he called it, in the bedroom in soft tones of green. MGM had been desperately trying to get him to sign another contract with them, but Clark had made up his mind this time not to renew. Early in January 1954, Clark went back into the studio to do some retakes and publicity shots. Then on March 3, with no farewell party or fanfare, he walked through the gates of the studio for the last time.

CHAPTER 25

KATHLEEN

One night Kay Spreckels' (nee Williams) phone rang. When she picked it up and heard the voice at the other end of the line, she felt as if ten years had dropped away. For some reason that even she professed she never knew for sure, Clark had decided to renew a friendship that had been interrupted when both of them married again unsuccessfully. Now Kay was the mother of two children, Bunker (who was never known by his given name, Adolph) and Joan, four and three years old, respectively. Clark asked Kay if she would like to have dinner with him. Kay warned him that she had developed an appetite over the last few years and that, seeing as how their last dinner had cost him hospital bills for the cook, cleaning bills for the rug, and had left Kay with china in her knee, perhaps it would be easier for everyone if Clark just sent money. "I'll take a chance if you will," Clark laughed. They both took that chance and never regretted it.[1]

Someone had once told Kay that Clark would never accept her because the children would scare him away but, on the contrary, for a man who had never had children of his own, Clark always had a soft spot for kids. He had been a good stepfather to Ria's children, always treating them as if they had been his own. Now he, Bunker, and Joan hit it off right

away, as did Clark and Kay, although it was more like fanning glowing coals than a brushfire. They were both older, she now thirty-six and he fifty-three, and had both been matured by time and experiences that were not entirely happy for either of them. Fortunately, neither seemed to have been embittered by what they had gone through. They were prepared to let the development of this relationship take time and let fate take its course.

Meanwhile, George Chasin's desk at MCA was becoming buried in offers of work for Clark. Now that he was wealthy and independent, Clark knew that he could pick and choose, and he wanted to choose only stories in which he would clearly be the hero. MGM story editor Samuel Marx approached him on behalf of Dore Schary about a script involving two Nevada gamblers in love with the same woman. Schary wanted Clark, Errol Flynn, and Lana Turner for the leads, but Clark turned him down, saying he wouldn't appear in a picture where the woman couldn't make up her mind which man to choose.[2] Finally, he signed with Darryl Zanuck of 20th Century–Fox on July 12, 1954, to do two pictures: *Soldier of Fortune* and *The Tall Men*. Clark would get ten percent of the gross and $400,000 up front for each film, prompting

Zanuck to comment wryly that Clark, "now owns half the studio."[3] Clark immediately asked for Grace Kelly as his costar for *Soldier* but Grace was busy making films with Hitchcock, so Susan Hayward got the part. When told the news, Clark made a memorable gaffe by not remembering who she was.

He would have cause to remember another actress, though, when he was invited as one of eighty guests to the wrap party for *The Seven Year Itch* at Romanoff's on the night of November 4. By the time the shoot ended, this film was already notorious for star Marilyn Monroe's famous publicity stunt of standing over a New York subway grate so her dress puffed up. When the scene was re-created back on the set, the studio camera only showed the dress lifting to her knees, but still shots of her taken in Lexington Avenue before a huge crowd of onlookers show her pleated dress blowing way up over her waist, clearly revealing her underwear. It had all been too much for her then-husband, Joe DiMaggio, who smacked her around for doing it. Monroe quickly filed for a divorce, which had been granted only a few days before on October 27. The party was organized by her agent, Charles Feldman, for two major reasons. He wanted to remind Zanuck at Fox how popular she was, and he wanted to ingratiate himself with Monroe by flattering her that she had finally been accepted by the Hollywood elite so she wouldn't sign with MCA, which she did anyway the following year.

As well as Zanuck and Gable, the guest list included Humphrey Bogart, Clifton Webb, Loretta Young, Susan Hayward, Gary Cooper, Claudette Colbert, Jack Warner, and Samuel Goldwyn. Monroe would later recall that somebody tapped her on the shoulder, and Clark's unmistakable voice asked whether he could have this dance. "I nearly collapsed," she said. "I'm sure I must have turned the color of my red chiffon dress. I don't remember what I said, or if I said anything. But I remember thinking, 'Wouldn't he be surprised to know how I really feel about him?'"[4] While they danced, according to biographer Donald Spoto, Monroe told Clark how much she admired him and that she had always wanted to work with him. Clark replied, "I ran *Gentlemen Prefer Blondes,* and I told my agent you have the magic. I'd like to do a picture with you too."[5] When they would finally work together, though, it would not be a party.

A few days later, on November 11, Clark finally put his fear of flying behind him and boarded a Pan Am flight for Hong Kong, acting as a surprise passenger greeter at the door, to begin location shooting for *Soldier of Fortune.* Director Edward Dmytryk was with him.[6] Together they stopped off in Tokyo for a press conference and some sightseeing. Once again, Clark found himself the center of female attention. When the women performers of the traditional Dance of Autumn spotted Clark in the Kokusai Theater audience one night, they were so overcome the show floundered to a halt.

Based on the novel by Ernest K. Gann, who also wrote the screenplay, *Soldier of Fortune* is the story of a photographer (Gene Barry) captured by the Chinese, who attempt to brainwash him. A mercenary smuggler (Clark) is asked by the photographer's wife (Hayward) to rescue her husband, which he does after being pursued by Chinese gunboats. The smuggler decides to go straight when the rescued photographer realizes his wife and his rescuer have fallen in love and gallantly leaves.

At the last minute, Susan Hayward was unable to leave the U.S. because her ex-husband objected when she filed a court motion to take their ten-year-old twin boys with her to Hong Kong. It was too dangerous there, he claimed. Haywood would not travel without them. Zanuck, knowing the box-office draw of her name, revised the script so that the interior scenes in which she appeared could be shot at the studio, using rear-projected footage for any external backgrounds. He sent director Edward Dmytryk, Clark, and the rest of the crew to Hong Kong to shoot all the external scenes.[7] The entire company took over the sixth floor of the Peninsula Hotel in Kowloon. It had already been noted by some, to Clark's displeasure, that his drinking and inactivity were catching up with him. Clark confessed to "going on the wagon" for the sake of the film and to cutting out starches to lose some fourteen pounds. Nevertheless, after a few weeks of Asian food the film company was feeling a tad nostalgic for some more traditional fare, so Clark went down to the docks, bought twenty pounds of hot dogs from the stewards of the liner *President Cleveland*, and put on a weenie roast for everybody by lighting a fire in a stove in his room.[8]

Returning to California in mid-December, Clark was met at the airport by Kay. He'd brought back gifts for her, a model ship for Bunker, a doll for Joan, and even a made-to-measure black silk housecoat for Jean Garceau. He continued with studio shooting for *Soldier* into the new year, and he and Kay now saw each other every day. Howard Strickling would later comment that Kay "made up her mind to be part of Clark's life, and she was. Whatever Clark wanted to do was fine with Kay. She learned to hunt and ride horseback and like it. She was more than a wife. She was Clark's favorite companion and friend."[9] They shared picnics, played golf, had quiet dinners together, and spent a lot of time with the children. Clark used to love reading to them at night and would often rush back from the studio without even taking the time to remove his makeup to spend this special period with them before their bedtime. While columnists had duly speculated on whether anything was developing between them, Clark and Kay were always careful to avoid any predictions of what might be and fell back on that old cliché: "We're just good friends." Between themselves, though, Clark and Kay realized their friendship had blossomed into love.

In April 1955, they faced another short separation while Clark would be in Durango, Mexico, for *The Tall Men*. They were sitting by the pool at the ranch one spring afternoon when Clark turned to Kay, whom he always called Kathleen, and said, "Kathleen, don't you think we've known each other long enough? We've really been in love so many years. Don't you think we should get this little job over and done with and become Mr. and Mrs.?"[10] After she got her breath back, Kathleen agreed. "I was walking on clouds," she wistfully recalled a few years later. "He had kept me on needles and pins for quite a few months, but I knew the chances for a wedding were pretty good when I heard him tell a friend, 'She has some good stuff in her. She can even run a tractor.' He liked independent women and I guess I qualified."[11] Clark wanted to go right out and buy her an engagement ring, but Kathleen said she didn't need one. He admitted that he'd wanted to ask her all year but had been waiting for just the right time; she reassured him that this was just the right time. They agreed to keep their wedding plans a secret. Once again, the ever-private Clark wanted to keep his life just that way.

Clark went to Durango, which had been chosen as *The Tall Men* location because the Mexican Crillo cattle around there looked similar to the scarcer Texas Longhorns. Fox had assembled three thousand head of cattle, three hundred horses and a company of seventy. Clark had done a lot of riding and roping practice at Palm Springs by way of preparation for his role as ex-Confederate outlaw Ben Allison, who is offered a trail-boss job and a share in the profits by the man he holds up (Robert Ryan). Directed by Clark's friend Raoul Walsh, who had been the original owner of his Encino ranch, *The Tall Men* was the most successful of a trio of Walsh movies and one of the best Western characterizations of Clark's career. Jane Russell is the woman rescued by the men from the Indians, and she takes up a lot of the movie to decide she'd rather have Clark than an unscrupulous Ryan.[12] Presumably, Clark felt that decision was more obvious in this script than in the Dore Schary deal he'd rejected.

When Howard Hughes sold RKO, where

Clark and Kathleen.

Russell had been made famous in the heavily promoted and subsequently banned 1943 Hughes film *Outlaw*, he had contracted a $1 million seven-year deal with Russell to be her independent employer who could loan her out to studios. Over five of those years, she would be loaned out for six pictures. Otherwise, she was free to make her own films, so she had formed a production company, Russ-Field, with husband Robert Waterfield. Their first movie was *Gentlemen Marry Brunettes*, the companion to Russell's earlier 1953 Howard Hawks film for Fox with Marilyn Monroe, *Gentlemen Prefer Blondes*.

Russell and Clark worked well together in *The Tall Men*, which was one of her loan-out pictures. They had known each other socially since the late 1930s, when they had met at the home of Fieldsie Lang, Carole Lombard's best friend, and her husband Walter. He was directing movies for John Payne, who was dating Russell at the time. There were the usual jokes on the set. In one scene where Clark has to pick Russell up and carry her to a carriage, she hid thirty to forty pounds of weights in the folds of her full-skirted period costume. He carried her without missing a beat. "Wasn't I just a bit heavy?" she asked later. "Well, I knew I had a real woman in my arms, but you weren't heavy," replied the gallant Clark.[13] In one scene, Clark calls Russell "Grandma," and the nickname stuck throughout the shoot. They called Raoul Walsh "Father." A tough-looking man who wore a patch over one eye, rolled his own cigarettes, and was known for snapping, "Take it before they forget it" after one rehearsal, Walsh was really a bit of a marshmallow with a sense of humor and a razor-sharp wit.[14]

When Clark walked out into the sun at Vicente Guerrero on the first day of the shoot, no one in the town had seen a movie to recognize who he was. "Guess I won't be signing any autographs today," he chuckled wryly.[15] He wrote letters to Kathleen in his spare time, and he called her every night at eight to talk about how the day's shoot had gone and to ask when she was sending him his American

cigarettes and the cans of red-skinned peanuts he loved to snack on.

Reunited after location shooting was over, Clark and Kathleen hatched plans to stage their secret wedding in Nevada. There was no way they were going to be able to marry anywhere in California without attracting a media stampede. Apart from Jean Garceau, who had known all along, they took into their confidence Clark's friends Al and Julie Menasco, who lived near St. Helena, to help plan the logistics. After some scouting around, Al recommended the small town of Minden, some forty-five miles south of Reno. He and Julie even purchased the simple wedding bands to maintain the secrecy. The night before the wedding, Kathleen's sister, Elizabeth Nesser, agreed to be matron of honor. Then they finally let Howard Strickling in on their plans, telling him not to release anything to reporters until they called him.

So, at 6 a.m. on July 11, 1955, Clark, Kathleen, and Elizabeth set out into the desert in Clark's new white station wagon, heading for the rendezvous with the Menascos at Gardnerville, Nevada. The car developed an oil leak but Clark, with his mind typically fixed on being punctual, merely stopped at a gas station to pick up six cans of oil, which they fed into the car every hundred miles or so. Arriving in Gardnerville, they needed to freshen up and change into wedding outfits. Kathleen suggested a grove of trees near a stream, not wanting to risk being recognized in town, but her sister flatly refused to rough it that much and insisted on a motel, saying she had a cunning plan. Walking into the motel office, she said that she, her mother, and her father were on their way to Lake Tahoe but just needed two rooms to rest in for a while. She and Kathleen took one. Then Clark, wearing dark glasses with his hat pulled low, hunched his shoulders and hobbled across the courtyard to the other room. Looking out of the window, Elizabeth said gleefully, "Look out the window at what's coming, Kay. It's not too late to change your mind."[16]

Dressed in their wedding outfits, they left a short time later. Kathleen wore a navy-blue Irene suit with white gloves and a pearl necklace; Clark wore a dark blue pinstripe suit with a white shirt and dark tie. They applied in Minden for their license, bargaining the clerk's silence for an autograph for her daughter. They arrived at the tiny cottage of the justice of the peace, Judge Walter Fisher, just before six p.m. When it came time for the ring, everyone's hands were shaking. Kathleen couldn't slide the ring on Clark's finger until she remembered that he'd injured that knuckle. They had agreed he would wear it on his little finger.

After the wedding, Al flew the newlyweds back to the Menasco house in the Valley of the Moon that he and Julie had agreed to loan them so they could have a peaceful honeymoon. After five days, Clark told Kathleen he would take her anywhere in the world she wanted to go; she said she would be happy going back to the ranch in Encino. Clark offered to buy her a house in Beverly Hills, but his wife didn't want to go anywhere else. She knew Clark loved this house, and she did too. "I knew what Pa was thinking," she wrote later, "but I felt no jealousy, no rivalry with the past. I was haunted by no ghosts."[17]

So at last Clark was able to settle into a happy, harmoniously married life. It is quite possible that he would have had that life with Carole, but fate decided that neither history nor Clark would ever know that for sure. Perhaps, on the other hand, it all happened for him when it was the right time, and when all is said and done, that's the best time. Many people seem to have decided that Carole was Clark's only perfect wife and that Kathleen was merely an inferior copy, who caught him in the last few years of his life by deliberately modeling herself on Carole. However, that unfairly denigrates the role of a remarkably kind, loving, and unselfish woman who deserved the happiness she found with Clark just as much as he did with her. Kathleen said that she always had the greatest respect for Clark

and Carole's relationship and never sought comparisons from him between that and their own relationship. Clark may have appeared the social man-about-town with women at his beck and call, but since Carole's death he had been a lonely and often tortured man. Kathleen had not long emerged from her own private hell of being a battered wife, somehow made all the more ugly by the vast wealth involved. That both Kathleen and Clark could still find within themselves the unembittered wellspring of human kindness and love that they both proceeded to pour into the tragically short period of their marriage says much about the strength of their respective characters.

Kathleen made few changes around the property and in Clark's life. She believed that it was important to learn to like what her husband liked, so she learned to shoot, fish, and play golf. She found that before long she loved it all as much as Clark did. They were happy with each other's company and only entertained occasionally at home, feeling that they were no longer in need of a social life. As Clark put it, "Ma, we've both been to all those fires."[18] He wanted to know what it felt like to actually retire, so they spent the next twelve months together working on being a family. "They always looked like newlyweds," British society publicist Lee Anderson once said. "They had a happiness few of us are fortunate to know. In their home, love filled every room, and we were all warmed by the glow."[19]

Sometimes it seems as if sadness waits, lurking until people are the happiest before striking with swift sureness at the very heart of their joy. Clark had always wanted children of his own, and it seemed his wish had come true when, two months after their wedding, Kathleen's doctor confirmed she was pregnant. They tried to keep it secret, but Clark couldn't stop smiling. His wide grin eventually gave it away at a dinner party, and he had to admit that next May he'd be "handing out cigars." But during her tenth week, Kathleen fell ill with a virus she couldn't shake off, and ran a persistent high temperature and fever. At one point, she slipped into a brief coma. Doctors were called. Unfortunately, they prescribed medication that has since proved to be inappropriate for use by expectant mothers.[20] Although she rallied, Kathleen collapsed a short time later and was rushed to hospital, where doctors could not save the baby. Clark and Kathleen would have to wait a few more years, but they knew in their hearts they wouldn't wait in vain. They held onto their new-found love and their family through a joyful Thanksgiving and Christmas and into a new year.

Kathleen was very conscious of her role as Mrs. Clark Gable and of what that entailed. Throughout their marriage, she would consider it her role to anticipate what Clark's wishes might be before he had the chance to wish them. As Lyn Tornabene so wryly and aptly observed, "Kay Gable's job was not so much wife as custodian of a national treasure, and she took it very seriously."[21] For most of his film-acting career, Clark had been the property of the MGM studio, and it had acted as his parents, his advisers, and his guardians as well as being his employer. For all those years, he'd worked in the equivalent of a walled city insulated from the outside world, although not quite as insulated as some, with various people on hand to look after his life for him. When he left the studio and went independent, Kathleen pretty much stepped into the gap and continued on in the time-honored role of looking after the king. For her, that meant having everything in her home in order, so that in winter Clark would be warmed by an open fire and in summer cooled by the fans. She always made sure, too, that she looked her best for Clark. Her husband "never found me still wearing pin-curls or lounging around in a housecoat. At least, not if I could help it. I always tried to allow myself time to bathe and freshen up before Pa arrived home.... I have always taken pride in being neat, clean and well-groomed. Clark admired this in a woman. If it had been an extremely warm day, or if I knew Clark had been working on a hot, dusty set, I'd try to wear something that would be pleasing and cool for him to look at. I'd select a white linen dress, or a fresh blouse and skirt. Pa always noticed what I was wearing and if he didn't like a certain outfit, he'd diplomatically let me know."[22]

Clark ate simply, and he wasn't that concerned whether they ate at the table or out on the porch, but he was as much a stickler for having his meals on time as he was about starting work on time. Lunch was always at noon, and dinner was at 7 p.m. His favorite dish was a good steak with potato salad or dill pickles. They both loved knockwurst and sauerkraut, potato pancakes, sauerbraten, and Pennsylvania Dutch coleslaw. Clark's big passion, though, was for raw onion, which he'd slice thickly and eat with or without bread. That preference might have gone a long way to explaining those periodic comments various female costars made about his breath.

Basically the Gables settled into being a model, quiet, well-off married couple of the 1950s. They went to bed early after watching some television or reading scripts or books. Clark, who disapproved of having weapons in view of inquisitive little children, locked away his beloved collection of guns and knives and had the display cabinets dismantled and replaced with bookshelves. He had eclectic and avid reading tastes, and the library was filled to overflowing with everything from Thoreau to Shakespeare to Winston Churchill's memoirs. He would always tell the children that it was never too much trouble to take the time to look up something they didn't know.

Clark was very proud of Bunker and Joan, and he would spend all the time he could with them when he was not working, but he would never let them forget that they owed love to their biological father too. He would take them swimming, cycling, and on fishing trips, and after Bunker had joined the Little League would practice afternoons with him throwing grounders. John Lee Mahin recalled Clark's qualms about inheriting two children: "He always said he would make a lousy father because he was impatient and selfish. But if there were two things Clark wasn't, it was impatient and selfish. He was a very gentle man. And after he married Kay, he treated Bunker and Joan as if they were his very own. He talked about the kids like any father brags about his children."[23] Indeed, Clark found it fun being a parent at his age. "Everything is new to them," he explained to writer Vernon Scott. "Seeing things through their eyes gives me a fresh outlook on life, too. I couldn't be more pleased."[24]

By now, Clark could talk about himself as "fundamentally a man who doesn't want to work."[25] He had grown tired of not being his own man. "For twenty-four years I had to answer the call of the studio," he said. "When they cracked the whip, I jumped. When you've been jumping for twenty-four years, you get a little tired of it."[26] At last, at fifty-four, he could enjoy being his own boss, although nothing would ever stop this wealthy man from fretting he didn't have enough money. Despite occasional comments such as the one he'd made the year previously that he would only make three more movies and then quit the business, it's highly unlikely Clark could ever have let himself completely retire. He simply had too much fun doing what he did and being the actor he was. "I enjoy acting," he said. "I enjoy it today more than I ever did before because of the freedom I have now. First I find a story. If I don't find one, I play golf."[27]

When released in October 1955, *The Tall Men* had been well received and made money at the box office, unlike Russ-Field's *Gentlemen Marry Brunettes*, which went hopelessly over budget and lost money. Jane Russell and Clark had worked well together, had both recently left the studio system, and were interested in independent production. Russell's husband, Robert, had found himself out of his depth with movie production and Russell needed a more experienced partner. After some negotiation, Clark joined them to form Gabco-Russfield.[28]

During the following year, their first pro-

ject began to take shape. According to Russell, her friend David Hempstead had showed her his script, *Last Man at Wagon Mound*. She and Bob thought the lead role of desperado con-man Dan Kehoe would be ideal for Clark, who read it and agreed. Passing through the ghost town of Wagon Mound, Kehoe hears the story of Mother McDade and the four Mc-Dade wives who had married the four Mc-Dade outlaw brothers. Three of the brothers are reputed dead, with only one to return alive to say where their buried loot is hidden. Kehoe persuades the family to let him stay. Each of the wives makes a play for him, but when he finds one of them is a fake, too, the pair team up and find the gold. Clark's friend Raoul Walsh would direct again and United Artists agreed to distribute. Clark wanted Russell to play one of the four women, but she declined for tax reasons.[29]

Somehow, before its release in December 1956, the film acquired the unfortunate and exploitable title of *The King and Four Queens*, and things went downhill from there. The whole premise of the story relies on the audience accepting that four sisters-in-law of varying ages and cultural backgrounds would all find Clark equally as attractive, but mid-1950s audiences were becoming just a tad cynical about accepting an aging Clark Gable in this sort of situation. Not only that, but he makes little effort to sell himself as a proposition, seeming to walk through his role as if this situation is just how life should be and how he expects women to react. While he's not looking, Jo Van Fleet, as the embittered Mother McDade with the hopeless task of keeping four man-hungry young women away from Clark, steals the show with her strong character acting. Underneath all the romantic melodramatics, this film is a rather cynical look at how greed can cause people to screw over their fellow man, even kin, long before a more modern screen idol would shout, "Show me the money!"

The location shooting for *King and Four Queens* began about mid-May of 1955 in the

The King and his four queens intently check that they're not losing the plot. L-r: Jean Willes, Sarah Shane, Eleanor Parker, and Barbara Nichols.

desert country around St. George, Utah. It was miserably hot during the day, although it could turn quite cold at night. Leaving the children still in school in California, Kathleen and her maid, Louise Jones, went along with Clark and the eighty members of the film company. While the others took over the town's motels, the Gables rented a house. Kathleen only went out to the location once, during a night shoot, saying she didn't want "to interfere with my man's work." She was up at the crack of dawn every morning to prepare breakfast for him, though, and a home-made lunch and a thermos of coffee would be ready for Clark to take.[30] During the day, Kathleen would join neighbors to work on quilts or go shopping. She demonstrated needlepoint to Barbara Nicholls, one of the four "queens," showing her how she put tiny, meticulous stitches into a pair of slippers for Clark, commenting that "you have to love someone an awful lot to have this much patience."[31] Every evening when Clark got home, Kathleen

would have dinner on the table. At night they'd be the very picture of domesticity, he studying his script while Kathleen embroidered or read. On days off, Clark put in time teaching his wife to shoot skeet and roll her own cigarettes.

The local townsfolk were impressed by how much of a regular guy Clark was. They'd stop in the street to chat to him and ask how the fishing was going, or they would come by and knock on his door at night to ask for an autograph. One chilly night, he was doing a scene in which he had to go into the river. The water was like ice and as he emerged shivering, with his teeth chattering, the crew wrapped him in blankets right away. Next thing, a group of youngsters were crowding around him with their autograph books. Instead of waving them away, Clark just laughed and began signing. Children in the community adored him, and they would follow him everywhere.

Just as Clark had helped Ava Gardner

An affectionate Clark and Kathleen in Utah while making The King and Four Queens.

Kay sending Clark off to work on The King and Four Queens *from their Utah kitchen.*

with her lines, he also helped Barbara Nicholls with hers and sought to add to her confidence. Clark had interviewed and selected Barbara personally, after seeing her performance in the rushes of *Beyond a Reasonable Doubt*, her only other major film role.[32] Clark had liked her spirit. "How old are you?" he'd asked. "How old do you want me to be?" she'd replied. Clark nearly fell out of his chair, laughing. He took her under his wing, coaching her how to move, where to look, and how to be aware of where her key light was. "I had done a great deal of television in New York," she said, "and I had learned to appreciate helpful friendliness from most fellow actors and directors, but I didn't expect that kind of help from a star like Mr. Gable. When one particular scene bothered me, he took me aside and sat down with me, discussed the scene, and rehearsed the lines with me. It was a difficult bit in which little nuances, conveyed in only a few words and gestures, were all-important."[33]

Although reporters would still invariably write about how fit and healthy Clark was, it was around this time that people closer to him began to observe little things about him that made them concerned. Clark had been a steady drinker for most of his life, and he had drifted in and out of being a heavy drinker. While admitting this, friends would point out in the same breath how well Clark could hold his liquor, and how he could drink the average person under the table and never seem the worse for wear. But Clark wasn't young any more. *The New York Times* had commented on the "bluish-purple" color of his lips in *Soldier of Fortune*.[34] Renee Conley, who fitted his costumes for *King and Four Queens*, noticed that Clark's complexion was often gray and that he would sometimes shake so badly he had to sit down between fittings. The man who loved fast cars confessed to her during one fitting that he had been pulled over and ticketed for driving too slowly on the freeway.[35]

Ironically, it wasn't Clark who fell ill. By the time the Gables returned home in June,

Kathleen was not at all well. While on location, she had suffered from sharp chest and arm pain that had concerned Clark, even though she had tried to carry on regardless. She was hospitalized as soon as possible. After tests, Kathleen was diagnosed with angina pectoris, an extremely painful heart disease, and put on medication. For some three weeks Clark moved into a hospital room next to her and never left her side. She was eventually allowed to return home to convalesce with complete bed rest. She was told she would have to change her whole way of life. There would be no more hunting and location trips with Clark, no more golf, no more dashing around in the Thunderbird, no more riding or working around the farm. In short, she would have to give up those activities that had brought her closer to Clark and that had helped their marriage be so happy so far. Climbing stairs was out of the question, so the library was converted into a bedroom where she would remain for most of the several months until her August 7 birthday.

She was, however, a very unwilling patient. Kathleen figured she had married Clark to be beside him actively, not as an invalid, and with grim determination she began to push herself to be out of bed and around the house. Clark would leave her to take a nap, then return only to find her sorting the children's clothes. She was so determined, she started to push too hard. Finally, her friends took her aside and told her to take things more slowly or else she would wind up dead and no help to anyone, let alone the man she loved. Clark's fans loved her too, and hundreds of cards and letters arrived encouraging her to get well. She took strength from them all, and from the circle of her close friends, but most of all Kathleen took strength from the look in her husband's eyes. So Kathleen gradually learned what she could and couldn't do, how to take care of herself, and she grew stronger. Her willpower helped her pull through, but so did Clark's love.

In the middle of all this, some late script

changes to *The King and Four Queens* made it necessary for Clark to fly back to Utah for four days. Those four days seemed like four months without Kay. By the time they were over, Clark was missing her so much that he chartered a plane to fly him home. After that, he declared, there would be "no more separations. I've made a decision — I'm not going to take any more pictures where I have to go on location. Life is too short. All I want to do is to sit home with 'Ma' this summer. We have a wonderful life here on our little ranch. We're going to take it easy together and be happy. Why, we're just as relaxed and contented as two new-born babies."[36]

By the fall, Kathleen had improved a great deal. She was able to appear in public with Clark again for the premiere of *Giant* in late October. It was Clark's first chance for them both to appear in his new Mercedes 300SL two-door coupe with tan leather upholstery and matching leather luggage. According to Kathleen, Clark hesitated for weeks about buying the car, examining it, test-driving it, then coming home to fret about the money until she insisted he buy it as a present to himself. He let Kathleen drive it once; she was so nervous she kept clashing the gears until Clark took over from her. After that, she wasn't even allowed to clean the ashtrays in his pride and joy.[37] Nevertheless, the Gables had successfully weathered their first major crisis. Kathleen's theory about why their happy marriage was going to last was that, aside from being deeply in love with each other, she and Clark also had a wonderful friendship. They truly enjoyed living together. Most important of all, for her, was that "there's no living in the past. No throwing things up to each other. Whatever either of us did before doesn't count now. We look ahead to all the happy things awaiting us. What more in the world can a woman ask? I have everything I want. I'm going to be all right. You can bet on that."[38]

The year 1957 marked Clark's twenty-fifth anniversary as a film actor. On Thursday,

January 10, Congressman Hon. Wayne L. Hays, state representative of Ohio, paid tribute on the floor of the House of Representatives to one of "Ohio's proud sons," declaring that Clark had "contributed much to the enjoyment of millions." Yet, he said, Clark had remained "one of the friendliest and approachable of all Hollywood stars, and the personification of all that is best in American manhood. He is an example of how a young American lad can advance himself and become famous…. Mr. Gable still reigns unchallenged as one of the world's most popular and best-known movie personalities. Time cannot wither nor custom stale 'King' Gable's infinite appeal…. Long live the king!"[39]

Through MCA, Warner Brothers made Clark an offer he should have refused, starring in their production of *Band of Angels* for ten percent of the gross. Perhaps he was discouraged by the failure of his efforts at independent production, perhaps he was attracted to the project because Raoul Walsh would be directing again. It certainly wasn't that he needed the money. In any event, he agreed to star with Yvonne de Carlo in this poor man's *Gone with the Wind,* and he and Kay left for location shooting in Louisiana in mid–January.

En route, the Gables stayed at the Roosevelt Hotel in New Orleans, where Clark discovered that the "international suite" put at their disposal was all of sixty feet long and thirty-five feet wide, and then drove on to the film's location in Baton Rouge. While Clark was working, Kathleen followed her usual pattern of shopping and socializing with the city's important families, including Governor Long and his wife, from whom there was no shortage of invitations. She was asked to visit Natchez, where she was presented with the keys to that city. When cloudy weather would hold up film shooting, Clark would go off shooting quail. On February 1, Kathleen threw a birthday party for Clark to which all the cast members were invited at the Baton Rouge Country Club. There they found that all the dishes on the menu were named after someone at the party.

Based on the novel by Robert Penn Warren, the story concerns a reformed slave trader, Hamish Bond (Gable), who sees a plantation owner's daughter put up for sale as a slave because her mother was one. Hamish, who has already reared and educated a slave, Rau-Rau (Sidney Poitier) as his son, buys Amantha (de Carlo) and brings her to his house, where he treats her as a lady. They fall in love, which was a bold and controversial move for a film in the less-than-multicultural 1950s. When the Civil War breaks out, Rau-Rau goes North and joins the Union Army, which had its own prejudices about African Americans (see the film *Glory*). The title of the book, in fact, referred to the short life expectancy of African American soldiers in the war, although there is no reference to that in the film. When New Orleans falls, Rau-Rau is there to denounce Hamish, but he finds he cannot and instead helps he and Amantha to escape.

Clark couldn't escape the critical mauling *Band of Angels* received when it was released in August. Once again, the gap between a rather tired-looking Clark and a young de Carlo is a bit much to be credible. In fact, it seems that just about everything that should have been done simply does not happen. No sparks strike between the lovers, there is no frisson of danger over the race issue, or indeed any attempt to deal with it as an issue, and the rest of the two-dimensional roles are pretty much wasted. *Newsweek* summed it up very succinctly: "Here is a movie so bad it must be seen to be disbelieved."[40]

Much of the film was shot at The Cottage, a nineteenth-century plantation house, and on the river paddleboat *Gordon C. Green*. The crew had a lot of problems with crowds of fans turning up to see the ever-popular Clark. Complaining about them brought he and Yvonne de Carlo, who had up until then respectfully kept her distance, together. "We were walking by the honey wagon one day," she recalled. "That was as near to the set as the fans could get and they were always lined up to watch whoever went in. I said to Clark, 'They take pictures of me zipping up my fly — so to speak — every time I come out of the wagon.' He loved it. After that he felt he could talk frankly and openly and use earthy language. He liked that kind of humor."[41]

No sooner had Clark returned from Louisiana when William Perlberg and George Seaton at Paramount, who had made a string of successful films, offered him the lead in *Teacher's Pet* with Doris Day. After a long stint of drama, Clark was eager to try some comedy again, especially back on his home ground of journalism and newspapers. He accepted for his usual ten percent of the gross. Clark would play a cynical, self-made newspaper journalist who hates cadets straight out of journalism school. He turns down an invitation to address a journalism class but is ordered to do it by his boss. Once he sees the teacher (Day), he is inspired to enroll as a student. As such, he gains new insight into what it means to study his profession, and he eventually falls for and marries the teacher. The cast also included Mamie Van Doren, Gig Young, and Nick Adams.

When shooting started in April, the cast was boosted by sixty-seven working newspaper columnists and journalists from all over the United States, who were invited to play themselves in the newspaper-room scenes. Of course, this also guaranteed the shoot would get lots of free publicity and column space.

Although audiences liked Day and Clark together, and the film collected the largest grosses of a Doris Day film since 1955's *Love Me Or Leave Me*, the film could have been more attractive and stylish to watch. It was shot in black and white when it could have been shot in color, giving it a gritty atmosphere rather than a lighthearted one, and to make matters worse George Seaton's direction had little finesse. Although *Variety* thought it was one of Clark's best performances in years, other critics thought that the role was not suited to either Clark's age or style. "Clark

Gable is feeling and showing his age," said Ellen Fitzpatrick in *Films in Review*. "The masculine self-confidence he has projected for thirty years has gone. Gable himself seems to know it has gone and resorts in this film to mugging of so stereotyped a kind that it is heartbreaking to see.... Film historians can perceive the beginning of the end of Gable's great career."[42] She would, in time, be proved wrong on that point.

Clark's relationship with Day was "smooth," George Seaton would comment later, because of their professionalism. "Clark was the kindest and fairest actor with whom I had ever worked," he said. "All he asked was that an actress playing opposite him was equally as fair, without resorting to those cheap tricks designed to gain an edge. Also Clark could never condone anyone being ill-prepared or late. Since Doris was always fully prepared, on time, and never caused a delay by primping between takes, they got along splendidly. There were times when Doris seems a bit nervous playing opposite the great Gable, but Clark always found a way to put her at ease."[43]

Doris Day and her husband, Marty Melcher, had only just bought a house in Beverly Hills and were having it decorated by Bruce Alan Clark. The Gables so liked his work there that they asked him to redecorate the Encino house, so Clark and Kathleen chose colors for walls and fabrics for upholstery and draperies. It was really the first complete redecoration of the house since Carole's time. Clark and Kay were settling into a wealthy domesticity. Between movies they traveled, often internationally. Kathleen always took her wardrobe and her maid, Louisa, and the children had a nanny. When work on *Teacher's Pet* was over, Clark and Kathleen saw Bunker off on his first summer camp, then they left for Del Monte Lodge at Pebble Beach, near Carmel, to get some rest and to celebrate their second wedding anniversary. They came back in mid-July, and then went to Maui where Bunker and Joan joined them later in August.

The Gables returned in September, and on the sixteenth Clark started work on *Run Silent, Run Deep* with Burt Lancaster. Clark plays a World War II submarine skipper, Commander Richardson, who has persuaded the Navy to give him another command after his previous boat was sunk by a Japanese destroyer. Richardson's arrival thwarts the promotion expectations of Lt. Bledsoe (Lancaster), and his increasing animosity escalates into confrontation with Richardson when he pursues the same Japanese destroyer against orders. Their first attack fails, and when their submarine is depthcharged Richardson is injured. They repair the ship and attack again, sinking the destroyer. A Japanese submarine chases them. After an intense cat-and-mouse pursuit, it is finally destroyed but at the cost of Richardson's life.

Produced by Lancaster, Harold Hecht, and James Hill for United Artists, *Run Silent, Run Deep* was directed by Robert Wise.[44] It was based on the best-selling book by thirty-year naval officer Commander Edward L. Beach, who acted as technical advisor. Lancaster and Wise were keen to maintain the authenticity of the book. "Every bit of dialogue is real submarine talk," Lancaster pointed out, "and every piece of equipment is in the right place and used the right way. Even the combat incidents in the John Gay screenplay ... are taken from naval archives." Don Rickles, cast as one of the crew, recalls that Lancaster took the technical aspects seriously: "He'd say, 'Don, do you know what you're looking at?' I had no idea what I was looking at, but to humor him I'd always say, 'Yes, I do, I do.'"[45]

Robert Wise believed that the most powerful method of portraying human emotions onscreen was to have a film's crucial moments enacted in a compact space, explaining that, "When a clash occurs between humans confined in such a manner, the intensification of emotion is terrific."[46] To achieve this claustrophobic atmosphere in *Run Silent, Run Deep*, Wise had his art director, Edward Carrere, build a submarine interior to exact scale so that the cast would get a true sense of just how the real thing felt. Clark and Lancaster also visited the Naval Training School at San Diego and went out on the *USS Redfish*, which would "play" the *USS Nerka* for the exterior shots. They were briefed on equipment and procedure and taken down on practice dives. Clark was given turns at the helm and the periscope, and it all gave the film just that added touch of gritty realism.

What threatened to sink Wise and Clark's ship, however, was not a submarine but a script that was being continuously rewritten. As the shoot wore on, Harold Hecht and screenwriter John Gay worked on one version of the script, while Lancaster and screenwriter James Hill worked on theirs. Every morning, pages would be altered. Clark, who would study his script the previous night to be ready for work, hated last-minute changes. Despite this, Clark and Lancaster got along fine, but Clark eventually became concerned that the script was being rewritten by Lancaster's writers to favor Lancaster. About three weeks into the shoot he balked at a scene in which he was supposed to commit a judgmental error in a major encounter with the Japanese destroyer, prompting Bledsoe to take command. "I'm not going to do it," Clark asserted. "He's not going to take over the boat." Production came to a halt for two days while Jim Hill and John Gay tried to figure out something that would appease Clark's insecurities, until they came up with the solution of having him be injured and unable to carry on. Satisfied, the king resumed his throne and went back to work.[47]

As many directors would, Wise later commented on Clark's professionalism and contractual nine-to-five punctuality, but Wise might well have been the only director to once persuade Clark to work a little later. Wise recalled that, "I'd spent the whole afternoon rigging up a very difficult shot with water tanks and things pouring. These shots are very time consuming to set up. It was just getting ready to be shot a few minutes before five, and I

knew that if I didn't get it that day I just had to start over in the morning and line it up again. Clark had a couple of chums who had been with him for years, watching out for him, taking care of his clothes. I went to them, explained the situation, and asked them to convince Clark to stay a few minutes just to get this shot, and he did it. He said, 'Don't ask again,' but he stayed. One of the guys said to me, 'I'd never seen him do that before, no matter who.'"[48]

Run Silent, Run Deep was received well by critics and audiences. The final version technically wasn't Wise's final cut, but Lancaster's. In keeping with the film's setting, the official premiere on April 1, 1958, took place on the submarine *USS Perch* before an invited audience of senior Navy officers. Bosley Crowther in *The New York Times* praised Clark's "strong" and "rugged" performance that was, he wrote, reminiscent of that in *Command Decision* and "revealing of a fiercely self-disciplined man." Clark, he wrote, was "one of Hollywood's genuine, changeless 'pros'" who could "act like the top-notch 'pro' he is." Crowther thought that both *Teacher's Pet* and *Run Silent, Run Deep* concentrated "his mature talents, and they may fetch forth a new respect for him." He observed that Clark "has always been able to handle a cynical wise-cracking role, particularly when it puts him in the way of being kidded himself," and that *Teacher's Pet* followed a similar theme to *It Happened One Night* where "the tough guy, scornful of class and education, comes to realize his attitude is wrong. On the other hand, the young lady … is made to see the extent of her own smugness and latent snobbery." Clark played the editor role, Crowther concluded, "so naturally, it looks simple. Don't believe it. Let's pay him the respect he is due."[49] Clark was so impressed that he commented the article was "the best vote of confidence I've ever had."[50]

After Carole died, Clark stopped going to premieres of his movies and would delegate Jean Garceau to appear on his behalf. He'd wait at home for her to phone in her report on what she thought of the finished film and on the audience reaction. Kathleen had begun to encourage him to go, however, and in March 1958, they appeared at the premiere of *Teacher's Pet*, Kathleen in a black satin Mainbocher gown and matching stole. Not only had Kathleen been working on Clark, so had George Seaton and producer William Perlberg, who finally persuaded him to appear onstage for the 1957 Academy Awards at the RKO-Pantages Theater on Hollywood Boulevard. Clark and Doris Day were introduced by Bob Hope to present the Screenwriter's Award to Pierre Boulle for *The Bridge on the River Kwai* and to George Wells for *Designing Woman*.

Clark and Kathleen then left for Chicago, the starting point of a rare promotional tour for *Teacher's Pet* that went on to Washington and Cleveland, spending two days in each. Perlberg and Seaton, along with Seaton's executive assistant Ted Taylor, accompanied Clark and Kathleen. In Washington, the Gables were being shown through the White House by a senator when President Eisenhower heard they were there. He invited them into his office for a chat. The two men had met during the war, so they sat and talked golf for a while. The president asked them to excuse his absence from the film's preview that night because he had offered to baby-sit so his son and daughter-in-law could attend. Then he called an aide to take them through the rest of the White House.

When they reached Cleveland early in April, Taylor later told Jean Garceau how impressed he was at the public reaction and how amazed he was that so many teenage girls turned out to see Clark. "His walk, his carriage, his dignity commanded respect everywhere," Taylor said. "As we walked down the street together it was interesting to watch people turn to look after Clark, or simply stand in awe as we went by. Huge crowds would gather, but he was never mobbed; they just wanted to look at him."[51]

One young woman was particularly impressed. Journalists from Ohio who had appeared in the film were brought together at a press conference and reception in Cleveland. Miles Welter, amusement editor of the Ohio State University's *Lantern* newspaper, thought it would be great publicity to get a photograph of Clark reading the *Lantern*. He managed to get himself and his then fiancé, journalism student Christi Galvin, invited to the reception. Seeing her at the press conference, William Perlberg was impressed by Christi's close resemblance to actor Jean Peters, who had also been an Ohio State student, and offered her a screen test if she came out to Hollywood. Christi, however, was determined to become a journalist. She was explaining this to Perlberg when Clark came into the room with Kathleen on his arm, saw at a glance what was happening, and came over to talk to her. Taking her hand and smiling down at her, he asked her a few questions. "Are you sure you don't want to come to Hollywood? You'd like it," he asked, leaning closer to her and looking at her intently. "I looked at him," she remembers, "and his eyes were kind. The rough rogue of filmdom I'd read about wasn't present that day. At my age, he seemed an older man, but still handsome and charismatic, someone with whom I felt safe. I knew immediately why women fell in love with him. 'I really want to be a reporter,' I explained, but softly this time. 'You're an egghead,' he almost whispered. Startled, I wondered if he were making fun of me. Seeing my look, he smiled and whispered again, "See the movie, you'll understand." When she did, Galvin realized he was using the nickname he gives to Doris Day's character, a journalist with ethics and commitment.[52]

Arriving back at Encino exhausted by the strain of so much public relations over that distance in such a short space of time, the Gables were glad to accept Marion Davies' invitation to recuperate at her Palm Springs house. Clark got in some golf, of course, and played a lot with his new Mercedes 300

Teacher's Pet *producer, William Perlberg (left),* Lantern *journalist Christi Galvin, and Clark Gable at the Cleveland press conference in April 1958.* (Photograph courtesy of Christi Welter.)

Gullwing, observing that he had bought this model so he'd be kept fit climbing in and out.

In July, Clark agreed to star in another Perlberg-Seaton film, *But Not for Me,* and shooting began early the following year. A remake of *Accent on Youth,* the film costarred Caroll Baker, Lee J Cobb, and Lili Palmer. "This is the first time I've thought of myself as a movie star," said Caroll. "I first saw Clark as a girl. I've dreamed about him ever since."[53] Even though the director was Walter Lang, husband of Carole Lombard's best friend Fieldsie, it was the first time he and Clark had worked together, but they got along well.[54] Clark liked his businesslike attitude. Once again, too, Clark had his old crew of Lew Smith, Don Roberson, and wardrobe man "Swede" along with him.

When this picture was over, Jean Garceau finally decided it was time she retired and spent more time with her family. After twenty years as Clark's personal assistant, it was a hard decision to make. She had been thinking about it for some time, but had put it off because of Clark's pleas that no one else could do the job as well as she could. But Clark had a wonderful wife and a good agent now, and Jean felt that she needed to claim her own life back. They interviewed a number of people before finally selecting Margareta Gronkwist as Jean's replacement.

Clark was all too aware of his role as father and provider for his family, despite not getting any younger. Never one to sit around for very long, he quickly signed with Paramount to star in *It Started in Naples* with twenty-five-year-old Sophia Loren, who was just getting into stride with her Hollywood career and would go on to win an Oscar in 1961 for the Italian film *Two Women.* Directed by Melville Shavelson, *It Started in Naples* is the story of a Philadelphia lawyer who arrives in Rome to settle the estate of his late brother and finds himself becoming involved with an Italian mother (Loren) and child.

The film would be shot on location in Italy. So in late June 1959, the entire Gable family sailed from New York for Holland. From there they traveled to Austria, where Clark and Kathleen stayed in a chalet to celebrate their fourth wedding anniversary. Kathleen had occasion to be reminded of Clark's universal appeal to women of all ages when their sixteen-year-old Austrian maid dressed in a red bikini to serve them strudel. "Our cook went into shock and I threw a lap robe over the girl," she recalled. "Clark thought the whole thing was hilarious."[55] Then, in early August, the family moved to Rome and settled into a villa just outside the city.

One day Clark opened the mail to find a script titled *The Misfits,* recommended to him by George Chasin and written by another of Chasin's clients, Arthur Miller. Clark read it over and over. Although moved by it, he had trouble coming to grips with a script essentially driven by the development of the characters rather than by the action, and action was what his films had traditionally been all about. People came to Clark Gable films to see what he would do, not who he would be. They knew who he would be: Clark Gable. In changing times, people wanted the security of knowing that they would see the man they felt was almost one of the family after all these years doing exactly what he'd been doing all these years: punishing the bad guys and rewarding the good women. Certainly there would be a woman in this film, played by Miller's wife Marilyn Monroe, and there would be action, but on the whole this would be a far more complex and cerebral film than anything Clark had previously tackled. He was flattered to be offered it, but although he didn't want anyone else to take the part, he had trouble seeing himself in it and wanted more time to think it over.

When they returned to America in November, the Gables purchased a home in the Bermuda Dunes development at Palm Springs as a recreational residence where Clark could relax between pictures. One of the main attractions of this property was that it abutted the one-hundred-and-sixty acres of the Bermuda Dunes Golf Club. Clark and Kathleen had both begun to take their golf seriously now, with Clark shooting in the high seventies. Because of the hot, dry climate and relaxed lifestyle, Palm Springs had become a thriving city with several chic hotels, where many of the film elite went to unwind. William Holden and his wife Brenda Marshall, Cary Grant, and Zeppo and Barbara Marx were neighbors.

Compared to some of the other celebrity homes, the Gable house was modest and unpretentious. It was a white, contemporary-styled brick house on a lot about an acre in size. From their patio, which opened onto the pool area, they could enjoy a vista of beautiful desert scenery with a backdrop of glowing sunrises and sunsets. Harry and Edlene La Chance, two of the film colony's leading interior designers, washed the inside of the house in desert colors of white, beige, and cactus green, accented with deep-burnt oranges and sunny yellows. The center of the dining room was a large marble-topped table with a fluted pedestal, with two smaller matching tables placed along the floor-to-ceiling windows. Bamboo, lattice-back chairs were placed by each table. Kathleen decorated the house with tasteful objects d'art and silver serving pieces, including complete silver tea and coffee services given to them by Louis B. Mayer as wedding presents. Their growing collection of paintings filled the walls; a large portrait of Carole hung over the living room fireplace. Yet this house, much like the Encino house, looked uncluttered inside, simple, full of light and wide-open space.[56]

In January 1960, after meeting with and talking to Arthur Miller about the role of Gay Langland, Clark finally signed with Seven Arts for *The Misfits*. His friends all cautioned him about doing this film, which by all appearances was set for disaster. He would be working with two troublesome actors, Monroe and Montgomery Clift, an egotistic director, John Huston, and Miller, who had never written a screenplay before. In the end, as it often did with Clark, it came down to money; he felt that he simply couldn't pass up the $750,000 plus ten percent of the gross that he'd been offered for a sixteen-week period with a stipulated nine-to-five shooting day. In the case of delays, Clark would collect $48,000 a week. It made him the highest-paid actor of his time.

After that, Clark's golf took on an added edge, along with a crash diet. He had to get seriously fit, having ballooned to some 230 pounds after all that Italian pasta. He had to lose thirty-five pounds by March 3. He made it and was ready to go, but Monroe wasn't, having run into an actors' strike on her current film, *Let's Make Love*. Clark kept playing golf, and neither he nor Kathleen showed any signs of being bothered by the Nevada heat, staying on at the house long after neighbors had fled back to a cooler climate. As long as he had some of Kathleen's sun-brewed iced tea waiting for him, Clark was fine.

Finally, *Let's Make Love* wrapped on July 1, and a starting date of July 18 was set for *The Misfits*. Clark and Kathleen decided this would be the perfect chance to celebrate their fifth wedding anniversary in Minden, where they had been married, on the way to the Reno location. They asked the Menascos to once again meet them at the same grove of cottonwood trees as they had back then. The Gables stopped at the same motel to freshen up. As Al and Julie looked down the road as they had five years ago, they saw Clark and Kathleen chug into view in the motel owner's 1914 Model T Ford with Kathleen nursing the champagne. "When does the honeymoon end?" asked Al, shaking his head in bemusement. "Never," replied Kathleen, "with us — never."[57]

CHAPTER 26

THE MISFITS

Clark once said that the story was the crucial factor for him in a movie. It is no wonder he was immediately interested in *The Misfits*, for it began as a story told to a group of children by a master storyteller about real people that he had met. In March 1956, Arthur Miller was living in a small rented shack at Pyramid Lake, about fifty miles northeast of Reno, Nevada, to fulfill residency requirements to obtain a divorce from Mary Slattery. One day he rode with a neighbor to pick up some cooking pots from a woman living in an isolated house in nearby Quail Canyon. When they arrived, she was being visited by two itinerant cowboys who made a living rounding up wild mustangs. Before the war, the older cowboy had rounded up mustangs to sell as ponies for children and circuses, but by 1956 that market had all but gone. The cowboys were now forced to sell the few remaining horses they caught for pet food. Miller became so interested in this pair and by the changes in traditional values represented in their life style that he spent some time with them, even going along on roundups.

Ever the writer in search of a story, Miller sensed potential with these characters. Here were two men who, with typical nineteenth-century Western stereotyping, would be cast in the role of caring about horses as much as they cared for themselves. As such, they were icons of traditional, old-fashioned "white-hat" Western values. However, they were living in the twentieth century. To survive, they had taken on "black-hat" villain roles in which they trapped magnificent wild horses and sold them to pet-food manufacturers. So the traditional cowboy ethic that would have once given their lives focus and meaning had been overtaken by a modern materialistic ethic. As a result, the cowboys had become itinerants for hire whose lives had been rendered largely meaningless as they lost that still point of their ethic. They survived, but their method of survival went against the very essence of who they were.

While Miller could see it all there in front of him, at the time he could not see how he could do these themes justice. He lacked context for these characters around which to construct a compelling narrative that would pull all the disparate elements together.

A year later in England, with time on his hands while his new wife Marilyn Monroe was costarring with Laurence Olivier in *The Prince and the Showgirl*, Miller realized that the character of the older cowboy was still there in his mind. The passage of time had now given him perspective. Whereas before he had been too close, with distance Miller understood more about those cowboys and their lives, so he set out to write it down. What he wrote became a short story called "The Misfits," which was eventually published in *Esquire* magazine.

Another year went by. Monroe was now ill and in Doctors Hospital in New York. While Miller was visiting her there, Sam Shaw, a New York photographer they knew, came to visit. As he and Miller talked about potential projects, the idea of *The Misfits* as a movie began to form in Miller's imagination. Over the next six months he worked intermittently on the screenplay, but as other projects gained priority, it was put aside.

Then, he was invited to dinner at the home of his friend and former publisher, Frank Taylor. During the course of that evening, he found himself telling *The Misfits* to their four children, playing each of the roles from memory with their distinctive characters and voices. His audience was captivated. So was Taylor, who persuaded Miller to give him a copy and in turn passed it on to director John Huston. Having read it through, Huston was also intrigued by the possibilities in the screenplay and forwarded it to Elliott Hyman of Seven Arts, a subsidiary of United Artists. Hyman asked if he could produce it, so what Taylor would one day call "the ultimate movie" was born.

Discussions began between MCA, who represented Miller, and United Artists. As far as Miller and Taylor were concerned, only two people could play the lead roles of the older cowboy, Gay Langland, and the young woman: Clark Gable and Marilyn Monroe. Both were also clients of MCA. Frank Taylor, who was invited to produce the film, told Bill Davidson later that they had felt "there was only one actor in the world who expressed the essence of complete masculinity and virility that we needed for the leading role — and that was Gable. At fifty-nine, he was still a contemporary image of virility. I see no one coming along in his class in this respect. Marlon Brando is virile to women but not to men. Gable was virile to both women and men.

Brando is a symbol of both sensuality and sexuality. Gable had no sensuality about him. His essential maleness is right on the surface."[1]

At the time Clark was busy in Rome shooting *It Started in Naples*, so George Chasin sent him a copy of the script there. Clark read it and immediately felt drawn to the role, even though he was not familiar with Miller's work. He asked director Mel Shavelson what he knew about Miller, and Shavelson replied, "Well, he's written several great plays, including *Death of a Salesman*, and many people consider him to be the greatest writer in the English language today." Clark scratched his head and said, "I read his script here and it's all right. I guess he's a pretty good writer at that."[2] Taylor, Miller, and John Huston quickly put together the rest of the cast: Montgomery Clift as the younger cowboy, Perce; Eli Wallach as Langland's partner, Guido; and Thelma Ritter as a Nevada divorcee, Isabelle. None of them had ever worked together before. By the time the movie was finished they would become an ensemble that happily adopted the movie's name for themselves.

By September 1959, Taylor and Huston had assembled a crew of over two hundred and were ready to begin location shooting around Reno, Nevada. Then they ran into their first real hitch. Clark couldn't complete his work on *It Started in Naples* before Monroe signed her contract for Fox to play in *Let's Make Love* with Yves Montand on September 30. *The Misfits* was sidelined until spring of 1960. While Monroe was working, Miller went to Ireland until mid-March to work on script revisions at John Huston's house.

By now, Miller was in an entirely different relationship with Monroe than he had been when he started writing the script. What became continuous revisions to the script throughout the entire project demonstrated his increasing bitterness and sadness over their deteriorating relationship. Monroe would, in the end, play out on-camera

Clark and Kathleen in England. (Spicer Collection.)

through her character, Rosalyn, a public exposure of their private grief. Miller wrote lines lifted straight from Monroe's childhood, her divorce from Joe DiMaggio, her conversations and philosophy, and from the rise and fall of Miller's romance with her. Bearing that in mind, it was small wonder that there were days she found it extremely difficult to face the camera and hear herself saying those words. Not only that, but she'd be saying many of them to the man she had adopted as a fantasy father figure during her childhood, when she had told relatives and friends that Clark Gable was her real father, attempting to replace the parents who had abandoned her.[3] It is more than likely that Miller knew of this connection, and he may well have used the character name Gay as a deliberate abbreviation of Gable.

Miller wrote much of his own "older man meeting a younger woman" situation into Gay's role, and he put many of his own words, such as: "What makes you so sad? I think you're the saddest girl I ever met," into Gay's mouth. Rupert Allan, a *Look* magazine writer and publicist who later became consul general of Monaco for Grace Kelly, recalled that Monroe was desperately unhappy at having to read lines that were written by Miller that were so obviously documenting the real-life Marilyn: "Just when she might have expected some support, she was miserable.... She felt lonely, isolated, abandoned, worthless, that she had nothing more to offer but this naked, wounded self.... It was the picture that was her enemy."[4] In many ways, as Frank Taylor would say, each of the characters was the person they played.

Miller returned to Hollywood to work on the script of *Let's Make Love,* which had been forced to stop production when the Screenwriters Guild joined the Actors Guild on March 7, 1960, in a strike over additional payments to actors and writers for television broadcasting of their earlier films. Monroe considered Miller's return to work a violation of his own ethics for the sake of a few thousand dollars, and it became more of a catalyst in the breakup of their marriage than her brief affair with the married Yves Montand a short time later, which happened while Miller was location scouting for *The Misfits* with Huston from mid-April into June.

Because *Let's Make Love* then ran way over schedule, it wasn't until July 18 that shooting began in Reno for *The Misfits.* Unlike most films, Huston planned to shoot this one in strict script sequence so that his actors could remain in context and retain a sense of continuity in the story's unfolding and development. Clark appears very early in the movie, and his first scene started shooting on July 20. In it he is saying goodbye to a divorcee, played by Marietta Tree, with whom Gay has had a brief affair. She is in tears as she leaves on the train, trying to persuade him to come to St. Louis to join her. Marietta was being shown around by her friend Huston the day before, when they had wandered into a room where Clark was interviewing some local women for the bit part. They had watched him interview a couple when he turned around, saw Marietta, and told her she would be ideal. When she protested she wasn't an actress, Clark merely said it would be the easiest thing in the world; all she would have to do was stand with him and take his lead. Nervously she agreed, and they rehearsed the scene three times.

So the next morning Clark and Marietta waited at the Southern Pacific train station with the rest of the film crew for the Overland Limited to pull in. The cost of a special train would have been prohibitive, so Huston had decided to use the real west-bound train on its way between Chicago and San Francisco. At 8:25 a.m. the train pulled in and was held for a few minutes while the scene was shot. "I felt like a very young ballet dancer being wafted across the stage by Nijinsky," she said. "Gable was so accomplished, I was never nervous. He played the part so completely that he became the man, and I became the girl. When the time came for me to turn, I couldn't leave and he put me on the train."[5]

Clark and Marilyn Monroe having a quiet moment off-camera while filming The Misfits.

That afternoon Marilyn Monroe arrived in Reno on a United DC-7 to be greeted by Miller, some photographers and press, and two hundred fans. They had to wait thirty minutes for her to emerge from the plane, by which time she had been made up and was in character as Rosalyn. She rode down Virginia Street to the Mapes Hotel sitting triumphantly on the back of Taylor's bright red Ford Thunderbird convertible. Monroe started work the next day, July 21, supported by her coach, her masseur, her secretary, her personal makeup artist, an expert in full body makeup, her hairdresser, her wardrobe assistant, and her driver.[6]

Alfred Hitchcock, who was one of the most meticulously planned and controlled of directors, once expressed his wonder that films got made at all. "I have lived," he said, "in a constant state of astonishment that we ever completed even one picture. There is so much that can go wrong, and it usually does."[7] *The Misfits* would prove to be absolutely no ex-

ception. The heat, that could reach 120 degrees Fahrenheit out in the open, the alkaline dust that would require constant cleaning of lenses and equipment, the ever-present journalists and photographers, the entire days when hardly any film was shot, the constantly changing script, and the constantly late Monroe all combined to make *The Misfits* an experience as about as close to hell as anyone there wanted to experience.

Every night, Clark would sit and read his script through, attempting to find his character. He had never been involved in a film before where he had so little to say and yet so much to convey. What was important here was what the characters were thinking rather than doing, and he realized that every one of those few words carried meaning.[8] He told *Life* reporter James Goode, "I would not have taken the *Misfits* part, even if I liked the man, if the rest of it was weak. But it's a strong play. One actor never made a picture. The play must have something to say. I've never played a part

exactly like this fellow. He interested me. As I saw it, there's not too many of these fellows who refuse to conform to the group around."[9]

On July 27, shooting moved to the Stix ranch in Quail Canyon, about fifty miles northeast of Reno, which would serve as the set for Guido's house. The film company quickly settled into a routine. The crew would leave Mapes Hotel in Reno at nine a.m. in a chartered bus. At nine-thirty Huston, his staff, Miller, and Taylor would walk over to the Crest Theater to watch the daily rushes. Everyone else who was awake had breakfast in the hotel coffee shop, where they would swap news and stories, the first question of the day always being, "Is Marilyn working today? " At 9:45 a.m., Huston and his entourage would return and the scramble would begin for transportation to the location. Although Clark had driven his Mercedes 300SL to Reno, he used a tan Cadillac as his work car for this shoot. He would usually take his stand-in Bob Davis, Frank Prehoda, and Lew Smith with him. By ten-thirty the group of about one hundred would be set up on location and Huston would attempt to start shooting around eleven. Lunch break was usually at 1 p.m. Shooting would begin again around three and wind up around 6 p.m., when everyone would rush for vehicles to be back in Reno by seven.

John Huston's fifty-fourth birthday and Kathleen Gable's birthday were both within the first week in August. Huston's private secretary had been making preparations for what was, even under normal circumstances, a social event of international proportions since long before work had started on *The Misfits*. For the "surprise" party, guests were jammed into the Fable Room of Mapes Hotel and the occasion was highlighted by the ninety-five-year-old chief of the Paiutes, Thunderface, conferring the titles of Long Shadow on Huston and Princess Laughing Eyes on Kathleen.

The shoot moved to Dayton a week later, where Montgomery Clift would first appear in the film. Clift had actually been doing some rodeo riding by way of preparation for his role as a cowboy, and the cut over the bridge of his nose that he wears in the film is a real one donated for the cause by a bad-tempered Brahmin bull. Shooting the ride down the main street of the town in the car while managing four hundred extras in the street took thirteen takes, and by now the interminable delays were getting on Clark's nerves. "You'll probably see a lot of fire and smoke before we're through with this picture," he prophesied gloomily.[10]

By now, Miller and Monroe's relationship had deteriorated to the extent that they had moved into separate rooms. They were barely speaking to each other and were even driving to locations in different vehicles. The strain of all this was beginning to show on Monroe, who was having increasing problems with her voice and with remembering such details in lines as people's names. That was hardly surprising because Miller would sometimes rewrite whole scenes at night and give them to her to learn by the morning. Monroe, who didn't have Clark's years of experience and discipline that enabled him to cope with this situation, if only barely, was badly panicked. To cope with the stress, which made her violently ill and caused insomnia, Monroe increased her dosages of Nembutal and Seconal way beyond safe levels. She sometimes could not be woken in time to start work even by noon. To save time, her makeup man, Allan Snyder, took to working on her while she was still lying down. Huston complained that "we get so little done. It's unthinkable for an actor not to start at nine in the morning."[11]

Huston, however, had worries of his own. He would often be paralyzed by coughing fits due to his heavy smoking, and he drank heavily. His worst problem, though,

Opposite: Clark in his gull-wing Mercedes 300SL at the time he was filming The Misfits.

was his increasing gambling addiction that was steadily sucking the production's funds dry. He would gamble in Reno most of the night, usually losing, and then fall asleep while on the job in his director's chair. On August 16, he lost $16,000 in one night, bringing his total losses to some $50,000. As Arthur Miller so aptly put it, "Chaos was on us all."[12] There was no way this could continue. Sure enough, on August 25, *The Misfits'* money well ran officially dry. Production was shut down for a week while meetings were held with United Artists to find further funds.

According to Monroe biographer Donald Spoto, it was this situation, more than any real concern for her welfare, that prompted Huston to suggest that Monroe take advantage of the shutdown to have some medically supervised rest. On arriving in Los Angeles, Monroe checked into the Beverly Hills Hotel and attended a dinner party. On August 28 she met with her doctors, who incidentally were the same ones supplying her with barbiturates in the first place. They pointed out that United Artists' insurance company would cover her care if it took place in a hospital rather than a hotel. Monroe duly checked into Westside Hospital.[13] The flood of media publicity that ensued swept attention from the real reason for the shutdown, as Huston meant it to. He would later heroically claim that although Marilyn was undoubtedly a genius, her physical and mental condition had deteriorated so much at that time that he had developed serious doubts about her ability to finish *The Misfits*. Consequently, Huston said, it was he who had her hospitalized in Los Angeles and weaned off her barbiturates for her own good.[14]

For the rest of her life, largely because of such manipulations of truth, Monroe was haunted by accusations that it was her drug habit and her constant reluctance to put in a full day's work on the set that contributed to stress on Clark's heart and, thus, to his death. She certainly held up production some days, but so did the heat, the horses, the wind, the cloudy skies, and Huston's three collapses due to his bronchitis.

Shooting resumed on Monday, September 5. The rising tension that had culminated in Monroe's departure had largely dissipated now, and the atmosphere on the set was a lot calmer. It needed to be; by now the film was $400,000 overbudget. Monroe certainly seemed to be the better for her rest. She was now able to stay up nights and study Miller's endless revisions without pharmaceutical assistance. Three days later they shot the scene in front of the saloon on the main street of Dayton where a drunken Clark brings Rosalyn, Perce, and Guido out of the bar looking for his children. He had to climb to the top of a car as he called for them, then fall drunkenly into the street. In five lines of dialogue he had to capture paternal pride and desire for his children, frustrated rage and despair that they had left before he could have them meet Rosalyn, drunkenness, and finally, oblivion. The entire *Misfits* company, the population of Dayton, and Kathleen Gable, with her eyes full of love and pride, turned out to watch him do the scene. When Huston declared the last take perfect, the street rang with the first applause given to any member of the cast so far.

Five days later, the company's first unit moved to a dry lake some twenty miles east of Dayton to shoot the scenes involving the roundup and roping of the mustangs. From here, standing out on the salt flat, Clark could look south-east towards the mountain that claimed the life of his beloved Carole. One can imagine that, as he gazed out at the treacherous Nevada terrain, memories of that tragic time so many years before came flooding back. Perhaps he pondered how life had ironically brought him full circle.

Monroe fell ill, so they shot scenes of Clark and Clift roping horses from the back of a truck. When it came time to shoot throwing the mare, the three stars decided to do it themselves and not use any stunt doubles. Gable, Wallach, and Clift held onto the uncooperative mare for all they were worth, trying to dodge flying hooves while at the same time remaining in camera range. The mare dragged them all around the dry lake bed until Clift's hands were torn and bleeding. Four days later, the original finish date, they were still there, and estimates for completion were anywhere from another month to Christmas. Clark felt that despite the shoot dragging out "to be an endurance test, you just have to keep at it."[15]

At Clark's insistence, the company moved back to the Stix house to reshoot the scene where he comes into the bedroom in the morning to kiss the sleeping Rosalyn awake. Clark felt he hadn't shown enough love and tenderness the first time around. As she did in real life, Monroe was shown sleeping nude during the nine takes. Reaching up for her robe, she would expose her naked back. In the seventh take she also exposed her right breast, prompting some earnest discussion about which take to use. They decided to keep it in. After all, *The Misfits* had already been denied the Motion Picture Association's seal of approval due to "an excessive amount of swearing" and because the "illicit relationship involving Gay and Roslyn seems to lack effective compensating moral values."[16] In other words, the script accepted the relationship of an unmarried couple rather than condemning it. In the end, however, take seven would not make it onto the screen but would be replaced by take nine, and the film would eventually receive its seal from the Association. Taylor would say that his consolation was that the film might have been remembered only as the movie in which you could see Monroe's breast; now both the film and Monroe would be assessed on their own merits.[17]

The company returned to the lake bed and resumed shooting the mustang scenes. When Kathleen Gable drove out to the location on September 29 with an antique cradle in the back of the new Chrysler station wagon Clark had given her as a birthday present, the word was out that she was expecting again. Clark and Kathleen had been told by her doctor on August 7, Kathleen's forty-third birthday, and the jubilant Clark thought it was nothing short of a miracle. "Between us we're 102 years old and here we are having a baby," he had laughed.[18] Wary of publicity too soon in case anything went wrong again, the Gables had kept their happy secret to themselves until Kathleen just had to show him the vintage 1815 cradle she had found. Two days later columnist Louella Parsons broke the story in the *Los Angeles Examiner*, announcing she would be the godmother. The news was out, but Clark was too happy now to care. "It's wonderful," he grinned to reporters. "I guess there's some life in the old boy yet.... I just want to be with Kay. I want to be there when the baby arrives."[19] John Lee Mahin later recalled that "My wife and I spent a week with Clark and Kay up there. Boy, were they excited. They bought a book, and we spent hours looking up names for the baby. Clark changed his mind every few minutes."[20] For Clark, the prospect of finally being a father to his own child was a blessing that he simply had never expected so late in his life.

At Kathleen's instigation, the Gables became part of the Reno community while Clark was working on this picture, much as they had in St. George, Utah, during *King and Four Queens*. They transplanted much of their Encino life to the house in Reno along with some of their furniture. Kathleen did her shopping in the town, Clark would sit around and talk about automobiles, and Bunker and Joan joined them. Kathleen loosened up Clark from his usual shyness a lot, even to the extent that he would pose for camera-toting fans, but Bunker would flatly refuse to pose with his famous stepfather. "It's my fault," Clark would explain to disappointed photographers. "I told him never to have his picture taken with an actor."[21]

By October 5, tensions had risen again within the *Misfits* company. Huston had entered into a prolonged difference of opinion with Miller over the order in which the last three horses were captured in the final part of the film. Also, both Monroe and Clark had finally had enough of the continual script rewrites, and Huston was notified that Clark would accept no more changes after September 26. Neither was anyone looking forward to the forthcoming scenes involving Clark's roping of the stallion. Huston had a renowned mean streak when it came to demanding realism on his set. In 1955, for example, there had been a number of injuries and Gregory Peck had nearly drowned during the shooting of *Moby Dick* because of Huston's insistence on shooting in fog and during real storms with fifteen-foot waves. There was some thoughtful trepidation of what Huston might be considering this time around.

For some days Tom Shaw had been directing the second unit as they shot scenes of Boots the stallion attacking Clark, with Jim Palen standing in as Clark's stunt double. Palen would lie on the dry lake bed in front of the camera while handler Corky Randall would crack a whip in front of Boots' nose or even hit him in the nose with buckshot (the SPCA had a representative on set) to make Boots rear back and try to stomp the prone Palen. Dressed in the same clothes Clark would be wearing, Palen would roll back and forth, attempting to dodge those flailing front hooves but he had already been struck on the head twice. Clark was looking on the day Palen's luck ran out and he was kicked hard in the face a third time, stunning and bloodying him. Disgusted at the chances being taken, Clark turned and walked away, exclaiming, "You can all go to hell. I'll see you later. If you want me to do that, I'll phone it in." Miller and Shaw caught up with him. Miller jokingly suggested that the script read well. Clark shot back that he wondered who was going to do it. Standing well back behind the camera, Clark stated emphatically that he was about as close to Boots as he was ever going to get and that if they didn't watch it they would lose a camera lens. No sooner were the words out of his mouth than one of Boots' hooves struck the camera, knocking off the

viewfinder. When the dust settled, Palen said dryly that was the fastest he'd moved in thirty years.[22]

Clark's declaration about script changes was of great concern to Miller, who had been busy trying to find the right ending for the script. By now he'd rewritten the final twenty pages three or four times, and both he and Huston were afraid that Clark would stand by his statement and accept none of the revisions. Miller had, in fact, taken Huston's advice and reversed the order in which the men capture the horses so that the colt was now last, emphasizing Roslyn's concerns. However, when they all met on the lake bed that October 5 morning, Clark laid any fears to rest by reassuring Miller and Huston that he approved of the new ending.

As the project drew towards its inevitable close Miller, finding it difficult to distinguish between Clark the man and the role he played, finally understood the extent to which Clark's personal integrity was inherent in the character of Gay Langland. For his part, Clark had always believed in Miller's story and felt real kinship with the man he portrayed. The three men, Clark, Huston, and Miller, whatever their momentary differences, had agreed on "the major statement of the screenplay and the common denominator of Clark Gable and Gay Langland: the necessity of personal dignity in a society bent on destroying individuality."[23]

For the next five days the company battled winds and increasingly overcast weather to shoot Clark, Wallach, and Clift trying to rope horses and fend off Rosalyn's protests over their actions. Then the weather closed in, and to their despair it began to rain. Given any sizeable rainfall, the dry alkaline lake bed could turn to muddy slush within thirty minutes. Asked if he couldn't do anything about the delays, Miller suggested he write in Clark holding up his hand to feel the rain and then saying, "We'd better get out of here."[24] They all returned to Reno to wait it out and discuss options. As per his contract, Clark went onto overtime on October 10, and *The Misfits* budget rose to $35,000 a day. They had already spent $3,805,000.[25] The following day the weather cleared and they went back to work on the lake bed. It was the seventy-third shooting day, and they were twenty-three days over schedule.

They began to shoot Clark's most physically taxing scenes, in which he struggles with the roped stallion, on October 14. They needed to shoot some twenty-eight cuts that would be matched to Shaw's second-unit footage, including close-ups of Clark being dragged across the lake bed on the end of a rope by the horse. The camera was mounted on the back of a truck, and the rope was attached to an outrigger on the left side so that Clark could be shot from an angle as he was dragged on his side for four hundred feet. When Huston was queried about suitable speed for the truck he replied, "About thirty-five, the speed of a horse, or until Clark begins to smoke."[26] They did it twice, then once again the next morning. Then Clark took a well-earned break and went duck-hunting for the weekend.

October 18 turned out to be the last day of location shooting. Even Miller was heard to say that he never thought it would take this long. It was Slate 456, take one, and Guido screams: "Gay, where are you going?" In the script, Gay doesn't answer, but Clark couldn't help himself and shouted back: "Home!" with a great deal of conviction. The next day, having put Kathleen on a plane, Clark climbed into his Mercedes drove the 477 miles home very quickly.

There were just the process shots to be done at Paramount now, work involving head shots and close-ups inside the vehicle cabs against rear-projection so dialogue could be taped. Once again Monroe and Clark successfully resisted potential Miller script and scene changes. Finally, on November 4, Huston placed Marilyn and Clark in the front seats of the station wagon for a retake of the film's last scene. It was the ninetieth production day,

forty days over schedule, and at $3,955,000 they were $500,000 over their budget. Clark looked out the windshield and said, "Just head for that big star."

Marilyn Monroe later said that on the next-to-last day of shooting, Clark had watched a rough cut of the film and that he had been "so excited as he told me how well it had turned out. He told me that he thought it was the best thing I had ever done and that it was the best thing he had done since Rhett Butler."[27]

What nobody knew was that Clark hadn't been well that Friday but had reported for work anyway. On Sunday morning he was taken to hospital after suffering a heart attack. Later, while editing, Huston watched the scenes where Clark ropes the stallion and is dragged. Huston commented heavily, "Everyone is going to think this is why Clark had a heart attack."[28] Thelma Ritter had already been hospitalized for exhaustion after she had finished shooting. Then Marilyn Monroe officially announced her separation from Miller on November 11.

Huston hoped that editing could be done so that the picture would be in final-print form by December 31, enabling it to be shown in a theater and thus qualify for Academy Award consideration, and he continued cutting work with this objective in mind. However, work on the soundtrack slowed them down. *The Misfits* was finally released on Clark's birthday, February 1, 1961. United Artists was concerned over the reaction of Clark's fans to the film, lacking enough confidence in the quality of the picture to consider that it would stand as an ensemble piece. The studio ordered an unprecedented 1,300 prints to be mass-released into theaters across the country to give the film as much chance for audience exposure as possible, and it allocated $1 million for advertising.

Arthur Miller saw the final version of the film on January 11, before its release. He was still shaking his head in amazement a week later over how miraculously the film had turned out so like his original vision and about how Clark and Gay Langland were so much the same person. He no longer knew "where one leaves off and the other begins. Clark is a hero in the mythical sense of the word as well as being real.... Clark, the picture, have a majesty about them that is deeply moving to me. I felt proud that we could create it."[29] Clark had, he said, accomplished "his elegy, his requiem."[30]

CHAPTER 27

IN DEATH, LIFE

Clark came home to the Encino ranch on the night of Friday, November 4, 1960, after studio work on *The Misfits* was completed. He looked so worn out, Kathleen said, that "my heart ached for him."[1] He was thinking of going up to the duck club at Stockton to do some hunting, but it started to rain, and he changed his mind. He spent that Saturday afternoon working his hunting dog and playing with the children, but he was so tired by that evening that he went to bed early on Kathleen's insistence.

About 4 a.m. he woke with a bad headache, took some aspirin, and went back to bed. Kathleen was kept awake by a heavy thunderstorm and vague disquiet about Clark that she couldn't quite put her finger on. She awoke from a restless night about 8 a.m. to see Clark standing in the doorway. Gray-faced and wet with perspiration, he complained of severe pain and said he thought it must be indigestion. Kathleen took one look at him and, despite Clark's protests, called a doctor immediately, who in turn called an ambulance and the fire-department rescue unit. It was, the doctor said, almost certainly a heart attack.

Kathleen had been diagnosed with heart problems some time before, and as Clark was wheeled out he was more concerned about the effect his illness would have on his pregnant wife than his own condition. However, Kathleen was from the same tough Pennsylvania Dutch heritage and insisted on riding along with him to the hospital and on staying there by his side once they arrived. For the first few days she slept on a small bed at Clark's feet, but then after the room started to fill up with equipment and nursing staff, she moved into an adjoining room. It frightened her to see the husband whom she had always thought of as being so healthy in a hospital bed. Clark remained more concerned for her and the baby than himself.

Typically, he informed the doctors that he wanted to know the truth about his prognosis and how much damage had been done. They predicted he would recover well. The tenth day after the attack would be a crucial recovery point, they said, and after that he would need a long rest and recuperation period. Clark seemed to take it all in his stride, and he talked about when he'd be back at the ranch and up and about. He read books that Kathleen brought in for him, joked with nurses and visitors, and confided to the now five-months pregnant Kathleen how much he was looking forward to the baby. One day he borrowed the doctor's stethoscope and, placing it on Kathleen's abdomen, listened to his baby's heartbeat.

Clark Gable and Roy Rogers playing golf with a limited set of options in the bag. (Photograph courtesy of Patrick Curtis.)

Nine days after Clark was admitted, Kathleen went home for the first time to collect some personal effects he needed. She had been concentrating so much on being strong in front of Clark that she had not really had time for her own feelings about all this. As she moved about the bedroom it all suddenly overwhelmed her. She locked herself in the bathroom and wept as though her heart would break. Then she took a deep breath and drove back to the hospital. When she walked in the door to Clark's room, he said, "Oh God, Ma, don't leave me again. I don't want to be alone."[2]

The next day, Wednesday, November 16, Kathleen brought in some of the hundreds of supportive letters and telegrams she had received for Clark to read. She sat and watched him, thinking how much younger he looked. His color was back, he looked fit, rested and at peace with the world. Rufus Martin, Clark's devoted house manager, came by to visit, and he left saying that Clark looked so well he wouldn't be worrying any longer about him. Clark and Kathleen sat together into the evening, having dinner and talking together.

Suddenly, just after 10 p.m., Kathleen felt an angina attack coming on, something that hadn't bothered her for two years. She didn't want to concern Clark and went to her room to lay down for a few minutes until she felt better. As she left, Kathleen leant over and said to Clark, "Sweetheart, I'll be back after the nurses get you ready for the night. Then we'll drink our buttermilk together. I love you."[3]

At 10:50 while he was reading a magazine and one of the nurses was talking to him, Clark looked up with a smile, turned a page, then laid his head back on the pillow, closed his eyes, and was suddenly gone. By the time the emergency team reached his bedside, there was nothing they could do. A doctor and nurse rushed into Kathleen's room and woke her to a nightmare. She tried to get up and fainted. When they revived her, all they could say was that the man she loved would never see their child. It would be the only time Kathleen would let herself submit to the overpowering sense of loss she felt. She stood up, refused the doctors' offers of medication, and walked into Clark's room to tearfully say goodbye to him and their life together.

When it was all over, Kathleen drove home, climbed the stairs to Clark's study, and sat in his chair. She stayed there the rest of the night thinking about him and what had to be done. When morning came, she called the children in and told them their beloved stepfather wouldn't be coming home.

Like Carole, Clark had never forgotten the media circus that surrounded his friend Jean Harlow's funeral all those years ago. It had made an indelible impression on him, and he left strict instructions that his closed-casket funeral was to be quiet and respectful. Kathleen carried out his wishes.

By nine in the morning on Saturday, November 19, a sad, reverent crowd of about three hundred people had gathered outside the Church of the Recessional at Forest Lawn Memorial Park, Glendale, to say goodbye to their hero. Inside, a short list of five hundred friends and important Hollywood people was seated to hear U.S. Air Force chaplain Johnson E. West conduct a simple Episcopal service alongside the coffin that was blanketed in red roses. On top rested a small crown of miniature, darker red roses. The pallbearers included Spencer Tracy, Robert Taylor, and Jimmy Stewart, who was still a brigadier general in the U.S. Air Force Reserve. Mourners included a tearful Norma Shearer, Marion Davies, Virginia Gray, directors Frank Capra, John Huston, and Mervyn LeRoy, comedian Jack Oakie, Arthur Miller, Van Johnson, Roy Rogers, Robert Stack, Robert Wagner, and restaurateurs Mike Romanoff and Dave Chasen. The chaplain read from Psalms 46 and 121, then asked the congregation to pray silently. While they bowed their heads, an air force bugler sounded the mournful notes of "Taps." As the notes died away, an air force honor party and color guard lowered the flag from a standard and folded it. The chaplain then presented it to Kathleen, who was sitting with the children in a family chapel off to one side from the body of the church. Carrying the flag and supported by the chaplain and Howard Strickling, Kathleen and the others quietly filed out. When the last person had left, the attendants closed the chapel doors, leaving the coffin there in peace. "Now," Norma Shearer said, "he is on the right side of eternity."[4]

At the time of Carole Lombard's death, Clark had purchased crypts for them both alongside each other in the Great Mausoleum at Forest Lawn. There he was laid to rest on November 23, with only Chaplain West and Kathleen present, dressed in his blue wedding suit and bearing his last Christmas gift from the children: his St. Jude medal. "It was a terribly difficult day," wrote Kathleen later. "I needed the memory of Clark's love and courage to get through it."[5]

A lot of other people needed a memory of Clark too, and many tributes were given by way of preserving that memory. "The King Is Dead" headlined *Newsweek*.[6] Producer Walter Wanger said, in words echoed by John Wayne, "He was a personification of everything that makes the motion picture industry great." The United States Ambassador to the United Kingdom, John Hay Whitney, voiced the sentiments of many of the ordinary moviegoing public when he commented that "To me he will always be Rhett Butler of *Gone with the Wind*. For this is the way he was: kind, considerate, with powerful charm, and truly modest. He was everybody's gentleman." Vivien Leigh said simply: "I am sadder than I can tell."[7]

Despite advice from her friends, Kathleen decided to stay at the Encino ranch. "I could never think of leaving this place," she said. "Sitting here seeing the things that were ours, I have the feeling Clark knows what we are doing and that he wants us to stay."[8] The following February, she attended church on Clark's birthday and commented that she still felt her late husband's presence with her. "It is still impossible for me to believe he is gone," she said. "It's like losing one half of yourself. But Clark didn't marry me because I was a weak woman. He sustains me. The baby will be along in a few weeks.... You'll have to ex-cuse me if I talk about Clark as if he were still alive, but I can't help feeling that, somehow, he is looking down on us."[9]

It was Marilyn Monroe who, apart from Kathleen, probably contributed the most immediate and extended personal insight into what Clark's death meant to any one person. In the months following Clark's death, rumors had begun to circulate placing a lot of blame for his heart attack at her feet. It had been brought on, critics said, because of added stress due to her chronic lateness or because her lateness had caused him to become bored with sitting around and he had performed hard physical work that would otherwise have been left to a stunt double or stand-in.

In February of the following year Monroe was interviewed by journalist Victor Sebastian for *Family Weekly* about her working relationship with Clark Gable. She had, she said, always meant to tell Clark how much he had meant to her one quiet evening when Clark, Kathleen, and Marilyn would be sitting around the fire together. By establishing in this interview that she and Kathleen were friends, Monroe carefully implied that Kathleen would not have regarded Monroe as a possible factor in Clark's death. She had, after all, received flowers from both of them when she had been in hospital. During the shoot, Monroe revealed, Kathleen and she had become "very close. She used to come out to the set and call to me, 'Hey, how did Our Man do today?' I'd laugh, 'Our Man? I must say you are generous, Kay.' And it was a joke between us always — Our Man!" Monroe pointed out that, "There was never any impatience or annoyance in Clark. There was only concern — real concern for me.... I'll remember his cheerfulness arriving at work early in the morning when nobody is cheerful. And his jokes — he always had a joke for me. I looked forward to them. He appreciated women. I think that was one of the strongest elements of his attraction to them. No one was more of a man's man than he was — but he *appreciated* women. Most of all he was a man. I don't mean just that he was virile, exciting vibrant — he was all of those things. But he had sensitivity, too, and tenderness, and he wasn't afraid of those qualities.... He understood me. I don't know why. He cared about everything. I think he knew that I cared too."[10] On the last day of shooting, Clark had done something Monroe had considered "valiant." She walked over to him and said, "Do you know something? You're my hero. And I never had a hero before."[11]

Clark's will, dated September 19, 1955, and admitted to probate December 9, 1961, left an estate calculated in 1964 at $1,464,866 entirely to his beloved wife Kathleen with one exception. He gave to Josephine Dillon the title of the house that he had bought for her, 12746 Landale, North Hollywood. The financial bulk of Clark's estate was made up of his interests in his last nine films, beginning with *Soldier of Fortune* and *The Tall Men* in 1954, most significantly his nearly $500,000 interest in *The Misfits*. Among the minor claims for expenses made against the estate was a $2,021 claim by United Artists for reimbursement of advance payments they had made to *The Misfits* caterers.

There was, however, one major claim against the estate, and there apparently lay a story. When Otto Winkler was killed in that 1942 plane crash with Carole Lombard, his widow Jill had intended suing the airline for compensation in the area of $100,000. Clark, however, persuaded her not to go down that route, saying that he did not want to become involved in a legal wrangle with Carole's brothers. That may have been because he was concerned they would sue for a larger share of her estate, or that they might persuade a court that Clark bore some of the responsibility for her death, which could also mean they would be awarded more money. Instead, Jill would always claim that Clark had verbally promised he would provide a $100,000 annuity for her. Consequently, she had never sought compensation of any kind. On June 12, 1961, the claim was rejected.

Nearly shattered by grief, Kathleen focused all her energy on her pregnancy during the lonely months that followed. "The tragedy that he would never hold his baby at times nearly defeated me," she wrote, "but I was determined not to give in to grief."[12] She didn't. Kathleen carried on, smiling for cameras, giving the occasional interview, reaffirming her faith in God, and above all caring for the two children she had and the one she was about to have.

On March 20, 1961, John Clark Gable was born in the same hospital, Hollywood Presbyterian, in which his father had died. "I'm happy, but a little sad," Kathleen had said when she checked in. "It's awfully lonesome here without Clark. I'd been counting on him being here."[13] Typically, Kathleen insisted on being conscious for the birth, watching her eight-pound baby's arrival reflected in the overhead lamp cover. In those days mothers didn't get to hold their baby until the nurses brought them in when the patient was back in bed. Never doubting that their baby would be a son, Clark had chosen John's name himself. "Movie fans all wanted a Clark Jr.," Kathleen said later, "but Pa felt it would have been too much of a handicap for the child to bear."[14] As she finally held their child, experiencing "such a mixture of grief and gratitude, of unbearable sadness and great joy," Kathleen could once again feel Clark's presence in the room.[15]

John Clark was christened by the Reverend Michael Lalor in Encino's St. Cyril's Roman Catholic Church on June 11, 1961, before 150 joyous guests. He was only fourteen days old when his picture appeared on the cover of *Life*. His siblings adored him. Everyone agreed how much he looked like his father. "Children and love give life real meaning," wrote Kathleen, "and each day I am so grateful for mine. Still, there are many bad hours, many days when I battle loneliness and despair, finding them the most formidable opponents. I will always sorrow for Clark, but I will always find comfort in the remembrance

Above: The Clark Gable Memorial in Cadiz, Ohio, next to his reconstructed birthplace. (Courtesy of Mary Ocheltree.) *Opposite: Kathleen and new baby John Clark Gable, 1961.*

of his love. Now I have his son. God blessed me very well."[16]

As summer approached, Kathleen supervised the construction of a wing on the house for the children. It had been something that she and Clark had always wanted to do, and Clark had worked on the plans himself. She felt it would give her another link with him. "If he could have held the baby just five minutes," she said at the time. "Just five minutes, so he could have seen his dream come true. My son, Bunker, helped me so much the other day when I told him how wonderful it would have been if Clark had had a few moments with John in his arms. He said, 'Mother, who do you think John is smiling at when he looks up at the sky and grins? He's smiling at Pa.'"[17]

John would grow up smiling at the memories of his famous father. Many years later he commented that, "It's strange having a famous father you've never met. I have seen all his movies, read books about him, and listened to my mother's stories. So, I feel I do know him."[18] After a kidnap threat during John's first year, Kathleen tightened security around the Encino estate, and John Clark Gable grew up very quietly, often with a bodyguard as company. In 1973, when he was twelve, Kathleen sold both their half-interests in the estate to a development company to cope with rising maintenance costs and property taxes, and most of the land was eventually subdivided.

Bunker, meanwhile, had left home and retreated to the North Shore of Oahu where he had become an itinerant surfer and revolutionary board designer, pioneering a short, hard-edged planing board that could be ridden lying down, kneeling or standing. He died suddenly four years later, aged only 27. In 1983 at the end of May, Kathleen lost her long battle with heart disease.

By then John had also left home. Preferring to follow in his father's tire tracks rather than stand under the klieg lights, he quickly built a reputation for racing motorcycles, competing frequently in the Baja 1000 despite a bad accident that damaged both knees when he was twenty. In 1988 Clark James Gable was born to John and his first wife Tracy. "Clark is a good name," they said.[19]

Despite the fame and wealth that eventually came his way, Clark Gable always knew that he was just a lucky farmboy from Ohio who'd had some good breaks and a lot of help. Only a month before his death, he commented to journalist Bill Davidson: "You know, this King stuff is pure bullshit. I eat and sleep and go to the bathroom just like everyone else. There's no special light that shines inside me and makes me a star. I'm just a lucky slob from Ohio. I happened to be in the right place at the right time and I had a lot of smart guys helping me.... I suppose by now there may be such a thing as a Clark Gable legend. If there is, it took a lot of people to make it. Yes, sir, one helluva lot of people."[20]

CLARK GABLE FILMOGRAPHY

Clark Gable Character Screen Roles

White Man (P. B. Schulberg Prod., 1924) — Lady Andrea's brother

Forbidden Paradise (Paramount, 1924) — Extra — uncredited

The Pacemakers (FBO, 1925) — Extra — uncredited

Declassee (First Nat'l Pictures, 1925) — Extra — uncredited

The Merry Widow (MGM, 1925) — Extra — soldier — uncredited

The Plastic Age (FBO, 1925) — College student athlete

North Star (Assoc. Exhibitors, 1926) — Archie West

The Painted Desert (Pathe, 1931) — Rance Brett

Night Nurse (First Nat'l Pictures, 1931) — Nick the chauffeur

The Easiest Way (MGM, 1931) — Nick the laundryman

Dance Fools, Dance (MGM, 1931) — Jake Luva

The Finger Points (First Nat'l Pictures, 1931) — Louis Blanco

The Secret Six (MGM, 1931) — Carl Luckner

Laughing Sinners (MGM, 1931) — Carl Loomis
    Original title: Complete Surrender

A Free Soul (MGM, 1931) — Ace Wilfong

Sporting Blood (MGM, 1931) — Tip Scanlon

Susan Lennox : Her Rise and Fall
    (MGM, 1931) — Rodney Spencer

Possessed (MGM, 1931) — Mark Whitney

Hell Divers (MGM, 1931) — Steve

Polly of the Circus (MGM, 1932) — Rev. John Hartley

Red Dust (MGM, 1932) — Dennis Carson

Strange Interlude (MGM, 1932) — Dr. Ned Darrell

No Man of Her Own (Paramount, 1932) — Babe Stewart

The White Sister (MGM, 1933) — Giovanni Severia

Hold Your Man (MGM, 1933)	Eddie Nugent
Night Flight (MGM, 1933)	Fabian
Dancing Lady (MGM, 1933)	Patch Gallagher
It Happened One Night (MGM, 1934)	Peter Warne
Men in White (MGM, 1934)	Dr. George Ferguson
Manhattan Melodrama (MGM, 1934)	Edward "Blackie" Gallagher
Chained (MGM, 1934)	Mike Bradley
Forsaking All Others (MGM, 1934)	Jeff Williams
After Office Hours (MGM, 1935)	Jim Branch
Call of the Wild (Fox, 1935)	Jack Thornton
China Seas (MGM, 1935)	Captain Alan Gaskell
Mutiny on the Bounty (MGM, 1935)	Fletcher Christian
Wife vs. Secretary (MGM, 1936)	Dan Sanford
San Francisco (MGM, 1936)	Blackie Norton
Cain and Mabel (Warner Bros., 1936)	Larry Cain
Love on the Run (MGM, 1936)	Michael Anthony
Parnell (MGM, 1937)	Charles Stewart Parnell
Saratoga (MGM, 1937)	Duke Bradley
Test Pilot (MGM, 1938)	Jim Lane
Too Hot to Handle (MGM, 1938)	Chris Hunter
Idiot's Delight (MGM, 1939)	Harry Van
Gone with the Wind (MGM, 1939)	Rhett Butler
Strange Cargo (MGM, 1940)	Verne
Boom Town (MGM, 1940)	"Big John" McMasters
Comrade X (MGM, 1940)	McKinley B. Thompson
They Met in Bombay (MGM, 1941)	Gerald Meldrick
Honky Tonk (MGM, 1941)	Candy Johnson
Somewhere I'll Find You (MGM, 1942)	Jonathon "Johnny" Davis
Adventure (MGM, 1945)	Harry Patterson
The Hucksters (MGM, 1947)	Victor Norman
Homecoming (MGM, 1948)	Colonel Ulysses Delby "Lee" Johnson
Command Decision (MGM, 1948)	General K.C. "Casey" Dennis
Any Number Can Play (MGM, 1949)	Charley King
Key to the City (MGM, 1950)	Steve Fisk
To Please a Lady (MGM, 1950) a.k.a. Red Hot Wheels	Mike Brannan
Across the Wide Missouri (MGM, 1951)	Flint Mitchell
Lone Star (MGM, 1952)	Devereaux Burke
Never Let Me Go (MGM, 1953)	Philip Sutherland
Mogambo (MGM, 1953)	Victor Marswell
Betrayed (MGM, 1954)	Colonel Pieter Deventer
Soldier of Fortune (Fox, 1955)	Hank Lee
The Tall Men (Fox, 1955)	Ben Allison

The King and Four Queens (United Artists, 1956)	Dan Kehoe
Band of Angels (Warner Bros., 1957)	Hamish Bond
Run Silent, Run Deep (United Artists, 1958)	Commander Richardson
Teacher's Pet (Paramount, 1958)	Jim Gannon
But Not for Me (Paramount, 1959)	Russell "Russ" Ward
It Started in Naples (Paramount, 1960)	Michael Hamilton
The Misfits (United Artists, 1961)	Gay Langland

Films in Which Clark Gable Appears as Himself

A Christmas Story (1931)

The Christmas Party (1931)

Screen Snapshots (1932)

Jackie Cooper's Christmas Party (1932)

Hollywood Hobbies (1934)

La Fiesta de Santa Barbara (1935)

Northward, Ho! (1940)

You Can't Fool a Camera (1941)

Show Business at War (1943) Also titled: The March of Time, Vol. 9, Issue 10

Combat America (1943)

Wings Up (1943) as narrator

Screen Actors (1950)

Callaway Went Thataway (1951)

Compilations in Which Clark Gable Appears

MGM's Big Parade of Comedy (1964)

The Love Goddesses (1965)

That's Entertainment (1974)

That's Dancing (1985)

Stage Productions in Which Clark Gable Appeared

Bits of Life (Astoria Players Stock Company, July 19, 1922)	A detective, and Billy Dressuitcase — a baby
When Women Rule (Astoria Players Stock Company, July 1922)	Eliza Goober, the cook
Corinne of the Circus (Astoria Players Stock Company, July & August 1922)	Village doctor
Blundering Billy (Astoria Players Stock Company, July 1922)	Sea captain
Mr. Bob (Astoria Players Stock Company, July 1922)	Uncle from Japan
Romeo and Juliet (West Coast Rd. Co., 1925)	Extra — Soldier, Mercutio
What Price Glory? (West Coast Rd. Co., 1925)	Kiper, Sergeant Quirt
Lullaby (West Coast Rd. Co., 1925)	Drunken Sailor
Madame X (West Coast Rd. Co., 1926)	Prosecuting Attorney
Lady Frederick (West Coast Road Co., 1926)	Unknown role
Lucky Sam McCarver (West Coast Road Co., 1926)	Nightclub manager
Copperhead (West Coast Rd. Co., 1926)	Unknown role
Chicago (West Coast Rd. Co., 1927)	Jake

Various appearances in stock productions with the Gene Lewis Stock Company, Houston, Texas, 1928.

Machinal (Plymouth Theater, Sept. 1928)	A Man
Gambling (George M. Cohn Prod., 1929)	Unknown role
Hawk Island (Howard Irving Young Prod., 1929)	Gregory Sloane
Blind Windows (David Belasco, 1929)	Unknown role
Love, Honor, and Betray (A.H. Woods., 1930)	Alice Brady's Lover
The Last Mile (West Coast Rd. Co., 1930)	John "Killer" Mears

Radio Plays in Which Clark Gable Appeared

Date	Title	Stars
11–11–1935	His Misleading Lady [Lux Radio Theatre]	Clark Gable
6–1–1936	Legionnaire and the Lady [Lux Radio Theatre]	Marlene Dietrich, Clark Gable
8–1936	Men In White [Camel Caravan radio series]	Clark Gable, Madeleine Carroll
10–20–1936	Valley Forge	Clark Gable
4–05–1937	A Farewell to Arms [Lux Radio Theatre]	Clark Gable, Josephine Hutchinson, Jack LaRue
9–27–1937	Cimarron [Lux Radio Theatre]	Clark Gable, Virginia Bruce
5–5–1938	Good News of 1938 [NBC]	C. Gable, R. Young, J. Garland, U. Merkel, F. Rice
10–27–1938	Good News of 1939 [NBC]	C. Gable, L. Barrymore, R. Morgan
11–14–1938	The Buccaneer [Lux Radio Theatre]	C. Gable, O. Bradna, A. Tamiroff, C. Blandick
12–4–1938	Danger Lights [CBS Silver Theater]	C. Gable, P. Winslowe
3–20–1939	It Happened One Night [Lux Radio Theatre]	Claudette Colbert, Clark Gable
10–1–1939	Imperfect Lady [CBS Gulf Screen Guild Theater]	Clark Gable, Ginger Rogers, Harriet Lindsey
10–6–1940	Red Dust [CBS Gulf Screen Guild Theater]	Clark Gable, Ann Southern, Jeffrey Lynn, Rita Johnson
2–8–1941	America Calling [CBS, NBC]	C. Boswell, M. Carroll, R. Colman, M. Douglas, C. Gable, F. Holden, C. Laughton, B. Hope, M. Loy, M. Martin, G. Marx, F. Morgan, M. Oberon, R. Owen, D. Powell, T. Power, M. Rooney, A. Rutherford, B. Stanwyck, L. Stone, R. Taylor, S. Temple

1943	Command Performance	C. Gable, J. Bushkin, P. Lind Hayes, C. Stroud.
1943	Mail Call	C. Gable, B. Hope, C. Rains, M. O'Brien, M. Whitty.
8–12–1943	London Broadcast [NBC]	
12–4–1944	China Seas [CBS The Screen Guild Theater]	Clark Gable, Lucille Ball, Anna Lee, Douglas Dumbrill
10–06–1949	Homecoming [CBS The Screen Guild Theater]	Lana Turner, Clark Gable
12–11–1949	Command Decision [NBC the Screen Guild Theater]	Clark Gable, Walter Pidgeon, John Hodiak, Van Johnson, Brian Donlevy, Edward Arnold

Notes

Chapter 1— Billy the Kid

1. Tornabene, L., *Long Live The King.* G. P. Putnam's Sons: New York, 1976, p. 31.

2. Ibid., p. 29.

3. Wallace, Charles, *The Young Mr. Gable.* Harrison County Historical Society: Cadiz, Ohio, 1983, p. 4–5.

John Gable (d.1866) married Sarah Frankfield (b. 1794 in LeHigh Co.) who died 1872 in Meadville, Pa. Gable is not an unusual name in Pennsylvania. Although highly unlikely, it is possible that an original form of the name Gable back in Germany may have been Goebel. If that ever was the case, it was certainly some centuries prior to MGM's Second World War claim that Clark's name had been changed from Goebel to avoid any links with the infamous German Propaganda Minister. (See Davidson, *The Real and the Unreal*, p. 87.)

The Gable House was previously known as the Lion Tavern, built in 1830 for John E. Smith.

The Gable farm was located in Vernon Twp at the top of Gable Hill on Highway 322 between Meadville and Conneaut Lake. The property was eventually sold and subdivided and the farm buildings, which stood near the Vernon Fire Hall have now gone.

4. Clark's mother was always known by the abbreviated first name Addie. Her headstone gives the full version of her first name as Adeline, but census records refer to her as Adelia.

5. Wallace, pp. 5, 7.

6. Rosetta Clark died October 20, 1886, and was buried in Chestnut Corners, St. Peters Church Cemetery, Vernon, Pa.

7. Wallace, p. 7.

8. Samuels, Charles, *The King.* Coward-McCann Inc.: New York, 1961, p. 15.

9. US Government, *Census of 1900,* Vernon Twp, Crawford County, Pa., enumerated June 6, 1900. Household No. 42 gives John Hershelman as head of household. It included Adelia J. Gable, daughter, born January, 1870, aged 30, years of marriage 0. No record of Addie and Will's marriage has been found, so a definite date has yet to be established.

10. *Cadiz Republican,* October 19, 1899.

11. Samuels, p. 17.

12. This house on Charleston Street was torn down in the 1960s and a seven-foot granite memorial eventually erected there. In 1997 work was begun on a replica of this house on the same site courtesy of a $300,000 bequest to the Clark Gable Foundation from schoolteacher Isabelle Clifford. Designed by Jack Harden, the Clark Gable Birthplace and Museum was dedicated on January 30, 1998, by his son John Clark Gable.

13. Wallace, pp. 8–9.

14. Harold V. Knight, "Clark Gable's Father Tells on His Son," *Hollywood Magazine,* undated, p. 14.

15. Wallace, p. 10.

16. Immaculate Conception Church of Dennison, Ohio, *Baptismal Record,* p. 2.

17. John C. Moffitt, "Yokel Row Yields Second Valentino," *The Sunday Oregonian*, September 25, 1932, p. 2.

18. Bill Davidson, *The Real and the Unreal.* Lancer Books: New York, 1962, p. 88.

19. Wallace, p. 14.

20. Ibid., p. 16.

21. John C. Moffitt, "Clark Gable Baby When Mother Dies," *The Morning Oregonian,* September 26, 1932, p. 4.

22. Samuels, p. 19.

Chapter 2 — Growing Up

1. John C. Moffitt, untitled, *The Morning Oregonian*, September 27, 1932, p. 18.
2. Joe McCarthy, "Clark Gable: Part 3 — How he became King of Hollywood," *Look,* November 1955, p. 100.
3. Davidson, p. 89.
4. Wallace, p. 23.
5. Harrison County, Ohio, *Deed Records*, Vol 2, p. 116.
The house still stands in excellent condition on Mill Street in Hopedale, looking much the same as when Clark lived there.
6. Wallace, p. 32.
7. Tornabene, p. 42.
8. Myrna Loy and James Kotsilibas-Davis, *Myrna Loy: Being and Becoming.* Bloomsbury Publishing Ltd: London, 1987, p. 148.
9. John C. Moffitt, September 27, 1932, p. 18.
10. John C. Moffitt, "Gable Falls Down as Master Lover," *The Morning Oregonian*, September 28, 1932, p. 12.
11. Wallace, p. 40.
12. Ibid, p. 38.
13. Jean Garceau and Inez Cocke, "*Dear Mr. G—*": *A Biography of Clark Gable*. Little, Brown and Co.: Toronto, 1961, p. 21.
14. Wallace, pp. 53–4.
15. Garceau & Cocke, p. 21.
16. Samuels, p. 22.
17. Knight, p. 54.
18. Wallace. p. 47.
19. McCarthy, p. 100.
20. Wallace, p. 54 The house was sold to Frank and Olga Loulan, August 6, 1917.
21. The Ensinger-Gable farm was on State Route 225, Yale, now Alliance Road in the township of Palmyra. According to Vol. 224, p. 358 of the Portage County Deed Records, the deed for the property was signed September 14, 1917. Although a smaller acreage now, the farm with its big red barn is still there and the house is little changed except for added window shutters and porch siding.
22. I am indebted to Don Evans, formerly assistant principal of the South-East High School, Ravenna, for locating copies of Clark Gable's Edinburg school record. The two-storied, brick school had only just been built a few years prior to Clark's enrollment after the first school had been destroyed by fire. Its role was subsequently superseded by the South-East High School and the building was eventually demolished.
23. Eleanor McConnell, "Edinburg Family Recalls Associations with Gable," *Record-Courier* (Ravenna, Ohio*)*, undated, February, 1968.
Mr. and Mrs. Ensinger had been married 61 years when Wesley died in 1975. Mary died in 1991, aged 101, still living in the same area.

24. Moffitt, September 28, 1932, p. 12.
25. Tornabene, pp. 45–6.
26. Helen Waterhouse, "Gable 'Afraid of His Shadow' as a Farm Boy Near Akron But Had a Way with the Girls, Old Neighbors Reminisce," *Beacon Journal* (Akron, Ohio), January 31, 1940, p. 26.
27. Figures from: Karl H.Grismer. *Akron and Summit County*. Summit County Historical Society: Akron, 1952, pp. 378–9, 392.
28. Tornabene, p. 49.

Chapter 3 — The Player

1. Samuels, pp. 31–2
2. John C. Moffitt, "Young Trio Start in Quest of Jobs," *The Morning Oregonian*, September 29, 1932, p. 20.
3. From Vicki Baum's *The Weeping Wood*, quoted in George W. Knepper's *Akron: City at the Summit*. Continental Heritage Press: Tulsa, Ok., 1981, p. 104.
4. Grismer, p. 379.
5. Ken Nichols, "Old Clark Gable Haunt in Akron Is Being Razed," *Beacon Journal* (Akron, Ohio), June 20, 1980, and "Clark Gable," *Beacon-Journal*, April 13, 1975.
None of these buildings remain. The Grether house was razed to make way for the Firestone Memorial Bridge, and the Haun drugstore was burned out and then demolished in 1980.
6. Garceau and Cocke, p. 23, and Moffitt, September 29, 1932, p. 20.
7. Knight, p. 54.
8. Jim Tully, *A Dozen and One*. Murray & Gee Inc.: Hollywood, California, 1943, p. 33.
The Akron Music Hall stood until 1929 on the current site of the *Beacon-Journal* newspaper office at the corner of High and Exchange, Akron.
9. Samuels, p. 38.
10. Tornabene, p. 51.
11. Knight, p. 54.
12. Adela Rogers St. Johns, "The Great God Gable," *Liberty*. March 24, 1932, p. 22.
13. Ibid, p. 54.
14. Davidson, p. 88.
15. John C. Moffitt, "Gable Quits Stage For Temporary Job," *The Morning Oregonian*, October 2, 1932, p. 2.
16. The town of Bigheart, in Osage County, was established around 1906 and named after the Osage chief James Bigheart. On November 22, 1921, its name was changed to Barnsdall.
17. Garceau and Cocke, pp. 24–5.
18. Davidson, p. 88.
19. Samuels, p. 41.
20. Tornabene, p. 54.
21. Davidson, p. 91.
22. Moffitt, October 2, 1932, p. 1.

23. Samuels, p. 44; Wallace, p. 55.
24. Ibid, p. 42.
25. Davidson, p. 91.
26. Samuels, p. 45.
27. Tornabene, p. 56.
28. Samuels, p. 30.
29. Davidson, p. 92.

Chapter 4 — Franz Dorfler

1. Samuels, p. 51
2. Don Murtha, "Clark Gable and Frances Doerfler: The Great Romance of Silverton," *Silverton Appeal-Tribune*, January 10, 1980, p. 12. Frances went to the one-room school in the McAlpin district, then to high school at the Sacred Heart Convent in Salem. She was around 80 and in a nursing home in Portland when this article was written. Although she had received a number of proposals, she never did marry.
3. Samuels interviewed Jewell many years later, when Jewell was living in semi-retirement in Palo Alto, California, with his wife Rita Cordero, who had begun her stage career at age three. They both agreed that Gable demonstrated such an appalling lack of stage experience in 1922 that he could not possibly have spent any time acting onstage previously.
4. Schumann was a young actress who later became a radio performer in San Francisco. Silvey was a theater usher, and Chinn was an electrician. They had just started in vaudeville only a few weeks before with a tumbling act, but they had wound up tending the snake pit in a carnival after getting drunk with the owner one night. They fled to Portland as soon as they could, where they joined the Astoria Players. They too were tracked down by Samuels and interviewed about this part of Gable's life.
5. Samuels, p. 56
6. Essoe, Gabe, *The Complete Films of Clark Gable*. Carol Publishing Group: New York, 1990, p. 69. This is a later edition of the Citadel Press publication of 1970. It contains an article by Franz Dorfler, "I Was Billy Gable's Sweetheart," which may have been written by her especially for this book. Essoe does thank Dorfler personally in the acknowledgements and, as yet, I've found no record of the article appearing anywhere else.
7. Essoe, p. 71.
8. "Show at Astoria Theater Is Liked," *The Morning Astorian*, July 16, 1922, p. 4.
9. "Mock 'Melodrammer' at Astoria Theater," *The Morning Astorian*, July 19, 1922, p. 5.
10. "Astoria Show Pleases," *The Morning Astorian*, July 25, 1922, p. 3.
11. Essoe, p. 71.
12. Better known as Margaret Mayo's very popular play *Polly of the Circus*, but renamed to avoid copyright problems. In one of life's little twists of fate, Gable eventually got his turn to play the lead, albeit unhappily, when MGM turned *Polly* into a film in 1932 costarring Marion Davies, but he should have stayed with the lesser part. Many critcs didn't find him believable as a pious preacher.
13. "Circus Play Pleases," *The Morning Astorian*, July 28, 1922, p. 2.
14. Samuels, p. 67.
15. Essoe, p. 72.
16. Samuels, p. 68.
17. Earle Larimore did go to New York, where he eventually became a distinguished actor, famous for his roles in O'Neill's *Mourning Becomes Electra* and *Days Without End* (1931), as Wang Lu in *The Good Earth* (1932), and in *Dark Victory* (1934) with Tallulah Bankhead. In 1932 he married and later divorced actress Selena Royle. Sadly, he died a penniless alcoholic in October 1947, at the age of forty-eight. (See *The Oregonian*, November 4, 1934, Sec.4, p. 4.)
18. Essoe, p. 72.
19. Ibid.
20. Samuels, p. 74.
21. Marie Canel, "Clark Gable One Actor Who Keeps His Feet on the Ground," *The Oregonian*, November 4, 1934, Section 4, p. 4.
22. John C. Moffitt, "Gable's First Love Is Still Good Friend," *The Morning Oregonian*, October 7, 1932, p. 6.
23. Richard H. Syring, "Young Clark Gable in Oregon," *The Oregonian Northwest Magazine*, Sunday, September 18, 1977, p. 11.
24. Samuels, p. 88.
25. John C. Moffitt, "Gable Takes Job on the Oregonian," *The Morning Oregonian*, October 8, 1932, p. 18. Also, "Gable Routed Out of Bed for Interview," *The Oregonian*, 17 January 1935, p.6.
26. Canel, Section 4, p. 5.
27. Essoe, p. 75.
28. Ibid. This is how Franz Dorfler said they met and there isn't any reason to doubt her. A story, the earliest version of which I've found so far dates from 1932, has often been repeated that Gable met Dillon when he was called out to her studio on a job for the telephone company, but neither Gable nor Dillon ever told it that way, either.
29. Essoe, p. 76.

Chapter 5 — The Apprentice

1. The Dillon family had moved to Los Angeles about 1906. Josephine had one brother, James, who became a lawyer, and four sisters: Fannie, a noted composer; Enrica Clay Dillon, an opera singer and voice teacher; Viva, a painter and opera singer, and Josephine's twin Anna Hood Dillon who was the only other sister to be married.

2. Tornabene, p. 82.

3. Samuels, pp. 89–90.

4. Garceau and Cocke, p. 31.

Portland's Broadway Theater now stands on the site.

5. Tornabene, p. 85.

6. Ibid, p. 82.

7. For reference to this manuscript, see Tornabene, pp. 82–95.

8. Essoe, p. 78.

9. Gable played Chang Lee in *East Is West*, and Harry Haydock in *Main Street*.

Chapter 6 — Becoming Clark Gable

1. Samuels, p. 102.

2. Samuels, pp. 104–5.

3. *Forbidden Paradise* starred Pola Negri, Rod LaRocque, and Adolphe Menjou.

4. Samuels, p. 104.

5. Samuels, p. 110.

6. Tornabene, p. 103.

7. Samuels, p. 112.

8. Born Grace Bailey in 1883, Cowl would also gain fame as a playwright when it was revealed that she and her friend Jane Murfin were jointly Alan Langdon Martin, the author of *Smilin' Through* which had run for 1170 performances from 1919–22. It had been produced by her husband, *New York Times* drama critic Adolph Klauber. She would write a number of other successful plays and appear in seven motion pictures until her death from cancer in 1950. On the plaque over her grave is inscribed, "Here Lies Juliet."

9. Essoe, p. 102.

10. Samuels, pp. 118–9.

Eddie Woods, who had become an actor while a student at the University of California, was Gable's closest friend in the *Romeo and Juliet* company, and they remained friends for years after. They worked together in *What Price Glory?* and *Madame X*, and most famously in *The Last Mile*. He later became a New York theater manager.

11. Written by Maxwell Anderson and Laurence Stallings, this was a play about U.S. Marines in World War One that had made Broadway history. It debunked the popular Teddy Roosevelt picture of fighting Americans and showed professional soldiers as rough men living by their own codes.

12. Samuels, p. 119.

13. Originally known as the Lincoln House, the Upham Hotel was built in 1871 to a design by Peter Barber for Amasa Lyman Lincoln, a cousin of President Abraham Lincoln. The oldest continuously operated hotel in Southern California, it still stands with its cottages in an acre of gardens on the corner of De La Vina and Sola. It was purchased by Carl Johnson of Vintage Hotels in 1982 and has been lovingly restored.

14. Essoe, p. 79.

15. Samuels, p. 127.

16. Pauline would not have much longer to enjoy the effects of her beauty, dying in 1938 at the age of 55 as a result of an asthma attack. Born Pauline Beatrice Libby in Boston, she had shown early promise on the stage and in music, and had rapidly made a name for herself on Broadway. The first of her thirty-six films was *The Emerald City* in 1915.

17. Samuels, p. 128.

18. Ibid, p. 122.

19. St Johns, "The Great God Gable," p. 24.

20. "Young Actor Has Great Time in Reporter Role," *Los Angeles Times*, May 22, 1927, Part 3, p. 19.

21. The handsome, pipe-smoking Wesley Ruggles (1889–1972) was the brother of actor Charles Ruggles, and started his work in film as a Keystone Kop. He began directing in 1927 and worked until 1946, mostly for Paramount. His films include *Cimarron* (1931), *I'm No Angel* with Mae West (1933), and *The Gilded Lily* with Claudette Colbert (1935). He later worked at Columbia, and then at MGM where he would direct Clark again in *Somewhere I'll Find You* in 1942. Ruggles would be the only director to work with both Carole Lombard and Clark in the same film when he directed *No Man of Her Own* in 1932.

22. David Stenn, *Clara Bow: Runnin' Wild*. Ebury Press: London, 1989, pp. 51–55.

23. *North Star* was directed by Paul Powell. The human costar was Virginia Lee Corbin.

24. Samuels, p. 130.

25. Born Ann Veronica Lahiff in New York City in 1903, the pretty, round-faced, redheaded Carroll was quickly dubbed "The Baby Cherub" or "Baby Face" during her early stage appearances. She married Jack Kirkland in 1924, and they moved to Los Angeles after their daughter Patricia was born the next year. After the success of *Chicago*, she was put under contract by Paramount. She made 42 films before returning to New York City and live theater in 1939, and she may well have been the first female actor to sing and dance in a motion picture. She was still working, in a production of *Never Too Late*, when she died suddenly in 1965.

26. Samuels, p. 131.

27. Tornabene, p. 113.

28. Ibid, p. 114.

29. Ibid, p. 115. Zita Johann's Broadway debut had been in 1924. She would wait until 1931 before her first film role in D. W. Griffith's last work, *The Struggle*. Her greatest fame would be as Boris Karloff's co-star in *The Mummy* (1932). However, nothing as good was offered her again, and

she returned to the stage two years later after appearing in only eight films. Her first marriage was to actor John Houseman. She died in 1993.

30. Essoe, p. 105.

31. Tornabene, p. 116.

Chapter 7 — Clark and Ria

1. Tornabene, p. 117.

2. John C. Moffitt, "Clark Gable Divorced by Miss Dillon," *The Morning Oregonian*, 13 October, 1932, p. 13.

3. Ibid.

4. St Johns, "The Great God Gable," p. 23.

5. Samuels, pp. 145–7.

6. Samuels, p. 149.

7. Garceau and Cocke, p. 39.

8. Produced by A.H. Woods, it opened on March 13.

9. Garceau and Cocke, p. 40.

10. John C. Moffitt, "Clark Gable Divorced by Miss Dillon," p. 13.

11. *The Last Mile* was written by actor John Wexley, 24, who based much of the story on real-life events. The first act was taken from a diary written by condemned murderer Robert Blake, while he was on death row. Blake had been executed in the Huntsville, Texas, penitentiary in April 1929. The rest of *The Last Mile* was based on events surrounding the Canyon City, Colorado, prison break that had also occurred in 1929. Wexley donated twenty percent of his royalties to be shared between Blake's mother, who had eight children to care for, and Blake's widow. (See, "The Last Mile Scores Hit in Los Angeles," *San Francisco Chronicle*, June 8, 1930, p. 2D.)

12. Tornabene, p. 124.

13. Essoe, p. 106.

14. Edwin Schallert, "The Last Mile Superthriller," *Los Angeles Times*, June 3 & 4, 1930.

15. Essoe, p. 106.

16. Alma Whitaker, "Murder Role Career Climax," *Los Angeles Times*, June 8, 1930, Part 3.

17. Lionel Barrymore as told to Cameron Shipp, *We Barrymores*. Appleton-Century-Crofts Inc.: New York, 1951, pp. 244–45.

18. Clark Gable, "Slap 'Em for Luck," *American Magazine*, September 1936, p. 76.

19. Pete Martin, "I Call on Clark Gable," *Saturday Evening Post*, May, 1957, p. 66.

20. Essoe, p. 85.

21. Martin, p. 66.

22. Tornabene, p. 131.

23. St Johns, "The Great God Gable," pp. 16–17.

24. Gable, p. 76.

25. Samuels, p. 154.

26. Tornabene, p. 130.

27. Through some four decades of filmmaking, the feisty, spiky and irreverent Wellman's career remains one of the most unconventional, diverse, and critically widely-debated in Hollywood history. Born in 1896, he was an ambulance driver for the French Foreign Legion, an ace pilot, and a stunt wing-walker before becoming an actor. Being an actor, he said, was the only job that really scared him, and so in 1923 he turned to directing. Some of his notable films were *Wings*, the first film to win the Academy Award for Best Picture (1927); *Public Enemy* (1931) which made a star of James Cagney; *Nothing Sacred* (1937) with Carole Lombard; the original 1937 Janet Gaynor version of *A Star Is Born*, *The Ox-Bow Incident* (1943), *Battleground* (1949), and *The Story of G.I. Joe* (1945). He would direct Gable again in *Call of the Wild* in 1935. He died in 1975.

28. Born Ruby Stevens in Brooklyn in 1907, Stanwyck became a dancing star on Broadway in the 1920s and entered the movies in 1927. Her second marriage was to Robert Taylor in 1939. She would make one other movie with Gable, *To Please a Lady* (1950). Stanwyck was famous for her strong, independant female characters who could still be tender on the inside though hard-boiled on the outside, such as she portrayed in *Union Pacific* (1939), *Ball of Fire* (1941), *Double Indemnity* (1944), *Sorry Wrong Number* (1948), *Clash by Night* (1952), and *The Big Valley* television series (1965–1969).

29. Axel Madsen, *Stanwyck: A Biography*, Harper Paperbacks: New York, 1995, p. 70.

30. Tornabene, p. 133.

31. Much of this information concerning MGM's financial status and executive salaries is drawn from chapter 3 of Douglas Gomery's *The Hollywood Studio System*, St. Martins Press, New York, 1986.

Chapter 8 — New Man, New World

1. Samuels, pp. 159–160.

2. Jack Conway directed his first film in 1909 and twenty years later had fifty feature films to his credit and a reputation as one of Hollywood's most reliable and dependable directors. Apart from the six Gable movies, his films include Crawford's first sound film, *Untamed* (1929), Harlow's *Red Headed Woman* (1932), and *A Tale of Two Cities* (1935).

Constance Bennett (1904–1965) was the spoiled, headstrong, eldest daughter in an acting family. Both her parents were actors on the stage, her sister Barbara appeared in films, and her other sister Joan Bennett also had a film career. Constance made her first acting appearance at age eleven in one of her father's films, and by mid–1925 she was a star. In her prime, she was a brilliant and sophisticated comedienne. She appeared in fifty-seven films, the last of which (*Madam X*) was released in 1966 after her death from cancer. She married five times; her last husband was Brigadier-General John Coulter and so she was buried in Arlington National Cemetery. Probably her two most well-known films are *What Price Hollywood?* (1932), and *Topper* (1937). She would work again with Clark in *After Office Hours* (1935).

3. Essoe, p. 80.

4. Tornabene, p. 139.

5. Ibid, p. 140.

6. Harry Beaumont (1888–1966) began performing in Edison Studios films in 1912 and made his directorial debut with Essanay in 1915. Quickly picking up a reputation for competence, he worked at all the major studios of the 1920s and continued on through the sound era until 1948, directing some eighty films. He directed the first film version of *Main Street* (1923), and MGM's first all-talking, all-singing movie, *The Broadway Melody* (1929), for which he received an Academy Award nomination. Some of his others are *Beau Brummel* (1924), *Babbitt* (1924), *Our Dancing Daughters* (1929), and MGM's "Masie" series during the 1940's starring Ann Southern.

7. From *A Portrait of Joan* by Joan Crawford and Jane Ardmore, Doubleday, 1962, as extracted in Essoe, p. 88.

8. Jane Ellen Wayne, *Clark Gable: Portrait of a Misfit*. St. Martins Press: New York, 1993, p. 74.

9. Essoe, p. 117.

10. Born Marion Benson Owens in San Francisco in 1888, she began her movie writing career at the age of twenty-six. A close friend of Mary Pickford, Marie Dressler and writer Adela Rogers St. Johns, Marion would eventually be credited with writing 325 scripts and directing and producing half-a-dozen films. She was the first Allied woman across the Rhine in World War 1, was the vice-president and only woman on the first board of the Screen Writers Guild, spoke several languages fluently, and she was a painter, sculptor, and pianist. While involved in all that, she somehow found the time for four husbands, two sons, and dozens of lovers including writer A.J. Cronin. She received two Academy Awards, and in 1966 she was awarded the University of Southern California's first Pioneer Film Award. She died in 1973.

11. Cari Beauchamp, *Without Lying Down: Frances Marion and the Powerful Women of Early Hollywood*. University of California Press: Los Angeles, 1998, pp. 270–1.

12. Rene Jordan, *Clark Gable*. Galahad Books: New York, 1973, p. 29.

13. Beauchamp, p. 271.

14. J.P. McEvoy, " Joe Lucky," *Saturday Evening Post,* May 4, 1940, p. 23.

15. Essoe, p. 96.

16. Wayne, p. 77.

17. Essoe, p. 119.

18. Clarence Brown probably directed more Gable movies than any other director. Born in 1890, he started out as an automotive engineer, but became interested in the movies in 1915. Becoming assistant director to Maurice Tourneur, Brown inherited his artistic touch for romance, aesthetics and stunning picture quality. MGM put him under contract in 1926, and he remained with them for the rest of his career. His last work was as producer of the 1953 Gable film *Never Let Me Go*. Brown became Garbo, Shearer, and Crawford's favorite director because of his discretion, diplomacy, and gentle manner. Some of his major work was *Flesh and the Devil* (1927), *Anna Karenina* (1935), *National Velvet* (1945), *The Yearling* (1947), and *Intruder in the Dust* (1950). Nominated six times for the Best Director Academy award, Brown died in 1987 without ever winning it.

19. L. Quirk, *Norma*. St. Martins Press: New York, 1988, p. 126.

20. Ibid., p. 127.

21. Adela Rogers' parents separated when she was two, and she was raised by her adored father and a succession of tutors. Her father introduced her to William Randolph Hearst by way of preventing her from becoming an actor, and so she began her writing career at 18 for the *Los Angeles Herald Examiner*. She thrived, writing screenplays and short stories as well as columns for a number of papers, feature star articles for magazines such as *Photoplay* and *Liberty*, and later an autobiography and two volumes of reminiscences about Hollywood. She remained a lifelong friend of Hearst, of Richard Nixon who awarded her the Medal of Freedom in 1970, and of Clark Gable, Frances Marion, Colleen Moore and Mary Pickford. When she died in 1988, her three husbands and son Bill had gone before her, but three children, ten grandchildren, fourteen great-grandchildren and five great-great-grandchildren remained.

22. Born Cecil Pringle in 1899 in Utah to an actress mother who abandoned him, John Gilbert became the greatest, and the highest paid, romantic actor of the silent screen. He married three times, but had long-standing associations with Greta Garbo and Marlene Dietrich. However, his unsuitable voice ruined Gilbert's chances of making a smooth transition into sound films, although rumors have persisted that his career was deliberately sabotaged. His health declined after 1932 because of his drinking and the sodium amatol injections he needed to sleep. He subsequently lost the lead in *Red Dust* to Gable, and died in 1936.

23. Clark's visit to Adela Rogers St. Johns' home that night and their conversation was recorded initially in her article for *Liberty* magazine, "The Great God Gable," pp. 19–20, and later in her

memoirs, *Love, Laughter, and Tears: My Hollywood Story*. Doubleday: New York, 1978, pp. 315–16.

24. Barrymore always said that although he was given the Award, it should have gone to director Clarence Brown. Shrewdly assessing that Barrymore's first rendering of his magnificent and emotive courtroom speech would be unique, Brown had ordered all eight cameras running for the first take so another would not be necessary — without telling Barrymore. Brown was proved right; Barrymore was exhausted when the take was over.

25. Quirk, p. 130.

26. Ibid.

27. Tornabene, p. 145.

28. The release of *Night Nurse* might also have been delayed by the merger of First National with Warner Bros.
Sporting Blood was directed by Charles Brabin who became Colleen Moore's favorite director. This competent veteran directed over 50 films between 1911 and his retirement in 1933, some fourteen of which he wrote. After directing two of Theda Bara's films in 1919, they were married in 1921 and he may have been responsible for influencing her retirement from acting soon after. He sued MGM for a half-million dollars after they fired him from the first *Ben-Hur* in 1925. His best known films were *Babette* (1917), *Twinkletoes* (1926), *Beast of the City* (1932), and *Mask of Fu-Manchu* (1932).

29. Madsen, pp. 70–71.

30. Tornabene, p. 150.

31. Her first husband, in 1928, had been director Kenneth Hawkes who was killed in a plane crash in 1930. Dr Thorpe would become famous in turn as the "wronged party" in his and Mary's 1936 divorce case, when he used the existence of a notorious diary to allege her unfitness as a mother. The diary allegedly contained intimate revelations of her affairs with playwright George S. Kaufman and a number of actors.

32. St. Johns, "The Great God Gable," p. 18.

33. Samuels, p. 177. Jack Butler was the guide and his wife Mary would cook for the outfit. Butler became ill with appendicitis on one of their trips. When it became apparent that Butler had no money to pay for an operation, Clark instructed that the best surgeon in the area be found for him immediately and paid Butler's hospital bill himself.

34. For information about the history of the Weasku Inn and Clark's association with it, I am greatly indebted to the current owners, Vintage Hotels, and to Laura Kath Fraser, author of *Weasku Inn: Oregon's Legendary Rogue River Resort*, Vintage Publishing: Santa Barbara, California, 1998.

35. Tornabene, p. 153.

Chapter 9 — Possessed

1. The film was based on the best-selling, two-volume novel by David Graham Phillips. He had been murdered in 1911 by a crazed fan, who believed Phillips had slandered his sister in a previous novel.
This would be the first of four Gable films that Robert Zigler Leonard (1889–1968) would direct. He began his career in 1914 and his long list of work includes the best of Jeanette MacDonald and Nelson Eddy in *Maytime* (1937), and Olivier and Garson in *Pride and Prejudice* (1940). He was married to two silent film stars, Mae Murray and Gertrude Olmstead.

2. The reclusive and legendary Garbo was born Greta Lovisa Gustafson in Sweden in 1905. A budding stage actor, her first starring film role was in the 1924 Swedish film, *The Saga of Gosta Berling*, and it was this film that brought her to the attention of L. B. Mayer. Garbo's first film for MGM was *Torrent* (1926). She starred in another ten silent films until audiences first heard her voice in *Anna Christie* in 1930, but she would make only a further fourteen. *Two Faced Woman* (1941) was not a success and, after difficulties in finding another project, she released MGM from their contract in 1943. Garbo subsequently moved to New York and did not return to acting. She never married. After her death in 1990, it was nine years before her ashes returned to her beloved homeland.

3. Jordan, p. 32.

4. Barry Paris, *Garbo*. Alfred A. Knopf: New York, 1995, p. 205.

5. *Red Dust* casting evolved from Garbo-Menjou, to Garbo-Gilbert, to Garbo-Gable, and finally to Harlow-Gable. See: Paris, p. 205.

6. Samuels, p. 175.

7. St. Johns, "The Great God Gable," pp. 20–21.

8. Samuels, p. 176.

9. Tornabene, p. 164.

10. Ibid, p. 161.

11. Crawford's personal account of her romance with Clark during the filming of *Possessed* is from her autobiography, *A Portrait of Joan*, as extracted in Essoe, pp. 88–89.

12. Gregory D. Black, *Hollywood Censored*. Cambridge University Press: New York, 1994, p. 6.

13. Ibid., p. 10.

14. Ibid., p. 40.

15. Ibid., p. 60.

16. Marion Davies had been born Marion Douras in Brooklyn in 1897, and she was a Ziegfeld Follies girl by 1917. She started making movies the same year. Her stammer made her nervous once sound was introduced, though, and she made her last film in 1937. She stayed with Hearst until his death in 1951, and died in 1961.

17. Marion Davies, *The Times We Had*. Ballantine Books: New York, 1989, p. 133.

18. Tornabene, p. 159.

19. Eve Golden, *Platinum Girl: The Life and Legends of Jean Harlow*, Abbeville Press: New York, 1991, pp. 79–80, 98.

20. Ibid., p. 98.

21. Barry Norman, *The Hollywood Greats*. Arrow Books, London, 1988, p. 192.

Harlow, like Carole Lombard, dyed her pubic hair so there'd be no shadow under the sheer white gowns she so loved, but under which she'd more often than not be wearing nothing at all. Lombard once referred to the practice as making sure that your collar and cuffs matched.

22. Wayne, p. 102.

23. Golden, p. 100.

24. Norman, p. 192.

25. Paul Bern left his entire estate to Jean. When Millette's body was found on the day Jean returned to work, Jean paid for her burial in East Lawn Cemetery, Sacramento.

26. Norman, p. 202.

27. Lucille Vasconcelles Langehanke, better known as Mary Astor, was born in 1906. She was a charismatic and intelligent actress for over 40 years. After being a well-known, silent-movie actress alongside such stars as Barrymore and Fairbanks, her career was in stasis after the introduction of sound when graphic excerpts from her diary were leaked to papers in 1936 during her divorce hearing. Her career was re-vitalized out of notoriety, and she stole an Academy Award from Bette Davis for *The Great Lie* in 1941. Her last film was again alongside Bette in the 1965 *Hush, Hush, Sweet Charlotte*, but her pinnacle was as the deceptively helpless Brigid O'Shaughnessy in *The Maltese Falcon*.

28. For some of the key thoughts in this discussion I am indebted to chapter 6 of William Rothman's, *The "I" of the Camera: Essays in Film Criticism, History, and Aesthetics*. Cambridge University Press: New York.

29. Essoe, p. 137.

30. Ibid.

Chapter 10 — Quiet Interlude

1. L. Quirk, p. 137.

2. Ibid.

3. Ibid.

4. Quirk, p. 138.

5. G. Lambert, *Norma Shearer: A Life*. Alfred A. Knopf: New York, 1990, p. 133.

6. Quirk, p. 138.

7. Essoe, p. 139.

8. Quirk, p. 140.

9. Tornabene, pp.175–76.

10. Warren G. Harris, *Gable and Lombard*. Simon and Schuster: New York, 1974, p. 44.

11. Harris, p. 45.

12. Not to be confused with the 1949 film *No Man of Her Own*, starring Barbara Stanwyck. Originally known as *I Married a Dead Man*, it was retitled at the last minute before release.

13. See Black, p. 60, for Lord's comments.

14. *Variety*, January 10, 1933, p. 8.

15. David Thomson, *Showman: The Life of David O Selznick*. Knopf: New York, 1992, p. 154.

16. Sam Wood (1883–1949), a man of extreme right-wing politics, would be remembered for his two classic Marx Brothers comedies, *A Night at the Opera* (1935) and *A Day at the Races* (1937), even if he'd made no other films. But during a long career he directed a series of professionally crafted classic movies that often evoked honest, heartwarming sentiment across a wide spectrum of genres, including *Goodbye Mr. Chips* (1939), *Our Town* (1940), *The Devil and Miss Jones* (1941), *The Pride of the Yankees* (1941), and *For Whom the Bell Tolls* (1943). He would direct Gable again in *Command Decision* (1949).

17. Golden, pp. 120–21.

18. Both Barrymores had legendary reputations for stealing scenes from each other. Director Clarence Brown bet Jack ten dollars that Lionel would not be able to steal a scene from him in this movie. After being bawled out by his brother as the supervisor, Lionel shuffled dumbly towards the door with his back to the camera. Just before he went through the door, he reached around and rubbed his bottom. Jack turned to Clarence and declared: "Now, there is a brother to be proud of!"

19. James Kotsilibas-Davis and Myrna Loy, *Myrna Loy: Being and Becoming*. Donald I. Fine Inc: New York, 1988, p. 84.

Night Flight was Myrna Loy's first film in a starring role, after one of the longest apprenticeships in movie history. Born Myrna Williams in Helena, Montana, in 1905 (but named after Myrna, Nebraska), she moved to Los Angeles with her mother after her father died in the 1918 influenza epidemic. She started acting in small movie roles in 1925. Given a five year contract by Warners, Loy became typecast as an exotic Eastern maiden because of her almond-shaped eyes, after appearing in *Desert Song* in 1929. *Night Flight* was her sixty-ninth picture in a career of over one hundred and ten.

20. Kotsilibas-Davis and Loy, p. 84.

21. Samuels, p. 179.

22. Tornabene, p. 182.

23. Tornabene, p. 177.

24. Tornabene, pp. 180–81.

25. Stanislas Pascal Franchot Tone was born in Niagara Falls in 1905, the son of the president of the Carborundum Company. After graduating

from Cornell University, he had a distinguished stage career. His first film appearence was in *The Wiser Sex* with Claudette Colbert in 1932, and not long after he was offered a five-year contract with MGM during which he achieved his two best film performances, in *Mutiny on the Bounty*, and in *Lives of a Bengal Lancer*. He would marry Joan Crawford in 1935, but they would divorce four years later, remaining good friends. He would marry another three times, equally unsuccessfully, and would continue to appear in films and on stage until his death in 1968.

26. Bob Thomas, *Joan Crawford*. Bantam Book/ Simon & Schuster: New York, 1979, p. 94.

27. Essoe, p. 149.

Chapter 11— It Happened One Year

1. Frank Capra, *The Name Above The Title*. W. H. Allan: London, 1972, p. 160.

2. Ibid. The other story, "Last Trip," had appeared in the earlier March edition of *Colliers*. It was about a forlorn and somewhat suicidal young secretary, who gains a more positive outlook on life when she meets an equally unhappy young man on her bus.

3. Joseph McBride, *Frank Capra: The Catastrophe of Success*. Simon & Schuster: New York, 1992, p. 285.

4. Kotsilibas-Davis and Loy, p. 94.

5. Capra, p. 165.

6. Clark Gable, "Slap 'Em for Luck," *American Magazine*. September 1936, p. 80.

7. Pete Martin, "I Call on Clark Gable," *The Saturday Evening Post*, May 1957, p. 64.

8. After her family arrived in New York from France when she was three, Colbert intended to be a painter, but she was bitten by the acting bug after appearing in a school play when she was fifteen. By 1927 she was famous for her performance in *The Barker* at the Biltmore, and Walter Winchell had dubbed her "Legs" Colbert. That was also the year she made her film debut, *For the Love of Mike*, and had been so appalled at Capra's direction. Paramount offered her a contract, however, and her first talkies were *The Hole in the Wall*, with Edward G. Robinson, and *Young Man of Manhattan* (1930), which was Ginger Rogers' first movie.

9. Amy Fine Collins, "A Perfect Star," *Vanity Fair*, January 1998, p. 102.

10. Garceau and Cocke, p. 56.

11. Capra, p. 166.

12. Ibid.

13. Garceau and Cocke, p. 56.

14. Ibid., p. 57

15. Elizabeth Kendall, *The Runaway Bride: Hol-*

lywood Romantic Comedy of the 1930's. Anchor Books/Doubleday: New York, 1991, p.44.

Kendall is of the opinion that this cabin scene is a reprise of a similar scene with Barbara Stanwyck in the penthouse in Capra's earlier *Lady of Leisure*.

16. Ibid.

17. McBride, p. 307.

18. Capra, p. 170.

19. Ibid.

20. Collins, p. 105.

21. Capra, p. 167.

22. Ibid.

23. Kendall, p. 45.

24. Colbert and Gable teamed up one more time for *Hony Tonk* in 1940. In 1938, the Treasury Department listed her, at $426,944 a year, as the second-highest Hollywood wage earner after L. B. Mayer. That figure also ranked her as the fourth-highest paid corporate employee in the U.S., a position that would next be surpassed by Gable himself. Much awarded, including the Legion of Honor in 1988, Colbert continued to work on the stage and screen until ten years before her death in 1996.

25. That year, Capra had been sure the Oscar for Best Director would be his, for *Lady for a Day*. When Will Rogers called out, "Come up and get it, Frank!," Capra was almost onto the stage when he realized that they did not mean him, but Frank Lloyd.

26. Tornabene, pp. 191–2.

27. Kotsilibas-Davis and Loy, p. 85.

28. Tornabene, p. 195.

29. McBride, p. 309.

30. Norbert Lusk, "Stage Appearance Smart Stuff," *Los Angeles Times*, March 4, 1934.

31. This was the first film in which Loy and Powell worked together. Apparently, Van Dyke was never a great one for introductions, so Loy had not met Powell until a scene where she runs out of a building and leaps into a car in which Powell is sitting, landing on his lap. "Miss Loy, I presume?" commented the ever-nonchalant Powell. They went on to be partners in fourteen movies, many of them part of the *Thin Man* series.

32. Mollie Merrick, "Clark Gable's Talents Smothered by Bad Role in a Maudlin Picture," *San Francisco Chronicle*, April 30, 1934.

33. Essoe, p. 154.

34. Mankiewicz worked on nine Crawford movies, producing most of them. Mayer claimed Mankiewicz was the only one who knew what to do with her.

35. Essoe, p. 161.

36. Martin, p. 64.

37. In fact, one of the great Academy Award controversies was the Academy's denial of an official Best Actress nomination for Davis in this film, making her a write-in candidate only. Davis considered she got even when, years later, she was

given the role of Margot Channing in *All About Eve.* Claudette Colbert had injured her back and couldn't take up the role when it was initially offered to her. (See: *Vanity Fair,* January 1998, p. 108.)

38. William Powell, born in 1892, had a thirty-two-year career spanning nearly a hundred movies, beginning in 1922. His first movie for MGM was his only appearance with Clark Gable, in *Manhattan Melodrama* in 1934. He was more closely associated with Clark as Carole Lombard's first husband, from 1931 to 1933, and as Jean Harlow's close friend at the time of her death. His second Oscar nomination would be for *My Man Godfrey,* with Lombard, and his third would be for *Life with Father* as Clarence Day.

39. In a career that spanned over thirty years and nearly a hundred movies, Frank Morgan remains probably best-known today for his portrayal of the Wizard in *The Wizard of Oz.* He would gain his second Oscar nomination for his role as "the pirate" in *Tortilla Flat.* He was born Frances Philip Wupperman in 1890, one of the eleven sons of the cofounder of the company that marketed Angostura bitters. After starting on the stage, he appeared in his first movie in 1916. He appeared in three movies with Clark Gable: *Saratoga, Boom Town,* and *Honky Tonk.*

40. *It Happened One Night, The Barretts of Wimpole Street, Cleopatra, Flirtation Walk, The Gay Divorcee, Here Comes the Navy, The House of Rothschild, Imitation of Life, One Night of Love, The Thin Man, Viva Villa, The White Parade.*

41. Lyle Abbott, Los Angeles *Herald-Express,* 28 February, 1935.

42. Samuels, p. 181.

43. *One Flew Over the Cuckoo's Nest* (1975) and *Silence of the Lambs* (1991) each won only the five top awards. Of the three notable Oscar sweeps, neither *Gone with the Wind* nor *Titanic* received Best Actor awards, and *Ben-Hur* did not receive Best Actress. On the other hand, films in which Oscars for both Best Actress and Best Actor were awarded but that did *not* win all five top awards were: Peter Finch and Faye Dunaway in *Network* in 1976, Jon Voigt and Jane Fonda in *Coming Home* in 1978, Henry Fonda and Katharine Hepburn in *On Golden Pond* in 1981 and Jack Nicholson and Helen Hunt in *As Good as It Gets* in 1997.

44. On December 14, 1996, Steven Spielberg purchased Gable's Oscar at a Christie's auction for $550,000 ($607,500 including auction fees), then donated it back to the Academy, which had tried unsuccessfully to obtain a court order to prevent its sale. Spielberg's bid topped the previous record price of $510,000 set in 1993 for Vivien Leigh's *Gone with the Wind* award. Spielberg also bought Gable's *Gone with the Wind* script for $220,000 ($244,500 after fees), and Clark's passport went to

another bidder for $10,000. Spielberg's record was broken in June 1999, when Michael Jackson bid $1.5 million for David O. Selznick's Best Picture Oscar for *Gone with the Wind.*

Chapter 12 — Call of the Wild

1. Its original title was *Town Talk.*

2. "Gable Routed Out of Berth for Interview," *The Oregonian,* January 17, 1935, p. 6.

3. Peter Lawford tribute program to Clark Gable.

4. Judy Lewis, *Uncommon Knowledge.* Pocket Books/Simon & Schuster: New York, 1995, p. 43.

5. Lewis, p. 47.

6. Colleen Moore was the prototype movie "flapper" of the 1920s who became a star with her appearance in *Flaming Youth* (1923). Her celluloid standards of dancing and drinking inspired daughters and distressed mothers. Born Cathleen Morrison in Port Huron, Michigan, in 1900, she began her prolific film career under the direction of D. W. Griffith in 1916, making most of her films for First National. Her last major film was *The Sound and the Glory* with Spencer Tracy in 1933. Wealthy when she retired, she invested money wisely and wrote three books, including a guide to the stock market. She was a collector of miniatures which were housed in what became known as Colleen Moore's Fairy Castle which still delights children and amazes adults in the Chicago Museum of Science and Industry.

7. In a major Academy Awards upset, Young won the Best Actress Oscar for her role as a Swedish farm girl who becomes a congresswoman in *Farmers Daughter* in 1947.

8. After a failed marriage, affairs with Tracy and Gable, reported involvements with Tyrone Power and Jimmy Stewart, and a failed engagement to William Buckner, Loretta would marry Tom Lewis in 1940. Her final marriage was at the age of 80 to long-time friend Jean Louis.

9. Lewis, pp. 25–6.

10. Bob Thomas, "Forever Young," *The Idaho Statesman,* November 24, 2000, p. 1D.

11. Lewis, p. 29.

12. Adela's comments and Ria's words are from Adela Rogers St. John's article "Love, Fame and the Clark Gables," *Photoplay,* February 1936, pp. 14–16.

13. Lewis, p. 58.

14. Ibid., p. 231.

15. Ibid., p. 109.

16. Joan Wester Anderson, *Forever Young.* Thomas More: Allen, Texas, 2000.

Chapter 13 — Uncharted Seas

1. After the stone was erected, by John Gizzie

Memorials in Meadville, it was noticed that an inscription error had Addie's death taking place in 1900 instead of in 1901.

2. St. Johns, "The Great God Gable," p. 24.

3. Collins, p. 105.

4. Tornabene, p. 190.

5. Ibid., p. 201.

6. This was all duly reported in the *Dallas Morning News* of March 18, 1935, but credit needs to go to writer Clay Reynolds and journalist Kent Biffle who rediscovered the incident and reported it in the *Morning News* of February 2, 1997, p. 47A.

7. Tornabene, p. 202.

8. Tay Garnett (1894–1977) first worked as a writer for silent films with the likes of Mack Sennett and Hal Roach before starting to direct in 1928. He moved from studio to studio and genre to genre over the years, finally moving into films of larger scope and more elaborate costumes with MGM in the forties. His best work is probably the 1946 Garfield-Turner version of *The Postman Always Rings Twice*. Some of his others were *One Way Passage* (1932), *Bataan* (1943), *Mrs. Parkington* (1944) with Greer Garson, and *Valley of Decision* (1945).

9. Rosalind Russell had worked with Clark in her third picture *Forsaking All Others* (1934). She typically played a strong, determined woman who often took on men at their own games on their own ground in a film career that extended over thirty years. Born in 1908, she graduated from the American Academy of Dramatic Art, worked in stock, and had then signed for seven years with MGM in 1934. MGM tended to use Russell as a threat to Myrna Loy, bringing her in whenever Loy was holding out for more money. So, Russell primarily played second lead except on loan-outs until she went freelance. *China Seas* was her seventh film.

10. This was the last of the three movies Beery made with Clark, the others being *The Secret Six* (1931) and *Hell Divers* (1931). Beery would die in 1949 of a heart ailment after a career that began with him appearing in silent shorts in 1915. Starting with MGM in 1930, he became popular teamed with Marie Dressler in *Min and Bill*, and in two magnificent performances in *Grand Hotel* and *Viva Villa*. One of the screen's most lovable rogues during the 1930s and 1940s, it was said he was so similar in real life that Mayer paid him $150,000 a year to work *only* twelve weeks.

11. Eve Golden, *Platinum Girl*. Abbeville Press: New York, 1991, p. 168.

12. Essoe, p. 164.

13. Golden, pp. 169–70.

China Seas was the last movie in which the Platinum Girl would appear with her trademark platinum hair. Thereafter, she refused to be typecast because of her hair color and reverted to her natural honey-blond.

14. "These Are Not Poison at the Box Office," *Look*, July 5, 1938, pp. 20–21.

15. See Tornabene, pp. 403–9.

16. Tornabene, p. 209.

17. Only officers in the British Navy are allowed the privilege of facial hair, although it is traditionally extended to submariners while on sea duty.

18. Martin, p. 64.

19. Charles Laughton, who began his film career in 1929, was the greatest character actor in the cinema at that time. He had started out successfully on stage where he continued to appear. His film characterizations of Bligh, Henry the Eighth, Nero, Rembrandt, and the Hunchback of Notre Dame are definitive ones. His last role was the Machiavellian Southern senator in *Advise and Consent*, just before his death in 1962.

20. Martin, p. 64.

21. Frank Lloyd (1888–1960) was born in Scotland. He came to the U.S. in 1913, working briefly as an actor before becoming a director, initially with silent films. His last silent film, *The Divine Lady* (1929), earned him a Best Director Oscar, and *Cavalcade* (1933) gained him his next Award (and two others), but his best film remains *Mutiny on the Bounty*. Although he skillfully directed scores of films over four decades, most of them were comparatively unpretentious and did not gain him the critical attention of these three.

22. Simon Callow, *Charles Laughton: A Difficult Actor*. Methuen Drama: London, 1988, p. 97.

23. Clark Gable, "Slap 'Em for Luck," *Amercian Magazine*, September 1936, p. 80.

24. Frank Westmore and Muriel Davidson, *The Westmores of Hollywood*. J.B. Lippincott; New York, 1976, pp. 62–63.

Mont Westmore was the eldest of the six Westmore brothers. They all became senior personnel in the make-up departments of various studios, and they were also involved with their salon, The House of Westmore. Mont had started out as Rudolph Valentino's personal valet and make-up artist.

25. Gable, p. 80.

26. Callow, p. 98.

27. Ibid., p. 100.

28. Essoe, p. 168.

29. Martin, p. 64.

30. Ibid.

31. "Clark Gable? I Like Johnny, Says Lupe," *San Francisco Chronicle*, October 21, 1935, p. 5.

32. "Clark Gable, Wife Break; She Plans Divorce Action," *San Francisco Chronicle*, November 15, 1935.

33. Kotsilibas-Davis and Loy, p. 124.

34. Golden, p. 183.

35. Like Gable, the twenty-three-year-old James Stewart, whose father ran a hardware store in Indiana, Pa., had come to movies from acting on the stage. He had only been under contract with

MGM since June. He had appeared in two movies for them, *Murder Man* and *Rose Marie*, and had then been loaned to Universal for his first lead role in *Next Time We Love* opposite Margaret Sullavan. He would have to wait another few months until his first MGM lead in *Speed*, in March 1936. The rest, as they say, is film history.

36. Gary Fishgall, *Pieces of Time: The Life of James Stewart*. Scribner: New York, 1997, p. 86.

Chapter 14 — Lift Up Your Golden Gate

1. Tornabene, p. 207.
2. Ibid., p. 208.
3. Ibid.
4. Black, p. 168.
5. "Home Town Arises to Back Gable," *San Francisco Chronicle*, March 10, 1935.
6. "Clark Gable Religious, But Can't Be Himself.," *San Francisco Chronicle*. August 13, 1935.
7. Edward Baron Turk, *Hollywood Diva: A Biography of Jeanette MacDonald*. University of California Press: Los Angeles, 1998, p. 177.
8. Anita Loos, *Kiss Hollywood Goodbye*. Viking Press: New York, 1974, p. 52.
9. Gary Carey, *Anita Loos: A Biography*. Bloomsbury Publishing Ltd.: London, 1988, p. 163.
10. Loos, p. 129.
11. MacDonald was the youngest of three sisters. The eldest, Elsie, eventually ran a Philadelphia dance school. However, middle sister Blossom was also a singer and dancer, and she and Jeanette appeared on stage together very early in their respective careers. It was not as a singer that she would be remembered by modern audiences though; Blossom Rock became famous as Granny of *The Addams Family*.
12. MacDonald would eventually have her chance when *I Married an Angel* was finally made in 1942. It was the last of the eight movies in which MacDonald teamed with Nelson Eddy.
13. Jordan, p. 74.
14. Bill Davidson, *Spencer Tracy: Tragic Idol*. Sidgwick and Jackson: London, 1987, p. 10.
15. Ibid., p. 67.
16. Turk, p. 181.
17. Ibid., p. 181.
18. Carey, p. 165.
19. Turk, p. 184.
20. MacDonald would eventually fall out of favor with Mayer when she went over his head, again, to Schenck so that she could dub her own voice in foreign-language versions. She married Gene Raymond in 1937, eventually sang opera, made some postwar movies, and sang at Mayer's funeral in 1957. She passed away eight years later due to heart problems.

21. Polish-born and Warsaw Conservatory-trained, Bronislaw Kaper (1902–1983) was a conductor, arranger and composer for Hollywood films from the 1930s to the 1960s. He collaborated with lyricist Gus Kahn to write such well-known film songs as "Someone to Care for Me," and "The One I Love." After 1940, he scored entire films, such as *Johnny Eager, The Chocolate Soldier, Somewhere I'll Find You, Gaslight, The Red Badge of Courage, Butterfield 8*, and *Lord Jim*. He won the Academy Award in 1953 for the score of the film *Lili*, known for its theme song, "Hi-Lili, Hi-Lo" with lyrics by Helen Deutsch.
22. Warren G Harris, *Gable and Lombard*. Simon & Schuster: New York, 1974, p. 20.
23. Ibid., p. 23.
24. Tornabene, p. 221.
25. A. E. Hotchner, *Choice People: The Greats, Near-Greats, and Ingrates I Have Known*. William Morrow and Company, Inc.: New York, 1984, p. 45.
26. Lloyd Bacon (1890–1955) was often overshadowed by his dance director Busby Berkeley in such films as *42nd Street, Footlight Parade* (1933), and *Gold Diggers of 1937*. Bacon was a veteran and extraordinarily prolific director turning out some fifty movies in fifteen years for Warner Brothers. He started out directing comedy shorts for Mack Sennett, and he directed *Singing Fool* (1928), Warner's first all-dialogue production. In the 1940s he moved to Fox and then to Columbia, where he directed two Lucille Ball comedies.
27. Westmore, pp. 76–77.
28. Marion Davies, *The Times We Had*. Ballantine Books: New York, 1989, p. 258.
29. Ibid., pp. 350, 351, 356.
Marion stayed with Hearst until his death in 1951 at eighty-eight. She was not mentioned in the will, but she was left voting control of the Hearst organization, which she later relinquished. Later that year she eloped to Las Vegas with Captain Horace Brown. She then lived quietly in California until her death in 1961 at sixty-four, leaving an estate of some $8 million.
30. Harris, p. 59.

Chapter 15 — Who Do You Think You Are? Clark Gable!

1. Tornabene, p. 227.
2. Ibid., p. 228.
3. "1935 Garbo Salary Totalled $332,500," *The New York Times*. January 28, 1937. As you can see by the headline, Clark was still well down the list of Hollywood salaries for that year with his $211,533. On the top rung was Greta Garbo with $332,500, followed in order by Wallace Beery's $278,749, Joan Crawford's 241,000, and William Powell's $238,750.

4. "These Are Not Poison at the Box Office," *Look*, July 5, 1938, pp. 20–21.

According to this poll, Shirley Temple had topped the list since 1935, while Clark was second in 1934, third in 1935, second again in 1936 and 1937. Third in 1937 was Robert Taylor, followed in order by Bing Crosby, William Powell, Jane Withers, Fred Astaire and Ginger Rogers, Sonja Heinie, Gary Cooper, and Myrna Loy.

5. John M. Stahl (1886–1950) was another veteran director who had started with silent movies in 1914. He gathered a reputation in the sound era for making even the most blatant tear-jerkers interesting, such as *Magnificent Obsession* (1935), by allowing the audience to become involved in the emotional upheavals of lead women roles. *Parnell* would be his sole work for MGM, after which he went to Fox where some of his major films were *Holy Matrimony* (1943*), The Keys of the Kingdom* (1944), and *Leave Her to Heaven* (1945).

6. Kotsilibas-Davis and Myrna Loy, p. 145.

7. Ibid.

8. Douglas Fairbanks, Jr., p. 208.

9. Anthony Quinn and Daniel Paisner, *One Man Tango*. Headline Book Publishing: London, 1995, pp. 139–40.

10. "Mr. Gyble: I'm Fully of Pep, So Let's Run Aw'y (sic) ," *San Francisco Chronicle*, January 28, 1937.

11. "Gable Love Child Fraud Case Closed," *San Francisco Chronicle*, April 22, 1937, p. 1.

12. *San Francisco Chronicle*, January 28, 1937.

13. John Fricke, *Judy Garland: World's Greatest Entertainer*. Little, Brown: London, 1992, pp. 28–29.

"Dear Mr. Gable"/"You Made Me Love You" and Judy Garland would go on to bigger and better things. She sang it in public and on radio to such acclaim that the song was written into *Broadway Melody of 1938*, where she sings it to her scrapbook of Gable photos. The song was the turning point in her relationship with MGM and in the creation of her public persona. On September 24, 1937, she recorded "You Made Me Love You" for Decca.

14. David Shipman, *Judy Garland: Secret Life of an American Legend*. Hyperion: New York, 1993, p. 223.

15. Essoe, p. 80.

16. These cases are documented in Clark Gable's FBI files 9–3178, 9–3482, 9–4005, 9–6434, 9–7006, 95–2996.

17. Garceau and Cocke, p. 70.

18. Ibid., p. 72.

19. Kotsilibas-Davis and Loy, p. 144–5.

20. Golden, p. 205.

21. Ibid., p. 211.

22. Jean Harlow's estate would total only $41,000. She was only leasing her house, and she left all her possessions in it to her mother. Contrary to popular rumor, Jean's mother was not a Christian Scientist nor did she prevent medical care for Jean.

23. Harlow would certainly not, however, be the last to do so. Kay Kendall and Natalie Wood would both die before their last movies were completed, for example, as would male stars James Dean and Vic Morrow. Bela Lugosi's mid-film death was made all the more tragic by that last movie being Ed Wood's nil-budget shocker *Plan Nine from Outer Space*.

24. Garceau and Cocke, p. 74.

Chapter 16 — The King

1. Kotsilibas-Davis and Loy, p. 146.

Chapter 17 — Frankly My Dear...

1. Anne Edwards, *Road to Tara: The Life of Margaret Mitchell*. Dell Publishing Co.: New York, 1984, pp. 228, 273. Mitchell's contract with Selznick expressly stated she would have nothing to do with film casting or publicity, nor did she have final script approval. However, much correspondence went between her and Selznick over his script rewrites.

2. Martin, p. 66.

3. Thomson, p. 213.

4. C. Cameron and C.J. Christman, *The Art of Gone with the Wind*. Prentice-Hall: New York, 1989, p. 52.

5. Tornabene, p. 239.

6. Thomson, p. 268.

7. Information on the history of the Marcoux-Bromberg racing plane and its pilot, Earl Ortman, courtesy of the New England Air Museum, Bradley International Airport, Windsor Locks, Connecticut. The restored Marcoux-Bromberg has been on exhibition there since October 30, 1984.

8. Harris, p. 94.

9. Kotsilibas-Davis and Loy, pp. 148–9.

10. Tornabene, p. 240.

11. Davidson, *Spencer Tracy: Tragic Idol*, p. 73.

12. Kotsilibas-Davis and Loy, p. 155.

13. Cameron and Christman, p. 37.

14. Hugo Vickers, *Vivien Leigh*. Pan Books: London, 1990, p. 83.

15. Alexander Walker, *Vivien: The Life of Vivien Leigh*. Wiedenfeld & Nicolson: London, 1987, p. 90.

16. Vickers, p. 95.

17. Black, p. 285.

18. Esperanto is an artificial language constructed in 1887 by a Polish oculist, L. Zamenhof, that was intended to become a neutral, international second language. It is relatively easy for Eu-

ropeans to learn as its roots are in the Romance languages, all words are pronounced as written, grammar is simple and regular, and nouns have no gender. Its popularity has waned a little in the last couple of decades, from an estimated 300,000 speakers in the U.S. alone in the late 1930s to perhaps 100,000 internationally now. There are still some fifty national Esperanto associations with more than 30,000 books having been published in the language. The president of the Esperanto Association of North America at the time, Joseph Scherer, was a technical advisor for *Idiot's Delight*.

19. Lupton Wilkinson, "Shearer and Gable Take a Dare," *Movie Mirror*, March 1939, p. 33.

20. Black, p. 287.

21. Jan Stokes, "Making Gable Dance," *Detroit Free Press*, January 15, 1939, p. 13.

22. The other chorines were: Lorraine Krueger from St. Louis, who had been on stage since she was three and had been on Broadway at ten; Paula Stone from New York, daughter of stage and film comedian Fred Stone; Virginia Dale from Charlotte, North Carolina; Joan Marsh, the only small town girl, from Porterville, California; and Bernadine Hayes from St. Louis, a beautiful radio blues singer who had been on the stage since she was eleven. They were chosen from over 200 applicants.

23. Stokes, p. 13.

24. Wilkinson, p. 33.

25. Tornabene, p. 245.

26. Garceau and Cocke, p. 11.

27. This article is quoted in: Martin Levin (ed.), *Hollywood and the Great Fan Magazines*. Harrison House: New York, 1991, pp. 168, 222.

28. Stewart Granger, *Sparks Fly Upward*. Granada Publishing Ltd.: London, 1982, p. 44.

29. Thomson, p. 278.

30. Ibid., p. 284. Her contract covered two films a year, building her salary to $6,250.

31. Walker, p. 120

32. Thomson, p. 291

33. James Reid, "Here's Rhett. You Asked for Him," *Motion Picture*, March 1940. In a *Photoplay* article by Ruth Waterbury, "Vivien Leigh, Rhett Butler, and I," February, 1940, Clark identifies this woman as Alicia Rhett, who eventually played the role of India Wilkes after having originally auditioned for Scarlett.

34. Unlike California, where one had to be resident for a year before a divorce became legal, Nevada only required six months in 1906, then three months in 1927, and finally six weeks in 1931. So quite a large industry developed in Nevada around dude ranches, where divorcing parties would stay and vacation for that crucial six weeks. Clark would have his turn some years later when divorcing Lady Sylvia. Ironically, Nevada divorce would feature in *The Misfits*.

35. Harris, p. 101.

36. Cameron and Christman, p. 47.

37. Roland Flamini, *Scarlett, Rhett, and a Cast of Thousands: The Filming of Gone with the Wind.* Macmillan: New York, 1976, p. 232.

38. Thomson, p. 291.

39. Ibid.

40. Ibid., p. 290.

41. This rumor about Clark's "dark past" was apparently started by Billy Haines, a gay MGM leading man of the 1920s who was fired when his sexual liasions at the YMCA became too blatant. He then became one of Hollywood's prominent interior decorators and, in that capacity, a confidant of Joan Crawford, whose home he redecorated a number of times. It was to her that Haines allegedly gossiped that Clark and he had shared certain sexual favors in exchange for Haines getting him work as an extra in his films. This unlikely and unconfirmed tale was then apparently passed on by Crawford before her death to author Jane Ellen Wayne.

42. Cameron and Christman, p. 182.

43. Flamini, p. 229.

44. Ruth Waterbury, "Vivien Leigh, Rhett Butler, and I," *Photoplay*, February 1940, p. 13.

45. Ibid, p. 221.

46. From a letter written by Myrick to Margaret Mitchell, February 14, 1939, recounting what Cukor had told Myrick personally. Published in: Susan Myrick and Richard Harwell (eds.), *White Columns in Hollywood: Reports from the Gone with the Wind Sets*, Mercer University Press: Macon, Georgia, 1994 (3rd ed.), p. 127.

47. Flamini, p. 232.

48. Thomson, p. 291.

49. Born in California in 1883, Fleming was at various times a race-car driver, pilot, hunter, and a Signal Corps photographer. He got his start as cameraman for Douglas Fairbanks, Sr. His first major film was *The Virginian* (1929), which made a star of Gary Cooper. Fleming became renowned as the poet of masculine pride and virtues, a man's man. He was also a ladies' man, though, whom directors and actors emulated and with whom stars such as Clara Bow, Norma Shearer, Lupe Velez, and Ingrid Bergman fell in love. His other major works were *Red Dust* (1932), *Bombshell* (1933), *Treasure Island* (1934), *Captains Courageous* (1937), *Dr. Jekyll and Mr. Hyde* (1941), *A Guy Named Joe* (1943) which was remade by Spielberg as *Always* (1989), and *Joan of Arc* just before his death in 1949.

50. Thomson, p. 294.

51. Ibid., p. 296.

52. Tornabene, p. 196.

53. Flamini, p. 250.

54. "Star's Wife Gets Decree," *San Francisco Chronicle*, March 8, 1939.

55. Tornabene, p. 256.

56. From a rough draft of an article by Gladys Hall, "Clark and Carole Gable," evidently intended for publishing in *Picture Play* in May, 1939. It is held in the Margaret Herrick Library, Academy of Motion Picture Arts and Sciences. Hall claimed to have personally interviewed Gable and Winkler not long after the events.

57. Harris, p. 106.

58. Ibid., p. 107.

59. Myrick, p. 193, quoting an article written by Gladys Hall.

60. Thomson, p. 297.

61. Ibid., p. 298.

62. Flamini, p. 250.

63. Although this game has sometimes been used as an example of Vivien's unstable state of mind, it apparently was not an uncommon game of that period. Gary Fishgall notes in *Pieces of Time*, p. 89, that 1936 roommates Jimmy Stewart and Henry Fonda are captured in home movies playing "killing babies." On one occasion, they pantomime putting a baby's head out of a car window and then cranking it up.

64. Walker, p. 130.

65. Harris, p. 111.

66. Ibid., p. 112.

67. Myrick, p. 105–6.

68. Ibid., p. 274.

69. Thomson, p. 319.

70. "How Movies Are Censored," *Look*, August 2, 1938, p. 13.

71. Cameron and Christman, p. 215.

72. Ibid., p. 225.

73. Ibid., p. 229.

74. Ibid., p. 230.

75. Davies, pp. 226–7.

76. In June 1999, Michael Jackson paid $1,500,000 for David Selznick's Best Picture Oscar for *Gone with the Wind*. One of Scarlett's dresses went for $90,500, an annotated script sold for $40,000, and Ashley's Confederate uniform jacket sold for $18,400.

77. Cameron and Christman, p. 232. Irene and Vivien would meet again when Leigh would play Blanche in Irene's production of *A Streetcar Named Desire*.

Chapter 18 — The House of the Two Gables

1. Martin, p. 62.

2. Harris, p. 113.

3. Ibid., p. 109.

4. Ibid., p. 113.

5. Garceau and Cocke, p. 82.

6. The 1938 Packard has been fully restored and was offered for sale in 1999.

7. The Duesenberg Automobile Company, founded in 1920 in Indianapolis, was purchased in 1926 by E. L. Cord's Auburn Automobile Company. From 1929 to 1937 they made only 481 Model J Duesenbergs. The usual practice was that they would manufacture the chassis, engine, grille, and front sheet metal, then the body would be custom-built by one of several coachbuilders to the customer's order. Thus many "Duesies" were one-offs or part of a very small group of similar design.

8. Also built by Auburn, the L-29 Cord was first released in 1929 as America's first front-wheel-drive production car. In 1935 the revolutionary design of the new 810 Cord resulted in it being called the "car of the future."

9. Both these fully restored Roadsters still exist, as do some 75 percent of all Duesenbergs. They were built on extra-short, 125-inch wheel-bases with dual-carburetor supercharged engines. The bodies, designed by J. Herbert Newport, were built by Central under the LaGrande name. Clark's roadster, known as 2595/J-567, is now owned by Alfred Ferrara of Gates Mills, Ohio, and was recently on display at the Auburn-Cord Museum in Auburn, Indiana. I would like to express my thanks to the Museum for much of this information

10. After Clark's death, the Mercedes Gullwing was eventually bought by Paul Newman and fully restored. It was offered for auction in 1998. The Cabriolet was bought from Kay by classic car collector Bruce Meyer, the former owner of Gearys of Beverly Hills. It had traveled only 32,000 miles. It is frequently on display at the Peterson Automotive Museum on Wiltshire Boulevard.

11. Tornabene, p. 263.

12. Ibid.

13. Harris, p. 121.

14. Frank Borzage (1893–1962) began as an actor for the Ince Studio playing bit parts as a heavy in westerns. He began acting and then directing at Universal in the early 1920s. He developed the use of soft-focus photography as a signature, giving his work a lush, gauzy, romantic atmosphere that made it a blueprint for other directors of romantic films. He was also a great believer in character development, no matter how small the role. He won his first Oscar for Best Director with *Seventh Heaven* (1927), which gained Janet Gaynor a Best Actress award. He then guided Gaynor to her next Oscar in *Street Angel* (1928). He won his second Oscar for *Bad Girl* (1931). Some of his other work was with Gary Cooper and Helen Hayes in *A Farewell to Arms* (1932), Marlene Dietrich and Gary Cooper in *Desire* (1936), Joan Crawford and Spencer Tracy in *Mannequin* (1937), and Ginger Rogers and David Niven in *The Magnificent Doll* (1946). His last film was *The Big Fisherman* with Howard Keel and Susan Kohner (1959). Shortly before his death, he received the D.W. Griffith Award for his outstanding contribution in the field of film directing.

15. Born in Hungary in 1904 as Laszlo Loewenstein, the Jewish Lorre was ironically reputed to be Goebbel's favorite actor for his role as the child killer in Fritz Lang's *M* (1931). Arriving in Hollywood in 1933, Lorre specialized in roles where he was hated, feared, and despised. Apart from his eight films as Mr. Moto, he was probably best known for his characters in Hitchcock's *The Man Who Knew Too Much* (1934) and *Secret Agent* (1936), as Joel Cairo in *The Maltese Falcon* (1941) and for his role in *Casablanca* (1943). He worked in films until his death in 1964.

16. Thomas, p. 83.

17. Douglas W. Churchill, "Metro Signs Gable in $2,000,000 Deal," *The New York Times*, January 26, 1940.

18. McEvoy, p. 85.

19. Henry Pringle, "Mr. and Mrs. Clark Gable," *Ladies' Home Journal*, May 1940, pp. 20, 99. Unlike many stars, Carole made no attempt to avoid her tax payments and made that known publicly. In 1937 she said that she was glad to pay her country's taxes because she considered that it was not too high a price to pay for all her country had done for her and for its citizens.

20. "The Big Money and Where It Goes," *Look*, December 30, 1941, pp. 30–31.

21. Born Hedwig Kiesler in Vienna in 1914, the teenage Lamarr gained early notoriety for her nude appearance in the film *Symphony of Love*, later released as *Ecstasy* in 1932. Unable to resist the lure of an MGM contract, she fled her first husband, Austrian munitions magnate Fritz Mandl, and came to Hollywood in 1937. He was the first of six husbands, mostly millionaires. She debuted with Charles "Come wiz me to de Cazbah" Boyer in *Algiers* (1938), starred in *White Cargo* and *Tortilla Flat* in 1942, and was history's most unwelcome hairdresser in DeMille's *Samson and Delilah* (1949) with Victor Mature. Billed as "the most beautiful woman in the world," she was also very intelligent and is credited with inventing the principle of "spread spectrum" technology, later used in missile guidance, mobile phones, and military radio and computer links. Having lived to see a new millennium, she died in January 2000.

22. Harris, p. 126.

23. Arriving penniless in California in 1915, King Vidor (1894–1982) was determined to become a director. After working on a number of minor films, his reputation was firmly established with the release of *The Big Parade* in 1925, by which time he was working for MGM. At his best in his early work, Vidor used innovative camera techniques, and he demonstrated a mastery of the epic vision and a talent for depicting steamy love affairs. He received his first Oscar nomination for *The Crowd* (1928). His second nomination was for *Hallelujah* (1929), in which he extended the possibilities of the new sound technology with his juxtaposition of sound and image. His third nomination was for *The Champ* (1931), and his fourth was for *War and Peace* (1956). In 1979 he received an honorary Oscar for his creative and innovative achievement. Some of his other films are: *Stella Dallas* (1937), *The Citadel* (1938), *Northwest Passage* (1940), *Duel in the Sun* (1947), *The Fountainhead* (1949), and his last film, *Solomon and Sheba* (1959).

24. Garceau and Cocke, p. 123.

25. Ibid., p. 127.

26. Garceau and Cocke, p. 129.

27. Tornabene, p. 275.

Chapter 19 — As Good As It Gets

1. Loos, pp. 169–171. Loos would stay busy and healthy, writing novels, reminiscences, and an autobiography, working with Colette turning *Gigi* into a play, and of course writing the screenplay for *Gentlemen Prefer Blondes*, until she died aged 88 in 1981. She never did divorce Emerson who, despite his years of proclaimed illness, had lived until his middle eighties, dying in 1956.

2. Essoe, p. 203.

3. Tornabene, p. 227.

4. Garceau and Cocke, pp. 119–120.

5. Essoe, p. 204.

6. Lana Turner, *Lana: The Lady, the Legend, the Truth*. Pocket Books/Simon & Schuster: New York, 1983, p. 62.

7. Harris, p. 136.

8. "Gable and Lombard Have Poor Luck, to Try at Coast," *Grants Pass Courier*, May 15, 1941.

9. Garceau and Cocke, p. 138.

10. Harris, p. 137.

11. Pringle, "Mr. and Mrs. Clark Gable," p. 20.

12. Harris, p. 137. A shorter, earlier version of this oft-repeated story can be found in Bill Davidson, *The Real and the Unreal*, Lancer Books: New York, 1962, p. 99.

13. Harris, p. 138.

14. Garceau and Cocke, pp. 142–43.

15. Harris, p. 148.

16. Garceau and Cocke, p. 144.

17. Harris, p. 149.

18. Tornabene, p. 284.

19. "Carole Lombard Dies in Crash," *Look*, February 4, 1942, p. 25

20. Ruth Waterbury, "What the Loss of Carole Lombard Means to Clark Gable," *Photoplay*, unknown month, 1942, p. 68.

21. Tornabene, p. 286.

22. Garceau and Cocke, p. 144.

23. Samuels, p. 253.

24. Ira Galdner, "Toy Plane Smashed to Bits," *San Francisco Chronicle*, January 19, 1942, p. 20.

25. Robert C. Miller, "Carole Lombard and 21 Others Are Found Dead!" *San Francisco Chronicle.* January 18, 1942, p. 6.

26. Garceau and Cocke, p. 147.

Chapter 20—After the Dance

1. Tornabene, p. 314

2. "Roosevelt Lauds Carole Lombard," *The New York Times,* January 20, 1942.

3. "Carole Lombard," *The New York Times,* January 19, 1942.

4. Thomas F. Brady, "Notations from the West," *The New York Times,* January 25, 1942.

5. "Plane Tragedy Stuns Hollywood," *The New York Times,* January 18, 1942, p. 38.

6. Last Will and Testament of Carole Lombard, Book 324, p. 314, No. 211–018, dated August 8, 1939.

7. Harris, p. 154.

8. "Simplicity Marks Lombard Funeral, *The New York Times,* January 22, 1942, p. 18.

9. "$112,000 Film Pay to Go to Charities," *The New York Times,* January 29, 1942. Of the $112,500, Red Cross received $50,000, the President's Infantile Paralysis Drive $25,000, the Motion Picture Relief Fund $25,000, and the Navy Relief Fund $12,500.

10. Fraser, p. 20.

11. Turner, p. 67.

12. Ibid., p. 68.

13. Tornabene, p. 339.

14. Essoe, pp. 89–90. Extracted from Joan Crawford and Jane Ardmore's *A Portrait of Joan.*

15. Garceau and Cocke, p. 158

16. "Lombard Plane 7 Miles Astray," *The New York Times,* January 21, 1942.

17. Garceau and Cocke, p. 158.

Chapter 21—Captain Gable

1. Henry H. Arnold, born 1886, graduated in the West Point class of 1907 where he was given the lasting nickname "Hap." After service in the infantry, he was sent to Dayton, Ohio, for personal instruction in the Wright bi-plane by the Wrights themselves. Consequently, in 1911, he became one of the first military aviators. As a pilot, teacher, and commanding officer he rose rapidly through the ranks of the developing air forces. He achieved the rank of brigadier-general in 1935, and command of the First Wing of General Headquarters Air Force, where he encouraged the development of the B-17 Fortress and B-24 Liberator bombers. In 1938, as major-general, he was appointed Chief of Air Corps, which became the Army Air Force in 1941. In 1942 Arnold became commanding general. Retiring in 1946, he died in 1950. Under him,

the air arm grew from 2,200 men and 3,900 planes to 2,500,000 personnel and 75,000 aircraft.

2. "Mayer's $704,425 Tops 1941 Salaries," *The New York Times,* May 29, 1942, p. 19.The Securities and Exchange Commission's figures showed Clark's 1941 income from MGM to be $357,500, which would place his weekly pay check at around $7500 for 48 weeks. However, Gable was beaten out in the salary stakes by James Cagney over at Warner Brothers, who in 1940 received $368,000 and in 1941 $362,500. By comparison, Bette Davis received $271,000, Charles Boyer $220,000, Ginger Rogers $215,000, Deanna Durbin $208,000, and Tyrone Power $188,000.

3. Harris, p. 160.

4. Samuels, p. 262.

5. Harris, p. 163.

6. "Room-mate Lauds Gable," *The New York Times,* September 4, 1942.

7. Hotchner, p. 42.

8. Ibid., p. 44.

9. Ibid., p. 45.

10. Roy Hoopes, *When the Stars Went to War: Hollywood and World War Two.* Random House: New York, 1994, p. 152.

11. Ibid.

12. Garceau and Cocke, p. 166.

13. "Gable Gets His Wings," *The New York Times,* January 7, 1943.

14. The activities of the busy 351st would follow the progress of the war in Europe. Formed in November 1942 at Geiger Field, Spokane, Washington, the 351st consisted of four squadrons of B-17 bombers—the 508th, 509th, 510th, 511th. Lt. Colonel William A. Hatcher was commanding officer until December 1943. After training in the US, they embarked for the UK and arrived at Station 110 near Polebrook in East Anglia in April, 1943.Their first successful mission was on May 14, 1943, bombing Courtrai Airfield in Belgium. Their final mission was on April 20, 1945, bombing the Brandenburg marshalling yards in Berlin. Between those dates, they flew 311 credited missions using 6,913 men and 9,075 aircraft that dropped 20,778 tons of bombs and fired 2,776,028 rounds of ammunition. Of their aircraft, a total of 175 B17's were lost in action with their crews, including two men who were later posthumously awarded the Medal of Honor. 351st gunners were credited with downing 303 enemy planes.

15. Hoopes, p. 153.

16. Eighth Air Force operations from Polebrook had actually begun in the summer of 1942. The 97th Bomb Group flew the first Eighth mission of the war from Polebrook on 17 August to bomb the Rouen marshalling yards. Copilot of the leading aircraft was Major Paul Tibbets, who later piloted the *Enola Gay* over Hiroshima. In October 1942 the 97th were transferred to the Mediterranean.

An advance party of 351st administration personnel arrived on April 15, 1943, and the rest of the group arrived the next day.

17. The 303rd Bomb Group, consisting of the 358th, 359th, 360th, and 427th Squadrons, had arrived at Molesworth in September 1942 and flown their first mission on November 17. Their B-17 *Hells Angels* was the first in the Eighth Air Force to survive 25 missions, and the 303rd took the name as their own. In January 1945, the 303rd would become the first Eighth Air Force Heavy Bomber Group to fly 300 missions from a US base in the UK. They were deactivated on June 11, 1945, having flown 364 missions, dropped 26,346 tons of bombs, and destroyed 378 enemy planes at a cost of 210 B-17s and 841 personnel killed in action.

18. This was the second B-17 with that name. The first *8-Ball*, named after the ball on the pool table that does all the work, had been one of the original planes of the group, a B-17F 41–24581. Calhoun had been forced to belly land the bomber in December 1942 due to battle damage, and it was declared a total loss. He was then given B-17F 41–24635, and as the second *8 Ball* this plane had a distinguished career, leading the group on many missions until it was retired in 1944. The third *8 Ball* was B-17G 42–97781. William R. Calhoun would also have a distinguished career, eventually reaching the rank of Lt. Colonel and command of the 359th Squadron for most of 1943. He flew 25 missions and was awarded a Silver Star.

19. Much like car models, successively improved versions of the B-17 were produced from 1939 onwards as the war progressed, and these were designated alphabetically. Some 3,405 B-17F's were produced between early 1942 and mid–1943, and this would have been the version Clark flew in. Of those, only three B-17Fs remain. The famous *Memphis Belle* has been fully restored and is on display in Memphis. B-17F 42–3374 became the property of MGM and is now in storage at Offutt Air Force Base in Nebraska awaiting restoration. 42–29782 is the only B-17F still flying, and it has appeared in a number of films including, ironically, the remake of the film *Memphis Belle* in which the plane was named the *Kathleen*.

20. For the information about Clark Gable and Oundle I am indebted to Michael Downes who graciously offered me his assistance and information from his book *Oundle's War*.

21. Ibid.

22. George Frazier, "The Man Behind the Gable Fable," *Collier's*, February 12, 1949, p. 24.

23. "Capt. Clark Gable Making Training Movies in England," *San Francisco Chronicle*, June 6, 1943.

24. "Battle of Europe," *Time*, August 23, 1943, p. 26.

25. "Gable Wins Air Medal," *The New York Times*, October 5, 1943, p. 3.

26. Capra, p. 353.

27. One of these four was *Be Careful*, which took combat fliers through routine aircraft checks and combat survival techniques. The other three dealt with general aspects of life and training in the AAF.

Chapter 22 — Somewhere I'll Find You

1. Beauchamp, p. 351.

2. Adela Rogers St. Johns, *The Honeycomb*. Doubleday: New York, 1969, p. 178–9

3. Louella O. Parsons, "Mister 'King,'" *Photoplay*. September 1947, p. 90.

4. Tornabene, p. 325.

5. David Niven, *Bring on the Empty Horses*. Coronet/Hodder and Staughton: London, 1976, p. 86.

6. Gary Fishgall, *Pieces of Time: The Life of James Stewart*. Scribner: New York, 1997, p. 173.

7. Parsons, "Mister 'King,'" p. 90.

8. Beauchamp, p. 353.

9. Irish-born redhead Greer Garson had won an Oscar for her performance as the plucky English housewife Mrs. Miniver in the 1942 film of the same name. At the time, she was married to Richard Ney, who played her son. L. B. Mayer had seen Garson performing on stage in London in 1937 and had signed her for MGM, but her first major film role would still be in England in *Goodbye Mr. Chips*. She would be nominated seven times for an Academy Award during a long career. A prominent philanthropist, she helped fund the Greer Garson Theater and Film Archive at Southern Methodist University in Dallas. She died aged 92 in Dallas in 1996.

10. Davidson, *The Real and the Unreal*, p. 103.

11. Dan C. Fowler, "Clark Gable: Big Money Man Gets Lucky Again," *Look*, undated, p. 64.

12. "Cinema: The New Pictures," *Time*, February 11, 1946, pp. 94–96.

13. Fraser, p. 21. Clark would continue his association with the Inn for the rest of his life. Many other famous people were Weasku guests, too, including David Niven, Herbert Hoover, Zane Grey, Bing Crosby, and Henry Hathaway whose movie *True Grit* was filmed on the Rogue. Peggie and Ced sold the Inn in 1962 and, sadly, it gradually declined during the following years. In 1993 it was purchased by Carl Johnson of Vintage Hotels and, fully restored to its former glory, was re-opened in 1996.

14. The Harley-Davidson is now part of the Imperial Palace Auto Collection in Las Vegas.

15. Nina Padgett, "Clark Gable: Actor, Ad-

venturer, Motorcyclist," *Cycle World*, August 1993, p. 48.

16. Tornabene, p. 327.

17. In 1945, Navy veteran Frederic Wakeman, originally from Seranton, Kansas, quit a $25,000 a year plus bonuses advertising job to write. His 1944 book *Shore Leave*, based on his experiences as a Navy lieutenant in Air Combat Intelligence, was a resounding success, and in 1946 *The Hucksters* followed suit. His third book was *The Saxon Charm,* about a novelist who writes a play that is picked up by an egocentric theatrical producer. It was sold to Universal for $400,000 and a profit share before publication. *Shore Leave* became the Broadway play *Kiss Them for Me.*

18. Thomas Brady, "Sifting the Hollywood News," *The New York Times*, January 19, 1947, p. 33.

19. Garceau and Cocke, p. 187.

20. Brady, p. 33.

21. Fowler, p. 69.

22. Frazier, p. 40.

23. Ava Gardner, *Ava: My Story*. Bantam Press/ Transworld: London, 1990, p. 102.

24. Parsons, "Mister 'King'," p. 90.

25. Gardner, p. 104.

26. Essoe, p. 211.

27. Mervyn LeRoy (1900–1987) had a long directing career working in every genre. After starting out as an actor, gag writer, and comedian, he became a director in 1927. He worked mostly for Warners, directing such big-budget musicals as *Gold Diggers of 1933* (1933), and such memorable gangster movies as *Little Caesar* (1930) and *The Public Enemy* (1931). His *I Am a Fugitive from a Chain Gang* (1932) was a forceful indictment of the penal system.

28. Vernon Scott, "Life Without Clark," *Coronet*, October, 1961, p. 108.

29. Kathleen Gable, *Clark Gable: A Personal Portrait*. Prentice Hall: Englewood Cliffs, New Jersey, 1961, p. 19.

30. Elza Schallert, "The Girl in Clark Gable's Life," *Photoplay*, June,1944, p. 29.

31. Scott, p. 107

32. Kathleen Gable, pp. 32–35.

33. The Spreckels family virtually invented the modern sugar industry. Klaus Spreckels was a personal friend of the last absolute Hawaiian monarch, King David Kalakaua. At one point, the family had proprietary title to the island of Maui. Amongst other things, they founded the Hawaiian Steamship Company (later the Matson Line), built the Hotel Del Coronado in San Diego, and founded the Palace of Fine Arts Museum in San Francisco.

34. Tornabene, p. 332.

35. Hedda Hopper and James Brough, *The Whole Truth and Nothing But*. Doubleday & Co.: Garden City, New York, 1963, pp. 251–252.

36. Ibid., p. 253.

37. Tornabene, p. 334.

Chapter 23 — Lady Sylvia

1. Niven, p. 74.

2. Ibid., p. 83.

3. Ibid., p. 85.

4. Slim Keith and Annette Tapert, *Slim: Memories of a Rich and Imperfect Life*. Simon and Schuster: New York, 1990, pp. 98–101, 134–139.

Mary Raye (Nancy) Gross was born in 1917 in Salinas, California. Her father knew Steinbeck and owned some of the canneries on Cannery Row. Dubbed "Slim" by William Powell, she became a friend of the Hearsts, of Ernest Hemingway and Truman Capote, and of Lauren Bacall whom she helped create her distinctive screen image. Known for her style and taste, Slim graced a number of *Harper's Bazaar* covers. She was married to director Howard Hawks, agent Leland Hayward, and to Sir Kenneth Keith. She died in April 1990, survived by Kitty and seven step-children.

5. Garceau and Cocke, p. 200.

6. Tornabene, p. 339.

7. Kenneth Lloyd Billingsley, *Hollywood Party*. Forum/Prima Publishing: Rocklin, California, 1998, p. 121.

8. Tornabene, p. 341.

9. Ibid., p. 340.

10. Hedda Hopper, "Gable Tells Hedda of Women in His Life," *Los Angeles Times*, undated, circa early 1949.

11. I am indebted to Patrick Curtis for this story, who is perhaps better known to legions of fans as "Baby Beau" in *Gone with the Wind*.

12. George Sidney (b. 1906) worked his way up the ladder at MGM from messenger boy to film editor to director in 1941. He was one of their best and most innovative directors of musicals. For *Bathing Beauty* (1944) he created equipment that could photograph underwater ballet, and his *Anchors Aweigh* (1944) featured Gene Kelly's dance with the animated Jerry the Mouse. Some of his other great musical work can be seen in *The Harvey Girls* (1946), *Annie Get Your Gun* (1950), *Kiss Me Kate* (1953), and *Show Boat* (1951). He also directed *The Three Musketeers* (1948) and *Scaramouche* (1952). In the late 1950s he became an independent producer and director working mostly for Columbia with such films as *The Eddie Duchin Story* (1956) and *Pal Joey* (1957).

13. Hopper, "Gable Tells Hedda of Women in His Life."

14. "Clark Gable Weds Widow of Fairbanks," *San Francisco Chronicle*, December 21, 1949, pp. 1, 14.

15. Elsa Maxwell, "Gable in Love Again," *Photoplay*, October 1952.

16. Cynthia Miller, "Fit for a King," *Modern Screen*, circa. January 1950, p. 58.

17. "Near Riot Mars Sailing of Gables on Honeymoon," *New York Times*, December 24, 1949, pp. 1, 14.

18. Carolyn Anspacher, "The Gables Sail," *The San Francisco Chronicle*, December 24, 1949, p. 1.

19. Lucille Warren, "Clark Gable Was 'Best Friend' for Hillsboro Man," *Hillsboro (Or.) Argus*, December 3, 1987, p. 6A. Ted Scott became a good friend of Clark's, with whom he'd often go fishing. He went on to have quite a career as a movie stuntman, including being Robert Mitcham's driving double in *Thunder Road*. Scott retired from movie work when Clark died, returning to Oregon to become a boat salesman.

Chapter 24 — A Lone Star

1. "Gable Organizes Producing Firm," *The New York Times*, September 28, 1950, p. 13.

2. Garceau and Cocke, p. 220.

3. Ibid., p. 221.

4. Vincent Sherman (born 1906) started out as an actor and writer, turning to directing in 1939. He spent most of the 1940s at Warners, where he specialized in films where leading ladies suffered and then turned to strong leading men to cry on their shoulders. Some of his best work is in *The Hard Way* (1942) with Ida Lupino, *Mr. Skeffington* (1945) with Bette Davis, *The Hasty Heart* (1949), *The Damned Don't Cry* (1950) with Joan Crawford, and *The Naked Earth* (1959) with Juliette Greco.

5. Hedda Hopper, "Why Does Gable Leave His Women?" *Look*, August 28, 1951, p. 32.

6. "Gable's Separation Is Doubted," *The New York Times*, April 18, 1951.

7. Hopper, p. 32.

8. "Mrs. Clark Gable in Honolulu," *The New York Times*, June 13, 1951.

9. Niven, p. 88.

10. Hopper, pp. 32–34.

11. Vincent Sherman, *Studio Affairs*.

12. Bosley Crowther, "Clark Gable and Ava Gardner in 'Lone Star' at Capitol," *The New York Times*, February 2, 1952.

13. Clark and Sylvia's comments are from "Gable Scores on Alimony," *The New York Times*, October 6, 1951.

14. Hopper, p. 34.

15. Garceau and Cocke, pp. 229–230.

16. Hopper, pp. 32, 34.

17. Scott Eyman, *Print the Legend: The Life and Times of John Ford*. Simon and Schuster: New York, 1977, p. 419.

18. Gene Tierney and Mickey Herskowitz, *Self-Portrait*. Wyden Books/Simon and Schuster, 1979, p. 175. Tierney's dance master for *Never Let Me Go* was Anton Dolin. She was doubled in long shots by ballerina Natalie Leslie. Tierney was subsequently offered the role in *Mogambo* later played by Grace Kelley, but declined because she didn't want to take her small daughter Tina with her to Africa. In 1955, after starring in *The Left Hand of God*, Tierney was hospitalized because of her declining mental condition for four years. She made only three other movies, *Advise and Consent* (1962), *Toys In the Attic* (1963), and *The Pleasure Seekers* (1964), and then she retired. She died of emphysema in Houston, Texas, in 1991.

19. Garceau and Cocke, p. 234

20. Gardner, p. 178.

21. Ibid., p. 179.

22. Ibid., p. 182.

23. James Spada, *Grace: The Secret Lives of a Princess*. Dell: New York, 1988, p. 74.

24. Spada, p. 68.

25. Ibid., p. 69.

26. Gardner, p. 183.

27. Spada, p. 69.

28. Ibid.

29. Eyman, p. 421.

30. Spada, p. 73.

31. Gardner, pp. 183–4.

32. Spada, p. 70.

33. This was just before Ava's thirtieth birthday, while Sinatra was in the U.S. successfully testing for *From Here to Eternity*. Ava decided that, because of her lifestyle, she wasn't ready to have a child and had the pregnancy terminated in London. Ava returned to Africa, but then so did Sinatra and in the New Year she was pregnant again. She hadn't told him about the first time, but he knew about the second. Even so, when *Mogambo* was finished, Ava made the same decision about her pregnancy.

34. Eyman, pp. 421–22.

35. When he arrived back in London, Ford had his eyes checked. He had cataracts in both of them. On June 30, 1953, he had an operation to remove both the cataracts, but while the left eye rebounded fine, the right remained light-sensitive. Ford would take to wearing what became a trademark eye patch.

36. Dan Ford, *Pappy: The Life of John Ford*. Prentice-Hall, Inc.: Englewood Cliffs, New Jersey, 1979, pp. 256–57.

37. Eyman, p. 422.

38. Ibid., p. 424.

39. Spada, p. 71.

40. Garceau and Cocke, p. 242.

41. Ibid.

42. "Who, Gable?" *Collier's*, January 8, 1954, p. 26.

Chapter 25 — Kathleen

1. Kathleen Gable, p. 45.

2. Tornabene, p. 374.

3. Helen Gould, "The King's Footnotes to the Gable Fable," *New York Times,* February 27, 1955.

4. Victor Sebastian, "I Remember Clark Gable," *Family Weekly,* February 26, 1961, p. 17.

5. Donald Spoto, *Marilyn Monroe: The Biography.* Chatto and Windus: London, 1993, p. 326.

6. After starting as a film editor, Edward Dmytryk (b. 1908) was a prolific RKO director until found guilty of communist affiliation by the House Un-American Activities Committee in 1947. Two of his best-known works from this period are the splendid film noir classics *Murder My Sweet* (1945) and *Crossfire* (1947). He went into self-imposed exile in England, but was jailed for several months upon his return to the U.S. He recanted his previous position and named names for the Committee, an action that overshadowed his career for the rest of his life. He resumed film making in the early 1950s and into the 1960s with bigger budgets but less originality and conviction. Some of his later work was *The Caine Mutiny* (1954), *Raintree County* (1957), *The Young Lions* (1958), *Walk on the Wild Side* (1962), and *The Carpetbaggers* (1964). From 1976 to 1981 he was a professor of film theory and production at the University of Texas at Austin. In 1981 he was appointed to a chair in filmmaking at the University of Southern California. He died recently.

7. Robert LaGuardia and Gene Arceri, *Red: The Tempestuous Life of Susan Hayward.* MacMillan Publishing Company: New York, 1985, p. 99.

8. Gould, p. 33.

9. Scott, p. 110.

10. Kathleen Gable, p. 49.

11. Scott, p. 108.

12. Eight years younger than Clark, Ryan didn't make his film debut until 1940, after successful boxing and stage careers. He was a fine and intelligent actor, who seemed to most enjoy playing unmitigated bad guys with no redeeming features. He brought to those memorable characters some truly nasty elements, such as the Jew-hating murderer in *Crossfire* (1947), a killer in *Bad Day at Black Rock* (1955), and Claggart in *Billy Budd* (1962). He was really good at portraying those on vengeful missions, such as the chief bounty hunter in *The Wild Bunch* (1969). He died of cancer in 1973.

13. Garceau and Cocke, p. 255.

14. Jane Russell, *My Path and My Detours.* Franklin Watts Inc.: New York, 1985, p. 158.

15. Garceau and Cocke, p. 254.

16. Kathleen Gable, p. 53.

17. Kathleen Gable, p. 61.

18. Ibid., p. 62.

19. Scott, pp. 109–110.

20. Tornabene, p. 378.

21. Ibid., p. 376.

22. Kathleen Gable, pp. 73–75.

23. Scott, p. 111.

24. Ibid.

25. Louis Berg, "Clark Gable ... Still the King!" *Los Angeles Times This Week,* May 24, 1953, p. 18.

26. "The King: He Was Leery of Playing Rhett Butler," *Newsweek,* December 24, 1955, p. 70.

27. Ibid.

28. Garceau and Cocke, p. 257.

29. Russell, p. 173. Russell declines to mention in her autobiography that Gable was actually in partnership with them for this film's production.

30. Earl Theisen, "Clark Gable: The King Has Four Queens," *Look,* September 4, 1956, p. 61

31. Frances Kish, "She Calls Him 'Pappy,' But She Calls Him 'Darling,'" *Photoplay,* February 1957, p. 68.

32. *Beyond a Reasonable Doubt* was a Fritz Lang–directed crime thriller released in 1956, starring Dana Andrews and Joan Fontaine, towards the end of both of their careers.

33. Kish, p. 86.

34. Gould, p. 33.

35. Tornabene, p. 378.

36. Dinter, Charlotte, "The Brave Lovers," *Modern Screen,* October 1956, p. 70.

37. Kathleen Gable, p. 112.

38. Dinter, p. 70.

39. From the *Congressional Record — House of Representatives,* January 10, 1957.

40. Essoe, p. 240.

41. Tornabene, p. 380.

42. Ellen Fitzpatrick, "Teacher's Pet," *Films in Review,* March 1958, p. 145.

43. Alan Gelb, *The Doris Day Scrapbook.* Grosset & Dunlap: New York, 1977, p. 101.

44. Robert Wise (b. 1914) began as an assistant cutter with RKO, becoming one of their best editors who worked on Welles' *Citizen Kane* (1941) and *The Magnificent Ambersons* (1942). He became a director in 1944, starting out in horror movies of which the best was probably *The Body Snatcher* (1945). His last film for RKO was *The Set-Up* (1949), an exposé of the brutal side of boxing. He then moved on to Fox, MGM, and other studios. The pinnacle of his achievement was probably *West Side Story* (1961), which won an Oscar for Best Picture and won Wise an Oscar for Best Director. Yet that film was eclipsed only a few years later by the phenomenal popularity of *The Sound of Music* (1965). His career extended into the seventies with *The Hindenburg* (1975) and *Audrey Rose* (1977), and even in a sense into the future with *Star Trek — The Motion Picture* (1979).

45. Gary Fishgall, *Against Type: The Biography of Burt Lancaster.* Scribner: New York, 1995, p. 169.

46. Sergio Leeman, *Robert Wise on His Films.* Silman James Press: Los Angeles, 1995, p. 148.

47. Fishgall, pp. 168–9.

48. Leeman, p. 147.

49. Bosley Crowther, "Mr. Gable Is Able," *New York Times*, March 30, 1958.

50. Garceau and Cocke, p. 280.

51. Ibid., p. 279.

52. Now Christi Welter, and living in San Jose, she did indeed go on to become a journalist. She kindly consented to talk with me and share her reminiscences and photographs. See also the *San Jose Mercury News*, Thursday, June 5, 1997, Zone 4, p. 1E.

53. "The Love Story of Caroll Baker," *Look*, November 24, 1959, p. 132.

Born in Pennsylvania, Caroll Baker had worked as a dancer and magician's assistant. After a small part in *Easy to Love* (1953), she studied at New York's Actor's Studio where she met director Jerry Garfein whom she later married. From a small role in *Giant* (1956), Baker become famous for her controversial thumb-sucking lead role in Elia Kazan's *Baby Doll* (1956) for which she had an Oscar nomination. She went on to play George Peppard's trashy step-mother in the wonderfully melodramatic *The Carpetbaggers* (1964) and then the lead in *Harlow* (1965). Moving to Europe to work, Baker returned to American movies in the early eighties, marrying Donald Burton, and she has worked steadily since, recently appearing in Michael Douglas' *The Game* (1997). Her daughter Blanche Baker is also an actor.

54. Walter Lang (1898–1972) directed mostly musicals and comedies for Fox. Some of his more notable work was *The Blue Bird* (1940), *Mother Wore Tights* (1947), *The King and I* (1956), and *Cheaper by the Dozen* (1950).

55. Scott, p. 110.

56. Some excellent black-and-white photographs of this house appear in Anne Edwards' article "Clark Gable: Desert Sunset for the Star of *The Misfits*," *Architectural Digest*, April 2000, pp. 256–59, 364.

57. Kathleen Gable, p. 115.

Chapter 26 — The Misfits

1. Davidson, p. 107.

2. Ibid.

3. Spoto, pp. 49, 58–59.

4. Ibid., p. 481.

5. James Goode, *The Making of The Misfits*. Limelight Editions: New York, 1986, p. 104.

6. Spoto, p. 476.

7. Ibid.

8. Goode, p. 47.

9. James Goode, "Revealing Talk of an Old Pro," *Life*, January 13, 1961, p. 54B.

10. Goode, *Making of The Misfits*, p. 105.

11. Ibid., p. 125.

12. Ibid.

13. Spoto, p. 491.

14. Goode, *Making of The Misfits*, p. 302.

15. Ibid., p. 150.

16. Ibid., p. 183.

17. Ibid., p. 304.

18. Kathleen Gable, p. 127.

19. Goode, *Making of The Misfits*, p. 201.

20. Vernon Scott, p. 111.

21. Ibid.

22. Goode, *Making of The Misfits*. p. 209.

23. Ibid., p. 293.

24. Ibid. p. 228.

25. Ibid., pp. 230–31.

26. Ibid, p. 241.

27. Victor Sebastian, p. 17.

28. Goode, *Making of The Misfits*, p. 290.

29. Ibid., p. 331.

30. Ibid., p. 294.

Chapter 27 — In Death, Life

1. Kathleen Gable, p. 131.

2. Ibid., p. 135.

3. Ibid., p. 136.

4. "Clark Gable Is Dead — A Last Intimate Look," *Life*, November 28, 1960, p. 93.

5. Ibid., p. 141.

6. "Gable: The King Is Dead," *Newsweek*, November 28, p. 27.

7. These tributes are from: "Rites Tomorrow for Clark Gable," *New York Times*, November 18, p. 31.

8. Scott, p. 112.

9. Ibid., p. 108.

10. Sebastian, p. 5.

11. Ibid., p. 17.

12. Kathleen Gable, p. 121.

13. Scott, p. 112.

14. Ibid.

15. Kathleen Gable, p. 142.

16. Ibid., p. 153.

17. Scott, p. 112.

18. Michael Small, "With His Father's Drive and His Mother's Looks, John Clark Gable Finally Races Out of Hiding," *People Weekly*, February 6, 1984, p. 88.

19. "John Gable, who never knew his dashing dad, shows off the king's grandson — the new Clark Gable!" *People Weekly*, November 14, 1988, p. 202. John Clark Gable and Tracy are now divorced. He married Lex on February 1, 1999, in a sunset ceremony on the beach at Malibu.

20. Davidson, pp. 81, 108.

BIBLIOGRAPHY

Biographical Works on Clark Gable

Cahill, Marie. *Clark Gable: A Hollywood Portrait.* Smithmark Publishers Inc.: New York, 1992.

Carpozi Jr., George. *Clark Gable.* Pyramid Books: New York, 1961.

Essoe, Gabe. *The Complete Films of Clark Gable.* Citadel Press: New York, 1970.

Gable, Kathleen. *Clark Gable: A Personal Portrait,* Prentice-Hall Inc.: Englewood Cliffs, New Jersey, 1961.

Garceau, Jean, and Inez Cocke. *Dear Mr. G.: A Biography of Clark Gable.* Little, Brown & Co.: Boston, 1961.

_____. *Gable: A Pictorial Biography.* Grosset & Dunlap: New York, 1977.

Harris, Warren G. *Gable and Lombard,* Simon & Schuster: New York, 1974.

Jordan, Rene. *Clark Gable.* Galahad Books: New York, 1973.

Morella, Joe, and Edward Epstein. *Gable & Lombard & Powell & Harlow.* Dell Publishing Co.: New York, 1975.

Samuels, Charles. *The King: A Biography of Clark Gable.* Coward-McCann, Inc.: New York, 1962.

Scagnetti, Jack. *The Life and Loves of Gable.* Jonathon David Publishers, Inc.: Middle Village, New York, 1982.

Tornabene, Lyn. *Long Live the King: A Biography of Clark Gable.* G. P. Putnam's Sons: New York, 1976.

Wallace, Charles B. *The Young Mr. Gable.* Harrison County Historical Society: Cadiz, Ohio, 1983.

Wayne, Jane Ellen. *Clark Gable: Portrait of a Misfit.* St. Martin's Press: New York, 1993.

Williams, Chester. *Gable.* Signet/ New American Library, Inc.: New York, 1975.

Other Books

Anderson, Joan Wester. *Forever Young.* Thomas More: Allen, Texas, 2000.

Beauchamp, Cari. *Without Lying Down: Frances Marion and the Powerful Women of Early Hollywood.* University of California Press: Los Angeles, 1998.

Billingsley, Kenneth Lloyd. *Hollywood Party: How Communism Seduced the American Film Industry in the 1930s and 1940s.* Forum/Prima: Rocklin, California, 1998.

Black, Gregory D. *Hollywood Censored: Morality Codes, Catholics, and the Movies.* Cambridge University Press: New York, 1994.

Bruccoli, M. J., ed. *San Francisco: A Screenplay by Anita Loos.* Southern Illinios University Press: Carbondale, 1979.

Callow, Simon. *Charles Laughton: A Difficult Actor.* Methuen Drama: London, 1988.

Cameron, C., and C. J. Christman. *The Art of Gone with the Wind.* Prentice-Hall, Inc.: Englewood Cliffs, New Jersey, 1989.

Capra, Frank. *The Name Above the Title.* W. H. Allan: London, 1972.

Carey, Gary. *Anita Loos: A Biography.* Bloomsbury Publishing Ltd: London, 1988.

Davidson, Bill. *The Real and the Unreal.* Lancer Books, Inc: New York, 1962.

_____. *Spencer Tracy: Tragic Idol.* Sidgwick and Jackson: London, 1987.

Davies, Marion. *The Times We Had: Life with William Randolph Hearst.* Edited by Pamela Pfau

333

and Kenneth S. Marx. Ballantine Books: New York, 1989.

Davis, R. *The Glamor Factory*. Southern Methodist University Press: Dallas, 1993.

Edwards, Anne. *Road to Tara: The Life of Margaret Mitchell*. Dell Publishing Co., Inc.: New York, 1984.

Essoe, Gabe. *The Complete Films of Clark Gable*. Citadel Press: New York: 1970.

Eyman, Scott. *Print the Legend: The Life and Times of John Ford*. Simon and Schuster: New York, 1999.

_____. *The Speed of Sound: Hollywood and the Talkie Revolution 1926–1930*. Simon & Schuster: New York, 1997.

Finch, Christopher, and Linda Rosenkrantz. *Gone Hollywood*. Doubleday & Co.: New York, 1979.

Fishgall, Larry. *Against Type: The Biography of Burt Lancaster*. Scribner: New York, 1995

_____. *Pieces of Time: The Life of James Stewart*. Scribner: New York, 1997.

Flamini, Roland. *Scarlett, Rhett, and a Cast of Thousands: The Filming of Gone with the Wind*. Macmillan Publishing Co., Inc.: New York, 1976.

Ford, Dan. *Pappy: The Life of John Ford*. Prentice-Hall, Inc.: Englewood Cliffs, New Jersey, 1979.

Fraser, Laura Kath. *Weasku Inn: Oregon's Legendary Rogue River Resort*. Vintage Press: Santa Barbara, California, 1998.

Fricke, John. *Judy Garland: World's Greatest Entertainer*. Little, Brown & Co.: London, 1992.

Gardner, Ava. *Ava Gardner: My Story*. Bantam Press/ Transworld: London, 1990.

Gelb, Alan. *The Doris Day Scrapbook*. Grosset & Dunlap: New York, 1977.

Golden, Eve. *Platinum Girl: The Life and Times of Jean Harlow*. Abbeville Press: New York, 1991.

Gomery, Douglas. *The Hollywood Studio System*. St. Martin's Press: New York, 1986.

Goode, James. *The Making of the Misfits*. Limelight Editions: New York, 1986.

Granger, Stewart. *Sparks Fly Upward*. Granada Publishing Ltd.: London, 1982.

Grismer, Karl H. *Akron and Summit County*. Summit County Historical Association: Akron, Ohio, 1952.

Hoopes, Roy. *When the Stars Went to War: Hollywood and World War I*. Random House: New York, 1994.

Hopper, Hedda, and James Brough. *The Whole Truth and Nothing But*. Doubleday & Co., Inc.: Garden City, New York, 1963.

Hotchner A. E. *Choice People*. William Morrow & Co.: New York, 1984.

Keith, Slim, and Annette Tappert. *Slim: Memories of a Rich and Imperfect Life*. Simon & Schuster: New York, 1990.

Kendall, Elizabeth. *The Runaway Bride: Hollywood Romantic Comedy of the 1930s*. Anchor Books/ Doubleday: New York, 1991.

Knepper, George. *Akron: City at the Summit*. Continental Heritage Press: Tulsa, Oklahoma, 1981.

Kotsilibas-Davis, James, and Myrna Loy. *Myrna Loy: Being and Becoming*. Primus/Donald I. Fine, Inc.: New York, 1988.

Lacey, Robert. *Grace*. Sidgewick & Jackson: London, 1994.

LaGuardia, Robert, and Gene Arceri. *Red: The Tempestuous Life of Susan Hayward*. Macmillan Publishing Co.: New York, 1985.

Lambert, G. *Norma Shearer: A Life*. Alfred A. Knopf: New York, 1990.

Leeman, Sergio. *Robert Wise on His Films*. Silman James Press: Los Angeles, 1995.

Levin, Martin, ed. *Hollywood and the Great Fan Magazines*. Harrison House: New York, 1991.

Lewis, Judy. *Uncommon Knowledge*. Pocket Books / Simon & Schuster Inc.: New York, 1995.

Loos, Anita. *Kiss Hollywood Goodbye*. Viking Press: New York, 1974.

Madsen, Axel. *Stanwyck: A Biography*. Harper Paperbacks: New York, 1995.

McBride, Joseph. *Frank Capra: The Catastrophe of Success*. Simon & Schuster: New York, 1992.

Myrick, Sue, and R. Harwell, eds. *White Columns in Hollywood: Reports from the Gone with the Wind Sets*. Mercer University Press: Macon, Georgia, 1994, (3rd Ed.)

Niven, David. *Bring on the Empty Horses*. Coronet/Hodder and Staughton: London, 1976.

Norman, Barry. *The Hollywood Greats*. Arrow Books Ltd.: London, 1988.

Paris, Barry. *Garbo*. Alfred A Knopf: New York, 1995.

Parish, James, and Ronald Bowers. *The MGM Stock Company: The Golden Era*. Arlington House: New Rochelle, New York, 1973.

Quinn, Anthony, and Daniel Paisner. *One Man Tango*. Headline Book Publishing: London, 1995.

Quirk, L. *Norma*. St. Martin's Press: New York, 1988.

Ray, Robert R. *A Certain Tendency of the Hollywood Cinema*. Princeton University Press: Princeton, New Jersey, 1985.

Russell, Jane. *Jane Russell: My Path and My Detours*. Franklin,Watts Inc.: New York, 1985.

St. Johns, Adela Rogers. *Love, Laughter and Tears: My Hollywood Story*. Doubleday & Co, Inc.: New York, 1978.

Sherman, Vincent. *Studio Affairs: My Life as a Film*

Director. University Press of Kentucky: Lexington, 1996.

Shipman, David. *Judy Garland: Secret Life of an American Legend*. Hyperion: New York, 1993.

Spada, James. *Grace: The Secret Lives of a Princess*. Dell Publishing Co.: New York, 1988.

Spoto, Donald. *Marilyn Monroe: The Biography*. Chatto & Windus: London, 1993.

Stenn, David. *Clara Bow: Runnin' Wild*. Ebury Press: London, 1989.

Thomas, Bob. *Joan Crawford: A Biography*. Bantam Book/Simon & Schuster: New York, 1979.

Thomson, David. *Showman: The Life of David O. Selznick*. Alfred A. Knopf: New York, 1992.

Tierney, Gene, and Mickey Herskowitz. *Self-Portrait*. Wyden Books/Simon & Schuster: New York, 1979.

Turk, Edward B. *Hollywood Diva: A Biography of Jeanette MacDonald*. University of California Press: Los Angeles, 1998.

Turner, Lana. *Lana: The Lady, the Legend, the Truth*. Pocket Books / Simon & Schuster : New York, 1983.

U.S. Government. *Census of Crawford County, Pennsylvania*. 1900.

Vickers, Hugo. *Vivien Leigh*. Pan Books Ltd.: London, 1990.

Wakeman, Frederic. *The Hucksters*. Rinehart & Company, Inc.: New York, 1946.

Walker, Alexander. *Vivien: The Life of Vivien Leigh*. Wiedenfeld & Nicolson: London, 1987.

Walters, James, and Jean Howard. *Jean Howard's Hollywood: A Photo Memoir*. Harry N. Abrams, Inc.: New York, 1989.

Westmore, Frank, and Muriel Davidson. *The Westmores of Hollywood*, J. B. Lippincott Company: New York, 1976.

Magazine Articles

"The Big Money and Where It Goes," *Look*. December 30, 1941, pp. 30–31.

"Blood in His Eye: Clark Gable Wants Action," *Look*. March 23, 1943, pp. 36–40.

Canfield, Alyce. "This Week Clark Gable," *Collier's*. January 19, 1946, pp. 56–61.

_____. "What Keeps Gable Clicking?" *Coronet*. August 1950, pp. 55–60.

Clarens, Carlos. "Clark Gable 1901–1960," *Films in Review*. December 1960, pp. 577–597.

"Clark Gable and Rosalind Russell," *Look*. July 1, 1941, p. 5.

Clark Gable Is Dead — A Last Intimate Look," *Life*. November 28, 1960, pp. 92–7.

"Clark Gable Takes His Lady on Vacation," *Look*. November 21, 1950, pp. 13–20.

"Clark Gable: The Lonely Man: His Life Story in Pictures," *Look*. September 7, 1954, pp. 60–65. Also: Letters, *Look*. September 21, p. 22.

Collins, Amy Fine. "A Perfect Star," *Vanity Fair*. January 1998, pp. 96–111.

Crow, James F. "Honky Tonk," *Look*. November 4, 1941, p. 52.

Davidson, Bill. "Clark Gable in His 60th Year," *McCall's*. November 1960, pp. 66–7, 224–8.

Dinter, Charlotte. "The Brave Lovers," *Modern Screen*. October 1956, pp. 49, 70–71.

Edwards, Anne. "Clark Gable: Desert Sunset for the Star of *The Misfits*," *Architectural Digest*. April 2000, pp. 256–59, 364.

Fitzpatrick, Ellen. "Teacher's Pet," *Films in Review*. March 1958, p. 145.

Fletcher, Adele. "Return to Romance," *Photoplay*. October 1946.

Fowler, Dan. "Clark Gable: Big Money Man Gets Lucky Again," *Look*, pp. 64–9.

Frazier, George. "The Man Behind the Gable Fable," *Colliers*. February 12, 1949, pp. 24, 40.

Gable, Clark. "Slap 'Em for Luck," *American Magazine*. September 1936, pp. 35, 74–80.

_____ "Why Janet Gaynor Walked Home," *American Magazine*. April 1941, p. 42.

"Gable Does It Again," *Look*. November 5, 1940, p. 16.

"Gable: The King Is Dead," *Newsweek*. November 28, p. 27.

"Gone with the Wind: Atlanta Premiere Stirs South to Tears and Cheers," *Life*. December 25, 1939, pp. 9–11.

Goode, James. "A Famous Pair — And a Finale," *Life*. January 13, 1961, pp. 53–6.

Hall, Gladys. "Clark and Carole Gable," draft manuscript marked to be published in *Picture Play*. May 1939.

Hopper, Hedda. "Why Does Gable Leave His Women?," *Look*. August 28, 1951, pp. 30–33.

Horton, Susan. "The Six-Week Cure," *Nevada*. November/December 1981, pp. 27–8.

"How Movies Are Censored," *Look*. August 2, 1938, pp. 12–19.

"Idiots Delight," *Life*. February 13, 1939, p. 45.

"John Gable, Who Never Knew His Dashing Dad, Shows Off the King's Grandson — The New Clark Gable!" *People Weekly*. November 14, 1988, p. 202.

"The King: He Was Leery of Playing Rhett Butler," *Newsweek*. December 24, 1955, p. 70.

Kish, Frances. "She Calls Him 'Pappy,' but She Calls Him 'Darling,'" *Photoplay*. February 1957, pp. 67–68, 86–87.

"The Love Story of Carole Lombard and Clark Gable," *Look*. May 11, 1937, pp. 34–41.

"The Love Story of Carroll Baker," *Look*. November 24, 1959, pp. 128–132.

Martin, Pete. "I Call on Clark Gable," *Saturday Evening Post*. May 1957, pp. 24, 62–8.

Maxwell, Elsa. "Gable Fable," *Photoplay*. c. 1949 (undated). pp. 52, 97.

_____. "Gable in Love Again," *Photoplay*, October 1952.

McCarthy, Joe. "Clark Gable: His Life Story," *Look*. October 4, 1955, pp. 63–70.

_____. "Clark Gable: How He Became King of Hollywood," *Look*. December 4, 1955, pp. 96–105.

_____. "The Five Wives of Clark Gable," *Look*. November 4, 1955, pp. 103–114.

McEvoy, J. P. "Joe Lucky," *The Saturday Evening Post*. May 4, 1940, pp. 22–23, 82–5.

Miller, Cynthia. "Fit for a King," *Modern Screen*. 1950 (undated).

"Mission Accomplished," *Screen Guide*. undated, pp. 40–1.

Padgett, Nina. "Clark Gable: Actor, Adventurer, Motorcyclist," *Cycle World*. August 1993, p. 48.

"Parnell," *Life*. June 14, 1937, pp. 43–51.

Parsons, Louella. "King Clark Returns," *Cosmopolitan*. October, 1953, pp. 10–12.

_____. "Mister 'King,'" *Photoplay*. c. 1947 (undated). pp. 40, 90.

Pringle, Henry F. "Hollywood's Selznick," *Life*. December 18, 1939, pp. 76–85.

_____. "It's a Living," *Collier's*. December 8, 1934, pp. 17, 49.

_____. "Mr. and Mrs. Clark Gable," *Ladies' Home Journal*. Vol 57, May 1940, pp. 20, 99.

Reid, James. "Here's Rhett — You Asked for Him," *Motion Picture*. March 1940.

Rocha, Guy Louis. "Gable vs. Gable," *Nevada*. November/December 1981, pp. 29–30.

St. Johns, Adela Rogers. "Gable Today," *Movie Stars Parade*. c. 1948 (undated), pp.51–3, 84–5.

_____. "The Great God Gable," *Liberty*. March 24, 1932, pp. 13–24.

_____. "Love, Fame and the Clark Gables," *Photoplay*. February 1936, pp. 14–16.

Schallert, Edwin. "The Girl in Clark Gable's Life," *Photoplay*. June 1944, p.29.

Scott, Vernon. "Life Without Clark," *Coronet*. October 1961, pp. 106–112.

Sebastian, Victor. "I Remember Clark Gable: Marilyn Monroe Tells," *Family Weekly*. February 26, 1961, pp. 5, 17.

Shipp, Cameron. "The Gable Saga," *Cosmopolitan*. January 1954, pp. 18–25.

Small, Michael. "With His Father's Drive and His Mother's Looks, John Clark Gable Finally Races Out of Hiding," *People Weekly*. February 6, 1984, p. 88.

Theisen, Earl. "Clark Gable: The King Has Four Queens," *Look*. September 4, 1956, pp. 60–64.

"These Are Not Poison at the Box Office," *Look*. July 5, 1938, pp. 20–1.

Waterbury, Ruth. "Vivien Leigh, Rhett Butler and I," *Photoplay*. February 1940, pp. 13–16.

_____. "What the Loss of Carole Lombard Means to Clark Gable," *Photoplay*. Unknown month, 1942, pp. 29–30, 68ff.

"Who, Gable?" *Collier's*. January 8, 1954, p. 26.

"Who's a Misfit?" *Newsweek*. September 12, 1960, p. 102.

Wilkinson, Lupton. "Shearer and Gable Take a Dare," *Movie Mirror*. March 1939.

Newspaper Articles

Anspacher, Carolyn. "The Gables Sail," *San Francisco Chronicle*. December 24, 1949, p.1.

"Astoria Show Pleases," *The Morning Astorian*. July 25, 1922, p. 3.

"Battle of Europe," *Time*. August 23, 1943, p. 26.

Berg, Louis. "Clark Gable … Still the King," *Los Angeles Times — This Week*. May 24, 1953, pp. 10–11, 18.

_____. "Clark Gable Today," *Los Angeles Times — This Week*. May 31, 1953, pp. 11–12, 21.

Biffle, Kent. "Gable Barely Escaped with His Pants," *The Dallas Morning News*. February 2, 1997, p. 47A.

Brady, Thomas F. "Notations from the West," *The New York Times*. January 25, 1942.

_____. "Sifting the Hollywood News," *The New York Times*. January 19, 1947.

Canel, Marie. "Clark Gable One Actor Who Keeps His Feet on the Ground," *The Oregonian*. November 4, 1934, Sect. 4, p. 4.

"Capt. Clark Gable Making Training Movies in England," *San Francisco Chronicle*. June 6, 1943, p. 13.

"Carole Lombard," *The New York Times*. January 19, 1942.

Churchill, Douglas. "Metro Signs Gable in $2,000,000 Deal." *The New York Times*. January 26, 1940.

"Circus Play Pleases," *The Morning Astorian*. July 28, 1922, p. 2.

"Clark Gable," *Beacon-Journal* (Akron, Ohio). April 13, 1975.

"Clark Gable Weds Widow of Fairbanks," *San Francisco Chronicle*. December 21, 1949, pp. 1, 14.

Crowther, Bosley. "Clark Gable and Ava Gardner in *Lone Star* at Capitol," *The New York Times*. February 2, 1952.

_____. "Mr Gable Is Able," *New York Times.* March 30, 1958.

"Gable and Lombard Have Poor Luck, to Try at Coast," *Grants Pass Courier.* May 15, 1941.

"Gable Disputes Suit," *The New York Times.* June 6, 1951, p. 33.

"Gable Gets His Wings," *The New York Times.* January 7, 1943.

"Gable Love Child Fraud Case Closed," *San Francisco Chronicle.* April 22, 1937, p. 1.

"Gable Organizes Producing Firm," *The New York Times.* September 28, 1950, p. 13.

"Gable Remembered as Amateur Actor Here," *The Morning Oregonian.* September 28, 1932, p. 12.

"Gable Routed Out of Bed for Interview," *The Oregonian.* January 17, 1935, p.6.

"Gable Wins Air Medal," *The New York Times.* October 5, 1943, p. 3.

"Gables' Separation Is Doubted," *The New York Times.* April 18, 1951.

Galdner, Ira. "Toy Plane Smashed to Bits," *San Francisco Chronicle.* January 19, 1942, p. 20.

Gould, Helen. "The King's Footnotes to the Gable Fable," *The New York Times.* February 27, 1955, p. 33.

Harris, Eleanor. "The King Talks," *Los Angeles Times — This Week,* undated, circa 1947.

Hopper, Hedda. "Gable Tells Hedda of Women in His Life," *Los Angeles Times,* undated, circa early 1949.

Kaufman, Gerald. "Olivia de Havilland: Grand Dame," *The Weekend Australian—Review.* June 12–13, 1999, pp. 4–6.

"The Last Mile Scores Hit in Los Angeles," *San Francisco Chronicle.* June 8, 1930, p. 2D.

"Lombard Plane 7 Miles Astray," *The New York Times.* January 21, 1942.

Lusk, Norbert. "Stage Appearance Smart Stuff," *Los Angeles Times.* March 4, 1934.

"Mayer's $704,425 Tops 1941 Salaries," *The New York Times.* May 29, 1942.

McConnell, E. "Edinburg Family Recalls Associations with Gable," *Record-Courier* (Ravenna, Ohio), undated, February, 1968.

Merrick, Mollie. "Clark Gable's Talents Smothered by Bad Role in a Maudlin Picture," *San Francisco Chronicle.* April 30, 1934.

Miller, Robert C. "Carole Lombard and 21 Others Are Found Dead!" *San Francisco Chronicle.* January 18, 1942, pp. 1, 6.

"Mr. Gyble: I'm Fully of Pep, So Let's Run Aw'y," *San Francisco Chronicle.* January 28, 1937.

"Mock 'Melodrammer' at Astoria Theater," *The Morning Astorian* (Astoria, Oregon). July 19, 1922, p. 5.

Moffitt, John C. "Yokel Row Yields Second Valentino," *The Sunday Oregonian.* September 25, 1932, pp. 1–2.

_____. "Clark Gable Baby When Mother Dies," *The Morning Oregonian.* September 26, 1932, p. 4.

_____. "Few Pals in Boyhood Revealed," *The Morning Oregonian.* September 27, 1932, p. 18.

_____. "Gable Falls Down as Master Lover," *The Morning Oregonian.* September 28, 1932, p. 12.

_____. "Young Trio Start in Quest of Jobs," *The Morning Oregonian.* September 29, 1932, p. 20.

_____. "Gable Bluffs Way Into Job Keeping Time," *The Morning Oregonian.* September 30, 1932, p. 12.

_____. "Clark Gable's First Acting Role," *The Morning Oregonian.* October 1, 1932, p. 6.

_____. "Gable Quits Stage for Temporary Job," *The Sunday Oregonian.* October 2, 1932, pp. 1–2.

_____. "Clark Gable's First Show," *The Morning Oregonian.* October 3, 1932, p. 4.

_____. "Clark Gable Gets Tip on Riding Rods," *The Morning Oregonian.* October 4, 1932, p. 6.

_____. "Gable Rides Rods Into Bend, Oregon," *The Morning Oregonian.* October 4, 1932, p. 13.

_____. "Frances Doerfler Takes Gable Eyes," *The Morning Oregonian.* October 6, 1932, p. 9.

_____. "Gable's First Love Still Is Good Friend," *The Morning Oregonian.* October 7, 1932, p. 6.

_____. "Gable Takes Job on *The Oregonian,*" *The Morning Oregonian.* October 8, 1832, p. 18.

_____. "Josephine Dillon Gable's Life Star," *The Sunday Oregonian.* October 9, 1932, pp. 1–2.

_____. "Gable Lands First Part in Picture," *The Morning Oregonian.* October 10, 1932, p. 13.

_____. "Stage Gable's Hope for Future Work," *The Morning Oregonian.* October 11, 1932, p. 7.

_____. "Gable Makes Two-Year Fight on Film Lots," *The Morning Oregonian.* October 12, 1932, p. 5.

_____. "Clark Gable Divorced By Miss Dillon," *The Morning Oregonian.* October 13, 1932, p. 13.

_____. "Gable Takes with Public and Filmdom," *The Morning Oregonian.* October 14, 1932, p. 6.

"Mrs. Clark Gable in Honolulu," *The New York Times.* June 13, 1951.

Murtha, Don. "Clark Gable and Frances Doerfler: The Great Romance of Silverton," *Silverton Appeal-Tribune.* January 10, 1980, p. 12.

"Near Riot Mars Sailing of Gables on Honeymoon," *New York Times.* December 24, 1949.

Nichols, Ken. "Old Clark Gable Haunt in Akron is Being Razed," *Beacon Journal* (Akron, Ohio). June 20, 1980.

"1935 Garbo Salary Totaled $332,500," *The New York Times.* January 28, 1937.

"$112,000 Film Pay to Go to Charities," *The New York Times.* January 29, 1942.

"Plane Tragedy Stuns Hollywood," *The New York Times.* January 18, 1942, p. 38.

"Rites Tomorrow for Clark Gable," *New York Times.* November 18, p. 31.

"Roommate Lauds Gable," *The New York Times.* September 4, 1942, p. 13.

"Roosevelt Lauds Carole Lombard," *The New York Times.* January 20, 1942.

Schallert, Edwin. "The Last Mile Superthriller," *Los Angeles Times.* June 3 and 4, 1930.

"Show at Astoria Theater Is Liked," *The Morning Astorian* (Astoria, Oregon). July 16, 1922, p. 4.

"Simplicity Marks Lombard Funeral," *The New York Times.* January 22, 1942, p. 18.

"Star's Wife Gets Decree," *San Francisco Chronicle,* March 8, 1939.

Stokes, Jan. "Making Gable Dance," *Detroit Free Press.* January 15, 1939, p. 13.

Syring, Richard H. "Young Clark Gable in Oregon," *The Oregonian's Northwest Magazine.* Sunday, September 18, 1977, p. 11.

Thomas, Bob. "Forever Young," *The Idaho Statesman.* November 24, 2000, pp. 1D–6D.

Waterhouse, Helen. "Gable 'Afraid of His Shadow' as a Farm Boy Near Akron but Had a Way with the Girls, Old Neighbors Reminisce," *Beacon Journal* (Akron, Ohio). January 31, 1940, p. 26.

Welter, Christi. "He Made Her Love Him," *San Jose Mercury News.* Thursday, June 5, 1997, Zone 4, p. 1E.

Whitaker, Alma. "Murder Role Career Climax, *Los Angeles Times.* June 8, 1930, Part 3.

"Young Actor Has Great Time in Reporter Role," *Los Angeles Times,* May 22, 1927, Part 3, p. 19.

INDEX

*Films preceded by an * are films in which Gable appears. Page numbers in italics indicate photographs.*